# Springer Texts in Business and Economics

Springer Texts in Business and Economics (STBE) delivers high-quality instructional content for undergraduates and graduates in all areas of Business/Management Science and Economics. The series is comprised of self-contained books with a broad and comprehensive coverage that are suitable for class as well as for individual self-study. All texts are authored by established experts in their fields and offer a solid methodological background, often accompanied by problems and exercises.

More information about this series at http://www.springer.com/series/10099

Laurent Gauthier

# Securitization Economics

## Deconstructing the Economic Foundations of Asset Securitization

Springer

Laurent Gauthier
SPE GmbH
Offenburg, Germany

ISSN 2192-4333 ISSN 2192-4341 (electronic)
Springer Texts in Business and Economics
ISBN 978-3-030-50325-3 ISBN 978-3-030-50326-0 (eBook)
https://doi.org/10.1007/978-3-030-50326-0



This Springer imprint is published by the registered company Springer Nature Switzerland AG
The registered company address is: Gewerbestrasse 11, 6330 Cham, Switzerland

ἀεὶ ὁ θεὸς ὁ μέγας γεωμετρεῖ τὸ σύμπαν

τῇ Ὀυικτωρίᾳ τῷ Ιουλιανῷ τῇ Αλεξάνδρᾳ καὶ τῇ Ελεονώρᾳ

# Preface

This monograph focuses on the economics of securitization, that is, the understanding of securitization by modeling and analyzing the motivations of the participants in that process. This focus differs from that of other books or manuals on securitization, which have tended to concentrate on either practical methods or the quantitative aspects of securitized product valuation. It also differs from existing academic literature because it includes detailed and formal descriptions of the core mechanics of securitization, loan modeling, and cash flow structuring, and relates these descriptions to fundamental economic models of securitization.

This work is not intended to be comprehensive in terms of economic models pertaining to securitization. I strive to present a wide range of such models and to narrow down on some that can be expanded or related to other models to some extent, but all cannot be covered. As such, I have made choices, some of them arbitrary, in selecting which research or results to discuss in detail. I have also used my own discretion in presenting existing research: in most cases, I retained the parts which I believed were relevant and appropriate, in both empirical and theoretical models. In addition, I extended some existing models when I thought it would help in understanding securitization or structures better. There is no central model from which more detailed or advanced models have been developed. In addition, as we will see, the models often make contradictory assumptions, and the empirical tests are rarely consistent. Hence, to understand the current research in securitization economics, one necessarily must adopt a deconstructive approach, comparing and contrasting these various models. Besides, economics, like other social sciences, is not a uniform body of Truth but a set of theories that do not have to be consistent with each other.

This book is not either intended to be comprehensive in terms of securitization techniques, which are extremely diverse, but to provide an understanding detailed enough that readers can go well beyond the simplified stylized facts that have often been used in academic research on securitization. My perspective as a practitioner, in analyzing, trading, structuring, or marketing securitized products over a quarter of a century, differs quite substantially from that of most academics and economists who have carried out research in securitization. Hence, I seek to understand securitization in the light of economics techniques, rather than to illustrate economics theories with securitization. Note that in light of the multiplicity of models and empirical results, I do not believe these economic models at the moment could capture enough details on securitization so that one could directly derive from them recipes to make securitization better.

Because of the dispersed nature of existing research, I have devoted significant time and effort in streamlining the material from two perspectives. First, I have centralized notations and approaches to the extent possible, both as they relate to modeling choices and in terms of mathematical treatment (I have tried to systematically follow a probability-inspired perspective). Second, I have scrutinized every step in the proofs to make sure they were absolutely clear and correct. In research papers, proofs are often quite summarized and are only sketches or intuitions of proofs, and I therefore expanded them in order to make them as clear as possible and be able to catch a few approximations and errors. In many cases, I entirely rewrote the proofs to bring them up to my standards for clarity and rigor, or to make them less heuristic. I aimed to cap the required mathematical level to that of a BS in mathematics or mathematical economics, approximately: one needs some knowledge of probability and measure theory, optimization, functional analysis, and game theory.

I have written parts of this book as a visiting professor at Konstanz University and as an adjunct at Toulouse Business School. This book has been composed initially of lecture notes for business Masters and economics Ph.D.-level classes on securitization, which I have taught since 2010, substantially augmented with recent research, others or mine. Although this course had started with a more practical focus, in particular on valuations, it evolved toward a more economics grounded overview, as the need for a thorough understanding of the underlying drivers of securitization became clear to me. Over the years, the course was taught to students at Toulouse Business School, EPFL, Bordeaux University, Nancy University, and Konstanz University, and also at Kanerai, the structured finance analytics company. I am grateful to the many students who followed these courses for their questions, remarks, and participation, which all helped me improve this work.

I owe a great debt to my friend and former colleague Sharad Chaudhary, an expert in asset- and mortgage-backed securities analysis, who carefully read parts of my manuscript and offered countless suggestions. All remaining errors are mine.

Offenburg, Germany Laurent Gauthier

# Contents

# List of Figures

# List of Tables

# 1 Introduction to the Economics of Securitization

Asset securitization is the partial or complete segregation of a specific set of cash flows from a corporation's other assets and the issuance of securities based on these segregated cash flows. It has also recently acquired a bad name, as the mortgage crisis of the late 2000s has been mostly attributed to its existence.

In this work, one important question we will seek to answer is to what extent securitization is inherently bad. To be able to address it, we will need to first define, characterize, and understand securitization, then explain why it exists in its particular and complex form. Then, we will look into the conditions in which securitization would have negative consequences. We do not address the mechanisms that could be designed in order to improve the working of securitization. As we will see, there is such a wide gap between the complexity of the securitization process and the economic models that can represent it that it appears difficult to use these models for detailed policy design.

Before laying out the plan for this endeavor, one may wonder how securitization is defined as an academic field of study.

## 1.1 Securitization as an Academic Field

Securitization as an academic field of study is not clearly defined. The study of securitization depends on more diverse inputs than other more traditional fields in finance, such as stocks, corporate debt, or options. Figure 1.1 illustrates this point by showing how one could see it in relation to other academic domains.

The study of securitization in financial economics can be seen as a part of corporate finance, and there has been a good amount of literature focusing on the reasons why securitization exists. Research in security design has led to fundamental explanations for the simplest structures, but the peculiar complexity of actual securitization



L. Gauthier, *Securitization Economics*, Springer Texts in Business and Economics,
https://doi.org/10.1007/978-3-030-50326-0_1

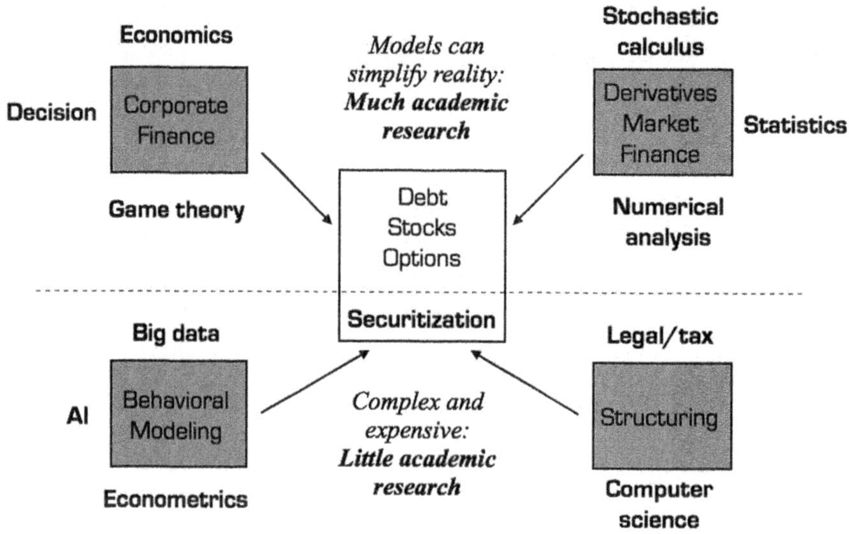


**Fig. 1.1** Simplified perspective on securitization as an academic field. *Source* compiled by the author

structures has not yet been accounted for in any way. In addition, there is no overarching theory or common agreement or single angle that can explain securitization in its wide-ranging complexity. As a result, we cannot follow a single approach as the "right" one, but rather compare and contrast a set of different perspectives.

A consequence of the fact that there is no unified theory is that the existing academic knowledge in securitization economics is dispersed in research articles and working papers rather than in unified monographs or manuals. Texts on corporate finance generally do not address securitization or only in passing. This reflects the general knowledge of this field, which is not very deep away from those who specialize in it: most people know what a bond is, few know what a CMO is.

In this book, we will effectively define securitization economics as a field of study, as the range of stylized securitization and structuring mechanics and the formal models that account for them, including empirical analysis.

## 1.2 Book Structure

The book is organized in nine chapters, and attempts to cover most of the economics aspects related to securitization, from its simple existence to complex structuring.

Discussing the economics of securitization is rather pointless without first having established a good understanding of how securitization works. As such, Chap. 2 is a rapid tour of the basics of securitization. We define a few terms and follow the cash flows in a typical securitization. Then we see how the various types of securitized products are generally categorized, and that the securitized bond markets are very sizable. We step through an overview of the types of securitized bonds that are most common, without yet going into the details of their structures. We also take a look at the trading mechanics applicable to these bonds, as they are quite particular and in some cases fairly complex. Finally, we briefly address some valuation techniques for securitized bonds and stress the importance of negative convexity.

Still at a rapid pace, we delve into the analysis of loan portfolios in Chap. 3. As one of the main inputs of securitization, large portfolios of loans require specific formal and practical tools for their analysis and we go through the main ones in this part of the book. The first section categorizes the various types of loans that one might encounter, and explains why at the core all these sorts of loans can be analyzed in a similar way. We nevertheless contrast corporate and consumer loans and how their differences lead to a differential treatment in securitization. Then we look into a loan's life cycle and how that can be represented as a transition matrix. Next, we discuss loan performance metrics and a few conventions. We then address loan behavior and discuss the drivers of prepayments and defaults, without going into the details of advanced modeling. We apply the general framework of loan behavior analysis to loan-level data on agency mortgages. We study refinancing and other forms of prepayment patterns, delinquencies and loss severities, and propose basic empirical models that capture their salient features. Next, we lay out practical methods for modeling loan cash flows, which are essential as an input into structures. Finally, we take a look at some formal ways of representing loan performance.

Chapter 4 addresses the economics of securitization at a fundamental level. We first see how, in theory, securitization should not exist. Then we look into various economic models that can explain not only why securitization actually exists, but also why it makes uses of certain fundamental structuring tools. We effectively decompose the notion of the existence of securitization into the existence of its fundamental components. First, for securitization to exist, selling assets needs to be optimal. Second, for securitization to exist as debt issuance, there has to be some optimality in debt versus equity or other forms of securities issuance. To address the first part of the question, we look through various explanatory factors such as taxes, bankruptcy, or regulatory costs, and certain synergies and asymmetries in information. We analyze a range of models and discuss their relevance in light of empirical studies. Then, we turn to the justification of debt financing in securitization. We study various models explaining how the optimal financing security that will not be mispriced by investors takes the form of debt. Finally, we look into how well these models account for reality, going through several empirical studies.

Having understood some of the drivers of securitization, we look into some of the problems that it raises from an economic standpoint in Chap. 5. We begin by characterizing some of the issues with securitization using loan-level performance data on agency mortgages. In particular, we quantify the massive jump in delinquencies on loans that were thought to be of the best quality. Then, we walk through theoretical and empirical models that explain how securitization would have favored a decline in the quality of the loans that were originated. Finally, we explain how securitization may have been used as a regulatory arbitrage tool and examine some empirical research on the subject.

At this stage, we will have a good grasp of the core mechanics of securitization, and some of the problems it raises in relation with loan origination. However, securitization is also well known for the seemingly arbitrary complexity of its structures. Hence, we then switch to the study of cash flow structuring, an essential aspect of securitization, as the focus of Chap. 6. The cash flows from the assets in a securitization are allocated to various bonds, following particular rules. These rules allow for the creation of bonds that have better or worse characteristics than the underlying collateral. We first discuss the underlying logic of structuring and the broad tools of the trade. Then, we offer a simplified taxonomy of structure types, and in the subsequent sections go through these various methods. These include subordination, over-collateralization, sequential payments, and many others. Then we address how different types of structuring approaches are usually combined in a securitization, and cover a few examples. We explain the logic with which various layers of structures are applied. We provide simple algorithmic descriptions of most of the structuring techniques we discuss, and we measure their efficiency across a large range of simulated scenarios.

How can one make sense of this structural complexity? We examine the economics of securitization structures in Chap. 7. We first go through several economic models that can explain certain general aspects of securitization structures, in particular, the pooling of assets, and the creation of layers of comparably structured bonds but with different degrees of risk. Then, we look into the handling of interest and principal specifically, in order to account for some non-trivial structuring techniques. We explain securitized product investor's desire for par-priced bonds, and show how this may drive the use of complex interest and principal allocation methods. Finally, we walk through several empirical studies on structuring, which put the theoretical models to the test.

While the existence of complex structures can be justified, in Chap. 8 we look into some of the problems raised by structuring. First, we characterize some symptoms of why structuring may not work for the benefit of investors. Then we drill down into the issues related to structure complexity. We examine the behavior of certain complex bonds and show that their structure effectively amplifies the exposure to risks that are difficult to measure. We follow some empirical studies that also show that more complex structures have tended to underperform simpler ones. Finally, we look into ratings following several empirical research papers that show evidence of rating shopping and influence. Chapter 9 concludes the book.

## 1.3 Notations

We will follow traditional probability-inspired notations:

Given two numbers or functions $a$ and $b$, we write $a \wedge b$ for the minimum between the two and $a \vee b$ for the maximum between the two.

We will often use the indicator function $\mathbb{I}$ in different contexts. For $x \in S$ for some set $S$, we write for $A \subset S$ $\forall x \in A : \mathbb{I}_A(x) = 1$ and $\forall x \notin A : \mathbb{I}_A(x) = 0$. In a probability space $(\Omega, \mathcal{F}, \mathbb{P})$, one sometimes writes $\mathbb{I}_B$ for a measurable set $B$, which effectively is a random variable defined for all $\omega \in \Omega$: $\mathbb{I}_B(\omega)$. If $X$ is a random variable taking values in a set $S$, we may also write an indicator function on an event defined based on $X$, for example, $\mathbb{I}_{X \in A}$ where $A \subset S$. We write $\overline{A} = \{x \in \Omega : x \notin A\}$.

For a random variable $X$ and a function $f$, we will write the expectation $\mathbb{E}[f(X)] = \int f(x)\mathbb{P}[X \in dx]$ where we may be able to write $\mathbb{P}[X \in dx] = q(x)dx$ for some measurable function $q$ if the density of $X$ is absolutely continuous relative to the Lebesgue measure. For an event $B$, we have $\mathbb{E}[\mathbb{I}_B] = \mathbb{P}[B]$.

We will sometimes use the Dirac mass function $\delta$ in order to be able to describe a large set of possible distributions without much specification. The Dirac mass measure is not absolutely continuous relative to the Lebesgue measure but we will write $\int f(x)\delta_a(dx) = f(a)$ for all measurable functions $f$. Note that the rigorous treatment of the Dirac mass implies the notion of a Dirac measure $\delta(dx)$. Hence, if a random variable $X$ has a discrete distribution its density will be a sum of Dirac masses. For example, if $Y$ takes value $y_1$ with probability $p$ and $y_2$ with probability $1 - p$ we will write $\mathbb{P}[Y \in dy] = (p\delta_{y_1}(dy) + (1 - p)\delta_{y_2}(dy))$. Using this form of expression efficiently synthesizes sometimes complex probabilistic models and avoids any ambiguity.

For conditional expectations relative to an event $B$, we write

$$\mathbb{E}[f(X)|B] = \frac{\mathbb{E}[f(X)\mathbb{I}_B]}{\mathbb{P}[B]}.$$

In order to treat the case of an event with a null probability, for example, $Y = y$ where $Y$ has a continuous distribution, we define it using a limit:

$$\mathbb{E}[f(X)|Y = y] = \lim_{\varepsilon \to 0} \frac{\mathbb{E}\left[f(X)\mathbb{I}_{y-\varepsilon \leq Y \leq y+\varepsilon}\right]}{\mathbb{P}[y - \varepsilon \leq Y \leq y + \varepsilon]}.$$

Through the text, certain terms have been bolded when they are used the first time, because they are important concepts or vocabulary items, and are generally used elsewhere.

Basic fixed-income concepts such as duration, average life, or price and yield relationships are not systematically defined in this text, see Tuckman and Serrat (2012) for example.

## 1.4 Data and Code

In order to illustrate a few points, I will refer to Fannie Mae and Freddie Mac's loan-level data in a few instances. These agencies provide detailed historical data, at the loan-level, on an extensive subset of their risk exposures, see Loan Performance Data (2018) and Single Family Loan-Level Dataset (2018). The extraction, processing, handling, and aggregation of this data, and the publication of the results fall under the academic and research purpose exemption in the Fannie Mae and Freddie Mac loan performance data use terms and conditions.

The data represents over 3 billion rows and hundreds of fields, and requires substantial processing in order for the two datasets to be merged in a congruent manner. In addition, to be properly exploited it needs to be joined with detailed home price indices (at the zipcode level), interest rates, or other external information sources. The necessary processing, which would have required the resources of an investment bank and a team of computer science professionals in the early 2000s, remains complex, but can nowadays benefit from distributed computing. In particular, using Amazon's Elastic Compute Cloud combined with Spark and the Athena database engine, creating and managing such a dataset is possible without such extensive resources. Creating this dataset has nevertheless been a substantial development project. Querying from this large loan-level dataset, I created various bucketed aggregates in order to illustrate the specific points I wish to address. The resulting pre-aggregated data usually amounts to less than 1 million lines, which makes it possible, if not easy, to further process and analyze with R on a desktop computer.

The point in referring to this data is to shed some light on empirical studies; using this very large dataset covering a broad share of the US mortgage market allows us to see to what extent certain empirical conclusions may be generalized, and sometimes offer alternative interpretations.

A few illustrations of loan-level data aggregations are expressed in SQL, the *lingua franca* of data processing. All other illustrations of algorithms in the book make use of the R language. The code examples are written in as simple a language as possible, and do not make use of R's more complex language syntax. They are not designed to be fast or efficient, but to be as clear as possible.

## References

Loan Performance Data. (2018). Fannie Mae. https://loanperformancedata.fanniemae.com/lppub/index.html.

Single Family Loan-Level Dataset. (2018). Freddie Mac. http://www.freddiemac.com/research/datasets/sf_loanlevel_dataset.page.

Tuckman, B., & Serrat, A. (2012). *Fixed income securities* (3rd ed.). John Wiley & Sons.

# 2 Overview of Securitization and Securitized Products

In this chapter, we go over the fundamental mechanics of securitization and securitized products markets at warp speed. The goal is to equip the reader, through simple descriptions, with just enough knowledge of the details, to set the stage for the more involved economic analyzes of the subsequent chapters.

Either as stand alone pieces or as introductory parts of research articles, there are tens of references on the basics of securitizations, not even including Street research. Some examples of academic introductions to securitization include Schwarcz (2013), an encyclopedia entry, and Gorton and Metrick (2013) who provide a historical perspective as propaedeutics for their economic analysis. Fabozzi and Vinod (2008) is an example of an overview intended for practitioners, addressing the basic principles and market structure.

Our quick review of securitization is articulated in five steps: first, we define structured finance and securitization, in contrast with other modes of financing. Next, we walk through the way in which securitized products are categorized. This may sound trivial, but it is reasonably complicated, and this can lead to many misunderstandings in empirical research. Then, we discuss the size and importance of securitization markets: in a nutshell, they are huge. After that, we turn to the trading mechanics of securitized products, which are fairly diverse, and matter because they correlate with product complexity. Finally, we scratch the surface of valuation methods for these products; while this is not our focus in this work, a minimal knowledge is useful to understand some aspects of structuring.



L. Gauthier, *Securitization Economics*, Springer Texts in Business and Economics,
https://doi.org/10.1007/978-3-030-50326-0_2

## 2.1 Structured Finance and Securitization

In order to present structured finance and securitization in a simple and intuitive manner, it serves to consider what financing is. We know that an important function of banks (commercial or investment banks) is to get firms the financing they require to develop their projects. The simplest type of external financing is a bank loan, where a single bank lends money to a particular firm, as a general obligation of that firm. There are many other ways in which a firm can get external financing, and studying these many ways and which ones are optimal in which case is an important part of finance. For a firm, issuing bonds, stocks, getting a bank loan or using securitization are different ways of obtaining financing.

In many cases, standard equity or debt financing is not used because the firm and/or the investors do not want the financing to be attached to the general performance of the firm, but rather to a particular business or project.

In this section we first define structured finance and lay out its multiple embodiments, including securitization. Then, we narrow our focus on securitization, define it and describe its most basic mechanics.

### 2.1.1 Structured Finance

Beyond straight equity or bond issuance, the financing techniques that investment banks advise on are part of **structured finance**: financing that uses a particular legal entity, separate from the issuing firm, typically called a **special purpose vehicle** or **SPV**. The financing vehicle can sometimes be a joint-venture with the providers of financing. With structured finance, the firm that looks for financing is able to get financing attached to a specific project, activity or business, hence the need for some type of SPV.

At this stage it is useful to define the general notion of **collateral**: in the context of debt, it is some asset on which the lender could have rights in contractually-defined situations, such as if the borrower does not repay the debt. Debt is said to be **collateralized** if some collateral is contractually attached to it.

There is a continuum of ways in which particular projects or businesses may be financed. However if we look around the many floors the investment banking and debt capital markets division occupies at a bulge-bracket bank, we will find that there are particular ways of getting firms the financing they require using specific approaches, and they are segregated into separate business units at the bank. The continuum is cut up into these particular approaches based on a variety of reasons, from what the bank's clients need to the vagaries of managers coming or leaving and randomly reducing or extending the bank's expertise.

In general, we can find the following businesses as part of structured finance:

- **Leverage or project finance**, which concerns the financing for a specific project. The assets underlying that project are used as collateral for whomever brings the funding. In case of non repayment, the funding provider could get the assets back. The assets are not necessarily physical items, they may be contracts.

- **Commodity finance**, or more specifically energy or commodity trade financing. The assets in this case are particularly liquid, and can be exchanged on a market, with a more clearly identifiable valuation, unlike the assets in the case of project finance.
- **Corporate acquisition finance**, dealing with the specific financing for a corporate acquisition, generally in the form of debt. This debt may be collateralized by the target's equity or other liabilities, or directly by the target's assets once the equity has been acquired.
- **Asset finance**, that is collateralized lending for very specific purposes, such as purchasing equipment, an automobile fleet, real-estate, warehouses… In case of non repayment the assets may be repossessed. This differs from project finance because the assets are typically transverse and not project specific, and may be efficiently used by another company in a different sector entirely.
- **Covered debt**, which qualifies debt typically collateralized by loans held by the issuing firm. Investors however have a recourse to the issuing company if the loans do not perform.
- **Securitization or Asset-backed finance**, in which case the company sells cash flow generating assets to the SPV, which issues debt to raise its own funding. The debt securities issued by the SPV hold the entire economic risk from the assets, as well as their economic value added. The company may continue to exploit the assets.[1] There is normally no recourse for the investors, unlike in the case of covered debt.

Since of all these bank business lines securitization has been the most visible and is by far the largest in terms of issuance volume, the term "structured finance" has sometimes been held as synonym with securitization. In our discussion of the basics of securitization economics in Chap. 4, we will address some of the distinguishing features between securitization and other forms of structured finance.

### 2.1.2 Definition of Securitization

To **securitize** means to create securities, mostly bonds, from cash flows. Those with a financial mathematics background may wonder why it would matter that some cash flows are in the form of securities, bonds, or equity, or anything else if they are the same cash flows. This is an extremely important question, and we will address it mainly in Chaps. 4 and 7, but for the time being we will concern ourselves with the "how" more than the "why".

A **securitization vehicle** or **deal** is the SPV used in a securitization. An SPV is a legal entity separate from the issuer and from investors. It only holds the assets

[1]That is, continue to act as a servicer.

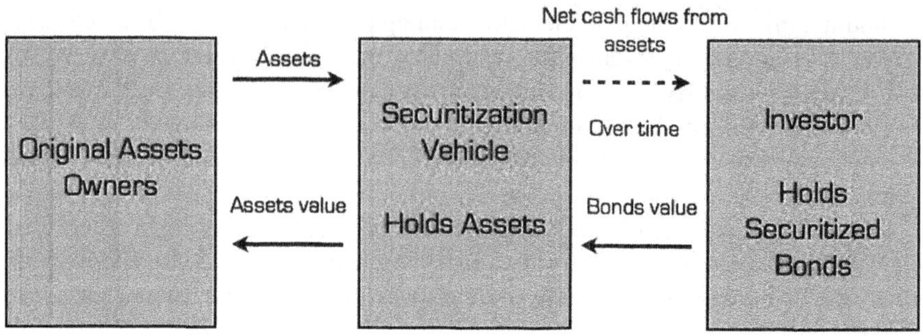


**Fig. 2.1** Flows of funds in a securitization. *Source* compiled by the author

(rights to future cash flows), and issues debt (bonds) as liabilities. As a company, the SPV does not have a "management" team, simply a set of rules describing how payments should be made. When the underlying assets are mortgage loans in the US, the deal normally takes the form of a special legal entity, a **REMIC** or real-estate mortgage investment conduit.

The bonds issued by the SPV are called **tranches**.[2] They are very different from traditional corporate debt: they are secured with assets, not with any future business growth or future valuation. The total face value of the bonds should equal the face value of the assets (since naturally, assets = liabilities).

The flows in a securitization are illustrated in Fig. 2.1. The corporation getting financing through securitization gets funding from the investors through the SPV. The issuer puts the assets in the SPV. These assets are called the **deal's collateral**. The SPV was originally an empty shell, so it needs to get funds to buy the assets from the issuer, and it gets these funds by issuing its liabilities to investors.

The important parties in a securitization, some of which are identified in Fig. 2.1, are as follows:

- The **issuer**, that is the original assets owner, sells assets into the SPV.
- The **investors** buy securities issued by the SPV.
- The **arranger** or **sponsor** or **dealer** is the investment bank which structures the securities and will sell them into the market.
- The **servicer** is in charge of managing the asset portfolio. The servicer collects the cash flows from the assets, aggregates them, and sends them to the SPV. If certain assets are not performing (delinquent loans for example), the servicer is in charge of using all available resources to recover payments. The servicer is typically paid as a function of the total balance, for example 50 bps of the deal outstanding amount. It is important to realize that a securitization could not exist without a servicer. Also, the servicer may or may not be related to the issuer.
- The **trustee** is in charge of managing the SPV. Every eventuality is in principle covered in the SPV's **pooling and servicing agreement** or PSA, akin to its

[2]From the French *tranche* meaning "slice", as a slice of cake.

statutes. The trustee is responsible for reporting, calculating and distributing the payments to the bond holders (from the amounts collected by the servicer). The trustee is usually paid 10–15 bps of the deal outstanding amount. In effect, the trustee is the SPV's management team, but has essentially no discretion and is entirely bound by the deal's PSA.
- In some cases[3] there may be a **deal manager** who can buy or sell some of the assets following specific rules. This manager is an asset management service provider, such as a hedge fund or a money manager and is tightly bound by the limits and rules set out in the PSA.
- There may be a **credit enhancement provider**, a third party that provides insurance on some of the securitized bonds that are issued by the SPV. This type of insurance is called a **wrap** on the bonds.
- One or several **credit rating agencies** may be involved, in order to give grades indicative of credit risk to the securitized bonds that are issued by the SPV.

While there are many businesses securitizing their assets, banks and financial companies constitute the majority of these issuers, and securitization fundamentally affects their business logic. Securitization effectively creates a shortcut between bank investors and bank assets. A bank has three traditional roles. First, extending loans and consequently being able to analyze the borrower's ability to repay the loan. Second, managing these loans, ensuring that the borrower's payments are collected over time, and using all legal means to recover principal when the borrowers are delinquent. Finally, holding a portfolio of loans, sometimes hedging some risks or not, acquiring more or less exposure to various sectors.

With securitization these three roles are dissociated. The initial lender is the entity selling the assets to the SPV, which could still be done by the bank, or by an independent mortgage company. The servicer is in charge of loan management, and may be part of the issuing bank. Finally, investors hold the rights to the assets through the SPV and therefore benefit from the economic interest in the assets, and the initial bank could also be an investor in an SPV.

Some legal aspects in securitization are particularly critical:

- **True sale**. The assets are truly sold to the SPV by the issuing company. There cannot be any contractual terms that would force the issuer to buy them back in certain conditions, and the issuer cannot retain too large an interest in the SPV, otherwise, in case of a bankruptcy of the issuing firm, the creditors could be allowed to take the assets out of the SPV. Hence the SPV is said to be **bankruptcy-remote**.
- **Tax exemption**. As a corporation the SPV should not pay taxes and should be transparent, and the investors should themselves pay taxes. In countries where securitization exists, there must be specific tax laws for securitization vehicles allowing this tax transparency.

[3]If the assets are not static, as will be discussed in more detail in Chap. 3.

- **No management**. An SPV cannot be managed like a "real" corporation. The behavior of the SPV's "management" must be entirely defined in its founding documents, and is administered by the trustee.
- **No SPV bankruptcy**. The SPV cannot be in bankruptcy because it can never pay less (or more) than exactly what it owes in the current conditions. The tranches may be affected by write-downs (balance reduction without a compensating principal payment) but they cannot be in default. As a result a securitization SPV could in no circumstance be bankrupt and suffer the costs associated with a restructuring. Note that while the SPV cannot be in bankruptcy, if its collateral consists of loans, the issuers of these loans could of course be in bankruptcy.
- Potential for **Reg Arb**, or regulatory arbitrage. Banks may be able, by using securitization, to benefit from lower **Reg Cap** (regulatory capital) requirements, while keeping their overall risk exposure and expected returns approximately constant.[4]

Of this extremely simplified presentation of securitization, the most important common thread is that securitization aims to create an isolated "box" in which the assets are moved, so that the securitized bonds that are issued only depend on these assets in a mostly deterministic way.

## 2.2 Categorization and Identification of Securitized Products

Having defined securitization, let us now turn to the infamous alphabet soup of securitized products acronyms. We first describe the market segmentation as a function, mainly, of the nature of the assets that are securitized. Then we discuss the manner and logic in which specific securitized bonds are identified. Next, in order to refine this categorization, we walk through a highly simplified view of different structuring dimensions[5] with more acronyms. Finally, we briefly discuss important acronym-like metrics: the ratings of securitized bonds.

### 2.2.1 Types of Securitized Products

In the same way as the continuum of project financing has been cut up in seemingly arbitrary silos, the continuum of assets that may be securitized has been categorized along an idiosyncratic taxonomy the intuitive logic of which only comes after many years of practice.

Over time, the definition of new product categories has stemmed from the need to clearly distinguish new kinds of collateral, in an effort to market them more

[4]We discuss regulatory arbitrage in detail in Chap. 5.

[5]The full discussion of structuring is in Chap. 6.

efficiently. The following list therefore, to a large extent, follows the chronology of the development of these new products.

- **MBS**, mortgage-backed securities, collateralized by real-estate loans. These include residential mortgage backed securities, **RMBS**, as well as commercial mortgage-backed securities, **CMBS**. MBS were the first securitized products to appear, in the 1970s. Until the early 1990s, development in securitized products was not through the extension of the range of assets being securitized, but through more complex structures. As we will discuss in the last section of the present chapter, mortgage loans exhibit a costly exposure to interest rates, which structuring has helped alleviate.
- **ABS**, asset-backed securities, collateralized by various non-mortgage cash flowing assets. This market began to grow in the early 1990s. These include loans such as Auto ABS, Student Loans ABS (**SLABS**), Dealer Floor Plan ABS and various other asset types. Certain assets that are technically not loans but instead **receivables** (rights to future cash flows) also fall under this category, such as Credit Card Receivables ABS, Tobacco Claims ABS, or Tax Liens ABS.
- **CDOs**, collateralized debt obligations, designate deals for which the assets are debt issued by corporations, and typically traded in the market. There are important subcategories in the CDO market and while some of them turned out fairly toxic for their investors, some have fared much better:
  - **CLOs**, collateralized loan obligations, where the assets are **leveraged loans**, loans made to corporations, and typically with below investment-grade ratings;
  - **CBOs**, collateralized bond obligations, for example
    - ⋆ Junk bond CBOs, where the assets are high-yield junk debt
    - ⋆ TruPS CBOs, where the assets are trust-preferred securities (junior debt issued by banks or insurance companies)
  - **CSOs**, collateralized synthetic obligations, where the assets are a combination of short-term money-market assets and credit derivatives
  - **SFCDOs**, structured-finance CDOs, where the assets are other securitized products. These products gave all CDOs their very negative reputation, because their performance through the 2008 crisis was abysmal:
    - ⋆ **ABS CDOs** where the assets are a combination of ABS and RMBS
    - ⋆ **CDO$^2$** where the assets are CDOs (typically SFCDOs)
    - ⋆ **CRE CDOs**, commercial real-estate CDOs where the assets are specifically CMBS.

All these types of securitization deals, MBS, ABS or CDOs, may be created in cash or synthetic structures, with a managed or static portfolio of underlying assets. They may also be issued as **arbitrage**, or as **balance-sheet** operations. In the case of a balance-sheet transaction, the issuer simply looks to shed some assets in order to free up capital for further development; this is the more fundamental driver of securitization, which we alluded to in the prior subsection. The issuer presumably originated the assets itself. In contrast, an arbitrage transaction consists of purchasing assets in the market for the specific purpose of securitizing them.

Residential MBS are such a gigantic market that they are further categorized as a function of the nature of their issuer:

- **Agency MBS** are issued by Ginnie Mae (GNMA), Fannie Mae (FNMA) or Freddie Mac (FHLMC). Ginnie Mae is a US Government agency, Fannie Mae and Freddie Mac are quasi-private **GSEs** (government-sponsored entities) and benefit from a Government guarantee. These agencies guarantee pools of loans for an insurance fee, so that the pools have a government credit guarantee (a wrap). Fannie Mae and Freddie Mac also issue large amounts of debt, in order to purchase MBS and carry out an arbitrage between the debt and MBS markets.
- **Non-agency MBS** or **Private-label MBS** are US MBS without outside credit protection, but use structuring techniques such as **credit enhancement** (manufacturing safer securities through the structuring of riskier securities) to create bonds with limited credit risk. Since the first private-label deals appeared in the 1980s, these products have been traded on different desks from agency MBS.
- **European MBS** are those backed by European mortgages, and use different structuring techniques to create bonds with limited risks.

In addition to the categorization based on issuer, RMBS are also categorized according to structure:

- **Passthroughs** are the simplest type of product: there is no structure apart from outside guarantees or credit structuring. Agency pools come in the form of passthroughs, and constitute the largest subset of securitized products.
- **CMOs**, collateralized mortgage obligations, use a complex structure to allocate principal and interest payments, in order to make some bonds longer or shorter, or riskier or safer relative to the timing of principal repayment, for example.

The A in ABS standing for assets, one might wonder why ABS would not include MBS, since mortgage loans are assets after all. The assets pooled in ABS historically exhibited very little exposure to interest rates, so that there was a clear incentive to market them separately from MBS. Different trading desks, often part of separate business units (rates products as opposed to corporate debt) handled these separate MBS and ABS markets. Some mortgage or mortgage-like loans such as subprime, home-equity or manufactured housing also exhibited the same low exposure to interest rates and were typically marketed as **mortgage ABS** from the mid 1990s. This apparent oxymoron, if "assets" are supposed to be distinct from "mortgages", was a simple marketing label. Since the 2008 mortgage crisis and subsequent RMBS and ABS market implosion, all mortgage related products, whether initially considered ABS or RMBS, have tended to be handled by the same trading desks.

Note that CDOs are often included as part of ABS in various statistics and reporting, so while they are structurally different and normally traded by different desks, they will often be lumped together.

One particular product based on agency passthroughs deserves to be discussed in more detail, as it is one of the most liquid markets in the world. To-beannounced (**TBA**) contracts are forward agreements to buy a certain amount of agency passthroughs with specific characteristics: agency, maturity, coupon, and delivery month. For example: $100 mm FNMA 30-year 4% for next month delivery. The seller then just needs to find approximately $100 mm of face value of Fannie Mae 4% net coupon 30-yrs before a delivery date next month. One can buy and sell these TBAs before the contract term without ever having to hold the actual pools. Liquidity is also facilitated because all the pools are made fungible through TBAs. There is a worst-to-deliver issue at play, where each market participant will strive to deliver, within the parameters, the pools with the lowest value. Because the worst pools are supposed to be delivered as TBAs, one can define better pools in contrast with the TBA market: this constitutes the **specified pools** market, precisely because by nature they have to be precisely identified, unlike the TBAs (which do not point to a particular pool). Note that most of these specified pools could technically be delivered as TBAs, but investors typically choose not to, because they are more valuable.

### 2.2.2 Identification of Securitized Products

An important concept in securitization is the notion of an issuance **shelf**. In general securities issuance, the SEC allows a so-called shelf registration whereby some issuer obtains a registration allowing it to issue several **series** of securities without requiring a new registration each time. The shelf acts as a template, off of which the subsequent series are issued. For corporate debt, an issuer might have registered documents that justify its standing, that is a shelf registration, and may issue several series of bonds (with different maturities, for example) on that shelf. When identifying a security, such as a bond, one can hence use its shelf and series to define it.

In the case of securitization, the equivalent process of shelf registration exists but is more complex. An issuer may register a shelf as a form of legal template that a sequence of securitization deals will follow, but every series in that sequence will substantially differ from the next one since the actual assets will not be the same, and the structure may not be exactly the same. In effect, a securitization shelf tends to specify a certain type of product (such as prime mortgages, auto loans, or credit cards for example), but every deal will be a clearly distinct entity from the others. The series are often grouped by years of issuance.

A shelf and a series identification hence specify a particular securitization deal. This SPV issues bonds, the tranches, which are identified by an acronym usually, but not always, cognate with their degree of credit enhancement and extension over time.[6] Combining shelf, series and tranche one fully defines a particular bond (but only on a particular information system: different data or information providers such as Bloomberg, Intex or Moodys may use different denominations or acronyms for the same shelf and series).

[6] More specifically, their average life.

For example on Bloomberg, the deal identified as "RAMP 2006-RS6" was issued on the RAMP shelf, with the series 2006-RS6. The bond "RAMP 2006-RS6 A2" was the securities A2 issued by this deal. The shelf RAMP was created by RFC (the now defunct Residential Funding Corp.) in order to issue so-called scratch-and-dent mortgage loans, that is loans which were almost of almost prime quality with some blemishes. Within the parameters of that shelf, the RS program (as opposed to RZ, for example) concentrated first-lien loans with a high loan-to-value ratio. The series of the tranche expresses a year, normally the issuance year of the deal, usually called the **vintage**. The tranche identification A2 normally signals an initially AAA-rated bond (as opposed to, say, bond B2), which may or may not have a longer average life than A1. Each fixed-income product has a unique identification character string, the CUSIP, but it is useless for an intuitive identification: this identification for "RAMP 2006-RS6 A2" is "7516QAB2".

In this example, the deal denomination conveys some information about the quality of the assets, and the tranche denomination some information about its structure, but that need not be the case. Many shelves combine securitizations of all sorts of assets, with series that do not distinguish issuance year or program type, and many bond denominations are simply arbitrary.

Even in the case, as with our example, where a security's identification conveys some information, one can only get a vague impression of the characteristics of the bond, a situation that markedly differs from typical corporate debt. Specifically, the identification of a securitized bond conveys absolutely no information on its expected cash flows. On the other hand, a corporate bond identification only requires an issuer, a coupon, and a maturity. For a standard bond, this is enough to determine its cash flows. In fact, given a handful of market prices for several bonds issued by the same corporation, one could build a yield curve and derived a reasonable valuation, albeit not exact, for another bond with comparable coupon and maturity characteristics. This type of exercise is absolutely impossible with securitized products: one would need to gather information on all the underlying assets, on the structures, build models and make assumptions in order to derive some kind of reasonable valuation.

The detailed description of what the assets are and how the structure functions is found in the prospectus supplement, a legal document related to the registration of the deal with the SEC. Figure 2.2 shows an excerpt from a subprime securitization listing the bonds in the deal and some of the language detailing the structure. The only way of analyzing a securitized bond involves parsing through such a document and, from the legal description of the structure (which will be applied by the trustee when carrying out payments), programming the structure's behavior. This is then combined with some representation of the collateral, either based on that same document, or on details on the assets provided in electronic format.

For agency MBS, identification follows a different logic. For particular pools, of which there are millions, one has to use an identification number akin to the CUSIP mentioned above. TBAs on the contrary are naturally much easier to identify since they are only defined by a few characteristics.

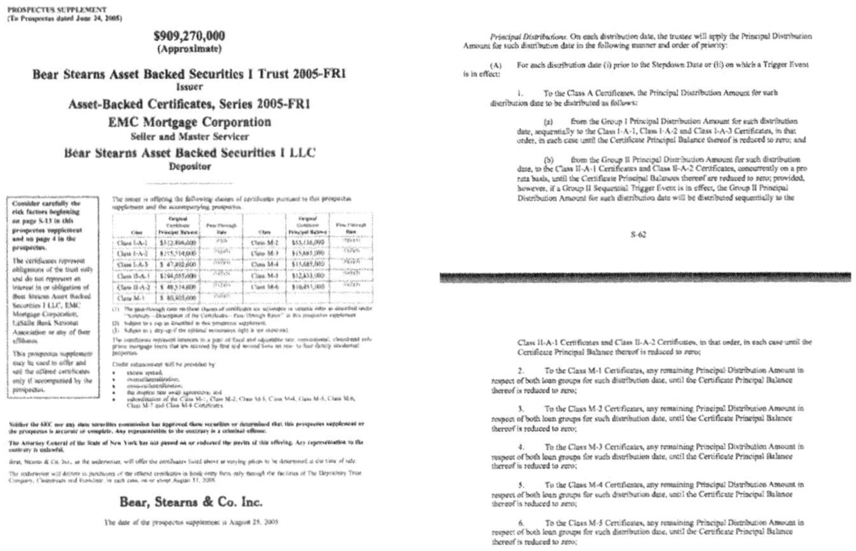

PROSPECTUS SUPPLEMENT
(To Prospectus dated June 24, 2005)

$909,270,000
(Approximate)

Bear Stearns Asset Backed Securities I Trust 2005-FR1
Issuer

Asset-Backed Certificates, Series 2005-FR1

EMC Mortgage Corporation
Seller and Master Servicer

Bear Stearns Asset Backed Securities I LLC
Depositor

Bear, Stearns & Co. Inc.

**Fig. 2.2** Subprime deal BSABS 2005-FR1. *Source* SEC Edgar

## 2.2.3 Ratings and Rating Agencies

The credit rating agencies or **CRA** are specialized entities that provide opinions on a debtor's ability to pay back debt (by making timely principal and interest payments) and on the likelihood of its default. These agencies rate the creditworthiness of issuers of debt obligations, or of debt instruments, and hence cover a large range of issuers and instruments. In particular, they give ratings on the bonds issued by securitization deals. Almost all ratings are produced by the three agencies, Standard and Poor's, Moody's and Fitch. In the US, the rating agencies are known as Nationally Recognized Statistical Rating Organizations, or NRSRO.

When an investment bank arranges a securitization, it obtains ratings for some or all of the bonds issued by the deal from one or several rating agencies, and pays them a fee. For structured finance, providing a rating requires a detailed analysis of the collateral and structure of the tranches in a deal, which represents a substantial amount of work. We will address the issues raised by ratings and so-called rating-shopping in Chap. 8.

While the rating scale of S&P and Fitch use the same acronyms, those of Moody's are different, as shown in Table 2.1. In addition, within each scale variations are noted with a "+" or "−" for S&P and Fitch, and with a number (1, 2, or 3) for Moody's: for example AA− maps to Aa3, and BB+ to Ba1. A simplified mapping of expected default risk as a function of rating level can be found in ("Commission Implementing Regulation (EU) 2016/1799 of 7 October 2016" 2016). AAA and AA ratings correspond to a 0.1% risk of default, single-A to 0.25%, BBB to 1%, BB to 7.5% and single-B to 20%.

**Table 2.1** Rating scales. *Source* compiled by the author

| Moodys scale | S and P scale |
|---|---|
| Aaa | AAA |
| Aa | AA |
| A | A |
| Baa | BBB |
| Ba | BB |
| B | B |

Note that if a debt instrument is sure to suffer a principal loss, even small relative to its overall size, as would be the case with a large portfolio of loans, then it cannot be rated. This is why in structures there is always a so-called unrated piece, while other bonds, which receive a rating, can obtain this rating because (in spite of having a degree of credit risk) they are in principle not very likely to suffer a loss.

It is particularly difficult to associate ratings to measures of risks for a variety of reasons. First, one might measure simply the risk of losing a single dollar, or the expected magnitude of loss, with different results. Second, ratings are supposedly forward-looking and hence can only be based on scenario analysis, themselves relying on countless assumptions. Changing these assumptions naturally leads to differing measures of risk. Looking at past data may provide some insights but, by nature, it is not forward looking.

### 2.2.4 Broad Types of Structured Bonds

Although we will walk through structuring in much detail in Chap. 6, it is helpful to get a first impression of the different types of bonds that are issued through a securitization deal. We have already mentioned the simplest kind, passthroughs, which simply pass the cash flows through unaffected.

The main structuring dimensions are as follows:

- **Senior/subordinated bonds** allocate losses following a particular order. Subordinated bonds receive losses before the senior bonds and hence are more at risk from a credit standpoint. Usually, the senior bonds have an "A" in their denomination; subordinated bonds have a "B" and mezzanine bonds, which stand between the two, are called "M".
- **Sequentials** are bonds structured so that they receive their principal in a certain order. A front sequential receives principal payment first. A back sequential receives principal payments last. This technique can be combined with senior/subordination in order to create junior back sequentials or senior front sequentials, for example.
- **PACs/Supports** are structures designed to dampen the impact from variations in principal repayment speed. PACs (planned amortization classes) aim to follow a

pre-determined principal amortization while supports absorb the difference with actual collateral repayments, up to a degree. These structures are common on MBS but much more rare on ABS or CDO.

- **Excess-spread and over-collateralization** can be used to create tranches akin to equity, which act as credit protection for all the other tranches and also use some interest rate cash flows in order to cover losses. These structures are very common on ABS and on CDO.
- **IOs and POs** (interest-only and principal-only) bonds can be created, and hence can help increase or decrease the coupon paid by other bonds in the structure to investors. They are common across all products.

Another manner in which bonds are usually categorized is in terms of their average life. For example one might have 2-year or 5-year sequentials, or 10-year PACs.

One enormously important distinction exists in structured bonds regarding the notion of how "long" the bonds are, and passes unnoticed in many academic papers: **average life** is not the same thing as (legal) **maturity**, and only the former really means anything in securitized products.

The legal maturity of a bond refers to the point in time when a bond will make its last principal payment. On a 30-year mortgage, for example, that would be 30 years. Hence, a 30-year mortgage has a legal maturity twice as long as a 15-year mortgage.

However many types of assets repay some principal over time, and are not supposed to repay it all at the end. In addition, when bonds are collateralized by pool of assets, nobody knows in advance if and when these assets will prepay or default over time, but some reasonable assumptions can be made about their propensity to return principal earlier than their schedules. As a result, the expected principal cash flows will be mostly paid much earlier than the legal majority, in the majority of cases. This is true even if some residual small cash flows are trailing for many years until the legal maturity. The average life of a bond computes, under some standardized collateral principal payment assumption, the time it takes to receive half of the initial balance. In the case of a simple debt that pays all its principal in one time at the end, it coincides with maturity.

From the perspective of valuation, risks, or any economic aspect related to a securitized bond's cash flows, the average life captures "how long the bond is". The legal maturity does not convey any economic meaning. For example, 15-year MBS with a 2.5% coupon would typically be considered to be much longer than 30-year MBS with a 5.5% coupon,[7] notwithstanding their legal maturities that would seem to imply the contrary. Empirical academic papers sometimes use legal maturity as a categorization input for securitized bonds instead of average life, which would be the appropriate method.

[7]Because the borrowers paying 2.5% would have little incentive to obtain new loans, and there would prepay slowly, while the borrowers paying 5.5% would have a greater incentive and would prepay fast, leading to a much shorter average life.

One additional concept for "how long a bond is" is **duration**,[8] which depends on interest cash flows and price in addition to principal cash flows. Duration depends on more inputs and assumptions than average life, which is why it is typically not used to categorize structured bonds. Duration does convey information about the bonds' interest rate sensitivity. For simplicity within our framework, and in accordance with market practical logic, we will interchangeably use duration and average life when dealing with bonds that do not use complex interest cash flow structuring.

All the distinctions above between products are made purely on the basis of structures. Within the private-label MBS market, there are important distinctions made in terms of the underlying type of loan:

- **Jumbo**[9] or jumbo prime RMBS are collateralized by so-called jumbo loans, residential loans of prime credit quality that do not satisfy the requirements for agency wraps, because of the loans' initial balance;
- **Alt-A** or alternative-A RMBS are backed by loans with a slightly worse credit quality than typical agency loans, which could be securitized as agency loans but for which a private-label securitization was more cost efficient;
- **Subprime** RMBS (also sometimes classified as ABS) pool loans with a substantially worse credit quality than typical agency loans.

These various categorizations can be combined, and one may talk of a "subprime 5-year sequential", or a "jumbo 2-year PAC", or an "Alt-A passthrough".

## 2.3 Securitized Bonds Markets

Since securitization entails issuing securities in the market, an activity that is highly regulated and tightly tracked, there are large volumes of data available on the issuance, outstanding amounts and trading of these securities. Up-to-date information on the market and on securitized products issuance can be found in SIFMA (2018) for the US, and in AFME (2018) for Europe. Securitization exists across the globe, from South America to Japan, but volumes are highly concentrated in the US and in Europe. As such we preferentially focus on the latter two.

We first examine total debt issuance in the US markets, then focus on securitized products more specifically, and finally briefly compare the US and European markets.

[8]See Tuckman and Serrat (2012) for example.

[9]They are also sometimes called whole-loans, which in fact simply refers to loans being traded unsecuritized. In the late 1980s and early 1990s, jumbos were the only non-agency market, so loans traded to be later securitized essentially consisted of jumbos.

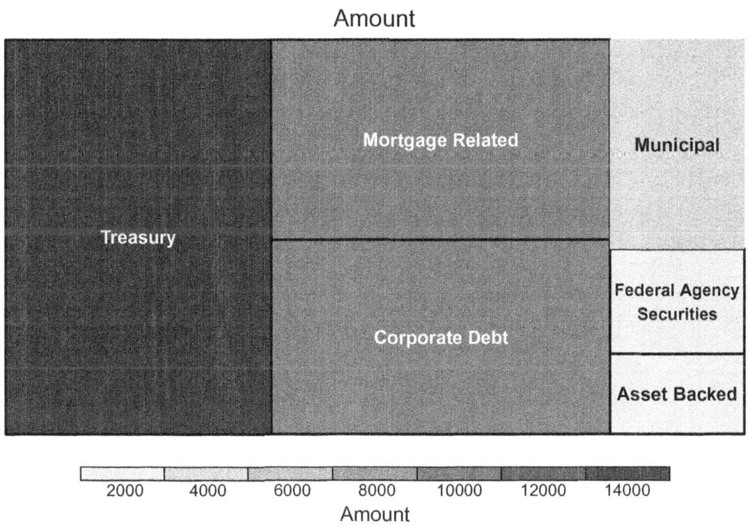


**Fig. 2.3** US bond market outstanding amounts ($bb), 2017. *Source* SIFMA statistics and author's own calculations

### 2.3.1 US Overall Debt Market Size

Figure 2.3 plots the outstanding amounts in the US bond market, according to the Securities Industry and Financial Markets Association. We can see that while Treasurys constitute the largest market, mortgage-related securitized paper weighs as much as all corporate debt. Asset-backed securities (which include CDOs) are markedly smaller. Note that the debt from the federal agencies (essentially Fannie Mae and Freddie Mac) serves to fund the purchase, by these agencies, of mortgage securities.

Looking at issuance instead of outstanding in Fig. 2.4, MBS and ABS appear even relatively larger, due to their typically faster rate of principal repayment than Treasury or corporate debt in aggregate. If we considered two sectors with the same outstanding amount, constant over time, a sector where principal repayment is faster would require larger issuance just to stay at that same constant outstanding amount. Being issued in large volumes, securitized products command a large market presence, and they are closely tracked by all large institutional investors.

### 2.3.2 US Securitized Debt Markets

Figure 2.5 plots the issuance breakdown of securitized products. Agency MBS represent the bulk of issuance, closely followed by agency CMOs. The issuance volume of CDOs is quite significant, but these are mostly composed of CLOs; the issuance of SFCDOs ground to a halt after the 2008 crisis.

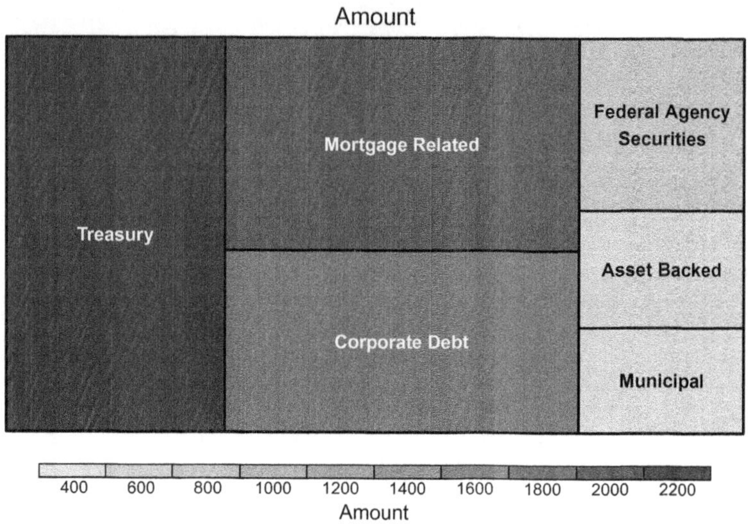


**Fig. 2.4** US bond market issuance ($bb), 2017. *Source* SIFMA statistics and author's own calculations

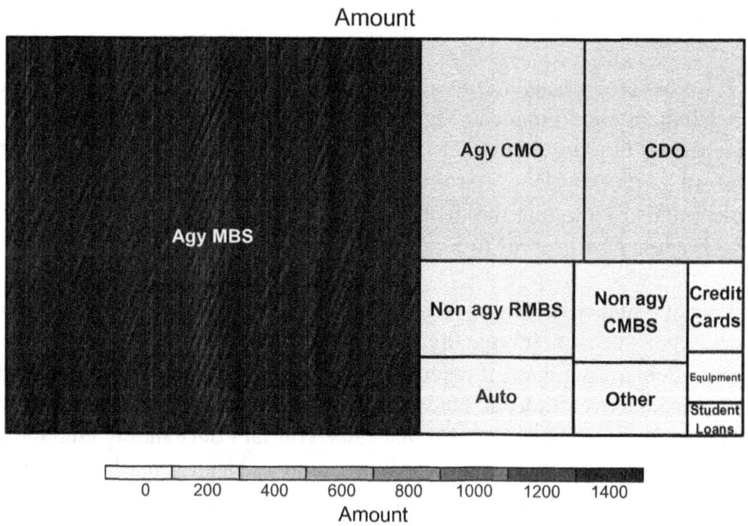


**Fig. 2.5** US securitized markets issuance amounts ($bb), 2017. *Source* SIFMA statistics and author's own calculations

Although they may look small on the chart, equipment lease ABS, Auto ABS, student loan ABS and credit card ABS all represent tens of billions of dollars in issuance.

The agency passthroughs that represent roughly half of all securitized products issuance benefit from the market's ability to trade most of them as TBAs. Being easily identifiable and fungible to a large degree, these products are traded in large volumes: issuers can easily bring them to market at a precisely determined price, and investors know they can rapidly acquire or sell significant amounts.

### 2.3.3 Evolution of US and European Securitized Debt Markets

The US securitized products market seems to dwarf the European market, as illustrated in Fig. 2.6, but this is mostly due to the size of the US MBS market, itself largely composed of Agency MBS.

The **GSEs** or Government-Sponsored Enterprises are mandated, and supported by the US Government, to not only wrap but also buy large amounts of MBS. By doing so they presumably help support a large and liquid mortgage market, and in turn the housing market. As there is no comparable guarantee mechanism in Europe, the European market is only composed of bonds using various structuring techniques to alleviate credit risk.

A more balanced comparison between the European and US markets can be made if we only consider private-label products without agency guarantee in the US.

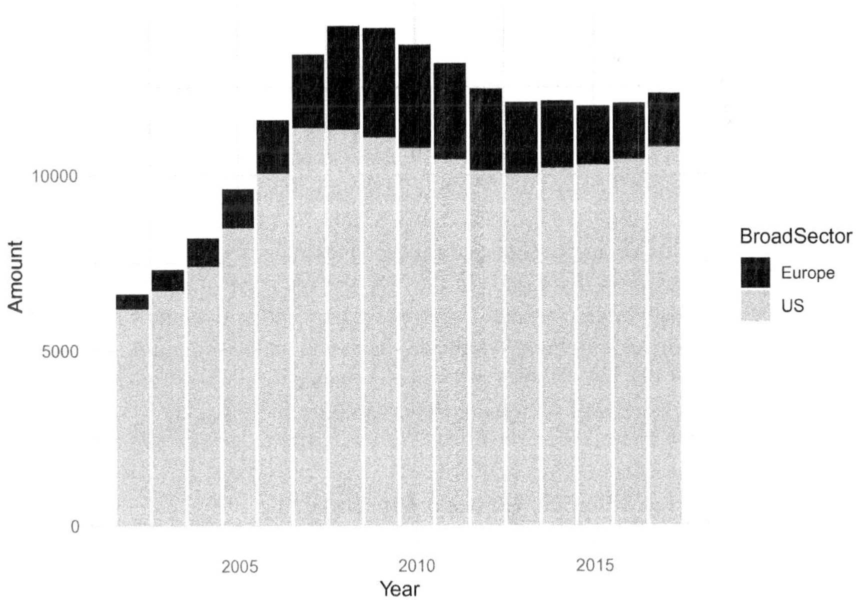


**Fig. 2.6** US and European securitized markets outstanding amounts ($bb). *Source* SIFMA statistics and author's own calculations

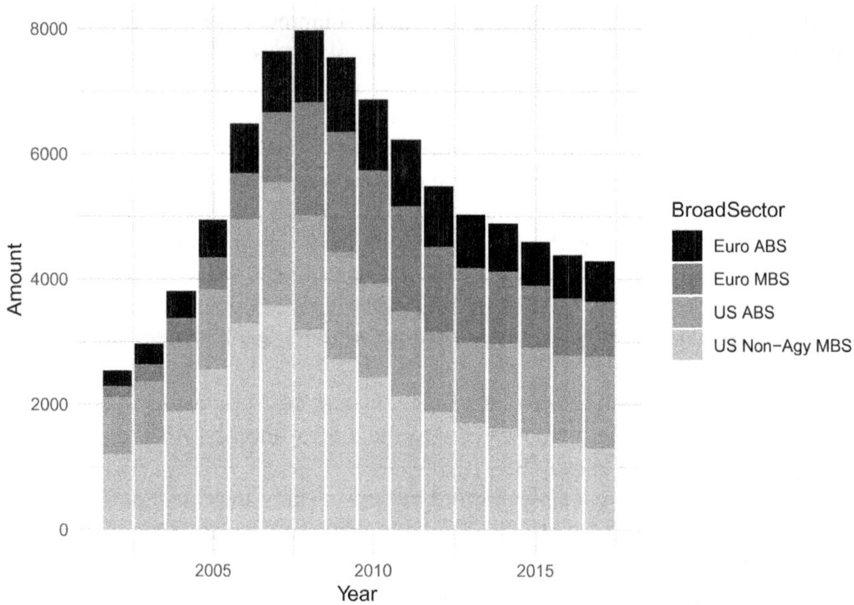


**Fig. 2.7** US and European private-label securitized outstanding history and regression ($bb). *Source* SIFMA statistics and author's own calculations

Figure 2.7 excludes agency securities, and distinguishes MBS and ABS. It appears that, while the US market remains larger than the European market, the difference is much less pronounced when we only consider products that are exposed to credit risk and rely on structuring for credit protection. In addition, in both cases we observe that MBS are larger than ABS. Mortgages, even without considering agencies, tend to be the most important market across the globe simply because that collateral is widely available and has a reputation of being well understood by lending institutions.

Considering the evolution of these markets through time, the run up in outstanding volume through the mid 2000s first in the US and then in Europe with a lag was essentially due to mortgage-backed securities. Since then, the amount of MBS has declined on both sides of the pond. In the US, the issuance of private-label MBS stopped in previously large markets such as subprime, and with no new issuance the high runoff rate due to defaults has depleted the assets on the remaining deals. Still, even these markets that have not seen any new issuance to speak of for over 10 years still account for hundreds of billions of dollars in outstanding debt.

## 2.4 Securitized Bonds Trading Mechanics

Securitized products, in spite of their complexity and checkered history, still represent roughly a third of all fixed-income issuance in the US, so it seems natural to wonder how these markets operate and how they trade. As we touched upon earlier, these bonds are more difficult to identify and to rapidly understand than plain vanilla corporate bonds, so we would anticipate the market mechanics to be somewhat influenced by these complications.

Most securitized bonds indeed trade **over-the-counter** or **OTC**, with no continuous public pricing. We can distinguish between **new issue** bonds, and **secondary trading**. Trivially speaking, new issue bond trading is akin to buying a new car, while secondary trading would be buying a used car.

When purchasing a new car, the buyers can specify some features they might like. In the same way in securitized bond markets, structurers discuss with investors the features they would need and reflect them in the design of the deal. New issue bonds are valued using two particular mechanisms. First, **Reverse inquiry**, when a single dealer is issuing the deal. The trading desk is in direct contact with customers and optimally structures the bonds according to their wishes and willingness to buy. Second, **Syndication**, when several dealers are working together on a deal, the structures are set by the lead manager reflecting the client requirements that are channeled back to them, and pricing is set so that the bonds clear the market.

In secondary trading, there are typically two sorts of ways in which bonds are traded. First, **bid lists**: clients give dealers list of bonds they would like to sell, and the dealers circulate these lists to their clients. The clients bid and the highest bidder gets the bonds. Second, **inventory**: dealers acquire positions for their own account, and offer out the bonds in their inventory at some clearly specified price.

Some bonds benefit from more organized markets, with continuous pricing. The more fungible or easy to value the product, the more liquid the market. Agency Passthroughs trade through bid lists, inventories and also pricing matrices. Agency Trust IOs/POs trade on screen, on bid lists and inventories. Finally, Agency TBAs trade on screen, like most stocks.

In the following subsections, we discuss the way in which securitized bonds are traded through these different channels, starting from the most liquid to the least liquid. A few examples also provide an opportunity to exercise one's product categorization recognition skills.

### 2.4.1 Securitized Products Trading on Screens

By far the most liquid market among securitized products, with trading volumes in the hundreds of billions of dollars a day according to SIFMA (2018), TBAs are said to trade "on screens". At every instant, broker/dealers and large institutional customers transmit bids and asks to an organized market platform, and transactions take place. Since there is a finite and low number of different TBAs (round coupons, a handful of maturities, etc) everyone of them can be tracked and market participants can provide markets for all of them.

As a result, the prices at which TBAs are traded constitute a continuous time series, as shown in Fig. 2.8, comparable to what can be observed with most stocks on an exchange or on-the-run Treasurys.

Certain products like IOs and POs created off of large pools of agency MBS, called **trust IOs and POs**, while being more structurally complex than passthroughs, trade

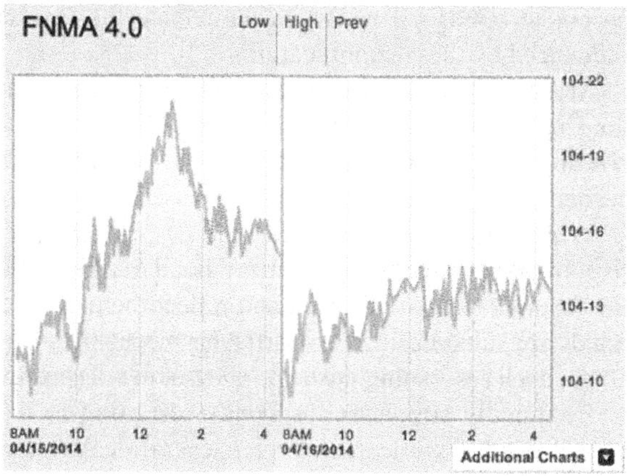


**Fig. 2.8** Agency TBA continuous pricing. *Source* mortgage news daily

with comparable mechanics. There are few of these products, so that the trading volume can be concentrated in these few and they can easily be tracked.

### 2.4.2 Offers and Inventory

The organized market platforms that show continuous TBA pricing reflect instantaneous bids and asks from the dealer and institutional investor community. Dealers and investors are also willing to bid and offer the specified pools that may underlie these TBAs, but there are so many of these pools that it has historically been deemed more efficient for market makers to simply distribute their **inventory**, that is the various positions they offer for sale, to their customers.

There are several ways in which market prices can be communicated by trading desks. On the more liquid products, in particular agency passthroughs, valuations are expressed relative to the corresponding TBAs in a so-called **pricing matrix**. We know the TBAs are liquid and their prices change all the time, so dealers value the specified pools they offer at a **pay-up** relative to TBAs. Figure 2.9 shows a screenshot from such a matrix. We can see, for example, that 30-year 4.5%-coupon MBS pools consisting of low loan balances (LLB) commanded a 38 ticks[10] pay-up over 4.5% TBAs, while 3%-coupon LLBs only commanded a pay-up of 6 ticks over 3% TBAs. For pools that can be delivered as TBAs, there cannot be a negative or zero pay-up, since in this case the pool would be simply sold as a TBA. The negative pay-ups in the chart apply to certain pool types that are precisely not deliverable as TBAs.

This pricing matrix would not constitute a binding offer; such an offer would consist of a list of pool identifications, characteristics and the offer pay-up. Matrices such as this one provide valuable information on market valuations, with which all the offers are normally assumed to be strongly consistent.

[10] 1 tick = 1/32 of a point.

| | LLB | MLB | HLB | INVST | NEW | 80-90 | 90-95 | 95-100 | 100-105 | CQ | CR | 10/20yr |
|---|---|---|---|---|---|---|---|---|---|---|---|---|
| FN3.0 | 6 | 4 | 2 | 0 | 0 | 0 | + | + | 1 | -10 | -28 | 97 |
| FN3.5 | 8 | 5 | 3+ | 1 | + | + | + | + | 1 | -13 | -31 | 67 |
| FN4.0 | 16 | 13 | 8 | + | + | + | 1 | 1+ | 2 | -8 | -22 | 45 |
| FN4.5 | 38 | 33 | 24 | 15 | 5 | 4 | 12 | 15 | 20 | 23 | 4 | 31 |
| | | | | | | | | | | | | |
| DW2.5 | 1+ | 1 | + | 0 | 0 | 0 | 0 | 0 | 0 | -16 | -28 | 70 |
| DW3.0 | 3+ | 2+ | 1 | 0 | + | 0 | 0 | + | 1 | -21 | -29 | 36 |
| DW3.5 | 7 | 4 | 2+ | + | + | + | + | 1 | 1+ | -18 | -23 | 12 |

**Fig. 2.9** Pricing matrix for agency PTs. *Source* dealer message

Front PAC

| WAL | Orig | Bond | Price | Spread | Speed | Desc |
|---|---|---|---|---|---|---|
| 4.67 | 74.00 | FNR 13-77 HP | 102-295 | 80 | 188PSA | 3.00 cpn 11 wala Jumbo 3s |
| 5.15 | 139.30 | FHR 4303 PA | 102-174 | 78 | 299PSA | 3.00 cpn 36 wala 5s |
| 6.12 | 50.00 | FNR 13-77 P | 101-021 | 85 | 185PSA | 3.00 cpn 11 wala Jumbo 3s |

Front SEQ/BPAC 30yr Collat

| WAL | Orig | Bond | Price | Spread | Speed | Desc |
|---|---|---|---|---|---|---|
| 1.70 | 4.70 | FHR 4109 KD | 103-076 | 70 | 410PSA | 3.00 cpn 47 wala Jumbo 4s |
| 2.00 | 95.00 | FNR 11-103 PB | 104-136 | 77 | 15CPR | 3.50 cpn 31 wala Jumbo 4s |
| 2.07 | 46.22 | FNR 12-65 JA | 103-154 | 125 | 628PSA | 3.50 cpn 47 wala Jumbo 5s |
| 3.60 | 1.28 | FNR 12-69 PL | 102-036 | 125 | 254PSA | 3.00 cpn 34 wala 4.5s |
| 3.68 | 8.00 | FHR 3312 PA | 111-143 | 100 | 359PSA | 5.50 cpn 87 wala HLB 6s |
| 4.60 | 160.73 | FNR 14-7 AG | 102-155 | 92 | 147PSA | 3.00 cpn 13 wala 3.5s |
| 4.60 | 199.24 | FNR 14-7 AJ | 104-214 | 90 | 147PSA | 3.50 cpn 13 wala 3.5s |

**Fig. 2.10** Agency CMO offers. *Source* dealer message

An example of an actual inventory offer is in Fig. 2.10 for agency CMOs. We can see "front" PACs (that is PACs that are currently paying principal), and sequentials, along with some of the bonds' characteristics. In particular, the identification shows that from a name like "FNR 13–77 HP", one could infer this is an agency CMO issued by Fannie Mae in 2013, but nothing more without further details. The prices[11] are the price at which this dealer is willing to sell the bonds. Normally the more invariant valuation metric in this offer is expected to be the spread: if markets move somewhat, the spread to swaps or to Treasurys would be expected to remain constant, while the price changes.

Dealers may sometimes provide both an offer and a bid, in a so-called "market". Figure 2.11 shows such markets on non-agency CMOs, all of them subprime MBS. The dealer states they are willing to buy a certain amount of a particular bond at a certain price, and willing to sell a certain amount at a certain price. Although the bottom four bonds are presumably AAA-rated bonds at issuance, because of the tranche names, the top one was a mezzanine bond (it shows, being offered under 30 cents on the dollar).

[11]Expressed here in points, ticks, and eighths: HHH-TTE means HHH + TT/32 + E/32/8.

**Updated Markets:**
BSABS 2005-FR1 M2 28-00/29-00 14+mm x 14+mm
SASC 2006-BC2 A3 51-16/53-16 35+mm x 35+mm
MSAC 2006-HE7 A2B 86-00/87-08 25+mm x 25+mm *New*
CMLTI 2006-NC1 A2B 82-00/84-00 18+mm x 18+mm *New*
SABR 2007-BR5 A2A 67-00/68-00 10mm x 620m *New*

**Fig. 2.11** Non-agency offers/market. *Source* dealer message

Given what we already know of the potential complexity of these structures, and the need to understand the collateral's behavior in order to properly analyze them, producing markets for five bonds represents a certain amount of work, and of risk as well. In spite of the two-point bid/ask spread on most of these in this example, a mistake in the analysis may well account for much more than that, and could be seen and exploited by other market participants. As a result, it is to be expected that there is no systematic market for the hundreds of thousands of unique bonds in the securitized markets. Participants rationally only invest effort in the analysis of the bonds they own, or that they are offered.

### 2.4.3 Bid Lists

Although the dealer offers we have examined above may seem coarse to those used to electronic markets, they have the strong advantage of providing a price. It may not be the case that the bonds trade at the offered price (just like used cars), but the offered price at least constituted a starting point for negotiations, known by both parties, and which both parties know many other parties know.

However, most of the trading in securitized products takes place through bid lists, also called **BWICs** for "bid wanted in competition", where there is very little to no price information. The clients of each dealer, when they are so inclined, send to the dealers lists of structured bonds they would like to sell. Dealers receive a large number of such lists, compile them and send them to all their clients. Then, among all these clients, the ones who may be interested submit bids to the dealers. Each one of the dealers, for each bond, sends the highest bid and the second highest back to the seller. The seller then gathers, for each bond, the highest bids from all the dealers to whom it had communicated the positions for sale; if the highest bid of all is above the seller's (unknown) reserve price, then the trade is done.

After that process, the seller communicates to all the participating dealers the second highest bid it saw for each bond that traded, and the dealers communicate it to their clients. This second-highest bid is the **cover**. Hence, if a bond does not trade (because the reserve price was too high), no cover is communicated back to investors. And if a bond trades, only the cover becomes public. The dealers however get to see the prices that investors they were in contact with bid for all the bonds.

Figure 2.12 shows a typical bid list in the non-agency CMO market, specifically on Alternative-A bonds, while bids are being gathered. There is an additional piece

| ORIGINAL | CURRENT | DESCRIPTION | CUSIP | PRICE TALK |
|---|---|---|---|---|
| 41,143,000 | 26,531,113 | AHM 2007-A 13A1 | 026931AC9 | M60S |
| 23,935,000 | 3,128,771 | BAFC 2005-A 5A2 | 05946XQZ9 | |
| 19,148,000 | 4,364,331 | BAFC 2007-1 TA1A | 05951FAA2 | |
| 19,148,000 | 19,148,000 | BAFC 2007-3 TA2 | 059515AC0 | H40S |
| 4,308,000 | 2,671,062 | BAFC 2007-8 2A1 | 05953LAD1 | |
| 35,508,000 | 35,508,000 | BOAA 2006-7 A4 | 059469AD8 | LM60S |
| 5,098,670 | 4,091,222 | CMLTI 2007-9 2A2 | 17313NAP0 | |
| 5,505,000 | 4,781,212 | CWALT 2007-J1 2A5 | 02149MAT6 | |
| 2,915,000 | 2,915,000 | FHAMS 2007-FA3 A4 | 32053GAD5 | |
| 25,938,540 | 10,523,275 | GSAA 2007-5 1AV1 | 3622ECAA4 | |
| 66,913,000 | 55,959,869 | INDX 2007-AR13 4A1 | 456681AE5 | LM 50S |
| 4,577,000 | 5,785,905 | MALT 2006-2 1A3 | 5764342E3 | |
| 23,556,000 | 23,556,000 | NAA 2006-AF1 1A2 | 65536PAC4 | LM50S |
| 4,308,000 | 4,308,000 | NCAMT 2006-ALT1 AF5 | 643528AE2 | |
| 6,429,000 | 6,221,834 | NCAMT 2006-ALT2 AF6A | 643529AF7 | |
| 23,935,000 | 19,776,885 | RAST 2007-A3 1A1 | 76113WAA1 | L40S |
| 26,438,000 | 17,540,347 | WFALT 2007-PA2 3A1 | 94985FAL2 | H30S |
| 4,000,000 | 4,000,000 | LXS 2007-12N 1A3A | 52524YAC7 | |

**Fig. 2.12** Non-agency bid list. *Source* dealer message

of information, not always present, the **price talk**. This is non binding information freely provided by the dealer: an estimate of where the bonds should trade, and cannot be precise (here, "mid 60s", "high 40s", "low to mid 60s" etc).

The lengths to which these market mechanics go in order to effectively protect and keep one's information on the value of the bonds correlate with the amount of effort required in order to obtain it, as well as with the risks entailed when it is wrong. In order to understand in more detail why it represents such an effort to properly evaluate these bonds, we turn to the analysis of securitized products, with a very basic overview.

## 2.5 Basics of Securitized Bonds Analysis and Valuations

In this section we present the basic intuitions behind various approaches to the valuation of securitized bonds, still at light speed. Analysis of securitized products, in particular mortgage-backed securities, is an entire field in itself, a specific part of mathematical finance and fixed-income modeling. There are many references on the subject, but some good starting points, ordered by their degree of focus on securitized products include:

- Tuckman and Serrat (2012), where securitized products are just a part of fixed-income products in general;
- Fabozzi (2016), focused on mortgage-backed securities and, although it is somewhat outdated, Fabozzi (2001) covering asset-backed securities, laying out practitioners' methods for the pricing of these bonds;
- Davidson and Levin (2014), which introduces advanced methods of valuation and synthesizes recent academic research and practitioners methods very well.

In the present work, our focus is not on valuing these structured products, but on explaining their existence and their features; nevertheless some intuition of the drivers of their value are necessary to form a proper understanding of these markets.

We first discuss what could be termed as the simplest and most traditional approach, using yields or spreads for valuation. Then we turn to the concepts of negative convexity and convexity costs, mostly applicable to mortgage-backed securities.

### 2.5.1 Simplified Approach: Yield/Spread Analysis

One first thing to note is that bonds that are considered by the market to bear very little credit risk and to have no particular interest rate risk will normally only trade as a function of their liquidity. These types of securities, like senior equipment lease bonds, or short senior subprime bonds before the mortgage crisis, tend to trade at fairly constant spreads to some reference curve. The stress scenarios that market participants apply to these bonds have little effect on them, and being hence considered insensitive to these risks, their valuations do not reflect changes in the underlying economic drivers.

The bonds that do exhibit a greater degree of exposure to risks such as credit risk, and which we will define later in Chap. 4 to be **informationally sensitive** bonds, require a thorough modeling of their collateral and structures. Market practitioners generally use the following logic to evaluate these bonds:

- Each underlying asset is modeled based on the available information. The term of "modeling" here is understood as any quantitative methodology that can relate future collateral cash flows to certain underlying economic metrics. This could be credit card defaults as a function of unemployment, mortgage delinquencies as a function of house prices, or loan prepayments as a function of interest rates.
- Collateral behavior is projected for various scenarios. These scenarios can represent variations in the underlying economic drivers or variations in the collateral behavior itself. For example, one may look at what happens if home prices declined by 10%, or one may look at what happens if defaults are 10% greater than initially anticipated.
- The bonds' yield or spread under these various scenarios give an indication in terms of safety thresholds to the investors. Given the nature of the most common structures, most bonds will tend to exhibit a binary behavior: up to a certain threshold, variations in stresses have little effect, while beyond the threshold, the bonds' cash flows are significantly affected.
- The scenarios are adapted to the degree of risk on the bond. A bond with a good degree of credit protection will be stressed more than one with less protection. The required yield or spread will also tend to be higher on bonds that have more credit exposure.

This raises a consistency issue: two bonds backed by the same collateral may be valued using different scenarios for that same collateral. It is hence not possible to really evaluate a bond that has a binary behavior with this approach, if one wants a degree of consistency between these valuations. Some methods have been developed to circumvent this consistency issue, see for example Levin and Davidson (2008) or Gauthier (2003) for an earlier but simpler approach. Nevertheless, the market practice is consistent enough "locally", when looking at bonds the risk of which is not substantially different, or when particularly leveraged structures are excluded.

When a structuring desk designs a new bond, they hence tend to work with a base-case scenario, maybe combined with some basic stresses, and typically do not resort to running large numbers of scenarios. To some extent, this design approach that only envisions few future outcomes affects the way securitized bonds are created. In our discussion of structuring in Chap. 6, we will consider both structural behavior in a controlled scenario as well as behavior across large sets of potential outcomes.

### 2.5.2 Negative Convexity and Convexity Costs in MBS

The notion of negative convexity is central in the valuation of many securitized products: all those whose cash flows are affected by interest rates. It is mostly prevalent in mortgages, where refinancing incentives are mostly driven by interest rates. Negative convexity is the materialization of the negative impact of the borrower's potential exercise of their prepayment option.

Although we will delve more closely into prepayment behavior in Chap. 3, it helps to have a basic understanding at this stage. A typical loan, in particular a mortgage, requires the borrower to make payments over time, at least covering interest and sometimes some part of principal. If, all else being equal (amount and maturity among other things), the borrower had the opportunity to get a new loan with a lower rate, it would allow them to fully repay the existing loan, and instead make lower payments on the new loan going forward. Hence, one expects that when people with a higher rate loan outstanding have access to a lower rate loan, they will want to refinance. The notion of "there are loans with lower rates offered in the market" is simply captured by the difference between the rate that people are paying on their loan, and the rates observed in the market for new loans.

Reciprocally, when rates are higher, then people that might have decided to refinance otherwise (if rates had stayed the same) will be less likely to do so. As a result, when rates go up, one expects to see less loan prepayments, and when rates go down one expects to see more loan prepayments. In other words, when rates go down, the cash flows become shorter (shorter average life and duration), and when rates go up they become longer.

Convexity is the second derivative of the price of a bond expressed as a function of its yield.[12] It is useful to first consider the case of **bullet** bonds, that is debt with

---

[12]See for example Tuckman and Serrat (2012) for a broad introduction to these notions.

**Table 2.2** 5-year duration 5% coupon bullet bond in various rates environments. *Source* compiled by the author

| Rates level (%) | Bond versus market (%) | Duration | Bond price |
|---|---|---|---|
| 6 | –1 | 5.0 | 95 |
| 5 | 0 | 5.0 | 100 |
| 4 | +1 | 5.0 | 105 |

a single principal payment at maturity. In the case of normal fixed-rate bullet bonds such as Treasurys, which cannot be prepaid in advance, the price/yield relationship is a simple hyperbolic function and exhibits a slightly positive convexity. At the first order, their value as a function of market yields changes proportionately to their duration, and that duration itself is reasonably stable. A 10-year Treasury will typically have a duration around 8 years, and if 10-year yields increase or decline a bit, that duration will stay roughly the same.

We can explain the way the price of a 5-year duration fixed-rate bond may move as follows: if the market required yield goes up, then that bond is paying less than the market requirement, and that difference persists for a number of years equal to the duration. So then the price has to go down roughly by the amount lacking in the bond's coupon times the number of years that this is going on for. If rates go down on the other hand, then the bond now pays more than what the market requires, by a certain amount over its duration, and that leads to a price increase of approximately the coupon/yield difference times duration. This case is illustrated in Table 2.2.

In fact, since a typical bullet has a slightly positive convexity then the price increase will be a little more than the rate change times duration, but we are neglecting this here. Since the movement in price is symmetrical, then in a risk-neutral environment whether volatility is high or low does not really matter for this bond, on average its value is 100.

Now we can look at how this simple setting would apply to a typical mortgage-backed security. We know that when rates increase, the underlying loans will prepay slower, while when rates decline they will prepay faster. Slower or faster prepayments will lead to a longer, or shorter, time until principal is returned on average. We could consider for example that in the base case, the MBS is valued at 100, pays a 5% fixed coupon, and the underlying loans pay principal with an average life of 5 years. If rates decline by 1% then there is a refinancing wave and the loans prepay very fast, so that the average life is only 1.5 years, while if rates increase by 1% then the loans stick around much longer on average, with an average life of 10 years. The MBS's structure could also amplify or reduce these effects, but we do not address this complication here. Now, applying the same logic as for the bullet bond above we can compute the numbers in Table 2.3.

The MBS's value increases much less than the comparable bullet when rates decline, and declines a lot more when rates back up. The under performance manifests itself as soon as rates move around. This is a prototypical example of **negative**

**Table 2.3** 5-year duration 5% coupon PAC support in various rates environments. *Source* compiled by the author

| Rates level (%) | Bond versus market (%) | Duration | Bond price |
|---|---|---|---|
| 6 | −1 | 10.0 | 90.0 |
| 5 | 0 | 5.0 | 100.0 |
| 4 | +1 | 1.5 | 101.5 |

**convexity**: an asymmetrical impact of movements in interest rates (convexity), to the detriment of the bond holder (negative).

How does one value the cost of the asymmetrical behavior of negatively convex bonds? This is carried out using complex **option-adjusted spread** models:

- Derive an **implied volatility** curve for interest rates: volatility of forward rates around the forward curve. Typically based on swaptions (for various combinations of maturity and tenor) and caps/floors (for short rates)
- The MBS can be seen as an exotic interest rate derivative. Using an option pricing replication argument one can hedge and price any kind of interest-rate exposed cash flow
- This would be formally correct if the MBS was a derivative contract with a pay off exactly derived from the prepayment model. In practice, there is a residual risk, the fact that given interest rates prepayments may be different from what the model expects. This residual risk is the **prepayment risk**.

One can also follow a simplified approach in the case of the example treated above, just to illustrate the logic. First, we estimate the chances that rates will rally or sell off: let's arbitrarily pick 20% of chances rates move up, 20% they move down, 60% they stay flat. The opportunity cost of prepayment directionality is the weighted average difference in value between the mortgage bond of interest and a Treasury bond of the same duration. In the example the cost is $0.2 \times 5 + 0.2 \times 3.5 = 1.70$.

We can also compute this cost in an annualized manner, as a yield reduction: in the example, it represents $1.70/5.0 = 34$ bps. The MBS should pay a yield higher by that much in order to fairly compensate for its negative convexity relative to a basic Treasury bond. This expression of the optionality cost as a yield give-up is called the **option cost** of the bond. The bond's spread over Treasurys minus the option cost is the **option-adjusted spread** (OAS).

## 2.6 Conclusion

In spite of the fact that this overview may not feel very deep and lacks any kind of formal analysis, the importance of being exposed to these stylized facts should be stressed. For example, the very essence of securitization as a sale of assets on which the issuer does not retain management discretion, and the necessity of not keeping a direct interest in these assets, will drive many aspects of the economics of securitization. The presence of negative convexity will drive very specific structuring and the creation of complex tranches. The granularity of many securitized markets will explain the costs investors face in acquiring information.

We now will drill down into the underlying assets in a securitization, and concentrate on loan portfolios.

## References

AFME. (2018). Data. https://www.afme.eu/en/reports/Statistics/.

Commission Implementing Regulation (EU) 2016/1799 of 7 October 2016. (2016). European Commission. https://eur-lex.europa.eu/legal-content/EN/TXT/HTML/?uri=CELEX:32016R1799&from=en#d1e32-12-1.

Davidson, A., & Levin, A. (2014). *Mortgage valuation models: Embedded options, risk, and uncertainty*. Oxford University Press.

Fabozzi, F. J. (Ed.). (2001). *Investing in asset-backed securities*. Frank J. Fabozzi series. John Wiley & Sons.

Fabozzi, F. J. (Ed.). (2016). *The handbook of mortgage-backed securities* (7th ed.). Oxford: Oxford University Press.

Fabozzi, F. J., & Vinod, K. (Eds.). (2008). *Introduction to securitization*. New York: Wiley.

Gauthier, L. (2003). Market-implied losses and non-agency subordinated MBS. *The Journal of Fixed Income*, *13*(1), 49–74.

Gorton, G., & Metrick, A. (2013). Chapter 1 - securitization. In G. Constantinides, M. Harris, & R. M. Stulz (Eds.), *Handbook of the economics of finance* (Vol. 2, pp. 1–70). Amsterdam: Elsevier.

Levin, A., & Davidson, A. (2008). The concept of credit OAS in valuation of MBS. *Journal of Portfolio Management*, *34*(3), 41–55.

Schwarcz, S. (2013). Securitization and structured finance. In G. Caprio (Ed.), *Key global financial markets, institutions, and infrastructure*. New York: Academic.

SIFMA. (2018). Research and data. http://www.sifma.org/resources/archive/research/.

Tuckman, B., & Serrat, A. (2012). *Fixed income securities* (3rd ed.). New York: John Wiley & Sons.

# Overview of Loan Portfolio Analysis

# 3

In this chapter we focus on an essential raw material of securitization: relatively homogeneous loan portfolios, still keeping our rapid pace. A good representation of the loans that go into a securitization deal is paramount, not only for the initial structuring and rating of the securities, but also for the secondary trading that takes place afterwards. The quality of this representation has evolved over time as a function of both the capabilities of technical tools, mainly computer storage and processing power, and the requirements of investors themselves. While at a time many market participants did not care too much about detailed information regarding the loans that went into a subprime securitization, they do a lot more today.

How to categorize and represent loans in order to structure a securitization deal is not a field that academic research has thoroughly investigated, and for these parts we will be guided by market practice and uses. The art of **tape cracking**, that is, the processing of large databases of loan information in order to model them for securitization purposes, has not attracted much academic interest. Nevertheless, the constraints related to the type of loan data available and the ease, or lack thereof, with which it can be manipulated, have affected the way in which the resulting securitized products could be analyzed.

The behavior of borrowers as they contemplate refinancing decisions or default have benefited from a very intense focus by market practitioners, and countless proprietary prepayment and default models have been developed by investment banks and institutional investors. This type of research is driven by the need to value bonds and measure their risks at the core, not by an effort to understand the borrowers' economic drivers. In contrast, academic research on this subject is less concerned with measuring the intensity of prepayments or defaults per se, and more concerned with explaining the strategic thinking that guides borrowers' decisions. In our discussion



L. Gauthier, *Securitization Economics*, Springer Texts in Business and Economics,
https://doi.org/10.1007/978-3-030-50326-0_3

of the drivers of loan behavior,[1] we will concentrate on the empirical approaches used in practice.

The chapter is organized as follows: we first discuss loan characterization: we distinguish corporate and consumer loans, various loan types, and the loan metrics of import. With these parameters, we're equipped well enough to qualify and differentiate various loans. Since in the economic literature addressing securitization many empirical studies focus on the performance of the underlying loans, it is essential to properly understand the true meaning of these metrics in order to detect sometimes fallacious results.

Then, we turn to the representation and the modeling of these loans. We keep the distinction between corporate and consumer loans, since their behavior is fundamentally not the same. We briefly discuss some academic research on applying Markov transition matrices to loan behavior.

Next, we address the measurement of loan performance. While this may sound trivial, the complexity of loan behavior in general implies that there are many facets in how to look at it to extract relevant measures. We cover the way in which the most common measures are computed: the ubiquitous CPRs, CDRs, severities, as well as the conventional scaling of these to define industry standards used in structuring. In our discussion of how to represent loans and measure their behavior, we also address the fundamental drivers of that behavior. We step through the usual stylized facts pertaining to loan prepayments or defaults. We do not focus on advanced economic research in that field, because it does not directly concern securitization. As a detailed illustration of these concepts, we drill down deep into the US agency market and walk through a loan-level analysis of prepayment and credit patterns, using the large database mentioned in the book's introduction.

Finally, we look into the details of projecting loan behavior. At the end of the day, all the analysis above leads to forming projections of loan cash flows, which will feed into securitization structures. We both address the practical way in which loan cash flows are most commonly projected, as well as useful simplifications to represent cash flows for economic modeling.

As can be understood by this chapter's relatively short length, the intention is not a detailed treatment of the practical techniques that relate to loan portfolio analysis. It is not either a discussion of the various economic underpinnings of loan behavior. Instead, the goal is to offer a certain cultural varnish which, even though it is superficial, gives enough structure and lines of thought so that some of the most important methods and notions in collateral analysis become accessible to the reader. This is an important step before discussing any deeper economic analysis of asset securitization.

[1]Note that we are discussing loan behavior, as opposed to borrower behavior. This might sound surprising, but the reason is that while the borrower will make decisions that are important to what happens to the loan, there are other entities, different from the borrower, which will play important roles. The behavior of the borrower and of those other entities, as they pertain to the loan, can be termed "loan behavior".

Note that in this chapter we will use the term of **loan** somewhat loosely, because in some cases we may in fact be discussing **bonds** as the underlying assets of a securitization.

## 3.1 Loan Characterization

Talking about "loans" in general hides an immense variety of debt contracts, and in that continuum we draw certain practical distinctions. As we will see, it makes sense to separate consumer and corporate loans. We can drill further down and categorize loans into broad types, depending on their nature and on how they are securitized. Then, within broad loan categories, we can explore the most important metrics or flags that define the loans.

### 3.1.1 Consumer Versus Corporate Loans

Every possible type of loan has been securitized in some way, but in this section we are focusing on the broad categories that are the most common. One important distinction is between **consumer loans** and **corporate loans** (or corporate bonds too). Consumer loans are those made directly to people, while corporate loans are made to institutions. Corporate loans are typically much larger than consumer loans, and hence for a given portfolio size one usually expect to have a much greater number of consumer loans than corporate loans. Table 3.1 summarizes some of the differences between the two. The dataset size here is understood for the typical cross-universe loan-level database.

The notion of the typical share of a loan held in a portfolio is one of the most important distinguishing features between corporate and consumer loans. In a loan portfolio, in a securitization context, one never holds a little share of a consumer loan. The loans are so small that they are held in whole. Corporate loans, on the other hand, are usually only held fractionally in a given portfolio, because they would be too large otherwise.

**Table 3.1** Main differences between consumer loans and corporate loans/bonds. *Source* Compiled by the author

| Metric | Consumer | Corporate |
|---|---|---|
| Nb of loans | Large | 50–500 |
| Share held | Whole | Fraction |
| Rating | Consumer credit | Rating agency |
| Pricing | Only at issue | Ongoing |
| Secured | Yes (mortgages), No (cards) | Generally not |
| Position size | ~5K to ~1 mm | Over 10 mm |
| Dataset | Billion rows | Million rows |

The rating that the loans get, in principle a measure of their credit quality, is typically a reflection of the borrower's standing. In the case of corporate loans, the company that issued the loans is given a rating by one or several rating agencies. The loan itself might carry a different rating than the company, for example, if it is a very junior or particularly senior obligation in the capital structure. For consumer loans the rating is typically some credit metric, such as the FICO score in the US.

The notion of pricing is important, as it typically is the most salient driver of loan behavior. For consumer loans, one only gets a true price at the loan's origination. After that, any kind of pricing tends to be model-derived. A single mortgage loan, for example, is too small for anyone to bother trading little pieces of it and from there get a market price. Corporate loans, on the other hand, are typically issued in a syndicated manner and, as we stressed earlier, there are many holders of the same loan. As a result, there can be a market between these holders, and prices can be established. Corporate bonds are issued into a market, so there is an even greater amount of competitive valuation taking place, and hence scrutiny into the quality of the debt.

Whether the loans are secured matters in terms of recoveries in the case of defaults or liquidations. Mortgages are a major example of secured loans: when the borrower does not pay, the lender can recover and sell the property. Unsecured consumer loans like credit cards have very low recovery rates on the other hand. The majority of corporate loans is not collateralized by a particular asset, but rather a general obligation of the issuing company. There can be gradations in how secure a loan is. For example, a second-lien mortgage would be repaid upon liquidation only after the first-lien mortgage has been paid. Also, as mentioned earlier, corporate debt may be more or less junior, which makes it less likely to be covered by a firm's assets upon liquidation.

### 3.1.2 Broad Loan Types Comparisons

Further than the corporate and consumer loan distinction, one also categorizes loans as a function of their broad sectors. Table 3.2 summarizes some characteristics of the main loan sectors.

**Table 3.2** Comparison of loan types. *Source* Compiled by the author

| Loan type | Static or Managed | Consumer or Corp | Secured |
|---|---|---|---|
| Mortgages | Mostly static | Consumer | Yes |
| Autos | Both | Consumer | Yes |
| Student loans | Both | Consumer | No |
| Credit cards | Revolving | Consumer | No |
| Leveraged loans | Managed | Corporate | No |
| Commercial Mtgs | Static | Corporate | Yes |
| Corporate bonds | Managed | Corporate | No |

The table illustrates another manner in which loans can be categorized: depending on whether their portfolios are typically held in a **static** or **dynamic** manner, in other words if a typical pool intended for securitization will be set forever, or **managed** over time. In the case of consumer loans we talk about a **revolving** portfolio. Assets that have an ongoing pricing mechanism, such as corporate loans, are often securitized as a managed portfolio, for the simple reason that they can be traded more or less efficiently. Assets that do not have a good pricing mechanism are in static portfolios. Credit card debt, for example, is normally in a revolving portfolio because the card accounts can be paid down and then reused. The fact that consumers would repay and sometimes re-borrow effectively is a pricing mechanism: these borrowers implicitly agree to the terms when they reuse the card. Some mortgage portfolios are also revolving, where loans that are paid down are replaced with new loans issued by an originator.

Note that commercial mortgages are taken by corporations usually but they do not tend to be traded, as they are not syndicated but rather directly securitized. It is worth noting that loans that are syndicated have been analyzed by an investment bank and by several competitive buyers at the time of origination. This is a different situation from when the entire loan is securitized because the syndication process adds a presumably efficient screening layer that does not necessarily exist with non-syndicated loans.

It is useful to discuss some of the dimensions along which various types of loans are characterized. It could appear as though there is not much in common between a subprime mortgage and a regional bank's trust preferred debt, and indeed they are tracked using very different metrics. Still, there are very similar aspects in how they are effectively analyzed and we will also discuss these common aspects.

### 3.1.3 Loan Metrics

Loan metrics can be thought of as the fields in the typically very large table, with one line per loan per period, representing the available data on some sector. Some of these fields will be found in all tables across all sectors, while some are very specific to some particular loan types.

As we segue into the notion of measuring loans, it is important to signal the notion of **hard information** and **soft information** on the loans or on the borrowers. When we imagine a table filled with information on the loans, we are implicitly considering the kind of publicly provided data on securitized products. These must respect some standards, and issuers, servicers and trustees generally do not provide more information than they have to based on these predefined templates. As such, this data may be termed hard information, a set of core metrics that must be filled with each loan. However, when lenders extend loans, and maybe when they maintain an ongoing relationship with the borrowers, they presumably obtain particular, potentially unstructured, information, that is not captured by the preexisting grid. This can be termed soft information. When we discuss loan screening and securitization decisions in Chaps. 4 and 5 we will see how these notions of hard and soft information play an important role in theoretical and empirical models. The metrics we discuss in this section are all hard information.

Among the important metrics that are found across all types of loans are the ones related to the very nature of these loans, that is, information about what the payments are and when they are due. These include the loan coupon, its maturity, its scheduled payments if any, and its amount.

- The loan coupon is probably the single most important measure in a loan portfolio, since it tells us how much interest one should expect from the loan. Some loans may have complex payment rules, for example, a floating rate with specific high and low bounds (called caps and floors). When aggregated across a portfolio of loans, this is called the weighted average coupon, or **WAC**, one of the most important acronyms when considering collateral. One further defines the **net WAC** and the **gross WAC**, respectively, after and before the payment of servicing (and other) expenses. In some cases, when most of the assets in a collateral pool pay floating rate coupons indexed off of the same reference rate, one may refer to the weighted average spread or **WAS** as well. The loan coupon is normally considered to be set as a function of the perceived risk of the loan.
- The **OMS**, or off-market spread,[2] is derived from the coupon: it is the difference with the coupon on the loan and the current reference market rate for loans of that type. For corporate loans, this may be the spread over the average loan spread in the market at that time. For mortgages, it is the difference between the coupon on the loan and the prevailing mortgage rate at the time of origination.
- The time to maturity normally measured in months[3] is another common and important metric. The aggregate is referred to as the **WAM** or weighted average maturity.
- A related metric, fairly ubiquitous, is the **WALA**, that is, the weighted average loan age, expressed in months. Since many of the important things that can happen to a loan take time to develop (responsiveness to prepayment incentives, or conditions for default for example), the WALA is a good first-order indicator of what may happen to a loan. The evolution of loan cash flows or repayment rates as a function of age is called **seasoning**, and any curve plotting some performance measure as a function of loan age is a **seasoning curve**.
- Each loan's initial and current outstanding principal are quite important too: they indicate the degree of exposure to a particular loan, and usually correlate with the borrower's financial condition. The aggregate is the average loan size, **ALS**, or if it is itself balance weighted, the **WALS**.
- In the case of amortizing loans, it is necessary to know the scheduled payment in order to derive the amount of principal recovered at each payment period.

[2]Also known as SATO, or spread at origination.

[3]As opposed to the average life, conventionally given in years.

These data points are held as quite important when looking at any loan portfolio, because with a few further assumptions on prepayments and defaults, one can use them to compute the cash flows from the loan portfolio. Let us now focus on corporate loans or bonds, and on some of the metrics that are specific to them, in addition to the ones we just discussed.

#### 3.1.3.1 Corporate Loans/Bonds Metrics

As we have mentioned earlier, one salient feature of corporate debt issues is that they are held by multiple investors, which effectively creates a market for them, and makes the availability of valuation information more likely. The following are some dimensions that one typically considers when analyzing corporate loan portfolios.

- **Seniority**: corporate loans are not all general obligations of the firm. They may be **second-lien** for example, which means in case of default they are paid only after the more senior loans are paid. Usually, loans are more senior than **bonds** issued by a firm. In some cases, this important information may not be available as such from loan tapes, and then market participants often use other correlated metrics such as the loan issuance spread.[4]
- The **rating**, issued by a rating agency gives information on the credit risk of the issuer of the loan or bond. The loans themselves can also have a rating, which depends on their seniority. Hence one distinguishes issuer ratings from loan or bond ratings.[5]
- The firm's **sector** or **industry** is an important driver of credit risk, and industry concentration can be a portfolio management constraint. Defining sectors or industries is somewhat arbitrary, and for it to be useful it needs to be consistent across all loans or bonds in the universe. This is why, usually, the most relevant industry or sector categorizations are those provided by the rating agencies.
- The loan's **price** is one of the most direct indicators of the likelihood of prepayment or default, as well as a loan portfolio manager's incentive to buy or sell a loan. Therefore, this metric is watched closely. The aggregate **WAP** or weighted average price provides an indication of credit risk across the portfolio. For leveraged loans, which do not trade on an organized market, monthly prices are obtained from market makers.
- The loan's type of **covenant** is an important metric. The lending contract includes a covenant between the firm and its lenders. This covenant will contain certain provisions that aim to protect the loan: for example, it may specify a maximum debt leverage that the issuer will be authorized to reach. It could also prevent the firm from issuing debt that would be senior to the loan. Some loans are referred to

---

[4]The idea being that if the spread was very large at issuance, the loan presumably is junior.

[5]To be perfectly clear we are talking about the potential assets in a securitization, which may be rated. The liabilities, or structured bonds, issued by an SPV may also be rated, but this is not what we are discussing here.

**Table 3.3** Rating factors as of 2007. *Source* Moody's CDO research data feed glossary of terms

| Rating | Rating Factor |
|---|---|
| AAA | 1 |
| AA | 20 |
| A | 120 |
| BBB | 360 |
| BB | 1350 |
| B | 2720 |

as **cov-lite**, when the covenants are deemed not to be very strong, which increases the credit risk on the loan.

- In the commercial mortgage market, a metric of paramount importance is the **debt service coverage ratio** or **DSCR**. This tracks, for every mortgage loan, the ratio of the property's rent minus expenses over the required mortgage payment. It naturally correlates with the likelihood of default: when rents coming in are too low, the borrower may not be able to make their loan payments anymore.

There is an oft-used metric associated to a loan's rating: its **rating factor**, a number that captures the credit risk numerically based on the rating. Table 3.3 shows the rating factors for various rating levels. They can be understood as multiples of default probabilities relative to that of a AAA issuer or security. Across a pool, the average rating factor is called the **WARF**, or weighted average rating factor.

#### 3.1.3.2 Consumer Loan Metrics

We list several metrics of import in consumer loan pools, focusing in particular on mortgages, since they are such a prevalent part of the entire market.

- The **FICO score** (Fair Isaacs & Co) is a measure of the borrower's credit quality between 300 and 850 based on the borrower's personal credit file. The score is calculated with a proprietary methodology, and uses detailed borrower information, such as payment history and use of credit cards (but not information on the borrower's income or assets). A lower score implies that a larger percentage of loans in that category will probably be delinquent. The score effectively ranks the borrowers as a function of their estimated probability of suffering a negative credit event (for example, missing a payment) within the following two years. These scores were originally introduced for consumer lenders to benchmark the credit worthiness of a borrower. Over time, the FICO score has become the standard credit measure in all mortgage underwriting. FICO scores play an important role in explaining not only the credit performance but also the prepayment speeds of a loan pool (since borrowers with better credit can more easily refinance). Delinquencies and losses of a pool are directly related to its FICO score distribution. In mortgages, one has generally considered that a FICO score above 620 was necessary for securitization through a prime channel.

- The **LTV**, or loan-to-value ratio, is the loan amount divided by the appraised property (for a mortgage) or collateral value. Note that one can only measure an LTV on a loan that is collateralized. At origination, the equity in the asset is simply 1 - LTV. LTV is one of the primary variables in credit performance. Standard mortgages at origination typically have LTVs under 80%, and a high LTV is often associated with weak credit indicators like a high debt-to-income ratio and may imply that the borrower is stretching to make monthly mortgage payments. A high LTV also means that the borrower has little equity in the property and is hence more likely to have negative equity in a housing market downturn. This increases the probability of being delinquent and the subsequently loss severity. Agencies[6] allow LTVs of up to 97%, but require loans with LTV greater than 80% to carry mortgage insurance. **CLTV** is the cumulative LTV, that is, the LTV also including other loans on the same property. Another related metric is the **current LTV**, which is the LTV computed with an updated estimate of the property value (rather than the appraisal or value at loan origination).
- The **lien** is the loan's seniority relative to other loans that may have been collateralized by the same property. In mortgages, a second-lien loan only gets repaid in case of liquidation after the first-lien has been repaid. Note that the LTV of a second-lien loan may be low (it is normally quite a small loan), although the CLTV on the property could be very high. Not accounting for this distinction often derails aggregate statistics on a pool combining first and second-lien loans.
- A mortgage loan's **occupancy** records whether the property backing the loan is to be occupied by the borrower or rented out, in which case the loan is called an **investor** loan. The occupancy status is a credit metric as defaults on investor properties are higher than those on owner-occupied properties. This is because the incentives and motives are different for the two different owners. A homeowner will have to face removal and other moral and social issues, whereas an owner of an investment property only suffers a loss in capital. Also, investor properties have higher loss severities as the maintenance of these properties is generally poorer relative to owned-occupied properties. In strong house price growth environments, investor properties have higher base rate prepayment speeds as these owners typically actively manage their investments and seek to maximize their returns leading to a refinancing at the next best opportunity.
- The loan's **rate type**: fixed-rate or floating rate, **FRM** (fixed-rate mortgages) and **ARM** (adjustable-rate mortgages) in the case of mortgages. The rate type naturally affects the projected cash flow on the loans, but they also induce different prepayment behaviors. Borrowers with fixed-rate loans will have an incentive to prepay when the rate on new mortgages declines, which tends to be driven by the long-end of the yield curve. ARM borrowers on the other hand will be affected by the evolution of the rate they are paying, usually based on short maturity indices, such as Libor. In addition, ARMS normally offer lower rates initially, which are expected to raise over time, in a normal upward-sloping yield curve environment.

[6]We're excluding GNMA in this statement.

As a result, the borrowers taking ARMs self select toward something cheaper right now, which can become more expensive later, and may signal a greater credit risk; see Posey and Yavas (2001), for example. Within ARMs, **option-ARMs** form a subcategory: the coupon is set lower than the loan rate so that the payment is lower than it should be, and the difference accrues, until a later date when the (higher) total amount amortizes as a normal mortgage. This feature is called **negative-amortization**.

- The loan's **purpose** for mortgages is the reason it was taken: due to a purchase, or to a refinancing, or a cash out (getting a larger loan than the prior one). Loan purpose does not directly affect credit performance or prepayments per se. However, cash-out refis may have a higher LTV and hence higher default rates. The different loan purposes also imply different evaluation methods for the underlying property. In the case of a purchase, the initial property valuation is based on an arms-length transaction, and should, therefore, be considered as a market price. In the case of a refinancing, there is no such transaction and the valuation is only an appraisal, which may be biased upward, see, for example, Leventis (2006). Historically, most loans in agency pools have tended to be purchase loans or refinancings without cash outs.
- Loan **documentation** is somewhat of a catch-all metric, because although as a flag (full, limited, or no documentation) it appears as a piece of hard information, it points to the existence of important soft information when it is not provided, or limited. Sometimes when homeowners have their own business, they either lack some documents such as income verification or do not want to fully disclose their income for privacy reasons. They may also not want to disclose information because they know it would hurt the loan application. As expected, default rates on non-full doc loans generally run higher than that on full doc loans.
- In the case of mortgages, the presence of **mortgage insurance** or **PMI** (private mortgage insurance), and the amount of coverage, is an important metric for two reasons: first, it has a direct impact on loss severities since upon liquidation the insurer will cover part of the loss, up to the guaranteed amount. Second, it correlates with other characteristics; on one hand the insurer will have carried out its own underwriting of the risk, on the other hand the lender may have a lesser incentive to perform due diligence on the loan, since it is insured. It is normally specified with a certain **LTV coverage**, in LTV terms. For example a loan with a 90% LTV might acquire insurance on 20% LTV, which is considered to reduce the LTV from the lender's standpoint to 70%. The mortgage insurance provider requires that certain processes to be followed by the servicer when handling delinquent loans, otherwise it may **rescind** the claims.

It is important to realize that apart from a few exceptions, the hard characteristics of a loan do not allocate it to a particular sector. In fact, one could argue there is no such thing as a subprime loan or a prime loan, because a single loan could be commingled with a pool of better or worse loans. The worst loan in a typical prime pool likely has characteristics making it look worse than the best loan in a subprime pool. Nevertheless, certain market segments have been traditionally defined, as a function of the pools' average characteristics more than as stringent characteristics of the loans themselves.

In the US mortgage market, the following securitization sectors were typically clearly distinguished up to the late 2000s mortgage crisis (these categorizations refer to what sector the deal would be said to belong):

- **Agency prime loans**, the bulk of mortgage issuance. First-lien FRMs, with FICO scores around 720 and LTVs around 70. Loan size is limited by charter, and loans above a certain limit cannot be guaranteed by the agencies.
- **Jumbo prime**, prime loans with a size above the agency limit. These have very good credit scores, low LTVs, mostly with full documentation, and are all first-liens.
- **Alt-A**, first-lien loans with agency-like characteristics but which could not be securitized due to expensive guarantee fees, typically caused by limited or low documentation, or the loans being investor loans.
- **Option-ARM**, first-lien loans with an adjustable rate, for which the actual mortgage payment is lower than required by the rate, and catches up at a later point. The aggregate credit characteristics in this sector resemble those of the Alt-A market.
- **Subprime**, borrowers with bad credit quality, with average FICO scores around 620, high LTVs, and low loan balances. Importantly, the subprime sector includes about 5% of second-lien loans, in balance.
- **Second-lien**, entirely composed of second-liens that were added to prime or Alt-A first-lien loans. Normally, second-lien loans to lower credit quality borrowers would be gathered in subprime deals.
- **Scratch and Dent**, loans that were delinquent previously and had to wait for some time before being securitizable, or loans with characteristics that prevented them to be securitized initially in their targeted sector.

Jumbos, Alt-A, subprime and option-ARMs each represented approximately $500bb of outstanding amounts at the beginning of the 2010s. The other non-agency sectors were smaller, around $100bb each. Since then, non-agency issuance has been mostly comprised of jumbo deals, with some special flavors of subprime (often resecuritization of seasoned loans). Table 3.4 presents a summarized view of the most important sectors in that list.

Now that we have a bird's eye view of loan characteristics, we are going to focus on the events that take place through a loan's existence. This will be a first step before studying how loan performance may be defined and measured.

## 3.2 Representation and Modeling of Loans

In this section, we are interested in what happens to loans over time. We are not yet concentrating on getting cash flows, but rather on why the cash flows would be what they are, or what fundamentally drives them. There is a whole continuum of actions

**Table 3.4** Overview of US mortgage securitization sectors in the mid 2000s. *Source* Compiled by the author

| Sector | Loan size range | FICO | FICO Cutoff | LTV | Pct Inv | Second-liens | Negam |
|---|---|---|---|---|---|---|---|
| Agency | \$250–400k | 720 | 620 | 70 | 1% | – | No |
| Jumbo prime | \$500–600k | 740 | 620 | 65 | – | – | No |
| Alt-A | \$300–500k | 700 | 620 | 75 | 15% | – | No |
| Option-ARMs | \$300–500k | 710 | 620 | 80 | 10% | – | Yes |
| Subprime | \$150–300k | 625 | 500 | 85 | 5% | 1–5% | No |

that a borrower or lender may take related to a loan, so they have to be summarized in order to make it possible to analyze the loans' behavior in a reasonably simple setting. Hence we will start with a more descriptive part, addressing the categorization of the states in which a loan might be.

First, we look at the typical loan life cycle, in a simplified setting, in order to show the important steps in a loan's life. There is a whole continuum of actions that a borrower or lender may take related to a loan, so they have to be summarized in order to make it possible to analyze the loans' behavior in a reasonably simple setting. The events that can take place in relation to a loan's situation are not the same whether that loan is a corporate loan or a consumer loan. In fact the very notion of default is different between corporate and consumer debt. We will first discuss the evolution of corporate loans, then consumer loans, and finally transition matrices, or rather **roll rate matrices** as they are known in market parlance. Note that while in modeling language, the transitions take place between various **states**, these are usually called **statuses** when they refer to loans.

### 3.2.1 Corporate Loan Evolution

The notion of default in corporate debt encompasses many complex strategies, but it is easily observed. Breaching the covenant, just like not paying interest or capital in time on this loan or on another loan, will put the issuer in default.

Hence, for corporate debt, default is a property of the issuer, not so much of the loan, because defaulting on any liability will normally force a restructuring of the company or even a liquidation. Default is also very clearly identifiable, since it is publicly declared. As a result, this can be a simple flag in a loan tape.

In the case of default, the lenders may agree to the issuer's trying to cure the situation, for example, by deferring interest payments for some time. The lenders may also decide to trigger bankruptcy, which may have to be agreed to by a judge. See Fig. 3.1 for a graphical depiction of these various steps.

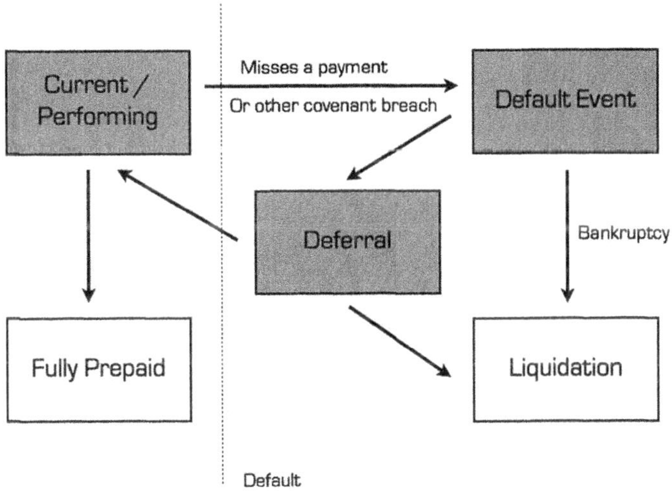


**Fig. 3.1** Simplified life cycle of a corporate loan. *Source* Compiled by the author

In corporate lending there are generally several loans or bonds issued by the same company. The company's default situation normally affects them all at the same time. If the issuer defaults on one of its loans, it will be considered in default by all the other loans. If the company is in default on a particular loan's payment, it will typically not have an incentive to continue paying its other loans since it will be in default with respect to them as well.

It is important to realize that the default rates that are typically reported on a portfolio of corporate loans (the MDR or CDR discussed in the next section) are not default rates in the sense of a corporate default, but rather liquidation rates.

### 3.2.2 Consumer Loan Evolution

There are many complex and detailed aspects in consumer loan servicing which we do not address here, in order to keep a fairly simple representation. We focus on mortgage loans, because they do cycle through a good variety of states. Figure 3.2 shows the possible statuses a mortgage may be in. Simpler loans such as credit cards would be represented with less states (some of the ones shown here not being applicable).

A mortgage may be in one of the following situations, or statuses, represented by darker boxes in the figure:

- A **current** or **performing** loan is one, that is, current on its payment obligations, or in other words it does not have a late payment. A current loan may have always been current, that is never skipped a payment, in which case it is generally termed **always current**. A loan that is current today but has missed payments in the

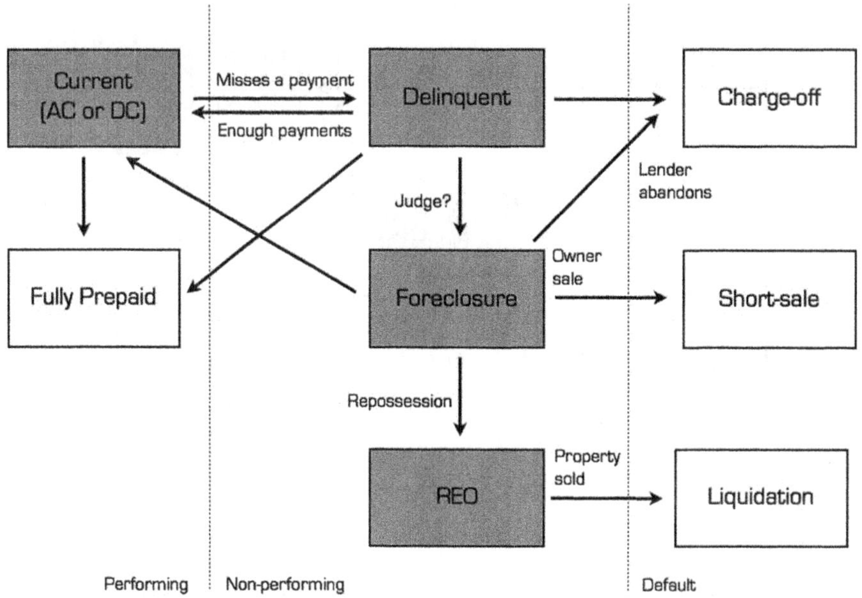


**Fig. 3.2** Simplified life cycle of a consumer loan. *Source* Compiled by the author

past would be called **dirty current**. Note that although a performing loan is not delinquent, we still may say that its "delinquency status" is current.

- A **delinquent** loan is one that has missed one or several payments and has not yet made up for them. The notion of delinquency is hence attached to a time-length which represents how many payments it has missed. Hence, one talks about a 30-day, or 60-day delinquent loan.[7] On a loan calling for monthly payments, that would represent, respectively, one and two months of payments that were skipped. Note that these missed payments need not have taken place last month and the month before. A loan that missed a single payment one year ago, but since then has been making scheduled payments, would still be today a 30-day delinquent loan. If fine buckets are created to represent delinquency (30-day, 60-day, etc) then a loan making regular payments but already delinquent would stay in the same status.
- The state of **foreclosure** applies to loans for which the lender has begun repossession proceedings. Depending on the jurisdiction, it might be necessary to go through court proceedings. The transition into this state is not directly driven by the borrower's decision but by the loan owner's or the servicer's acting on its behalf. Note that **bankruptcy** does not appear in Fig. 3.2, because it is a property

[7]There are two different conventions on reporting the number of days of delinquency in the US, the MBA's and the OTS's. When manipulating loan data across the mortgage spectrum one should always ascertain the consistency of delinquency reporting. Deal-level delinquency reporting is typically not consistent.

of the borrower. The borrower may be in legal bankruptcy, but still be current on this particular loan. Similarly, the borrower may not have declared bankruptcy but be fighting foreclosure. In the US, many borrowers declare bankruptcy when foreclosure proceedings are initiated against them. There is a clear distinction between jurisdictions where foreclosure requires a judgment, and where it does not, due to the significantly longer time required. In the US, this distinction between States is referred to as **judicial** versus **non-judicial** States. Empirical papers studying the relationship between lending and ease of recovery, or lack thereof, may use this as an important geographic marker.

- The status of **REO** refers to real-estate-owned: after foreclosure proceedings have been carried out, and the lender has obtained ownership of the property. In general, the foreclosure ends with a public auction, and if there are no bids above the loan owner's reserve, then the lender gets the property. It is in fact a misnomer as a loan status, because once the property's ownership has been transferred, the loan becomes extinct, and it is replaced by that property.

The figure also shows particular states in lighter color, which are absorbing states: once a loan enters them, it stays there. These states are in fact ways in which the loan exits the pool:

- A **full prepayment** is most often done from a performing situation, but may also take place for lightly delinquent loans. Apart from rare cases of inheritance, for example, full prepayments are typically the result of a loan refinancing or of the borrower's decision to move.
- A **charge-off** corresponds to just abandoning the loan. The servicer may deem that the potential recovery of cash from the collateral would not compensate the costs in carrying out that recovery, or simply that there is no recoverable collateral.
- A **short-sale** is a sale of the property by the owner for an amount that does not fully compensate the outstanding loan amount. A short-sale may take place while the loan is in foreclosure. In cases where it is not legally or practically feasible to personally sue the borrower in order to recover the shortfall, the servicer may accept the lesser amount that the home owner pays off by selling the house. Even though the recovered amount is less than the loan's outstanding amount,[8] it is usually much better than having to wait for an REO sale.
- A **liquidation** is the sale of the property by the servicer after it has acquired the rights to the property directly. Following a foreclosure sale, the loan owner has obtained the property and typically the servicer hires a realtor to sell it. The amount for which it ends up being sold is often much less than the loan's outstanding amount.

As signaled on Fig. 3.2, the states of delinquency, foreclosure and REO can be referred to the loan being **non-performing**. For consumer loans, missing a payment

[8]Otherwise it would be a straight prepayment, in fact.

or even being repossessed does not yet get termed a default. Default is usually considered to take place in the transition out of a serious delinquent state: when there is a charge-off, short-sale, or liquidation. Loan-level tapes generally do not contain any particular flag saying that a loan defaults, so it needs to be carefully defined. As we will see in the discussion of some empirical papers, some authors may define some of the serious delinquency states as "default". This is improper, because the loans are still in the pool at that time, and conventional measures of default rates require the loans to exit the pool.

It is worth noting that when the statuses represented in Fig. 3.2 are further broken down by delinquency level, the most commonly used statuses are: 30-day, 60-day, 90-day, and 90+-day. This last status pools all the loans that are significantly late. Nevertheless, the most commonly single measure of delinquency that is reported[9] is the 60+ delinquency bucket, that is all the delinquencies apart from the mildest ones.

Now that we have quickly covered all the various states the loans might be in, we turn to the analysis of their transitions among these states.

### 3.2.3 Loan Transitions

Since loans move from one status to another randomly, it seems natural to consider these transitions as driven by a transition matrix containing the probabilities for all possible movements.

Although this is a very widely used practice in the market, there is not much academic literature on the subject. With institutional investors in mind, Gauthier and Zimmerman (2006) give a simple presentation of the use of transition matrices in mortgage credit. More recently, Grimshaw and Alexander (2011) give a more detailed and formal analysis of these methods. Using transition matrices assume that the transition probabilities would be reasonably stable; however, they show empirically that in the case of subprime the matrices are not homogeneous nor stable. As a result, they propose to estimate separate transition matrices for different subgroups of loans which have different characteristics. This is the way in which, in practice, these transition matrices are used.

We will focus more specifically on consumer credit, as this is where this transition approach has been used the most in practice. In the corporate market, a subset of transitions of importance concerns ratings with the use of **rating migration matrices**. See, for example, Shao et al. (2016), although in this approach one does not specifically look at the loan's behavior, only at the issuer's rating. There are less data points on corporate loans than on consumer loans, and the shorter list of statuses for corporates limits the degree of accuracy with which these transitions can be modeled.

Loan behavior can be represented as a row-stochastic matrix. Each cell $(i, j)$ represents the probability that a loan will go from state $i$ to state $j$ over a given

[9]Because it has an impact on some structural features. The level of 60+ delinquencies can affect cash flows to subordinated bonds in some structures.

period. The following matrix represents such a case, where the transitions combine the "from" and the "to" states, selected from the five possible statuses of "current", "delinquent", "foreclosure", "REO", and "out", represented by their first initial. The status of "out" represents both voluntary and involuntary payoffs, and captures liquidations, short-sales, charge-offs as well as prepayments. The distinction between these types of payoffs is based on the status from which the loan transitions.

$$A = \begin{pmatrix} \mathbb{P}[CC] & \mathbb{P}[CD] & 0 & 0 & \mathbb{P}[CO] \\ \mathbb{P}[DC] & \mathbb{P}[DD] & \mathbb{P}[DF] & 0 & \mathbb{P}[DO] \\ \mathbb{P}[FC] & \mathbb{P}[FD] & \mathbb{P}[FF] & \mathbb{P}[FR] & \mathbb{P}[FO] \\ 0 & 0 & 0 & \mathbb{P}[RR] & \mathbb{P}[RO] \\ 0 & 0 & 0 & 0 & 1 \end{pmatrix}$$

The transitions $\{CF, CR, DR, RC, RD, RF\}$ are normally not possible and this is reflected in the transition matrix. The bottom row reflects the fact that once a loan is out of the pool it stays out of the pool. Note that in this example matrix we have not distinguished the states "always current" and "dirty current", nor differentiated among delinquencies.

The upper left corner of the transition matrix contains states that are effectively driven by the borrower (being current or delinquent), while the lower right corner contains states driven by the servicer (foreclosure or REO). They are usually referred to as the **front-end** and the **back-end** of the transition matrix, respectively.

How are these matrices filled with numbers? It depends on the nature of the available data. Loan data can be found to be structured in many different ways. Sometimes it is represented with just **one line per loan**, with a current date and an eventual prepayment or default date. It may also be with **one line per loan per period**, with a status field tracking the loan's delinquency. In all cases, the data should be converted to a structure allowing for a direct computation of transition probabilities through aggregation:

- One line per loan and at each row in the data one needs the loan's information for that time period as well as for the prior time period.
- Any transition probability can then be calculated by a direct sum in a basic database system.

For example, the expression in **SQL** shown in Table 3.5 would compute the average transition probability from current ("C") to delinquent ("D"). Since the typical datasets on which this would be applied could run in the billions of rows, an SQL engine is typically an efficient and practical way through which loan-level information may be exploited before pre-aggregation. The field "delq" represents the current delinquency status of a loan,[10] and "prior_delq" the delinquency status in the previous month.

[10] Remember that the delinquency status of a loan may be that it is current.

**Table 3.5** Example calculation of transition probabilities. *Source* Compiled by the author

```
select
  CurDate,
  sum(prior_balance * ((prior_delq = 'C') and (delq = 'D'))) /
    sum(prior_balance * (prior_delq = 'C')) as AvgCtoD
from loantable
group by CurDate
```

As we indicated earlier, even though the loans in a tape are normally homogeneous, one expects significant differences in loan behavior patterns based on their characteristics, in which case it makes sense to bucket the data according to these characteristics. Further, one can also directly model the relationship between continuous or categorical characteristics and the empirical probabilities in the transition matrix. Multinomial probit or logit models are common in practice. See, for example, the fully detailed model from HUD: Mosley (2019). There are countless such models both from academia and Wall Street research.

We now turn to the conventional metrics that are defined to capture loan performance.

## 3.3 Measuring Performance

In theory very diverse loan portfolios could be securitized, combining all sorts of assets ranging from credit cards to mortgages or corporate loans. However, as we have indicated, the practice over the years has been to gather loans of the same type.[11] This simplifies the representation of a securitization deal's asset portfolio, since this homogeneity implies that all these assets can be, in principle, represented following the same template. In other words, the "grid" that one may use to represent the loans' characteristics should be expected to be applicable in the same way to all the assets in a typical deal.

In this section we will first discuss the measurement of prepayments, defaults and severities. Then we will look into conventional scaled seasoning curves widely used in the market to express core prepayment or default assumptions. After that, we will go through the main drivers of prepayment and credit, in a descriptive fashion. There are as many empirical models on this subject as there are institutional investors and academics who have looked into it. Finally, we will dive deep into agency loan-level data in order to illustrate many of the main patterns in loan characteristics and behavior.

Before delving into the detailed analysis of loan portfolios, we need to define a few important terms related to mortgages. Mortgage loans are particular because

[11] In fact we will see some theoretical justification for this in Chap. 7.

unlike typical corporate loans or bonds, they repay some principal over time and not all at maturity, and the scheduled payments the borrower is supposed to make are constant (assuming a constant interest rate on the loan).

We consider a mortgage with an annualized interest rate $c$ expressed as a percentage, a maturity of $m$ periods, and an initial amount $B_0$, and we will be looking at the various payments at some point in time $0 \leq t \leq m$. Define the **scheduled payment** $\hat{S}$, which is constant. Note here we will use a "hat" notation for the scheduled payments, because later we will need to distinguish them from unscheduled payments. The interest and principal payments $I$ and $\hat{P}$ are such that $\hat{S} = I_t + \hat{P}_t$. The scheduled loan balance $\hat{B}$ is considered a the beginning of each period, so at maturity $\hat{B}_m = 0$. Given the coupon rate $c$, each monthly interest payment is equal to

$$I_t = \frac{c\hat{B}_t}{1200}$$

or if we write $r = \frac{c}{1200}$, $I_t = r\hat{B}_t$. At each period the ending balance satisfies

$$\hat{B}_{t+1} = \hat{B}_t + I_t - \hat{S}$$

or $\hat{B}_{t+1} = \hat{B}_t(1+r) - \hat{S}$. Hence

$$\hat{B}_m = B_0(1+r)^m - \hat{S}\sum_{k=1}^{m}(1+r)^k.$$

Rearranging we get

$$\hat{B}_m = B_0(1+r)^m - \hat{S}\frac{(1+r)^m - 1}{r}.$$

But since we have $\hat{B}_m = 0$, we can solve for $\hat{S}$ and obtain the fixed mortgage payment $\hat{S} = \frac{B_0 r}{1-(1+r)^{-m}}$.

The outstanding balance at the end of time $t$ can be derived as

$$\hat{B}_{t+1} = B_0(1+r)^t - \hat{S}\frac{(1+r)^t - 1}{r}.$$

The scheduled principal payment at time $t$ is simply derived as the total payment minus the interest payment: $\hat{P}_t = \hat{S} - r\hat{B}_t$.

### 3.3.1 Prepayments, Defaults, and Severities

As we look into the various ways of measuring prepayments, defaults or severities, recall that identifying a prepayment or a default is not always trivial,[12] but in all cases it is very important that at any point in time the flagging of which loan is in which category be consistent.

#### 3.3.1.1 Prepayments

**Single monthly mortality** or **SMM** is a monthly measure of prepayments. In the general context, loans are supposed to pay some amount of principal, the scheduled principal payment, each month. Prepayments should not count that scheduled amount, since it is supposed to be paid in any case. We need to distinguish between principal payments that are scheduled (which we wrote $\hat{P}$ earlier) and the principal payments that are unscheduled and **voluntary** (i.e., willingly made by the borrower), which we can write $\check{P}$, and unscheduled **involuntary** prepayments (that is, recoveries from liquidations typically) noted $\bar{P}$. The total principal payment collected at time $t$ is $P_t = \hat{P}_t + \check{P}_t + \bar{P}_t$. The prepayment on a loan at time $t$ is $\check{P}_t$, and we define the SMM, the monthly rate of prepayment, as $SMM_t = \frac{\check{P}_t}{B_t - \hat{P}_t}$.

In most cases, one wants to compute prepayments not at the level of a single loan but across an entire portfolio. So for loans indexed by $k \in \mathcal{L}$ for some loan portfolio $\mathcal{L}$, one could write

$$SMM(\mathcal{L})_t = \frac{\sum_{k \in \mathcal{L}} (\check{P}_k)_t}{\sum_{k \in \mathcal{L}} ((B_k)_t - (\hat{P}_k)_t)}$$

The measure above captures prepayments that are not necessarily full loan repayments. It captures both the situation of someone sending a few extra dollars, or rounding up their payment, as well as someone obtaining a full pay down of the loan from a lender in a refinancing. If we wanted to only measure these full pay downs then the expression for the SMM would become

$$SMM(\mathcal{L})_t = \frac{\sum_{k \in \mathcal{L}_t^P} ((B_k)_t - (\hat{P}_k)_t)}{\sum_{k \in \mathcal{L}} ((B_k)_t - (\hat{P}_k)_t)}$$

where $\mathcal{L}_t^P$ is the set of loans that fully prepay at time $t$.

Sometimes, for simplicity and without much impact on the resulting measures, SMM is not computed in terms of the effective balance of loans that get repaid, but as a weighted proportion of loans that fully repay, in the following manner:

$$SMM(\mathcal{L})_t = \frac{\sum_{k \in \mathcal{L}_t^P} (B_k)_t}{\sum_{k \in \mathcal{L}} (B_k)_t}$$

[12]For example, a transition from a serious delinquent state to a full repayment of the outstanding balance.

Monthly prepayment metrics are annualized into a **Conditional Prepayment Rate** or **CPR** as follows:

$$CPR = 1 - (1 - SMM)^{12}$$

This acronym is one of the most commonly pronounced in the securitized markets, because prepayments drive the collateral's average life, and in turn the time over which the structured bond's principal payments will extend.

#### 3.3.1.2 "Defaults"

The **Monthly Default Rate** or **MDR** is in fact a measure of liquidation rates, not so much defaults for consumer loans, as we have explained in the discussion of a loan's life cycle. As we stressed earlier, on corporate loans these MDRs or CDRs when annualized track liquidation rates, not defaults. One could compute a proper rate of occurrence of issue default on a pool of corporate loans, but that is not a conventional measure of loan performance in the context of securitization.

At a time when a given loan is liquidated one does not normally expect to be collecting principal payments or interest payments, but due to the mechanics of servicer advances, such payments might be recorded at the time of liquidation. Hence it is important to account for them. We write $\mathcal{L}_t^D$ the set of loans that are liquidated at time $t$. Then the MDR can be defined as

$$MDR(\mathcal{L})_t = \frac{\sum_{k \in \mathcal{L}_t^D}((B_k)_t - (\hat{P}_k)_t - (\check{P}_k)_t)}{\sum_{k \in \mathcal{L}}((B_k)_t - (\hat{P}_k)_t - (\check{P}_k)_t)}$$

So this measure of liquidations excludes principal amounts that were paid according to the scheduled payments or voluntary prepayments effectively made. The expression of the metric also effectively excludes the case of a liquidation happening only partially to a loan (unlike what we have with prepayments as we saw earlier). Along the same logic as for SMM, we can also define a simpler version of MDR as a weighted proportion of loans that are liquidated:

$$MDR(\mathcal{L})_t = \frac{\sum_{k \in \mathcal{L}_t^D}(B_k)_t}{\sum_{k \in \mathcal{L}}(B_k)_t}$$

However one chooses to represent defaults and prepayments, it is crucial that the metrics be consistent, so that they can be combined.

Monthly default rates are annualized into a **Conditional Default Rate** or **CDR** as follows:

$$CDR = 1 - (1 - MDR)^{12}$$

Note that while SMM and MDR may be added up in some cases in order to obtain the full amount of balance reduction, one cannot add CPR and CDR together, they first need to be converted back to SMM and MDR (since they are not linear as a function of the principal cash flows).

#### 3.3.1.3 Severities

The **severity** or **loss severity** on a loan is the amount of loss it generates upon liquidation, relative to the liquidated balance. One can also define the **recovery** as the amount recovered upon liquidation. So we would have $SEV = 1 - REC$. We have defined unscheduled involuntary payments as $\bar{P}$, so the definition of loss severity will depend on the way liquidations have been defined: either by looking at total loan balance, or looking at the balance once prepayments and scheduled payments have been accounted for. Accordingly, one can define severities either as

$$SEV(\mathcal{L})_t = 1 - \frac{\sum_{k \in \mathcal{L}_t^D} (\bar{P}_k)_t}{\sum_{k \in \mathcal{L}_t^D} (B_k)_t}$$

Or as:

$$SEV(\mathcal{L})_t = 1 - \frac{\sum_{k \in \mathcal{L}_t^D} (\bar{P}_k)_t}{\sum_{k \in \mathcal{L}_t^D} ((B_k)_t - (\hat{P}_k)_t - (\check{P}_k)_t)}.$$

#### 3.3.1.4 Example Expressions of Prepayments, Defaults, and Severities

We give some example code expressing the aggregations corresponding to the metrics we have defined above. All these metrics can be expressed in a single aggregation by careful conditioning:

- Prepayments are captured as loans exiting the pool which were performing before (it is an arbitrary decision of whether or not to include transition to full repayment from 30-day delinquencies).
- Severity is the amount of losses incurred at liquidation over the liquidated balance. There may be complexities related to the timing of the recoveries, if they are reported at later dates in the tape, for example.
- Defaults/liquidations are captured as loans exiting the pool which were delinquent before. These transitions may be further bucketed by the starting state, since we expect differences in severities between short-sales and REO exits. Note that although it is a faster exit, a charge-off will typically imply a very high loss severity since it is conditioned upon the servicer judging the collateral worthless compared to costs.

The example code in Table 3.6 shows the way such expressions would be computed in a simple fashion. The status "0" refers to the loan having exited the pool.

### 3.3.2 Alternative Performance Measures

Although CPR and CDR are the most commonly used measures, there are many more, which are sometimes preferred by the market because they supposedly better

**Table 3.6** Example calculation of prepayment, default, and severity metrics. *Source* Compiled by the author

```
select
  CurDate,
  sum(prior_balance * ((prior_delq = 'C') and (delq = '0'))) /
    sum(prior_balance) as AvgSMM,
  sum(prior_balance * ((prior_delq in ('D', 'F', 'R')) and (delq = '0'))) /
    sum(prior_balance) as AvgMDR,
  sum(loss * ((prior_delq in ('D', 'F', 'R')) and (delq = '0'))) /
    sum(prior_balance * ((prior_delq in ('D', 'F', 'R')) and (delq = '0')))
    as AvgSEV
from loantable
group by CurDate
```

capture the natural patterns in prepayments or defaults. The curves shown here are all indexed by each loan's age, since they attempt to capture particular patterns that are related to the time spent since origination. Reporting a prepayment or default measure on these age-based scales, therefore, nets out the assumed contribution of the loans' aging. These alternative scales are ubiquitous when reporting deal-level prepayments or defaults or to express structuring assumptions.

#### 3.3.2.1 PSA

The **PSA**, or Public Securities Association prepayment curve, starts at 0.2% CPR at month 1 and adds 0.2% every month until it reaches 6% CPR in month 30 after which it is flat. It was published in 1985 and represents an estimate of a standard mortgage prepayments due to people's propensity to move, that is turnover. Prepayment speeds expressed in PSA mean a multiple of this base curve, in percentage terms. So, for example, a prepayment speed of 300% PSA means prepayments ramping up to 18% CPR after 30 months and staying flat after. The chart in Fig. 3.3 shows the curves in CPR terms for 100% PSA as a dotted line, 200% PSA solid, and 50% PSA dashed.

#### 3.3.2.2 SDA

The **SDA** curve, or Standard Default Assumption, follows the same underlying notion as the PSA, but for credit. It is supposed to represent the default patterns of a standard mortgage over time. A default assumption of 100% SDA assumes an initial CDR of 0.02% for the first month, then ramping up by 0.02% each month until the 30th month where it reaches a CDR of 0.6%. It remains at 0.6% until the 60th month. Then it starts decreasing by 0.0095% each month until it reaches at month 120 a CDR of 0.03% and stays at that level afterward. The chart in Fig. 3.4 shows the curves in CDR terms for 100% SDA as a dotted line, 200% SDA solid, and 50% SDA dashed.

The SDA curve is supposed to capture the patterns generally observed in the data, whereby borrowers do not tend to default very soon after they just obtained their loan. And past a certain loan age, defaults are then less frequent because those borrowers who would have been most likely to default already have, and also because home

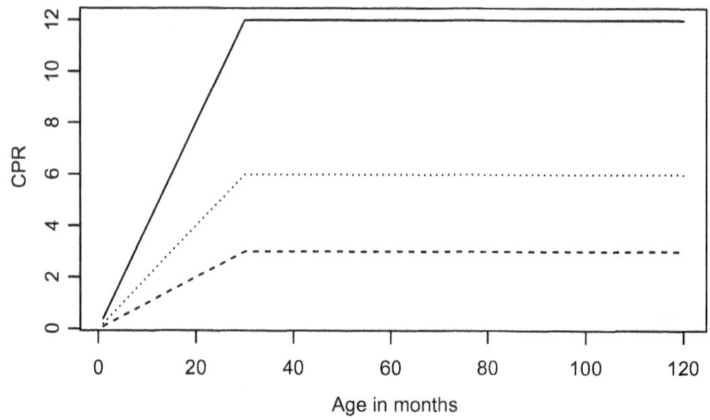


**Fig. 3.3** PSA curves. *Source* Compiled by the author

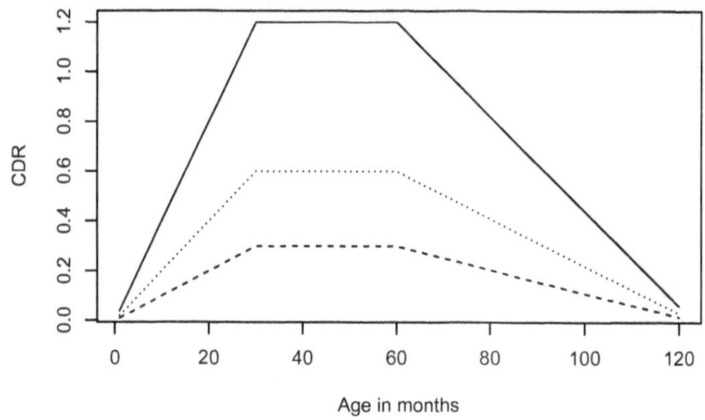


**Fig. 3.4** SDA curves. *Source* Compiled by the author

prices tend to increase, which increases the borrower's equity in the house and hence reduces their propensity to default.

#### 3.3.2.3 ABS

The so-called **ABS prepayment curve** is a particular metric often used in non-mortgage related asset-backed securities analysis or structuring. It differs from metrics like CPR or CDR in that the reference is not the current balance, but the initial balance. A prepayment speed of 2% ABS, for example, means that a fixed amount of 2% of the collateral's initial balance will prepay each year. Expressed in CPR terms, a constant ABS prepayment speed is therefore increasing over time. A constant volume of prepayments, in absolute terms, is deemed more representative of the typical behavior of non-mortgage assets like car loans, mostly because they have much shorter term than mortgage loans.

### 3.3.3 Drivers of Loan Behavior

We have seen how to empirically define and track prepayments or defaults on pools of assets, but it is also useful to have some basic intuition of what drives them. It is not our main focus, and there are massive amounts of literature on loan prepayment and defaults, both academic and from the industry. For US mortgages, see, for example, Fabozzi (2016) for an applied perspective, or Krainer and Laderman (2011), for an empirical study looking at both defaults and prepayments over the period of the mortgage crisis.

In this section, we go through an overview of the main drivers of loan behavior, as they are typically understood. The most basic explanation is as an option exercise, both for prepayments and defaults.

#### 3.3.3.1 Prepayments

The prepayment option can be seen as a **call** and the default option as a **put**. Both options are American, as they can be exercised at any time.

If prepayment is allowed without significant penalties, the borrower possesses indeed a prepayment option: if the loan value goes up (rates go down), the borrower can refinance into a new loan at the new market rate, this is akin to a call on the loan value. In theory, the borrower should refinance as soon as the loan's value goes above 100 (or rates drop below the rate that they are paying).

Generally in the literature, the incentive to refinance is not expressed as a function of the value of the loan, but as a function of available rates in the market. Expressing it as a function of the value of the loan is fundamentally the same thing,[13] but it is a more general framework since it also encompasses the case of corporate loans, for which a price is directly given.

When one considers prepayment behavior, it is common practice to distinguish two essential drivers, the **refinancing incentive** and **turnover**.

The refinancing incentive is a measure of how far higher than par the value of the loan is. The greater this refinancing incentive, the more one expect the borrowers to prepay.

- In the case of mortgage loans, one can look at the difference between the rate paid by the borrower and the rate in the market available to them. This is generally captured as the loan rate minus the prevailing market rate.
- In the case of callable corporate loans, this can be captured equivalently by the rate or spread paid on the loan minus the market rate or spread for the same rating and sector. One can also compute the difference between the loan's price (if it is traded) and 100.

[13] Valuing a mortgage relative to current available mortgage rates is done by simply computing the present value of that existing mortgage at the new mortgage rate.

In either case, one considers **refinancing curves**, that is some plot or analysis of prepayments as a function of the incentive measure.

Turnover is the part of prepayments that is not driven by a purely financial incentive:

- In the case of mortgages, turnover measures the prepayments due to people moving to a new house, a function of demographics and underlying economic trends.
- On corporate loans, this is driven by the necessity to secure financing before the loan's term. As the full payment becomes due on a loan it is common for a corporation to roll it into a new loan in order to keep permanent debt funding.

To analyze turnover, one considers prepayments on loans that do not have a refinancing incentive as a function of their seasoning. Many loan characteristics affect these patterns, and real-world prepayment models are very complex and go far beyond basic statistical models. In most cases every variable enters an adhoc non-linear expression designed to capture its contribution. The options-based perspective has been used mainly in academia: see, for example, Stanton (1995), a seminal paper on prepayments. Practitioners have generally stayed with purely econometric models, which can better capture minute differences in behavior that have an importance in terms of valuation.

#### 3.3.3.2 Defaults

The decision to default can also be looked at as an option. If lenders have limited recourse in the case of default, then the borrower possesses the following default option:

- If the value of the assets financed through the loan goes down, and the borrower's equity becomes negative they can default (and theoretically get a new, cheaper asset, and a new loan).
- In theory the borrower should default as soon as their equity is negative (barring strategic behavior regarding timing, or the cost of credit damage).

Neither the prepayment nor the default option can be exercised optimally as there are substantial frictions, in particular in the default process. Naturally, getting a new, cheaper, loan after having defaulted on a prior loan is fairly unlikely.

Regarding the modeling of defaults and credit, the landscape is comparable to that of prepayments. On one side, academic research has concentrated on explaining certain effects in default behavior. For example, studies by Guiso et al. (2013) and Gerardi et al. (2015) empirically examine the details of the default decision, and try to identify particular drivers at the individual level. Similarly, Gupta and Hansman (2015) look into the disambiguation between moral hazard and adverse selection in mortgage default. These models are tests of certain theoretical decision processes, in contrast with the models used by institutional investors or banks, which aim at predicting defaults in the most accurate manner possible given a set of observable inputs.

As we mentioned above, one can consider that whether on mortgages or corporate loans, the drivers of default are metrics related to declines in loan values. On mortgages, these drivers can be grouped into two broad categories:

- Deterioration of borrower credit: for example, missing payments, or increased rate of unemployment leading to a higher likelihood of missed payments.
- Deterioration in borrower equity: for example, an increasing loan balance due to negative amortization, or declining house prices, both leading to a reduced equity.

On loans, it revolves mainly around the factors leading to lower loan valuations:

- Issuer specific factors, for example, a rating downgrade and limited access to cash, leading to a drop in loan value, could trigger a default
- Industry-wide loan price declines can lead to the same outcome.

We can now apply these various considerations, combined with the loan characteristics descriptions we discussed earlier, to the US agency market.

### 3.3.4 A Drill Down into US Mortgages

Using the database mentioned in the introduction, we query 30-year fixed-rate loan-level monthly data on about 8.5 trillion dollars worth of mortgages issued and securitized between 2000 and 2018 in order to explore various aspects of mortgage loan characteristics, and prepayment and default behavior. The securitization rate of prime mortgages in the US is very high, so these loans represent a substantial sample of mortgages originated in the US over the period.

There are some particular quirks with the loan-level data provided by the agencies, which deserve mentioning. Since this data is given in support to the analysis of synthetic securitizations that were historically only exposed to some arbitrary notion of default (rather than to actual losses), the reporting does not conform to the long term uses in the non-agency market. Fewer details have been provided concerning the back-end of transitions. Further, the agencies have been able to put delinquent loans back to their sellers in many cases, which effectively translates into a sudden exit of the loan from the pool. As a result, one can get a relatively precise view of the front-end of the transition matrix, and of the liquidation of some loans, but the transition from moderate delinquency to the liquidation is less precise from the perspective of a transition analysis. In our use of this data we will, therefore, mostly focus on prepayments, 30 to 90-day delinquencies, and liquidations and loss severities. These minor issues are well compensated by the fact that combining both Fannie Mae and Freddie Mac data, this is by far the largest freely available loan-level dataset.

This drill down will bring us through loan origination, then refinancing and turnover prepayment curves, followed by the relationship between housing and delinquencies, with finally a close look into loss severities.

#### 3.3.4.1 Loan Origination

We begin by looking at the distribution of origination volumes. Figure 3.5 shows the relative frequency of origination along FICO scores (in vertical slices), as one changes the original LTV. We distinguish pre- and post-crisis origination, respectively, up to and including 2007, or after. The darker color represents a denser concentration of origination. We can see that in both cases, the dark shades move down as LTV increases. This means that loans with a higher LTV also tend to have a FICO distribution shifted downward. This may sound surprising, because one could have expected that the worse loans (from an LTV standpoint) would somehow compensate that with a better FICO. It is not the case, because the reality is that the borrowers who will borrow to a higher LTV, because they need to, tend to have a worse credit score than those borrowers who do not need to borrow as much. Hence, the landscape already contains a degree of risk layering.

We can also observe that this effect is less pronounced in post-crisis loans than before the crisis. The layering of risks, that is concentrating bad credit characteristics onto particular subsets of the loans, was more pronounced at the time. As lending constraints tightened after the crisis, more attention was paid to these risky pockets, but they have not been entirely limited. Note that the loans with an LTV above 80 have required to obtain MI in order to benefit from the agency guarantee, so there are differences in how they were underwritten, and in their eventual risks.

As we have seen above, lower credit scores were associated with higher LTVs. We may wonder to what extend this has been priced in. Figure 3.6 displays the average OMS of the loans at issuance as a function of LTV and FICO, and of the origination period. Recall that the off-market spread measures the difference between a loan's rate at origination with the market reference rate (here the Freddie Mac 30-year Survey Rate). We can see that while in pre-crisis origination the differences in rates were not strong and depended mainly on LTV, the loans that were originated afterward factored in the FICO score in a much stronger fashion. Although the relationship with LTV and OMS remained after the crisis, it has been dominated by the relationship between FICO and OMS. Note that the loan rates reported here do not include the cost of mortgage insurance.

#### 3.3.4.2 Prepayments: Refinancings and Turnover

Focusing now on prepayment behavior, we look into turnover and focus on one of its important drivers. In order to discuss turnover, as distinguished from refinancings, we need to properly define a measure of refinancing incentives. For our illustration purposes, we measure the refinancing incentive as the difference between each

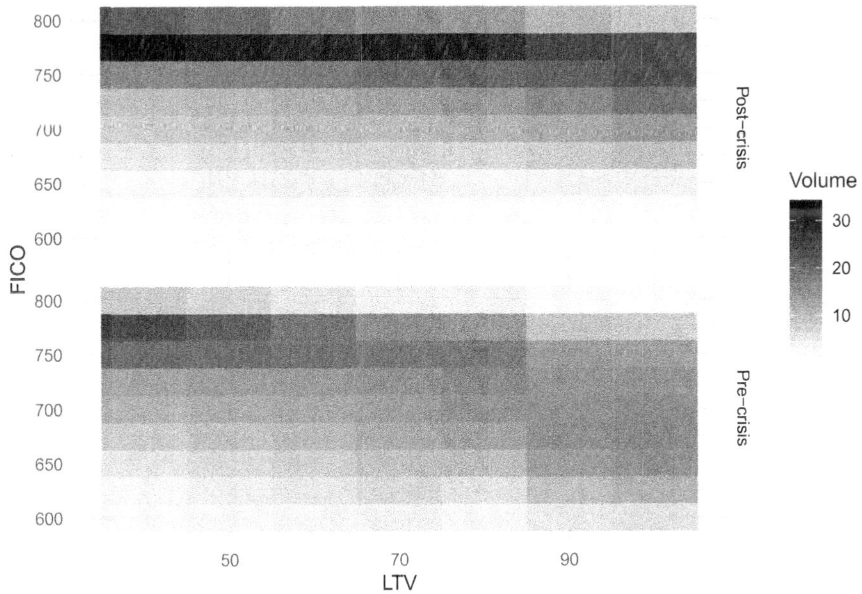


**Fig. 3.5** Evolution of the relationship between FICO and LTV in agency 30-year FRMs origination. *Source* Compiled by the author based on loan-level data from Fannie Mae and Freddie Mac

loan's rate and the prevailing market rate.[14] The seasoning curves in Fig. 3.7 show prepayments on loans with a negative refinancing incentive, and therefore whose prepayments are not expected to be driven by an interest rate related decision. We can see how prepayments ramp up, and in the post-crisis period stabilize more or less under 10% CPR after reaching a plateau around 3 years of seasoning. Recalling the shape of the PSA prepayment assumption, we can see it is not unreasonable.

The prepayment seasoning curves are bucketed by original LTV, and we can see that high LTV loans have been printing faster speeds by a handful of CPR. Presumably, the cost of mortgage insurance on these higher LTV loans creates an additional refinancing incentive for these borrowers, leading to faster prepayments.

We now shift gear and drill further into prepayments, and will seek to disambiguate between several correlated factors affecting the loans' negative convexity, by analyzing some refinancing patterns.

A loan's original LTV conditions its credit risk but also the borrower's access to refinancing opportunities. The refinancing curves in Fig. 3.8 display prepayments on loans, controlling for seasoning (between 18 and 36 months), as a function of the incentive. The various curves are bucketed by original LTV, and both sets of curves distinguish prepayments that took place in the pre-crisis period (defined as observations up to and including 2007), or post-crisis. The data combines loans

[14]We actually use the market rate shifted in time by several weeks to account for processing lags, in line with the usual practice.

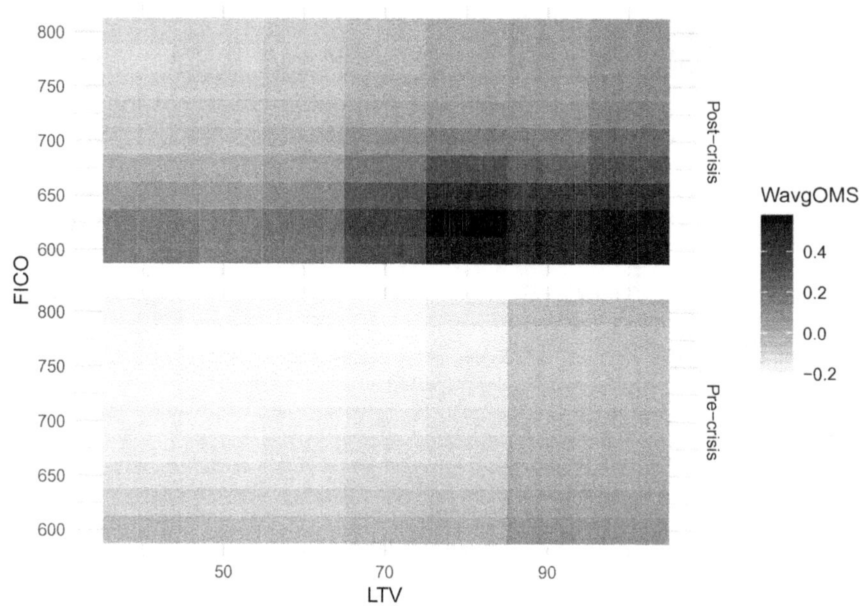


**Fig. 3.6** Evidence and evolution of risk-based pricing in agency FRMs origination. *Source* Compiled by the author based on loan-level data from Fannie Mae and Freddie Mac

with or without mortgage insurance. The slope of these curves is effectively an approximation for the negative convexity cost on these loans, something which gets structured as much as credit risk in securitization deals.

We can note the following patterns:

- Before 2008, the LTV did not appear to play a significant role in terms of refinancing behavior, but what little role it had, consistent with intuition, was that a greater LTV leads to slower prepayment speeds on loans that were in-the-money.
- After the crisis, the situation was markedly different: not only were prepayment speeds generally much lower, given the incentive, but the effect of LTV was stronger and depressed prepayments further.

These patterns are consistent with the mortgage crisis pushing lenders to look at loan characteristics much more closely, and in particular to offer less opportunities to borrowers who initially had a high LTV.

Somewhat in contrast with the impact of LTV, we can see that refinancings have been much more affected by the original credit score, as shown in Fig. 3.9. While we observe a similar pattern as in Fig. 3.8, with refinancings being muted in the post-crisis period, the curves are much more affected by the original FICO than by LTV. It is also clear that prepayments on low FICO loans that are out of the money are faster than on high FICO loans. This feature of credit-impaired borrowers (leading to a flatter refinancing curve overall) is referred to as **extension protection**, because

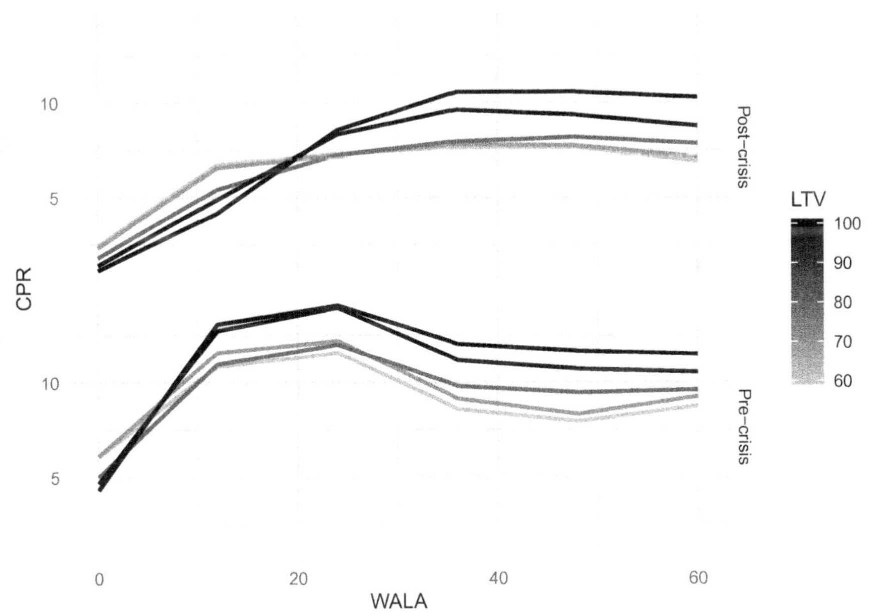


**Fig. 3.7** Turnover curves on agency 30-year FRMs by LTV. *Source* Compiled by the author based on loan-level data from Fannie Mae and Freddie Mac

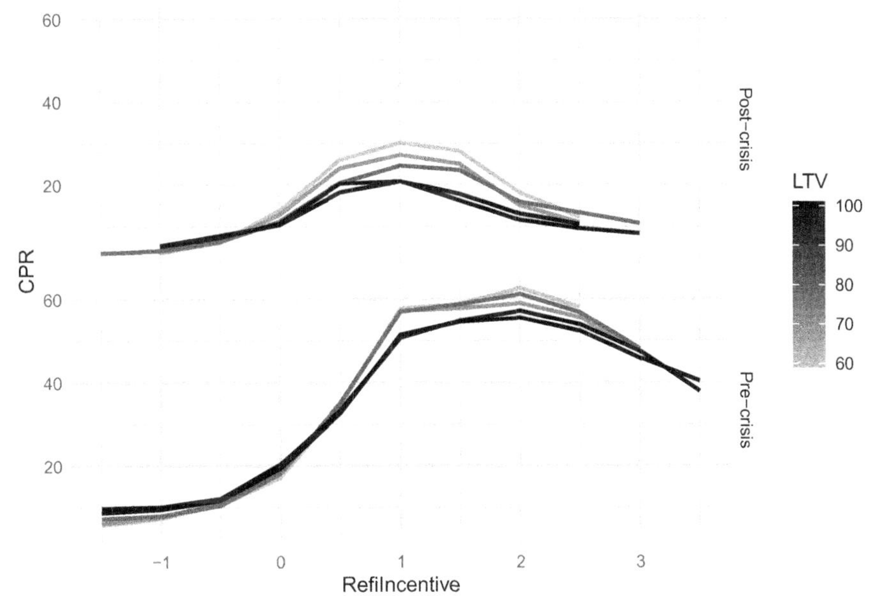


**Fig. 3.8** Refinancing curves on agency 30-year FRMs by LTV. *Source* Compiled by the author based on loan-level data from Fannie Mae and Freddie Mac

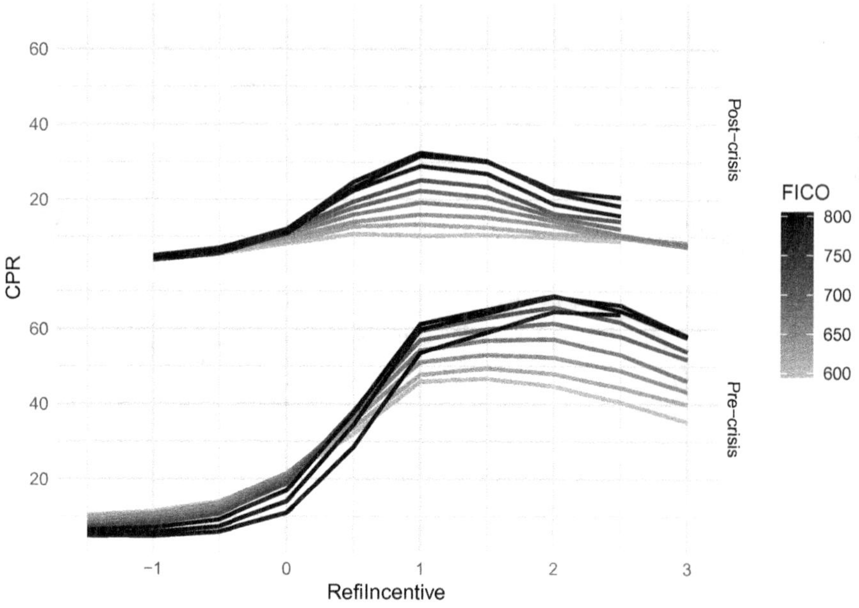


**Fig. 3.9** Refinancing curves on agency 30-year FRMs by FICO. *Source* Compiled by the author based on loan-level data from Fannie Mae and Freddie Mac

in situations where interest rates back up, the pool's average life does not extend as much as it does with high FICO loans.

Figure 3.9 stresses the importance of the original credit score as a driver of future prepayments, but in fact it needs to be adjusted to some extent. Indeed, the impact of FICO on refinancings is augmented by the fact that low original FICO scores lead to a greater proportion of delinquencies, as we will see further down, which in turn essentially bars these loans from seeking a refinancing, and hence reduces overall prepayment speeds on the pool even though it might be well in-the-money.

The FICO score strongly affects the likelihood that the loans will be delinquent in the future. When we plotted Fig. 3.9, looking at loans aged between 1.5 and 2.5 years, some of them had time to have become delinquent, which would be a function of the FICO score. In order to eliminate the impact of the relationship between FICO and future delinquencies on prepayments, Fig. 3.10 shows the same refinancing curves as Fig. 3.9, but only on loans that had never been delinquent. We can see that the contribution of FICO is less important, and the various curves are closer together in the pre-crisis period.

After the mortgage crisis, a low credit score, even without having been delinquent on the loan, became more of a handicap when applying for a new mortgage, and the post-crisis refinancing curves are more clearly separated.

Beyond the credit score, one of the most important drivers of refinancing behavior is the loan amount. Figure 3.11 shows prepayments as a function of initial loan size (in thousands), and it is striking how strongly refinancings are affected by that metric. On smaller loans, the fixed costs attached to a refinancing such as application or

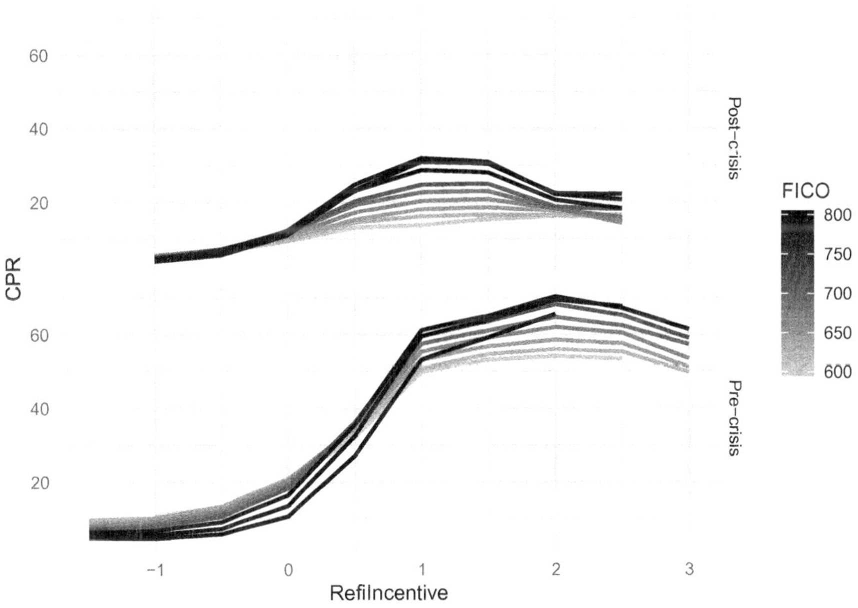


**Fig. 3.10** Refinancing curves on agency 30-year FRMs by FICO on loans never delinquent. *Source* Compiled by the author based on loan-level data from Fannie Mae and Freddie Mac

processing fees represent such a large amount relative to the loan amount and to the potential savings from refinancing, that they act as a form of deterrent. One traditional explanation has also been that borrowers who took out smaller loans, financing properties of lower-than-average value, had lower income than the rest and maybe less access to financial information. While this explanation may have been relevant 20 years ago, it seems less so today.

The importance of loan size as a driver of the prepayment curve slope, which in turn drives the cost of convexity, is reflected in the significant pay-ups at which agency pools with low loan balances trade.

In order to simply account for the contribution of various factors, Table 3.7 shows several empirical models (linear least-squares regressions) for the rate of delinquency (30-day to 90+) between seasonings of 18 and 36 months. The loan-level data was first aggregated along several bucketing dimensions (FICO, LTV, HPI…) in order to make the processing of the regression feasible. The four models presented in the table cover loans that were in-the-money (with a refinancing incentive between 1.75% and 2.25%), or out-of-the-money (with an incentive between −1.25% and −0.75%). The pre/post-crisis observations refer to those before and after 2008, respectively. Prepayments are measured in CPR terms, so that they are commensurate with the charts we have discussed so far, but note that SMM would be a more appropriate measure for modeling, undistorted by compounding.

The explanatory variables are not re-scaled or centered, so that the magnitude of their impact can directly be read from the coefficients. ALScap250 refers to the initial loan size, in thousands, capped at $250K. LTVgt90 is the LTV in excess of 90%.

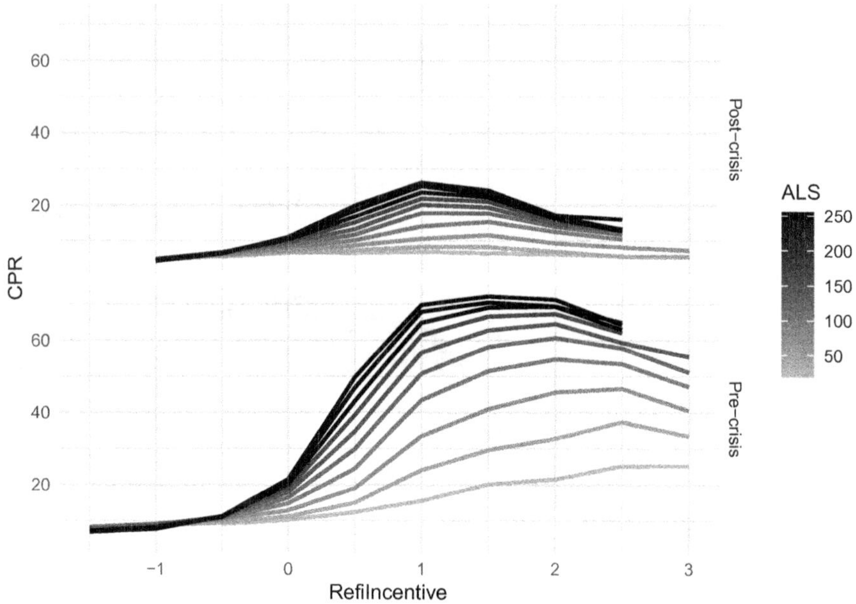


**Fig. 3.11** Refinancing curves on agency 30-year FRMs by loan size. *Source* Compiled by the author based on loan-level data from Fannie Mae and Freddie Mac

**Table 3.7** Empirical models for In-the-money and Out-of-the-money prepayments. *Source* Compiled by the author based on loan-level data from Fannie Mae and Freddie Mac

| Names | ITM Pre-crisis | OTM Pre-crisis | ITM Post-crisis | OTM Post-crisis |
|---|---|---|---|---|
| (Intercept) | −216.258 *** | 84.339 *** | −40.533 *** | −11.612 |
| | (12.702) | (5.279) | (4.089) | (7.504) |
| FICO | 0.343 *** | −0.106 *** | 0.10 *** | 0.016 |
| | (0.018) | (0.007) | (0.006) | (0.009) |
| ALScap250 | 0.198 *** | −0.015 *** | 0.084 *** | −0.008 *** |
| | (0.003) | (0.001) | (0.001) | (0.001) |
| DQ | −0.441 *** | −0.616 *** | −0.079 *** | 0.025 |
| | (0.064) | (0.067) | (0.013) | (0.084) |
| LTV | 0.126 *** | 0.035 *** | −0.286 *** | 0.065 *** |
| | (0.021) | (0.005) | (0.009) | (0.005) |
| HPI | 0.237 *** | 0.094 *** | 0.456 *** | 0.033 *** |
| | (0.025) | (0.002) | (0.01) | (0.004) |
| N | 2,517 | 3,846 | 3,954 | 2,295 |
| $R^2$ | 0.683 | 0.585 | 0.695 | 0.185 |

*** $p < 0.001$; ** $p < 0.01$; * $p < 0.05$

DQ is the percentage of loans that are 30 to 90+ days late and HPI is the property's reference zip code level FHFA home price index appreciation since origination, expressed as a percentage.

We can see that the R-squares are fairly high, apart from that for OTM loans after the crisis, for which several coefficients are also not significant. On these, prepayments may have been more a function of the credit environment than of the loan characteristics.

The credit score and loan amount are shown to be very strong drivers of refinancings in the pre-crisis period: an original FICO score greater by 50 points translates into about 15% CPR more in peak speeds, and an increase in $50K in loan balance under $250K translates into 10% CPR more. After the crisis, with prepayment speeds generally more muted, these sensitivities are more than halved. The share of delinquencies plays a role, since in the pre-crisis period a pool with 10% more in delinquencies would have shown peak speeds slower by about 5%. Still before the crisis, a higher LTV also translated into very sightly faster speeds (1.5% CPR for 10 points in LTV). The greater LTV indicated more leverage and a greater incentive to cash out, but also a slightly more difficult access to streamlined refinancings. Local home price appreciation also played a moderate role with an extra 10% leading to a pickup by less than 3% CPR in peak speeds.

Contrasting these coefficients with those for loans in the money after the crisis, most of them work in the same direction, with more muted responses; however, LTV then acted to slow down peak speeds, and home prices played a stronger role. Both are consistent with the credit environment post-crisis, where risk factors such as LTV, and the presence of negative equity, were naturally acting against fast prepayments, even for borrowers with an incentive.

On loans that were out of the money, most of the coefficients are small, even though they may be significant, and hence played little role. The HPI, however, as well as the share of delinquencies could both account for a couple of CPR points, which on slow prepaying pools (under 10% CPR), would be significant for valuation.

Now that we have looked into the prepayment behavior of these 30-year agency loans, we can focus on credit.

#### 3.3.4.3 Credit: Delinquencies and Severities

As we briefly mentioned earlier, given some uncertainty regarding the back-end of the roll rate matrix as we can reconstruct it from the data provided by the agencies, we use delinquency rates instead of transitions into or out of serious delinquencies in order to track credit performance.

While refinancings are naturally driven by movements in interest rates, mortgage credit performance is strongly affected by housing appreciation. Figure 3.12 shows delinquencies on 30-year agency loans, controlling for seasoning (2.5 to 5 years), as a function of local cumulative home price appreciation, for different LTV buckets. The real effect of negative home price appreciation is clear from the post-crisis data. For local cumulative home price growth under 10%, delinquencies appear to raise substantially as it declines.

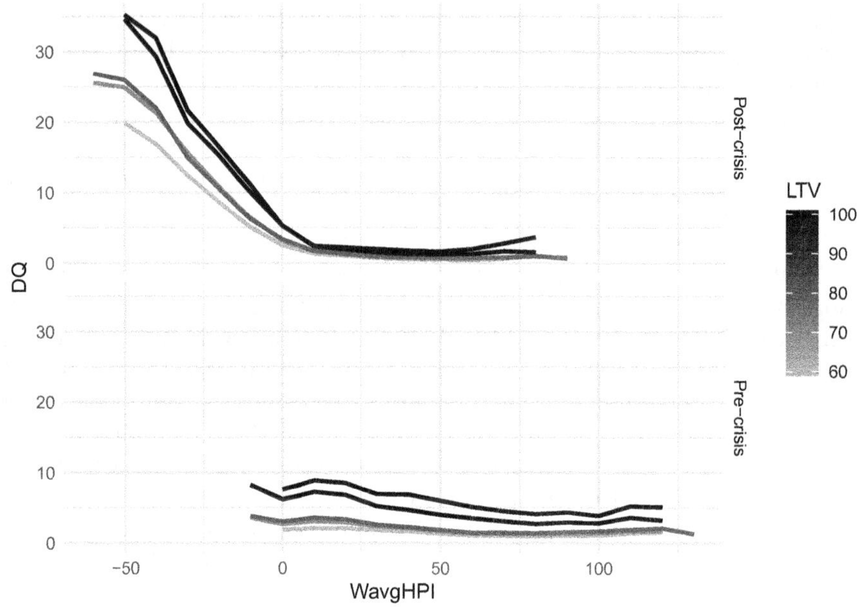


**Fig. 3.12** Delinquencies and home prices on agency 30-year FRMs by LTV. *Source* Compiled by the author based on loan-level data from Fannie Mae and Freddie Mac

Whether we look at observation periods before the crisis, or after, the impact of LTV on delinquencies also grows as home price appreciation declines. For a given housing market level, delinquencies are also clearly delineated as a function of original LTV.

An even more striking relationship is evidenced if we consider Fig. 3.13, where similar data is shown bucketed by original FICO score. Although for positive home price appreciation the higher ranges of credit scores show essentially no delinquencies,[15] these raise to about 10% (for 800 original FICO score borrowers) where home prices dropped by 50%. In the same situation, loans with the worst credit scores in the range displayed delinquency rates nearing 50%.

As we did with prepayments, we can illustrate the combined effect of many loan characteristics on delinquencies through a simple linear least-squares regression, as shown in Table 3.8. The loan-level data is pre-aggregated into buckets along the dimensions tested in the regression, in the same manner as for the prepayment regressions from Table 3.7. In addition to basic metrics such as FICO or LTV, we also included the loan's original rate and the monthly prepayment speed among the explanatory variables. The R-squares and significance of the other coefficients are not affected by this inclusion.

All the coefficients are significant, but several are of such a magnitude that they essentially have no impact. Interestingly, the coefficient for LTV is quite small, pre-

[15]Note that this would be the normal regime for prime mortgages in the US.

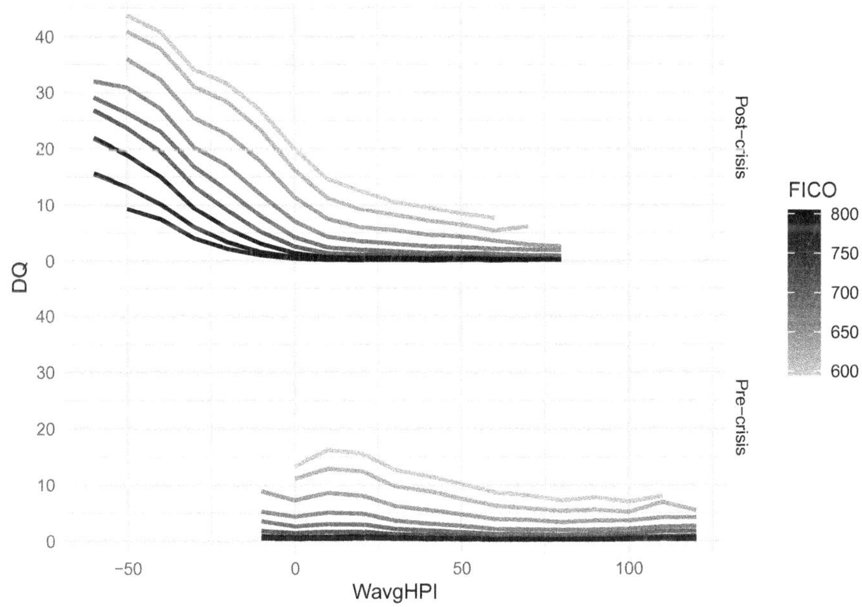


**Fig. 3.13** Delinquencies and home prices on agency 30-year FRMs by FICO. *Source* Compiled by the author based on loan-level data from Fannie Mae and Freddie Mac

sumably because it gets captured by the coupon. In contrast, original FICO both pre- and post-crisis plays a much stronger role, with a 50 points difference accounting for a change by 5 to 10% in delinquency rates. Interestingly, DTI has a clear positive impact post-crisis (where 10 points increase leads to 7% more delinquencies); however it has a counter-intuitive and slightly negative impact pre-crisis. This could be due to issues in the quality of loan documentation at the time. Home price appreciation does not come as a very strong effect pre-crisis, but, as could be expected, played a stronger role afterward.

Having empirically established some of the drivers behind delinquencies, we can turn to another aspect of overall credit performance, that is the outcome from liquidations. As we explained earlier, properties that have been repossessed by the servicer for the lender need to be sold into the market, and the proceeds from that sale, minus costs and potential advances by the servicer, are recovered.

The amount of loan outstanding balance that entered REO and that is not recouped after liquidation and costs is the loss severity. Figure 3.14 shows loss severities as a function of local home prices, bucketed by LTV, on loans that did not carry mortgage insurance.

Liquidation data on agency loans before the mortgage crisis was sparse, and it shows in the noise for that period in the chart. After more negative prints in home prices growth were observed, and many more liquidations, the data shows some clear patterns. One first thing should stand out: there is a clear and seemingly linear relationship between loss severity and local home price appreciation. The slope of that relationship in the data is approximately half a point of increase in severity for

**Table 3.8** Empirical models for delinquencies. *Source* Compiled by the author based on loan-level data from Fannie Mae and Freddie Mac

| Names | Pre-crisis | Post-crisis |
|---|---|---|
| (Intercept) | 130.422 *** | 47.861 *** |
| | (1.041) | (1.174) |
| FICO | −0.182 *** | −0.09 *** |
| | (0.001) | (0.001) |
| ALScap250 | 0.003 *** | 0.01 *** |
| | (0.00) | (0.00) |
| LTV | −0.003 * | −0.009 *** |
| | (0.001) | (0.001) |
| Seconds | 0.131 *** | −0.30 *** |
| | (0.012) | (0.01) |
| HPI | −0.014 *** | −0.112 *** |
| | (0.00) | (0.001) |
| DTI | −0.172 *** | 0.666 *** |
| | (0.006) | (0.008) |
| Coupon | 1.646 *** | 0.286 *** |
| | (0.024) | (0.036) |
| SMM | −0.241 *** | −0.933 *** |
| | (0.007) | (0.012) |
| N | 63,988 | 109,545 |
| $R^2$ | 0.733 | 0.703 |

*** $p < 0.001$; ** $p < 0.01$; * $p < 0.05$

each less point of home price growth. Another interesting pattern in this chart is that the LTV has some effect, but it is not as important as one might have believed.

Accounting for numerous effects at the same time, the linear least-squares regression shown in Table 3.9, also using pre-aggregated bucketed data, gives us some insights into the combined drivers of loss severity. First, note the R-squares come out at about half of those for delinquencies: this is a likely consequence of the smaller number of observations in each aggregation bucket.

The variable LTVcap80 represents the LTV capped at 80%. Indeed, we are also including MI, a variable that captures the amount of mortgage insurance coverage in the regression, which would normally be set in order to bring down the LTV to the 70s, on those loans with an initial LTV above 80. The variable REOtime tracks the number of months that the loan spent in REO before liquidation.

We can see that all the coefficients in the regressions shown in the table are significant, with signs that are congruent with intuition. The LTV, as we guessed from Fig. 3.14, plays a moderate role, with each 10 points of additional LTV adding a couple of points in loss severity. House price growth, or lack thereof, affects loss severity with a slope of approximately 1:2, as we indicated above. Mortgage insurance seems to lower loss severity by 50 to 70% of its coverage amount, which makes it quite significant. Every extra year in REO adds about 6 or 7% to loss severities,

**Table 3.9** Empirical models for loss severity. *Source* Compiled by the author based on loan-level data from Fannie Mae and Freddie Mac

| names | Pre-crisis | Post-crisis | All periods |
|---|---|---|---|
| (Intercept) | 45.064 *** | 16.029 *** | 9.466 *** |
| | (2.825) | (0.653) | (0.635) |
| LTVcap80 | −0.21 *** | 0.467 *** | 0.459 *** |
| | (0.036) | (0.008) | (0.008) |
| HPI | −0.552 *** | −0.55 *** | −0.628 *** |
| | (0.011) | (0.002) | (0.002) |
| MI | −0.72 *** | −0.683 *** | −0.716 *** |
| | (0.008) | (0.003) | (0.003) |
| REOtime | 0.734 *** | 0.594 *** | 0.593 *** |
| | (0.023) | (0.007) | (0.006) |
| ALS | −0.113 *** | −0.111 *** | −0.105 *** |
| | (0.001) | (0.00) | (0.00) |
| WALA | 0.281 *** | 0.033 *** | 0.09 *** |
| | (0.007) | (0.001) | (0.001) |
| N | 56,603 | 423,843 | 480,446 |
| $R^2$ | 0.298 | 0.323 | 0.361 |

*** $p < 0.001$; ** $p < 0.01$; * $p < 0.05$

either through the capitalization of maintenance costs, or to self-selection (the harder properties to sell being the ones that eventually sell for less). Note that straight loan age also has an impact, presumably because the older the loans, the more potential they have for having diverged from the local house price index estimates.

Now equipped with a broad understanding of what drives a mortgage loan's propensity to prepay or default, we can shift our attention to constructing cash flow projections based on particular state transitions, or CPR or CDR assumptions.

## 3.4 Projecting Loan Behavior

Given some set of assumptions, how does one derive the future cash flows of a loan portfolio? This is the first thing that a freshly minted analyst in securitized products trading or structuring needs to master. We will first briefly discuss how using transition matrices maps into projecting prepayments and defaults. Then we turn to the calculation of cash flows given assumed prepayments and defaults, following market practice. We will use these types of computations very extensively through our discussion of structuring in Chap. 6. Finally, we discuss how to represent simple loan cash flows for the purpose of economic modeling, something we will also use extensively in the following chapters focused on economic modeling.

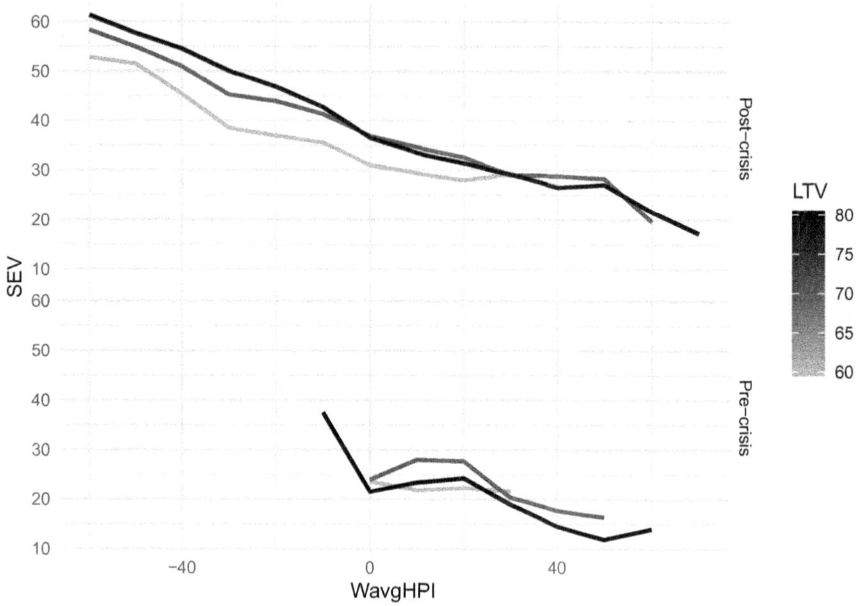


**Fig. 3.14** Loss severities and home prices on agency 30-year FRMs by LTV. *Source* Compiled by the author based on loan-level data from Fannie Mae and Freddie Mac

### 3.4.1 Using Transition Matrices

A transition matrix allows us to project the loan's status distribution over time. Recall that we have a matrix $A$ in which each cell $(i, j)$ represents the probability that a loan will go from state $i$ to state $j$ over a given period. Given a vector of starting conditions $V^0$ specifying the probability that a loan is in each status, we can compute the probability that the loan will be in each status $i$ at the next period:

$$\mathbb{P}[L \in i] = \sum_j V_j^0 A_{i,j}.$$

At an arbitrary time, and for a constant matrix, the distribution across statuses is given by $V^n = V^0 \cdot A^n$.

To each of the transitions corresponds a particular cash flow. Transitions from current to current, for example, imply a normal scheduled payment.[16] Transitions into a worse delinquency state correspond to a lack of payment. Transitions into prepayment correspond to a full loan payment, and transitions into a default state (for consumer loans) correspond to the recognition of a loss and some potential recovery of principal. Hence, to a set of future transitions correspond particular cash flows coming from the loans as a function of the states they are transitioning into.

[16]They may also imply some curtailments, that is additional payments that the borrower sends in, but we are neglecting them here.

Therefore, the volume of prepayment can be represented as the sum of all transitions into prepayments; the volume of "defaults" as the sum of all transitions into liquidation, short-sale, or charge-offs. From the transition matrix one can derive vectors of prepayment amounts and default amounts over time.

It may seem superfluous to model the behavior of loans in such detail when analyzing securitized products.[17] It is however important for two principal reasons:

- First, it is a concise way of reflecting the full information of the loans' delinquency status. A model that would not use each loan's status as an input would lose some information.
- Second, representing loan behavior in this manner allows for proper path-dependent dynamics in collateral cash flows. For example, if prepayment incentives increase and then come back down, one would observe a wave of prepayments on performing loans in good standing. Then, after the prepayment wave has passed, the remaining pool would have a greater proportion of low quality or non-performing loans, and would be expected to exhibit higher delinquency rates going forward, all else being equal. This situation would be very different from that of the same pool if it had not been through this prepayment wave.

### 3.4.2 Usual Market Practice

While we have tended to consider loans without much context so far, we are in fact focused on such loans within a securitization vehicle, and as such we need to account for various expenses that are necessary in setting up an SPV. One of the most important effects to account for is the servicer's advances, shifting interest shortfalls to principal losses.

When loans are delinquent, the servicer is normally supposed to advanced scheduled payments, so as not to disturb the functioning of the structure and preserve senior bonds. At the time of liquidation the servicer recoups their advances. Therefore, a continuous payment of the scheduled amount is assured at the cost of greater eventual losses. Reported losses by trustees include the withdrawal of the servicer advances on each liquidated loan.

However, the servicer may deem the loans to be non-recoverable in which case they can decide to not advance these cash flows. The collateral portfolio cash flows may be substantially affected by these decisions, in particular, and as is normally the case if the structure allocates interest in priority to senior bonds. The modeling of these decisions is complex, however, and for the purpose of our study of securitization not directly essential. It is simply important to be aware of these effects when studying the incentives of junior bonds holders, senior bond holders, and servicers.

In our loan portfolio cash flow representations used for the illustration of structures as well as in the present chapter, we consider these effects are already represented

[17] Although in some cases, some delinquency statuses are collapsed in order to simplify the analysis.

in the underlying cash flows in order to simplify the analysis: whatever servicer advancing takes place, it is assumed to be reflected in the interest and principal cash flows.

Prepayments and defaults are binary events (excluding rare partial prepayments). Hence a loan randomly defaults or prepays or does not, and one should in principle randomly simulate the behavior of each loan according to its transition probabilities, however, this would require too much compute power. In practice prepayments and defaults are treated as deterministic and progressive phenomena.

One considers that a certain probability of prepayment or default (SMM or MDR) translates into each loan prepaying or defaulting a little at each time period. One can show that if the number of loans is large enough, and prepayments and defaults are random then both calculations converge.

We note the collateral's total outstanding balance $B_t$ and its cash flow $CF_t$ at some discrete point in time $t \leq M$ (the balance is meant at the beginning of a period, and the cash flow takes place during that period). These are random variables apart from $B_0$ naturally which would be known. When we compute the cash flows on an asset portfolio, we are effectively looking at a particular realization of the future, that is, $(CF(\omega))_{t \geq 0}$ for $\omega$ an element in some probability space. Typically, one comes up with that particular realization by picking some set of assumptions that seems reasonable based on the analysis of the loans along the lines of what we have discussed in the present chapter. In our notations when we omit $\omega$, we mean something is valid for all possible realizations, in particular, in structuring.

The term $CF$ covers all types of cash flows aggregated together: there are naturally at least principal payments $P_t$ and interest payments $I_t$. However, these can also sometimes be decomposed into more categories, for example, principal payments could be coming from scheduled payments, prepayments and loss recoveries, and one might need to track these sources of cash flows differently. When we mention cash flows in our discussion, this can be understood as a pair of principal and interest payments $CF_t = (P_t, I_t)$. We will also note $CF = (CF_t)_{M \geq t \geq 0}$ that is the vector of future collateral or bond cash flows. We will use the equivalent notations for collateral or bonds outstanding balances $B$. For our purposes, an asset portfolio or a bond can be uniquely represented by a pair $(B, CF)$.

Given a coupon $c_t$ interest can be expressed as $I_t = \frac{c_t}{1200 B_t}$. But in a very general case where the cash flows are not coming from a loan, there might not be a notion of a coupon on the collateral, so we cannot generally define $c$ as a function of $I$.

One might wonder why, in this formal definition of cash flows, we do not track losses. Indeed, it could seem logical to have $L$ to represent write-downs, just as we have $P$ and $I$. The reason is that losses are easily defined from $P$ and $B$, and hence do not need to be specified separately. A loss, or a write-down, is simply a reduction in the balance of a bond that is not compensated by a principal payment. So we would always have $L_t = (B_t - B_{t+1}) - P_t$.

Nevertheless, when we discuss the allocation of losses within a structure, for example, it can be useful to use $L$ even if it is not a cash flow properly speaking, for the sake of simplicity.

**Table 3.10** Basic cash flow amortization

```
InitBal <- 100
Term <- 10
# Vector of sched principal payments vs initial balance
Sched <- (1:Term) / InitBal
Sched[Term] <- (1 - sum(Sched)) + Sched[Term]

basiccf <- function(cpr, cdr, sev, Cpn, InitBal, Term, Sched) {
  amort <- data.frame(Period = 1:Term, BegBal = NA, Int = NA,
    Prin = NA, Loss = NA, SchedPrin = NA, Ppay = NA, Dft = NA, Reco = NA)
  amort$BegBal[1] <- InitBal
  for (per in 1:Term) {
    amort$Int[per] <- amort$BegBal[per] * Cpn
    amort$Ppay[per] <- amort$BegBal[per] * cpr
    amort$Dft[per] <- amort$BegBal[per] * cdr
    amort$SchedPrin[per] <- (amort$BegBal[per] - amort$Ppay[per] -
        amort$Dft[per]) * Sched[per] / sum(Sched[per:Term])
    amort$Loss[per] <- amort$Dft[per] * sev
    amort$Reco[per] <- amort$Dft[per] * (1 - sev)
    amort$Prin[per] <- amort$SchedPrin[per] +
        amort$Ppay[per] + amort$Reco[per]
    if (per < Term) {
      amort$BegBal[per + 1] <- amort$BegBal[per] - amort$SchedPrin[per] -
        amort$Ppay[per] - amort$Dft[per]
    }
  }
  return(amort)
}
```

**Table 3.11** Example loan amortization with no prepayments or defaults. *Source* Compiled by the author

| Period | BegBal | Int | Prin | Loss | SchedPrin | Ppay | Dft | Reco |
|---|---|---|---|---|---|---|---|---|
| 1 | 100 | 5.0 | 1 | 0 | 1 | 0 | 0 | 0 |
| 2 | 99 | 5.0 | 2 | 0 | 2 | 0 | 0 | 0 |
| 3 | 97 | 4.8 | 3 | 0 | 3 | 0 | 0 | 0 |
| 4 | 94 | 4.7 | 4 | 0 | 4 | 0 | 0 | 0 |
| 5 | 90 | 4.5 | 5 | 0 | 5 | 0 | 0 | 0 |
| 6 | 85 | 4.2 | 6 | 0 | 6 | 0 | 0 | 0 |
| 7 | 79 | 4.0 | 7 | 0 | 7 | 0 | 0 | 0 |
| 8 | 72 | 3.6 | 8 | 0 | 8 | 0 | 0 | 0 |
| 9 | 64 | 3.2 | 9 | 0 | 9 | 0 | 0 | 0 |
| 10 | 55 | 2.8 | 55 | 0 | 55 | 0 | 0 | 0 |

The code in Table 3.10 illustrates how one builds an amortization table for a homogeneous loan portfolio.

Tables 3.11 and 3.12 show the result of the calculation of the loan or loan portfolio amortization with different prepayments and default assumptions.

We will use this type of collateral cash flow model in order to illustrate realistic structure behavior in Chap. 6, also including some simulations. Nevertheless, it is

**Table 3.12** Example loan amortization with prepayments or defaults. *Source* Compiled by the author

| Period | BegBal | Int | Prin | Loss | SchedPrin | Ppay | Dft | Reco |
|---|---|---|---|---|---|---|---|---|
| 1 | 100 | 5.00 | 14.3 | 0.60 | 0.86 | 12.0 | 2.00 | 1.40 |
| 2 | 85 | 4.26 | 12.9 | 0.51 | 1.48 | 10.2 | 1.70 | 1.19 |
| 3 | 72 | 3.59 | 11.5 | 0.43 | 1.91 | 8.6 | 1.43 | 1.00 |
| 4 | 60 | 2.99 | 10.2 | 0.36 | 2.19 | 7.2 | 1.20 | 0.84 |
| 5 | 49 | 2.46 | 8.9 | 0.30 | 2.35 | 5.9 | 0.98 | 0.69 |
| 6 | 40 | 2.00 | 7.8 | 0.24 | 2.43 | 4.8 | 0.80 | 0.56 |
| 7 | 32 | 1.60 | 6.7 | 0.19 | 2.44 | 3.8 | 0.64 | 0.45 |
| 8 | 25 | 1.25 | 5.8 | 0.15 | 2.39 | 3.0 | 0.50 | 0.35 |
| 9 | 19 | 0.96 | 4.9 | 0.11 | 2.32 | 2.3 | 0.38 | 0.27 |
| 10 | 14 | 0.71 | 14.1 | 0.08 | 12.17 | 1.7 | 0.28 | 0.20 |

useful to also discuss more formal models that may not be as realistic, but capture the essentials of loan cash flow for economic modeling.

### 3.4.3 Some Simplified Representations for Economic Modeling

The detailed representation of loan cash flows we have covered is realistic, but is difficult to capture in a concise manner with a formal expression. There are alternative approaches, more practical for the formal modeling required in security design models, for example. Although simpler and not requiring an algorithmic description, these alternative models are still able to incarnate the patterns of loan portfolio cash flows.

#### 3.4.3.1 Two-Period Loan Cash Flows

The simplest model that could account for a single loan's or a loan portfolio's cash flows is over one term. We assume there are 2 periods, 0 and $T$, and the loan's original balance is $B_0$. The total collateral cash flow $Y_T$ is decomposed into interest and principal, as well as losses (although they can be implicitly defined as we pointed out).

We have $B_T = 0$, and the loan principal payment and losses before the effect of servicing sum up to the initial balance $P_T^s + L_T^s = B_0$, with $P_T^s \in [0, B_0]$ a random variable. One can also model randomness in $L_T^s$. In addition, a coupon at the rate $c$ is paid. The servicing cost is noted $c_s$. Note that $c$ could also be a random variable, if one needs to account for floating rate loans, for example.

With this simple model, there are several ways of representing the portfolio cash flows depending on assumed servicer behavior: the simplest case with safe coupon, the case with a coupon at risk like principal, and the more complex case reflecting the servicer's advances transferring cash flows from principal to coupon.

First, in the simplest case we do not explicitly model servicer behavior and just consider the net coupon $c - c_s$. The coupon is considered to be paid by the loans before they go delinquent or default and hence we have $I_T = (c - c_s)B_0$, $P_T = P_T^s$ and $L_T = L_T^s$. This essentially makes the interest a risk-free cash flow.

Second, still not factoring in servicer advances, we can also consider the delinquent loans do not pay their coupon, and the coupon shortfall can be recovered at the same recovery rate as principal. Then the total cash flow is composed of the interest $I_T = cP_T^s - c_s B_0$ and $P_T = P_T^s$ and $L_T = L_T^s$. Note that even though the loans' coupons may not be recovered fully, the servicing cost is due.

Third, while delinquent loans would not be paying interest, as we have seen, the servicer would typically advance the payment and recover it as principal payment. Nevertheless, if losses were so high that the advances would account for more than the available principal, then there would be no further advancing. As in the case above we consider that the coupon is not entirely safe, so that before accounting for the impact of the servicer's actions the interest is $I_T^s = cP_T^s - c_s B_0$. Losses are augmented by the coupon that was advanced, but cannot exceed the total initial balance:

$$L_T = B_0 \wedge L_T^s(1 + c),$$

and principal is reduced as much:

$$P_T = 0 \vee (P_T^s - cL_T^s).$$

The full coupon is advanced, unless losses are too high and hence

$$I_T = (c - c_s)B_0 - (0 \vee (L_T - B_0(1 - c - c_s))) .$$

We can see that still with such a simple two-period model, one can represent many aspects of loan portfolio cash flows. Still, in the optimal funding or security design literature, such details of loan cash flows have been rarely addressed. These simple models may, however, be sufficient to look into servicer behavior, for example.

The main drawback of this model is the lack of dynamics, and we can address that with a more advanced approach.

#### 3.4.3.2 Dynamic Representation of Cash Flows

In order to capture many of the dynamic aspects of the cash flows from a loan portfolio, we turn to a continuous time representation. We consider a portfolio with a starting balance of $B_0$, in which loans may repay principal at a certain instantaneous rate $R_t$ relative to the current balance, and generate losses at an instantaneous rate $D_t$. Note that we do not need to distinguish between defaults and losses here: recoveries can be included as part of $R_t$. More formally, we equip ourselves with a probability space $(\Omega, \mathcal{F}, \mathbb{P})$ and assume $(R_t)_{t\geq 0}$ and $(D_t)_{t\geq 0}$ are two continuous and $\mathcal{F}$-adapted random processes taking positive values. The coupon that might be paid by this collateral is another continuous process $(c_t)_{t\geq 0}$. We consider a legal maturity of $T$.

The portfolio's instantaneous change in balance is expressed as

$$dB_t = -B_t(R_t + D_t)dt,$$

which describes a continuous and derivable stochastic process. With the initial condition this stochastic differential equation can be resolved:

$$B_t = B_0 \exp\left(-\int_0^t (R_s + D_s)ds\right).$$

The total amount of principal paid by the loan portfolio up to time $\tau \leq T$ is

$$P_\tau = \int_0^\tau B_t R_t dt = B_0 \int_0^\tau R_t \exp\left(-\int_0^t (R_s + D_s)ds\right) dt.$$

Losses and interest can be expressed in the same way:

$$L_\tau = \int_0^\tau B_t D_t dt = B_0 \int_0^\tau D_t \exp\left(-\int_0^t (R_s + D_s)ds\right) dt,$$

and

$$I_\tau = \int_0^\tau B_t c_t dt = B_0 \int_0^\tau c_t \exp\left(-\int_0^t (R_s + D_s)ds\right) dt.$$

Also, since principal and losses must eventually add up to the initial balance, we have

$$B_0 = P_T + L_T = \int_0^T B_t(R_t + D_t)dt.$$

## 3.5 Conclusion

With this chapter, we have now concluded the rapid overview of useful stylized facts that pertain to securitization. In our discussion of the characterization of loans and of the general patterns of loan behavior, the common thread has been to gain just enough details to make the close reading of many empirical papers in the field accessible, in addition to opening the door to an advanced discussion of structuring techniques. The high-level description of mortgage data, and of sometimes opaque characteristics or definitions for the uninitiated should come in handy when we drill into some empirical research. Clarifying (and explaining) how certain metrics should be computed is also important, as it forces us to critically think about what defaults really mean, and puts us in a position to judge the relevance of various alternative methods of default definition.

We hence are now in the right position to jump into the more formal economic analysis of securitization.

## References

Fabozzi, F. J., (Ed.). (2016). *The handbook of mortgage-backed securities* (7th ed.). Oxford University Press.

Gauthier, L., & Zimmerman, T. (2006). Mortgage credit quantified. In F. J. Fabozzi (Ed.), *The handbook of mortgage-backed securities* (6th ed.). McGraw-Hill Education.

Gerardi, K., Herkenhoff, K. F., Ohanian, L. E., & Willen, P. S. (2015). Can't pay or won't Pay? Unemployment, negative equity, and strategic default. In *Working Paper 21630. Working Paper Series, National Bureau of Economic Research*. Cambridge: National Bureau of Economic Research.

Grimshaw, S. D., & Alexander, W. P. (2011). Markov chain models for delinquency: Transition matrix estimation and forecasting. *Applied Stochastic Models in Business and Industry*, *27*(3), 267–279.

Guiso, L., Sapienza, P., & Zingales, L. (2013). The determinants of attitudes toward strategic default on mortgages. *The Journal of Finance*, *68*(4), 1473–1515.

Gupta, A., & Hansman, C. (2015). *Selection, Leverage, and Default in the Mortgage Market. Working Paper. SSRN.*

Krainer, J., & Laderman, E. (2011). Prepayment and delinquency in the mortgage crisis period. In *Working Paper Series 2011–25*. San Francisco: Federal Reserve Bank of San Francisco.

Leventis, A. (2006). Removing appraisal bias from a repeat-transactions house price index: A basic approach. In: *OFHEO Working Papers 06-1*. OFHEO.

Mosley, R. (2019). *Fiscal year 2019 independent actuarial review of the mutual mortgage insurance fund: Economic Net worth of forward mortgage insurance-in-force*. HUD. https://www.hud.gov/sites/dfiles/Housing/documents/ActuarialMMIFForward2019.pdf.

Posey, L. L., & Yavas, A. (2001). Adjustable and fixed rate mortgages as a screening mechanism for default risk. *Journal of Urban Economics*, *49*(1), 54–79.

Shao, J., Li, S., & Li, Y. (2016). Estimation and prediction of credit risk based on rating transition systems. arxiv:1607.00448.

Stanton, R. (1995). Rational prepayment and the valuation of mortgage-backed securities. *The Review of Financial Studies*, *8*(3), 677–708.

# 4 Incentives and the Economics of Securitization

There is reasonably extensive academic research on issues related to the economics of securitization. Detailed literature reviews on the subject include Elul (2005), Pinto and Alves (2016) and Gorton and Metrick (2013). As we pointed out in Chap. 1, securitization in and by itself is not quite an academic field of study, with an agreed upon set of assumptions that researchers in finance or economics could all use in order to study particular aspects. This is a different situation from subjects such as options valuation, credit risk modeling, or firms' optimal dividend policy. As a result, the literature on securitization has tended to be produced by specialists of various fields in financial economics or corporate finance, each with a particular angle, which is a consistent and logical extension of the existing models in each field, but not necessarily in relation to other works on securitization. This makes it difficult to present the various models that exist on securitization as an optimal financing tool under a single umbrella. In our discussion of these models, we try and set them on an equal footing by varying some of their assumptions and constructs, but it is not always entirely possible.

Theoretically, securitization should not exist. Under the traditional assumptions developed in Modigliani and Miller (1958), the mode of financing of a project should not affect that project's value, and there would therefore be no point in using securitization. It is useful to look at the main assumptions in Modigliani Miller, and try and understand which ones, by not being verified in reality, could account for the existence of securitization as such a widespread financing tool. In summary, these assumptions are that bankruptcy cost is less, debt is risk-free, there are no regulations, all securities have the same tax treatment, and investors are as informed as the firm or its managers.

Before we can delve into the relationships between these assumptions and securitization, we need to decompose the notion of the existence of securitization into the existence of its fundamental components. First, for securitization to exist it is nec-



L. Gauthier, *Securitization Economics*, Springer Texts in Business and Economics,
https://doi.org/10.1007/978-3-030-50326-0_4

essary that off-balance sheet (SPV) financing be optimal. Second, for securitization to exist as debt issuance, there has to be some optimality in debt versus equity.

The question of why firms might want to use SPV financing is related to the notion of **optimal funding**. The question often revolves around a study of banks' behavior, since they are by far the largest securitizers of assets. Some of the explanatory factors are considered to be taxes, bankruptcy, or regulatory costs, and certain synergies and asymmetries in information. We will look at a range of models developed in Gorton and Metrick (2013) and Gorton and Souleles (2007), Han, Park, and Pennacchi (2015), and Leland (2007). These models try to justify the existence of securitization typically without making specific assumptions about preference differences between issuers and investors, which would naturally lead to the assets going to those for which they are worth the most. They consider certain exogenous factors that make securitization optimal. Then, we examine the models proposed by Iacobucci and Winter (2005), which do not depend on particular assumptions on taxes, bankruptcy, or regulatory costs but explain securitization through improved manager agency and monitoring costs. Their approach draws from the **theory of the firm**, as introduced by Jensen and Meckling (1976), but systematically applied to securitization and hence addresses optimal funding questions. We conclude by examining the study by An, Deng, and Gabriel (2009) which attempted to quantify the funding cost reduction observed in securitization, and discuss the various optimal funding models in the light of practical experience.

We can then turn to the question of how to justify debt financing, which relates to the field of **security design** in corporate finance. Security design is the conception of an optimal financing security which will not be mispriced by investors. Debt and, on the other side, leveraged equity are specific types of securities or contracts; why do they exist in the form they have? Following Modigliani and Miller, this issue has received extensive attention in economics and finance over the past 60 years. The optimality of particular securities is generally considered to be a consequence of information asymmetries. The models focused on security design tend to make specific assumptions about issuers and investors, so that the issuers have to issue securities and then one can ask what the optimal form for these securities should be. We will focus on the works of Boot and Thakor (1993), DeMarzo and Duffie (1999), and Dang, Gorton, and Holmström (2015), which use information asymmetry between issuers and investors or among investors, building upon the original work by Leland and Pyle (1977) and Myers and Majluf (1984). We will see how the right balance between debt and equity can be struck when there are information asymmetries. We also look into some empirical evidence on the design of mortgage securities in Begley and Purnanandam (2017), in Park (2013), and in Franke, Herrmann, and Weber (2012).

There is a distinction between why securitization may exist as debt, and why it exists in its particularly structured and complex form. Research into the theoretical reasons for the particular complexity and shape of securitization structures will be discussed in Chap. 7, which specifically focuses on the economics of structuring. It is important indeed to go through the complex details of actual structuring (in Chap. 6) before discussing a theoretical perspective, so that we can understand the potential differences between real-life structures and the simplified versions discussed in the literature. As we will see in Chap. 6, securitization deals are so extremely complex that an argument just generally proving their existence is not satisfactory.

The models we discuss in this chapter do not make a distinction between securitizing assets that already exist on the issuer's balance sheet, or buying or originating assets for the purpose of securitization (originate-to-distribute model). This, and other potential sources of concern with securitization, will be addressed in Chap. 5, specifically focused on problems with securitization.

In our presentation of a few models from the literature, we have made some modifications: we set them in a probabilistic context when possible even when the original models were not conceived that way, because in spite of a little more formality, it helps to clearly express the underlying reasoning. Also, we unified notations and concepts, when possible.

## 4.1 Perfect Financing and the Existence of Securitization

The starting point in this discussion is the analysis in Modigliani and Miller (1958). The authors do not make many assumptions about the preferences of investors, mostly that they prefer more income than less and are rational. Equity or debt prices are implicitly affected by preferences, but of the market as a whole, and so the prices of future income streams can be treated as given. Information is supposed to be the same for all investors, they all agree on the expected returns, and trade shares and debt in perfect markets (where the prices of two assets providing the same returns are the same). Taxes are initially assumed to be null. Also, there is no distinction between dividends and retained earnings, as the managers of the firm are supposed to act in the shareholders' best interest.

Modigliani and Miller consider that firms can be grouped into sectors within which the ratio between expected returns and prices is constant, if there is no debt financing. So for all firms $j$ in sector $k$ with expected returns per period of $\bar{Y}_j$ and total stock value $E_j$, $\frac{\bar{Y}_j}{E_j} = r_k$ when there is no leverage, where $r_k$ is the capitalization rate for sector $k$ (the inverse of the PE ratio in a way).

Now allowing for the use of debt, we have a total firm value of $V_j = E_j + D_j$. The debt is assumed to be risk-free, and returns $r$, which is the same across the board, the market being perfect. Then, using a no-arbitrage argument the authors show the following:

**Proposition 4.1** (Modigliani–Miller) *Introducing financing by debt does not change the total value of the firm; in other words, at the equilibrium, the pricing of the firm relative to its assets' return is constant:* $\frac{\bar{Y}_j}{V_j} = r_k$. *Also, the expected return on stock* $j$ *is equal to the unlevered expected return for the sector plus a premium equal to the debt-to-equity ratio times the yield spread between sector return and risk-free return:* $i_j = r_k + (r_k - r)\frac{D_j}{E_j}$.

If taxes are introduced, they affect the result because interest paid on the debt would be deductible from the overall tax liability. If $\tau$ is the tax rate then define the capitalization rate reflecting taxes $r_k^\tau = (1-\tau)r_k$. Then Modigliani and Miller show that for any firm $j$ in sector $k$:

$$\frac{\bar{Y}_j}{V_j} = r_k\left(1 - \frac{\tau r D_j}{(1-\tau)r_k V}\right).$$

When there are taxes, even in perfect capital markets, the firm's value increases as debt increases because it reduces the overall cost of taxes.

With the assumptions in the proposition, securitization should therefore not exist, and even if for some reason firms sold assets into SPVs, there is no reason why these SPVs should issue debt. Indeed:

- If we focus on the firm that securitizes assets, such as a bank, then the conditions differ from the Modigliani–Miller world; in addition to taxes, there are regulations, frictions, and the company's management may not always act in the stakeholders' best interest. We will see how bankruptcy costs, risks, taxes, and certain information asymmetries can make securitization optimal for certain institutions. Without these frictions, there is no particular reason in the Modigliani–Miller world for an issuer to sell some of its assets to an SPV and securitize it.
- The notion of a firm as applicable in the Modigliani–Miller world is also closer to a securitization vehicle than to a bank or operating company. The no tax assumption is indeed applicable, as well as the assumption that the managers act in the interest of the stakeholders, since the SPV is not managed but driven by contractual terms. If the other assumptions held, then the returns on securitized bonds would all be determined in a linear fashion, and there would be no point in creating complex structures. We know this is not the case, so it is then a valid question to ask what the conditions could be that make it optimal to have particular levels of structure in securitizations. As we will see in the section on security design, one finds that information asymmetries can explain the importance of subordination in securitizations, in particular, adverse selection and moral hazard.

Practitioners sometimes argue that one reason for securitization is the lower cost of funding that it can afford issuers because the securitized bonds are, in principle, safe and well rated. The relatively safer assets that are securitized (versus a firm's business whose valuation is more volatile) are appreciated by investors and will trade at lower yields than what the firm itself would require. As is pointed out in Iacobucci and Winter (2005), this is however incorrect reasoning: Modigliani–Miller makes it clear that any gain in funding cost realized by segregating safer assets should be expected to be exactly compensated by a loss due to financing the remaining assets that are now riskier.

The main arguments in favor of securitization, as an improvement in market efficiency and investor welfare, that have generally been considered in the literature can be found in the overview by Franke and Krahnen (2008):

1. Improved risk allocation, as assets that are otherwise not tradable become accessible by the market. This leads to greater diversification and contributes to completing the market.
2. Disintermediation, which allows each entity in the securitization process to specialize in particular tasks and be more efficient at it.
3. Transparency of assets, necessary for the creation of informationally insensitive securities, which reduces information asymmetry.

The first two items, improved risk allocation and disintermediation, follow from securitization without any structuring being necessary. They are a consequence of securitization being an optimal funding strategy under particular assumptions, which we address in the next section. We will see how some models explicitly address the advantage gained from making an asset tradable that would otherwise only be accessible as part of the entire issuer's holdings. We will also see how some other models explain that securitization improves the effort invested by managers in running their operation, by being more focused on certain assets.

The third item concerns the design of securities with optimal features, and we will see in the following section on security design how issuers can structure their funding through securitization so that the negative effects of asymmetrical information on asset quality can be reduced.

## 4.2 Optimal Funding

We first look at the simple model presented in Gorton and Metrick (2013) as part of a literature review, because it frames the question of securitization in a recourse context, where the investors could have a recourse and therefore there is no structuring to speak of. Then we look at a more involved version of that model in Gorton and Souleles (2007) that considers the optimal strategies the issuer may follow in deciding whether to bail out or not a securitization vehicle. These authors also examined some empirical evidence. Next, we will go through the model in Han, Park, and Pennacchi (2015) which is more specifically focused on the impact of taxes and is tested against data across US states. Following that, we discuss the synergy model from Leland (2007), which gives some optimal conditions for securitization depending on a variety of factors, including the correlation between the securitized assets' evolution and the assets remaining in the firm's own portfolio. Finally, we discuss the models developed in Iacobucci and Winter (2005), using information asymmetry to justify securitization. In the latter article, the authors show how the optimality of securitization directly stems from asymmetrical information, while in the other research mentioned above, asymmetrical information could explain some issuer or investor choices but not securitization per se.

One important common feature among these models is that they consider securitization essentially separate from structures and do not address the question of structure optimality. As such, they are offer a very good perspective on some fun-

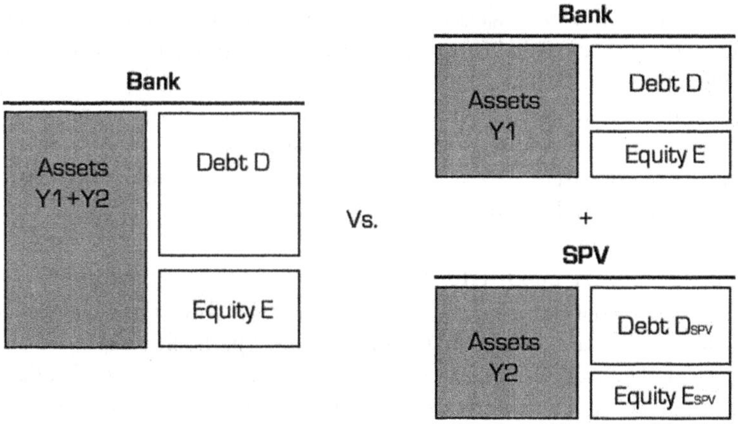


**Fig. 4.1** Banks With and Without Securitization. *Source* Compiled by the author

damental reasons for the existence of securitization independently from complex financial engineering.

Across these various models, the approach usually consists of comparing the situation with and without securitization, in a simplified setting. See Fig. 4.1 for a basic graphical explanation. Note that in some models such as Gorton and Metrick (2013) or Gorton and Souleles (2007), the bank may retain the SPV's equity part (or, in other words, the entire cash flow is not sold).

Finally, in the last subsection, we discuss and contrast some of the empirical findings from these models with practical observations and analyze the empirical study by An, Deng, and Gabriel (2009).

### 4.2.1 Securitization and Bankruptcy

In Gorton and Metrick (2013), the authors present a simple model exhibiting taxes and bankruptcy costs as drivers of securitization choice. We follow their model, with substantial modifications. The model looks at a bank's decision to securitize assets, rather than use debt financing and keep the assets on its balance sheet. As in Modigliani–Miller, debt financing reduces the cost of taxes relative to equity financing. Since securitization vehicles are risk-neutral, they do not benefit from this tax advantage and hence higher taxes would encourage debt funding rather than securitization. Bankruptcy costs work in the opposite direction: liquidation costs are null for the SPV, but not for the bank. In certain conditions, transferring assets to the SPV allows them to reach a better valuation than if they stayed on balance sheet thanks to these reduced liquidation costs. In addition to these drivers, Gorton and Metrick also include a convenience yield in the model, which is an extra cost that investors are paying to the issuer because the assets they are buying can be used as collateral to finance further asset purchases. Securitized debt is typically considered as good collateral and hence would command a higher convenience yield than comparable bank debt, which creates further incentives to securitize.

Agents are risk-neutral in the model (which can be reasonable if they are considered to be well diversified), and the risk-free rate $r$ is set to 0, which simplifies calculations. The market is competitive so borrowers and lenders must exactly break even, since they are all in competition within each activity.

There are two periods in the economy (0 and 1), and a bank has two loans, each with a principal of 1 monetary unit. The loans are to be repaid at period 1. Each loan may default with probability $p$, in which case repayment is null. If we write each loan's outcome as random variables $Y_1$ and $Y_2$, we have $\mathbb{P}[Y_i = 1] = (1 - p)$ and $\mathbb{P}[Y_i = 0] = p$ for $i \in \{1, 2\}$. Note, for consistency with other models, we could write these as continuous distributions using a Dirac "delta" distribution:

$$\mathbb{P}[Y_i \in dx] = p\delta_0(dx) + (1 - p)\delta_1(dx). \tag{4.1}$$

The bank finances its loan holdings with debt $D$ and equity $E$. The bank debt, which consists of deposits, is assumed to provide a convenience yield $\rho$ so that depositors actually pay in order for the bank to hold their funds. We are assuming $r = 0$ here, but if that was not the case it would mean the bank would pay its depositors a rate of $r - \rho$. We assume that there is not enough equity so some debt must be used to finance the loans. The debt repays $F$ at period 1, and the convenience yield is effectively integrated into $F$, so that if there were no risks (and $p = 0$) then $F = D(1 - \rho)$. The tax rate in the economy is $\tau$, and charges on debt are tax deductible. We consider that $D(1 - \rho) < 2$ must hold since there must be at least a positive probability that the debt gets repaid.

If the bank defaults, there is a bankruptcy cost $c$ that the creditors suffer, due to liquidation costs or frictions in liquidations. We will consider that $F > 1$, and both loans need to perform in order to repay the creditors, so that if either loan does not perform then the bank defaults. For simplicity, it is assumed that in case one loan defaults and the bank defaults, nothing can be recovered from the other loan even though it might be performing. This assumption increases the liquidation cost in effect: it is not only the direct cost $c$ but also the lost cash flow from the other loan in cases when it performs.

#### 4.2.1.1 Simple Depositor Model

Gorton and Metrick express the bank's expected profit that it seeks to maximize as

$$\Pi = 2(1 - p)^2 - (1 - \tau)F.$$

So the expected profit can be understood as the following expectation (using (4.1)), where the post-tax cost $F$ is incurred in all states of the world:

$$\mathbb{E}[(Y_1 + Y_2)\mathbb{I}_{Y_1=1,Y_2=1} - (1 - \tau)F].$$

This raises some issues and demands some clarifications. The bank's profit depends on the outcome of the loans' performance: either they both perform and debt can be repaid, or there is a default and the debt holders do not get anything.

- In the case of a loan defaulting, the bank's profit is shown as negative, but the debt holders do not get anything so there should be no negative cash flow for the bank. In addition, the tax advantage applied to the full cost in case of a default implies there would be tax credits that are usable by the banks' shareholders. Either the debt holders should be getting a payment, reaching beyond the bank's limited liability, or the bank's gain should be simply 0 in the bad state.
- In the case when both loans perform, the income is 2, from which the debt repayment must be deducted. However, in that case, one would expect the tax advantage to only apply to the interest charged on the debt $F - D$, not to the entire debt payment $F$. The tax rate $\tau$ is not used in a manner consistent with the Modigliani–Miller model. One would have expected that the post-tax debt repayment cost would be $(1-\tau)(F-D)+D=(1-\tau)F+\tau D$.

In order to make the tax treatment consistent with other models, we only apply it to the effective interest. In addition, we also correct the negative cash flows and give the bank limited liability consistent with the amount that debt holders recover. This also makes the model consistent with the other models we analyze in that respect. With these corrections, the bank's value now writes

$$\begin{aligned}\Pi &= \mathbb{E}\left[(Y_1+Y_2-(1-\tau)F+\tau D)\,\mathbb{I}_{Y_1=1,Y_2=1}\right]\\ &= (2-(1-\tau)F-\tau D)(1-p)^2.\end{aligned}$$

Relative to Gorton and Metrick's original model, the calculations are quite different but the end results are generally comparable. With these assumptions, we can show the following proposition. It is not an extension of Proposition 4.1 because the assumptions are more restrictive, but it does illustrate how the impact of taxes on financing gets limited by bankruptcy costs.

**Proposition 4.2** *In a competitive environment, the bank's debt level is*

$$D=\frac{2(1-p)^2-(1-\tau)cp(2-p)}{(1-\tau)(1-\rho)+\tau(1-p)^2}$$

*provided that* $0 < D(1-\rho) < 2$. *The amount of debt is decreasing in bankruptcy costs and increasing in convenience yield. The amount of debt is increasing in taxes if* $2(1-p)^2 < 2(1-\rho)+cp(2-p)$, *that is, if bankruptcy costs and the probability of default are high enough.*

***Proof*** From the standpoint of the depositors/investors, the expected repayment of debt must be high enough so that it compensates the potential costs related to a loss for investors in bank debt, accounting for the benefit from the convenience yield. The repayment to the debt holders is $F$ if all goes well, and nothing in all other cases although the debt holders do pay a liquidation cost:

$$\mathbb{I}_{Y_1-1,Y_2-1}F - (1 - \mathbb{I}_{Y_1-1,Y_2-1})c.$$

Therefore, the condition on the expected debt repayment is

$$(1-p)^2F - c\left(2p(1-p) + p^2\right) \geq D(1-\rho).$$

The bank will set $F$ at its lowest possible value and

$$F = \frac{D(1-\rho) + cp(2-p)}{(1-p)^2}.$$

Replacing $F$ in the expression for expected profit, we obtain

$$\Pi = 2(1-p)^2 - (1-\tau)(D(1-\rho) + cp(2-p)) - \tau D(1-p)^2.$$

One can look at the profit per share as well $R = \frac{\Pi}{2-D}$. Note that if $2(1-p)^2 - 2(1-\rho) - cp(2-p) > 0$ then $\frac{\partial R}{\partial D} > 0$.

Hence, we can observe the following:

- Bankruptcy costs reduce expected profits through a higher cost of financing $F$ for the bank.
- The impact of higher debt financing on profits is $\frac{\partial \Pi}{\partial D} = -\tau(1-p)^2 - (1-\tau)(1-\rho)$ which is negative.
- A higher tax rate reduces the negative drag of debt financing, as $\frac{\partial^2 \Pi}{\partial D \partial \tau} > 0$.
- A higher convenience yield also reduces the negative drag of debt financing, as $\frac{\partial^2 \Pi}{\partial D \partial \rho} > 0$.
- Increases in default probability lead to a greater loss in profit if debt increases, since the financing cost is increased in that case: $\frac{\partial^2 \Pi}{\partial D \partial p} < 0$.

The profit per share is increasing in $D$ and hence the bank would want the highest possible amount of debt financing. In a competitive environment where the adjustment variable is the amount of debt that can be raised, as all banks compete for it, the debt amount that is effectively raised will be such that the marginal entrant has a null profit. Hence, the debt amount raised at equilibrium is subject to the model's assumptions:

$$D = \frac{2(1-p)^2 - (1-\tau)cp(2-p)}{(1-\tau)(1-\rho) + \tau(1-p)^2}.$$

This expression is decreasing in $c$ and increasing in $\rho$, as we would expect. Also, the condition $2(1-p)^2 - 2(1-\rho) - cp(2-p) < 0$ implies that the debt amount is increasing as a function of $\tau$. □

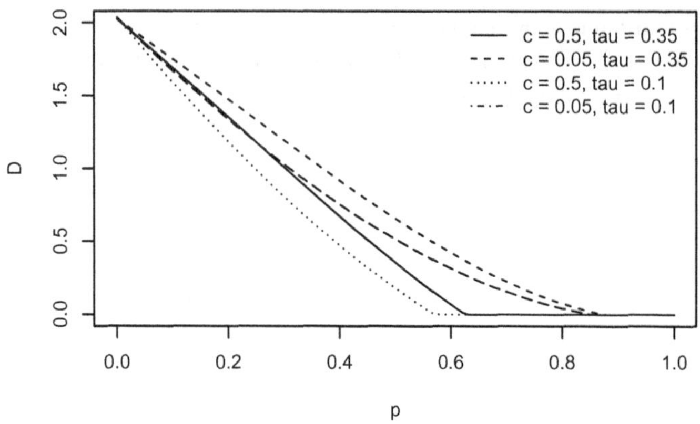


**Fig. 4.2** Debt Funding as a Function of Default Probability. *Source* Compiled by the author

Figure 4.2 shows the optimal debt level as a function of the probability of default $p$, for various values of $c$ and $\tau$. As the probability of default declines, funding is optimally carried out mostly through debt. With an increasing probability of default, the bank issues less debt depending on the tax rate (which tends to favor debt financing) and on bankruptcy costs (which tend to discourage debt financing by raising its cost).

Since we have $F = \frac{D(1-\rho)+cp(2-p)}{(1-p)^2}$, we can also derive the promised repayment when debt sets profits to zero:

$$F = \frac{2(1-\rho) + \tau cp(2-p)}{(1-\tau)(1-\rho) + \tau(1-p)^2}.$$

This expression is increasing in $c$ and increasing in $\tau$ if $2(1-p)^2 < 2(1-\rho) + cp(2-p)$.

#### 4.2.1.2 Including Securitization

Let us now see how things change once we introduce securitization. Gorton and Metrick consider securitization with recourse in this case, where the issuer of securitized debt would in fact be on the hook for losses of the securitized vehicle. This is not the most common case, but it has the advantage of specifically isolating the advantages of securitization from the advantages of credit structuring.

We now consider that one loan is securitized, and not the other. The bank sells one loan to an SPV, and the SPV issues debt in the market. The SPV is a new entity and has its own debt financing and debt characteristics. We write $D_S$ for the SPV's debt and $F_S$ for the SPV's promised repayment. The SPV also benefits from a convenience yield (since presumably its debt can be used as collateral), which we write $\rho_S$. In order to distinguish the bank's new metrics now that securitization is possible, we write $D_B$ for the bank's own debt, $F_B$ for its promised repayment, and $\rho_B$ for its convenience yield (in fact, we can assume $\rho_B = \rho$).

**Proposition 4.3** *If securitization is possible, the bank's profit changes by* $A + B + \Gamma + \Delta$ *with*

$$\begin{aligned} A &= 2p(1-p), \\ B &= cp(1-p), \\ \Gamma &= -\tau\left(cp(1-p) + D\left((1-p)^2 - \frac{1}{2}(p+\rho_B)\right)\right), \\ \Delta &= \frac{D}{2}(\rho_S - \rho_B). \end{aligned}$$

***Proof*** Buyers of the bank's debt now require

$$(1-p)F_B - cp \geq D_B(1-\rho_B)$$

and buyers of the SPV debt require

$$(1-p)F_S \geq D_S(1-\rho_S).$$

These expressions show that each entity is only exposed to the risk of one loan. Also, in the case of the SPV, there is no bankruptcy cost since it cannot enter bankruptcy.

From these we derive $F_B = \frac{D_B(1-\rho_B)+cp}{1-p}$ and $F_S = \frac{D_S(1-\rho_S)}{1-p}$. The required payment is lower on the SPV than on the bank, since there are no bankruptcy costs to reflect. Also note that if either loan performs but not the other, then the bank debt or SPV investors get some cash flow, which is in effect another reduction in liquidation cost.

We can express the bank's expected profit now as

$$\Pi_B = (1 - (1-\tau)F_B - \tau D_B)(1-p) + (1-p)(1-F_S).$$

Note that the SPV is not taxed and hence there is no tax advantage in its using debt financing.

Hence, the profit writes

$$\Pi_B = 2(1-p) - (1-\tau)(D_B(1-\rho_B) + cp) - (1-p)\tau D_B - D_S(1-\rho_S).$$

In order to derive simple results, Gorton and Metrick assume that the bank breaks down its financing equally on both sides, and sets $D_B = D_S = \frac{D}{2}$. This will allow us a direct comparison with the case without securitization. Now we can look at the difference in profit with or without securitization, $\Pi_B - \Pi$. After some simplifications, we can write

$$\Pi_B - \Pi = A + B + \Gamma + \Delta,$$

with the terms defined in the proposition. □

This decomposition helps us understand what drives the benefits of securitization in the context of this model. The model does not consider the optimal amount of debt being issued, but taking it as a given, it tells us that the bank benefits from resorting to securitization. The total amount of debt $D$ could be determined at the competitive equilibrium from Proposition 4.2 in the case where securitization is not yet available.

The term $A$ captures the fact that when using securitization, each loan may perform independently from the other and provide a benefit, unlike the case without securitization where both must perform in order to be able to face repayments. The securitized loan may default without forcing the bank into bankruptcy. This is also a consequence of the particular assumption that in the case of bank default, it was not possible to recover payments on a performing loan.

Note that the securitization benefit $\Pi_B - \Pi$ is increasing in $c$, which is expected since securitization bypasses bankruptcy costs. Focusing on term $B$ specifically, the direct bankruptcy costs directly increase the profit difference.

Finally, the impact of the convenience yield is shown in term $\Delta$. If the securitized debt does not pay a convenience yield then $\Delta$ is entirely negative, since the non-balance sheet debt convenience yield is a net positive for full on balance sheet funding. However, if the securitized debt is particularly useful as collateral and serves a high convenience yield then it needs to be high enough so that $\Delta$ becomes positive.

Term $\Gamma$ shows the impact of taxes, and its contribution depends on the amount of bankruptcy costs. Higher taxes will lead to preferring on balance sheet funding, since it affords tax savings (which are not available in the case of securitization). However, this reasoning is true for a given amount of debt $D$. Even if taxes make securitization less attractive, at an equilibrium condition where the amount of debt raised is such that profits are null, the amount of debt raised including securitization may be increasing as a function of $\tau$.

**Proposition 4.4** *In a competitive equilibrium, the amount of securitized debt raised is*

$$D_S = \frac{2(1-p)-(1-\tau)cp}{(1-\tau)(1-\rho)+(1-p)\tau+(1-\rho_S)},$$

*which is increasing in $\tau$ if $cp\left((1-p)+(1-\rho_S)\right) > 2(\rho-p)(1-p)$. The condition is true if $p > \rho$.*

The proposition shows that in spite of the fact that higher taxes may reduce the gains in securitization, if the probability of default is high enough, then the amount of securitized products that gets issued will increase as a function of taxes. This conclusion is in fact opposite to that of Gorton and Metrick's article, but it is consistent with the model and the empirical evidence exposed in Han, Park, and Pennacchi (2015) which we discuss further down.

***Proof*** Note that here $D_S$ is still defined as in Gorton and Metrick's approach, that is, $D_S = D_B = \frac{D}{2}$. In the case where securitization is possible, we determine the

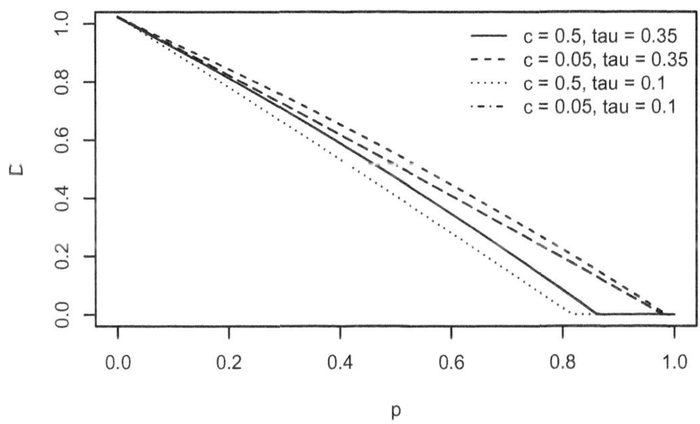


**Fig. 4.3** Securitization Funding as a Function of Default Probability. *Source* Compiled by the author

amount of debt that sets profits to zero. Solving $\Pi_B = 0$ for $D$ and dividing by 2, we get the expression in the proposition.

Then, we can compute $\frac{\partial D_S}{\partial \tau}$ and after simplifications we find that $\frac{\partial D_S}{\partial \tau} > 0$ is equivalent to $cp\left((1-p)+(1-\rho_S)\right) > 2(\rho - p)(1-p)$. □

Figure 4.3 shows the amount of debt financing as a function of the default probability. We can observe that with these parameters, a higher tax rate leads to a greater amount of securitization. The impact of project riskiness (which can be summarized by the probability of default $p$) on the gains from securitization is positive, from the expression of $\Pi_B - \Pi$. However, this does not necessarily mean that the volume of securitized debt will too be increasing since a higher probability of default also implies cheaper debt valuation. The chart clearly shows $D_S$ declining as $p$ increases.

This simple model has allowed us to capture the potential contribution of taxes and bankruptcy costs in securitization incentives. It did not, however, account for the control the bank may exert on the quality of the loans it originates.

### 4.2.2 Securitization, Bankruptcy, and Bailout

We now shift our focus to the model from Gorton and Souleles (2007), which in some ways extends the one we just walked through, focusing more specifically on the role played by bankruptcy costs in a richer strategic setting. They consider the case of recourse securitization, where a bank or financial company may offer some additional protection and effectively bail out the SPV in times of need. They also analyze a repeated game where the strategic decision by the bank to provide this protection is endogenously accounted for. Finally, the authors test some implications by the model against data on credit card securitizations.

In securitization, the buyers of securitized debt are always potentially subject to adverse selection by the issuer: the securitized assets may have been cherry picked. Even without securitization, one would need to establish whether the bank will have an incentive to carry out some loan screening in the first place. By modeling the bank's efforts (or lack thereof) in screening loans, Gorton and Souleles can account for the bank's optimal choices regarding the quality of loan production. Under certain conditions, the bank will screen the loans. In addition, if the bank still adversely selects the loans for securitization, it can nevertheless maintain an issuance program by providing an implicit recourse to the SPV. In this case, if the loans that were securitized turn out bad, then the original issuer bails out the SPV.

#### 4.2.2.1 Loan Screening Model

Some of the aspects of the model developed in Gorton and Souleles (2007) are very similar to the model in Gorton and Metrick (2013), but the major difference is that now the bank determines the rate that is offered to lenders as well as its own degree of effort in loan screening. The bank finances two projects, each requiring 1 monetary unit. The bank's equity $E$ is less than the total required funding so the bank uses debt. Agents are risk-neutral. Similarly as the model developed in the prior section, there is a bankruptcy cost $c$ borne by investors, and on balance sheet debt has a tax advantage.

The bank decides on how much effort it wants to spend on originating the loans backing the projects, either a high effort or a low effort. A high effort will lead to a better probability that the project provides good returns. There is a cost to the effort that the bank pays. Then depending on a random outcome each project will return either a high value $y_g$ or a low value $y_b$ with $y_h > y_b$. So the values that the project can return are always either good or bad, but the bank's efforts determine the likelihood that the loan ends up in the good or bad states. Define a project's total return $Y_i(e)$ a random variable as a function of the effort $e \in \{e_H, e_L\}$, with $i \in \{1, 2\}$ for each project. The $Y_i$ are independent. Then $\mathbb{P}[Y_i(e) = y_g] = e$ and $\mathbb{P}[Y_i(e) = y_b] = 1 - e$. In a continuous setting along the lines of (4.1), this could be written as

$$\mathbb{P}[Y_i(e) \in dx] = e\delta_{y_g}(dx) + (1 - e)\delta_{y_b}(dx). \tag{4.2}$$

The overall logic is comparable to the prior model we discussed but now the distribution of $Y_i$ is affected by the effort. The effort cost to the bank is $h(e)$. More generally, we can say that screening is defined by two functions, its distribution impact $I$ and its cost $C$ such that given an effort $e$,

$$\mathbb{P}[Y_i(e) \in dx] = I_i(e, x),$$

and a cost $C_i(e)$ is paid. In the case at hand,

$$\begin{aligned} I_i(e, x) &= e\delta_{y_g}(dx) + (1 - e)\delta_{y_b}(dx) \\ C_i(e) &= h(e). \end{aligned} \tag{4.3}$$

One considers that it is not possible for investors to determine the effort choice that was made from the outcome of the projects. This is a typical agency problem, **hidden action** more specifically. In other words, investors cannot observe enough outcomes to be able to figure from which probability the draws were made. This is important because it implies that they cannot observe the bank's actual choices.

The authors make several assumptions so that the analysis can be carried out and is not trivial:

- (**A1**) A high project screening effort leads to positive NPV relative to the debt amount: $\mathbb{E}[Y_1(e_H) + Y_2(e_H) - h(e_H)] > D$. In other words, $2(e_H y_g + (1 - e_H)y_b) - h(e_H) > D$.
- (**A2**) A low screening effort leads to a negative NPV relative to the debt: $\mathbb{E}[Y_1(e_L) + Y_2(e_L) - h(e_L)] < D$.
- (**A3**) Bank default is certain if each project returns the low amount, i.e., for $e \in \{e_H, e_L\}$ $2y_b - h(e) < F$.
- (**A4**) Default does not occur if either loan performs well, for $e \in \{e_H, e_L\}$ $y_h + y_b - h(e) > F$.[1]

Assumptions A1 and A2 imply that investors only buy the bank debt if they believe the bank will spend the high effort level. Also note that these assumptions are expressed relative to potentially endogenous variables: $F$, which will be decided by the bank, as well as $D$ if we let the degree of debt financing vary.

In effect, the authors write the bank's projects value in their article as

$$(Y_1(e) + Y_2(e) - h(e) - (1 - \tau)F)\,\mathbb{I}_{\{Y_1(e), Y_2(e)\} \neq \{y_b, y_b\}}.$$

According to this expression, the bank's profit in the case of default is assumed to be 0 in the bad state, so that it has limited liability (all the cash flows go to the debt holders). This expression also raises an issue comparable to the one we discussed in the Gorton–Metrick model regarding the treatment of taxes: debt is considered as entirely tax deductible (that is, not only the effective interest being charged but the whole principal as well).

Since in the discussion of the model as well as in the empirical tests the authors did not explicitly use the tax rate, we are setting $\tau = 0$ and hence avoiding the ambiguity in how taxes enter the issuer's optimal decision. The bank's project value is therefore:

$$(Y_1(e) + Y_2(e) - h(e) - F)\,\mathbb{I}_{\{Y_1(e), Y_2(e)\} \neq \{y_b, y_b\}}.$$

Debt investors collect a payment of $F$ when the bank does not default. If the bank defaults, then they collect whatever income the bank was getting, minus the bankruptcy costs and the bank's cost in screening the loans (basically they get the bank's net return in that case minus bankruptcy expenses). So payments to the debt investors are

$$R(y, e) = F\mathbb{I}_{\{Y_1(e), Y_2(e)\} \neq \{y_b, y_b\}} + (y_b(1 - c) - h(e))\mathbb{I}_{\{Y_1(e), Y_2(e)\} = \{y_b, y_b\}}.$$

[1] Note that this is different from the model in Gorton Metrick where if either loan did not perform there was a default.

In the optimization program, we will consider that the bank sets the repayment amount $F$ as a function of the investors' expectations (since they will have to agree to buying the debt). Hence, we will write $F(e_0)$ to make that dependency explicit, where $e_0$ is the investors' belief about the bank's choice of $e$. Further, the investors' belief is itself a function of $e$ and $F$, since it is driven by the bank's choices, so formally we could write $e_0(e, F)$.

We write the maximization program that the bank follows as

$$\begin{aligned}&\max_{e,F} V(e, e_0(e, F), F)\\&= \max_{e,F} \mathbb{E}\left[(Y_1(e) + Y_2(e) - h(e) - F(e_0))\, \mathbb{I}_{\{Y_1(e),Y_2(e)\}\neq\{y_b,y_b\}}\right].\end{aligned}$$

The optimization is subject to standard **participation constraints** and **incentive compatibility constraints** in principal-agent problems: the investors need to expect a positive outcome in order to participate

$$\mathbb{E}[R(y, e_0)] \geq D$$

and the bank behaves consistently with beliefs; it sees more value in a higher effort spending than on low spending, when investors expect a high spending

$$V(e_H, e_H, F) \geq V(e_L, e_H, F).$$

Gorton and Souleles derive the conditions for the existence of an equilibrium where the beliefs of investors are consistent with the bank's actions.

**Proposition 4.5** (Gorton–Souleles 1) *Without securitization there exists an equilibrium with consistent beliefs and the bank's value is* $V(e_H, e_H, F(e_H))$ *if*

$$\begin{aligned}&2y_g(e_H - e_L) + 2y_b(e_H(1-e_H) - e_L(1-e_L))\\&- (h(e_H)e_H(2-e_H) - h(e_L)e_L(2-e_L))\\&- D + (1-e_H)^2\,(2y_b(1-c) - h(e_H))\left(1 - \frac{e_L(2-e_L)}{e_H(2-e_H)}\right) > 0.\end{aligned}$$

***Proof*** First, note that we can write $V$ explicitly by expressing the success probabilities

$$\begin{aligned}V(e, e_0(e, F), F) &= e^2\left(2y_g - h(e) - (1-\tau)F(e_0)\right)\\&\quad + 2e(1-e)\left(y_g + y_b - h(e) - F(e_0)\right).\end{aligned}$$

Also, given an expectation of the bank's effort to be $e_0$, the debt investors's lowest accepted fixed payment verifies $\mathbb{E}[R(y, e_0)] = D$, therefore

$$(e_0^2 + 2e_0(1-e_0))F(e_0) + (1-e_0)^2(2y_b(1-c) - h(e_0)) = D,$$

and hence

$$F(e_0) = \frac{D - (1 - e_0)^2(2y_b(1 - c) - h(e_0))}{e_0(2 - e_0)}.$$

This expression can be substituted into the expression for $V$.

Now the incentive compatibility requires that at the optimum, the bank's effort choice should be the same as what investors believe, so that $e = e_0 = e_H$, for beliefs to be consistent. If that is the case then the bank's objective function would be

$$\begin{aligned}
&V(e_H, e_H, F(e_H)) \\
&= 2e_H y_g + 2e_H(1 - e_H)y_b - e_H(2 - e_H)h(e_H) \\
&- D + (1 - e_H)^2(2y_b(1 - c) - h(e_H)).
\end{aligned}$$

If, on the other hand, beliefs are inconsistent then the value to the bank is

$$\begin{aligned}
&V(e_L, e_H, F(e_H)) \\
&= 2e_L y_g + 2e_L(1 - e_L)y_b - e_L(2 - e_L)h(e_L) \\
&- e_L(1 - e_L)\left(\frac{D - (1 - e_H)^2(2y_b(1 - c) - h(e_H))}{e_H(2 - e_H)}\right).
\end{aligned}$$

Writing the inequality for the incentive compatibility and simplifying get us the condition from the proposition. If this condition is verified, then at the optimum investors believe $e_0 = e_H$ and the bank chooses $e = e_H$. The value of the bank is given by $V(e_H, e_H, F(e_H))$. One can verify that the value of $F(e_H)$ that is obtained satisfies Assumptions A3 and A4. □

If we set $e_H = e_L = (1 - p)^2$, $y_g = 1$, $y_b = 0$ and $y_b(1 - c) = -c$ (making bankruptcy costs fixed), and $h(e) = 0$ then the bank's expected gains become

$$2(1 - p)^2 - D - 2c(1 - (1 - p)^2)^2,$$

which resembles the expression we obtained in the Gorton–Metrick model. The advantage of the more complex model is that it makes the bank's decision to put in an effort to screen loans or not endogenous.

#### 4.2.2.2 SPVs and Moral Hazard

We now consider the case when bank decides on securitizing one loan and keeping the other. The decision of which loan is securitized is made *before* the bank makes an effort choice, and before the outcome of the random project performance is known. Investors in securitized debt will face a moral hazard problem associated with the bank's choice of effort.

The bank borrows $\frac{D}{2}$ for the loan on balance sheet and promises a repayment of $F^B$. The SPV issues debt for $\frac{D}{2}$ and will repay $F^S$. The bank holds the equity on the SPV, so that the bank's income from the SPV is $(y - F^S) \vee 0$, for a realization $y$ of the project in the SPV. We will consider that project 1 goes to the balance sheet and project 2 goes to the SPV.

We adjust some of the earlier assumptions and add a new one:

- **(A3a)** Default occurs for both the SPV and the bank if both project realizations are low: $2y_b - h(e) < F^B + F^S$.
- **(A4a)** If either loan performs, then the total collected cash flow should be able to repay both debt claims: $y_b + y_g - h(e) > F^B + F^S$.
- **(A5)** The expected return from the bank if both projects do not perform is not enough for it to repay its debt: $(1 - e_H)^2 y_b(1 - c) < \frac{D}{2}$.

Note that A4a specifies that if all the cash was commingled it would be sufficient to repay both claims, but if, for example, the project in the SPV turns out bad, the bank may not decide to support the SPV in which case it would default. With these assumptions, Gorton and Souleles show the following proposition related to the feasibility of securitization.

**Proposition 4.6** (Gorton–Souleles Feasibility of Securitization) *If securitization is possible, there exists an equilibrium where beliefs are consistent if*

$$\begin{aligned}
&2y_g(e_H - e_L) + y_b(e_H(1 - e_H) - e_L(1 - e_L)) \\
&- (h(e_H)e_H(2 - e_H) - h(e_L)e_L(2 - e_L)) \\
&- \frac{D}{2} + (1 - e_H)^2 \left(y_b(1 - c) - h(e_H)\right) \left(1 - \frac{e_L(2 - e_L)}{e_H(2 - e_H)}\right) > 0.
\end{aligned}$$

*With no taxes, securitization is feasible and it brings positive value to the bank.*

***Proof*** If $\{Y_1, Y_2\} = \{y_g, y_b\}$ the bank's project performs well but the SPV's does not and in that case the SPV defaults on its debt while the bank remains solvent. In the opposite case, $\{Y_1, Y_2\} = \{y_b, y_g\}$, the SPV's project performs well but not the bank's. However, the bank does not default because it gets the income from the SPV's equity and thanks to A4a, the bank is solvent. Finally, if both projects perform badly then neither the bank nor the SPV can honor their debt.

The bank's income depending on the realizations $Y_1$ and $Y_2$ can be written (again assuming that there is no negative income in the case of its default) as follows:

$$\begin{aligned}
&P(Y_1, Y_2, e, F^B, F^S) \\
&= \mathbb{I}_{\{Y_1(e), Y_2(e)\} = \{y_g, y_g\}} \left(2y_g - h(e) - F^B - F^S\right) \\
&+ \mathbb{I}_{\{Y_1(e), Y_2(e)\} = \{y_g, y_b\}} \left(y_g - h(e) - F^B\right) \\
&+ \mathbb{I}_{\{Y_1(e), Y_2(e)\} = \{y_b, y_g\}} \left(y_g + y_b - h(e) - F^B - F^S\right).
\end{aligned}$$

We write for the payments to the bank debt holders

$$R^B(y,e) = F^B(e)(\mathbb{I}_{Y_1(e)=y_g} \vee \mathbb{I}_{Y_2(e)=y_g}) + \mathbb{I}_{\{Y_1(e),Y_2(e)\}\neq\{y_b,y_b\}}(y_b(1-c)-h(e)).$$

And for the SPV debt holders

$$R^S(y,e) = F^S(e)\mathbb{I}_{Y_2(e)=y_g} + y_b\mathbb{I}_{Y_2(e)=y_b}.$$

The bank chooses its effort level as well as the promised repayment amounts. Using comparable notations as before the bank solves

$$\max_{e,F^B,F^S} V^S(e, e_0(e, F^B, F^S), F^B, F^S) = \mathbb{E}\Big[P(Y_1, Y_2, e, F^B(e_0), F^S(e_0)\Big]$$

with the following participation constraints:

$$\mathbb{E}[R^B(y,e_0)] \geq \frac{D}{2} \text{ and } \mathbb{E}[R^S(y,e_0)] \geq \frac{D}{2}.$$

The incentive compatibility constraint remains the same as before

$$V^S(e_H, e_H, F^B, F^S) \geq V^S(eL, e_H, F^B, F^S).$$

Solving the optimization problem is done the same way as before, by first saturating the constraints in terms of investors expected returns, and deriving the optimal repayments $F^B$ and $F^S$, and then showing that at the optimum the bank chooses the high effort rate (under certain conditions).

The bank's optimal value if beliefs are consistent simplifies into

$$\begin{aligned}&V^S(e_H, e_H, F^B(e_H), F^S(e_H))\\&= 2e_H y_g + e_H(1-e_H)y_b - e_H(2-e_H)h(e_H)\\&-\left(\frac{D}{2} - (1-e_H)^2\right)(y_b(1-c) - h(e_H)).\end{aligned}$$

The condition so that the investors believe $e_0 = e_H$ and the bank chooses $e = e_H$ is very close to the one that was obtained earlier in the case when securitization was not available. Gorton and Souleles show that it simplifies into

$$\begin{aligned}&2y_g(e_H - e_L) + y_b(e_H(1-e_H) - e_L(1-e_L))\\&-(h(e_H)e_H(2-e_H) - h(e_L)e_L(2-e_L))\\&-\left(\frac{D}{2} - (1-e_H)^2(y_b(1-c) - h(e_H))\left(1 - \frac{e_L(2-e_L)}{e_H(2-e_H)}\right)\right) > 0.\end{aligned}$$

The bank's optimal value when SPVs are available $V^S$ can then be shown to be higher than the bank's optimal value $V$ when securitization is not available, if $(1-e_H)^2 y_b c > 0$, which is always true. This is shown simply by looking at the difference $V^S - V$ at their respective optima, $V$ being given in Proposition 4.5. □

In the same way we analyzed the sensitivities to various parameters in the previous section we can look at what drives the preference for securitization in the current model. The main parameters are, in fact, comparable to the ones we had previously, although they play slightly different roles here. In summary, the gains in resorting to securitization increase with bankruptcy costs and increase in project riskiness.

- Relative to bankruptcy costs $\frac{\partial(V^S - V)}{\partial c} = (1 - e_H)^2 y_b$ which is positive.
- To capture project risk let us define $p = (1 - e_H)^2$ as a measure for that risk, then $\frac{\partial(V^S - V)}{\partial p} = c y_b$ which is positive.

In the same manner as for the model derived from Gorton and Metrick (2013), the fact that there are higher gains in securitization when the default probability is higher does not necessarily imply the volume of securitization would be higher.

#### 4.2.2.3 SPV, Moral Hazard, and Adverse Selection

So far, we considered that the bank was choosing its effort level, but not selecting which loan went to which program based on their actual realized performance. Now we consider that the bank can select the attribution of the loans based on their actual quality. Investors in the SPV debt then will have two issues to resolve: the moral hazard in the bank's effort choice, plus the adverse selection in terms of project allocation.

Gorton and Souleles add another assumption:

- **(A6)** The expected income from an adversely selected project is less than the debt: $e_H^2 y_g + (1 - e_H^2) y_b < \frac{D}{2}$.

Conditional upon the projects' random realization, if both are the same then the outcomes do not change from the prior model. If both projects perform, the bank and the SPV are able to repay their debt. If both projects fail, neither the bank nor the SPV can honor their debt. However, if one project performs and the other fails, then the bank keeps the good project and allocates the bad one to the SPV, which then defaults.

Previously, the SPV defaulted when $Y_2 = y_b$, notwithstanding what $Y_1$ was doing. Now, the SPV will default when $Y_2 = y_b$ or when $Y_1 = y_b$. Because of Assumption A6, the financing of an adversely selected project will be NPV negative, and therefore debt investors will not purchase it. In that case, the bank would want to guarantee in some way that they would allocate projects before knowing their outcome, but this is not verifiable since the investors cannot directly observe the probability.

One manner to address this issue is for the bank to commit to subsidize the securitization vehicle if the SPV fails and the bank has a performing project. This would give to the SPV recourse to the bank, as an extra protection. In that case, the bank's profit will be changed as follows. We note $F^{BR}$ and $F^{SR}$ for the promised payments for the bank and SPV, in the case of a recourse arrangement.

- If both projects perform well, then the bank's gain is as before;
- If both projects fail, then the bank's gain is zero, also as before;
- If the bank's project performs well and the SPV's project performs badly, then the bank is solvent and subsidizes the SPV so that neither defaults on its debt. In that case, the bank's gain will be $\mathbb{I}_{\{Y_1(e),Y_2(e)\}=\{y_g,y_b\}}(y_g + y_b - h(e) - F^{BR} - F^{SR})$; and
- If the bank's project fails and the SPV's performs well, then as before the bank is able to use the cash flow from its equity stake in the SPV to face its own debt payment. In fact, the amount is the same as above but the justification differs (and so does the order of the $Y_1$ and $Y_2$): $\mathbb{I}_{\{Y_1(e),Y_2(e)\}=\{y_b,y_g\}}(y_g + y_b - h(e) - F^{BR} - F^{SR})$.

Hence, the bank's income can now be written as a function of the effort choice:

$$
\begin{aligned}
&P^R(Y_1, Y_2, e, F^{BR}, F^{SR}) \\
&= \mathbb{I}_{\{Y_1(e),Y_2(e)\}=\{y_g,y_g\}}(2y_g - h(e) - F^{BR} - F^{SR}) \\
&+ (\mathbb{I}_{\{Y_1(e),Y_2(e\}=\{y_b,y_g\}} + \mathbb{I}_{\{Y_1(e),Y_2(e)\}=\{y_g,y_b\}})\times \\
&(y_g + y_b - h(e) - F^{BR} - F^{SR}).
\end{aligned}
$$

The income of the debt holders is expressed the same way as before

$$
\begin{aligned}
R^{BR}(y, e) = F^{BR}&(e)(\mathbb{I}_{Y_1(e)=y_g} \vee \mathbb{I}_{Y_2(e)=y_g}) \\
&+ \mathbb{I}_{\{Y_1(e),Y_2(e)\}\neq\{y_b,y_b\}}(y_b(1-c) - h(e)).
\end{aligned}
$$

Though for the SPV debt holders it is different now, reflecting a full payment in all cases except when both projects fail

$$
R^{SR}(y, e) = F^{SR}(e)\mathbb{I}_{\{Y_1(e),Y_2(e)\}\neq\{y_g,y_b\}} + y_b\mathbb{I}_{\{Y_1(e),Y_2(e)\}=\{y_g,y_b\}}.
$$

The bank seeks to maximize its profit or value

$$
\max_{e,F^{BR},F^{SR}} V^{SR}(e, e_0(e, F^{BR}, F^{SR}), F^{BR}, F^{SR})
$$

with:

$$
\begin{aligned}
&V^{SR}(e, e_0(e, F^{BR}, F^{SR}), F^{BR}, F^{SR}) \\
&= \mathbb{E}\left[P^R(Y_1, Y_2, e, F^{BR}(e_0), F^{SR}(e_0)\right]
\end{aligned}
$$

and with the following participation constraints

$$
\mathbb{E}[R^{BR}(y, e_0)] \geq \frac{D}{2} \text{ and } \mathbb{E}[R^{SR}(y, e_0)] \geq \frac{D}{2}.
$$

The incentive compatibility constraint remains the same as before

$$V^{SR}(e_H, e_H, F^{BR}, F^{SR}) \geq V^{SR}(eL, e_H, F^{BR}, F^{SR}).$$

The participation constraints, for investors' beliefs of $e_0$, lead to

$$F^{BR}(e_0) = \frac{\frac{D}{2} - (1-e_0)^2(y_b(1-c) - h(e_0))}{e_0(2-e_0)},$$

and

$$F^{SR}(e_0) = \frac{\frac{D}{2} - (1-e_0)^2 y_b}{e_0(2-e_0)}.$$

Then, assuming beliefs are consistent, the authors derive the expression for the maximal bank value and show that at the optimum $V^S = V^{SR}$ ($V^S$ is given in Proposition 4.6), although the valuation of the debt may be different, i.e., $F^S \neq F^{SR}$ and $F^B \neq F^{BR}$. There are no changes to bankruptcy or taxes through the possibility of recourse, and hence the total bank net value has no reasons to change.

Hence, recourse allows to compensate for the potential impact of adverse selection due to the bank's potentially cherry-picking the projects for securitization. However, as has been explained in Chap. 2, there needs to be a true sale in a securitization and such a recourse commitment would put that into question. The SPV would not be bankruptcy remote in that case. A hard contractual recourse is therefore out of the question in reality. However, one may have an implicit "soft guarantee", that is, the bank may decide to help the SPV without it being a contractual constraint.

#### 4.2.2.4 Repeated Game and Implicit Recourse

Without recourse, in a single period, we have seen that investors would not purchase the SPV debt for fear of adverse selection. However, would that still be the case if we consider the dynamic aspects of a repeated game, where the bank looks at its financing over time? Gorton and Souleles point out that in economics, oligopoly collusions are also non-contractual, but a form of optimal commitment, and can be resolved with repeated games.

We will assume that in cases when the bank does badly and loses its equity, it can reissue new equity and there is not frictions in that. We also assume there is now a non-zero interest rate $r$, so that the NPV of future cash flows does not explode.

Now there is an additional decision variable for the bank, it can either support or not support the SPV. If the investors believe that the bank will support the SPV, then they price the debt as $F^{BR}$ and $F^{SR}$ with a belief $e_0 = e_H$. Then, if the bank's loan performs well but the SPV's performs badly, its realized profit would be expected to be $y_g - h(e_H) - F^{BR} + (y_b - F^{SR})$, where the latter term is the bank's cost in bailing the SPV out. However, if the bank does not support the SPV, then it collects instead $y_g - h(e_H) - F^{BR}$. Therefore, the one-time gain in not supporting the SPV is $F^{SR} - y_b$, which is positive. The bank has an interest in reneging on its implicit promise.

However, in a repeated setting the investors will punish the bank and not invest in the SPV debt anymore, say for $N$ periods. If the bank cannot securitize for $N$ periods then it loses

$$\sum_{t=1}^{N} \frac{V^S - V}{(1+r)^t}.$$

Therefore, if $N$ is large enough and the discount rate $r$ low enough, the disincentive to renege will be larger than the one-time gains in not bailing out the SPV. This optimization program is quite complex, with a large number of potentially optimal strategies, but the reasoning above shows the intuition of the trade-off between bailing out and not bailing out the SPV.

Gorton and Souleles cover a simpler example that is more tractable, assuming $N = \infty$, so that the investors would punish the bank forever. At each period, the bank and the SPV offer debt using the pricing of $F^{BR}$ and $F^{SR}$, and then the investors choose which debt they want to buy at these levels. If investors buy the SPV debt then the issuance proceeds in these terms, otherwise the bank finances the loans on balance sheet. If the SPV's project performs badly, the bank is supposed to bail it out. If it does not then there is no more securitization possible.

They show that there is a subgame perfect Nash equilibrium, so that in certain quadratic conditions on the interest rate, securitization will happen and is optimal for the bank, with an implicit commitment to honoring recourse from the SPV.

The bank will choose to honor that commitment at any point in time, provided that the present value of its future gains is higher than the one-shot gain, or in other words:

$$\frac{V^{SR} - V^{BR}}{r} > F^{SR} - y_b,$$

which gives a quadratic inequality after expliciting all the terms.

### 4.2.2.5 Empirical Evidence

Gorton and Souleles derived two testable hypotheses from their bank and SPV model. These hypotheses are purely focused on the effect of bankruptcy and do not factor in the contribution of taxes in the model.

- If the issuer/sponsor is very risky, then its ability to provide recourse will be limited and hence that should make their securitized products less attractive, in spite of the fact that in theory (due to bankruptcy remoteness) they should be independent.
- Since the profitability of securitization increases with bankruptcy costs and project riskiness, then riskier issuers should securitize more.

In order to test these hypotheses, they obtained data from various sources on credit card securitizations, for en empirical study. They used data on every Moody's rated credit card deal from 1988 to 1999, containing such things as amounts of credit protection, deal sizes, and various collateral measures. They also obtained the pricing levels for a subset of these deals (the spreads at which these bonds were sold into the market). They measured issuers' risk by using their ratings. So as to find out which banks securitize they used regulatory filings, along with Moody's bank ratings.

To address the first hypothesis, the authors analyzed the drivers of SPV debt pricing, in this case spreads on credit card ABS. Given a rating (say, AAA), if the risks were all the same, then they should trade at the same level. Differences in collateral quality would be adjusted by the SPV structure in order for the bonds to reach the rating in question. Regressing spreads over ratings and issuers, and controlling for a few other variables such as structure type, time and asset quality, they find that depending on the issuer the required spreads all else being equal can be up to 45bps higher on riskier issuers on AAA notes. On lower rated notes, they find that the riskier sponsors issue SPV debt paying 42bps more than the less risky, all else equal. Gorton and Souleles conclude that this supports their conclusion that the strength of the sponsor matters, because of the implicit recourse commitment.

If the actual risks to the bonds were dependent on the sponsor, then one might expect the ratings to reflect them. Still, these ratings may not be able to reflect non-contractual arrangements. In addition, it could also be that it is not so much the sponsor's risk per se that is at stake, but their ability to maintain a regular supply in the market. From the standpoint of investors, owning bonds from an issuer who will continue to issue bonds and maintain a market is more desirable than owning bonds from an issuer that will stop issuing bonds, notwithstanding bankruptcy risk. The sponsor strength matters, not necessarily because of recourse commitment, but rather simply because they are more likely to ensure an orderly market and supply of standardized securities.

For the second hypothesis, the question is whether riskier firms securitize more. The authors regressed the probability that a bank used securitization as a function of the bank's rating, in addition to control variables such as the bank's name, time, and some bank characteristics (like assets size, etc). The underlying data suggests scale effects, whereby larger banks resort to securitization more than smaller banks, for example, which tend to be highly rated. Hence, it is more appropriate to control for the bank, and look at variations in securitization within banks, over time. Then, excluding the larger well-rated banks, the authors find some degree of relationship between securitization level and bank rating, but not always monotonic.

The empirical results are hence reasonably consistent with the theory developed in the paper, although one could also argue there are other effects at play, such as sponsor size and strength driving the size and stability of their SPV-issued bonds, which would then be preferred by investors.

Note, however, that the second hypothesis is not necessarily a direct conclusion of the model. Indeed, the model shows that given an amount of debt funding a riskier firm would have more to gain from securitization than a less risky firm. However, the amount of debt that could be raised would be affected by the loans risk and will be lower if, for example, one sets it so that the gains are null as with the Gordon–Metrick model extension we discussed previously.

We have seen that loan risk and bankruptcy may account for some incentives toward securitization. We will now turn toward the combined effect of taxes and regulatory capital, another two factors that have traditionally been held as important drivers of securitization.

### 4.2.3 Securitization, Reg Cap, and Taxes

We now examine the impact of taxes and capital requirements while reflecting incentives in loan production and screening, following Han, Park, and Pennacchi (2015). These authors consider how a tax treatment asymmetry between securitization vehicles and banks leads to incentives for banks to sell loans into SPVs in certain cases, even if the loans are of lesser quality. They also show how higher capital requirements can lead to more loan selling by banks. Finally, they investigate empirical evidence and test their model. This model expands and tests the initial approach to bank funding including securitization that was developed in Greenbaum and Thakor (1987).

In the models presented so far, taxes initially appeared as a disincentive toward securitization, since issuing debt on balance sheet provided a tax reduction, but we saw that in a context where access to debt was competitive then higher taxes led to more securitization. In the present model, the authors consider the fact that loans held on balance sheet will generate returns that bear corporate taxes, while that would not be the case if they are sold to an SPV that does not bear these taxes, which makes the SPV attractive from a tax standpoint.

The model by Han, Park, and Pennacchi assumes that banks can screen and monitor the loans they make and improve their performance that way. The bank can also invest in market securities and fund loans through deposits or sell them to buyers who price in the bank's incentives to screen the loans. In this model, the degree of screening applied to the loans is a continuum, and the distribution of outcomes for the loans is also a continuum. In a sense, this generalizes the approach of Gorton–Souleles who considered two levels of screenings and two levels of possible outcomes. In the Han–Park–Pennacchi model, however, assume they the investors know the characteristics of the loans being securitized, and use them for valuation. While the optimality of loan screening is reached at equilibrium (when the bank optimizes its strategy), all the external market valuations (deposits or securitized loans) are done reflecting perfect information or exogenous assumptions about preferences (such as how the deposits or loans are priced). As a result, even though the model resembles that of Gorton–Souleles (and we will see how some of Gorton and Souleles' assumptions are a particular case of the present model), it does not have a strategic component. In fact, comparable results could be obtained with a much simpler specification of the loan screening parameters.

Han, Park, and Pennacchi use a valuation approach based on pricing densities: given some asset that pays a function of the state of the world $A(s)$, its value to a class of investors $i$ would be written $\int A(s)p^i(s)ds$ where $p^i$ is the pricing density for these investors. They also assume that if the asset returns 1 then $\int p^i(s)ds = \frac{1}{1+r_i}$

for some rate $r_i$, the certainty equivalent. Expressing the model that way allows them to only specify the investors' pricing density and not bother about the actual distribution of future outcomes. However, the model does not result in tractable results in any case, so in order to keep the analysis in line with other literature, we change the overall approach, so that investors are risk-neutral with different inter-temporal preferences. So for investors $i$ we will write the value of asset $A$ as $\frac{1}{1+r_i}\mathbb{E}[A]$. In terms of calculations, this does not change much since the expectation will be written as an integral too.

#### 4.2.3.1 Model Assumptions

1. A bank has multiple opportunities to make loans each period. Borrowers are heterogeneous and each loan made to borrower $i$ of 1 monetary unit returns a random amount $Y_i$ the distribution of which is considered a function of the screening effort $e_i$ applied to loan $i$. Using the notations from the prior section, there is a distribution related to each loan's screening effort $I_i$ so that $\mathbb{P}[Y_i(e_i) \in dx] = I_i(e_i, x)dx$ and hence the screening changes the shape of the loans' outcome distribution. Expressing screening this way we can see the screening or monitoring is the same notion as the effort measure that was used in the Gorton–Souleles model.
2. Credit screening or monitoring by the bank improves the loans so that $I_i$ net of costs is weakly increasing and concave in $e_i$. The bank's cost is $C_i(e_i) = ce_i$, and the amount of screening $e_i$ is not verifiable based on the observation of the outcomes, just as in the Gorton–Souleles model. This is important because it implies that the investors can only rely on what they believe the bank will do optimally, and not on any actual observation, which could be then used in an optimal contractual arrangement. Without this assumption there would be no moral hazard regarding loan quality.
3. The bank is subject to a corporate tax at a rate $\tau$. Note that the way the tax rate is used in this model differs from the original Gorton–Metrick or Gorton–Souleles models discussed earlier, because it is now applied to the gains on equity and therefore only the interest on the debt is tax deductible and this makes it consistent with the use of taxes in Modigliani–Miller. Regulations also require a minimal capital amount relative to deposits: $\kappa D \leq E$. In theory (see Proposition 4.1), banks would want the highest amount of leverage in order to reduce taxes to shareholders, but with the minimal capital requirement in place they cannot leverage beyond a point. We write $E$ for equity at time 0 and $D$ for debt at time 0. These quantities do not change and are not random.
4. The valuation of cash flows one period ahead is done using different actualization rates for equity and debt, $r_e$ and $r_d$, respectively. Equity and debt pricing can differ due to investor preferences or personal taxation differences. In addition, the certainty equivalent return on debt post-tax is less than the certainty equivalent required on equity: $r_d(1-\tau) < r_e$.
5. There are debt securities in the market that the bank can purchase, which have state-contingent returns. These bonds are not affected by the amount of screening the bank performs on its loans. The certainty-equivalent return on these bonds is

$r_d$ and in the competitive market they are valued so that $1 + r_d = \frac{\mathbb{E}[B]}{B_0}$ if $B$ is the total return at period 1 on these securities with an initial face value of $B_0$.

6. Competition is imperfect on deposits and hence the rate the bank pays on deposits can differ from $r_d$; more generally $r_D = r_D(D)$ is the bank's certainty-equivalent deposit rate, so that $r_D$ increases in $D$ since more debt would require to attract more customers with more attractive rates.
7. Deposits are insured by the government at a fair cost that reflects the bank's risk of failure. In reality, deposit insurance is typically subsidized, but in order for the model not to become distorted by an insurance subsidy it makes sense to factor out that issue. The bank will be assumed to pay a deposit insurance premium of $\phi D$ with certain conditions.
8. If the bank sells loans, this is done without recourse. This is a major difference with the Gorton–Souleles, in which the recourse was a core aspect of securitization. However, while that may hold true for ABS in a revolving structure, it is typically not the case for general assets, which are sold without any recourse whether explicit or implicit. One way of framing the current model in institutional practice is to consider that the loans are standard mortgages, sold to an agency for securitization, at a rational price that will reflect their plausible quality.

Using these assumptions, we now turn to the bank's optimal decisions.

#### 4.2.3.2 The Bank's Optimization Program

The bank's objective is to maximize after-tax return to shareholders' equity. It decides on how much funding it raises (deposits or equity, or even loan sales), how much screening it applies, and how many loans it makes or securities it buys. $N^h$ is the number of loans of 1 monetary unit that the bank originates and holds to maturity, each paying a cash flow of $Y_i^h(e_i)$ at the end of the period. $N^m$ is the number of loans that are sold into the market (securitized), and $Y_i^m(0)$ their cash flow, reflecting no effort in screening since they are sold away. The loans are sold to bond investors who value them as such and apply bond-specific discounting. $B_0$ is the amount of bonds purchased by the bank in the market, which will pay a random amount $B$ at the end of the period. The bank's initial net worth is $E$, the equity amount; we write $W$ for the bank's net worth at the end of the period (which is a random variable).

We can write $W$ as the sum of the starting equity, plus the gains $G$ net of taxes, i.e., $W = E + (1 - \tau)G$. The gain can be written explicitly

$$G = \sum_{i=1}^{N^h} \left( Y_i^h(e_i) - 1 - ce_i \right) + \sum_{i=1}^{N^m} \left( \frac{1}{1 + r_d} \mathbb{E}[Y_i^m(0)] - 1 \right) + B - B_0 - r_D D.$$

The terms $\mathbb{E}[Y_i^m(0)]$ are simply the amounts for which the securitized loans are sold.

Based on its net worth, the bank will pay the deposit insurance premium $\phi D$: if the net wort is sufficient then the full premium is paid and the end of period shareholder equity is $W - \phi D$. If $W < \phi D$ then bankruptcy occurs and the shareholders get nothing, and the insurer suffers the loss $-W$. The deposit insurer is risk-neutral and uses an actualization rate of $r$. The fair premium should satisfy

$$\frac{1}{1+r}(\phi D\mathbb{P}[W > 0] + \mathbb{E}[W\mathbb{I}_{W<0}]) = 0,$$

which gives us an expression for $D$, which does not depend on $r$. Note that by construction $\mathbb{E}[W\mathbb{I}_{W<0}]$ is negative.

Then note that the present value of the shareholder's end of period payoff is $\frac{1}{1+r_e}\mathbb{E}[(W - \phi D)\mathbb{I}_{W>0}]$. Hence replacing $D$, we write the shareholders' net present value as

$$\frac{1}{1+r_e}\mathbb{E}\left[\left(W + \frac{\mathbb{E}[W\mathbb{I}_{W<0}]}{\mathbb{P}[W > 0]}\right)\mathbb{I}_{W>0}\right] = \frac{1}{1+r_e}\mathbb{E}[W].$$

In other words, the fair cost of depositor insurance is canceled out. The fact that this insurance is necessary means that it is as if there was no limited liability floor in the drop in value, because the bank has to pay insurance for it.

The expected NPV of the shareholders' net worth increases, which is what the bank seeks to maximize, can be written out

$$\begin{aligned}
&\frac{1}{1+r_e}\mathbb{E}[W] - E = \frac{1}{1+r_e}\mathbb{E}[E + (1-\tau)G] \\
&= \left(\sum_{i=1}^{N^h}\left(\mathbb{E}[Y_i^h(e_i)] - 1 - ce_i\right) + \sum_{i=1}^{N^m}\left(\frac{1}{1+r_d}\mathbb{E}[Y_i^m(0)] - 1\right)\right)\frac{1-\tau}{1+r_e} \\
&+ (\mathbb{E}[B] - B_0 - r_D D)\frac{1-\tau}{1+r_e} + \frac{E}{1+r_e} - E.
\end{aligned}$$

The expected return on the debt securities can be simplified, and the whole expression can be scaled up by $(1 + r_e)$ without changing the optimal strategies. Therefore, we have the total expression for the maximization program

$$\begin{aligned}
\max_{N^h, N^m, B_0, D, E, (e_i)} &\sum_{i=1}^{N^h}\left(\mathbb{E}[Y_i^h(e_i)] - 1 - ce_i\right)(1-\tau) \\
&+ \left[\sum_{i=1}^{N^m}\left(\frac{1}{1+r_d}\mathbb{E}[Y_i^m(0)] - 1\right) + r_d B_0 - r_D D\right](1-\tau) - r_e E,
\end{aligned}$$

subject to the constraints for financing

$$N^h + B_0 \leq D + E + \sum_{i=1}^{N^m}\left(\frac{1}{1+r_d}\mathbb{E}[Y_i^m(0)] - 1\right),$$

and for leverage

$$\kappa D \leq E.$$

In the objective function, it is worth noting that the retained loans are effectively taxed at the corporate tax rate, and the loans that are sold/securitized immediately are valued in the market reflecting a debt-like rate for present-value calculation. The financing constraint states that the retained lending and market securities must be less than the amount of debt, equity, and gains from the immediate sale of non-retained loans. Note that the financing constraint also implies that the funds from selling the loans are available for investing in retained loans or in market securities; in other words, the sale happens at time 0.

If we were using the same type of assumptions as in Gorton–Souleles, then $Y_i$ would be explicitly specified, as well as the cost function as a function of efforts using (4.3). All the loans would have the same characteristics and we would write the following components of the value function:

$$\sum_{i=1}^{N^h} \left(\mathbb{E}[Y_i^h(e_i)] - 1 - ce_i\right) = \left(ey_g + (1-e)y_b - 1 - h(e)\right) N^h,$$

and

$$\sum_{i=1}^{N^m} \left(\frac{1}{1+r_d}\mathbb{E}[Y_i^m(0)] - 1\right) = \left(\frac{e_b y_g + (1-e_b)y_b}{1+r_d} - 1 - h(e_b)\right) N^m.$$

The effort could be made into a continuous choice, for example, given a lower bound $e_b$, with $e \in [e_b, 1]$ and $h$ a continuous function that may arbitrarily rise as $e$ nears 1.

#### 4.2.3.3 Bank's Optimal Behavior

**Proposition 4.7** (Han–Park–Pennacchi) *At the optimum, depending on the relative values of loans' expected returns and deposit costs, there are three possible equilibria for the bank without securitization characterized by the marginal financing rate:*

$$\frac{\lambda_f}{1-\tau} = r_d,$$
$$\frac{\lambda_f}{1-\tau} = \frac{r_e}{1-\tau},$$
$$\frac{\lambda_f}{1-\tau} = \frac{1}{1+\kappa} r_d + \frac{\kappa}{1+\kappa}\frac{r_e}{1-\tau}.$$

***Proof*** Recall that when facing an optimization program with inequality constraints one can equivalently solve a modified program using positive multipliers on the distance to the constraints (see Varian (1992)). We write $\lambda_f$ and $\lambda_k$ for the Lagrange multipliers for the financing constraints and leverage constraints. Also, we consider that at the optimum the $i$ are ordered so that loan $i = N^h$ is the marginal loan (the loan for which the optimum is reached by the smallest amount), and the same thing for the loans sold: $i = N^m$ is the marginal loan sold. The Kuhn–Tucker conditions for the problem are

For all $i$,

$$\left(\frac{\partial \mathbb{E}[Y_i^h(e_i)]}{\partial e_i} - 1 - c\right) e_i = 0.$$

For the discrete number of loans, we do not take a derivative for the first-order condition, but rather a discrete difference:

$$\left(\left(\mathbb{E}[Y_{N^h}^h(e_{N^h})] - 1 - ce_{N^h}\right)(1-\tau) - \lambda_f\right) N^h = 0,$$
$$\left(\frac{1}{1+r_d}\mathbb{E}[Y_{N^m}^m(0)] - 1\right)(1-\tau+\lambda_f)N^m = 0.$$

And for the other continuous variables and Lagrangians:

$$\left(\frac{1}{1+r_d}\mathbb{E}[Y_{N^m}^m(0)] - 1\right)(1-\tau+\lambda_f)N^m = 0,$$
$$\left(-(r_D + D\frac{\partial r_D}{\partial D})(1-\tau) + \lambda_f - \kappa\lambda_k\right) D = 0,$$
$$(-r_e + \lambda_f + \lambda_k)E = 0,$$
$$(r_d(1-\tau) - \lambda_f)B_0 = 0.$$

Han, Park, and Pennacchi first consider the case with no loans being sold, so $N^m$ is set to 0. Then the first-order condition for the $e_i$ determines the optimal levels $e_i^*$. The optimal quantity of loans is determined by solving for $N^h$. At the optimum, the net return on the marginal loan equals the tax adjusted marginal cost of financing $\frac{\lambda_f}{1-\tau}$. We assume $D > 0$ and $E > 0$ so that the conditions are binding and $E = \kappa D$. The financing cost $\lambda_f$ then can be written as

$$\frac{\lambda_f}{1-\tau} = \frac{1}{1+\kappa}\left(r_D + D\frac{\partial r_D}{\partial D}\right) + \frac{\kappa r_e}{(1+\kappa)(1-\tau)}.$$

In addition, if we assume that at equilibrium the bank purchases some market securities so that $B_0 > 0$, then we know that $\lambda_f = r_d(1-\tau)$.

The type of equilibria that can be reached in the model depends on which constraints are binding, which in turn depends on the parameters driving the aggregate returns from different activities: lending, or buying securities, or funding through deposits.

The authors identify several possible equilibria in this model without securitization, depending on the underlying model parameters. First, the so-called "loan-poor and deposit-rich" equilibrium: the $I_i$ and $r_D$ are such that the bank has limited lending opportunities (so the $I_i$ are not very strong, and the expected returns are low) but cheap deposit funding, thanks to a strong deposit market power. Then the bank makes loans until the least profitable loan's returns equal the return from investing in market securities:

$$\mathbb{E}[Y^h_{Nh}(e^*_{Nh})] - 1 - ce^*_{Nh} = r_d$$

The excess of cheap deposits that the bank has access to is then invested in securities, but since equity should be relatively expensive then the capital constraint will be binding, i.e., $\lambda_k > 0$. In that case, the weighted cost of funding equals the certainty equivalent securities return:

$$\frac{1}{1+\kappa}\left(r_D + D\frac{\partial r_D}{\partial D}\right) + \frac{\kappa}{1+\kappa}\frac{r_e}{1-\tau} = r_d,$$

where, since the capital constraint is binding, $\kappa = \frac{E}{D}$.

The second equilibrium the authors examine is "loan-rich and deposit-poor", where the bank sees many interesting lending opportunities but the cost of deposits is high. In that case, the bank issues deposits until their marginal cost balances the tax adjusted cost of equity, and further funding is done by equity and the capital constraint is not binding, so $\lambda_k = 0$.

Then the marginal cost of financing $\lambda_f$ verifies

$$\frac{\lambda_f}{1-\tau} = r_D + D\frac{\partial r_D}{\partial D} = \frac{r_e}{1-\tau}.$$

The number/amount of loans originated verifies at the optimum screening $e^*$

$$\mathbb{E}[Y^h_{Nh}(e^*_{Nh})] - 1 - ce^*_{Nh} = \frac{r_e}{1-\tau},$$

and the bank does not purchase market securities since their return is less than the marginal cost of funding (Assumption 4).

The third possible equilibrium is when deposits are not too expensive to the bank, and loans are attractive, in which case it is the capital leverage constraint that binds: $\lambda_k > 0$. In that case the bank's marginal cost of funding $\frac{\lambda_f}{1-\tau}$ is between the debt certainty equivalent return and the equity post-tax certainty equivalent return. It is not profitable for the bank to invest in debt securities. The authors stress a particular case where deposit demand would be competitively priced and deposits would exactly cost $r_d$. Then the bank's marginal cost of funding becomes a weighted average between equity and debt, at the maximal leverage:

$$\frac{\lambda_f}{1-\tau} = \frac{1}{1+\kappa}r_d + \frac{\kappa}{1+\kappa}\frac{r_e}{1-\tau}.$$

These are the three conditions mentioned in the proposition. □

#### 4.2.3.4 Impact of Securitization

Now we consider that loan selling may be positive, so that $N^m \geq 0$. At the optimum, the gain in retaining a loan on balance sheet, funded with equity and deposits at the marginal rate, can be written as follows:

$$\mathbb{E}[Y_i^h(e_i^e)] - 1 - ce_i^* - \frac{\lambda_f}{1-\tau}.$$

However this amount is realized at period 1, and we can make it comparable to a period 0 amount by considering the amount at time 0 which, invested in market securities, would have returned the net gain. Hence, at time 0, the certainty equivalent of the net gain in extending a loan and retaining it is

$$\frac{1}{1+r_d}\left(\mathbb{E}[Y_i^h(e_i^*)] - 1 - ce_i^* - \frac{\lambda_f}{1-\tau}\right).$$

On the other hand, the profit from selling that loan into a securitization is

$$\frac{1}{1+r_d}\mathbb{E}[Y_i^m(0)] - 1$$

and the excess gain from retaining a loan as opposed to selling it can be written

$$\frac{1}{1+r_d}\mathbb{E}[Y_i^h(e_i^*) - ce_i^* - Y_i^m(0)] - \frac{\frac{\lambda_f}{1-\tau} - r_d}{1+r_d}.$$

The first term is always positive since it is the increase in expected gain from applying screening, which we have assumed to be positive (Assumption 2). In a case where the bank has an easy access to deposits but few lending opportunities, the marginal financing cost net of taxes is $r_d$, so that the second term is null. In that situation, it is always optimal for the bank to retain the loans, and in no conditions would the bank sell them.

In the second case, where the bank sees many lending opportunities but has limited financing ability through deposits, the second term writes $-\frac{\frac{r_e}{1-\tau}-r_d}{1+r_d}$ which is always negative. Hence, if the net gains from monitoring are not sufficiently large, the bank will securitize the loans. The third case, where the bank maximizes its leverage, leads to a similar possible securitization since the marginal financing rate is strictly greater than $r_d$.

In summary, banks for which the funding cost exceed the minimal $r_d$ will want to securitize potentially, since it is more efficient for them to get others to finance these loans at $r_d$.

The authors stress that competition from mutual funds, for example, makes funding more expensive for banks, which in turn will make them more likely to securitize according to this model. Also, if the bank can optimally securitize, it may originate more loans than it would have when loan sales were not possible. This is the case if the gain in retaining the loan for the bank is negative (and hence it does not keep it), but the gain from selling is positive. In other words, if the difference in funding cost between the bank's and $r_d$ compensates for the worse valuation of the loans due to no screening.

In addition, increases in tax rates will raise the cost of capital for the bank when it is marginally resorting to equity rather than deposits. This will reduce the threshold over which the bank will sell the loans rather than retain them. Equivalently, in the equilibrium when the bank is fully levered, an increase in capital requirements will also lead to higher funding costs (less leverage), and in turn to a greater incentive to sell loans.

Finally, if the tax rate increases and more loans are sold rather than retained for a bank that is not yet at the maximum leverage, then its leverage will increase (using less equity funding for these loans).

#### 4.2.3.5 Empirical Evidence

Han, Park, and Pennacchi tested some of their model's predictions on empirical data, using filings on banks' origination volumes and loans sales at the metropolitan area level (MSA). They related these data to state-level taxes, and focused on banks that operate in a single state (so that from a tax perspective the bank's strategy was mostly driven by that state's tax level). They measured what they termed a mortgage sales ratio for each year and each bank, that is, the value of mortgages originated and sold, over the value of mortgages that were originated. They also distinguished between jumbo loans, which could not be securitized by the agencies and conforming loans. The asset sales may be less efficient on jumbos since they cannot be securitized in such a streamlined manner as conforming loans.

They collected demographics data across MSAs, so that the loan origination characteristics can be related to local demographics, employment, and other local dynamics. In addition, these demographics can help frame the degree of local deposit market competition.

The first hypothesis is that banks in markets with limited lending opportunities but substantial deposit market power will have little incentives to securitize loans, whatever the tax rate. The second hypothesis is that banks in areas with substantial lending opportunities but limited deposit market power will have an incentive to sell loans, and that incentive will be higher in high tax areas.

The notion of deposit power, and lending opportunities, is proxied by the proportion of seniors in the population. The underlying assumption is the more senior people there are in proportion, the greater demand for deposits, but at the same time the lesser demand for mortgages and less lending opportunities.

The average mortgage sales ratio on high tax environments is significantly higher for banks in high tax states than for banks in low tax states (19% vs. 14%). All else equal, taxes raise the cost of equity and provide an incentive to sell.

Also, they look at the same split, but further categorize by the proportion of seniors in the population. When that proportion is high (limited lending, cheap funding, in theory), then mortgage sales are not dependent on tax rates. In areas with a lower proportion of seniors, then there is a 9% difference in mortgage loan sales ratio between high and low tax states.

Then, the authors consider a fuller regression model: the mortgage sales ratio is regressed over tax rates, whether the proportion of seniors is higher than the median, and various bank-level metrics, MSA-level metrics, and time effects as controls. They find that controlling for many overall drivers of loan sales, tax rates, and deposit market power are significant drivers of loan sales, as the model predicts.

Using this model, we have seen that taxes and regulatory capital requirements were plausible drivers of securitization, in a way that could be supported by the data. We will now take a closer look at the contribution of limited liability, which as we have already seen played an indirect role.

### 4.2.4 Securitization, Leverage, and Liability

In Leland (2007), the author looks at securitization from the angle of the firm's scope. Sometimes, firms merge and create synergies which accrue value. Securitization is the opposite of that; in some conditions, it may make sense for a firm to separate itself from parts of its business (or assets), if the sum of the values of the parts is more than the value of the whole. This issue is related to the interesting question of where a firm optimally starts, and where it ends or, in other words, why do firms have the perimeter that we are familiar with. A particular business's financing may also not be optimal for all activities, and it might be easier to sell off some of these activities rather than find a more adapted financing.

#### 4.2.4.1 Capital Structure Model and Optimization

The economic actors are considered risk-neutral in this model, and there are two periods, times 0 and 1. In that respect, the model matches the ones that we have covered so far. Information is perfect, which matches the Han–Park–Pennacchi and Gorton–Metrick models. The risk-free rate over the period is $r$. A business activity generates a future random cash flow of $Y$, a random variable with a density $I$ such that $\mathbb{P}[Y \in dx] = I(x)dx$, which could be seen as the same expression as (4.3) but without any intervention or screening of the loans. This cash flow can be from a loan or a loan portfolio. The value of the future cash flow at time 0 is $Y_0 = \frac{1}{1+r}\mathbb{E}[Y]$ or, in other words, $Y_0 = \frac{1}{1+r}\int xI(x)dx$. The rights to these cash flows do not have to be traded. Leland explicitly assumes that the firm owners' thanks to limited liability are protected from negative cash flows, so that the pre-tax value of the activity with limited liability is $H_0 = \frac{1}{1+r}\mathbb{E}[Y\mathbb{I}_{Y>0}]$. The pre-tax value that limited liability brings is $L_0 = \frac{-1}{1+r}\mathbb{E}[Y\mathbb{I}_{Y<0}]$.

The tax rate is assumed to be $\tau$ at the investor level, so that the after-tax value of the unlevered firm is

$$V_0 = \frac{1}{1+r}\mathbb{E}[(1-\tau)Y\mathbb{I}_{Y>0}] = (1-\tau)H_0.$$

The present value of taxes paid by the firm with no debt is $T_0(0) = \tau H_0$.

Firms can finance their activity by issuing zero-coupon bonds at $t = 0$ paying a principal of $P$ at time 1. The debt's market value at time 0 is denoted $D_0(P)$. The interest payment is $P - D_0(P)$. Interest is explicitly assumed to be a tax deductible expense so that taxable income is $Y - (P - D_0(P))$, and the zero tax income level is $Y^Z(P) = P - D_0(P)$. Also, there are no tax credits, so if $Y < Y^Z$ no tax amount is recovered.

The present value of future tax payments for a levered firm is

$$T_0(P) = \frac{\tau}{1+r}\mathbb{E}[(Y - Y^Z(P))\mathbb{I}_{Y>Y^Z(P)}],$$

where the only random variable in the expectation is $Y$.

The future random equity cash flow $E$ from the project $Y$ is the maximum between 0 and the project's cash flows minus the tax liability and minus principal repayment (thanks to limited liability). So

$$E = 0 \vee \left(Y - P - \tau\left(0 \vee (Y - Y^Z(P))\right)\right).$$

Default occurs if the above term reaches zero, that is, if the cash flow $Y$ drops under a default threshold $Y^d$ such that $Y^d = P + \tau\left(0 \vee (Y^d - Y^Z(P))\right)$. We solve that equation by going through both cases, where either $Y^d - Z^Z \geq 0$ or $Y^d - Y^Z < 0$. In the first case, $Y^d = P + \frac{\tau}{1-\tau}D_0$, and in the second case, this would lead to $Y^d = P$ and $D_0 < 0$, which we assume is not possible.

Now, given $Y^Z$ and $Y^d$ we can determine the value of the debt $D_0(P)$ given the principal amount $P$. If the firm is solvent at the end of the period, then the debt holders receive $P$. If the firm is not solvent, we assume a severity fraction $\alpha$, so that a share $1 - \alpha$ of positive pre-tax cash flows is received. Bondholders also benefit from limited liability if $Y < 0$. Finally, the tax liability remains due if $Y^Z \leq Y \leq Y^d$. Hence, we have the net present value of the debt

$$D_0 = \frac{1}{1+r}\mathbb{E}\left[P\mathbb{I}_{Y>Y^d} + (1-\alpha)Y\mathbb{I}_{0<Y<Y^d} - \tau(Y - Y^Z)\mathbb{I}_{Y^Z<Y<Y^d}\right].$$

with $Y^d = P + \frac{\tau}{1-\tau}D_0$ and $Y^Z = P - D_0$, which makes the expression above an equation that may be difficult to solve depending on the density $f$.

The expected after-tax recovery rate on debt, conditional on default, is (as a function of $P$)

$$R = \frac{\mathbb{E}\left[(1-\alpha)Y\mathbb{I}_{0<Y<Y^d} - \tau(Y - Y^Z)\mathbb{I}_{Y^Z<Y<Y^d}\right]}{P\mathbb{P}[Y < Y^d]}.$$

Leland points out that on firms the parameter $\alpha$ is difficult to observe, but the recovery amount relative to debt outstanding, $R$, can be observed.

The value of the equity can also be expressed, and is also a function of $P$:

$$E_0 = \frac{1}{1+r}\mathbb{E}\left[(Y - P - \tau(Y - Y^Z))\mathbb{I}_{Y>Y^d}\right].$$

We can now look at the financing that maximizes the total firm value, $v_0(P) = D_0(P) + E_0(P)$, with the equity and debt value given above. The optimal debt $P$ is the one that maximizes firm value. As with the models of Modigliani–Miller or Gorton–Metrick, the gains from increased leverage $v_0(P) - V_0$ stem from tax savings in part. Further, Leland points out that the value of the levered firm can be written as

$$v_0(P) = V_0 + (T_0(0) - T_0(P)) - \frac{\alpha}{1+r}\mathbb{E}[Y\mathbb{I}_{0<Y<Y^d}],$$

that is, the unlevered value, plus the tax gains from using leverage, minus the present value of default costs. We can write this in summary as $v_0(P) = V_0 + TS_0(P) - DC_0(P)$.

The presence of default costs can be paralleled with the bankruptcy costs in the Gorton–Souleles and Gorton–Metrick models. Determining the optimal leverage is hence a question of determining the amount of borrowing that maximizes tax savings minus expected default costs.

The author then treats a particular case using a Gaussian distribution for the project's returns, that is,

$$I(x) = \frac{1}{\sigma\sqrt{2\Pi}}\exp\left(-\frac{1}{2\sigma^2}(\mu - x)^2\right).$$

The Gaussian distribution represents a reasonable choice to model random outcomes on projects, as they can be thought of the aggregation of multiple separate effects. However, the expressions for equity or debt value cannot be much simplified formally using Gaussians, because the cumulative probability is only known as an integral. Leland numerically computes many examples and illustrates that with reasonable parameters many types of corporate situations can be accounted for, such as a firm issuing unsecured debt with a BBB-like level of risk, reaching an optimal leverage of about 50% debt/50% equity, leading to a positive increase in value $v_0^* - V_0$ versus the unlevered firm.

#### 4.2.4.2 Measuring Financial Synergies

Leland then focuses on how to measure the benefits from financial synergies. Concentrating on financial, as opposed to operational synergies, means that the cash flows remain as they are and are simply added together, there are no economies of scale or other factors that would change the cash flows themselves. Considering two activities $i \in \{1, 2\}$, should they be kept separate and each levered optimally, or merged together in to a unique firm $i = M$ and that one firm levered optimally?

Leland defines the financial benefit of merger $\Delta = v_{0M}^* - v_{01}^* - v_{02}^*$. Based on the value decomposition between unlevered, tax savings and default cost, we can write $\Delta = \Delta V_0 + \Delta TS + \Delta DC$ where the components are simply the differences between the merged firm's value and the sum of the component firms.

Even though the project cash flows are simply added when merging, value may be created for the unlevered firm due to changes in the value of limited liability (consider, for example, the case where the projects are negatively correlated, this might greatly reduce the default probability of the merged cash flows). We have

$$\Delta V_0 = (1-\tau)(H_{0M} - H_{01} - H_{02}) = (1-\tau)(L_{0M} - L_{01} - L_{02}) = LL.$$

The remaining terms in $\Delta$ can be combined in a single leverage effect term $LE$, which may be positive or negative.

While a positive $\Delta$ would indicate that firms would benefit from merging, a negative $\Delta$ indicates that parts of a firm may optimally be sold off and segregated, as they would reach a better total value being separate entities.

#### 4.2.4.3 Financial Benefits of Securitization

Leland then specifically looks at how securitization may be optimal, depending on the parameters defining firms 1 and 2, the original firm and the part of its business that should be securitized. In a securitization the SPV raises funds by itself, and these funds are only backed by the assets in that SPV (we are assuming there is no recourse here).

The author considers the case of a bank with two sources of cash flows: mortgages with a low risk, and other banking activities with a high risk. The low risk assets are moved to an SPV, which will issue securities backed by these assets. The sponsor receives the proceeds from the SPV's issuance of securities, and does not retain any of the securities issued by the SPV.

For the numerical simulations, the mortgage assets are assumed to represent 25% of the total operational cash flows value, with a low annual volatility (4%), and a correlation with the remaining cash flows of 0.50. The bank's other banking activities have an annual volatility of about 29%. With these parameters, securitizing improves the value of the assets being securitized by about 14%. The optimal leverage rises from about 50% for the whole firm to 83% for the mortgage assets. The SPV debt has very low risk and a high value. Securitization allows the use of very high leverage on particular assets, and a majority of the benefit (increase in value) comes from gains due to leverage. The rest comes from the $LL$ effect, reflecting increased limited liability protection value.

When the originating firm is riskier, securitization is more attractive, which matches the results from Gorton and Souleles, both theoretical and empirical. In addition, reducing the default costs at the SPV level, which would make sense given that an SPV does not technically default, increases leverage, and the overall value of securitization. This is also in line with Gorton–Souleles, although the impact is less significant.

So far, we have seen how taxes, liquidation costs, regulatory capital, leverage, and limited liability all could contribute to explaining the existence of securitization. All these factors, however, are intrinsically external to a firm. We now shift our focus to factors that may explain securitization, but are endogenous to a firm.

### 4.2.5 Securitization and Asymmetrical Information

In Iacobucci and Winter (2005), the authors use **hidden action** and **hidden information** concepts in order to explain securitization without resorting to exogenous drivers. There have been further developments, for example, the approach proposed by Fan, Ong, and Sing (2006), but we focus on the original simpler models presented by Iacobucci and Winter.

The authors stress the fact that most explanations for securitization use some kind of external factor, such as regulations, differences in funding costs, or bankruptcy avoidance, and this justifies looking for truly endogenous sources for securitization. In particular, they argue that bankruptcy avoidance and judgment-proofing along the arguments developed by LoPucki (1996) are not very convincing reasons since the ex ante probability of bankruptcy is typically low on firms using securitization. One additional argument against bankruptcy cost reduction is that when assets are securitized, the proceeds need to be distributed otherwise they remain accessible to claimants.

Securitization effectively consists of a change in firm structure and as a result it is logical to look at the foundations of the theory of the firm, which is based on information asymmetry. There are two kinds of asymmetries that the authors delineate:

- Hidden action, which refers to the fact that investors do not have full information on what managers are doing and it raises an agency problem (investors do not see the managers' actions but only some of the results of their actions) and
- Hidden information, which refers to information differences between issuers and investors, or also between investors: some of them are experts and have better information than others.

In the whole analysis, there are two crucially important assumptions concerning securitization, which we consider to be generally verified:

- First, the cash flows that are securitized are little sensitive to managers' efforts. In most cases, they are receivables that already belong to the firm and have already been earned, so that managers cannot alter them.
- Second, the securitized assets are uncertain, they are never entirely risk-free. Some noise is taken out of the firm.

In other words, securitization takes some manager-independent noise out of the firm's output. Note that these assumptions about securitization make it very clearly distinct from secured debt. With secured debt financing, there is no true sale. The issuer's equity is not insulated from the fluctuations of the assets value or performance in the case of secured debt, since the collateral remains within the issuing firm. Also, the valuation of the assets is more precise when they are fully segregated from the issuing firm. In the case of secured debt, the value of the collateral will be affected by the firm's overall situation.

#### 4.2.5.1 Hidden Action and Agency Costs

The first type of information asymmetry that can explain the optimality of securitization is that between investors and managers. Managers are agents acting "for" investors, who are the principals. These principals do not see the actions taken by the managers (hence the notion of hidden action) and have to resort to indirect ways in order to incite the managers to act in the principals' interest. This asymmetry forces investors to monitor what they can observe from managers and to also limit managerial discretion. The agency cost is the loss in firm value due to individuals (the managers) following their own interest rather than that of the firm. Specifically, it is the cost of monitoring or the cost of the other mechanisms put into place in order to control the distortions created by the managers' following their particular interest. As we will see, securitization can reduce this agency cost.

In their seminal introduction of the theory of the firm, Jensen and Meckling (1976) described five mechanisms that can be used to limit agency costs: monitoring, managerial reputation, takeovers, explicit incentive pay, and the limitation of managerial free cash flows. Following Iacobucci and Winter, we describe how securitization can improve the efficiency of these mechanisms.

We begin with a formal model in the case of managers' reputation, which clearly shows how these core assumptions play a crucial role in making securitization a tool for agency cost reduction. Reputation is an important source of discipline for managers, since the firm's performance will affect their reputation. Effort and talent cannot be contracted, because they cannot be directly observed, and cannot either be disentangled from one another. A manager may work hard not to gain a reputation of hard worker per se, but rather in order to affect the future perception of their talent, which will be influenced by the greater firm output.

Reputation cannot perfectly resolve agency problems. Managers are rewarded in the future for actions taken today, so the rewards are discounted, while ideally they would not be. In addition, greater output could be attributed by the future labor market to luck rather than talent, and hence there will be less gain in hard work.

Securitization takes manager-independent noise away, which improves the precision of the reading of the manager's own performance. Iacobucci and Winter propose a version of the model from Dewatripont, Jewitt, and Tirole (1999) (see also Holmström (1999) for the initial work on this subject) in order to illustrate how securitization improves reputation-related agency costs.

**Proposition 4.8** (Iacobucci–Winter Benefits of Securitization for Manager Reputation Agency Costs) *In a context where managers are compensated as a function of* *their reputation and set their effort level in order to maximize their gains, securitization leads to a higher effort.*

***Proof*** We consider a two-period model, with periods 1 and 2. The firm's output or profit $Y_t$ is driven by the manager's talent $\Theta$, current effort $a$ which depends on the period and noise $\varepsilon$ which also depends on the period. The variables $\varepsilon$ are assumed to be iid Gaussians with mean 0 and variance $\sigma^2$. Talent is also assumed to be a Gaussian with mean $\theta_T$ and variance $\sigma_T^2$. We write the distributions for $\Theta$ and $\varepsilon_1$ as follows: $\mathbb{P}[\Theta \in d\theta] = \mu_{\theta_T,\sigma_T^2}(\theta)d\theta$ and $\mathbb{P}[\varepsilon_1 \in dx] = \mu_{0,\sigma^2}(x)dx$.

At first we consider a firm that has securitized some cash flows which were Gaussian and independent from managerial efforts or talent, and had a mean of 0 and variance $s^2$.

Talent is unknown by the manager and by investors, and the effort is set and known by the manager. The cost of effort $c$ is an increasing convex function of $a$. The shape of the cost function is known to all. Profits are also known to all at the end of each period.

The manager gets a wage $w$ at the end of each period, as a function of profit for the preceding period. For the first period, the wage $w_1$ is hence fixed (and could be set to 0). The manager discounts the wages at a rate $\delta$. Having observed $Y_1$, at the end of the second period the market will pay the manager $w_2$ as a function of $Y_1$, and the manager has no incentive to make any effort $a_2 > 0$ since there will not be any $w_3$ payment dependent on $Y_2$.

An equilibrium effort level $a^*$ in the first period is the effort level such that if the market anticipates the effort level $a^*$ from the manager, then that effort level maximizes the manager's interest. The market rationally anticipates $a_2 = 0$ for the second period, so that $w_2$ will be the market's expectation of the manager's talent given the firm's profit $Y_1$ and the manager's estimated effort level $a^*$. We write with a subscript the expectation or conditional expectation assuming a given effort level.

Hence, the market sets the wage as

$$w_2(a^*, Y_1) = \mathbb{E}_{a^*}[\Theta|Y_1]$$

and the manager chooses $a$ that maximizes

$$\max_a \delta\mathbb{E}_a[w_2(a^*, Y_1)] - c(a) = \max_a \delta\mathbb{E}_a\left[\mathbb{E}_{a^*}[\Theta|Y_1]\right] - c(a).$$

For an equilibrium to be reached, the first-order condition of this maximization program must be verified at the effort level assumed by the market:

$$\frac{\partial}{\partial a}\left[\delta\mathbb{E}_a\left[\mathbb{E}_{a^*}[\Theta|Y_1]\right] - c(a)\right]\Big|_{a=a^*} = 0.$$

Now we turn to the calculation of these expectations. First, we express the joint distribution of $Y_1$ and $\Theta$. Noting that $Y_1 = a + \Theta + \varepsilon_1$, for any measurable $f$:

$$\mathbb{E}_a[f(Y_1, \Theta)] = \int f(a+\theta+x, \theta)\mu_{0,\sigma^2}(x)\mu_{\theta_T,\sigma_T^2}(\theta)dx d\theta$$
$$= \int f(y, \theta)\mu_{0,\sigma^2}(y-(a+\theta))\mu_{\theta_T,\sigma_T^2}(\theta)dy d\theta.$$

Note that this density is in the form of a Gaussian density relative to $\theta$. Integrating with respect to $\theta$ we can express the distribution of $Y_1$ as $\mathbb{P}_a[Y_1 \in dy] = \mu_{\theta_T+a,\sigma_T^2+\sigma^2}(y)dy$.

Using the joint distribution we can also express the distribution of $\Theta$ conditional upon $Y_1$:

$$\mathbb{P}_a[\Theta \in d\theta | Y_1] = \frac{\mu_{0,\sigma^2}(Y_1-(a+\theta))\mu_{\theta_T,\sigma_T^2}(\theta)d\theta}{\int \mu_{0,\sigma^2}(Y_1-(a+\theta))\mu_{\theta_T,\sigma_T^2}(\theta)d\theta}$$
$$= \mu_{\frac{\sigma^2\theta_T+\sigma_T^2(Y_1-a)}{\sigma^2+\sigma_T^2}, \frac{1}{\frac{1}{\sigma^2}+\frac{1}{\sigma_T^2}}}(\theta)d\theta.$$

Hence, $\mathbb{E}_{a^*}[\Theta|Y_1]$ is easy to compute, so $w_2(a^*, Y_1) = \frac{\sigma^2\theta_T+\sigma^2(Y_1-a^*)}{\sigma^2+\sigma_T^2}$ and the first-order condition at equilibrium can be written as

$$\delta\frac{\partial}{\partial a}\mathbb{E}_a\left[\frac{\sigma^2\theta_T+\sigma^2(Y_1-a^*)}{\sigma^2+\sigma_T^2}\right]\Bigg|_{a=a^*} = c'(a^*)$$
$$= \delta\frac{\sigma^2}{\sigma^2+\sigma_T^2}.$$

Since $c'$ is assumed to be decreasing, the optimal effort level $a^*$ is decreasing in $\sigma$. If the additional cash flows had not been securitized then $\sigma$ would be higher and equal to $\sqrt{\sigma^2+s^2}$, and the optimal effort level would be lower. □

Securitization also improves monitoring costs for investors. Monitoring in this context means inferring the inputs or efforts of managers based on the corporation's outputs, which is fundamentally comparable to what the market was doing when estimating managers' talent. The manager's actions as observed through the firm's output are noisy. It does not require a formal model to realize that if a firm's output is less noisy, the managers' actions become more easily identifiable. Since the cash flows that are securitized are noisy, by assumption, then the output from the assets that remain within the firm will more directly reflect the managers' inputs. Taking out the securitized assets cash flows will also make the valuation of the firm more precise.

The reduction in the noise in firm output is also beneficial to takeovers as a source of discipline for managers. The quality of existing management can be better ascertained if the observable output is less noisy, and the market can better evaluate the firm.

Managers get typically paid a share of the residual claims: stocks or stock options for example. However, managers are typically more risk-averse than stock holders: managers are not as diversified (they have a greater share of their wealth invested in a single corporation), and if they were not risk-averse they would optimally buy the entire company and hence reduce all agency costs. Through securitization, exogenous noise not due to the manager's performance is reduced, and agency costs are hence reduced: the contracts that set pay based on the firm's output will more accurately reflect each manager's performance.

Finally, the agency cost of free cash flows is reduced by securitization. When in a firm there are small cash flows that are not needed for investment, there is a risk managers will use these cash flows to their own benefits because the fixed cost of monitoring these cash flows would be relatively high. Thanks to securitization, a stream of small cash flows can be turned into a large lump sum, for which monitoring costs will be relatively smaller.

#### 4.2.5.2 Hidden Information

With hidden information, we look into a situation where the information itself is not observed by every agent: issuers may have more information than investors, or different classes of investors may not all have the same information.

We first consider the case of general firm assets as opposed to securitizable assets. General firm assets are typically better known by the firm than by outside investors, while securitizable assets are well known and understood by investors as well as the firm, since they are fairly insensitive to managers' unobservable actions. In other words, there are more information asymmetries on general assets than on securitized assets. As a result, when general assets are financed by equity issuance there is a lemon premium to be paid.

As we will see, if there is an additional cost to using securitization as a means of financing, then securitization can act as a signal pointing to better quality assets. This hence makes securitization optimal in certain cases.

**Proposition 4.9** (Iacobucci–Winter Benefits of Securitization for Informed Issuer) *If issuers have privileged information on their core company assets, and securitizable assets are well known by the market, then securitization is optimal as it allows issuers with good quality core assets to avoid a lemon premium and also signal that quality to the market.*

***Proof*** In order to make the model in Iacobucci and Winter more consistent with the ones we have covered so far, we consider a setting comparable to the Gorton–Souleles model, without taxes or bankruptcy costs and with some differences. A bank has two loans of amounts $Y_1$ and $Y_2$, where the quality of $Y_2$ is perfectly known by the market, so that loan could be securitized, while the quality of $Y_1$ is dependent on an exogeneous amount of effort $e$ the bank made that is not known by the market.

This effort is random and drawn independently from other random variables such that $\mathbb{P}[e \in dt] = f(t)dt$, with the support of $f$ included in $[0, 1]$.

We follow the logic from (4.2) with some changes. The value of $Y_2$ is known with probability 1: $Y_2 = y_2$, while for $Y_1$ we have $\mathbb{P}[Y_1 \in dx] = e\delta_1(dx) + (1 - e)\delta_0(dx)$. Note that here we are not looking into how the bank decided on its effort in loan screening, but rather on how the market is going to react, given that effort.

The bank wants to raise a fixed amount of capital $Y_3$ in order to make a new loan that will return a NPV of $\delta$, so that $Y_3 = y_2$ (the value of the securitizable asset exactly matches the amount needed for investment). It can raise an equity amount of $y_2$ or securitize in order to get the necessary funds. In the case of securitization, there is an administrative cost $k$.

We can compare the payoff to the bank depending on its financing strategy. The expected payoff to the banks who choose securitization is $V_S = e + \delta - k$. For a bank choosing equity financing, we define $p_1$ as the market value of the asset $Y_1$ (which is not a function of each bank's observed $e$ since it is not known by investors), and $\lambda$ the share of equity that must be sold in order to finance the project. The financing condition must be verified: $\lambda(p_1 + y_2 + \delta) = y_2$; in other words, the amount of capital to be raised must be equal to the fraction of shares sold times the total value of the shares. The expected payoff for the bank choosing equity issuance knowing its own effort is, therefore, $V_E = (1 - \lambda)(e + \delta + y_2)$.

Given its known effort level $e$, a bank will choose equity issuance if $V_E(e) \geq V_S(e)$, which is equivalent to

$$\frac{p_1 + \delta}{p_1 + y_2 + \delta} \geq \frac{e + \delta - k}{e + y_2 + \delta}.$$

This is verified if $e \leq p_1$. The equality is verified for

$$\bar{e}(p_1) = \left(\frac{y_2 + \delta}{y_2} - \delta\right) p_1 + \left(\frac{y_2 + \delta}{y_2} + p_1\right) k,$$

so that securitization is optimal for the bank if the effort it exerted satisfies $e \geq \bar{e}(p_1)$, and equity issuance is optimal otherwise. If $\bar{e}(p_1) > 1$ then securitization is never preferred, which is the case if the securitization fixed cost $k$ exceeds $\frac{y_2\delta-(y_2+\delta)}{y_2 p_1+(y_2+\delta)}$. Note that we write the threshold as an explicit function of $p_1$ for the time being, but at the equilibrium it should only be a function of various parameters.

At the equilibrium, the market sets the price rationally as a function of what it knows: the fact that there exists $\bar{e}$ such that for $e \leq \bar{e}$ the bank will issue equity. Hence

$$p_1(\bar{e}) = \mathbb{E}[e|e \leq \bar{e}] = \frac{\int_0^{\bar{e}} tf(t)dt}{\int_0^{\bar{e}} f(t)dt}.$$

Hence, the actual threshold $\bar{e}$ can be determined by solving $\bar{e}(p_1(x)) = x$, which is equivalent to

$$x = \left(\frac{y_2 + \delta}{y_2} - \delta + k\right) \frac{\int_0^x tf(t)dt}{\int_0^x f(t)dt} + k\frac{y_2 + \delta}{y_2}.$$

Iacobucci and Winter look at the gains from securitization as the difference between $V_S$ and $V_E$, which is

$$V_S(e) - V_E(e) = y_2 \frac{e + y_2 + \delta}{\mathbb{E}[e|e \leq \bar{e}] + y_2 + \delta} - k.$$

The authors define the term separate from the cost $k$ as a "lemons premium avoidance benefit": the gain that the bank obtains by avoiding being categorized as a lemon.

However, this is looking at a context where securitization is possible, and a bank with a strong effort $e$ issuing equity would be assumed by the market to not have exerted a strong effort (since $Y_1$ is priced as $\mathbb{E}[e|e \leq \bar{e}]$). It would make more sense to compare the gain of a bank with a strong effort $e$ issuing equity when no securitization is possible, and when securitization is possible.

If there is no securitization possible, then the market's valuation of $Y_1$ is simply the expected effort, and the gain to the bank issuing equity is

$$V(e) = \frac{e + y_2 + \delta}{\mathbb{E}[e] + y_2 + \delta} \left(\mathbb{E}[e] + \delta\right).$$

After some simplifications, we find that

$$V_S(e) - V(e) = y_2 \frac{e - \mathbb{E}[e]}{\mathbb{E}[e] + y_2 + \delta} - k,$$

so that in order for securitization to be truly optimal, the issuer's effort needs to be larger than the average.

If after financing has been raised, but before the returns are realized, the original stock holders decide to sell shares, the price at which the transaction takes place will reflect the market's evaluation of the bank's core assets knowing the bank resorted to securitization or not.

If securitization was not possible, and after having raised equity the inside equity holders sell a given fraction $g$ of equity, the value of that sale is $(\mathbb{E}[e] + \delta)g$. In this case, the market has no information beyond the general distribution of $e$.

If securitization is possible, and a firm with $e \geq \bar{e}$ has used securitization, then the value of the equity sale will reflect the knowledge that the firm elected to securitize, and in this case the value of the sale reflecting market expectation is $(\mathbb{E}[e|e \geq \bar{e}] + \delta - k)\, g$. Hence, the difference to the securitizing firm between being able or unable to securitize is $(\mathbb{E}[e|e \geq \bar{e}] - \mathbb{E}[e] - k)\, g$. This amount represents an additional gain thanks to securitization, as a signaling benefit. □

Iacobucci and Winter also looked into the impact of hidden information when investors do not have the same information. When firms sell specialized assets, these assets require particular analysis and not all investors are able to carry it out. A part of the specialized assets is sold to these informed investors, and another part to the general market. By observing how much of the assets is sold to informed investors, the general market infers their quality, and the equilibrium leads to high-quality assets being preferably sold to informed investors. The authors consider that selling to specialized investors would be securitizing, while selling to the general market would be just like an equity sale, which is a questionable assumption. In addition, the initial core assumptions about securitization are not entering the reasoning in this case, since the assets that are securitized end up being riskier than the firm's core assets. Hence, we do not examine this formal model in detail.

#### 4.2.5.3 Empirical Results

Iacobucci and Winter looked at data on the patterns of choices for securitization. They ask whether firms the most vulnerable to agency costs are more likely to securitize. Unfortunately, there is no good measure for a firm's vulnerability to agency costs.

As an approximation for these agency costs, the authors use the power of incentive contracts for CEOs, that is, the non-wage part of their compensation. This assumes that firms with higher potential agency costs will have higher powered incentive contracts. Both compensation through these contracts and the decision to securitize are endogenous in the models discussed by Iacobucci and Winter, and hence they establish a correlation, not a causal relationship: higher agency costs would not cause securitization but rather they would both be optimally determined in an interconnected way at equilibrium.

Hence, one may expect a negative relationship between contract power and propensity to securitize: both strategies are attempts to mitigate agency costs by firms in a competitive environment. If given a firm's particular situation one is more efficient than the other, then the firm will first choose that approach, to the detriment of the other. For example, if due to managers' risk aversion high incentive contracts were difficult to impose, then the marginal value of securitization would be high, which would lead to low-power contracts and a high securitization rate.

However, the authors argue that the cost of adopting a particular mitigation strategy against agency costs (for example, the cost of risk aversion by managers or the transaction cost in carrying out a securitization) is less likely to vary across firms than the firms' vulnerability to agency costs. Hence, the variation in the magnitude of the agency problem across firms is more likely to drive the relationship between the use of both instruments, rather than the variation in the cost of each instrument. The differences in each instrument's cost would be what drives a negative relationship between them, while the (presumably large) variations in overall agency costs would be what drives a positive relationship between the occurrence of these instruments. Therefore, one expects to see a positive relation.

Looking at data across a large panel of over 1,100 firms through various industries, the authors found that 66% of CEO compensation was non-wage based, with a good degree of dispersion around this average. Then, the authors analyzed the occurrence of securitization as a function of the firm's contract power. They find a clear and positive relationship: on firms where CEOs are paid more than 80% of their compensation as participation, close to 10% used securitization. On firms where CEOs are paid less than 50% as participation, securitization occurred about 2% of the time.

These results could be due to biases, for example, size; since there are fixed costs in securitization, larger firms may be more likely to use it, which at the same time will tend to pay less wage-based compensation. Accounting for size and contract power in a regression, the authors find that the agency cost proxy is still a significant driver of securitization occurrence.

### 4.2.6 Discussion of Optimal Funding Models

The models we have gone through, focused on optimal funding, used a variety of approaches to explain the onset of securitization. Their assumptions were quite diverse, but they each found that under particular assumptions securitization was optimal, and to a degree that was empirically verified.

The models in Leland (2007) and Gorton and Souleles (2007) as well as the model we extrapolated from Gorton and Metrick (2013) imply that riskier firms will have greater benefits in securitizing. However, as we pointed out in the case of the models by Gorton and Souleles and Gorton and Metrick, even if for a given amount of debt firms will prefer securitization more if they are riskier, the total amount of securitized debt issued at some equilibrium may not be increasing as a function of default risk. The empirical evidence analyzed by Gorton and Souleles, for that particular effect, was not very strong.

The model developed in Han, Park, and Pennacchi (2015) showed that higher taxes would lead to more securitization, because it increased the capital funding cost for the loans. Indeed, banks must fund a certain share of their assets with equity, which makes a part of their funding exposed to tax costs. Fundamentally, this model explains securitization by the fact that investors would have better funding conditions than the bank itself. The empirical evidence that Han, Park, and Pennacchi analyzed strongly supported the model. In their original models, Gorton and Metrick and Gorton and Souleles found seemingly the opposite, namely, that firms benefit less from securitization when taxes are low. However, as we pointed out, this is valid for a given amount of debt funding. If the amount of debt funding is determined endogenously (as we showed with the model derived from Gorton and Metrick), then under certain conditions higher taxes will lead to more securitization. Finally, we saw that the empirical evidence presented in Iacobucci and Winter (2005) was consistent with information asymmetries driving the use of securitization, either by setting managers' interest more in line with investors' or as an efficient signal of good business quality.

Across these models, we can draw a distinction between those of Gorton and Metrick (2013), Gorton and Souleles (2007), and Leland (2007) on one side, and Han, Park, and Pennacchi (2015) and Iacobucci and Winter (2005) on the other side. The former group indeed at the core explains securitization by the risk of default of the issuing entity, through friction costs or a limited liability option. The latter group considers the existence of securitization through an improvement in funding efficiency or a reduction in information related inefficiencies. Considering all these competing potential explanations, an explanation of securitization that only hinges on an unlikely and remote event, the default of the issuer, appears somewhat inferior to an explanation that relies on a systematic improvement of efficiency.

Across all these arguments, bankruptcy costs, probability of default, taxes, or conflicts of interests between investors as drivers that may be explored, there are particular patterns, however, that cannot be directly explained, and we will go through a few examples. First, we ask what changed: why did securitization appear? There was not a sudden change in tax rate or bankruptcy costs in the 1980s that could have brought about securitization. Then, we look into so-called street shelves and wonder why they exist, and address so-called shelf specialization. With these discussions about how SPVs are set up we are not yet drilling down into the types of bonds or structures created by the SPVs, we are still only looking at securitization in general. Finally, following an empirical study by An, Deng, and Gabriel (2009), we look to measure the benefits brought by the existence of securitization in terms of reduced borrowing costs.

#### 4.2.6.1 What Changed?

Unlike debt or equity, securitization as a main source of funding has not existed for hundreds of years and therefore there must have been some fundamental changes that made its existence optimal at some point. Between the late 1970s and the late 1980s, securitization rose in the US as an important source of bank financing, and one can identify a few underlying trends that help understand this evolution. The literature review in Gorton and Metrick (2013) offers an overview of how securitization came about. An important evolution was a decline in bank profitability because of increased competition. The need to maintain profitability drove banks to become more efficient with their businesses, including how they funded themselves, and that led them to use securitization more.

Up to the beginning of the 1980s, banks operated in a protected environment, dating back to the depression era. Regulations limited competition across states, which favored the creation of local monopolies. There were barriers to entry in the banking business, because of the costs attached to obtaining a bank charter. There were ceilings on deposit rates, which allowed banks cheap funding. In addition, for most corporations, bank loans were the main source of funds.

Through the 1980s, corporations developed new ways to access funding without bank loans, by directly issuing bonds. This contributed to reduce the yield on banks' assets. The regulations against banking across states went away, which increased competition in lending and further reduced assets yields. In parallel, deposit rate ceilings disappeared and that led banks to price their deposits more aggressively. Money market mutual funds also appeared around that time, offering investors an alternative for safe investments, and further contributing to more expensive bank funding.

While banks, as the main users of securitization, had an incentive to be more efficient with their funding, there was an increase in market demand for high-grade debt paper. Institutional investors as well as bank themselves were able to generate incremental returns by using more leverage. In order to get levered financing, they had to post collateral, which must be well-rated debt paper. Before the advent of securitization, there was a limited set of bond types that could be used: highly rated corporate debt (which is not very common), or Government or agency paper. Securitization provided a much needed supply of AAA-rated bonds that could be used as collateral and increase leverage.

In the analysis of Iacobucci and Winter (2005), the assets that reduce information asymmetries when they are securitized possess two key features: they should be independent from manager intervention and have some uncertainty. Also implicit in that second feature, the uncertainty should be measurable for investors. In addition, in order to establish that the assets are not affected by the manager, investors need detailed information. The model proposed by Leland (2007) also implies that the investors in the segregated assets would be able to analyze these assets' risks in detail.

In the 1980s, the systems that were available to analyze mortgage securities were not very sophisticated. For example, see the discussion of the analysis of mortgage securities developed in Pinkus, Hunter, and Roll (1987). The characteristics of the underlying loans do not enter this analysis in much detail, since valuations rely on simple yield matrices. A few years later, the analysis in Schwartz and Torous (1989) used more complex modeling, in the form of a formal valuation methodology comparable to that of fixed-income derivatives. The loan performance data, although in a largely aggregated and cohorted form, entered the analysis in a much more significant way. As the ability to access data on the underlying loans grew, thanks to advances in technology, investors were increasingly able to properly study the loans, and the conditions for the optimality of securitization were more likely to be verified.

In the following years, we can also observe how certain types of mortgage collateral became good securitization candidates, as the tools to analyze them became available. Loan-level databases were developed in the mid- to late 1990s, which allowed increasingly precise understanding of loan behavior. See, for example, Banerjee and Mustapha (2000) on Alt-A loans or Banerjee et al. (2000) on subprime loans. The analyses were rather descriptive initially, which was already an important step relative to no analysis at all. Simply collecting, cleaning, and aggregating the data required advanced systems at the time. In parallel, securitization volumes of alternative or non-prime mortgages continued to increase.

More advanced analyses, for example, focused on the factors that explained credit performance and on the specific role the originator or servicer might play, were common in the early- to mid-2000s (see, for example, Gauthier and Zimmerman (2006) or Mansukhani and Qbbaj (2005)), as the securitization of these products continued to grow. These studies required computer tools that would not have been available a few years earlier or would have been prohibitively expensive.

It appears, therefore, that there was indeed specific evolution, both in the banking environment and in the ability for investors to analyze assets, which can directly explain why securitization grew along the lines of the models we have discussed so far.

#### 4.2.6.2 Street Shelves and Aggregators

From the late 1990s and, in particular, in mortgage securitizations, there was a clear evolution toward so-called **Wall Street shelves**, that is, securitization facilities created by investment banks (as opposed to mortgage originators or commercial banks). As Wall Street dealers invested in large loan conduits, they were able to buy whole loans directly from large and small originators or brokers, and securitize them. Many Wall Street dealers even bought mortgage originators and owned the entire mortgage lending process from borrower to securitization.

There were a few particular issuers following a comparable model, different from banks or mortgage lenders in the usual sense, acting as **aggregators**. They would simply acquire loans and securitize them, acting as a conduit, in a way comparable to investment banks. However, these aggregators would not arrange the deals by themselves and needed to work with investment banks to be able to issue their paper.

In all the models looking at securitization we have discussed in this optimal funding section, there was no clear distinction between the notions of selling the loans, or actually securitizing them. The existence of street shelves or aggregators can fulfill the function of turning loans that are sold into securities. The observed reality, therefore, allows us to not have to distinguish precisely between simply selling assets and securitizing them.

Nevertheless, the existence of street shelves or aggregators does raise the question of why the loan originators would not securitize them themselves. One easy argument could be that these originators are too small and the overhead costs in a securitization program would be too high. This is likely true for some small specialized lenders, however the loans securitized by street shelves are often originated by large lenders, which in most cases have their own securitization programs. These loans may be commingled with other loans, but may also be securitized as one large package. For example, MABS 2006-NC1, a subprime deal issued on UBS's shelf, was entirely collateralized by loans purchased from New Century, a mortgage lender which also had its own securitization shelf NCHET.

While the fixed costs in setting up a securitization program are most likely a factor in the existence of aggregators and street shelves, they do not explain why some issuers may have their own shelf and still securitize loans on another shelf (while, in all cases, the originator is clearly identifiable).

In Park (2013), which we discuss in more detail in the next section, the author argues that dealers use their own shelves in what is effectively a fixed-income market arbitrage: selling the securities for more than the collateral costs. In contrast, the originator shelf is used for funding, in order for the originator to satisfy certain capital requirements. By carrying out their own deal issuance, originators can, for example, retain a junior interest in the transaction. In effect, selling the senior tranches is a form of financing of the initial loan portfolio. However that does not explain why dealers would sometimes bring together loans from several sellers into a deal, or segregate them in separate deals. Presumably the arbitrage would be the same.

The distinction between issuer-specific and street shelves may also be related to the distribution cost. When a deal is issued on an originator shelf, there generally is a syndicate of investment banks (with one or several lead managers) who ensure the deal's distribution and share among themselves the task of selling the bonds to investors. A deal issued by a dealer shelf, however, is only distributed by that shelf's owner. The incentives for the investment banks are not the same: in the case of a syndicate they are in competition with each other, while that is not the case for one of their own deals.

The dealer also owns more underlying exposure to the collateral in the case of a street shelf, since they will typically retain a part of the tranches, which is retained by the originator in the case of an originator-issued deal. By holding to some tranches the dealer has an opportunity to buy bonds at a cheap price, but at the same time this creates potentially significant risk exposure. Hence, a deal issued on a dealer shelf will typically be thoroughly analyzed and fully underwritten. In addition, the dealer may or may not commingle the loans from different originators. The securities backed by loans with specific features are easier to analyze if these loans are not mixed with other loans with different characteristics, which would then incite the dealer to issue a deal backed by loans from a single originator.

Given these elements, when an originator securitizes reasonably generic collateral, which would be expected to be easier to sell, they may use their own issuance shelf. When, on the other hand, the collateral has a little more "story", then resorting to a dealer shelf may be optimal since the dealer will then have a vested interest in distributing the paper and thoroughly underwriting the deal. The full underwriting effort is better spent on collateral that requires it, rather than on loans that may be less difficult to analyze.

#### 4.2.6.3 Shelf Specialization

Although this has not been systematic in securitization markets in general, another important trend that was observed in the non-agency market in the late 1990s and early-2000s was the creation of very specialized and specific shelves. Issuers would not securitize all their mortgage loans on a single shelf anymore, but create dedicated shelves for certain products. For example, Bank of America used a shelf BOAMS for jumbo prime loans, and BOAA for Alt-A loans. Wells Fargo had WFMBS for jumbo-A paper, WFALT for Alt-A, or WFHET for subprime. Countrywide had CWHL (Jumbo), CWALT (Alt-A), or CWL (subprime). Within these shelves, specific series were sometimes created, for example, one could find the "Tier-1", "Tier-2", and "Conforming Balance" series within CWALT.

One striking example is GMAC/RFC, which in 2007 culminated with 12 separate series on 6 shelves (see Table 4.1). Each loan, according to its characteristics, would be securitized on one of these shelves, with in fact a "catch-all" series RAMP RS that would securitize loans between Alt-A and subprime that could not be sold into the specific RALI or RASC shelves.

The structures used by these various shelves were generally different and were adapted to the characteristics of these loans, in a sense as a consequence of the types of loans that were issued. The decision to create these particular vehicles was not a structuring decision per se.

**Table 4.1** Comparison of GMAC/RFC US Securitization Shelves. *Source* SEC Edgar, ResCap Investor Report 2007

| Broad category | Shelf | Series | Product type |
|---|---|---|---|
| MBS | RFMSI | SA | Jumbo-A ARM |
| | | A | Jumbo-A Fixed |
| | RALI | QA | Alt-A ARM |
| | | QS | Alt-A Fixed |
| | | QO | Option-ARM |
| | | QH | Hybrid Option-ARM |
| | RAAC | SP | Seasoned Portfolio |
| ABS | RAMP | RS | High LTV 1st |
| | | RZ | Conduit Assets |
| | RASC | KS | Subprime |
| | RFMS2 | HS | Home Equity 2nds |
| | | HI | High CLTV 2nds |

This trend toward shelf specialization was also followed by street shelves. The earliest Wall Street shelves dating back to the late 1990s did not differentiate between the various types of collateral. For example, Salomon Brother's SBM7, Lehman Brothers' SASC, or CSFB's CSFB shelves were used for all types of loans, from subprime to jumbo, even including commercial mortgages. However, many dealers that set up conduits in the early-2000s differentiated between their issuance shelves because they targeted clear product segregation. UBS created MASTR for jumbos, MALT for Alt-As, MARM for ARMs, and MABS for subprime.

We must then wonder why issuers would want to create these highly specialized issuance series. We are not questioning here why one would not want to securitize jumbo prime loans together with subprime loans,[2] but rather why a jumbo prime securitization would have to be done on a separate shelf from a subprime securitization.

One potential explanation is that investors value securitization programs with regular issuance, as regularly issuing relatively standardized products would be perceived to promote liquidity and help reduce asymmetrical information. By setting up dedicated shelves, which carries a cost, issuers signal that they will maintain regular issuance of product on that shelf. In their empirical study, Gorton and Souleles found that the spreads on securitized paper were wider on riskier issuers. Their conclusion was that this pattern was due to the impact of the issuer's risk on its ability to provide recourse, as posited by their model. However, as we mentioned earlier, this could also be due to the lesser degree to which the issuer would be able to ensure regular product issuance in the future, and hence promote liquidity.

[2]That is also an interesting question, but it is more related to structuring decisions. In fact, we show how the segregation of assets in securitizations makes sense in Chap. 7.

#### 4.2.6.4 Measuring the Gains from Securitization

In the present section, we have seen a variety of perspectives that could justify the existence of securitization. An empirical study by An, Deng, and Gabriel (2009), focused on the CMBS market, has directly looked into measuring the benefits of securitization, by comparing the borrowing costs on loans that were securitized with those that were not.

Throughout the 1990s, the commercial mortgage market evolved substantially as the presence of conduits grew. Commercial mortgage loans were increasingly made by these conduits, for the sole purpose of subsequent securitization, while some loans were still made by banks in order to be retained, as portfolio loans. The conduit loans are priced reflecting the sale into a securitization vehicle, while portfolio loans are priced reflecting the bank's own funding. These portfolio loans could be sold and securitized later on, but their initial valuation would not reflect a securitization-driven pricing.

In order to study the differences in loan rate due to securitization, An, Deng, and Gabriel chose to isolate a particular subset of the market, as homogeneous as possible: multifamily commercial mortgages securitized in the private-label market. Some of these loans were made as conduit loans and some as portfolio loans, later sold into a securitization deal.

The authors define the following regression:

$$R_{i,t} - R_{f,t} = D_i\alpha + X_i\beta + Z_t\gamma + \varepsilon_{i,t}.$$

The LHS is each loan $i$'s spread over the corresponding Treasury of maturity $f$ given its origination time $t$. On the RHS, we find the explanatory variables: $X$ is the vector of loan characteristics, $Z$ market conditions at the time, and $D$ the dummy variable reflecting whether the loan is a conduit or portfolio loan.

The data is composed of about 13,000 multifamily commercial loans originated between 1992 and 2003, with an average spread of 200 bps over Treasuries. The loan characteristics $X$ include region, term, amortization, LTV, quarter, and year of issuance. The history of prepayment and defaults on these loans is also available. The market environment $Z$ includes corporate credit spreads (the difference between corporate BBB and AAA spreads) as an indicator of the broad credit market environment, the Treasury curve slope from twos to tens, and the return volatility of 10-year Treasuries and of the real-estate investment trust index.

The regression as stated gives a coefficient $\alpha$ of $-11$bps, so that all else being equal, securitized loans had a rate 0.11% lower than portfolio loans. On a 10-year loan, this translates into a reduction in total cost of about 1% of the loan's balance.

It is worth noting that the other regression coefficients were generally significant, and their sign and magnitude appear reasonable:

- The greater the LTV, the higher the loan spread, as a riskier loan is required to pay a higher rate.
- Loan balance is negatively correlated with spreads, as larger loans are considered less risky than smaller loans.

- Corporate credit spreads play a role, with a coefficient of about 0.7.
- Higher interest rate volatility leads to a larger spread, as one would anticipate due to the effect of the embedded option valuation.[3]

The authors then address three potential problems with this first simple model.

1. The prepayment and default risks of the portfolio loans may be inherently different from those of conduit loans, and that could explain the difference picked up by $\alpha$ in the regression.
2. A lender effect may be at play, whereby large lenders which will tend to keep loans in portfolio benefit from a particularly strong pricing power, and are able to obtain higher rates all else being equal.
3. The contract terms may be endogenous, as they are negotiated at the same time as the rate, in particular, the borrower may have some leeway in determining the LTV, which in turn would affect the rate.

The first item is resolved by creating a simple prepayment and default model, using the available loan-level variables, including a dummy variable for conduit/portfolio loans. The coefficient for this variable is insignificant, while the other variables are both significant and with the anticipated magnitude. The authors conclude that there is no bias due to an ill-controlled prepayment or default risk effect in the original model.

In order to address the second item, the regression receives an additional set of dummy variables representing the lender. These lender-specific dummies all get small but significant coefficients (in the 0–20 bps range). Nevertheless, the conduit/portfolio loan dummy remains significant and actually increases in magnitude to 16 bps. Hence, differences in lenders do not account for the rate difference between loans funded through securitization and through the bank.

Finally, the third item requires the estimation of simultaneous equations for the loan spread and for LTV. The authors specify the following model:

$$\begin{aligned} R_{i,t} - R_{f,t} &= D_i\alpha + L_i\phi + Y_i\beta + Z_t\gamma + \varepsilon_{i,t} \\ L_i &= (R_{i,t} - R_{f,t})\theta + Y_i\rho + \eta_{i,t}. \end{aligned}$$

where $L$ is the LTV, taken separately from the rest of the loan characteristics, and $Y$ represents these remaining characteristics. This model expresses the fact that the LTV will be adjusted as a function of the conditions offered to borrowers. With this simultaneous equations model, the conduit/portfolio dummy coefficient $\alpha$ is significant, and even larger in magnitude at 20 bps.

It is important to point out, as An, Deng, and Gabriel do, that this estimate of the benefit of securitization in the order of 10–20bps is only measuring the benefit to the

[3] See Chap. 2 for a simplified description of negative convexity and the link between volatility and valuation.

borrower, although some additional value may have been extracted by other parties such as the originator or the securitization arranger.

In our analysis of securitization so far, we have focused on reasons why securitization might exist, as a separate vessel from the firm, into which the firm may sell some assets in order to gain better efficiency. The main reasons we studied were stemming from information asymmetries, taxes, capital requirements for banks, or bankruptcy costs avoidance. While all these may explain why some assets will find themselves segregated into a special vehicle, they did not explain why the securitization structures always looked to create debt-like securities, with a degree of credit protection. After all, equities are securities too, why don't securitization vehicles just issue plain old stocks? We will now focus on several models that seek to answer this question.

## 4.3 Security Design

In this section, we try to understand why securitizations always involve a level of credit protection being built in, or some guarantees. In fact, there has been a good amount of academic literature on the subject of security design; in other words, why are there particular contracts that allocate risks in a specific manner for investors?

In the general corporate finance literature, there are a few important papers that are somewhat applicable to securitization, see the literature reviews mentioned earlier. For example, Leland and Pyle (1977) look at the incentives for insiders to retain an equity stake in order to convince buyers of the quality of their securities. This can be applicable to securitization, where the issuer may retain an equity stake in order to show they "put their food where the mouth is". In spite of the fact that the general conclusions from this paper have some connections with securitization, we do not, however, look into the details of this model because the modeling of entrepreneurs' choices developed by Leland and Pyle is not readily transferable to the situation of a bank selling loans into an SPV. As a side note, corporate finance research is sometimes invoked to explain aspects of securitization without much of a regard for the very specific conditions under which an SPV and structured securities operate.

Another important work in corporate finance is Myers and Majluf (1984), where the authors considered that firms prefer to issue debt to outside investors, rather than stocks, because those investors would be suspicious of these stocks and would not value them correctly. Debt is **informationally insensitive**, and hence not exposed to privately known factors. This leads to a **pecking order** in financing choices. In securitization, this would imply that the risky part of securitized assets would not be valued correctly and hence would be best, detained by the issuer, or those with enough information to value it. We do not go through the model from Myers and Majluf in detail either because there again it is difficult to directly apply it to a different context than a firm issuing stock or risk-free debt.

In the following subsections, we will focus on a few specific models that offer some insights into the existence of senior debt structures. As with the preceding section, we rewrite parts of each model in order to make it roughly consistent with the other models presented in this chapter. We only look at models that assume risk neutrality and de facto exclude explanations derived from differences in utility function shapes, and focus on information asymmetries. Assuming risk neutrality, all else being equal, typically simplifies calculations and allows us to focus on other important factors than differences in preferences. We go through the inner workings of these models in a good amount of detail, not only because they are fundamental in understanding the nature of securitization, but also because extensions of these models will be used when we analyze the existence of complex structures in Chap. 7.

In the specific literature on security design, such as Boot and Thakor (1993), one can find explanations for why there may exist senior and junior securities, without the issuer necessarily retaining the junior securities. The segmentation encourages some investors to acquire information and knowledge, after which they are in a position to pay a fair price for these securities, and hence the whole capital stack is better priced.

The model developed in Axelson (2007) like the one in Boot and Thakor (1993) looks at the optimal design of securities for a firm effectively securitizing an asset, but assumes that investors are informed (with some noise), while the firm itself does not have particular information. The investors follow a competitive bid process that establishes the trading price. While this information asymmetry may sound extreme in the case of the usual firms issuing stocks, it is not an exaggeration when we consider the resources hedge funds have in the securitized products world, for example, compared to those of a typical mortgage bank. Axelson finds that it is optimal for the seller to issue securities that are informationally sensitive. The optimal security design is quite dependent on the shape of the distribution of the assets returns however, and may lead the issuer to retain junior, mezzanine, or senior securities.

Among the research that explicitly looks to address securitization, DeMarzo and Duffie (1999) examine securities backed by specific assets, not issued as general obligations of the whole firm's business. They consider asymmetrical information between investors and issuers and show that the issuers should optimally separate senior and junior exposure, and sell the senior bonds, which is more in line with what has been observed in securitization.

The model presented in Riddiough (1997) follows a technically simpler approach, without relying on a signaling equilibrium, but nevertheless accounts for the information asymmetries between an informed issuer and uninformed investors. In this case, the creation of safe securities is a way for the issuer of avoiding a lemons problem.

Focusing on the notion of information sensitivity, Dang, Gorton, and Holmström (2015) develop a model where uninformed investors propose an optimal security design which the issuer can choose to accept (effectively, a kind of reverse inquiry). They show that in the context of securitization, issuing senior securities is optimal, and, in particular, if the issuer has costless access to information, then standard debt is optimal.

In the following sections, we will concentrate on the models of Boot and Thakor (1993); DeMarzo and Duffie (1999); and Dang, Gorton, and Holmström (2015), covering a reasonably wide set of assumptions that lead to similar conclusions. Finally, we will look into empirical evidence beginning with the work of Park (2013), who shows that senior subprime bonds were structured to be informationally insensitive. Then we focus on Begley and Purnanandam (2017), who present some evidence that information asymmetries have driven differential pricing in the RMBS market. They show that deals where the equity tranches were larger incurred less losses, and that the senior bonds in these deals were generally priced higher than in other deals. Finally we discuss an empirical paper on CLOs.

### 4.3.1 Asymmetrical Information Between Investors

In their article, Boot and Thakor discuss a firm issuing securities in a market where there are liquidity traders, as well as uninformed traders who can decide to pay a cost and become informed. They show that in certain conditions, it makes sense for the firm to structure an equity and debt breakdown, rather than purely issuing equity. The context of the model they develop is fairly general, and we adapt it here specifically to securitization. We will consider that there is a loan, the quality of which is known by the bank, but on which eventual investors can acquire information. The performance of that loan is modeled with a simple binary outcome, along the lines of Gorton–Metrick, Gorton–Souleles, or Han–Park–Pennacchi. The various agents are considered risk-neutral, as with the models discussed so far. The bank issues securities collateralized by the loan: at first we will consider a simple unique security and then a senior and junior securities break down. We assume that there is an investment bank advising the issuer, which will also competitively price the securities so that their value is equal to their expected returns, for a non-informed trader.

In this model, the cost of asymmetrical information initially comes from the fact that securities from good issuers and bad issuers have to be priced the same if nobody acquires information, which therefore provides the bad issuers with a free ride. Introducing the ability to acquire information for some investors at a certain cost, we will see that they will tend to do so. Then, it becomes optimal for the good firms (the ones that know their loan is good) to issue debt and equity rather than pure equity, as it allows these informed investors to buy the junior equity with better returns. Then, the price difference between good and bad issuers is closer to the fully informed valuation.

#### 4.3.1.1 The Model

In this model, there are three classes of investors:

- Liquidity traders, who are uninformed and will buy a random volume of securities as price takers. This could represent mutual funds, for example, which will buy generic mortgage or asset-backed securities so that their portfolios roughly mirror the overall market. This may also represent commercial banks which will buy mortgage-backed securities sometimes as a substitute to their own loan origination. These investors do not purchase the securities because they are particularly attractive, but rather because they need exposure to the market as a whole. These liquidity traders buy a volume $L$ of securities (in dollars).

- Discretionary traders[4] who are originally uninformed but may decide to become informed at a cost. The uninformed traders will act as market makers (like investment banks) and set the price of the securities at the expected uninformed value. The uninformed traders are different from liquidity traders because they do not have to buy the securities, and hence set the price at its fair value. These uninformed traders will buy the securities that are not purchased by other types of traders (and potentially sell them short so that the market clears).
- Informed discretionary traders, who are discretionary uninformed traders who have decided to acquire information and become informed. Note that information here does not mean private or privileged information but rather expertise and systems. For example, an investment fund may decide to build complex models to value asset-backed securities, at a significant cost. These informed traders will buy a volume $D_I$ of securities, in dollars. Discretionary traders have a wealth of 1 plus the cost of information acquisition (which they can consume if they do not buy the information).

The bank sells its loan into an SPV, which issues securities backed by the loan. The bank looks to structure the securities it issues optimally, and maximize its revenue from selling the loan.

There are two periods, 0 and 1, and the risk-free rate is set to 0 for simplicity. The loan's cash flow $Y$ at period 1 is a random variable and will be either good or bad, just as in (4.2) but without an influence from screening:

$$\mathbb{P}[Y \in dx] = p\delta_{y_g}(dx) + (1 - p)\delta_{y_b}(dx),$$

with $0 < y_b < y_g$. The bank issues 1 unit of securities, and the positive demand from liquidity traders is $L$ such that $\mathbb{P}[L \in dl] = f(l)dl$, with $L$ independent from $Y$. We will write $D = L + D_I$ for the total demand, in dollars as well, coming from liquidity traders and informed traders. The demand from the uninformed discretionary traders in dollars is then simply the difference $P - D$ with $P$ the price of the securities (recall that 1 security is issued). The uninformed traders will only be able to observe $D$ in aggregate, and do not see the demand from liquidity traders separately from that of informed traders.

The cost of acquiring information is a constant $c$, and those who acquire this information receive a (perfect) signal about the actual quality of the project, so their decision are conditioned by the full knowledge of $Y$. We write $\theta$ for the share of discretionary traders who become informed. Traders who become informed know whether $Y = y_g$ or $Y = y_b$, and that the other market participants do not know the value of $Y$ and can only make inferences. In that case, they know that the equilibrium

[4] These are termed Uninformed Discretionary Traders (UDTs) by Boot and Thakor.

price set by the uninformed traders will be somewhere between the bounds $y_b$ and $y_g$ and therefore will always prefer not to invest in the bad state and rather consume their wealth. Therefore, $D_I = \theta \mathbb{I}_{Y=y_g}$ and the total demand is a random variable and can in fact be written as $D(Y, L) = L + \theta \mathbb{I}_{Y=y_g}$.

The uninformed traders will set the price at the $D$-measurable random variable $P$ such that $P(D) = \mathbb{E}[Y|D]$. The discretionary traders will look at the expected gains $V$ from becoming informed in order to decide whether or not they do become informed. As we explained above, if $Y = y_b$ then the informed traders will not buy the securities, and hence they will have gains only when $Y = y_g$:

$$V = \mathbb{E}\left[\mathbb{I}_{Y=y_g} \frac{Y - P(D)}{P(D)} - c\right],$$

where $\frac{1}{P(D)}$ represents the number of units purchased, since each informed trader invests all their remaining wealth of 1 after paying the cost to acquire information. Note that in this expression $V$ depends on $\theta$ through the expression of $D$ and in turn $\theta$.

The situation is a strategic game where the issuer and the discretionary traders act optimally each accounting for the others' rational choices. Boot and Thakor characterize the Nash equilibrium as follows:

- There is a $\theta^*$ so that $V = 0$ and each informed trader takes as given the equilibrium strategies of other traders, and assumes their own trades are small enough and do not affect the equilibrium.
- The aggregate demand from informed and liquidity traders is $D = L + \theta \mathbb{I}_{Y=y_g}$.
- The market-clearing price is determined by the uninformed discretionary traders so that supply and demand are equal and the expected gains from an uninformed trader given the total aggregate demand is 0.
- The structure of the securities issued by the bank maximizes its revenue.

#### 4.3.1.2 Single Security Case

First, we look at the equilibrium in the case when there is a single security, without any structuring, passing through all the cash flows from the loan. We can compute the price explicitly.

$$\begin{aligned}
P(D) &= \mathbb{E}[Y|D] \\
&= \mathbb{E}[\mathbb{I}_{Y=y_g} Y + \mathbb{I}_{Y=y_b} Y|D] \\
&= \mathbb{E}[\mathbb{I}_{Y=y_g} y_g + \mathbb{I}_{Y=y_b} y_b|D] \\
&= \mathbb{E}[\mathbb{I}_{Y=y_g} y_g + (1 - \mathbb{I}_{Y=y_g}) y_b|D] \\
&= y_b + (y_g - y_b)\mathbb{P}[Y = y_g|D].
\end{aligned}$$

The distribution of $D$ is continuous and therefore we write

$$\begin{aligned}
&\mathbb{P}\left[Y = y_g | D = \delta\right] \\
&= \lim_{\varepsilon \to 0} \frac{\mathbb{P}\left[Y = y_g \cap \delta \leq L + \theta \mathbb{I}_{Y = y_g} \leq \delta + \varepsilon\right]}{\mathbb{P}\left[\delta \leq L + \theta \mathbb{I}_{Y = y_g} \leq \delta + \varepsilon\right]} \\
&= \lim_{\varepsilon \to 0} \frac{\int \mathbb{I}_{y = y_g} \mathbb{P}[\delta \leq L + \theta \mathbb{I}_{y = y_g} \leq \delta + \varepsilon] \mathbb{P}[Y \in dy]}{\int \mathbb{P}[\delta \leq L + \theta \mathbb{I}_{y = y_g} \leq \delta + \varepsilon] \mathbb{P}[Y \in dy]} \\
&= \lim_{\varepsilon \to 0} \frac{p\mathbb{P}[\delta - \theta \leq L \leq \delta + \varepsilon - \theta]}{p\mathbb{P}[\delta - \theta \leq L \leq \delta + \varepsilon - \theta] + (1-p)\mathbb{P}[\delta \leq L \leq \delta + \varepsilon]} \\
&= \frac{pf(\delta - \theta)}{pf(\delta - \theta) + (1-p)f(\delta)}.
\end{aligned}$$

where we used the fact that $D = L + \theta \mathbb{I}_{Y = y_g}$, and conditioned by $Y$. From this, the price can be written (in a $D$-measurable fashion):

$$P(D) = y_b + (y_g - y_b) \frac{pf(D - \theta)}{pf(D - \theta) + (1-p)f(D)}.$$

Note that we do not write $P$ as an explicit function of $\theta$ since it is $D$ that actually depends on $\theta$.

**Proposition 4.10** (Boot–Thakor Single Security Optimal Information Acquisition) *If the following conditions are verified:*

- $f'(l + \theta) < 0$ *for all* $l > 0$,
- $\frac{p(1-p)(y_g + y_b)}{py_g + (1-p)y_b} > c$,

*then the good quality issuer's expected revenue is increasing in the fraction of traders who choose to become informed $\theta$, and there exists an optimal $\theta^*$ so that the marginal individual trader's gain in acquiring information is null.*

***Proof*** Based on the expression for the price, we can compute the value of acquiring information for discretionary traders $V$, which is a function of $\theta$. We use the fact that $D = \mathbb{I}_{Y = y_b} L + \mathbb{I}_{Y = y_g}(L + \theta)$.

$$\begin{aligned}
V(\theta) &= \mathbb{E}\left[\mathbb{I}_{Y = y_g} \frac{Y}{P(D)}\right] - p - c \\
&= \mathbb{E}\left[\mathbb{I}_{Y = y_g} Y \frac{pf(D - \theta) + (1-p)f(D)}{y_g pf(D - \theta) + y_b(1-p)f(D)}\right] - p - c \\
&= \mathbb{E}\left[\mathbb{I}_{Y = y_g} y_g \frac{pf(L) + (1-p)f(L + \theta)}{y_g pf(L) + y_b(1-p)f(L + \theta)}\right] - p - c \\
&= p\mathbb{E}\left[\frac{pf(L) + (1-p)f(L + \theta)}{pf(L) + \frac{y_b}{y_g}(1-p)f(L + \theta)}\right] - p - c.
\end{aligned}$$

From this, we can compute the derivative of the gains for an individual trader relative to how many traders acquire the information

$$\frac{\partial V}{\partial \theta}(\theta) = \mathbb{E}\left[\frac{(y_g - y_b)(1-p)f(L)f'(L+\theta)}{\left(y_g p f(L) + y_b(1-p)f(L+\theta)\right)^2}\right].$$

If we assume that for all positive $l$, $f'(l+\theta) < 0$ then the derivative of individual trader gains to $\theta$ is negative. As far as the distribution of liquidity demands declines past a certain point, each additional trader acquiring information reduces the benefit of acquiring information to the informed traders. For $\theta = 0$, the expression simplifies into

$$V(0) = \frac{p(1-p)(y_g + y_b)}{p y_g + (1-p) y_b} - c.$$

We assume that the distribution of $Y$ is such that $\frac{p(1-p)(y_g+y_b)}{py_g+(1-p)y_b} > c$ so that $V(0) > 0$. Therefore there is a certain level $\theta^*$ so that $V(\theta^*) = 0$ at the equilibrium, when the marginal informed trader is indifferent between acquiring or not the information.

Now we can look at the bank's expected revenue, if the loan is of good quality. Now we can see that at the equilibrium, this revenue is increasing as a function of the total demand of informed traders $\theta$. The expected revenue to the bank securitizing a good loan (as a function of $\theta$) is

$$\begin{aligned} R_g(\theta) &= \mathbb{E}[P(D)|Y = y_g] = \mathbb{E}[P(L+\theta)] \\ &= y_b + (y_g - y_b)\mathbb{E}\left[\frac{pf(L)}{pf(L) + (1-p)f(L+\theta)}\right]. \end{aligned}$$

Differentiating with respect to $\theta$, we get

$$\frac{\partial R_g}{\partial \theta}(\theta) = -(y_g - y_b)\mathbb{E}\left[\frac{p(1-p)f(L)f'(L+\theta)}{(pf(L) + (1-p)f(L+\theta))^2}\right]$$

and given our earlier assumption for $f'$, this is positive and the bank's revenue increases as the demand from informed traders increases. □

The bank securitizing a bad loan, on the contrary, has a declining revenue as a function of the demand from informed traders. This suggests that the seller of a good loan has an incentive to get more discretionary traders to become informed, and that can be done by structuring more securities.

#### 4.3.1.3 Senior and Junior Securities

The bank selling a loan of good quality into an SPV will want to create security structures issued by the SPV that maximize its revenue. For another bank selling a loan of bad quality, we will see that even if such an issuance structure is not as attractive as the single security from earlier, it is still a better choice to mimic the good loan structure. Indeed, if the issuer of a lower quality product selected a different structure then that signal would reveal the loan quality, and it would trade at the lowest bound.

Given the distribution of the loan's cash flows, a safe senior security can be created with a specific maximal size. The senior security, which we call $A$, promises a repayment of $y_b$. The subordinated security $S$ pays the difference between the loan's total cash flow and what was paid to $A$, hence $Y - y_b$. Given that $Y \geq y_b$, $A$ is sure to be repaid and there is no uncertainty about its payment. $S$ concentrates all the uncertainty. By creating an **informationally insensitive** security (the senior $A$), the issuer concentrates the benefit from informed trading into the junior security, which accrues gains to the informed traders and allows them to value the junior security closer to its fair price.

With the new security split, the liquidity demand is assumed to be spread out. A fraction $\alpha$ of the liquidity traders' demand $D$ is diverted toward the senior security $A$, so that $L_A = \alpha L$ and $L_S = (1 - \alpha)L$.

The informed traders gain nothing by buying $A$, since its value is perfectly known, and instead they concentrate on security $S$. The uninformed traders will set the price of $A$ equal to its (sure) value of $y_b$. In the same way, as earlier in the case of a single security, the uninformed discretionary traders will set the price of security $S$ to its expected return, conditioned by the knowledge of aggregate liquidity and informed demand $D_S = L_S + D_{IS}$ for that security. Hence, we have $P_S(D_S) = \mathbb{E}[Y - y_b|D_S]$. The informed demand is again based on a perfect signal and $D_{IS} = L_S + \theta_S \mathbb{I}_{Y=y_g}$.

As we did in the case of a single security, we can write the price explicitly:

$$\begin{aligned} P_S(D_S) &= \mathbb{E}[Y - y_b|D_S] \\ &= (y_g - y_b)\mathbb{P}[Y = y_g|D_S], \end{aligned}$$

and therefore properly writing the conditional probability (the calculations of that probability are the same, if not for the symbols indexed by $S$) as a limit, we obtain

$$P_S(D_S) = (y_g - y_b)\frac{pf_S(D_S - \theta_S)}{pf_S(D_S - \theta_S) + (1 - p)f_S(D_S)}.$$

**Proposition 4.11** (Boot–Thakor Optimality of Debt/Equity Split) *The total revenue to a good quality issuer when creating securities A and S is greater than when issuing a single security. The bad quality issuer's revenue is lower when splitting into A and S than when issuing a single security, but they still choose to split so that they do not signal their bad quality to investors.*

***Proof*** We define the gain for informed traders to acquire information for tranche $S$ as

$$V_S(\theta_S) = \mathbb{E}\left[\mathbb{I}_{Y=y_g}\frac{(Y - y_b) - P_S(D_S)}{P_S(D_S)} - c\right].$$

We use the explicit expression for the price $P_S$ and after simplifications using, in particular, the fact that $D_S = \mathbb{I}_{Y=y_b} L_S + \mathbb{I}_{Y=y_g}(L_S + \theta_S)$ we obtain

$$V_S(\theta_S) = p\mathbb{E}\left[\frac{pf_S(L_S) + (1-p)f_S(L_S+\theta_S)}{pf_S(L_S)}\right] - c.$$

However, we assumed that $L_S$ has the same distribution as $(1-\alpha)L$, and $f_S((1-\alpha)l) = f(l)$ for $l \geq 0$, so we may write the expression as a function of the distribution of $L$ rather than $L_S$:

$$\begin{aligned} V_S(\theta_S) &= p\mathbb{E}\left[\frac{pf_S((1-\alpha)L) + (1-p)f_S\left((1-\alpha)\left(L+\frac{\theta_S}{1-\alpha}\right)\right)}{pf_S((1-\alpha)L)}\right] - p - c \\ &= p\mathbb{E}\left[\frac{pf(L) + (1-p)f\left(L+\frac{\theta_S}{1-\alpha}\right)}{pf(L)}\right] - p - c. \end{aligned}$$

We can now compare $\theta^*$ such that $V(\theta^*) = 0$ and $\theta_S^*$ such that $V_S(\theta_S^*) = 0$. If for some $\theta$ we set $(1-\alpha)\theta = \theta_S^*$ then the expressions for $V(\theta)$ and $V_S(\theta_S^*)$ would only differ by the positive term $\frac{y_b}{y_g}(1-p)f(L+\theta)$ in the denominator for $V$, and that would hence make $V(\theta)$ strictly smaller than $V_S(\theta_S^*)$. However, $V_S(\theta_S^*) = 0$, which would then imply $V(\theta) < 0$. Since $V$ is decreasing in $\theta$, then we would necessarily have $\theta^* < \theta$, and therefore $(1-\alpha)\theta^* < \theta_S^*$. Hence, at the equilibrium when the marginal informed trader gains 0 by acquiring information, more information is being acquired relative to the amount of liquidity demand than if there is a single security.

Now we turn to the bank's revenue from securitizing good quality loans and issuing separate securities, $R_g^{AS}(\theta_S)$ and compare it with the bank's revenue when it issued a single security $R_g$. We have the following, where we can see that the expression for both revenues have very similar shapes:

$$\begin{aligned} R_g^{AS} &= y_b + \mathbb{E}[P_S(D_S)|Y = y_g]] \\ &= y_b + \mathbb{E}\left[(y_g - y_b)\frac{pf_S(L_S)}{pf_S(L_S) + (1-p)f_S(L_S+\theta_S)}\right] \\ &= y_b + (y_g - y_b)\mathbb{E}\left[\frac{pf(L)}{pf(L) + (1-p)f\left(L+\frac{\theta_S}{1-\alpha}\right)}\right]. \end{aligned}$$

Given the condition on $f'$ and assuming $\theta_S \geq (1-\alpha)\theta$, we know that $\frac{\partial R_g^{AS}}{\partial \theta_S} > 0$. In addition, if we set $\theta_S = (1-\alpha)\theta$ then $R_g(\theta) = R_g^{AS}(\theta_S)$. However, we have shown that $(1-\alpha)\theta^* < \theta_S^*$. Therefore, at the equilibrium, $R_g(\theta^*) < R_g^{AS}(\theta_S^*)$, and the bank with a good loan chooses the senior and junior structure over the single security. If the bank securitizing a bad loan does not choose that same structure it will be detected as such and hence also issues senior and junior securities with the same parameters. □

Under the particular assumptions we laid out, creating a senior bond hence alleviates the cost of asymmetrical information. We may, however, stress two major drawbacks of Boot and Thakor's model. First, the representation of loan performance and information structure is quite simplistic. Second, the range of possible structures is limited, and in effect we have not shown that creating an informationally insensitive senior bond is the optimal security design, but only that it is better than a pure pass-through. We will now turn toward a more realistic approach that can help us determine what the optimal design is, at the cost of increased mathematical complexity.

### 4.3.2 Asymmetrical Information Between Issuers and Investors

We propose a slightly simplified version of the model developed in DeMarzo and Duffie (1999), and adapt some of the logic to make it consistent with the other security design models discussed in this chapter. In effect, the overall setting can be made to resemble that of Boot and Thakor (1993). In particular, the agents in this model are considered risk-neutral, the risk-free rate is zero, and information and decisions follow a particular order, which we represent with two periods 0 and 1. We consider an issuer who owns an asset (such as a loan or portfolio of loans), and looks to issue securities based on the cash flows from the asset.

In this model, the issuer has private information on its assets and has an incentive to sell them (in full or in part in a structured form) due to some holding cost. It has a natural incentive to try and sell more assets if they are expected to perform poorly. However, while the investors do not have information, they know that the more the issuer will want to sell, the worse the performance would likely be. Given this situation, the issuer finds the optimal structure and size it wants to issue. Unlike in the model by Boot and Thakor, DeMarzo and Duffie look for the optimal structure across all possible functions and do not initially restrict the analysis to pure equity versus debt/equity. Then, it appears that in certain conditions, a debt/equity is optimal, in particular, when the underlying cash flow distribution has a so-called worst-case outcome. We reach the same conclusion as with Boot and Thakor's model, but with more general assumptions.

#### 4.3.2.1 The Model

The asset will return an amount $Y$ in period 1, and the issuer can create securities that depend on that cash flow. In the current model, the authors introduce a non-zero holding cost, so that while investors are in a zero risk-free rate environment, the issuer will have a slight preference to sell some of its cash flows. This cost can represent more expensive funding for the issuer, for example. Given some random cash flow $X$, the issuer is indifferent between a cash amount of $\frac{\mathbb{E}[X]}{1+r}$ and holding the cash flow.

We consider that the issuer benefits from private information, represented by a random variable $Z$ taking values in $\mathbb{R}$, on the future cash flow $Y$, but that information is not necessarily perfect. We define the conditional distribution $\mu$ of $Y$ given $Z$

so that for any measurable $f$, $\mathbb{E}[f(Y)|Z] = \int f(y)\mu(y, Z)dy$. The distribution $\mu$ is assumed to be continuous relative to $z$: given a series $z_n$ converging to $z$, $\mathbb{E}[f(Y)|Z = z_n]$ converges to $\mathbb{E}[f(Y)|Z = z]$.

The issuer designs a security paying a cash flow $S = g(Y)$: we consider that the eventual cash flow $Y$ is contractible. In their original article, DeMarzo and Duffie allowed the security to depend on other signals on which the issuer may have information and consider a complex information structure that can be contracted upon; we simplify the approach to keep the aspects that are the most relevant to structures found in securitization. We require that $g(Y) \leq Y$, since in any case if the promised payment was greater than the available cash flow from the assets, the investors would only get what is available. Also, we assume that $g$ is weakly increasing, as is normally the case with all securitization structures. This encompasses a debt-like payoff, equity-like payoff, and many other possible situations. Note that the issuer designs the optimal structure before being in a position to observe its privileged information.

For simplicity, we consider $\mathbb{R}$-valued $Y$ and $Z$, although the proofs essentially work the same way for the more general case of variables taking values in $\mathbb{R}^m$ and $\mathbb{R}^n$.

The issuer has an incentive to sell more securities if it knows the asset will not perform very well, and hence investors are expected to assign a lower price to the security if the issuer tries to sell more of it. Hence, given a security design $S$, the issuer assumes an inverse demand curve $P_S : [0, 1] \to \mathbb{R}$, so that for a given fraction of security sold $q$, the market price of the security would be $P_S(q)$. We note the $\mathcal{F}_Z$-measurable variable $\bar{S} = \mathbb{E}[S|Z]$.

The issuer chooses the optimal fraction $q$ of the security $S$ to sell to investors, given its private information and the demand these investors will have for the security. We can write the issuer's valuation of its portfolio at period 1 as follows, given a quantity $q$ of security sold:

$$\begin{aligned} &\frac{1}{1+r}\mathbb{E}\left[Y - S|Z\right] + \frac{1}{1+r}(1-q)\mathbb{E}\left[S|Z\right] + qP_S(q) \\ &= \frac{\mathbb{E}\left[Y|Z\right]}{1+r} + q\left(P_S(q) - \frac{\mathbb{E}\left[S|Z\right]}{1+r}\right). \end{aligned}$$

For each realization $s$ of $\bar{S}$, the issuer chooses the fraction $q$ to maximize the value of its holding, and solves

$$\Pi_S(s) = \sup_{q\in[0,1]} q\left(P_S(q) - \frac{s}{1+r}\right).$$

where $\Pi_S : \mathbb{R}^+ \to \mathbb{R}$ is the profit function given the demand function. The expected profit from selling the security $S$ can be written as

$$V(S) = \mathbb{E}\left[\Pi_S\left(\mathbb{E}[S|Z]\right)\right] = \mathbb{E}\left[\Pi_S\left(\mathbb{E}[g(Y)|Z]\right)\right].$$

Using the expectation here reflects the fact that the issuer does not yet know the details of $Z$, but creates a design that will be optimal depending on the observation of $Z$ when it becomes available. Hence, the security optimal design problem is to determine the function $g$ belonging in the space of measurable functions $\mathcal{M}$ that maximizes $\sup_{g\in\mathcal{M}} V(g(Y))$.

We will now assume that $\bar{S}$ is a positive bounded random variable and its distribution has the interval $[s_L, s_H]$ for its support.[5] This implies that the random variable is continuous and cannot be discrete. In turn, this implies that $Y$ must have a continuous distribution conditioned by $Z$, and that $g$ is continuous. If $g$ was not continuous, then there could be ranges of values that have a probability of 0 between the lower and higher bounds of $g(Y)$ conditioned by $Z$.

We derive certain properties of the profit function, given an assumed demand function taken as a given by the issuer. We also consider the security design $S$ as given.

**Proposition 4.12** (DeMarzo–Duffie Characteristics of the Profit Function) *For a given $Q : [s_L, s_H] \to [0, 1]$ suppose that for each $s \in [s_L, s_H]$ $Q(s)$ solves $\Pi_S(s) = \sup_{q\in[0,1]} q\left(P_S(q) - \frac{s}{1+r}\right)$. Then*

- *For any $s \in [s_L, s_H]$, $\Pi_S(s) \geq (P_S(1) - \frac{s}{1+r})^+$,*
- *$\Pi_S$ is decreasing and convex and*
- *For any $s \in [s_L, s_H]$, if $\Pi_S$ is differentiable at $s$ then $\Pi'_S(s) = -\frac{Q(s)}{1+r}$,*
- *$Q$ is weakly decreasing.*

***Proof*** The first point comes from the fact that $\Pi_S$ is necessarily greater than the function value taken for specific choices of $q$, namely, 0 and 1.

Given $q$, the function $s \mapsto m_q(s) = q\left(P_S(q) - \frac{s}{1+r}\right)$ is affine and decreasing. Hence, $\Pi_S = \sup_{q\in[0,1]} m_q$, as its upper envelope, is convex and decreasing.

The third point is a direct application of the envelope theorem: the derivative of the optimum is equal to the function's derivative taken at the optimal argument.

We pick $t_1$ and $t_2$ in $[s_L, s_H]$, and write for $i \in 1, 2$ and $i \neq j$,

$$Q(t_i)\left(P_S(Q(t_i)) - \frac{t_i}{1+r}\right) \geq Q(t_j)\left(P_S(Q(t_j)) - \frac{t_i}{1+r}\right)$$

if $Q$ solves the optimization problem. Indeed, by our assumptions, $Q(t_i)\left(P_S(Q(t_i)) - \frac{t_i}{1+r}\right)$ is maximally determined given $t_i$ and hence $Q(t_j)\left(P_S(Q(t_j)) - \frac{t_i}{1+r}\right)$ for $t_j \neq t_i$ could not be greater. Then adding these expressions for indices 1 and 2 yields $(Q(t_1) - Q(t_2))(t_1 - t_2) \leq 0$ and hence $Q$ is weakly decreasing. At the core, the fact that $Q$ is decreasing as a function of the issuer's private valuation of the security comes from the expression for what the issuer is

[5] Note that we are not saying its support is contained in the interval, bur rather that it is the interval.

maximizing: quantity sold times the difference between sale price and private valuation. The greater the private valuation, the lesser the incentive to sell the security. Since $Q$ is decreasing investors know that whatever the issuer's expectation regarding demand, the optimal sales decision implies a larger quantity when the expected outcome is low. □

#### 4.3.2.2 Signaling Equilibrium

We now focus on the signaling equilibrium for the price schedule and quantity of security sold, where investors use the amount of sales to infer the issuer's private valuation $\bar{S}$. We look for an endogenous relationship between $Q(\bar{S})$ and $P_S(Q(\bar{S}))$. Investors are only able to see the fraction of security sold to the market. The equilibrium price function $P_S$ will need to be decreasing as a function of quantity sold, since the investors through rational inference reflect the fact a lower private valuation leads to a higher sales volume ($Q$ being decreasing). Note that if there was no uncertainty regarding the issuer's conditional valuation, i.e., $s_L = s_H$, then we would expect that $P_S(q) = s_L = s_H$ for all $q$, which is (weakly) decreasing. Also, we expect that $P_S(1) = s_L$, since in this case the issuer is offering the entire security for sale and the investors must infer that the issuer's private expected valuation is the worst case.

We consider a signaling game where the uninformed investors compete to purchase the securities created by the issuer. The issuer is informed of $Z$ and computes $\bar{S} = \mathbb{E}[S|Z]$, and then chooses a quantity $Q(\bar{S})$ put up for sale to the investors. Then investors bid the securities. The fact that the issuer might retain some of the securities is a credible signal due to the higher funding cost the issuer faces. We call this game the liquidation game as it concerns the sale of securities.

An outcome of the liquidation game is an element $(s, q, p) \in \Theta = [s_L, s_H] \times [0, 1] \times [s_L, s_H]$ where $s$ is the realization of $\bar{S}$ known to the issuer, $q$ is the quantity put up for sale, and $p$ is the market price paid by investors. The payoff function for the issuer is $U : \Theta \to \mathbb{R}$ with $U(s, q, p) = q\left(p - \frac{s}{1+r}\right)$.

A Bayes–Nash equilibrium for the liquidation game is a pair $(P, Q)$ of measurable functions satisfying

- $Q(\bar{S}) \in \arg\max_q U(\bar{S}, q, P(q))$,
- $P(Q(\bar{S})) = \mathbb{E}[\bar{S}|Q(\bar{S})]$ almost surely,
- and the equilibrium $(P, Q)$ is separating if $P(Q(\bar{S})) = \bar{S}$ almost surely.

When for every given $(p, q) \in (0, 1] \times \mathbb{R}^+$, the function mapping from $s$ to

$$u(s) = -\frac{\frac{\partial U}{\partial q}(s, q, p)}{\frac{\partial U}{\partial p}(s, q, p)}$$

is strictly monotone, then there exists a separating equilibrium, a condition known as the "single crossing property". This property is verified in our case, since $u(s) = -\frac{1}{q}\left(p - \frac{s}{1+r}\right)$ is indeed strictly monotone in $s$.

The condition that the support of $\bar{S}$ is a given interval is essential in obtaining an equilibrium, and this assumption is fairly standard in this case. With the monotonicity of the quantity and price functions, it implies that an optimum can be found. In the following proposition, we show that a particular expression for $Q^*$ is optimal. In order to find this expression in the first place, one has to express the first order conditions for the maximization program and substitute the rational expectations equality. This requires the quantity function to be invertible. The boundary condition for the differential equation that is then obtained is itself a consequence of the existence of a lower bound to the distribution of $\bar{S}$: if the security design outcome (conditioned on the information the issuer has) turns out to be the worst case $s_L$ then the issuer offers everything for sale, and the market anticipates that everything is offered for sale and values it accordingly. Without the lower bound, it would not be possible to establish the conditions in this worst case.

**Proposition 4.13** (DeMarzo–Duffie Equilibrium Solution) *Let* $Q^*(s) = \left(\frac{s_L}{s}\right)^{\frac{1+r}{r}}$ *and* $P^*(q) = s_L q^{-\frac{r}{1+r}}$, *then* $(P^*, Q^*)$ *is a separating equilibrium.*

***Proof*** Based on the expression given, we can compute that for all $s \in [s_L, s_H]$ $P^*(Q^*(s)) = s$ and therefore $P^*(Q^*(\bar{S})) = \bar{S}$, so if it is an equilibrium $(P^*, Q^*)$ is separating. Also, note that $Q^*$ is strictly monotonic and invertible and hence $\mathbb{E}[\bar{S}|Q^*(\bar{S})] = \mathbb{E}[\bar{S}|\bar{S}] = \bar{S}$ and hence $P^*(Q^*(\bar{S})) = \mathbb{E}[\bar{S}|Q^*(\bar{S})]$.

To show the optimality condition is verified, we need to show that for all $s \in [s_L, s_H]$, we have $Q^*(s) \in \arg\max_q U(s, q, P^*(q))$. Thanks to the single crossing condition, we only need to show that first-order conditions are verified at the optimum. Precisely, we need to show that

$$0 = \frac{d}{dq}\left[q\left(P^*(q) - \frac{s}{1+r}\right)\right]\bigg|_{q=Q^*(s)}.$$

However, $q = Q^*(s)$ implies $P^*(q) = s$ since $P^*(Q^*(s)) = s$. Hence, we need to verify that for all $q \in [Q^*(s_H), Q^*(s_L)]$,

$$P^*(q) + q\frac{d}{dq}P^*(q) - \frac{1}{1+r}P^*(q) = 0.$$

Considering that $P^*(q) = s_L q^{-\frac{r}{1+r}}$ and hence $q\frac{d}{dq}P^*(q) = -\frac{rS_L}{1+r}q^{-\frac{r}{1+r}}$, the equality is verified. □

It is typical of a signaling equilibrium that the equilibrium depends on the particulars of the distribution of $Z$ or $Y$ only through the minimum value taken by $\bar{S}$. This is a concern in terms of realistic modeling, in fact voiced in DeMarzo (2005) when he developed an extension of the present model and proposed a way of addressing this issue.

The profit function can now be expressed, using $Q^*$:

$$\Pi_S(s) = U(s, Q^*(s), s) = \frac{r}{1+r} s_L^{\frac{1+r}{r}} s^{-\frac{1}{r}}.$$

Although we are considering that the investors do not apply a discount rate for simplicity, note that assuming a non-zero discount rate $r' < r$ would not materially change the subsequent results. Indeed, with a discount rate $r'$ then investors value a generic security design $S$ so that $P^*(Q^*(\bar{S})) = \frac{1}{1+r'}\mathbb{E}[\bar{S}|Q^*(\bar{S})]$. As a result, the optimal expression for the price becomes

$$P^*(s) = \frac{s_L}{1+r'} q^{\frac{-r}{1+r}},$$

and the expression for the optimal quantity does not change:

$$Q^*(s) = \left(\frac{s_L}{s}\right)^{\frac{1+r}{r}},$$

so that $P^*(Q^*(s)) = \frac{s}{1+r'}$.

Then the expression for $\Pi_S(s)$ is modified as it reflects the investor's discount rate:

$$\Pi_S(s) = Q^*(s)(\frac{s}{1+r'} - \frac{s}{1+r}) = \frac{r-r'}{(1+r)(1+r')} s_L^{\frac{1+r}{r}} s^{-\frac{1}{r}}.$$

The form of the expression remains the same, it is simply scaled by a constant.

We can push this generalization further by considering that the timing of the cash flows is itself random. We assume the payment takes place at a time $T$ following a continuous distribution so that $T \geq 0$, independent from $Z$ and independent from $Y$. Note this is not a very realistic assumption: total collateral cash flows would normally depend on the maturity, for example, if a coupon is capitalized.

The value of a future cash flow $X$ to the issuer then writes $\mathbb{E}\left[\frac{X}{(1+r)^T}\right] = \mathbb{E}\left[(1+r)^{-T}\right]\mathbb{E}\left[X\right]$. Therefore, we have

$$U(s, q, p) = q\left(p - s\mathbb{E}[(1+r)^{-T}]\right),$$

and

$$P^*(Q^*(\bar{S})) = \mathbb{E}[(1+r')^{-T}]\mathbb{E}[\bar{S}|Q^*(\bar{S})]$$

as well.

Solving the optimization with these modified expressions, we find

$$P^*(q) = \mathbb{E}[(1+r')^{-T}] s_L q^{\mathbb{E}[(1+r)^{-T}]-1}$$

and

$$Q^*(s) = \left(\frac{s_L}{s}\right)^{\frac{1}{1-\mathbb{E}[(1+r)^{-T}]}}.$$

As a result, the profit function is altered as follows:

$$\Pi_S(s) = \left(\mathbb{E}[(1+r')^{-T}] - \mathbb{E}[(1+r)^{-T}]\right) s_L^{\frac{1}{1-\mathbb{E}[(1+r)^{-T}]}} s^{\frac{\mathbb{E}[(1+r)^{-T}]}{\mathbb{E}[(1+r)^{-T}]-1}}.$$

Again, it is only a change in scale and therefore does not affect the following analysis and conclusions. The complex exponent expressions have the same form as in the simple case with an altered rate $r_0$, if we write

$$r_0 = \frac{1}{\mathbb{E}[(1+r)^{-T}]} - 1.$$

#### 4.3.2.3 Security Design

We can now search for the optimal ex ante structure for the security sold by the issuer.

In order to make the dependency explicit on the distribution of $\bar{S}$, we define $\Pi(s, s_L) = \Pi_S(s)$. $\Pi$ is homogeneous of degree 1: $\Pi(\alpha s, \alpha s_L) = \alpha \Pi(s, s_L)$ and hence $\Pi(s, s_L) = s_L \Pi\left(\frac{s}{s_L}, 1\right)$. Also note that we can also express the first derivative of $\Pi$:

$$\frac{\partial}{\partial s}\Pi(s, s_L) = -\frac{1}{1+r}\left(\frac{s_L}{s}\right)^{\frac{1+r}{r}}.$$

The derivative therefore verifies $-\frac{1}{1+r} < \frac{\partial}{\partial s}\Pi(s, s_L) < 0$.

In effect, the optimal quantities and prices in the liquidation problem do not depend on the full definition of $g$ where $S = g(Y)$, but only on $s_L = \min_z \mathbb{E}[g(Y)|Z = z]$. Also, we can write the value of a given security design $V(g(Y)) = \mathbb{E}[\Pi(s, s_L)]$, where for ease of notation $V$ is to be understood as a functional depending on $g(Y)$, not a $g(Y)$-measurable function. $V$ depends on the entire definition of $g(Y)$ and operates somewhat like an expectation operator.

The security design problem now boils down to solving $\sup_{g\in\mathcal{M}} \mathbb{E}[\Pi(\bar{S}, s_L)]$ given $s_L = \min_z \mathbb{E}[g(Y)|Z]$ and $\bar{S} = \mathbb{E}[g(Y)|Z]$. In fully developed form, this means solving

$$\sup_{g\in\mathcal{M}} \mathbb{E}\left[\Pi(\mathbb{E}[g(Y)|Z], \min_z \mathbb{E}[g(Y)|Z = z])\right].$$

In order to analyze optimal securities that may be created, we will express the marginal benefit from adding some positive cash flow $e(Y)$ to $g(Y)$, such that $g(Y) + e(Y) \leq Y$, as a directional derivative, for $1 \geq k \geq 0$:

$$\nabla(g, e) = \frac{d}{dk}V(g(Y) + ke(Y))\bigg|_{k=0}.$$

We define the directional derivatives of the issuer's private valuation, noting that it is $\mathcal{F}_Z$-measurable:

$$\gamma(g,e)(Z) = \frac{d}{dk}\mathbb{E}\left[g(Y)+ke(Y)\middle|Z\right]\bigg|_{k=0}$$

and minimum private valuation:

$$\gamma_L(g,e) = \frac{d}{dk}\min_z \mathbb{E}\left[g(Y)+ke(Y)\middle|Z=z\right]\bigg|_{k=0}.$$

The following proposition allows us to express the impact on the issuer's private valuation of altering a given security design, and, in particular, shows that the change in the issuer's minimal valuation of the resulting design only depends on the alteration. The proof relies on a kind of envelope theorem extension (to move the directional derivative inside the minimum).

**Proposition 4.14** (DeMarzo–Duffie Security Design Directional Derivatives) *We have*

$$\gamma(g,e)(Z) = \mathbb{E}\left[e(Y)|Z\right]$$

*and*

$$\gamma_L(g,e) = \min_{z\in\mathcal{L}} \mathbb{E}\left[e(Y)|Z=z\right]$$

*with* $\mathcal{L} = \{z : \mathbb{E}[g(Y)|Z=z] = s_L\}$. *Also if* $s_L > 0$ *and* $\gamma_L(g,e) > 0$ *then*

$$\nabla(g,e) = \gamma_L(g,e)\mathbb{E}\left[\Pi\left(\frac{\bar{S}}{s_L},1\right) + \frac{\partial}{\partial s}\Pi\left(\frac{\bar{S}}{s_L},1\right)\left(\frac{\gamma(g,e)}{\gamma_L(g,e)} - \frac{\bar{S}}{s_L}\right)\right].$$

***Proof*** We know that $g(Y)+ke(Y)$ conditioned on $Z$ is bounded and positive since $Y$ conditioned on $Z$ is bounded. Hence, through dominated convergence we can move the derivative under the integration and write

$$\gamma(g,e)(Z) = \mathbb{E}\left[\frac{d}{dk}(g(Y)+ke(Y))\middle|Z\right]\bigg|_{k=0} = \mathbb{E}\left[e(Y)|Z\right].$$

We write $c(z,k) = \mathbb{E}\left[g(Y)+ke(Y)\middle|Z=z\right]$, which is continuous with respect to $k$ and $z$ since we have assumed that the conditional distribution $\mu(y,z)$ was continuous relative to $z$. $c$ is also linear with respect to $k$. We define $\mathcal{L}^*(k) = \arg\min_z c(z,k)$ and $c^*(k) = \min_z c(z,k)$, and we note $c_k$ and $c_k^*$ for the derivatives with respect to $k$. We want to show that

$$\gamma_L(g,e) = c_k^*(0) = \min_{z\in\mathcal{L}^*(0)} c_k(z,0).$$

First, we know that by definition $c^*(k) \leq c(z,k)$, and for $z \in \mathcal{L}^*(0)$, $c^*(0) = c(z,0)$. Hence, for $z \in \mathcal{L}^*(0)$ and for all $k \geq 0$:

$$c^*(k) - c^*(0) \leq c(z,k) - c(z,0).$$

Dividing by $k$ and taking the limit, this implies that $c_k^*(0) \leq c_k(z,0)$ for $z \in \mathcal{L}^*(0)$, and hence $c_k^*(0) \leq \inf_{z\in\mathcal{L}^*(0)} c_k(z,0)$. This gives us a first relationship involving the desired quantities.

As the minimum of linear functions, we know that $c^*$ is concave. For any integer $n$ and $z_n \in \mathcal{L}^*(\frac{1}{n})$, we know that $c^*(\frac{1}{n}) = c(z_n, \frac{1}{n})$ and $c(z_n, 0) \geq c^*(0)$. Also, due to the definition of $c$, we have $c_k(z_n, 0) = \mathbb{E}[e(Y)|Z = z_n]$. We can write

$$\begin{aligned} c_k(z_n,0) &= \mathbb{E}[e(Y)|Z = z_n] \\ &= n\left(c\left(z_n, \frac{1}{n}\right) - c(z_n, 0)\right) \\ &\leq n\left(c^*\left(\frac{1}{n}\right) - c^*(0)\right) \\ &\leq c_k^*(0), \end{aligned}$$

the last inequality being due to the minimum's concavity. So can write that for all $n$: $c_k^*(0) \geq c_k(z,0)$ for all $z \in \mathcal{L}^*(\frac{1}{n})$. By continuity of $c_k$, we get that $c_k^*(0) \geq c_k(z,0)$ for all $z \in \mathcal{L}^*(0)$, and hence $c_k^*(0) \geq \min_{z\in\mathcal{L}^*(0)} c_k(z,0)$. Since we've shown this inequality was valid in the other direction, we infer that $c_k^*(0) = \min_{z\in\mathcal{L}^*(0)} c_k(z,0)$.

In order to express $\nabla(g,e)$, we first compute the derivative with respect to $k$, and then take the value at $k = 0$. Thanks to the profit function's homogeneity we have

$$\begin{aligned} V(g(Y) + ke(Y)) &= \mathbb{E}\left[\Pi\left(c(Z,k), \min_z c(z,k)\right)\right] \\ &= \min_z c(z,k)\mathbb{E}\left[\Pi\left(\frac{c(Z,k)}{\min_z c(z,k)}, 1\right)\right]. \end{aligned}$$

Then by deriving with respect to $k$, using dominated convergence since all the quantities are bounded and positive, we obtain

$$\begin{aligned} &\frac{\partial}{\partial k} V(g(Y) + ke(Y)) \\ &= \frac{\partial}{\partial k}\min_z c(z,k)\mathbb{E}\left[\Pi\left(\frac{c(Z,k)}{\min_z c(z,k)}, 1\right)\right] \\ &+ \mathbb{E}\left[\frac{\partial}{\partial s}\Pi\left(\frac{c(Z,k)}{\min_z c(z,k)}, 1\right)\left[\frac{\partial}{\partial k}c(Z,k) - \frac{c(Z,k)\frac{\partial}{\partial k}\min_z c(z,k)}{\min_z c(z,k)}\right]\right]. \end{aligned}$$

Taking the values at $k = 0$, we note that $c(Z,0) = \bar{S}$, $\min_z c(z,0) = s_L$, $\frac{\partial}{\partial k}\min_z c(z,k)\big|_{k=0} = \gamma_L(g,e)$, and $\frac{\partial}{\partial k}c(Z,k)\big|_{k=0} = \gamma(g,e)(Z)$, and obtain the result. □

The ratio of $\frac{\bar{S}}{s_L}$ can be interpreted as an information sensitivity of the security design, because it captures how much the issuer's private information matters relative to the lowest possible private valuation. The ratio $\frac{\gamma(g,e)}{\gamma_L(g,e)}$ gives the marginal information sensitivity of adding cash flow $e$ to cash flow $g$. Since $\Pi$ is decreasing in its first argument, we can see that based on the expression for the directional derivative when $\frac{\gamma(g,e)}{\gamma_L(g,e)} < \frac{\bar{S}}{s_L}$ then one gains by adding the cash flow $e$ when the marginal information sensitivity is always less than the information sensitivity of $g$.

Therefore, one would expect that it should be optimal to sometimes exhaust all the available cash flows: if some security was such that always $g(Y) < Y$, then one could add a risk-free payment to improve it, which would not be information sensitive. In other words, risk-less debt is not optimal.

**Proposition 4.15** (DeMarzo–Duffie Probability of Full Cash Flow) *If $g$ is an optimal design, then $\mathbb{P}[\exists a > 0 : \forall y, y - g(y) > a] = 0$.*

***Proof*** Let us assume there exists $a > 0$ such that for all $y$, $y - g(y) > a$. We consider an additional cash flow $e(Y) = a = \inf_\omega (Y - g(Y))(\omega)$. Then $\gamma(g, e) = \gamma_L(g, e) = a$. Using the formula for $\nabla(g, e)$, we obtain

$$\nabla(g, e) = a\frac{V(g(Y))}{s_L} + a\mathbb{E}\left[\frac{\partial}{\partial s}\Pi\left(\bar{S}, s_L\right)\left(1 - \frac{\bar{S}}{s_L}\right)\right].$$

Since $\bar{S} \geq s_L$ and $\frac{\partial}{\partial s}\Pi \leq 0$, the term in the expectation is positive. Hence, $\nabla(g, e) > 0$ and $g$ cannot be optimal. □

We can also easily show that if one pays a pass-through like proportional cash flow, then a full equity-like cash flow is optimal.

**Proposition 4.16** (Optimality of Full Pass-Through) *Of all cash flows of the form $g(y) = \alpha y$ for $\alpha \in [0, 1]$, the full equity payment $g(y) = y$ is optimal.*

***Proof*** Consider $g(y) = \alpha y$ and $e(y) = \beta y$ with $\beta \geq 0$ such that $\alpha + \beta \leq 1$. Then $\gamma(g, e) = \beta\mathbb{E}[Y|Z]$ and $\gamma_L(g, e) = \beta \inf_z \mathbb{E}[Y|Z = z]$. Note that we have

$$\frac{\gamma(g, e)}{\gamma_L(g, e)} - \frac{\bar{S}}{s_L} = \frac{\mathbb{E}[Y|Z]}{\inf_z \mathbb{E}[Y|Z = z]} - \frac{\mathbb{E}[Y|Z]}{\inf_z \mathbb{E}[Y|Z = z]} = 0.$$

As a result, the expression for $\nabla(g, e)$ simplifies to

$$\beta \inf_z \mathbb{E}[Y|Z = z]\mathbb{E}\left[\Pi\left(\frac{\bar{S}}{s_L}, 1\right)\right],$$

which is positive and increasing in $\beta$. Therefore, the optimal security of the form $g(y) = \alpha y$ is the one with $\alpha = 1$. □

Following the same logic, one can see that adding risky cash flows could also improve the security design as far as they are not too informationally sensitive. For example, even if the initial security had no information sensitivity, adding a contingent payment will improve the issuer's value function as long as $\gamma_L(g,e) > \frac{1}{1+r}\gamma(g,e)$: the signaling cost of adding the cash flows is less than the funding cost of retaining them.

DeMarzo and Duffie propose a measure for the informational sensitivity of the asset cash flow to the private information. Taking events $B$ in the set of all $\mathcal{F}_Y$-measurable sets, and $z_1$ and $z_2$ in the support of the distribution of $Z$, they define the information sensitivity as

$$\epsilon_Y = \sup_{B,z_1,z_2} \frac{\mathbb{P}[B|Z=z_1]}{\mathbb{P}[B|Z=z_2]} - 1,$$

where if $\mathbb{P}[B|Z=z_1] = \mathbb{P}[B|Z=z_2] = 0$ then $\epsilon_Y = 0$. This new metric represents the largest possible ratio of conditional densities of $Y$ knowing $Z$. When this metric is small, it means that conditioning by $Z$ never changes $Y$'s probability distribution very much, and therefore there is little cost to the informational asymmetry. In that case, we can show that it becomes optimal to issue equity-like payoffs.

Note that conditions on the information sensitivity are reflected on the private valuation's distribution relative to its minimum. Define $z_L$ as a conditional value that minimizes the issuer's private valuation of the security, such that $\mathbb{E}[g(Y)|Z=z_L] = s_L$. The assumption $\epsilon_Y \leq r$ implies for $B$ $\mathcal{F}_Y$-measurable:

$$\sup_B \frac{\mathbb{P}[B|Z]}{\mathbb{P}[B|Z=z_L]} < 1+r.$$

Hence,

$$\mathbb{P}[B|Z] < (1+r)\mathbb{P}[B|Z=z_L]$$

and since $Y$ is bounded, for any positive and measurable $f$,

$$\int f(y)\mathbb{P}[Y \in dy|Z] < (1+r)\int f(y)\mathbb{P}[Y \in B|Z=z_L].$$

Since this is true for all possible $z_L$, we can write

$$\frac{\mathbb{E}[f(Y)|Z]}{\min_{z\in\mathcal{L}} \mathbb{E}[f(Y)|Z=z]} < 1+r.$$

If we set $f = g$ then we have $\bar{S} < (1+r)s_L$ almost surely. Also, this implies that $\gamma(g,e)(Z) < (1+r)\gamma_L(g,e)$.

**Proposition 4.17** (DeMarzo–Duffie Optimality of Equity Security) *Assume $\epsilon_Y \leq r$. Then, $g$ is optimal if and only if $g(Y) = Y$ almost surely.*

***Proof*** We define $e(Y) = Y - g(Y)$, so that $e$ complements $g$ to turn the entire cash flow into equity. We assume that $g$ is optimal.

Thanks to the information sensitivity assumption, we know that almost surely $\gamma(g, e) < (1+r)\gamma_L(g, e)$ and $\bar{S} < (1+r)s_L$. However we do not know whether $\frac{\gamma(g,e)}{\gamma_L(g,e)} > \frac{\bar{S}}{s_L}$ or not.

First, let is consider the cases where $\frac{\gamma(g,e)}{\gamma_L(g,e)} > \frac{\bar{S}}{s_L}$. Thanks to the bounds for the first derivative of $\Pi$, then to the first item in Proposition 4.12, and then to the fact that $\gamma(g, e) < (1+r)\gamma_L(g, e)$, we can write

$$\begin{aligned}
&\Pi\left(\frac{\bar{S}}{s_L}, 1\right) + \frac{\partial}{\partial s}\Pi\left(\frac{\bar{S}}{s_L}, 1\right)\left(\frac{\gamma(g,e)}{\gamma_L(g,e)} - \frac{\bar{S}}{s_L}\right)\\
\geq&\Pi\left(\frac{\bar{S}}{s_L}, 1\right) - \frac{1}{1+r}\left(\frac{\gamma(g,e)}{\gamma_L(g,e)} - \frac{\bar{S}}{s_L}\right)\\
\geq&\frac{1}{s_L}\left(s_L - \frac{1}{1+r}\bar{S}\right)^+ - \frac{1}{1+r}\left(\frac{\gamma(g,e)}{\gamma_L(g,e)} - \frac{\bar{S}}{s_L}\right)\\
\geq&\left(1 - \frac{1}{1+r}\frac{\bar{S}}{s_L}\right)^+ - \left(1 - \frac{1}{1+r}\frac{\bar{S}}{s_L}\right).
\end{aligned}$$

Since $\bar{S} < (1+r)s_L$ almost surely, then the above quantity is almost surely strictly positive.

Let us now consider the alternate case, where $\frac{\gamma(g,e)}{\gamma_L(g,e)} \leq \frac{\bar{S}}{s_L}$. Then, again thanks to Proposition 4.12:

$$\begin{aligned}
&\Pi\left(\frac{\bar{S}}{s_L}, 1\right) + \frac{\partial}{\partial s}\Pi\left(\frac{\bar{S}}{s_L}, 1\right)\left(\frac{\gamma(g,e)}{\gamma_L(g,e)} - \frac{\bar{S}}{s_L}\right)\\
\geq&\Pi\left(\frac{\bar{S}}{s_L}, 1\right) \geq \left(1 - \frac{1}{1+r}\frac{\bar{S}}{s_L}\right)^+.
\end{aligned}$$

For the same reason as in the previous case, this quantity is almost surely strictly positive.

Therefore, taking the expectation we find that $\nabla V(g, e) > 0$ and the security design $g$ cannot be optimal. This implies that $e$ must be null, and $g(Y) = Y$. □

The information sensitivity measure presented above is captured across all possible measurable sets $B$. DeMarzo and Duffie also define the informational sensitivity specific to a $\mathcal{F}_Y$-measurable set $B$:

$$\epsilon_{Y,B} = \sup_{z_1,z_2} \frac{\mathbb{P}[B|Z = z_1]}{\mathbb{P}[B|Z = z_2]} - 1,$$

so that $\epsilon_Y = \sup_B \epsilon_{Y,B}$. Now we can show that when is possible for the issuer to strictly increase the payoff of the security on outcomes the informational sensitivity of which is less than $r$, then the issuer should add these cash flows.

**Proposition 4.18** (DeMarzo–Duffie Optimality of Partial Equity Cash Flow) *Suppose $g$ is an optimal security design and $B$ is a measurable outcome of $Y$ so that $g(Y) < Y$ on $B$ (i.e., $B \subset \{g(Y) < Y\}$). Then the informational sensitivity of $B$ verifies $\epsilon_{Y,B} \geq r$.*

***Proof*** We consider $B$ to be given. Note that with $\mathbb{E}[g(Y)|Z = z_L] = s_L$, we have for all $z$ $\mathbb{P}[B|Z] < (1+r)\mathbb{P}[B|Z = z_L]$. Hence, for any measurable function $f$:

$$\int_B f(y)\mathbb{P}[Y \in dy|Z] < (1+r)\int_B f(y)\mathbb{P}[Y \in dy|Z = z_L].$$

Therefore, we can write that for any security design $g$ and $\mathbb{I}_B e$,

$$\mathbb{E}[\mathbb{I}_B e(Y)|Z] < (1+r)\min_z \mathbb{E}[\mathbb{I}_B e(Y)|Z = z]$$

and

$$\gamma(g, \mathbb{I}_B e) < \gamma_0(g, \mathbb{I}_B e).$$

Using these results, we can follow the proof for Proposition 4.17 by setting $e(Y) = (Y - g(Y))\mathbb{I}_B$, where $g$ is assumed to be optimal. Hence, $e$ must be null and therefore $g(Y) = Y$ on $B$. Equivalently, if $g(Y) < Y$ then it implies that $\epsilon_{Y,B} \geq r$. □

Based on this result, if a security design $g$ is optimal and if for a measurable set $B$ $\epsilon_{Y,B} \leq r$, then on $B$ $g(Y) = Y$. If $\epsilon_{Y,B} \leq r$ then

$$\sup_{z_1,z_2} \frac{\mathbb{P}[B|Z = z_1]}{\mathbb{P}[B|Z = z2]} - 1 \leq r,$$

and hence

$$\inf_z \mathbb{P}[B|Z = z] \geq \frac{1}{1+r}\sup_z \mathbb{P}[B|Z = z].$$

If according to the proposition this is true for all $B$ on which $g(Y) = Y$, then we can write that for all $y$ such that

$$\inf_z \mu(y,z) \geq \frac{1}{1+r}\sup_z \mu(y,z),$$

then $g(y) = y$. In other words, in local outcomes where the private information does not condition much, the optimal design behaves like equity.

#### 4.3.2.4 Standard Debt

We have seen some of the characteristics of optimal security designs, and, in particular, how a full equity cash flow may be optimal. We now turn to the conditions that may make standard debt optimal. We define standard debt with face value $D$ as a payment $g(Y) = D \wedge Y$. If we were making this a straight debt security it would imply that the issuer would not either retain the unsold fraction of the security $(1-q)$ in the case of default. If these securities were retained then the payment definition would need to be adjusted to reflect the debt holder's right to the extra assets remaining on the issuer's balance sheet: $g(Y) = D \wedge \left(\frac{Y}{q}\right)$. This type of cash flow cannot be accounted for in the model developed by DeMarzo and Duffie. For our purposes related to securitization, however, this is not an issue since the cash flows to investors are contractually determined, and there would not be a notion of default or bankruptcy on behalf of the SPV. The bond holders would have a right to the cash flow as defined in the bonds' prospectus, not more and not less. So, even if only a fraction of the securities were sold to investors that does not constitute an issue in terms of applicability to the creation of securitized bonds.

While the security design problem we have tackled so far was in the infinite-dimensional space of all possible measurable functions, we will see now that thanks to some particular assumptions, we can reduce it to a single dimension problem.

Notion of Uniform Worst Case

The authors define a worst-case outcome for the information $Z$: an outcome $z_L$ of the variable $Z$ is a uniform worst case if, for any other outcome $z$ and any interval $I \in \mathbb{R}^+$ of outcomes of $Y$,

- if $\mathbb{P}[Y \in I | Z = z] > 0$ then $\mathbb{P}[Y \in I | Z = z_L] > 0$, or equivalently, $\mu(y, z)dy$ is absolutely continuous with respect to $\mu(y, z_L)dy$ (and hence the Radon–Nikodym derivative of $\mu(y, z)dy$ relative to $\mu(y, z_L)dy$ exists) and
- the conditional of $Y$ knowing $Z = z$ given $Y \in I$ has first-order stochastic dominance over the conditional of $Y$ knowing $Z = z_L$ given $Y \in I$, or equivalently, the Radon–Nikodym derivative of $\mu(y, z)dy$ relative to $\mu(y, z_L)dy$ is an increasing function.

This technical definition essentially says that $z_L$ is such that the distribution of $Y$ conditioned by that realization is worse than for other possible private information observations $z$. The Radon–Nikodym derivative in this case is the positive function $\nu$ such that for any measurable set $B$,

$$\mathbb{P}[B | Z = z] = \int_B \nu(y) \mathbb{P}[Y \in dy | Z = z_L].$$

We can also write that for any measurable positive function $g$, $\int g(y)\mu(y, z)dy = \int g(y)\nu_z(y)\mu(y, z_L)dy$. This Radon–Nikodym derivative is required to be increasing, so that the higher outcomes count more relative to the worst case. Note that $\nu_z(y)$ naturally depends on $z$, but we want it to be increasing with respect to $y$.

If the distribution of $Y$ conditional on $Z = z$ verifies the maximum likelihood ratio property (MLRP) relative to the distribution of $Y$ conditional on $Z = z_L$, then the uniform worst-case property is verified. Indeed, the MLRP requires that the ratio of the densities be an increasing function. This property effectively says that the greater an observation, the more likely it is drawn from the first distribution rather than from the second one, and reciprocally, the lower the observation of $Y$, the more likely it was drawn from the worst-case condition $Z = z_L$.

To illustrate the uniform worst-case notion, we could define $Y = h(Z) + W$ for some continuous function $h$ and an independent random variable $W$, with distribution $k(w)dw$. Then for any measurable function $g$, and for all outcomes $z$ of $Z$,

$$\mathbb{E}[g(Y)|Z = z] = \int g(w + h(z))\mathbb{P}[W \in dw].$$

By change of variable, this equals $\int g(y)k(y - h(z))dy$. There exists a worst-case outcome $z_L$ if for all $z$ and for all $g$, there exists an increasing function $\nu$ such that

$$\int g(y)k(y - h(z))dy = \int g(y)\nu_z(y)k(y - h(z_L))dy.$$

Hence, we need $\nu_z(y) = \frac{k(y-h(z))}{k(y-h(z_L))}$ to be increasing.

If we take $W$ to be Gaussian (not truncated, centered, and reduced for simplicity), then

$$\nu_z(y) = \exp\left(y(h(z) - h(z_L)) + \frac{1}{2}\left(h^2(z_L) - h^2(z)\right)\right),$$

which is increasing if $h(z) \geq h(z_L)$ for all $z$. In this case, the uniform worst case is defined as the minimum argument to $h$.

Note that if $g$ is increasing, then $\mathbb{E}[g(Y)|Z = z]$ is minimal at the uniform worst-case $z = z_L$, and therefore $s_L = \mathbb{E}[g(Y)|Z = z_L]$.

Optimality of Debt Contract

We begin by showing the following lemma, which tells us that given any security design one can find a better design as a debt contract in some sense.

**Lemma 4.1** (Defining a Superior Debt Contract) *If there is a uniform worst case, given a security design $g$ there exists a standard debt contract $d(y) = y \wedge D$ such that $\mathbb{E}[d(Y)|Z = z_L] = \mathbb{E}[g(Y)|Z = z_L]$ and $\mathbb{E}[d(Y)|Z] \leq \mathbb{E}[g(Y)|Z]$.*

***Proof*** We assume the uniform worst case is $z_L$, and we consider a generic security design $g$ (increasing, as per our initial assumptions). Thanks to the monotonicity of $g$, we know that

$$\min_z \mathbb{E}[g(Y)|Z = z] = \mathbb{E}[g(Y)|Z = z_L] = g_L.$$

Now we consider a standard debt contract $d(Y) = D \wedge Y$. We know that $\mathbb{E}[D \wedge Y|Z = z_L]$ is continuous in $D$ thanks to dominated convergence. Hence, we can choose $D$ so that

$$g_L = \min_z \mathbb{E}[g(Y)|Z = z] = \min_z \mathbb{E}[D \wedge Y|Z = z] = d_L,$$

since varying $D$, $d(Y)$ can take all the possible values between a uniform 0 and the full cash flow $Y$.

Now we define $e$ as the difference between $d$ and $g$: $e(Y) = (g(Y) - d(Y))$. This variable may therefore be negative. We write $h(Z) = \mathbb{E}[e(Y)|Z]$, and note that $h(z_L) = 0$ given how $D$ has been set. Since $g(y) \leq y$ and $g$ is increasing, there exists $y^*$ such that $e(Y) > 0$ is equivalent to $Y > y^*$. This threshold represents the case when the generic security pays more than the debt contract. Then for all $z$, thanks to the definition of the Radon–Nikodym derivative introduced earlier,

$$h(z) = \mathbb{E}[e(Y)|Z = z] = \mathbb{E}[e(Y)\nu_z(Y)|Z = z_L].$$

Now note that we can write

$$\begin{aligned} h(z) &= \mathbb{E}\left[\mathbb{I}_{e(Y)>0} e(Y)\nu_z(Y)|Z = z_L\right] + \mathbb{E}\left[\mathbb{I}_{e(Y)\leq 0} e(Y)\nu_z(Y)|Z = z_L\right] \\ &= \mathbb{E}\left[\mathbb{I}_{Y>y^*} e(Y)\nu_z(Y)|Z = z_L\right] + \mathbb{E}\left[\mathbb{I}_{Y\leq y^*} e(Y)\nu_z(Y)|Z = z_L\right]. \end{aligned}$$

However, the first term is positive and the second term is negative, and since $\nu_z$ is increasing we have

$$\mathbb{E}\left[\mathbb{I}_{Y>y^*} e(Y)\nu_z(Y)|Z = z_L\right] \geq \mathbb{E}\left[\mathbb{I}_{Y>y^*} e(Y)\nu_z(y^*)|Z = z_L\right]$$

and

$$\mathbb{E}\left[\mathbb{I}_{Y\leq y^*} e(Y)\nu_z(Y)|Z = z_L\right] \geq \mathbb{E}\left[\mathbb{I}_{Y\leq y^*} e(Y)\nu_z(y^*)|Z = z_L\right].$$

Therefore, combining both terms, we get

$$h(z) \geq \nu_z(y^*)\mathbb{E}[e(Y)|Z = z_L] = \nu_z(y^*)h(z_L)$$

and that last term is zero, as pointed out earlier. We infer that $\mathbb{E}[g(Y)|Z] \geq \mathbb{E}[d(Y)|Z]$ since $h(Z) \geq 0$. □

We can now show the following proposition.

**Proposition 4.19** (DeMarzo–Duffie Optimality of Debt Security) *If there is a uniform worst case then a standard debt contract is optimal.*

***Proof*** We know thanks to Lemma 4.1 that given a security design $g$ we can find a standard debt contract $d$ with the same worst-case expected outcome, and such that $\mathbb{E}[d(Y)|Z] \leq \mathbb{E}[g(Y)|Z]$. We write $e = g - d$.

We also know that the profit function with respect to the generic security $g$ is decreasing and hence

$$\begin{aligned}\Pi\left(\mathbb{E}[g(Y)|Z], g_L\right) &= \Pi\left(\mathbb{E}[e(Y) + d(Y)|Z], g_L\right) \\ &= \Pi\left(\mathbb{E}[e(Y) + d(Y)|Z], d_L\right) \\ &\leq \Pi\left(\mathbb{E}[d(Y)|Z], d_L\right).\end{aligned}$$

Integrating with respect to $Z$, we obtain that $V(d(Y)) \geq V(g(Y))$. Given an arbitrary $g$, we defined a superior security, the debt, by setting its face value as a function of the characteristics of $g$. Hence, an optimal security is standard debt at the face value $D^*$ maximizing $V(D \wedge Y)$. □

As the proof illustrates, the logic behind this result is that using a face value based on the worst-case outcome, thanks to the stochastic dominance of any other outcome then we know that all higher outcomes will be above the face value. Any more promised cash flows than the debt's face value would not be expected to be available in the worst-case scenario.

We can express the value to the issuer of issuing a standard debt contract. Recall that

$$V(S) = \mathbb{E}\left[\Pi_S\left(\mathbb{E}[g(Y)|Z]\right)\right],$$

and

$$\Pi_S(s) = \frac{r}{1+r} s_L^{\frac{1+r}{r}} s^{-\frac{1}{r}}$$

where $s_L = \inf_z \mathbb{E}[g(Y)|Z = z]$. In the case at hand, we have $g(y) = y \wedge D$. Since $g$ is increasing, then $s_L = \mathbb{E}[Y \wedge D|Z = z_L]$ and we therefore have an explicit expression for $V(D \wedge Y)$:

$$\begin{aligned}V(D \wedge Y) &= \mathbb{E}\left[\frac{r}{1+r}\mathbb{E}[Y \wedge D|Z = z_L]^{\frac{1+r}{r}}\mathbb{E}[Y \wedge D|Z]^{-\frac{1}{r}}\right] \\ &= \frac{r}{1+r}\mathbb{E}[Y \wedge D|Z = z_L]\mathbb{E}\left[\left(\frac{\mathbb{E}[Y \wedge D|Z = z_L]}{\mathbb{E}[Y \wedge D|Z]}\right)^{\frac{1}{r}}\right].\end{aligned}$$

We can see that the value to the issuer has a term for the expected security cash flow assuming the worst outcome, $\mathbb{E}[Y \wedge D|Z = z_L]$, which would increase as the face value $D$ increases, but also a term $\mathbb{E}\left[\left(\frac{\mathbb{E}[Y \wedge D|Z = z_L]}{\mathbb{E}[Y \wedge D|Z]}\right)^{\frac{1}{r}}\right]$ that will be lower when the expected security cash flow conditioned upon the worst outcome is low relative to the expected cash flow without such conditioning. The first term is the basic cash flow that investors expect to receive and the second one is a discount related to how bad the worst case would be relative to the average, in a sense.

According to Proposition 4.19, debt is optimal if the distributions driving the asset returns and the private information possess certain characteristics. However, as we saw in Proposition 4.17, if the informational sensitivity of the asset's return distribution is less than $r$ then an equity cash flow is optimal. How can these two opposite types of securities be optimal at the same time? Debt is, in fact, the same thing as equity for asset returns that are less than the face value, so the difference resides in asset returns above the debt's face value. If a security design is optimal, but on some subset of all outcomes it is less than equity, then it means that the information sensitivity on that subset of outcomes is greater than $r$, thanks to Proposition 4.18. Note that a form of security that would correspond to debt plus a positive amount is defined as quasi-debt in the next section, and shown to be optimal in the model developed in Dang, Gorton, and Holmström (2015).

More formally, Proposition 4.18 implies that if debt with a face value of $D^*$ is optimal, setting $B = \{Y > D^*\}$ then

$$\sup_{z_1,z_2} \frac{\mathbb{P}[Y > D^*|Z = z_1]}{\mathbb{P}[Y > D^*|Z = z_2]} \geq 1 + r$$

and hence the cash flows going beyond the face value in the worst-case scenario are limited:

$$\inf_{z} \mathbb{P}[Y > D^*|Z = z] \leq \frac{1}{1+r}.$$

One can therefore study how the optimal face value for the debt varies as a function of the characteristics of the conditional distribution of $Y$ given $Z$, and the issuer's funding constraints as captured by $r$. The highest the funding cost, the strongest the issuer's demand for funding and hence the larger the debt, potentially even to the point of being simply equity (when the face value increases beyond a certain point). If the funding cost is low, then the issuer prefers holding a larger share of assets, and may issue a smaller amount of debt (which would hence be more likely to be repaid).

Using the Demarzo–Duffie model, we have qualified the conditions for the optimality of creating senior securities in a fairly general setting. We will now look into an approach allowing us to account for the possibility of acquiring information at a cost, in a somewhat different and slightly less general setting, and we will see how it affects the conditions for the optimality of debt contracts.

### 4.3.3 Information Sensitivity

In this section, we look at security design that explicitly addresses information sensitivity, and follow the approach from Dang, Gorton, and Holmström (2015). The proofs have been entirely rewritten in order to make them less heuristic.

The core model setup is kept similar to that of Boot–Thakor or DeMarzo–Duffie. We consider assets that generate an underlying cash flow $Y$ in period 1, a random variable. Securities can be created off of this cash flow, and they may be traded at period 0. We will define a security as a function $g$, so that the promised cash flow is

$g(Y)$. The variable $Y$ is assumed to be positive, to have its support in $[y_b, y_g]$, and the security cannot pay more than the assets generate, and can only pay a positive amount so that for all $y \in [y_b, y_g]$, $0 \leq g(y) \leq y$. The security is assumed to have a price which we will write $p$ (the price at which it is traded, if at all, at period 0). Note that we are not aiming to calculate the price of the security, so the price is not explicitly written as a function of the characteristics of the security, rather we will consider this price as a variable and we do not write explicitly the expression of $Y$'s density.

Dang, Gorton, and Holmström first consider a rather general notion of security design based off of a cash flow, and study its characteristics and derive various properties. Then, they focus on optimal contract design using these securities, in an economy where one agent (akin to an issuer) has a project and can issue a security, and another agent (akin to an investor) has a preference for future consumption. The issuer can also choose to acquire information in order to better value the security. The authors show that when the cost of information acquisition is null (i.e., the issuer is informed) then the optimal contract structure is debt.

#### 4.3.3.1 The Value of Information

We define the space of possible security designs as

$$\mathcal{L} = \{f \in C([y_b, y_g]) : \forall x, 0 \leq f(x) \leq x\},$$

where $C([y_b, y_g])$ is the set of real continuous functions with support in $[y_b, y_g]$. Dang, Gorton, and Holmström define the information sensitivity of a security $g$ at a price $p$ in the loss (left) region as follows, for $(p, g) \in \mathbb{R}^+ \times \mathcal{L}$:

$$\Pi_L(p, g) = \mathbb{E}\left[(p - g(Y))^+\right] = \mathbb{E}\left[(p - g(Y))\mathbb{I}_{g(Y)<p}\right],$$

and the information sensitivity in the gain (right) region as

$$\Pi_R(p, g) = \mathbb{E}\left[(g(Y) - p)^+\right] = \mathbb{E}\left[(g(Y) - p)\mathbb{I}_{g(Y)>p}\right].$$

We can express the security design problem as determining the optimal designs $g$ that will lead to desirable characteristics in terms of information sensitivity.

**Lemma 4.2** *Given $g \in \mathcal{L}$, we have*

*i.* $\Pi_R(p, g) - \Pi_L(p, g) = \mathbb{E}[g(Y)] - p$;
*ii.* $\Pi_L(\mathbb{E}[g(Y)], g) = \Pi_R(\mathbb{E}[g(Y)], g)$;
*iii.* $\frac{\partial \Pi_L}{\partial p}(p, g) \geq 0$ *and* $\frac{\partial \Pi_R}{\partial p}(p, g) \leq 0$ *with strict inequalities if* $\Pi_L$ *and* $\Pi_R$ *are non-zero; and*
*iv. If* $\Pi_L(p, g)$ *and* $\Pi_R(p, g)$ *are non-zero, then if* $p > \mathbb{E}[g(Y)]$ *then* $\Pi_L(p, g) > \Pi_R(p, g)$ *and if* $p < \mathbb{E}[g(Y)]$ *then* $\Pi_L(p, g) < \Pi_R(p, g)$.

***Proof*** The first result is obtained by calculating the difference

$$\begin{aligned}\Pi_R(p,g)-\Pi_L(p,g)&=\mathbb{E}\left[(g(Y)-p)\mathbb{I}_{g(Y)>p}\right]-\mathbb{E}\left[(p-g(Y))\mathbb{I}_{g(Y)<p}\right]\\&=\mathbb{E}\left[\mathbb{I}_{g(Y)>p}(g(Y)-p)-(1-\mathbb{I}_{g(Y)>p}(p-g(Y))\right]\\&=-\mathbb{E}[p-g(Y)]=\mathbb{E}[g(Y)]-p.\end{aligned}$$

The second result is a direct application of the first one, with $p=\mathbb{E}[g(Y)]$.

For the third result, we write

$$\begin{aligned}&\frac{\partial\Pi_R}{\partial p}(p,g)\\&=\lim_{\varepsilon\to0}\frac{1}{\varepsilon}\mathbb{E}\left[(g(Y)-p-\varepsilon)\mathbb{I}_{g(Y)>p+\varepsilon}-(g(Y)-p)\mathbb{I}_{g(Y)>p}\right]\\&=\lim_{\varepsilon\to0}\left(-\frac{1}{\varepsilon}\mathbb{E}\left[\varepsilon\mathbb{I}_{g(Y)>p+\varepsilon}\right]+\frac{1}{\varepsilon}\mathbb{E}\left[(g(Y)-p)(\mathbb{I}_{g(Y)>p+\varepsilon}-\mathbb{I}_{g(Y)>p})\right]\right)\\&=-\mathbb{P}[g(Y)>p]-\lim_{\varepsilon\to0}\left(\frac{1}{\varepsilon}\mathbb{E}\left[(g(Y)-p)\mathbb{I}_{p+\varepsilon>g(Y)>p})\right]\right)\\&=-\mathbb{P}[g(Y)>p]-\lim_{\varepsilon\to0}\left(\frac{1}{\varepsilon}\mathbb{E}\left[g(Y)-p\middle|g(Y)\in(p,p+\varepsilon)\right]\mathbb{P}[g(Y)\in(p,p+\varepsilon)]\right)\\&=-\mathbb{P}[g(Y)>p]\leq0.\end{aligned}$$

If $\Pi_R(p,g)>0$, which implies that $\mathbb{P}[g(Y)>p]>0$, then this a strict inequality. Following the same approach, we can show that

$$\begin{aligned}&\frac{\partial\Pi_L}{\partial p}(p,g)\\&=\lim_{\varepsilon\to0}\frac{1}{\varepsilon}\mathbb{E}\left[(p+\varepsilon-g(Y))\mathbb{I}_{g(Y)<p+\varepsilon}-(p-g(Y))\mathbb{I}_{g(Y)<p}\right]\\&=\mathbb{P}[g(Y)<p]+\lim_{\varepsilon\to0}\left(\frac{1}{\varepsilon}\mathbb{E}\left[p-g(Y)\middle|g(Y)\in(p,p+\varepsilon)\right]\mathbb{P}[g(Y)\in(p,p+\varepsilon)]\right)\\&\geq0.\end{aligned}$$

For the fourth result, note that $\Pi_L$ is increasing in $p$, $\Pi_R$ is decreasing, and they are both equal at $p=\mathbb{E}[g(Y)]$. Therefore, for $p>\mathbb{E}[g(y)]$, $\Pi_L(p,g)>\Pi_R(p,g)$, the first term being increasing and the second one decreasing. Symmetrically, for $p<\mathbb{E}[g(y)]$, $\Pi_L(p,g)<\Pi_R(p,g)$. □

We are now looking at how different actors with different utilities might behave. We consider that there could be security buyers and security sellers. The buyers or sellers will buy/sell if the value of the security to them is higher/lower than the given market price, based on their information. In a general context, we can define the utility for buyers as $U_B(p,g)$ and for sellers as $U_S(p,g)$. The payment or collection of the price $p$, if it happens, takes place at time 0, and the realization of the utility from the cash flows comes at time 1, which may imply inter-temporal differences.

With our general setting, we need to express the fact that if the price is not right (if it is too high for a buyer or too low for a seller) for the agents, given their information, then they do not trade and will have a zero utility. We consider there is information $Z$, a random variable that is not independent from $Y$. The informed agents can observe $Z$, while the uninformed cannot. For an uninformed agent, the utility of security $g$ at price $p$ would be $\mathbb{E}[U(p,g)]\mathbb{I}_{\mathbb{E}[U(p,g)]>0}$, that is, the agent will not buy or sell a security that would lead to a negative expected utility. In the case of an informed agent, the utility of security $g$ at price $p$ will reflect the choice that the agent makes to transact, depending on information $Z$: $\mathbb{E}[U(p,g)\mathbb{I}_{\mathbb{E}[U(p,g)|Z]>0}]$.

Dang, Gorton, and Holmström define the notion of the **value of information** as the difference between the utility for an informed agent, and that for a non-informed agent. We can define this concept precisely as the difference:

$$V(p,g) = \mathbb{E}[U(p,g)\mathbb{I}_{\mathbb{E}[U(p,g)|Z]>0}] - \mathbb{E}[U(p,g)]\mathbb{I}_{\mathbb{E}[U(p,g)]>0}.$$

In the particular case of risk neutrality, no inter-temporal preferences, and full information for insiders, we will see that the value of information coincides with the information sensitivity as we have defined it earlier.

We assume that $Z = Y$ so that when informed agents obtain information, they get full information on the underlying cash flow $Y$. In addition, we assume for buyers $U_B(p,g) = g(Y) - p$ and $U_S(p,g) = p - g(Y)$. Reflecting these assumptions we can write the value of information for buyers and sellers as

$$V_B(p,g) = \mathbb{E}\left[(g(Y) - p)\mathbb{I}_{g(Y)-p>0}\right] - \mathbb{E}\left[(g(Y) - p)\right]\mathbb{I}_{\mathbb{E}[g(Y)]-p>0},$$

and

$$V_S(p,g) = \mathbb{E}\left[(p - g(Y))\mathbb{I}_{p-g(Y)>0}\right] - \mathbb{E}\left[(p - g(Y))\right]\mathbb{I}_{p-\mathbb{E}[g(Y)]>0}.$$

**Proposition 4.20** (Dand–Gorton–Hölmstrom Value of Information) *Given a security design $g$ at a price $p$, the value of information to the buyer and to the seller is the same, $V_B(p,g) = V_S(p,g) = V(p,g)$ and is equal to $\Pi_L(p,g) \wedge \Pi_R(p,g)$. Besides, when $p \leq \mathbb{E}[g(Y)]$ then $V(p,g) = \Pi_L(p,g)$ and when $p \geq \mathbb{E}[g(Y)]$ then $V(p,g) = \Pi_R(p,g)$.*

***Proof*** In order to show the first part of the statement, we calculate $V_B - V_S$ and we obtain the result

$$\begin{aligned} V_B(p,g) - V_S(p,g) &= \mathbb{E}\left[(g(Y) - p)\mathbb{I}_{g(Y)>p} - (1 - \mathbb{I}_{g(Y)>p})(p - g(Y))\right] \\ &\quad - \mathbb{E}\left[(g(Y) - p)\mathbb{I}_{\mathbb{E}[g(Y)]>p} - (1 - \mathbb{I}_{\mathbb{E}[g(Y)]>p})(p - g(Y))\right] \\ &= 0 \end{aligned}$$

after a few simplifications. We will hence simply write $V$ for the value of information.

For the second part of the statement, note that

$$V(p,g) = V_B(p,g) = \Pi_R(p,g) - \mathbb{E}\left[(g(Y) - p)\right]\mathbb{I}_{\mathbb{E}[g(Y)]>p},$$

and since we know that $\Pi_R - \Pi_L = \mathbb{E}[g(Y)] - p$, $V$ can also be written as

$$V(p, g) = \Pi_L(p, g) - \mathbb{E}[(p - g(Y))] \mathbb{I}_{\mathbb{E}[g(Y)]<p}.$$

The second term in the first expression of $V$ vanishes when $p \geq \mathbb{E}[g(Y)]$ so that in that case, $V = \Pi_R$. The second term in the second expression of $V_B$ vanishes when $p \leq \mathbb{E}[g(Y)]$ and in that case $V = \Pi_L$. At the same time, we know that when $p \geq \mathbb{E}[g(Y)]$, then $\Pi_R \leq \Pi_L$, and when $p \leq \mathbb{E}[g(Y)]$ then $\Pi_R \geq \Pi_L$. Hence, we can write $V = \Pi_L \wedge \Pi_R$. □

We define the minimum and maximum cash flow values

$$g_m = \inf_{y \in [y_b, y_g]} g(y), \quad g_M = \sup_{y \in [y_b, y_g]} g(y).$$

We can derive the following corollary:

**Lemma 4.3** *The following hold for any security design $g$:*

*i. If $p \leq g_m$ or $p \geq g_M$ then $V(p, g) = 0$.*
*ii. $V$ is maximum as a function of $p$ for $p = \mathbb{E}[g(Y)]$.*

***Proof*** If $p \leq g_m$ then $g(y) - p \geq 0$ for all $y$ in the support of $Y$, and hence $\Pi_L(p, g) = 0$ and $V(p, g) = 0$. Symmetrically, if $p \geq g_M$ then $g(y) - p \leq 0$ and $\Pi_R(p, g) = 0$, and $V(p, g) = 0$.

We know that for $p < \mathbb{E}[g(Y)]$, $V(p, g) = \Pi_L(p, g)$ and therefore $V$ is increasing in $p$. When $p > \mathbb{E}[g(Y)]$ then $V(p, g) = \Pi_R(p, g)$, which is decreasing. Therefore, $V$ is maximal at $p = \mathbb{E}[g(Y)]$. □

#### 4.3.3.2 Quasi-debt and Security Design

We can now look into the problem of security design more specifically. We have already defined the space of possible designs $\mathcal{L}$ and are now going to define a few additional subspaces.

First, the set of quasi-debt securities consists of securities that behave like the underlying collateral up to a point, a given threshold, and then always stay above that threshold. More formally we define the set of quasi-debt securities $\mathcal{L}_a^{QD}$, depending on a positive threshold $a$, as all the functions $f$ in $\mathcal{L}$ such that there exists a continuous positive $z$ with $z(0) = 0$ such that for all $x$,

$$f(x) = \mathbb{I}_{x \leq a} + (a + z(x - a))\mathbb{I}_{x > a}.$$

As far as the total underlying cash flow amount is less than $a$, then the quasi-debt pays it entirely. Above that limit, it pays more than this limit and less than the entire available amount.

We now define the set of standard debt securities with a threshold $a$ quite simply as

$$\mathcal{L}_a^{SD} = \{f \in \mathcal{L} : \forall x \in [y_b, y_g],\ f(x) = x \wedge a\}.$$

Finally, we define the set of security designs such that their expected payoffs are a given constant:

$$\mathcal{L}_w^0 = \{f \in \mathcal{L} : \mathbb{E}[f(Y)] = w\}.$$

We are going to look for particular designs that solve

$$\min_{f \in \mathcal{L}_w^0} \Pi_L(p, f)$$

or

$$\min_{f \in \mathcal{L}_w^0} \Pi_R(p, f),$$

and minimize the informational sensitivity or the value of inside information.

The following result tells us that quasi-debt contracts minimize the information sensitivity in the loss region.

**Lemma 4.4** *Given $p$ and $w$ so that $p \le w$, for any $f \in \mathcal{L}_w^0$, it is possible to find a design $f_p^{QD} \in \mathcal{L}_p^{QD} \cap \mathcal{L}_{w^*}^0$, with $w \le w^* \le \mathbb{E}[Y]$, such that $\Pi_L(p, f_p^{QD}) \le \Pi_L(p, f)$.*

***Proof*** First, let us establish that one can find $f_p^{QD} \in \mathcal{L}_p^{QD} \cap \mathcal{L}_w^0$. We use the definition of $\mathcal{L}_p^{QD}$ and write that there must exist some continuous positive function $z$ with $z(0) = 0$ so that for $x \in [y_b, y_g]$:

$$f_p^{QD}(x) = x\mathbb{I}_{x \le p} + (p + z(x - p))\mathbb{I}_{x > p}.$$

For $f_p^{QD}$ to belong to $\mathcal{L}_w^0$, we have the requirement that $\mathbb{E}[f_p^{QD}(Y)] = w$. Hence, there must exist $z$ such that

$$\mathbb{E}[Y\mathbb{I}_{Y \le p} + (p + z(Y - p))\mathbb{I}_{Y > p}] = w,$$

which is equivalent to

$$\mathbb{E}[z(Y - p)\mathbb{I}_{Y > p}] = w - \mathbb{E}[Y \wedge p].$$

The function $z$ is positive, so for it to exist we must have $w \ge \mathbb{E}[Y \wedge p]$. Since we have assumed $p \le w$, we know that is the case. Otherwise, it may not be possible to find a general quasi-debt contract satisfying these constraints.

Now let us see whether we can find a $z$ so that $f_p^{QD} \in \mathcal{L}_{w^*}^0$. We would need to set $z$ so that

$$w^* = \mathbb{E}[z(Y - p)\mathbb{I}_{Y > p}] + \mathbb{E}[Y \wedge p].$$

The maximal $z$ that can be chosen is the identity (for $f_p^{QD}$ to remain a proper security design), in which case the RHS term can be written as

$$\begin{aligned}&\mathbb{E}[(Y-p)\mathbb{I}_{Y>p}]+\mathbb{E}[Y\wedge p]\\&=\mathbb{E}[(Y-p)\mathbb{I}_{Y>p}]+\mathbb{E}[(Y-p)\mathbb{I}_{Y\leq p}]\quad=\mathbb{E}[Y].\end{aligned}$$

Therefore, since $w^*\leq\mathbb{E}[Y]$, it is possible to find $z$ such that $f_p^{QD}\in\mathcal{L}_{w^*}^0$.

Note that for $f_p^{QD}\in\mathcal{L}_p^{QD}$, by definition for all $y$ in its domain of definition $f_p^{QD}(y)<p$ is equivalent to $y<p$, and if $y<p$ then $f_p^{QD}(y)=y$. Hence, we have

$$\begin{aligned}\Pi_L(p,f_p^{QD})&=\mathbb{E}\left[(p-f_p^{QD}(Y))\mathbb{I}_{f_p^{QD}(Y)<p}\right]\\&=\mathbb{E}\left[(p-Y)\mathbb{I}_{Y<p}\right].\end{aligned}$$

Now let us consider a security design $f$ that belongs to $\mathcal{L}_w^0$ but not to $\mathcal{L}_p^{QD}$. There are two possible reasons why a function $f$ would not be a quasi-debt (and these reasons are not mutually exclusive): there exists some $x\leq p$ such that $f(x)<p$ or there exists some $x>p$ such that $f(x)<p$.

In this first case, we can further distinguish between whether $f(p)=p$ and $f(p)<p$. When $f(p)=p$ then for all $y$ in the relevant domain, $f(y)<p$ is equivalent to $y<p$. If $f(p)<p$ then $\{y:y<p\}\subset\{y:f(y)<p\}$. Hence, $\mathbb{I}_{f(Y)<p}\geq\mathbb{I}_{Y<p}$. In addition, since for all $y$, $f(y)\leq y$, we have $p-Y\leq p-f(Y)$ and therefore $(p-Y)\mathbb{I}_{Y<p}\leq(p-f(Y))\mathbb{I}_{f(Y)<p}$. Integrating, we obtain that

$$\Pi_L(p,f_p^{QD})\leq\Pi_L(p,f).$$

In the second case, let us define the set $A_p^f=\{x\geq p:f(x)\leq p\}$. Also, we are considering that for all $x\leq p$, $f(x)=f_p^{QD}(x)=x$ since if that is not the case we have seen above that it contributes to increasing the information sensitivity. We can write for all $y$:

$$\mathbb{I}_{f(y)<p}=\mathbb{I}_{\{y<p\}\cup\{\{y\geq p\}\cap y\in A_p^f\}}$$

and therefore

$$(p-f(y))\mathbb{I}_{f(y)<p}=(p-y)\mathbb{I}_{y<p}+(p-f(y))\mathbb{I}_{y\in A_p^f}.$$

Integrating, we can write

$$\Pi_L(p,f)=\Pi_L(p,f_p^{QD})+\mathbb{E}\left[(p-f(Y))\mathbb{I}_{Y\in A_p^f}\right].$$

The term in the expectation is positive and this concludes the proof. □

We can now derive a comparable result for the information value in the gain region.

**Lemma 4.5** *Define $D_w$ as a solution to $\mathbb{E}[Y \wedge D_w] = w$.*

*i.* $\Pi_R(p, f)$ *where* $f \in \mathcal{L}_w^0$ *and* $w \leq p < D_w$ *is minimal for* $f \in \mathcal{L}_p^{QD}$*;*
*ii. with* $p = D_w$*, it is minimal for* $f \in \mathcal{L}_{D_w}^{SD}$*;and*
*iii. with* $p > D_w$*, any security with* $g_M \leq p$ *has information sensitivity of 0.*

***Proof*** To show the first statement, we compare $\Pi_R(p, f)$ for a generic $f$ with $\Pi_R(p, f_p^{QD})$ where both $f$ and $f_p^{QD}$ and in $\mathcal{L}_w^0$ and $f_p^{QD} \in \mathcal{L}_p^{QD}$.

By definition there exists a positive continuous $z$ with $z(0) = 0$ such that for all $x$

$$(f_p^{QD}(x) - p)\mathbb{I}_{f_p^{QD}(x) \geq p} = (p + z(x - p))\mathbb{I}_{x \geq p}.$$

At the same time, since $f_p^{QD} \in \mathcal{L}_w^0$ we have the constraint that $\mathbb{E}[f_p^{QD}(Y)] = w$. A first question is whether one can find a quasi-debt security with these constraints. The constraint is equivalent to

$$\mathbb{E}[z(Y - p)\mathbb{I}_{Y \geq p}] = w - \mathbb{E}[Y \wedge p].$$

Since $D_w = \mathbb{E}[Y \wedge D_w]$ and $p < D_w$, $\mathbb{E}[Y \wedge p] \leq \mathbb{E}[Y \wedge D_w]$ and therefore $w - \mathbb{E}[Y \wedge P] \geq 0$ and a function $z$ satisfying the conditions can be found.

Assuming that $f$ is not in $\mathcal{L}_p^{QD}$, as in the proof of Lemma 4.4 we can consider two cases:

1. For all $x \leq p$, $f(x) = x$ and there exists $y > p$ such that $f(y) < p$ or
2. There exists $x \leq p$ such that $f(x) < x$.

In the first case, note that $f(x) \geq p$ implies $x \geq p$. Given $x \geq p$, we can define $f$ as follows for some continuous and positive functions $h$ and $k$ such that $h(0) = k(0) = 0$, and $k$ is not uniformly equal to 0:

$$f(x) = p + h(x - p) - k(x - p).$$

Hence, we have

$$\begin{aligned}
\Pi_R(p, f) &= \mathbb{E}[(f(Y) - p)\mathbb{I}_{f(Y) > p}] \\
&= \mathbb{E}[(f(Y) - p)\mathbb{I}_{f(Y) > p}\mathbb{I}_{Y > p}] \\
&= \mathbb{E}[(h(Y - p) - k(Y - p))\mathbb{I}_{f(Y) > p}] \\
&= \mathbb{E}[h(Y - p)\mathbb{I}_{f(Y) > p}].
\end{aligned}$$

By setting $z = \frac{h}{2}$, we can find a quasi-debt $f_p^{QD}$ such that $\Pi_R(p, f_p^{QD}) < \Pi_R(p, f)$. If $f$ is defined in such a way that $h = 0$, then the inequality is weak.

We now turn to the second case, and consider there exists $x \leq p$ such that $f(x) < x$, which also includes the possible case where $f(p) < p$. For $x > p$, $f$ behaves like a quasi-debt security so we can consider that using the same decomposition as before for $x > p$ and $f(x) \geq p$, $f(x) = p + h(x)$. If $f(p) = p$,

$$\Pi_R(p, f) = \mathbb{E}[h(Y - p)\mathbb{I}_{Y>p}].$$

If $f(p) < p$ then setting $h(y) = 0$ when $f(y) < p$,

$$\Pi_R(p, f) = \mathbb{E}[h(Y - p)\mathbb{I}_{f(Y)>p}].$$

In both cases, if we define $f_p^{QD}$ by setting $z = \frac{h}{2}$ then $\Pi_R(p, f_p^{QD}) < \Pi_R(p, f)$.

For the second statement in the lemma, we consider a standard debt security $f_{D_w}^{SD}$. We have $f_{D_w}^{SD}(x) = x \wedge D_w$ by definition. We can write

$$\Pi_R(D_w, f_{D_w}^{SD}) = \mathbb{E}[(Y \wedge D_w - D_w)\mathbb{I}_{Y \wedge D_w > D_w}] = 0.$$

Therefore, if $p = D_w$ then $f_p^{SD}$ minimizes $\Pi_R$.

Now turning to the third statement, we use Lemma 4.3 and note that if $p \geq g_M$ then for any security design $f$, $V(p, f) = 0$. Besides, with the assumptions for our proof,

$$\mathbb{E}[Y \wedge D_w] = w = \mathbb{E}[f(Y)]$$

hence $D_w \geq w$ and since $p > D_w$, $p \geq \mathbb{E}[f(Y)]$.

Using Proposition 4.20, we know that when the price is under the security design's expected payoff, $\Pi_R \leq \Pi_L$. Therefore, $V(p, f) = 0$ implies $\Pi_R(p, f) = 0$. □

Thanks to Lemmas 4.4 and 4.5 we have established that quasi-debt minimizes the value of information on both sides, for $\Pi_L$ and for $\Pi_R$. This result does not depend on the specific form of the distribution of $Y$. When the price is set at the face value, then standard debt is the unique solution that minimizes information sensitivity.

**Proposition 4.21** (Dang–Gorton–Holmström Quasi-Debt Minimizing Information Sensitivity) *Within $\mathcal{L}_w^0$, quasi-debt minimizes the value of information $V = \Pi_L \wedge \Pi_R$ for all prices.*

#### 4.3.3.3 Optimal Contract Design

Equipped with the prior results, we can now turn to an application to an optimal contract design. So far, we have discussed securities, that is, some payoff function relative to an underlying asset, without factoring in a specific price. We will now focus on the notion of optimal contract, which specifies a security as well as a price. The price will be endogenously determined by the agents.

We consider two agents A and B, which are risk-neutral but differ in inter-temporal preferences. There are two periods 0 and 1. Given two cash flows $X_0 = X_1$ taking place at periods 0 and 1, agent A is indifferent: $\mathbb{E}[U_A(X_0)] = \mathbb{E}[U_A(X_1)]$. However, Agent B has a preference for later consumption: there is $\alpha > 1$ such that $\alpha\mathbb{E}[U_A(X_0)] = \mathbb{E}[U_A(X_1)]$.

Agent A is endowed with a project that returns $Y$ in period 1, with $Y$ following the same distribution as in the prior subsections. Agent A can acquire information on the project at the cost of $\gamma$, and if it acquires information then it can observe $Y$ directly. Agent B is endowed with perishable goods in period 0. Given Agent B's preferences, there is value in trading whereby Agent B could exchange some of its wealth at time 0 for a contract promising some return at time 1.

A contract is a pair $(p, f) \in \mathbb{R}^+ \times \mathcal{L}$ that specifies the amount of wealth $p$ transferred from Agent B to Agent A at period 0, and the amount $f(Y)$ transferred from Agent A to Agent B at period 1. An optimal contract is a contract that maximizes Agent B's utility given that Agent's A utility from the contract is greater than its reserve utility $\mathbb{E}[U_A(0, Y)]$ (of not trading). We will assume the agents are risk-neutral, so that $U_A$ and $U_B$ are the identity function.

Hence, we are looking for a Nash equilibrium in the following game played at period 0:

1. Agent B makes a take-it-or-leave-it offer of $(p, g)$ to Agent A,
2. Agent A chooses whether or not to acquire or produce private information, and
3. Agent A accepts or not.

The fact that B proposes a certain contract is similar to the notion of reverse inquiry in new issuance that we have pointed out in Chap. 2. If A accepts, then it gets $p$ units of goods at time 0, while B consumes $w - p$ at that time. At time 1, Agent A consumes $Y - g(Y)$ and B gets $g(Y)$. If there is no trade, then the agents consume what they have, respectively, $Y$ at period 1 for A and $w$ at period 0 for B. We assume that $w > y_b$ in order to avoid the trivial case where Agent B's entire wealth can be invested in a guaranteed cash flow.

Note that Agent A in this context is a seller, while B is a buyer. The values of information metrics defined earlier as $V_B$ and $V_S$ are applicable. Recall that the value of information gives us the gain in obtaining perfect knowledge of the underlying cash flow. For the seller, who is risk-neutral without inter-temporal preferences, we have $V_S = V_B = V = \Pi_L \wedge \Pi_R$. If a contract $(p, f)$ is such that $V(p, f) < \gamma$, then the benefit of acquiring the information does not compensate for its cost, and Agent A will not decide to acquire that information.

We define the entire project security design $e$ in a straightforward fashion: $e(x) = x$ for all $x$. We consider the contract $(\mathbb{E}[Y], e)$, where B would buy the whole project at its expected payoff. Let us consider some generic contract $(p, g)$, with $p \leq \mathbb{E}[g(Y)]$. We can write

$$V(p, g) = \Pi_R(p, g) = \mathbb{E}[(g(Y) - p)\mathbb{I}_{g(Y) \geq p}].$$

Since by definition $g \leq e$, we know that for all possible $g$ $\Pi_R(p, g) \leq \Pi_R(p, e)$. In addition, we know $V$ is maximal with $p = \mathbb{E}[Y]$ thanks to Lemma 4.3 and therefore

$V(\mathbb{E}[Y], e)$ is the maximal information value across all contracts (prices and security designs). We can now define the maximum information value as $\bar{\gamma} = V(\mathbb{E}[Y], e)$.

**Lemma 4.6** *Suppose $\bar{\gamma} < \gamma$. Any contract $(p, f)$ so that $\mathbb{E}[f(Y)] = \mathbb{E}[Y] \wedge w$ and $p = \mathbb{E}[f(Y)]$ maximizes $\mathbb{E}[U_B(w - p, f(Y))]$.*

***Proof*** Since the cost of acquiring information is greater than the maximum benefit that can be derived from this information, Agent A will not decide to acquire information. If Agent B proposes contract $(\mathbb{E}[Y], e)$ then it is a best response for Agent A to not acquire information, sell, and get paid $\mathbb{E}[Y]$.[6]

If $w \geq \mathbb{E}[Y]$ then Agent B can pay for everything and it is optimal for trade to take place with contract $(\mathbb{E}[Y], e)$. Indeed, let us consider that Agent B proposes a contract $(\mathbb{E}[f(Y)], f)$. As far as the price paid by B verifies $p = \mathbb{E}[f(Y)]$ then Agent A's reserve expected utility constraint is met since

$$\mathbb{E}[U_A(\mathbb{E}[f(Y)], Y - f(Y))] = \mathbb{E}[Y] = \mathbb{E}[U_A(0, Y)].$$

Agent B's expected utility can be written as

$$\begin{aligned}\mathbb{E}[U_B(w - p, f(Y))] &= \mathbb{E}[w - \mathbb{E}[f(Y)] + \alpha f(Y)] \\ &= w + (\alpha - 1)\mathbb{E}[f(Y)].\end{aligned}$$

This quantity is increasing in $f$ and hence maximized by $e$. In this case, Agent B increases its utility by $(\alpha - 1)\mathbb{E}[Y]$ through trading.

If $w < \mathbb{E}[Y]$ then B buys what it can afford. Indeed in that case Agent A's reserve expected utility constraint is still the same but in addition we must have $\mathbb{E}[f(Y)] \leq w$. Agent B's utility is written the same way as above but now the maximum is reached for any $f \in \mathcal{L}_w^0$. Agent B's utility is increased by $w(\alpha - 1)$ through trading in this case. □

If information acquisition is very expensive, then it does not act as a constraint on the security design. Note that one can interpret the security design $e$ as a form of degenerate debt: $e = f_{y_g}^{SD}$.

In order to better express the optimization problem solved by the agents, we now define a few contract sets. First, the set of all possible contracts is

$$\Lambda = \{(p, f) \in \mathbb{R}^+ \times \mathcal{L}\}.$$

Then, define the set of contracts that do not trigger information acquisition

$$\Lambda_\gamma^N = \{(p, f) \in \Lambda : V(p, f) \leq \gamma\}.$$

[6]Another best response would also be not to trade.

Let us also define the set of security designs such that they do not trigger information acquisition when priced at the expected payoff value

$$\mathcal{L}_\gamma^N = \{f \in \mathcal{L} : (\mathbb{E}[f(Y)], f) \in \Lambda_\gamma^N\}.$$

Finally, we define the set of security designs for which the expected cash flow is within a budget constraint:

$$\mathcal{L}_{w-}^0 = \{f \in \mathcal{L} : \mathbb{E}[f(Y)] \le w\} \supset \mathcal{L}_w^0.$$

**Lemma 4.7** *Assume* $\gamma < \bar{\gamma}$ *and* $\Pi_L(w + \gamma, e) \ge \gamma$. *Let* $\nu$ *verify* $\gamma = \Pi_L(\nu, e)$. *Then* $\mathbb{E}[f(Y)]$, *with* $f \in \mathcal{L}_\gamma^N \cap \mathcal{L}_{w-}^0$, *is maximal for* $f \in \mathcal{L}_\nu^{QD}$ *with* $\mathbb{E}[f(Y)] = w \wedge \nu$.

This lemma expresses that the maximal amount that Agent B can acquire without triggering an information acquisition (value of information less than $\gamma$) and without giving out free rents to Agent A (trading at a "fair" price such that $p = \mathbb{E}[f(Y)]$) is a quasi-debt contract that satisfies particular conditions. The constraint that relates the budget with information acquisition cost has been added in order to ensure that certain solutions exist.

***Proof*** Since $\gamma < \bar{\gamma}$, then $\Pi_L$ is not maximal and for any security design $f$ one can find $\nu$ such that $\gamma = \Pi_L(\nu, f)$.

In order to show the lemma, we will pick a generic security design $f \in \mathcal{L}_\gamma^N \cap \mathcal{L}_{w-}^0$ and show that its expected payoff is less if it is not a quasi-debt security with the particular features from the lemma.

First, one needs to show that one can find some $f \in \mathcal{L}_\gamma^N$ such that $(\nu, f) \in \Lambda_\gamma^N$. In other words, setting the price as the smallest between $\nu$ and $w$, one can still find a security design that will not trigger acquisition information and that is priced at the expected cash flow. The following need to be verified:

$$\begin{aligned} \gamma &= \Pi_L(\nu, f), \\ \gamma &\ge V(\nu \wedge w, f), \\ \nu \wedge w &= \mathbb{E}[f(Y)]. \end{aligned}$$

The first equation is the definition for $\nu$, the second one expresses that the contract does not trigger information acquisition, and the third one that the contract is priced at its expected payoff.

Given any $\nu$ and $f$ we know that if $\gamma = \Pi_L(\nu, f)$ then $\gamma \ge V(\nu \wedge w, f)$ since $\Pi_L$ is increasing. Therefore, $V(\nu \wedge w, f) \le \Pi_L(\nu \wedge w, f) \le \gamma$, and the second equation is verified.

In order to find a security design that can verify the first and third equations, we first consider $\nu_\gamma$ that solves $\gamma = \mathbb{E}[(\nu_\gamma - Y)\mathbb{I}_{Y<\nu_\gamma}]$, or equivalently, $\gamma = \Pi_L(\nu_\gamma, e)$. This $\nu_\gamma$ is determined by the distribution of $Y$ and by $\gamma$. For any quasi-debt $f_{\nu_\gamma}^{QD} \in \mathcal{L}_{\nu_\gamma}^{QD}$ we have $\gamma = \Pi_L(\nu_\gamma, f_{\nu_\gamma}^{QD})$ since this expression does not depend on the shape of

$f^{QD}_{\nu_\gamma}$ on its domain above $\nu_\gamma$. Hence, all these quasi-debt contracts verify the first equation.

Now we can express the expected payoff from any one of these security designs, and use the expression of $\gamma$ as a function of $\nu_\gamma$. As per the definition of quasi-debt, the following is true for any positive $z$ such that $z(0) = 0$ and $\nu_\gamma + z(x - \nu_\gamma) \leq x$:

$$\begin{aligned}\mathbb{E}[f^{QD}_{\nu_\gamma}(Y)] &= \mathbb{E}[Y\mathbb{I}_{Y\leq\nu_\gamma}] + \mathbb{E}\left[(\nu_\gamma + z(Y-\nu_\gamma))\mathbb{I}_{Y>\nu_\gamma}\right] \\ &= \mathbb{E}[Y\mathbb{I}_{Y\leq\nu_\gamma}] + \nu_\gamma(1-\mathbb{P}[Y\leq\nu_\gamma]) + \mathbb{E}\left[z(Y-\nu_\gamma)\mathbb{I}_{Y>\nu_\gamma}\right] \\ &= \nu_\gamma - \gamma + \mathbb{E}\left[z(Y-\nu_\gamma)\mathbb{I}_{Y>\nu_\gamma}\right].\end{aligned}$$

The values of $w$ and $\nu_\gamma$ are fixed, based on the characteristics of Agent B and the project's return distribution. There are two cases to consider, either $w > \nu_\gamma$ or $w \leq \nu_\gamma$.

In the first case, one then needs to set $z$ so that

$$\mathbb{E}\left[z(Y-\nu_\gamma)\mathbb{I}_{Y>\nu_\gamma}\right] = \gamma,$$

so

$$\mathbb{E}[f^{QD}_{\nu_\gamma}(Y)] = w \wedge \nu_\gamma = \nu_\gamma.$$

The function $z$ could be set maximally so that $z(x - \nu_\gamma) = x - \nu_\gamma$. In that case, using the expression that defines $\nu_\gamma$, we have

$$\begin{aligned}\mathbb{E}\left[(Y-\nu_\gamma)\mathbb{I}_{Y>\nu_\gamma}\right] &= \mathbb{E}\left[Y-\nu_\gamma\right] - \mathbb{E}\left[(Y-\nu_\gamma)\mathbb{I}_{Y\leq\nu_\gamma}\right] \\ &= \mathbb{E}\left[Y\right] - \nu_\gamma + \gamma.\end{aligned}$$

Separately, since we have assumed that $\gamma < \bar{\gamma}$, we know that

$$\Pi_L(\nu_\gamma, e) < \Pi_L(\mathbb{E}[Y], e),$$

and therefore $\nu_\gamma \leq \mathbb{E}[Y]$ since $\Pi_L$ is increasing in its first argument. As a result, the maximal $z_M$ that can be chosen is such that

$$\mathbb{E}\left[z_M(Y-\nu_\gamma)\mathbb{I}_{Y>\nu_\gamma}\right] \geq \gamma,$$

and hence one can find a $z$ so that $f^{QD}_{\nu_\gamma}$ satisfies all three equations.

In the second case, where $w \leq \nu_\gamma$, one can set $z$ so that

$$\mathbb{E}\left[z(Y-\nu_\gamma)\mathbb{I}_{Y>\nu_\gamma}\right] = w - \nu_\gamma + \gamma,$$

in order to have

$$\mathbb{E}[f^{QD}_{\nu_\gamma}(Y)] = w \wedge \nu_\gamma = w.$$

We already know that $z_M$ can be chosen so that

$$\mathbb{E}\left[z_M(Y-\nu_\gamma)\mathbb{I}_{Y>\nu_\gamma}\right] \geq \gamma \geq w - \nu_\gamma + \gamma.$$

However, if $w - \nu_\gamma + \gamma$ was negative, it would not be possible to find a $z$ small enough. This condition effectively forces a relationship between $w$ and $\gamma$, which are given. Agent B's endowment needs to be large enough, otherwise it is not possible to purchase a contract that would pay enough quasi-debt and not trigger information acquisition. Using the fact that $\Pi$ is increasing and $\Pi_L(\nu_\gamma, e) = \gamma$, we can express this particular constraint without involving $\nu_\gamma$ as $\Pi_L(w + \gamma, e) \geq \gamma$.

Now that we have shown there exists security designs that belong to the space in which we are looking for an optimal design, we can turn to the actual optimality proof.

Assume we are given a security design $f \in \mathcal{L}_\gamma^N \cap \mathcal{L}_{w-}^0$, with $\gamma = \Pi_L(\nu, f)$ and $\mathbb{E}[f(Y)] = \nu \wedge w$. We treat two cases: $w < \nu$ and $\nu \geq w$.

Consider $\nu^*$ solving $\gamma = \Pi_L(\nu^*, f^*)$ for some security design $f^* \in \mathcal{L}_\nu^{QD}$, such that $\nu^* \geq \nu$. We must have $\Pi_L(\nu^*, e) \leq \bar{\gamma}$ and therefore $\nu^* \leq \mathbb{E}[Y]$. Thanks to Lemma 4.4, we can find $f^* \in \mathcal{L}_\nu^{QD} \cap \mathcal{L}_{\nu^*}^0$ such that $\Pi(\nu, f^*) \leq \gamma$, and $\Pi(\nu^*, f^*) = \gamma$ with $\nu^* \geq \nu$, and $\mathbb{E}[f^*(Y)] = \nu^*$. The lemma's result hence holds in this first case.

Now, in the second case, we have $\mathbb{E}[f(Y)] = w$, and since $\Pi_L$ is increasing and $\Pi_L(\nu, f) = \gamma$, we have $\Pi_L(w, f) \leq \gamma$. We can also apply Lemma 4.4 but keeping the expectation constant: we find $f^*$ in $\mathcal{L}_w^{QD} \cap \mathcal{L}_w^0$, so that $\mathbb{E}[f^*(Y)] = w$ and $\Pi_L(w, f^*) \leq \gamma$, and the lemma holds as well in this case. □

**Lemma 4.8** *Given an arbitrary price $p$, a contract that gets traded $(p, f) \in \Lambda_\gamma^N$ such that $f \in \mathcal{L}_p^{QD} \cap \mathcal{L}_{p-}^0$ maximizes Agent B's utility at that price.*

In order to show this lemma, we start from a generic security design and see how it gets successively improved in terms of utility through alterations that turn it into a quasi-debt with the characteristics detailed in the statement. With a given trade price, and given that the contract is traded, we know that Agent B's utility increases with the expected amount of cash flow it can recover at period 1.

***Proof*** First, let us consider a contract $(p, f) \notin \Lambda_\gamma^N$. In this situation, since $V(p, f) > \gamma$, Agent A pays $\gamma$ and acquires information. Define $T_{(p,f)}$ as the event "a trade takes place with contract $(p, f)$". In this current situation, $T_{(p,f)} = \{f(Y) \leq p\}$. We have

$$\mathbb{E}[f(Y)|T_{(p,f)}] = \frac{\mathbb{E}[f(Y)\mathbb{I}_{f(Y)\leq p}]}{\mathbb{P}[f(Y) \leq p]}.$$

We can construct an alternative security design $\bar{f}$ so that $\bar{f}(x) = f(x) \wedge p$. In this case, we have $\mathbb{E}[\bar{f}(Y)] \leq p$, and hence thanks to Proposition 4.20, $V(p, \bar{f}) = \Pi_R(p, \bar{f})$. We have

$$\Pi_R(p, \bar{f}) = \mathbb{E}[(\bar{f}(Y) - p)\mathbb{I}_{\bar{f}(Y)\geq p}] = 0,$$

and Agent A does not acquire information. In addition, Agent A agrees to trade $(p, \bar{f})$ since the price is higher than the expected payoff, so $\mathbb{P}[T_{(p,\bar{f})}] = 1$. Let us now look at the expected payoff to B conditional upon trading:

$$\begin{aligned}\mathbb{E}[\bar{f}(Y)|T_{(p,\bar{f})}] &= \mathbb{E}[\bar{f}(Y)] = \mathbb{E}[f(Y) \wedge p] \\ &= \mathbb{E}[f(Y)\mathbb{I}_{f(Y)\leq p}] + p\mathbb{P}[f(Y) > p].\end{aligned}$$

Note that one always has $p \geq \mathbb{E}[f(Y)|f(Y) \leq p]$. Hence

$$\mathbb{E}[f(Y)\mathbb{I}_{f(Y)\leq p}] + p\mathbb{P}[f(Y) > p] \geq \frac{\mathbb{E}[f(Y)\mathbb{I}_{f(Y)\leq p}]}{\mathbb{P}[f(Y) \leq p]}.$$

This shows that

$$\mathbb{E}[\bar{f}(Y)|T_{(p,\bar{f})}] \geq \mathbb{E}[f(Y)|T_{(p,f)}].$$

Now, let us see how we can even further improve our security design by making it into standard debt $f_p^{SD}$. The design $\bar{f}$ was already somehow debt-like, by having a maximum payoff set to $p$, but now we maximize the amount of cash flow paid that is less than $p$. Let us assume that $\bar{f}$ was not already a standard debt security: there exists $x$ such that $\bar{f}(x) < x$ for some $x \leq p$. Hence,

$$\mathbb{E}[f_p^{SD}(Y)] \geq \mathbb{E}[\bar{f}(Y)].$$

In addition, we know that $\mathbb{E}[f_p^{SD}(Y)] \leq p$ and as a result trading takes place: $\mathbb{P}[T_{(p,f_p^{SD})}] = 1$. The value of information is also unchanged relative to $\bar{f}$ and stays at zero.

Finally, we show that a quasi-debt design further improves Agent B's utility. Given the price $p \geq \mathbb{E}[f_p^{SD}(Y)]$, the design $f_p^{SD}$ results in a zero seller information sensitivity. By allowing the information sensitivity to increase right to the level that triggers information acquisition, we can increase the expected payoff. We define another design $f_p^{QD} \in \mathcal{L}_p^{QD}$ as $f_p^{QD}(x) = f_p^{SD}(x) + z(x-p)\mathbb{I}_{x\geq p}$, with $z$ a positive function as in the prior proof.

The value of information for the seller is $V(p, f_p^{QD}) = \Pi_R(p, f_p^{QD})$. Using our definition for the new design, we have

$$V(p, f_p^{QD}) = \mathbb{E}[z(Y-p)\mathbb{I}_{Y\geq p}],$$

and

$$\mathbb{E}[f_p^{QD}(Y)] = \mathbb{E}[f_p^{SD}(Y)] + \mathbb{E}[z(Y-p)\mathbb{I}_{Y\geq p}],$$

with the constraint that $\mathbb{E}[f_p^{QD}(Y)] \leq p$ (so that $\mathbb{P}[T_{(p,f_p^{QD})}] = 1$) and $V(p, f_p^{QD}) \leq \gamma$ (so that there is no information acquisition), which as we have seen are necessary for Agent B's utility to be optimal.

As functionals, $V$ and $\mathbb{E}[f_p^{QD}(Y)]$ are increasing relative to $z$ therefore at the maximum one of the two constraints is binding: either $z$ is such that $V(p, f_p^{QD}) = \gamma$ and $\mathbb{E}[f_p^{QD}(Y)] < p$, or $V(p, f_p^{QD}) < \gamma$ and $\mathbb{E}[f_p^{QD}(Y)] = p$. Note we do not consider the case where $\mathbb{E}[Y] \leq p$ in which case both constraints could be slack. In either case, we have found a $z$ so that

$$\mathbb{E}[f_p^{QD}(Y)] \geq \mathbb{E}[f_p^{SD}(Y)],$$

and this concludes the proof. □

We now turn to defining the optimal contract for the uninformed buyer Agent B. In order to do this, we characterize two possible strategies, which both involve quasi-debt securities.

- Strategy I: Agent B offers a contract $(p_I, f_I)$ with $f_I \in \mathcal{L}_{p_I}^{QD}$ and $p_I = \mathbb{E}[f_I(Y)]$ such that $\gamma = \Pi_L(p_I, f_I)$. The expected utility is $w + p_I(1 - \alpha)$.
- Strategy II (a "bribe"): Agent B offers a contract $(p_{II}, f_{II})$, $f_{II} \in \mathcal{L}_{p_{II}}^{QD}$, and with a price $p_{II} > \mathbb{E}[f_{II}(Y)]$, that maximizes $\sup_{p,f}(w + \alpha\mathbb{E}[f(Y)] - p)$, such that $\gamma = \Pi_R(p_{II}, f_{II})$.

With these strategies defined we can now show how the optimal prices and cash flows are determined.

**Proposition 4.22** (Dang–Gorton–Holmström Optimal Contract Design as Quasi-Debt) *At equilibrium, Agent B proposes to Agent A the contract $(p, f)$ such that*

*i. If $\bar{\gamma} \leq \gamma$, then $p = w \wedge \mathbb{E}[Y]$, and $f$ is any security design in $\mathcal{L}_p^0$.*
*ii. If $0 < \gamma < \bar{\gamma}$ then depending on the parameters $\alpha$, $\gamma$, $w$, and $\mathbb{P}[Y \in dy]$, Agent B buys quasi-debt according to either Strategy I or II.*

*Agent A does not acquire information in any equilibrium.*

***Proof*** If $\bar{\gamma} \leq \gamma$, then Lemma 4.6 is applicable: Agent A does not acquire information and the contract proposed in the Lemma maximizes Agent B's utility.

If $0 < \gamma < \bar{\gamma}$, then Lemmas 4.7 and 4.8 are applicable. We know thanks to Lemma 4.8 that a contract $(p, f)$ that maximizes utility does not trigger information acquisition. Hence, if the cost of information acquisition is not null then inducing its acquisition is a strictly dominated strategy.

Also, thanks to Lemma 4.7 if Agent B wants to avoid inducing information acquisition and wants to pay a fair price $p = \mathbb{E}[f(Y)]$ (and does not give any surplus to Agent A), then the maximal amount that can be traded is a quasi-debt contract $f_I$ with the price $p_I = \mathbb{E}[f_I(Y)] = w \wedge w$, where $\gamma = \Pi_L(\nu, e)$.

Agent B may be able to extract more utility, depending on the parameters, by "bribing" Agent A: Agent B can pay a higher price $p_I I$ such that $p_I I > \mathbb{E}[f_I I(Y)]$

where $f_I I$ is an alternate quasi-debt security design so that $\mathbb{E}[f_I I(Y)] > \mathbb{E}[f_I(Y)]$, and so that the expected utility from buying this alternate contract is maximal, still without triggering information acquisition. In other words, $p_{II}$ and $f_I I$ maximize $\sup_{p,f} (w + \alpha\mathbb{E}[f(Y)] - p)$, such that $\gamma = \Pi_R(p_{II}, f_{II})$. □

Agent B's optimal strategy is to avoid adverse selection: either by reducing the amount traded (in which case the constraint is to keep the value under that which would trigger information acquisition), or by agreeing to pay a higher price and offer a rent to Agent A. In the first case, quasi-debt is optimal because it minimizes $\Pi_L$ for a security priced at expected cash flows, without triggering information acquisition. In the second case, quasi-debt is also optimal because it has the lowest $\Pi$ for any price above expected cash flows.

As a consequence of Proposition 4.22 in the case where information acquisition cost is null, we can show that the optimal contract is standard debt. We note $F$ the inverse cumulative distribution of $Y$, so that $F(\mathbb{P}[Y \leq y]) = y$.

**Corollary 4.1** (Dang–Gorton–Holmström Optimal Contract Design as Standard Debt) *If* $\gamma = 0$, *and* $p_0 = w \wedge F\left(1 - \frac{1}{\alpha}\right)$, *then the following holds:*

*i. The optimal contract is unique: Agent B buys standard debt* $f_{p_0}^{SD}$ *with price* $p_0$.
*ii. For* $\alpha$ *large enough, Agent B buys standard debt* $f_w^{SD}$ *at price* $w$.

***Proof*** With $\gamma = 0$, Agent B follows Strategy II, and hence the optimal contract $(p, f)$ verifies the following: $f \in \mathcal{L}_p^{QD}$ and $0 = \Pi_R(p, f)$. These constraints are uniquely verified by $f = f_p^{SD}$.

Since the constraints force a relationship between $f$ and $p$, Agent B maximizes its utility over $p$ as $\sup_p \left(\alpha\mathbb{E}[f_p^{SD}(Y)] - p\right)$. If $p_0 = \arg\max_p (\alpha\mathbb{E}[Y \wedge p] - p)$, then this utility is maximized by $p_0$.

Note that $\frac{\partial}{\partial p}\mathbb{E}[Y \wedge p] = \mathbb{P}[Y \geq p]$ and hence the first-order condition for the optimal price is $\mathbb{P}[Y \geq p_0] = \frac{1}{\alpha}$. The second-order condition is $-\alpha\mathbb{P}[Y \in dy] \leq 0$ and is always verified. If the first-order condition can be verified for a $p_0 \leq w$ then this sets the price, otherwise Agent B chooses the maximal possible price, that is $w$. Hence, if the price $p_0$ verifies

$$p_0 = w \wedge F\left(1 - \frac{1}{\alpha}\right),$$

then it solves the maximization.

Given $\alpha$, one can always find $p$ small enough so that $\alpha \geq \frac{p}{\mathbb{E}[Y \wedge p]}$, hence the total value of the utility is always greater than $w$ and trading always takes place. □

Note that in the case where $w < F\left(1-\frac{1}{\alpha}\right)$, the maximal utility at the optimal price $F\left(1-\frac{1}{\alpha}\right)$ can be written as a conditional expectation:

$$\begin{aligned}
&\alpha\mathbb{E}\left[Y \wedge F\left(1-\frac{1}{\alpha}\right)\right] - F\left(1-\frac{1}{\alpha}\right) \\
&= \alpha\mathbb{E}\left[Y\mathbb{I}_{Y \leq F\left(1-\frac{1}{\alpha}\right)}\right] \\
&= (\alpha-1)\mathbb{E}\left[Y | Y \leq F\left(1-\frac{1}{\alpha}\right)\right].
\end{aligned}$$

The analysis of this model has shown that when issuing a claim, a company will prefer to structure debt (either pure debt or a variation thereof) in order to alleviate the costs related to asymmetric information. If it is informed without costs, then the optimal contract is pure debt, while if information is costly the optimal contract is quasi-debt. We will now examine the degree to which these security design models capture reality, by discussing some empirical research and practical considerations.

### 4.3.4 Discussion of Security Design Models

Given the existence of securitization, the security design models we analyzed so far have provided us with various explanations for typical senior/junior structuring as well as some reasons why securitized paper is mostly issued as debt.

Within these models, the greater the information asymmetry, the more the issuer needs to retain equity. Similarly, the greater the underlying loan risk (such as the worst case of the distribution of loan performance), the more the issuer also needs to retain equity. In other words, loans with greater risks or on which the investors have less information cost more, all else being equal, to the issuer if they want to securitize them. Hence, one would expect, in the context of these models, that lenders retain the riskier loans and securitize the safer ones, for which the market will be willing to pay a comparatively better price. The lender will also factor in their analysis the rate on the loans.

First, we discuss the degree of realism of the security design models we have presented in the prior section. These are theoretical models, and should not be expected to perfectly reflect reality, but it is important to at least compare them to some extent in that regard.

We then turn to some empirical analysis, focusing first on mortgage securities, in order to question whether securitizations in the mid-2000s were structured in manners consistent with the security design literature we have discussed. We examine two empirical papers focused on MBS, Park (2013), and Begley and Purnanandam (2017). After that, we discuss Franke, Herrmann, and Weber (2012), who carried out an empirical analysis of CDOs (in particular, CLO and CBO structures) in the European market.

As we have mentioned earlier, we are not discussing complex structures in this chapter and hence it might seem surprising that we would discuss mortgage securities, which are usually known to be extremely complex, in this section. The papers by Park (2013), Begley and Purnanandam (2017), and Franke, Herrmann, and Weber (2012) look into MBS or CDO structures, but they do not focus on the complexities in the structures, and restrict the analysis to collateral characteristics and simple senior/subordination considerations. They, therefore, constitute direct illustrations and applications of our discussion of security design as it applies to broad securitization structures. As we will see, these empirical papers provide support to the conclusions of the theoretical models we have examined: informationally insensitive securities are created and sold to the broader market, while more sensitive tranches are retained or sold to more informed investors. Looking into various aspects of securities performance also creates an opportunity to further introduce some of the aspects of structuring which will be addressed in detail in later chapters.

#### 4.3.4.1 Realism of Security Design Models

Notwithstanding the empirical validations of the security design concepts, it is worthwhile to address the degree of "realism" of these various models. As is often the case in theoretical economics, the focus is not so much on accurate valuations (as it might be in finance), but on the existence and shape of various equilibria. Hence, researchers do not try to build realistic models specifically. In the models we have discussed so far, we can nevertheless identify differences, in particular, if we look at the way in which the assets that are to be securitized are represented.

In the model from Boot and Thakor (1993), the assets returned $Y$ taking the value of $y_g$ with probability $p$ and $y_b$ with probability $1 - p$, and the informed party knew the outcome. While this type of distribution makes the calculations simpler, in spite of which the overall model is still far from trivial, it cannot be used to represent the outcome from a loan portfolio barring with the most extreme simplifications.

The model developed in Dang, Gorton, and Holmström (2015) allows greater flexibility, as $Y$ follows a continuous distribution, but bounded by $y_b$ and $y_g$. The issuer's information is the full observation of $Y$. Using a continuous distribution allows for a more refined representation of losses on a loan portfolio. However, the full information that the issuer can acquire is also not representative of how one would apprehend the risk of a loan portfolio.

In that respect, the model from DeMarzo and Duffie (1999), where the cash flow $Y$ simply follows a continuous distribution conditioned on some observation which itself could be considered bounded, appears to provide a framework that could be adapted to capture the uncertainty around loan performance as well as the kind of inside information an issuer could reasonably have. For example, while the loan originator may have information about the borrower's propensity to become delinquent, the borrowers' propensity to prepay would be affected by many external factors on which the issuer does not have privileged information. As a result, eventual losses would be random, but presumably conditioned by the private information of the issuer.

The fact that these models remain reasonably simple also implies that they can be more readily used as stepping stones to study more complex aspects of securitization or structuring. As we will see in Chap. 7, all three models can be extended to address some aspects of pooling and tranching, and, in particular, the model by DeMarzo and Duffie (1999), combined with DeMarzo (2005), can be usefully extended to account for certain structural complexities along the lines of Gauthier (2019).

Finally, it should be noted that the models that explain the existence of securitization, of which we discussed a few in the section on Optimal Funding, cannot always be directly plugged into the security design models we presented above. To explain both why securitization would take place and why it would be in the form of debt requires the development of a broader model. This broader model needs to encompass the effects explaining both securitization and debt structuring. For example, the optimal funding model in Leland (2007) includes a form of debt issuance, and would therefore interact strongly with any of the security design models we have discussed. The models in Gorton and Metrick (2013) and Gorton and Souleles (2007) also assume the issuer would retain equity.

In the cases where the optimal funding model does not include any residual cash flow retention by the issuer, then securitization and debt structuring are cleanly separated and connecting the optimal funding model with a security design model is more straightforward. In particular, the models from Iacobucci and Winter (2005) and Han, Park, and Pennacchi (2015) explain that assets would be sold for various reasons. We can then consider that the entity owning these assets issues the structures, and apply to it the security design models we have discussed.

#### 4.3.4.2 Subprime Securities and Information Sensitivity

In Park (2013), the author examines the ex ante information sensitivity of subprime securities, in order to test security design theoretical models. The main questions are first whether the structure of subprime bonds reflected the underlying collateral's risk, and second whether the market recognized the senior bonds as informationally insensitive and the subordinated bonds as informationally sensitive. We will see that Park's article illustrates that until the onset of the mortgage crisis in 2007, senior mortgage securities were not considered as having credit risk—they were informationally insensitive.

Dataset, Assumptions, and Setup

The author gathered a large database of subprime deals issued between 2004 and 2007. The data included the following:

- Collateral-related metrics, such as weighted-average coupon (WAC), FICO credit scores, loan-to-value ratios (LTV), occupancy, loan purpose, limited documentation, house type, and some other characteristics. The collective collateral characteristics are vectors $H_i$, where $H_{i,F}$ may be FICO score, $H_{i,L}$ may be LTV, etc.

- Collateral performance subsequent to issuance, at the deal level, including delinquency and loss rates.
- Tranche information at issuance, including originator name, issuer name, spread, average life, rating, and credit support. We will write credit support as $c_i$ for the various observations, rating as $r_i$, and spread as $s_i$. The collective deal and tranche characteristics are denoted $X_i$. Issuer and originator are also important and will be noted $u_i$ and $o_i$, respectively

For clarification, note that we can represent the collateral metrics data as having one line per deal (and many columns). The tranche information data has one line per deal per tranche. The two are joined by repeating the same collateral information for each tranche in a given deal. The index $i$ is meant to represent every combination of tranche and deal. For fixed effects, we note $d_x$ for effect "$x$".

Borrower credit scores and the loan-to-value ratio are obvious indicators of each loan's credit risk. Loan size, as we know, is also expected to have an impact on credit risk. Occupancy matters too, one expects that a borrower is less worried by eviction in the case of non-payment when they do not live in the house. Also, with refinancing as loan purpose, there is a risk of optimistic appraisal that could drive the LTV down artificially, also potentially indicating a worse credit.

The tranche spread collected in this dataset was the margin paid by the bonds over the floating rate index (normally 3-month Libor). The average life is calculated in a conventional simplified base-case scenario.

In the framework of the security design models, we have discussed so far, credit support would translate into the following: set $Y \in [0, 1]$ some random variable that describes the principal return from the collateral. We neglect interest here for the sake of simplicity. The loss $l$ would be the random variable $l = 1 - Y$. A straight-debt-like security design $g_c$ (for a credit support of $c$) would be $g_c(x) = (1 - c) \wedge x$. In this case, as far as the collateral returns more than $(1 - c)$, or in other words $l \leq c$, then $g_c$ gets its full face value. The "remainder" $Y - g_c(Y)$ is effectively a junior (leveraged) security exposure, since it only gets a positive cash flow if $Y > c$.

In all the security design models we have analyzed, Boot–Thakor, DeMarzo–Duffie, or Dang–Gorton–Holmström, we observed that

- The optimal design depended on the characteristics of the distribution of $Y$ and
- The valuation of the debt (the optimal security) should not be very sensitive to the collateral characteristics, while that of other, more junior, securities should be more sensitive.

In order to validate these theoretical results, Park uses the dataset discussed above to first test to what extent senior bond support is sensitive to collateral characteristics, and then measure the sensitivity of the valuation of senior and junior bonds to collateral characteristics. In addition, issuance and pricing at the time when the crisis began provide additional insights into the transition of some securities from informationally insensitive to informationally sensitive.

Tests and Analysis

The first test is to measure the impact of collateral characteristics on credit support, by computing the following regression where $\varepsilon$ is the residual:

$$c_i = \beta_0 + \beta_1 \cdot H_i + \gamma u_i + \delta d_y + \varepsilon_i.$$

Here $d_y$ is a fixed effect for the year of issuance, in order to capture trends in credit enhancement requirements over time. The focus is on the credit support for the most senior bonds and hence the regression is carried out only on the subset of AAA-rated tranches. In addition, in order to exclude the stress period from mid-2007s, only deals issued before August 2007 are included.

Trying various combinations of collateral characteristics and fixed effects, Park finds that collateral characteristics always have a significant effect on credit support at the AAA level. LTV, WAC, % of ARMs, % of California contribute to increasing subordination, while credit score and the presence of insurance wraps contribute to decreasing subordination. These variables explain about 60% of the variations in credit enhancement. Note that further down we discuss some issues in the analysis, and show that it may be possible to explain more of the variance.

Interestingly, the year and issuer fixed effects have little explanatory power, which would indicate that the credit support amount is mostly driven by collateral characteristics, and not by time trends or who the issuer was.

The author also tested a variation of this regression with an additional term $d_{u=o}$, a fixed effect for when the issuer is the same as the originator. As we have pointed out earlier, in some securitizations, the originator hires a syndicate of dealers, issues securities, and may retain some tranches, while, in other cases, the collateral is sold to a dealer who then brings the deal to market itself. There could potentially be an adverse selection where the collateral sold, rather than the one securitized, by the originator would be riskier. It turns out that the coefficient is not statistically significant.

The second test is to see to what extent senior securities are informationally insensitive. Focusing on AAA securities, are the spreads related to collateral characteristics? Using the same subset of the data as before (AAAs, before the crisis), Park computed the following regression:

$$s_i = \beta_0 + \beta_1 c_i + \beta_2 \cdot H_i + \beta_3 \cdot X_i + \gamma u_i + \delta d_q + \varepsilon_i.$$

The spread captures the valuation of the AAA securities, and the regression relates it to credit support, all the collateral characteristics, and all the tranche characteristics. The fixed effect for issuer is also included, and $d_q$ captures a quarterly fixed effect.

The first interesting outcome of the regression is that the amount of credit support is not statistically significant: provided that a bond was AAA, the market did not care about the amount of credit support that afforded it that rating. Most variables in the regression have a non-zero coefficient, and hence are economically significant, but they are not statistically significant. Variations in FICO score, LTV, and other collateral characteristics did not matter in terms of AAA bond valuations.

Certain tranche or deal-specific characteristics play an economically and somewhat statistically significant role. The bond's average life has a clear impact on spread, as one could expect: there is a spread curve whereby longer bonds tend to pay a higher spread than shorter bonds. In addition, bonds that were issued as private placements also paid a few basis points more in spread, presumably because of a smaller distribution base. Overall, the regression can explain about 60% of spread variations.

The results above show that senior bonds effectively were informationally insensitive. What about the remainder of the cash flows? Tranches rated at BBB do not fully reflect the full remainder of the cash flows, but they are a useful proxy for junior securities, much more leveraged than the AAA-rated bonds even though they do benefit from some credit support (albeit much less than the AAAs). The author hence carried out the same regression as above, but on BBB-rated tranches instead of AAAs, and still before August 2007. This regression yields very different results from the prior one:

- The amount of subordination is economically and statistically significant: the more subordination there is, the tighter the issuance spread and the more valuable the bonds.
- Average life is not significant anymore. We know that subordinated bonds were typically structured around a tighter average life target than senior bonds. While senior bonds may have been structured anywhere from 1 to over 7 years in expected average life, junior securities were usually very concentrated around 5 years.
- Collateral characteristics play a significant role, in the expected direction: a higher credit score decreases spread, a higher LTV increases it, etc.
- Issuer fixed effects are more important than on senior securities.

In spite of the fact that BBB-rated bonds benefited from credit enhancement, they were perceived to have enough residual credit risk that their valuation was strongly driven by collateral and structural characteristics: they were informationally sensitive.

Finally, Park focused on the bonds issued after August 2007, over a few months until the subprime market entirely shut down. These transactions took place at a time when there was much uncertainty about credit risk in the mortgage market. Spreads on AAA securities widened suddenly and massively over the summer of 2007. Starting with the same regression as before, but now on AAA securities again, restricting the dataset to deals issued after August 2007, she finds that the results are not robust across alternate specifications (unlike for the prior regressions). Nevertheless, she found that certain factors, such as issuer fixed effects, explain more of the variance than on issues before 2007. Beyond the lack of data (less than 35 deals were issued at that time), the lack of clarity in spread drivers could be pointing to the market's confusion at the time, whereby, on one hand, participants were realizing that the AAA securities were not informationally insensitive, but, on the other hand, it was very difficult to understand and quantify the risks. In a sense, one could not readily acquire information in order to value these then informationally sensitive securities.

Discussion of the Findings

As we indicated earlier, there are certain issues in the way the data is gathered, which do weaken the conclusions because they make the data fuzzier than it should be. These issues concern the precise definition of LTV and the presence of second-lien mortgages.

It is not specified whether the LTV that is extracted is the aggregate loan-to-value ratio, or the aggregate cumulative loan-to-value ratio (the CLTV). The latter adds to the LTV the LTV of more junior loans written on the property, and is more representative of the actual credit risk that each loan is exposed to and that the market would value. In the mid-2000s, in particular, in the non-agency market, the share of "piggyback" second-lien loans was substantial. One would not expect the same credit performance at all between a 75% LTV loan without any additional mortgages and a 75% LTV loan on top of which the borrower has taken a 25% second-lien loan. Some deal documents reported LTV, some CLTV, and some both. As a result, there may be a substantial amount of noise around the LTV that is used in the analysis.

The share of second-lien mortgages in the collateral is not tracked as one of the collateral metrics. In subprime securitizations, there usually was a 0–15% share of second-lien mortgages, which naturally carried significantly greater credit risk than other, first-lien, mortgages. This share would have been likely to impact credit enhancement requirements as well as the valuation of credit risk. In addition, the other characteristics of these second-lien loans (such as credit score, CLTV, or occupancy) tended to be milder than those of the first-lien mortgages in the pool. This would hence affect the relationship between the average FICO or LTV on the pool, and the expected credit risk (by rating agencies or by the market). By extension, it is also unclear whether the analysis reflected pure second-lien deals, which may be categorized as subprime.

These issues we raise here somewhat weaken Park's conclusions, but they are probably not at the first order.

#### 4.3.4.3 RMBS Risks and Equity-Like Exposure

The empirical study in Begley and Purnanandam (2017) looks at the same fundamental question as that of Park (2013), but with a different approach. Instead of focusing on senior bonds in the subprime market, they look at the so-called equity tranche; in other words, the equity-like exposure in securitizations, across RMBS deals, including subprime but also prime and alternative credit qualities.

Begley and Purnanandam address the following questions:

1. Given the risk characteristics of the underlying assets, does the size of the equity increase with information asymmetry between investors and securitization sponsors?
2. Given these risk characteristics, does the collateral in deals with a large share of equity perform better ex post relative to these with a smaller equity tranche?

3. Do securities buyers pay a higher price for the bonds issued in deals with a larger equity size?

It is interesting to note that questions 1 and 3 would seem very similar to some of the questions addressed in Park (2013). Indeed, the larger the equity tranche, the more one could expect the senior bonds to have credit support, and reciprocally. According to the analysis by Park, the riskier the underlying collateral, the greater the credit support (and hence the greater the equity), which would give a positive answer to question 1. Also, we saw that senior securities valuations were not sensitive to the underlying collateral's risk measures, which would point to a negative answer to question 3. As we will see, however, these questions require a more nuanced analysis.

Dataset and Tests

The authors gathered deal and loan-level data on close to 200 non-agency US RMBS deals issued in 2001, 2002, and 2005. They also tracked subsequent performance up to the end of 2011. They used the share of loans without documentation as a proxy for the degree of information asymmetry between the entities securitizing the loans and the investors. The "no-doc" category here refers to loans on which no income and no assets verification was provided.

Based on data on each of the deals they tracked, the authors computed the equity tranche size by subtracting the face value of all the bonds sold in the securitization from the total collateral amount. This implicitly assumes that the collateral was valued at par.

The first test the authors carry out is to measure the empirical drivers of the equity tranche size. Begley and Purnanandam find that deals with a greater proportion of NINA loans, after controlling for other explanatory variables, had significantly larger equity tranches. This would be consistent with the notion that on issuance with greater informational asymmetry, the issuer finds it optimal to create a larger equity exposure, as we saw in our discussion of the DeMarzo–Duffie model. This could be loosely interpreted as the fact that more underlying risk results in more credit support, however that is not the case.

Indeed, Begley, and Purnanandam also find that other credit characteristics such as FICO score and LTV affect the sizing of senior bonds (and hence credit support), while the share of no-doc loans affects the size of the equity tranche, and not the sizing of the senior bonds, giving a very particular role to that metric. Observable credit characteristics, the effect of which is known and understood by issuers and investors alike, affect the amount of credit support that is required to create informationally insensitive securities such as the AAAs. Unobservable credit characteristics such as on loans without documentation, that embody the asymmetric information between issuer and investors, drive the size of the equity tranche.

It is worth noting, however, that if observable credit characteristics impact performance in an unequivocal way, and if the issuer has no privileged information on these characteristics or on their impact on performance, according to the various models of security design we have discussed there would be no need to create informationally insensitive securities. In other words, the informationally insensitive securities (such as AAAs) should only exist because there is some asymmetrical information about loan documentation, and generally speaking the size of these securities would depend on the range of possible future performance distribution depending on documentation outcomes.[7]

Then, the authors decompose the ex post pool performance into three components: one part that is driven by observable information (such as credit scores, LTV, etc), one part that is driven by macroeconomic conditions (interest rates driving the incentive and ability to prepay, house prices, …), and a residual part. Then, the relationship between this residual part and the size of the equity tranche should show whether defaults are abnormally lower on deals with a larger equity size. In effect, the authors need to build a loan default model. They actually build two different models:

- A first more traditional and econometric model that predicts default rates as a function of the loans' observable characteristics and
- A second entirely empirical model: for each deal's collateral, they reconstruct an equivalent pool from a large sample of loans, matching all the deal collateral's observable characteristics (average and standard deviation of FICO, LTV, and other such characteristics). Then, they use the actual performance of the loans thus selected and that constitutes a projection of how that deal's collateral "should" have performed.

They find that pools with a larger equity tranche performed better than deals with a smaller equity tranche, after accounting for the impact of known characteristics. They find that collateral in deals with larger equity tranches perform about 25% better using the econometric model in order to establish the base-case expected performance. Using the empirical pool replication model, they find very similar results, with high equity deals performing 27% better than those with smaller equity tranches.

Finally, they find that the spreads on senior securities issued by deals with larger equity pieces were tighter than on deals with a smaller equity tranche. This would indicate that the uninformed investors in the senior securities value the greater share of exposure to the deal that the issuer retains.

Discussion of the Findings

In our discussion of Park (2013), we pointed out some issues with the data, which mostly pertained to the representation of the collateral. In Begley and Purnanandam (2017), the collateral data appears to have been more thoroughly analyzed. For example, CLTV is reported along with LTV.

There is, however, an issue in how certain structure information is manipulated and analyzed. In order to derive the size of the equity tranche, the authors subtracted the deal's liabilities (senior and junior bonds) from the deal's collateral. The differ-

[7]Considering the issuer would be able to know the "real" documentation outcome through soft information, while the investors would only know there is no documentation.

ence is held as the equity size, representing the sponsor's involvement in the deal. Technically, on deals with non-prime collateral, this quantity is the **upfront over-collateralization**.[8] Intuitively, there is more collateral than bonds issued, and hence the term of over-collateralization ("OC"), and it is upfront because it is the amount at the issuance of the deal.

Unfortunately, the value of the deal's equity (the sponsor's "skin in the game") could be much higher than just the upfront OC. A deal's equity tranche fairly systematically also contains **excess-spread**, that is, the difference between the interest collected on the collateral (high) and the interest paid on the bonds (low). For example, on a subprime deal this excess-spread could represent over 3% a year of the deal's balance. Hence, a deal with 1% upfront OC but a low excess-spread might actually have much less equity than a deal with 0.5% upfront OC, with 3% of excess-spread. In addition, there can be substantial structural variability in how this over-collateralization is eventually returned to the deal sponsor and when there could be an **OC release** early on, or not. A sponsor who agrees to a large amount of OC that is expected to be returned in 2 years is actually signaling less of a commitment than the sponsor of a deal with less OC, but that gets returned in many years.

The only proper way of measuring the size of the equity is to value it the way the sponsor would. One has to project its cash flows (reflecting excess-spread and eventual OC releases), compute an NPV and subtract the "acquisition cost" of that equity, i.e., the upfront OC. The greater the amount, the more economic value there is in this particular deal for the holder of the equity tranche. Carrying out this valuation would effectively amount to pricing the deal's collateral at issuance, which was typically not par priced.

On deals with prime collateral, OC structures are typically not used, and the difference between the collateral and offered bonds effectively correspond to the junior-most security, which one could assumed to be retained by the issuer or sponsor. However, the issuer would also typically retain a **WAC IO** and **WAC PO**,[9] a complex stream of interest or principal loosely comparable to excess-spread. As a result only considering the junior-most bond as a measure of their exposure is misleading.

In addition to the difficulty in measuring the right amount of equity, one cannot escape the fact that non-agency equity tranches have been very largely securitized, as net interest margin ("**NIM**") securitizations.[10] Sponsors would typically only retain the equity of the equity tranche, called the **baby equity**, which naturally raises the question of how that influenced the impact of the equity tranche sizing as a signaling device. Begley and Purnanandam mention the fact that if the equity tranche was resold, it would most likely be to an informed investor, not fundamentally different from the sponsor itself in terms of information, and hence the signaling aspect of the equity size would be the same whether it is fully retained or sold. In the case of NIMs, however, senior bonds are structured and receive an investment grade rating,

---

[8]See Chap. 6 for a detailed study of over-collateralization.

[9]Refer to Chap. 6 for a discussion of WAC IOs/POs and their structuring logic.

[10]Here again, refer to Chap. 6 for a detailed study of NIM structures.

and presumably do not go to informed investors. In the prime market, the junior-most bonds were also typically resecuritized, for example, in so-called **zebra** structures.

A second potential issue in the analysis comes from the relationships between equity size and expected spread on senior bonds. First, the equity size is related to the sector. At one side of the spectrum, unrated bonds in jumbo prime deals (which the authors identify as retained equity) are very small, in the order of 0.10 to 0.25% of the whole deal, because the overall credit quality of the underlying loans is considered to be extremely high. At the other end of the spectrum, even the cleanest subprime deal had some upfront OC, typically around 0.5%.

At the same time, the floating rate securities issued on prime deals (whether the underlying collateral was fixed or floating) structurally had to contain a cap to their interest.[11] The effect of this cap is that if interest rates increase beyond a certain point, then the bond locally becomes a fixed-rate bond. At the same time, borrowers behind prime loans exercise their option to refinance or not efficiently. Combining efficient refinancings and a bond that will become akin to a fixed rate in certain conditions, the cost of this cap in terms of **negative convexity**[12] is far from negligible. As a result, it is entirely normal to see wider spreads on such floating rate securities backed by prime loans than on securities backed by more credit impaired loans, all else being equal in terms of bond-level credit risk (AAA in the case at hand). Therefore, the tighter spreads on senior bonds in deals with a larger equity tranche may have nothing to do with information asymmetry. The proper way of comparing spreads on senior securities on a large cross section of the mortgage market (from prime to subprime) would be to compute the **option adjusted spread**, which would have factored out the negative convexity. It does requires a full prepayment model for all the underlying loans as well as a full deal structure model.

While the conclusions in Begley and Purnanandam (2017) make sense intuitively and appear to confirm the main conclusions of security design models as applied to securitization, the flaws in how they measure the equity interest and in associating securities spread to credit risk weaken these conclusions.

#### 4.3.4.4 CLO/CBO Risks and Equity Size

In two related analyses, Franke, Herrmann, and Weber (2012) and Franke, Herrmann, and Weber (2007), we can find further empirical confirmation of the core ideas from security design applied to securitization. This research took place earlier than that of the other two empirical papers we have just discussed, and although it focused on a smaller market, its findings were to some extent more significant because it did not suffer some of the potential methodological flaws of these other papers. CLOs and CBOs not only benefit from simpler structures than MBS, but their collateral's behavior (bullet bonds with limited prepayments) renders the subordinated tranches' amounts more directly related to their risks.

---

[11] See Chap. 6 for floater structures.

[12] See Chap. 2 for a basic introduction to the analysis and valuation of negatively convex securities.

Franke, Hermann, and Weber consider **first-loss pieces** (FLP), another name for a deal's equity. They also look into third-loss pieces, which in our discussion so far correspond to senior bonds, debt-like securities.

While in the case of mortgage-backed securities one needs to look at a series of loan-level characteristics such as FICO scores or LTVs; in the case of CLOs and CBOs, these characteristics are mostly encapsulated in so-called weighted-average default probabilities (WAPD) and diversity scores (DS), provided by rating agencies. The weighted-average default probability is based on a detailed analysis of each loan or bond in a deal's collateral in order to derive a rating and an estimated default probability. Once these metrics are known for all the assets, the weighted average is calculated at the portfolio level. The diversity score is a measure of how widespread the portfolio's exposure is to various industries.

CLOs and CBOs are types of CDOs, as we explained in Chap. 2. These deals may be cash or synthetic, managed or static, and may be arranged by banks or by investment management companies.

Dataset and Tests

The authors used a sample of 169 CBOs/CLOs issued between 1997 and 2005 in the European market, on which they had the categorization information mentioned above as well as WAPDs and DSs. The data excluded structured finance CDOs, whose underlying assets would have been of an entirely different nature.

In addition to these metrics, they also tracked for each deal the size of the equity and the size of the senior tranches. They computed the ratio of the WAPD to the size of the equity, defined as the *loss share*.

The equity sizes observed on the sample of deals are fairly dispersed: bucketed by loans/bonds and cash/synthetic, the average equity size ranges from 1.9% to 13.2%, reflecting large differences in underlying asset quality.

The authors set out to test several hypotheses, of which we retain a few:

1. Does lower quality collateral lead to a larger equity?
2. Is the loss share invariant?

Testing the first hypothesis shows that indeed a higher expected default and a lower diversification both lead to a greater equity size. As would be expected, the equity, typically retained by the issuer, is larger on deals for which there is more credit risk. The securitization issuers keep a greater exposure on collateral with worse quality, as implied by the various security design models we have discussed.

The regression coefficient relating the WAPD with the equity size is around 30%, so that an increase of the expected default probability by 1% in absolute terms leads to an increase in the equity size by 0.3%. The authors consider that the market's expectation of loss given default is 50% and hence the slope of the relationship is less than one would expect.

Based on the typical range of diversity scores that have been observed in the market, one can see based on the regression coefficients that the typical impact on equity size is in the order of 2–3% in absolute terms. It is worth pointing out that using a 0% expected default and a very high diversity score, the regression projects an equity size of 1%. This extrapolation stresses that the market would likely still apply a minimal assessment of an information asymmetry risk.

For the second hypothesis, it appears that the loss share is empirically unaffected by the weighted-average default probability, but is related to the diversity score. Given the same expected loss, lack of diversification will increase the probability than an extreme loss number is reached, and that the senior tranches suffer a loss. It is logical, hence, that the equity would be sized somewhat larger in order to reduce that risk. The coefficient for the diversity score in this second regression is about the same as in the first one, so that the absolute impact of diversity on the loss share is much less than on the equity size itself in the prior regression.

Discussion of the Findings

One first thing to note is that looking at the size of the equity tranche, in the case of CLOs and CBOs, is much less flawed than in the case of RMBS. CLOs and CBOs also may use over-collateralization, but have typically not used that mechanism to build OC as much as in RMBS. Indeed, the loans or bonds used as collateral in these CDOs do not tend to prepay fast, and even when they do, their speed is low early on. As a result, there is less of a structural need to rapidly extract excess-spread and "store" it in reserve, as is typically the case with RMBS. As a result, the size of the equity is more directly related to the actual degree of exposure it has in the deal's performance, and to the degree of credit protection to senior bonds it provides. Differences in equity size, therefore, are likely to be more relevant on CLOs and CBOs.

Still, CLOs and CBOs do use excess-spread as part of credit enhancement, and the residual excess-spread will normally accrue to the equity holder. As a result, the absolute level of equity may not fully capture the economic exposure retained by the issuer or the protection provided to other tranches. The slope of equity size to default probability was appearing to be too low, as we pointed out earlier. The difference of 0.2 could be due to the contribution of excess-spread.

## 4.4 Conclusion

In this long chapter, we have begun to explore the economic drivers of the existence of securitization and of the issuance of senior and junior structured products. We first saw how securitization should not exist in theory and how a series of plausible explanations in terms of optimal funding could justify its existence, in contrast with the simple Modigliani–Miller model. We found some empirically motivated benefits in securitization. Then, we turned our attention to the reason why securitized products should be structured. A few security design models, with various assumptions, all showed that information asymmetries explained the necessity for equity and debt structures. Empirical research offered some validation for these theoretical models.

Now that we understand the economic justifications for securitization and minimal structuring, we should ask ourselves what could explain such a spectacular failure as the mortgage crisis from the late 2000s. Our next chapter, drilling into some of the problems of securitization, will try and offer some perspective on this complex issue.

## References

An, X., Deng, Y., & Gabriel, S. (2009). Value creation through securitization: Evidence from the CMBS market. *Journal of Real Estate Finance and Economics*, *38*(3), 302–326.

Axelson, U. (2007). Security design with investor private information. *Journal of Finance*, *62*(6), 2587–2632.

Banerjee, S., & Mustapha, E. (2000). RALI alternative-a mortgages. In F. J. Fabozzi (Ed.), *The handbook of mortgage-backed securities* (2nd ed.). McGraw-Hill Education.

Banerjee, S., Gauthier, L., Tan, W., & Zhu, D. (2000). A study of RASC subprime loan prepayments, delinquencies, and losses. *The Journal of Fixed Income*, *10*(3), 47–67.

Begley, T. A., & Purnanandam, A. (2017). Design of financial securities: Empirical evidence from private-label RMBS deals. *The Review of Financial Studies*, *30*(1), 120–161.

Boot, A., & Thakor, A. (1993). Security design. *Journal of Finance*, *48*(4), 1349–1378.

Dang, T. V., Gary, G., & Holmström, B. (2015). The information sensitivity of a security. Working Paper. Columbia University.

DeMarzo, P. (2005). The pooling and tranching of securities: A model of informed intermediation. *The Review of Financial Studies*, *18*(1), 1–35.

DeMarzo, P., & Duffie, D. (1999). A liquidity-based model of security design. *Econometrica*, *67*(1), 65–100.

Dewatripont, M., Jewitt, I., & Tirole, J. (1999). The economics of career concerns, part I: Comparing information structures. *The Review of Economic Studies*, *66*(1), 183–198.

Elul, R. (2005). The economics of asset securitization. *Business Review*, no. Q3, 16–25.

Fan, G.-Z., Ong, S. E., & Sing, T. F. (2006). Moral hazard, effort sensitivity and compensation in asset-backed securitization. *The Journal of Real Estate Finance and Economics*, *32*(3), 229–251.

Franke, G., & Krahnen, J. P. (2008). The future of securitization. Working Papers 2008/31. Center of Financial Studies, Göethe Universität Frankfurt.

Franke, G., Herrmann, M., & Weber, T. (2007). Information asymmetries and securitization design. Working Paper. SSRN.

Franke, G., Herrmann, M., & Weber, T. (2012). Loss allocation in securitization transactions. *Journal of Financial and Quantitative Analysis*, *47*(5), 1125–1153.

Gauthier, L. (2019). Securitization structures and security design. Working Paper. SSRN.

Gauthier, L., & Zimmerman, T. (2006). Mortgage credit quantified. In F. J. Fabozzi (Ed.), *The handbook of mortgage-backed securities* (6th ed.). McGraw-Hill Education.

Gorton, G., & Metrick, A. (2013). Chapter 1 - Securitization. In G. Constantinides, M. Harris, & R. M. Stulz (Eds.), *Handbook of the economics of finance* (vol. 2, pp. 1–70). Elsevier.

Gorton, G., & Souleles, N. (2007). Special purpose vehicles and securitization. In *The risks of financial institutions* (pp. 549–602). National Bureau of Economic Research, Inc.

Greenbaum, S. I., & Thakor, A. (1987). Bank funding modes: Securitization versus deposits. *Journal of Banking & Finance*, *11*(3), 379–401.

Han, J., Park, K., & Pennacchi, G. (2015). Corporate taxes and securitization. *Journal of Finance*, *70*(3), 1287–1321.

Holmström, B. (1999). Managerial incentive problems: A dynamic perspective. *The Review of Economic Studies*, *66*(1), 169–182.

Iacobucci, E. M., & Winter, R. A. (2005). Asset securitization and asymmetric information. *Journal of Legal Studies*, *24*(1), 161–206.

Jensen, M. C., & Meckling, W. H. (1976). Theory of the firm: Managerial behavior, agency costs and ownership structure. *Journal of Financial Economics*, *3*, 305–60.

Leland, H. (2007). Financial synergies and the optimal scope of the firm: Implications for mergers, spinoffs, and structured finance. *The Journal of Finance*, *62*(2), 765–807.

Leland, H., & Pyle, D. H. (1977). Informational asymmetries, financial structure, and financial intermediation. *Journal of Finance*, *32*(2), 371–387.

LoPucki, L. M. (1996). The death of liability. *The Yale Law Journal*, *106*(1), 1–92.

Mansukhani, S., & Qbbaj, M. (2005). *CSFB's starter kit for non-agency residential mortgage-backed securities*, Research Report. CSFB.

Modigliani, F., & Miller, M. H. (1958). The cost of capital, corporation finance and the theory of investment. *The American Economic Review*, *48*(3), 261–297.

Myers, S. C., & Majluf, N. S. (1984). Corporate financing and investment decisions when firms have information that investors do not have. *Journal of Financial Economics*, *13*(2), 187–221.

Park, S. (2013). The design of subprime mortgage-backed securities and information insensitivity. *International Economic Journal*, *27*(2), 249–284.

Pinkus, S., Hunter, S. M., & Roll, R. (1987). *An introduction to the mortgage market and prepayment analysis*, Research Report. Goldman Sachs.

Pinto, J., & Alves, P. (2016). The economics of securitization: Evidence from the European markets. *Investment Management and Financial Innovations*, *13*(1), 112–126.

Riddiough, T. (1997). Optimal design and governance of asset-backed securities. *Journal of Financial Intermediation*, *6*(2), 121–152.

Schwartz, E. S., & Torous, W. N. (1989). Prepayment and the valuation of mortgage-backed securities. *The Journal of Finance*, *44*(2), 375–392.

Varian, H. R. (1992). *Microeconomic analysis*. Norton International Ed. Norton.

# 5 Problems with Securitization

As we have extensively shown in the prior chapter, asymmetrical information has been an essential concept in explaining the existence of securitization, and its most basic forms. Differences in access to information, for example, between the stockholders of securitizing firms and their managers or between securitized products investors and issuers, were shown to be a reasonable explanation for the existence of securitization, and differences in information between issuers of securitized products and investors could explain, both theoretically and empirically, that securitized products should be structured as debt.

We now shift our focus to the problems that the existence of securitization raises. The prior chapter showed how securitization may be economically optimal, but it has been no mystery that there could be significant shortcomings in securitization, since the economic crisis of the late 2000s is largely ascribed to mortgage securitization in the US. It is important to draw a distinction between structuring, that is, the manner in which securitization is carried out,[1] and its simple existence or its reasons for being. In the present chapter, we aim to discuss issues with the very existence, or the very essence, of securitization rather than the way in which structured products are created, which raises its own series of problems.

As much as asymmetrical information helped explain the existence and form of securitization, we will see that it also provides grounds for many of the issues raised by securitization through **agency problems**. There are numerous literature reviews and research papers on the problems with securitization, and we loosely follow Paligorova (2009), Frame (2017), and Goodman (2016), which all effectively illustrate that agency conflicts can exist at every stage of the securitization process. The first paper considers the asymmetrical information problems affecting securitization at

[1]This will be extensively discussed in Chaps. 6 and 8.



L. Gauthier, *Securitization Economics*, Springer Texts in Business and Economics,
https://doi.org/10.1007/978-3-030-50326-0_5

large, the second more specifically focuses on mortgage securitization, and the third discusses the problems of the US non-agency mortgage market, in particular, from the perspective of an experienced research analyst.

Paligorova (2009) classifies the problems with securitization into two kinds: those related to **adverse selection** and those related to **moral hazard**. Adverse selection in this context is raised if the issuer possesses more information than investors on the assets it securitizes: in an originate-to-distribute model, there is a low incentive to screen the loans. While there are arguments why this could be alleviated by the fact that investors would rationally factor in the potentially lower quality of securitized loans, empirical studies can shed light on whether worse assets are securitized than are retained. Frame (2017) in his review raises more specific questions from this standpoint on mortgage securitization: have riskier US mortgages been securitized? Are securitized loans more likely to default, controlling for known risk factors? Do investors price the potential information asymmetry?

The problem of moral hazard in securitization is concerned with the incentives of the different parties to ensure the performance of the assets. The originator or servicer may have no economic exposure to the performance of the assets, because they are paid a fixed fee, and hence engage in behavior that is detrimental to investors. The compensation schemes of bank managers may also lead them to take tail risks, effectively selling options.

According to Goodman (2016), the negative effects mentioned above were most prevalent in the non-agency mortgage market. Indeed, she argues the private-label mortgage market in the late 2000s should be distinguished from other securitized markets. First, it suffered by far the most significant dislocation and delinquencies in this market increased the most in relative terms. Flaws in the securitization process became most apparent: weakness in loan underwriting, lack of consistent loan-level information, and sloppy due-diligence. Second, the interests of investors and issuers were more properly aligned in other asset classes: little equity was retained in mortgage securitizations (by trading out or hedging with CDS) while in other markets equity was more often retained, and servicing was more integrated, leading to a greater benefit in extended processing of delinquent loans.

In the following section, we first characterize the mortgage crisis more precisely. We know that bad things happened and the performance of securitized loans was bad. Looking at data on agency prime loans, we will assess how bad that was. Then we will analyze problems in the very existence of securitization from two different angles: agency problems and regulatory problems.

In the second section, we discuss some of the agency problems mentioned above: we first address the moral hazard potentially raised in securitization and whether proper loan screening was enforced, following the theoretical model developed by Plantin (2011) and the empirical study by Keys et al. (2010). Next, we examine the theoretical model proposed in Rajan et al. (2010) and its empirical tests from Rajan et al. (2015), showing how the lack of screening can lead to underestimates of future performance problems, in a snowball effect. Finally, we discuss adverse selection or whether securitized products may be a lemons market, following Downing et al. (2009).

The third section addresses the question of whether securitization might just be a way around regulatory requirements, first following Jones (2000) to describe regulatory arbitrage, we then look into the empirical results from Ambrose et al. (2005) and Efing (2016). If securitization is beneficial to issuers as a regulatory work-around, are its theoretical benefits diminished?

## 5.1 Characterizing Some Problems with the Mortgage Crisis

Before delving into the detailed modeling and analysis of the issues with securitization we have mentioned above, it makes sense to simply characterize the mortgage crisis of the late 2000s. For this purpose, we use the agency loan-level database we have mentioned earlier. These agency loans were expected to be mostly good quality prime mortgages.

Figure 5.1 shows the aggregate prepayment speeds, in CPR, the aggregate share of delinquent loans (30 to 90+ days late, excluding foreclosures and REO), and the rate of transition into REO or foreclosure exit, over time. The data essentially covers the universe of 30-year fixed-rate single family agency mortgages. We can see fairly clearly that as prepayments reached a low, delinquencies and transitions to REO began to ramp up significantly. Although the transitions to REO look low on this scale, over the years from 2008 to 2014 they amount to approximately 7% of the whole universe, a staggering volume. Before and after that period in this dataset, the total transitions amounted to less than 2%.

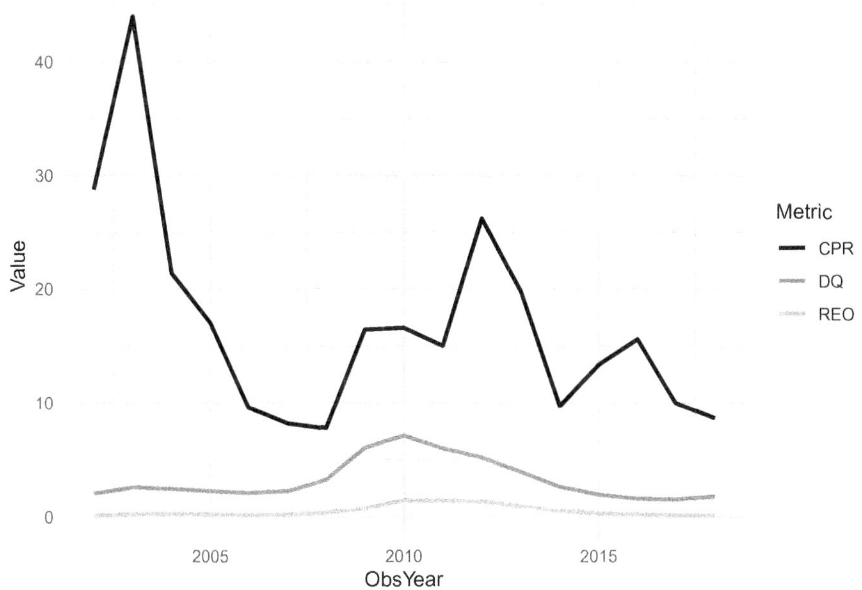


**Fig. 5.1** Historical prepayments and delinquencies on agency 30-year FRMs. *Source* Compiled by the author based on loan-level data from Fannie Mae and Freddie Mac

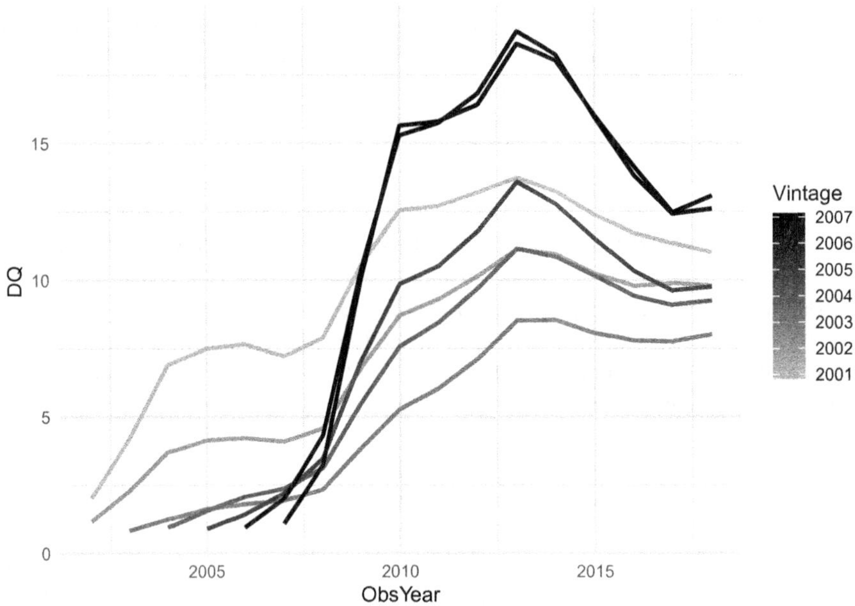


**Fig. 5.2** Historical delinquencies on agency 30-year FRMs by Vintage. *Source* compiled by the author based on loan-level data from Fannie Mae and Freddie Mac

However, the plot across the universe hides significant differences across vintages. As Fig. 5.2 illustrates, delinquencies jumped much more significantly on loans originated toward the end of the run-up period. The 2006 and 2007 vintages turned out particularly bad. Also, note that the jump in delinquencies on earlier vintages after 2008 was relative to a then much lower balance due to the prepayments that had been taking place since their origination.

Some of the worsening in credit performance should be attributed to external factors, such as declining home prices at the time: one can clearly see in Fig. 5.2 how the earlier vintages suffered a sudden jump in delinquency rates after they had apparently already peaked. However, the speed at which delinquencies jumped on the later vintages suggests that there was something about these loans that made them just worse.

One of the major issues raised by the deterioration in credit that started to take place in 2007 is that it affected many loans which were considered to be of very good credit quality. See Fig. 5.3 for a comparison of delinquency rates on agency loans, scaled by the average delinquency during the low of 2005–2007. The delinquency rate is measured controlling for seasoning, on loans aged between 30 and 36 months. The three lines on the chart capture loans with a particularly good set of credit characteristics (high FICO above 725 and low LTV under 65), those with a particularly bad set of characteristics, for agencies, (low FICO under 650 and LTV above 75), and the rest of the loans. The chart shows us two very clear patterns.

First, we can see that the rise in delinquencies on all three groups of loans took place at very much the same time. The lower credit quality loans did not lead the way,

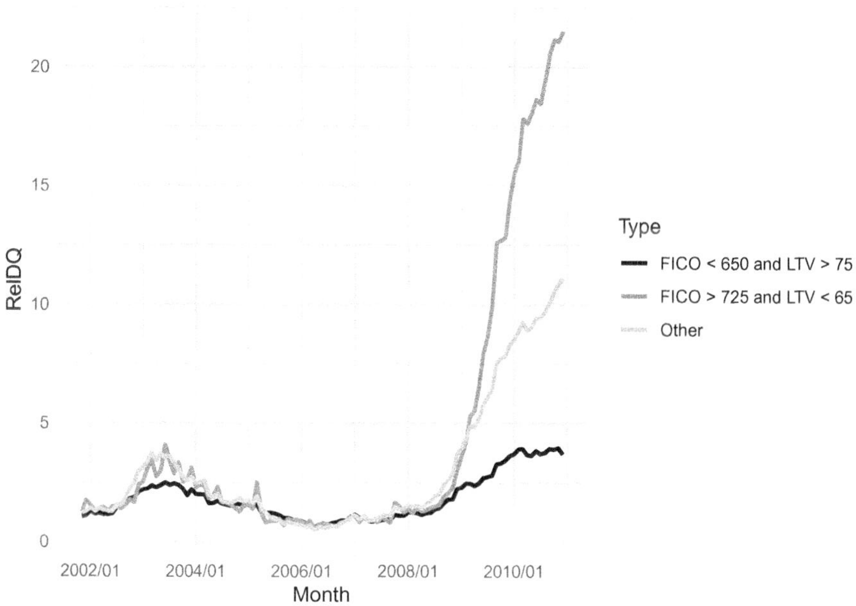


**Fig. 5.3** Timing of credit degradation on good and bad 30-year agency loans. *Source* Compiled by the author based on loan-level data from Fannie Mae and Freddie Mac

in relative terms. It implies that the lower end of the spectrum, for agencies, did not act as a trigger for the higher end of the spectrum. Although we are not displaying subprime loan performance here, it is generally known that these delinquencies started to increase substantially in 2007, which would put them well ahead of the agency loans illustrated on the chart. This pattern would be consistent with the broad prime sector not suffering a deterioration in performance due to much worse underwriting quality, but to declining house prices, as was the case in early-2009s when the curves jump up.

Second, it is clear that the relative increase in delinquencies for the lower end of the credit spectrum was much more moderate than on the higher end. While delinquencies on lower credit quality paper doubled or tripled relative to their baseline, they raised by a multiple of 20 on very high-quality paper.

We should also stress that the rise in liquidations and defaults is not the only component of losses for investors: loss severities have also increased, quite significantly, as shown in Fig. 5.4. This rise has been largely driven by increased expenses related to liquidations, as the time during which the loans were in liquidation extended. As we know, loss severities are significantly affected by house prices, and the trend we observe in severities over time is consistent with their evolution over the period.

Now mindful of these broad patterns, we are going to look into theoretical and empirical justifications for this narrative, where worse loans would have been produced, because of securitization.

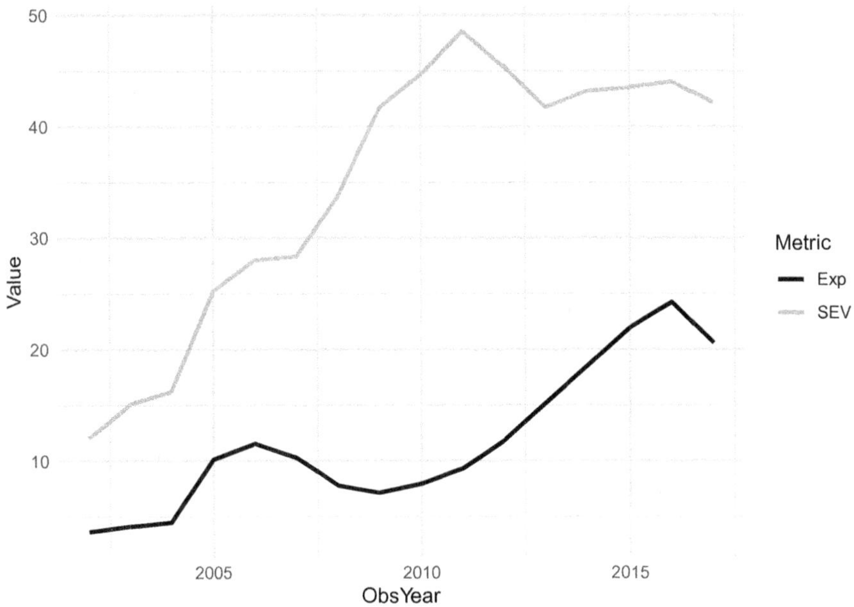


**Fig. 5.4** Historical loss severities and expenses on agency REO loans. *Source* Compiled by the author based on loan-level data from Fannie Mae and Freddie Mac

## 5.2 Some Agency Problems in Securitization

In this section, we focus on the negative aspects of securitization brought about by the fact that it involves selling the loans. The originate-to-distribute model has been criticized principally because it may lead lenders to not care about the loans that are made. We saw in the prior chapter, for example, with Gorton and Souleles (2007), that under some conditions the interest of lenders is aligned with that of investors. We now see the (seemingly more common) situations where they are not.

Some models have considered how some of these agency problems spilled into the market as well. Informationally insensitive securities are normally created in order to alleviate information asymmetry problems in securitization. These safe securities are valued more fairly by investors, and it is hence in the issuer's interest to create them. What if there were too many of them? Hanson and Sunderam (2013) addressed this question with a theoretical model. They looked at the interaction between issuer security design decisions and investor's decisions on information acquisition. We know that from the investor standpoint, the costs of sourcing and processing information on deals and bonds are quite high; if bonds are structured based on the information analysis of other investors, it may make sense for a particular investor to save on these costs and rely on the others' work, leading to a lack of production of information.

This approach can be contrasted with that of Pagano and Volpin (2012), who also considered information in the market for securitized products, but focus on the opaqueness of the market, based on assumptions leading issuers to restrict the information they provided on the collateral or on the structures. Their model shows conditions in which investors would have limited information and ability to evaluate securitized products. However, many banks and investors exerted substantial effort before, during, and after the crisis to acquire and analyze extremely detailed data on the underlying assets, as well as on the structures. Hence, that this information flow would have been effectively controlled by the issuers does not appear to be capturing reality.

We begin our discussion with a model that stresses the relationship between excessive securitization and low incentives for the lender to monitor and improve the quality of the loans.

### 5.2.1 Good and Bad Securitization

In Plantin (2011), the author proposes a simple but interesting theoretical model of bank origination and securitization, with rational screening, or lack thereof. He stresses that a bank's under-screening of loans resulting in a later increase in delinquencies may not be negative. However, if the increase in securitization comes with a reduction in information efficiency, then there is a risk of excessive securitization and broad inefficiencies.

The model considers securitization as a transaction where the markets sell issuing banks insurance against future liquidity or solvency constraints. Indeed, being able to securitize assets through a true sale frees up the bank's capital and reduces the risk it may run into liquidity constraints in the future. Also, the larger the gains from securitization (purchasing future liquidity insurance at some cost), the greater the incentive for the bank to increase its securitization volume and hence originate lower quality loans.

In this logical chain, greater investor appetite for risk leads to greater gains for banks in securitization, which leads to more securitization, which leads to a lowering of screening or monitoring standards, and which leads to more defaults. In and by itself, this process is not bad, but we will see how some changes in the conditions of the securitization can make it suboptimal.

We first discuss the model setup, then the first application to the case of "good" securitization, which is optimal. Next, we see how changing certain conditions in the securitization process makes it "bad", because it becomes excessive and induces a suboptimal lack of monitoring. Finally, we briefly discuss the application of this model to the narrative of the subprime crisis.

#### 5.2.1.1 The Model

We consider three dates at times [0..2], and two types of agents: a single bank and several investors, which are all risk-neutral. Given a cash flow stream $(c_0, c_1, c_2)$, investors attach a value $c_0 + c_1 + c_2$ to it, and the bank $c_0 + c_1 + \frac{c_2}{1+r}$ where $r > 0$ is some discount rate, and can be held to represent the bank's funding cost relative to that of the investors (which is set to 0, effectively). Discounting the later payment makes the bank more willing to sell out assets and adds inherent value in the bank's trading with the market. This is very comparable to the assumptions in DeMarzo and Duffie (1999) or Dang et al. (2015), as a realistic way of inducing a need for securitization without having to resort to more detailed explanations such as those from Iacobucci and Winter (2005) for example.

Investors receive endowments at all times. With our usual notations inspired from the discussion of Gorton and Metrick (2013) in Chap. 4, at time 0, the bank owns a loan that pays off a cash flow of $Y_2$ at time 2. The bank may or may not monitor the loan between times 1 and 2, an event which we denote by $M$. The payoff writes, using the Dirac mass,

$$Y_2 = ((1-p)\delta_0 + p\delta_F)\,\mathbb{I}_M + ((1-p+\Delta p)\delta_0 + (p-\Delta p)\delta_F)\,\mathbb{I}_{\overline{M}},$$

where $F$ is the total loan payment (which could be understood as its face value for a zero coupon). The bank incurs a benefit $\gamma = B\mathbb{I}_M$ if it does not monitor, in the form of cost savings. If the bank monitors the loan, it knows the realization of $Y_2$. We assume that $(1+r)B < F\Delta p$, which states that the monitoring efficiency needs to be above a minimal level.

#### 5.2.1.2 The Good Securitization

Let us assume that the bank, which is protected by limited liability, offers a contract to the investors at time 0 where it sells all or part of the future loan cash flow to investors. Considering that investors cannot observe whether the bank monitored the loan or not and monitoring is not contractible, this is a prototypical moral hazard problem, comparable to some of the problems we discussed in Chap. 4. If the bank does not have an incentive to monitor, the investors will assume it does not and reflect the greater probability of default, thus lowering the amount for which they are willing to buy into the contract.

We have the following proposition:

**Proposition 5.1** (Plantin Good Securitization Optimal Contract) *If* $r \leq \frac{\Delta p(F\Delta p - B)}{pB}$ *then the optimal contract specifies that the bank retains a share of the loan and monitors, and the probability of default is* $1-p$. *If* $r > \frac{\Delta p(F\Delta p - B)}{pB}$ *then the entire loan is sold and the probability of default is* $1-p+\Delta p$.

***Proof*** If the bank kept the entire loan until the end of period 2, it would not benefit from trading and would incur the discounting cost related to waiting over two periods to obtain the terminal cash flow. If the bank sold the entire loan at date 1, then it would have no incentive to monitor the loan, which may be suboptimal (consider that the monitoring efficiency may be very high and its cost very low).

Since the outcome from the loan takes values in a set with two elements, one of them being 0, and because the bank benefits from limited liability flooring its income at zero, the optimal contract can be specified as a single value $F_B \geq 0$, corresponding to the stake of the bank in the loan. The contract cash flow is hence $C_2 = \frac{F_B}{F} Y_2$.

For the bank to have an incentive to monitor, the bank's expected gain when monitoring needs to be greater than when it is not monitoring:

$$\mathbb{E}\left[\frac{C_2}{1+r}+\gamma|M\right] \geq \mathbb{E}\left[\frac{C_2}{1+r}+\gamma|\overline{M}\right]$$
$$\frac{pF_B}{1+r} \geq \frac{(p-\Delta p)F_B}{1+r}+B,$$

which is equivalent to $F_B \geq \frac{B(1+r)}{\Delta p}$, a positive amount by assumption. In these conditions, the investors rationally assume that the bank is monitoring, and value their share of the loan at $p(F - F_B)$ and pay the bank that amount for the contract.

Hence, the bank's valuation of the loan $L_M$ becomes the investors' valuation of their cash flows plus its own valuation of its cash flows:

$$L_M = p(F - F_B) + \frac{pF_B}{1+r} = p\left(F - \frac{rB}{\Delta p}\right).$$

If the share retained by the bank is null and it does not monitor, the valuation of the loan becomes

$$L_{\overline{M}} = (p - \Delta p)F + B$$

The bank's decision to offer a contract where it does not retain anything versus a contract where it retains a certain share and monitors hence hinges on the comparison of both loan valuations:

$$L_M \geq L_{\overline{M}}$$
$$p\left(F - \frac{rB}{\Delta p}\right) \geq (p-\Delta p)F + B$$
$$\Delta p(F\Delta p - B) \geq pBr,$$

which is the expression in the proposition. □

The result shows that the bank's discount rate, if it is too high, creates such an incentive for trading that the bank simply does not want to hold on to the loan, notwithstanding the induced gains from monitoring. Within this model's setup, there is no negative effect attached to securitization: if the issuer has an incentive to monitor, then this is reflected in market valuations, and if it does not, the lower valuations are also reflected. In the case where default rates are higher than they could otherwise be due to the lack of monitoring, this loss is compensated by the bank's lower cost.

Note that the bank's private information about the loan quality does not have any effect, only the fact that it does monitor (and improves quality) or it does not. Also, the fact that the bank may shirk and cannot be contractually forced to monitor is reflected in the optimal contract, as investors rationally analyze the cases when this may happen.

Since uncertainty is modeled as a discrete variable, there are only two outcomes in the optimal contract; in a continuous setting, we would expect to see a continuous relationship between the differential funding cost $r$ and the bank's effort level.

#### 5.2.1.3 The Bad Securitization

How does the above model evolve into a negative situation? Plantin first considers simple ways in which the model could accommodate the subprime lending boom and bust form the late 2000s, noting that the situation was characterized by three particular measures which increased substantially:

- structured products valuations,[2]
- the rate of securitization of subprime,
- and loan delinquency rates.[3]

Within the model, we assume that the differential cost of holding loans increased so that lenders were made less willing to hold these loans on balance sheet, which is consistent with market yields on securitized products declining more than the lenders' funding costs. According to Proposition 5.1, if that increase is large enough then the bank will switch to selling the entire loan without retaining a share, and stop monitoring: the situation evolves toward a pure originate-to-distribute model.

An increase in the bank's funding cost $r$ relative to the market's required yield would reflect the increase in structured products valuations, all else being equal. This simple effect illustrates quite well the relationship that one has posited between general market liquidity (pushing yields down) and the decline in loan monitoring incentives.

In order to account for the bad side of securitization within this model, we assume that instead of monitoring between periods 1 and 2, the bank now may monitor the loan between periods 0 and 1. The contract is still offered at time 0, as before. The bank thus privately learns the loan's quality (and affects its outcome) if it decided to monitor. The loan's payoff still takes place at period 2. Now, the bank's private information and the fact that it may shirk will have a more profound impact on the optimal contract design. The following proposition characterizes the negative outcome in this situation.

**Proposition 5.2** (Platin Bad Securitization Optimal Contract) *If* $p < \frac{1}{1+r}$ *then securitization is always optimal. Further, Proposition 5.1 applies in this case, monitoring and retaining part of the loan depend on the level of* $r$. *If* $p \geq \frac{1}{1+r}$, *then the bank does not monitor and sells the entire loan. This is suboptimal if* $r \leq \frac{\Delta p(F\Delta p-B)}{pB}$.

***Proof*** First, we note that after period 1, when the bank has or has not monitored the loan, there is no additional incentive that could play a role.

At period 1, if the bank had decided not to monitor at period 0, then it is optimal to sell the entire loan for $(p - \Delta p)F$, since conditional on the lower performance it is optimal to trade, as the market and the bank valuation's hypotheses coincide. If,

[2]In other words, spreads on subprime RMBS reached historical lows.

[3]This, more specifically from the late 2007s.

on the other hand, the bank had monitored the loan, then it must be because it had an incentive and therefore had a stake $F_B$ in the loan. The bank in this case would, at period 1, know the outcome of the payoff $Y_2$. Platin then calls, in this situation, the bank that knows the loan will perform a "good" bank, and the one that knows the loan will not perform a "bad" bank. This then resembles the model setup in Boot and Thakor (1993) discussed in Chap. 4, where the good and bad issuers were competing to issue products, although the information structure differs.

Assume that the bank knows the loan will perform, after monitoring. This good bank possesses some cash, from the sale of part of the loan, that is $p(F - F_B)$. Indeed, if the bank monitored then the investors must have rationally anticipated this monitoring and would have reflected this knowledge in the valuation, using the probability of $p$ conditional on monitoring.

The bank would want to sell more of the loan in this case, as its funding cost drives a trading incentive. This cash could be used in order to sell a greater part of the loan, as collateral for a sale with recourse: sell the loan, but make investors whole if it does not perform. As such, the bank could at time 1 offer a contract whereby it sells its retained claim $F_B$ and is committed to pay an amount $cF_B$ at time 2 if the loan does not perform. This strategy is also fully consistent with the main results in Boot and Thakor (1993): the bank in the case at hand provides equity in the contract. This amount would be collateralized by the available cash mentioned above. A bad bank would not be willing to offer that same contract (and the good bank hence would be in a position to signal itself) if $c > 1$. In other words, bad loan performance has to be punishing enough in the contract to deter the bad bank for contemplating offering it.

So, the good bank considers the choice of offering such a contract: if it does so, it collects $F_B$ at period 1, but needs to put $cF_B$ aside (so, since $c > 1$, a net cash outlay) and gets it back at period 2. In the alternative, the bank can consume this cash $cF_B$ at period 1, and this is worth more to the bank since for all $c$ and $r$, $F_B + \frac{cF_B}{1+r} < cF_B + \frac{F_B}{1+r}$. As a result, the good bank never signals its information to the market by selling the sure cash flows of period 2, due to its internal funding cost for the necessary collateral it would have to post.

Since there is no signaling at period 1, the bank's optimal strategy is easier to represent and is a basic example of a lemon market. For a good bank, its stake at time 1 is worth $\frac{F_B}{1+r}$, and it is worth 0 for the bad bank. Investors in the market are willing to pay $pF_B$ for that stake, so trading will take place if this value is greater than the bank's value. Hence, if $p < \frac{1}{1+r}$ then the good bank will not be willing to trade, and only bad loans (with a value of 0) would be offered for sale. If $p \geq \frac{1}{1+r}$ then both the good and the bad banks are willing to trade at the investor's valuation. If the probability of performance is high enough, then the occurrence of a bad bank is low enough that the market's uninformed valuation of the loan is high enough to entice the good bank to trade.

Then, based on these various outcomes at time 1, we can determine the optimal contract at time 0.

If $p < \frac{1}{1+r}$ then there is no trading of good loans at period 1. Then, the stake $F_B$ such that the bank has an incentive to monitor is the same as in the conditions of Proposition 5.1: $F_B \geq \frac{B(1+r)}{\Delta p}$. The bank's valuation of the loan is also the same depending on monitoring, and monitoring and retaining a share of the loans follow the same logic as in that proposition.

If $p \geq \frac{1}{1+r}$ then there will be trading at period 1 and the informed bank, whether the loan is performing or not, will sell its residual stake for $pF_B$. Note that we are still under the assumption there would be a stake $F_B$ such that the bank had an incentive to monitor from period 0. We express the loan valuation at time 0 as a function of monitoring given this retained share $F_B$:

$$L_M = p(F - F_B) + pF_B = pF,$$

where the first term is the contribution from selling part of the loan at time 0, and the second from trading at time 1, and

$$L_{\overline{M}} = B + (p - \Delta p)F.$$

By assumption, $(1 + r)B < \Delta pF$ so necessarily $B < \Delta pF$ and as a consequence we always have $L_M < L_{\overline{M}}$ for all $F_B$, and there never is any monitoring. □

The bad securitization outcome stems from the fact that, relative to the prior "good" case, there is a situation where the funding cost differential between the bank and the market verifies

$$\frac{1-p}{p} \leq r \leq \frac{\Delta p(F\Delta p - B)}{pB},$$

and there is no monitoring although it is inefficient, because the bank would be better off if it could credibly commit to not trade its stake at period 1, and hence monitor the loans, as in the prior "good" case. Plantin interprets this outcome as excessive securitization (selling the entire stake) and lax screening (lack of monitoring). If the benefit in loan performance improvement due to monitoring is significant, then the higher limit for $r$ for this situation to happen is increased.

#### 5.2.1.4 Application to the Subprime Boom/Bust Narrative

Before the subprime boom, we can consider that the differential funding cost $r$, being small enough, verified $r \leq \frac{1-p}{p}$ and $r \leq \frac{\Delta p(F\Delta p-B)}{pB}$. In this situation, partial securitization was optimal and banks had an incentive to monitor the loans. As market yields declined more than bank funding costs, $r$ increased and reached above $\frac{1-p}{p}$, at which point we observe excessive securitization (sale of the entire stake) combined with no monitoring, which leads to increased default rates, both consistent with the subprime market dislocation from the late 2000s.

Further, note that if monitoring costs go to zero, the ratio $\frac{\Delta p(F\Delta p-B)}{pB}$ goes to infinity and as a result the inequation characterizing inefficient securitization is always verified. So even if the cost of monitoring vanishes, and one would have hoped that banks would chose to monitor, there will still be too much securitization and the bank will not retain a share of the loans as $r$ increases.

The overall approach hinges on three important assumptions in explaining the bad side of securitization, which are reasonably consistent with our understanding of subprime lending:

- Banks cannot credibly commit to a contractual risk transfer. They will try and shirk a commitment to monitor loans if they can.
- Monitoring takes place early in the life of the loans.
- The bank can obtain valuable private information by monitoring the loans.

While the model in Plantin (2011) gives us interesting insights into the onset of the subprime crisis, it cannot account for the significant compounding effect the effective relationships between $r$ and $p$ exerted. Indeed, since a large majority of subprime loans were securitized, the rates that the borrowers themselves paid on their loans were driven by the securitization market yields, which in our narrative were going down. Directly (by lowering mortgage payments) or indirectly (by pushing home prices up), the decline in secondary yields, and not their level, pushed default rates down. Borrowers were generally able to continuously refinance into cheaper loans or based off of higher house estimates. When the secondary yields stopped declining, borrowers could not refinance cheaply anymore, and having to face their payments were more likely to default. Hence, one could represent this as a relationship between $p$ and the change in $r$ (assuming the banks' funding costs did not evolve as much as the market yields). Because if this relationship holds, then the increase in default rates was greater than simply $\Delta p$, and as defaults increased and markets priced them in, the yields on secondary rates gaped out further, feeding further increases in defaults by the same mechanism.

It is worth stressing that the early monitoring assumption, or lack thereof, seems particularly relevant. Indeed, at the onset of the mortgage crisis, there was an unprecedented raise in early payment defaults or **EPDs** in the low end of the non-agency market, where loans would make very few or even no payment before becoming delinquent. These EPDs had been subdued up to that point. Such EPDs would have been limited by early monitoring and control of the borrowers by the bank.

We now turn to an empirical study that sheds some light on the phenomena we just discussed in a theoretical framework.

### 5.2.2 Securitization Led to Low Screening Efforts

In their paper, Keys et al. (2010) study securitization in the private-label mortgage market to determine whether the fact that loans could be securitized led to worse performance, all else being equal, because of less screening. Measuring the performance of loans depending on their securitization channel while keeping characteristics constants is far from trivial, so these authors had to devise a smart way of carrying out this analysis.

In the 2000s, as we pointed out in Chap. 2, loans with a FICO score under 620 normally could not be securitized through the agencies' wraps or in prime or Alt-A private-label deals. Hence, lenders making loans to borrowers with a FICO score under this threshold either had to keep these loans on their balance sheet or, due to the greater difficulty in placing them, hold them longer than the other loans.[4]

Starting from this realization, the main idea in the paper is to consider loans that were right under or right above that 620 FICO threshold: from the standpoint of credit characteristics they were presumably very similar, with the main difference being that the ones slightly above could be securitized as prime or near-prime paper, while the others could not. This constitutes an appropriate test case in order to assess whether a greater ability to securitize led to differences in loan screening and subsequent performance. Implicitly, one assumes (reasonably) that screening is costly, and hence would be only done to the extent that the lender benefits from it.

#### 5.2.2.1 Data and Analysis

The authors used data on non-agency securitized loans across the credit spectrum, originated between 2001 and 2006. During this time period, the subprime market had grown enough, and the securitization volume of these loans was sufficiently large to provide enough data points in this very narrow FICO band of interest. Note that there is no publicly available detailed information on the loans that originators may retain on their balance sheet, so comparing the loans that were securitized with those that were not would not be possible across a large universe. The comparison can be made between loans that satisfied the minimal constraint to access a larger securitization channel (with FICO greater than 620), and those that could only be securitized as subprime.

The loans' performance can be measured 2 years after issuance,[5] by tracking delinquency statuses. This gives an indirect measure of screening. A more direct measure is the loan documentation categorization, normally provided in non-agency loan tapes. The argument is that the relationship between credit scores and observed default rates or degree of screening should be smooth, and not change much for minimal variations in FICO scores; if it is not the case then this would be a consequence of less stringent lending standards on the loans right above the threshold.

Keys et al. first show that the volume of low- or no-doc loans jumped significantly at the 620 FICO threshold. They run a regression in order to document the jump as the FICO score moves from 619 to 621. They aggregate the origination loan-level data by FICO score on low- and no-documentation loans, so that for every FICO score $F_i$ there is a corresponding metric $Y_i$, the total volume of issuance of low- and no-doc loans with that score. They estimate the following generalized additive regression equation:

$$Y_i = \alpha + \beta T_i + \theta f^0(F_i) + \delta T_i f^1(F_i) + \varepsilon_i,$$

where $T_i = \mathbb{I}_{F_i \geq 620}$, and $f^0$ and $f^1$ are seventh-order polynomials which should fit both sides of the volume distribution. The variable $\beta$ captures the magnitude of

[4]Time during which they would incur the loans' credit risk.

[5]Recall that the FICO score is intended as a measure of the risk of a credit event within 2 years.

the jump in volume at the threshold. Running this regression for a range of other possible threshold values, they confirm that the jump at the particular threshold of 620 is significant for each origination vintage: at the 1% significance level, there is on average an increase by 110% of low/no-doc issuance at the threshold. This jump in securitization volume stresses that the loans right above the threshold are easier to securitize than the ones right below.

Although this strong relationship between documentation and FICO score can be observed around the threshold, this is not the case for other important loan terms: the distribution of LTV and interest rates on low/no-documentation loans, in particular, does not exhibit any discontinuity. This is confirmed with regressions along the lines of the one mentioned above, where the corresponding $\beta$ is not significantly different from zero.

Then, the authors turn to the performance of the low/no-documentation loans. They measure the delinquency rates approximately 1 year after the origination on the loans, bucketed by FICO score, and qualify as defaulted all the loans in 60+ delinquencies. Running the regression, they find that the magnitude of $\beta$ is large relative to the average default rate. On average, defaults on loans just above the threshold are 20% higher than those just below the threshold, which paradoxically have a slightly lower FICO score.

These results clearly point toward looser screening by mortgage originators on the loans that can be more easily securitized. This effect is further confirmed by two specific analyses using the same broad dataset:

- In 2002, the states of New Jersey and Georgia implemented restrictive anti-predatory lending laws, which almost brought the securitization of subprime loans from these states to a halt. This took away the advantage that loans with a FICO over the threshold had over the other loans in terms of ease of securitization. The data shows that the issuance distribution of no/low-documentation loans in these states as a function of FICO became smooth, as did the subsequent performance.
- Focusing on full-doc loans rather than low/no-doc loans, a threshold can be identified around a FICO score of 600: because of the greater ease with which loans above that threshold could be securitized, there is a significant jump in the loan issuance distribution. However, the subsequent performance does not show that same jump, and remains smooth across the threshold. This is consistent with the fact that on fully documented loans, there is less additional valuable information that can be acquired by more careful screening. As a consequence, there is no opportunity for a lax, cheaper screening strategy on the loans right above the threshold.

Although the data studied in Keys et al. (2010) only pertains to a subset of the mortgage market, at a particularly point in time, it clearly points to an undesirable consequence of the lack of incentives for loans to be screened when they are earmarked for securitization. Both theoretically and empirically, we've shown that having the opportunity to securitize led the lenders toward looser screening and monitoring.

#### 5.2.2.2 Extending the Approach to Agency Loans

Can we empirically verify these results in a much broader universe, with the agency loan-level data? It has the benefit of capturing a larger section of the whole market than did Keys et al., although the logic cannot be the same: the agencies do not provide documentation information (mostly because the loans are supposed to be well documented enough), and by construction the loans on which we have data have been securitized. Instead of using documentation information, we can consider the presence of mortgage insurance and its relationship with LTV. The loans with mortgage insurance are such that their characteristics forced the lender to have them insured so that they may be securitized. We may hence anticipate seeing a common moral hazard in insurance, where the lender would not care much for the underwriting quality on loans they know will be insured. Here, we would not be considering the fact that the loans may be sold into a securitization as in Keys et al. (2010), but rather the fact that the loans' credit risk be effectively sold to the insurer. Lenders would hence not carry all the risk of loans with an LTV above 80, if they were not securitized. On the other hand, lenders would carry all the risk on loans with an LTV under 80 if they were not securitized. On the loans that were securitized, the lender had little risks.

Figure 5.5 shows several metrics (delinquency rate observed 2.5 years after, OMS, percent of retail origination, DTI and FICO) as a function of LTV in pre-crisis loan origination, as a function of LTV. The curves are bucketed as a function of the vintage: early (before and including 2004) or later (from 2005 to 2007). Figure 5.6 is similar, but is bucketed by the presence of mortgage insurance instead of origination period.

It is apparent from both charts that measures such as DTI, percentage of retail origination, or OMS are reasonably smooth across the 80% LTV threshold and as a function of the presence of PMI. The credit score, however, is about 20 points lower right as the threshold is passed, and the observed delinquency rate doubles from about 4 to 8%. This jump in delinquencies is roughly consistent with the regression coefficients from Table 3.8, which would call for an increase of 3.6% in delinquencies in relation with that jump in FICO. Some differences in the observed cumulative home price appreciation, which is declining in the sample as LTV increases, would further explain the much higher delinquencies.

Hence, it appears that the loans on which agency lenders obtained mortgage insurance had worse credit characteristics, which would be consistent with a pattern of lenders being less stringent if they know they can shed off the risk. However, the credit characteristics of these loans do not make them significantly worse than would be expected, given these characteristics. The ex ante probability that a loan may be securitized is presumably high, and as a result there would be less risk to price in into the cost of retaining the loans as there may have been in the below 620 FICO subprime sample that Keys et al. (2010) considered.

After this close look into how the capacity of selling the loans led to less monitoring or screening, we will take the securitization rate as a given, and see how screening becomes suboptimal for the issuer, as securitization rises.

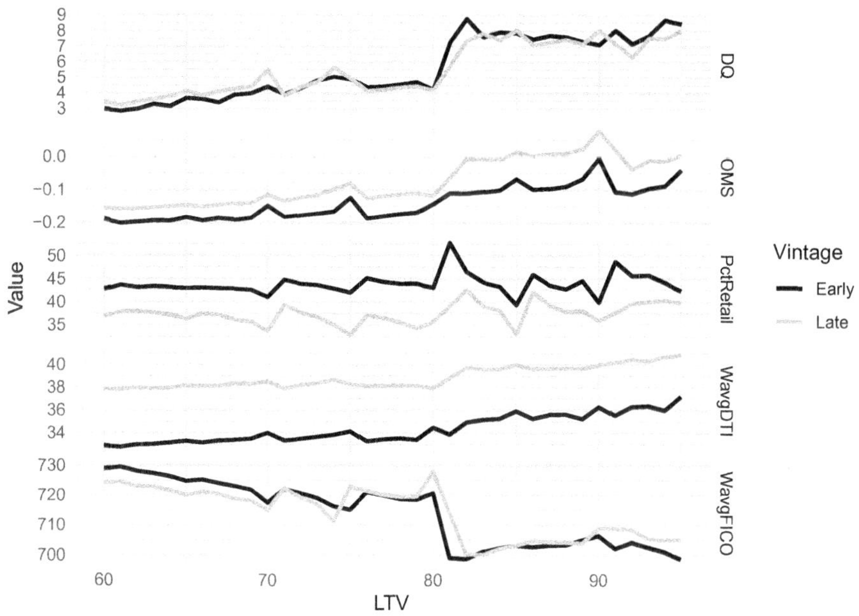


**Fig. 5.5** Analysis of LTV thresholds by origination period.*Source* Compiled by the author based on loan-level data from Fannie Mae and Freddie Mac

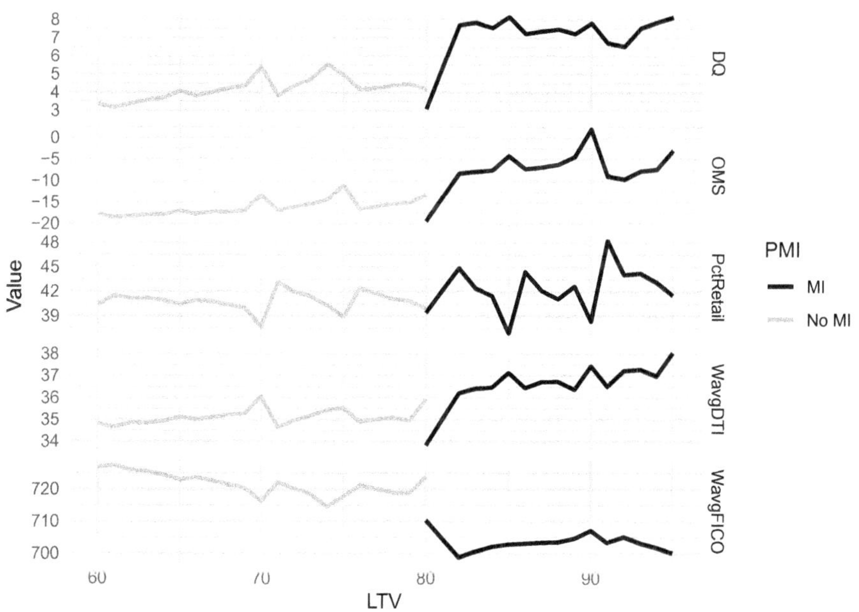


**Fig. 5.6** Analysis of LTV thresholds by PMI presence. *Source* Compiled by the author based on loan-level data from Fannie Mae and Freddie Mac

### 5.2.3 Worsening of Borrowers

In Rajan et al. (2010; 2015), the authors address the relationship between monitoring incentives, issuance volumes, and loan quality, following a different angle from Plantin (2011) which we discussed earlier. Indeed, instead of considering the securitization rate is driven by the bank's cost of funding, they developed a theoretical model explaining the degree of screening as a function of the share of loans that are securitized.

The model shows that, as securitization volumes explode, the loans are not screened anymore based on soft information. However, the statistical models of loan performance used to establish bank capital requirements and many other such limits are based on past data generated by loans that had been screened based on soft information. As a result, once can expect these models to underestimate future losses.

Then, using subprime loan-level data, they carry out an empirical study and verify the model's predictions.

#### 5.2.3.1 A Model for the Deterioration of Screening as Securitization Increases

We follow the model presented in Rajan et al. (2010) as a stand-alone publication. We consider a single bank, a population of borrowers, and multiple investors, in a two-period economy. All are assumed to be risk-neutral. The bank can offer loans of 1 unit to borrowers, who have to pay the interest at the end of the period. The loan interest is set to $r$, assumed to be the maximum amount that the borrowers will accept to repay, and that will not push them into default. We assume there is no discounting applied by any agent.

Each borrower is assumed to be of a random type expressed as a random variable $P$, one of two types, high and low: $P \in \{p_l, p_h\}$ such that $\mathbb{P}[P = p_h] = p$. The type affects the future loan performance: if they obtain a loan, a borrower of type $P$ will repay $(1 + r)$ at time 1 with probability $P$. In this setting, a unique rate is optimal since the lender will not know for sure the borrower's type, if we assume the borrower's acceptance of a rate and sensitivity to this rate in terms of default risk also depend on type.

Borrowers have both hard and soft credit characteristics, $H$ and $S$, which in both cases can be of high or low type. Hence, each borrower is defined by characteristics drawn from some random distribution $C = (H, S)$ such that $H \in \{h_l, h_h\}$ and $S \in \{s_l, s_h\}$. The hard characteristics are observable by the bank and by investors and contractible, while soft characteristics are only observable by the bank at a cost $c$ for each loan, and not contractible.

We consider that the random characteristics and types are independent across borrowers, and as a result will only carry out our analysis for the bank considering a single borrower. In addition, we will write the events of the form $M = m_i$ simply $M_i$, to simplify notations, so that, for example, $P_h = \{P = p_h\}$. The borrowers' characteristics affect the their types in the following manner:

- For $j \in \{l, h\}$, the probability that the borrower is of type $p_h$ conditioned by having hard information $h_j$ is $\mu_j = \mathbb{P}[P_h | H_j]$. We assume that $\mu_h > p$, so that knowing the hard characteristics are of type $h_h$ the borrower is more likely to be of type $p_h$ than without conditioning.
- For $j \in \{l, h\}$, the probability that the borrower shows soft information $s_h$ given that it is of type $p_j$ is $\gamma_j = \mathbb{P}[S_h | P_j]$. We assume $\gamma_h > \gamma_l$, so that the probability of observing soft characteristics of type $s_h$ is greater when the borrower is of type $p_h$ than when it is of type $p_l$.
- For $i \in \{l, h\}$ and $j \in \{l, h\}$, we define the probability that the borrower is of type $p_h$ condition by its characteristics $\lambda_{ij} = \mathbb{P}\left[P_h | H_i \cap S_j\right]$.

Also, conditioning on borrower type, the hard and soft characteristics are independent, so that for $m$, $i$, $j$ in $\{l, h\}$, $\mathbb{P}\left[H_i \cap S_j | P_m\right] = \mathbb{P}\left[H_i | P_m\right] \mathbb{P}\left[S_j | P_m\right]$. We have the following useful result.

**Lemma 5.1** *The probability of a high soft characteristics observation given a low hard characteristics observation is*

$$\mathbb{P}[S_h | H_l] = \mu_l \gamma_h + (1 - \mu_l)\gamma_l = \frac{\mu_l \gamma_h}{\lambda_{lh}}.$$

*The conditional probability $\lambda_{lh}$ that the borrower is of high type given that $H_l$ and $S_h$ are observed verifies*

$$\lambda_{lh} = \frac{\mu_l \gamma_h}{\mu_l \gamma_h + (1 - \mu_l)\gamma_l}.$$

***Proof*** We observe the following, due to the conditional independence:

$$\mathbb{P}[P_h \cap S_h | H_l] = \mathbb{P}[S_h | P_h] \mathbb{P}[P_h | H_l] = \mu_l \gamma_h,$$

and

$$\mathbb{P}[P_l \cap S_h | H_l] = \mathbb{P}[S_h | P_l] \mathbb{P}[P_l | H_l] = (1 - \mu_l)\gamma_l.$$

As a consequence:

$$\begin{aligned}
\lambda_{lh} &= \frac{\mathbb{P}[P_h \cap H_l \cap S_h]}{\mathbb{P}[H_l \cap S_h]} = \frac{\mathbb{P}[P_h \cap S_h | H_l]}{\mathbb{P}[S_h | H_l]} \\
&= \frac{\mathbb{P}[P_h \cap S_h | H_l]}{\mathbb{P}[P_h \cap S_h | H_l] + \mathbb{P}[P_l \cap S_h | H_l]} \\
&= \frac{\mu_l \gamma_h}{\mu_l \gamma_h + (1 - \mu_l)\gamma_l}.
\end{aligned}$$

Rearranging the terms gives the expressions in the lemma. □

We will assume that the lender makes a profit if it lends to a borrower of type $p_h$, but loses otherwise: $p_h(1+r) > 1 > p_l(1+r)$. The expected present value of a loan to a borrower of type $i$ is $v_i = p_i(1+r) - 1$, and $v_h > 0 > v_l$.

Once a loan has been extended it may be sold in a securitization, with a probability $\alpha$ exogenously provided. The investors select the loans randomly on the bank's balance sheet, and hence there is no strategic decision related to the selection of loans that get securitized. The price at which the loans are acquired by the investors only reflect the loan's hard information $H$, since they cannot observe $S$. Pricing is assumed to be competitive, so that it equals the expected loan cash flows. If, given hard information $H_i$, investors believe that the probability of the loan to be of type $p_h$ is $z(H_i)$, then the market price is

$$p(H_i) = v_l + z(H_i)(v_h - v_l).$$

If the bank retains a loan, its value to the bank will only depend on the hard information if it decides to never acquire soft information (noted $nc$):

$$\pi_B^{nc}(H_i) = v_l + \mu_i(v_h - v_l).$$

If the bank uses a screening strategy, then it will first observe the hard characteristics, and then decide to acquire the soft characteristics, and exclude the loans with $S_l$ (since if no loans were ever excluded, it would not make sense to spend the screening cost). If the bank uses the hard characteristics to decide whether to screen (we denote this strategy $lc$) and grants loans to hard characteristics $H_h$, and screens loans with $H_l$, we have the following expression for its expected profit when $H_h$ is observed:

$$\pi_B^{lc}(H_h) = v_l + \mu_h(v_h - v_l).$$

We define the expected profit on a retained loan, excluding screening costs, conditional on $(H_i, S_j)$ as

$$\pi_B^{x}(H_i, S_j) = v_l + \lambda_{ij}(v_h - v_l).$$

Using Lemma 5.1 we know that $\mathbb{P}[S_h|H_l] = \frac{\mu_l \gamma_h}{\lambda_{lh}}$ and as a consequence the expected profit when $H_l$ is observed can be written

$$\pi_B^{lc}(H_l) = \pi_B^{x}(H_l, S_h)\frac{\mu_l \gamma_h}{\lambda_{lh}} - c = (v_l + \lambda_{lh}(v_h - v_l))\frac{\mu_l \gamma_h}{\lambda_{lh}} - c.$$

In this case, the screening cost is always incurred when observing a loan of hard characteristics $H_l$, but the loan is only extended on the condition that it has soft characteristics $S_h$. As all the loans have the same interest rate, the only benefit in screening comes from the increased probability of repayment.

**Lemma 5.2** *If*

$$\lambda_{ll} < -\frac{v_l}{v_h - v_l} < \lambda_{hl}$$

*and*

$$c < -\left(1 - \frac{\mu_l \gamma_h}{\lambda_{lh}}\right) v_l - \mu_l (1 - \gamma_h)(v_h - v_l),$$

*then the bank will acquire soft information if the hard information signal is $H_l$ but not otherwise.*

***Proof*** For the bank, retaining a loan, to find it optimal to screen out borrowers with characteristics $(H_l, S_l)$ but not those with $(H_l, S_h)$, the expected profits from these alternatives should be on either side of zero:

$$\begin{aligned}
\pi_B^x(H_l, S_h) > 0 &> \pi_B^x(H_l, S_l) \\
v_l + \lambda_{lh}(v_h - v_l) > 0 &> v_l + \lambda_{ll}(v_h - v_l) \\
\lambda_{lh} > -\frac{v_l}{v_h - v_l} &> \lambda_{ll}.
\end{aligned}$$

For the bank, retaining a loan, to gain more by lending to borrowers with $(H_l, S_h)$ than by lending to all borrowers $(H_l, S_h)$ and $(H_l, S_l)$ (and therefore not screening), we need to have:

$$\begin{aligned}
\pi_B^{lc}(H_l) &> \pi_B^{nc}(H_l) \\
(v_l + \lambda_{lh}(v_h - v_l)) \frac{\mu_l \gamma_h}{\lambda_{lh}} - c &> v_l + \mu_l(v_h - v_l) \\
-\left(1 - \frac{\mu_l \gamma_h}{\lambda_{lh}}\right) v_l - \mu_l(1 - \gamma_h)(v_h - v_l) &> c.
\end{aligned}$$

If both these conditions are verified, then it is optimal for the bank to acquire soft information when $H_l$ is observed, and to then exclude loans for which $S_l$ is observed. □

The main theoretical result from Rajan, Seru, and Vig then states that in equilibrium, the rate of securitization needs to be sufficiently low for the lender to have an incentive to acquire soft information and screen the loans.

**Proposition 5.3** (Rajan–Seru–Vig Impact of Securitization on Screening Incentive) *Assuming that the conditions in Lemma 5.2 hold, there exist thresholds $\alpha_h, \alpha_l \in (0, 1)$ such that $\alpha_l < \alpha_h$, such that there is an equilibrium where the bank acquires soft information and screens loans only if $\alpha \leq \alpha_l$ and $H_l$ is observed, and an equilibrium where the bank does not acquire soft information if $\alpha \geq \alpha_h$.*

***Proof*** In order to characterize the equilibrium, we need to consider the investors' beliefs, which will affect how they value the loans. These beliefs, embedded in the term $z(H_i)$ which we defined earlier, may be that the lender screens, or that it does not.

The case where $H_h$ is observed does not raise any particular difficulty since in this case there is no soft information acquisition, because thanks to the first condition in Lemma 5.2, $\pi_B^x(H_h, S_l) > 0$ and even if the soft information was $S_l$, the bank would make a profit by lending. The loan's valuation for the bank and for the investors would be consistent: we always have $\pi_B^{lc}(H_h) = \pi_I(H_h) - 1$. Hence, we place ourselves in the case where $H_l$ is observed.

First, we consider the case where investors believe that the bank will acquire soft information (which we denote as before by $lc$), and screens out borrowers for which $S_l$ is observed. Indeed, due to the first condition in Lemma 5.2, we know that $\pi_B^x(H_l, S_l) < 0$ and hence if the bank does acquire information it has no incentive to lend to borrowers for which $S_l$ is observed. Hence, for the investors in this case $z^{lc}(H_l) = \lambda_{lh}$, or in other words based on their knowledge and information the probability that the loan is of type $p_h$ is $\lambda_{lh}$, and the loan market price is $p^{lc}(H_l) = 1 + v_l + \lambda_{lh}(v_h - v_l)$. If the bank sells the loan, it collects a sure payoff equal to

$$p^{lc}(H_l) - 1 = v_l + \lambda_{lh}(v_h - v_l).$$

However, the loan needs to have been made, and the screening cost has to be paid in all cases, and that only happens with probability $\mathbb{P}[S_h|H_l] = \frac{\mu_l \gamma_h}{\lambda_{lh}}$, and as a result the expected gain from selling a loan is

$$\left(p^{lc}(H_l) - 1\right) \frac{\mu_l \gamma_h}{\lambda_{lh}} - c.$$

This is the case notwithstanding what the bank actually does (it may deviate and not screen in fact).

If the bank does not deviate and carries out the screening strategy as anticipated by the investors, then its expected profit on a loan conditioned by the fact that it is retained (and recalling that we are still in the case where $H_l$ is observed) writes

$$\pi_B^{lc}(H_l) = (v_l + \lambda_{lh}(v_h - v_l)) \frac{\mu_l \gamma_h}{\lambda_{lh}} - c,$$

with assumptions that are consistent with the investors' beliefs. In this situation, the bank's total gain on the loan $\Pi_B^{lc}(H_l)$ when it applies screening, including the benefits from securitization at the rate $\alpha$, can be written as follows:

$$\begin{aligned}
\Pi_B^{lc}(H_l) &= \alpha\left(\left(p^{lc}(H_l) - 1\right) \frac{\mu_l \gamma_h}{\lambda_{lh}} - c\right) + (1-\alpha)\pi_B^{lc}(H_l) \\
&= (v_l + \lambda_{lh}(v_h - v_l)) \frac{\mu_l \gamma_h}{\lambda_{lh}} - c.
\end{aligned}$$

When the bank acts as the investors anticipate, the total expected profit per loan does not depend on $\alpha$, since the loan valuation is the same, based on the same expected cash flows, whether the loan is retained or sold.

If, on the contrary, the bank deviates and offers loans on all borrowers when $H_l$ is observed, there is no incentive to acquire any information. The expected profit on a retained loan is simply

$$\pi_B^{nc}(H_l) = v_l + \mu_l(v_h - v_l).$$

In this case, the total expected profit as a function of whether the loan is sold (a fraction $\alpha$ is securitized) can be written as

$$\begin{aligned}\Pi_B^{cd}(H_l) &= \alpha\left(p^{lc}(H_l) - 1\right) + (1-\alpha)\pi_B^{nc}(H_l) \\ &= v_l + \mu_l(v_h - v_l) + \alpha(\lambda_{lh} - \mu_l)(v_h - v_l).\end{aligned}$$

where $\Pi_B^{cd}(H_l)$ is defined as the bank's total gain including securitization, where it is assumed to screen but deviates (denoted by the exponent $cd$).

It is optimal for the bank to follow the screening strategy, as assumed by investors, if and only if $\Pi_B^{cd}(H_l) \leq \Pi_B^{lc}(H_l)$. This condition can be hence written as

$$(v_l + \lambda_{lh}(v_h - v_l))\frac{\mu_l\gamma_h}{\lambda_{lh}} - c \geq v_l + \mu_l(v_h - v_l) + \alpha(\lambda_{lh} - \mu_l)(v_h - v_l),$$

and after some simplifications

$$\alpha \leq \frac{-\left(1 - \frac{\mu_l\gamma_h}{\lambda_{lh}}\right)v_l - \mu_l(1-\gamma_h)(v_h - v_l) - c}{(\lambda_{lh} - \mu_l)(v_h - v_l)}.$$

We define $\alpha_l = \frac{-\left(1 - \frac{\mu_l\gamma_h}{\lambda_{lh}}\right)v_l - \mu_l(1-\gamma_h)(v_h - v_l) - c}{(\lambda_{lh} - \mu_l)(v_h - v_l)}$. Since the conditions in Lemma 5.2 hold, we know that $-\left(1 - \frac{\mu_l\gamma_h}{\lambda_{lh}}\right)v_l - \mu_l(1-\gamma_h)(v_h - v_l) > c$ and hence $1 > \alpha_l > 0$.

Now, we consider the case where the investors assume that the bank does not screen (which we denote by $nc$), still under the assumption that the hard information is $H_l$. Then $z(H_l) = \mu_l$, and the loan market price is

$$p^{nc}(H_l) = 1 + v_l + \mu_l(v_h - v_l) = 1 + \pi_B^{nc}(H_l).$$

The lender gets this price when they sell the loan, whether they actually acquire soft information or not.

If the bank does not deviate, and, as assumed, does not screen, then its own valuation of the loan is consistent with the market price and we have

$$\Pi_B^{nc}(H_l) = \pi_B^{nc}(H_l) = v_l + \mu_l(v_h - v_l),$$

and the total gain does not depend on $\alpha$, as in the prior case.

If the bank does deviate, then it can only sell the loans if it makes them, so that the gains from selling the loan can only be collected with probability $\mathbb{P}[S_h|H_l] = \frac{\mu_l\gamma_h}{\lambda_{lh}}$. As a result, the total gain from retaining or selling the loan is

$$\Pi_B^{ncd}(H_l) = \alpha\left(\left(p^{nc}(H_l) - 1\right)\frac{\mu_l\gamma_h}{\lambda_{lh}} - c\right) + (1-\alpha)\pi_B^{lc}(H_l).$$

In this case, where investors assume no screening, it is therefore optimal for the bank to not screen (i.e., not deviate in this case) if and only if $\Pi_B^{ncd}(H_l) \leq \Pi_B^{nc}(H_l)$, which writes

$$v_l + \mu_l(v_h - v_l) \geq \frac{\mu_l\gamma_h}{\lambda_{lh}}\left(v_l + \lambda_{lh}(v_h - v_l) - \alpha(v_h - v_l)(\lambda_{lh} - \mu_l)\right) - c,$$

which simplifies into

$$\alpha \geq \frac{-\left(1 - \frac{\mu_l\gamma_h}{\lambda_{lh}}\right)v_l - \mu_l(1-\gamma_h)(v_h - v_l) - c}{\frac{\mu_l\gamma_h}{\lambda_{lh}}(\lambda_{lh} - \mu_l)(v_h - v_l)}.$$

We use this term to define $\alpha_h$, and since $\mu_l\gamma_h < \lambda_{lh}$, $\alpha_h > \alpha_l$.

From the above, we can gather that

- If $H_h$ is observed, there is no information acquisition;
- If $H_l$ is observed and $\alpha \leq \alpha_l$, there is an equilibrium where investors' expectations are aligned with the bank's strategy to screen the loans and reject them if $S_l$ is observed;
- If $H_l$ is observed and $\alpha \geq \alpha_h$, there is an equilibrium where investors' expectations are aligned with the bank's strategy not to screen the loans;

and the proposition is proved. □

This proposition shows that, as the volume of securitization grows from an initial low level, a threshold will be reached where the originating bank's incentives lead it to not screen any loans, although it did have an incentive to screen loans in the low securitization setting. As a result, all else being equal, worse loans are originated when the securitization rate is high than when it is low. The market correctly values these worse loans. This also entails that statistical models that may have been estimated using data from a low securitization environment should overestimate the quality and future performance of loans originated in a high securitization regime.

#### 5.2.3.2 Empirical Tests

Detailed empirical tests of the theoretical model were presented in Rajan et al. (2015), as a separate publication, where testable predictions are confronted with subprime loan-level data.

Although the theoretical model does not formally account for the lender's setting of different interest rates based on the loans' hard characteristics, we can carry out an informal extension, by considering that the lender can decide on the binary variable of making the loan or not, as well as on the continuous variable of setting the rate. The rate is among the hard characteristics of the loan, also observed by investors. In the low securitization regime, since the lender potentially applies screening, then the approval decision and the rate depend on hard and soft information. In the high securitization regime, then both approval decision and rate depend only on hard information. In consequence, given the hard information there should be more variability in rates in a low securitization regime (due to the variability in soft information being reflected) than in a high securitization regime.

This gives us a testable prediction: as a function of an increasing securitization rate, the loans' interest rate should rely more on hard characteristics or the variables from the tape.

The second prediction is a straight consequence of Proposition 5.3: when the securitization is in a high regime, there is less screening and therefore given the same hard characteristics there will be a higher default rate. It is worth noting that this is true, even if investors know that the quality is worse, the difference being that they would have purchased the loans at cheaper prices (as is reflected in the theoretical analysis), and that cheaper price itself is reflected in the lender's strategy.

**The Data**

Rajan, Seru, and Vig gathered an interesting dataset. They used loan-level data from LoanPerformance, but complemented it with data from a single lender, New Century. The data from New Century includes information on loans that were extended as well as on loans that were rejected, and it also includes more detailed information on the loans than the tape fields passed to investors.

In LoanPerformance's data, they used its own categorization of subprime loans, which is itself derived from the issuers' own categorization (mainly a function of shelf and structure). All the usual loan-level characteristics, as well as information on the shelf and deal, are available. The authors also mention they only use data on owner-occupied purchases. They also exclude loans with particular features, such as VA guarantees or pledged properties. One worrying aspect is the lack of mention of anything related to lien. Since the authors specifically considered pools flagged as subprime that would have excluded pools categorized as second lien. But this would only exclude loans belonging to pools entirely composed of second liens; as we know, subprime pools generally held a few percentage points of exposure to second-lien mortgages. The issue with not filtering out seconds is that they will likely be reported with a low LTV (these loans are small), which creates a bias in the relationship between rates and LTV, which is one of the most important drivers of risk-based pricing. Also, looking at the evolution of the average LTV may not mean much, due to this bias.

The data from New Century tracks loans that were made or rejected as well as whether the loans were retained or sold for securitization. In addition, it contains various internal variables, among which a private rating, which can be used to represent the essence of soft observations.

Rajan, Seru, and Vig report the increase in securitization rate over time in the subprime market from the publication Inside B&C Lending, covering the entire subprime market, and show it raised from 37% in the late 1990s to 85% in 2006. Looking at the data from New Century specifically, the securitization rate raised from 41 to 96% over the period. This clear trend allows them to carry out the tests bucketing by issuance year, which captures significant differences in securitization rates.

**Drivers of Loan Interest Rate**

The first prediction to test is whether the loans' interest rate has been set with a greater reliance on hard characteristics reported to investors as securitization increased. More specifically, the following loan-level model is fitted for every year:

$$r_i = \alpha + \beta \cdot X_i^{FL} + \varepsilon_i,$$

where $r_i$ is the loan's rate, $X_i^{FL}$ is a vector of the loan's FICO score and LTV, and $\varepsilon_i$ is a residual error. For the whole subprime market, the R-square of this regression increases dramatically from 9 to 47% over the period.

Adding a series of dummy flags for loan type (FRM/ARM), documentation, or presence of a prepayment penalty, there is little impact: the R-square still raises from 11 to 50% over time. These variables do not account for much variability in interest rates.

The authors raise an important remark. It could be the case that there are new lenders entering the market and some exiting, and they follow different screening strategies, and the evolution that we observe empirically would simply be a consequence of a shift in the lenders set composition. This is addressed by fixing the set of lenders for which the regression is run; the results are essentially unchanged.

Overall, the authors confirm that before the early-2000s, it was very difficult to measure risk-based pricing in the subprime market, with a very large degree of dispersion in interest rates given some hard characteristics such as the ones available in a tape.

Narrowing the universe of loans but greatly expanding the available information, they analyzed the data from New Century with the same logic. The same model as the one mentioned above was fitted on the data for new loans,[6] and the R-square rises from 10 to 28% over the period, comparable to the numbers observed on the whole market.

In another regression, they added the internal rating as an explanatory variable. Adding this rating massively improves the R-square in the earlier periods, by 50%, which is consistent with the notion of the lender carrying out a detailed analysis of

[6]Interestingly, the authors mentioned they used only first-lien loans in this case.

soft characteristics. In the later years, the gain in R-square from reflecting the internal rating drops to 5%, which is consistent with this lender resorting almost exclusively to hard characteristics to extend loans.

As we mentioned in Chap. 4 when we discussed the evolution of securitization, the available systems to represent loan information have significantly evolved over time. In the early-2000s, most street dealers began using loan-level data, and investors also began to accustom themselves to using some of that data. Providers such as Loan-Performance helped to establish a standardized way of accessing and representing this information. Once this data was available, it was not necessary anymore to try and gather loan-level data directly from lenders. However, before that time, it was still possible to gain access to ad hoc loan-level data directly provided by lenders, and many investment banks used such data in order to carry out analyses. This data typically included many internal measures. See, for example, Banerjee et al. (2000), which shows how certain internal credit grades were used to analyze subprime credit performance. In consequence, there may not have been be such a clear dichotomy between internal, soft, and hard data initially. The soft information being by nature lender specific, it was very difficult to analyze across the entire market, and hence did not make its way into the cross-universe tapes used in the 2000s.

**The Failure to Predict Failure?**

The second test we discuss is whether the relationship between observed variables and credit performance did change over time, as securitization increased. The approach is to fit a statistical model of loan performance using data from a low securitization regime, and measure the quality of its projections on loans originated in a high securitization regime.

The model using the low securitization regime data is fitted as follows:

$$\mathbb{I}_{D_i} = \phi\left(\beta \cdot X_i + \mathbb{I}_{l_i}\beta^l \cdot X_i\right) + \varepsilon_i,$$

where $D_i$ is an eventual default situation, defined as reaching 90+ delinquencies within 2 years of origination, $\mathbb{I}_{l_i}$ is a flag for the loan having low documentation, $\phi$ is the logistic function, and $\varepsilon_i$ an error term. $X_i$ is a vector with all relevant loan characteristics from the tape (FICO, LTV, etc). The R-square is not very high, as can be expected with a typical loan-level credit model, at 7%.

The coefficients from this model are then plugged into the data on origination after 2001, to estimate the default probability and compare it with the actual outcomes. The model prediction error, defined as the actual default minus the predicted default, increased from about 4% for the 2001 vintage to 25% for the 2006 vintage. In relative terms, the prediction error is a quarter to half of the projected default. This seems to indicate that the model estimated using data from the low securitization regime significantly underestimated defaults on the high securitization regime loans.

One major critique that could be raised in the discussion of this result is that the evolution of home prices, understood to be one of the major drivers of loan performance, was not included in the default prediction model. Looking at higher defaults in the high securitization regime, all else being equal in terms of origination characteristics, may very simply by a reflection of slower home price growth. Another extremely important driver would be the credit environment: depending on interest rates and the accessibility of refinancing opportunities for credit impaired borrowers, prepayments may be much higher or lower, which in turn affects the observed credit performance, since the loans that have refinanced, if they eventually defaulted, would do so outside of the pool.

While the initial model does not include these important inputs, Rajan, Seru, and Vig did also run a model with home price appreciation as one of the drivers. Accounting for home prices, the mean prediction error relative to the projected default magnitude is approximately halved. They conclude that the mean prediction errors remain large and significant, and could be explained by the difference in securitization regime.

They used state-level, not MSA-level or ZIP-code-level, home prices, however, which do not capture as much variability as one would ideally want. In particular, home price appreciation in the late 1990s did not exhibit significant declines at the state level, and one would presumably have needed to dig to a more granular level to find pockets of negative home price appreciation. The impact of slowing home price growth on credit is explosive,[7] and it may well be that the model as parameterized does not capture this effect, which prevents it from accounting for the impact of the substantial slowdown in house prices after 2006. Combined with the lack of a factor to capture prepayment opportunities and incentives, we could argue the conclusion on the under prediction of defaults is not entirely convincing.

Rajan, Seru, and Vig do show, both empirically and theoretically, that as the rate of securitization increases, the degree of screening and use of soft information decline substantially over time. This may not prove a causal relationship per se. However, if we consider the evidence from Keys et al. (2010) at the same time, the hypothesis that securitization had a negative impact on screening and monitoring finds some very strong support.

#### 5.2.3.3 A Comparison with Agency Loans

We can test to what extent prime loan-level agency data confirms these patterns. We extracted a random sample of 500,000 loans, and look at these loans' OMS as a function of a few basic variables.

Table 5.1 shows the results from linear least-squares regressions, relating the off-market spread to a wealth of metrics. Three models are shown, the first one only using FICO and LTV, termed as "Basic" only on loans without MI; the second one using many more variables; and the third one including loans with MI. The data encompasses the entire production from 2000 to 2018 and as such covers a large variety of different environments.

The coefficients are all significant, but exhibit generally low magnitudes. For example, a difference of 100 points in FICO score only results in a difference of 10 bps in OMS. The variable Seconds measures the difference between CLTV and

[7] Recall the shape of the delinquency curves from Chap. 3.

**Table 5.1** Empirical models for off-market spread. *Source* Compiled by the author based on loan-level data from Fannie Mae and Freddie Mac

| Names | Basic | Combined | With MI |
|---|---|---|---|
| (Intercept) | 0.394*** | 0.419*** | 0.431*** |
| | (0.01) | (0.01) | (0.009) |
| FICO | −0.001*** | −0.001*** | −0.001*** |
| | (1.241e-5.00) | (1.269e-5.00) | (1.118e-5.00) |
| LTV | 0.002*** | 0.002*** | 0.002*** |
| | (4.663e-5.00) | (4.873e-5.00) | (4.764e-5.00) |
| ALS | | 0.00*** | 0.00*** |
| | | (4.896e-6.00) | (4.477e-6.00) |
| Broker | | 0.043*** | 0.047*** |
| | | (0.002) | (0.002) |
| Retail | | 0.046*** | 0.037*** |
| | | (0.001) | (0.001) |
| MH | | 0.173*** | 0.168*** |
| | | (0.013) | (0.01) |
| Purchase | | 0.013*** | 0.012*** |
| | | (0.001) | (0.001) |
| SFR | | −0.007*** | −0.011*** |
| | | (0.002) | (0.001) |
| Condo | | 0.035*** | 0.047*** |
| | | (0.003) | (0.002) |
| Seconds | | −0.003*** | −0.003*** |
| | | (0.00) | (0.00) |
| MI | | | 0.002*** |
| | | | (6.653e-5.00) |
| N | 388,549 | 388,538 | 499,989 |
| $R^2$ | 0.02 | 0.027 | 0.041 |

***$p < 0.001$; **$p < 0.01$; *$p < 0.05$

LTV, and capture the presence of additional loans backed by the same property. Flags such as the property being categorized as manufactured housing (MH), origination channel, or purchase versus refi have a significant but small impact, in the order of a few basis points. This is a markedly different situation from the regressions reported in Rajan et al. (2015), and the R-squares appear to be much lower as well.

Using all three types of regressions for each observation year, we plotted the resulting R-squares in Fig. 5.7. Although they started quite low, they increased significantly over time. Compared to the results from Rajan, Seru, and Vig, we see that the R-squares increased, but to a lower level overall.

This trend loosely matches the evolution of the securitization share through the agency channel, which increased dramatically after 2008, as shown in Fig. 5.8. For

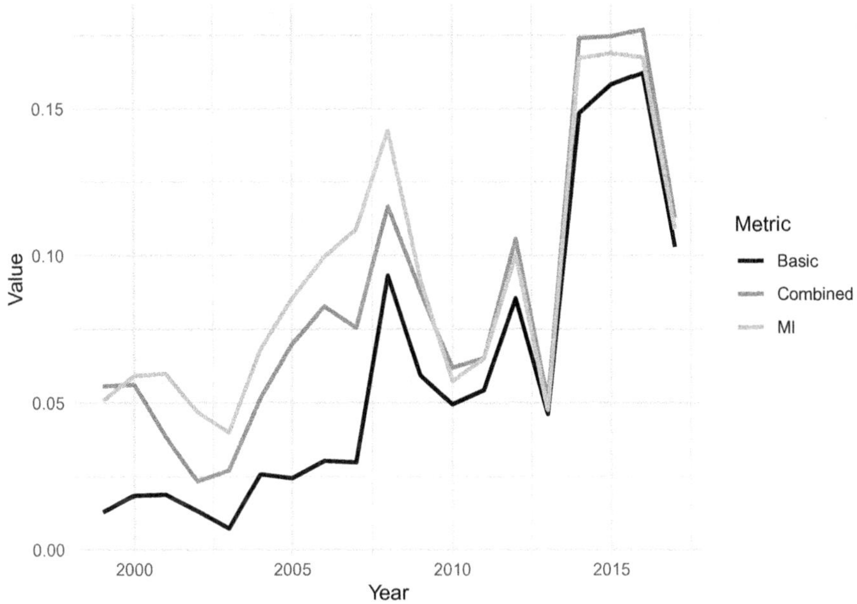


**Fig. 5.7** R-squared of mortgage OMS regressions through time on 30-year agency loans. *Source* Compiled by the author based on loan-level data from Fannie Mae and Freddie Mac

the types of loans that are captured in the agency dataset, we can consider that given their generally high securitization rate, the choice was less between whether to retain the loans or securitize them, but rather between securitization through the agencies or through a private-label deal. The choice to securitize loans as non-agencies was driven in part by the greater costs they would have incurred as agencies due to higher guarantee fees.

While the evolution in securitization channel may explain the similar increasing trend in R-squares between agencies and subprime, it does not account for the generally low level of R-squares. It simply appears as though the pricing of risk was less a function of hard characteristics in the agency market.

Another angle through which we can shed light on these patterns is to consider structure execution. As we will discuss in Chap. 6, and as we have alluded to in the discussion of security design in Chap. 4, a high coupon rate can be efficiently used for credit enhancement through the technique of excess-spread. In the subprime market, the coupon must be commensurate with the credit enhancement requirements set by the rating agencies, themselves a function of the loans' hard characteristics. In the agency market, on the other hand, once a loan has received a wrap, its valuation will depend on the market's assessment of its negative convexity. A subprime-like loan with a high coupon but with an agency wrap would have to trade at a very high price, because of the high coupon, compounded by the lower refinancing sensitivity brought about by its low credit quality. Hence, it is unlikely this would be fairly priced by the market. In other words, even if loan coupons were mostly randomly set as a function of their characteristics (or mostly driven by local competition and soft information

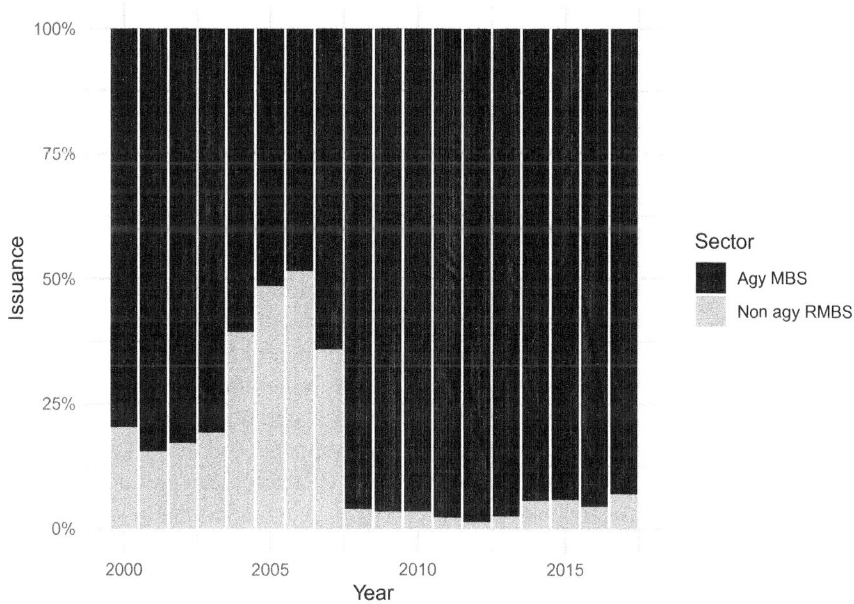


**Fig. 5.8** US agency and non-agency historical securitization issuance share ($bb). *Source* SIFMA Statistics and author's own calculations

as well), then the ones that would end up being securitized as non-agencies and subprime, in particular, would have to observe that coupon/risk relationship, while this would not be such a factor for agency securitizations. As a result, the trend in the coupon/risk relationship in the subprime market could be due to an increase in the attention paid to the efficiency of structuring in private-label deals, while at the same time a less strong relationship would be observed in the agency market. Note that it is possible that the subprime market would have been particular in that respect due to the fact that agency wraps on these loans would have been essentially prohibitive.

Having shown how securitization lead to the production of lower quality loans, we now examine a related issue, which is whether, given a set of loans on balance sheet, issuers would have picked the worst ones for securitization. We are not considering the way in which the loans are made anymore, only how they are selected.

### 5.2.4 Cherry-Picking in Securitization

When issuers decide to securitize certain assets, are these assets systematically worse than the others? Downing et al. (2009) look into this question, using data on agency CMO issuance. Although agency pass-throughs and CMOs do not have credit risk, we know they do suffer from negative convexity, which represents a true cost.[8]

[8]See the introductory description in Chap. 2.

Agency CMOs are created off of pass-throughs, which may be initially purchased as TBAs (hence reflecting the lowest available quality) or as specified pools. One can wonder if, for the purpose of further securitization through CMOs, worse pools have been purchased than those that were generally in the market. Downing et al. study the characteristics of CMO pools in order to answer this question.

#### 5.2.4.1 A Model for Cherry-Picking

According to the security design models we covered in Chap. 4, an informed issuer who needs to sell assets will optimally create informationally insensitive securities and retain part of the risk, in order to maximize its wealth. This is therefore applicable to structured securities, where one may design an arbitrarily complex contract allocating the cash flows. However, if we are constrained to the issuance of pass-throughs, the problem takes on a different shape, as by definition there cannot be any structure, and the decision for each asset (pool of mortgages) is binary: keep it or sell it at the market price. The whole-or-none trading decision is key in this approach, otherwise we know based on the various security design models that it is optimal to structure debt and retain equity.

We use the same overall model and notations as in our analysis of DeMarzo and Duffie (1999) from Chap. 4, with some important simplifications.[9] The issuer holds a series of assets which will return an amount $Y_i$, for $i \in [1..I]$ in period 1, and they can sell these assets. There is a holding cost, which can represent more expensive funding for the issuer, for example. Given some random cash flow $X$, the issuer is indifferent between a cash amount of $\frac{\mathbb{E}[X]}{1+r}$ and holding the cash flow. Issuers and investors are risk-neutral, and investors do not apply a discount rate.

We further consider that the issuer benefits from private information, represented by variables $Z_i$, for $i \in [1..I]$, taking values in $\mathbb{R}$, on the future cash flow $Y_i$. For simplicity, we consider the special case where $Y_i = Z_i + W_i$, such that $\mathbb{E}[Y_i|Z_i] = Z_i$ and there is a worst-case outcome $z_L^i = \sup\{z \in \mathbb{R} : \mathbb{P}[Z_i \geq z_L^i] = 1\}$, with $z_L^i > 0$.

Since the issuer values future cash flows less than investors, trading may happen at time 0. If $p_i$ is the market price for the asset $i$, then the issuer will be willing to sell if and only if $p_i \geq \frac{Z_i}{1+r}$. This price, at the equilibrium $p_i^*$, is assumed to verify rational anticipations so we have

$$p_i^* = \mathbb{E}\left[Z_i | Z_i \leq (1+r)p_i^*\right].$$

If $r > 0$ and $Z_i$ has a continuous support, and the above equation can be solved, all assets for which $Z_i \in [z_L^i, p_i^*(1+r)]$ will be traded.

For example, if $Z_i$ follows a uniform distribution over $[z_L^i, z_H^i]$, we can write

$$\mathbb{E}\left[Z_i | Z_i \leq (1+r)p_i^*\right] = z_L^i + \frac{1}{2}\left(p_i^*(1+r) \wedge z_H^i - z_L^i\right),$$

[9]Note also that this model resembles that of DeMarzo (2007) which is discussed in Chap. 7.

and solving for $p_i^*$, we obtain $p_i^* = \frac{z_L^i}{1-r}$ if $z_L^i \frac{1+r}{1-r} \leq z_H^i$ and $p_i^* = \frac{1}{2}(z_H^i + z_L^i)$ otherwise.

In the case of the securitization of pools of mortgages through the agencies, applying this model implies that the pools that are securitized should have worse characteristics than the ones that are kept by the issuing institutions. There is also another stage at which such a model is applicable. Indeed, the agencies themselves also benefit from private information through their analysis of the pools for the purpose of offering their guarantee. As a result, if they use that information when deciding on MBS purchases for their own balance sheets, they will further filter better assets. Finally, if the MBS pools for agency CMO structuring are purchased through the TBA market, there is further selection through the delivery option, which does not reflect private information but rather the picking of the pools with the worst characteristics given the market environment at the time of delivery.

#### 5.2.4.2 Empirical Tests: Are CMOs Lemons?

The empirical test to be carried out is whether the pools that back agency CMOs are worse, from the standpoint of negative convexity (which we know has a cost for bondholders), than pools that are not thus resecuritized (and potentially held by the original issuer or by a GSE).

The difficulty lies in measuring the degree of negative convexity that various pools exhibit, because, as we saw, convexity depends on the potential for directionality in prepayments as a function of interest rates. Hence, it is a measure of how things could change as a function of interest rates, which is not the same thing as measuring how they have changed. Nevertheless, we can only observe the pools' characteristics and their historical prepayment rates. Downing et al. measure prepayment speeds relative to interest rates[10] in order to capture the degree of adverse prepayment behavior shown by these pools. To be precise, the authors do not actually consider monthly prepayment rates but rather cumulative prepayment rates, relative to cumulative refinancing incentives, presumably in an effort to smooth out typically very volatile data.

Using the usual drivers of prepayments in a regression (WAC, cumulative home price appreciation, and cumulative interest rates incentives), the authors add an additional dummy variable for whether the pool was securitized as a CMO, both as a constant and for the interaction with the contribution from interest rates variations. It appears that the pools that are resecuritized exhibit a significantly larger sensitivity to interest rates than pools that are not securitized. In addition, the interaction between the CMO flag and home price appreciation over longer periods (4 or 5 years) indicates that pools securitized in CMOs are more sensitive to home price appreciation, in a manner consistent with these borrowers exhibiting a greater efficiency at exercising their options. In that respect, the pools that are securitized as CMOs can be qualified as lemons. Adding fixed effects for vintage or issuers, as well as alternate measures of interest-rate-related incentives, these results are found to be robust.

---

[10]Or in other words, prepayment speeds relative to the refinancing incentives.

One important question is the valuation of this greater prepayment directionality. Downing et al. chose not to use the actual pricing data on specified pools relative to TBAs (from pricing matrices for example), and instead use a form of OAS model, pricing the prepayment option, in order to derive a theoretical value impact from the more efficient prepayment option exercise in the pools underlying CMOs.

Depending on coupon (and on the overall moneyness of these prepayment options), they find a difference of around 5 bps in yield terms, which, if we spread it over a 4- to 5-year base-case average life, amounts to a fifth to a quarter-point in upfront value.

This significant difference clearly shows that the pools targeted for further securitization were worse than those that were more likely to be retained, in agreement with the cherry-picking model. It is worth noting that in an earlier study, which we discuss further down in this chapter, Ambrose et al. (2005) found that from a credit risk standpoint safer bonds were securitized.

We should stress that the fact that the pools going into CMOs were worse than the others gets priced by the market. Besides, there is an alternative explanation for the patterns observed above, although it may be difficult to prove empirically.[11] We will see in Chap. 6 how finely structured agency CMOs are, with very complex allocation of prepayment risk among various tranches. This tranching creates many bonds that are safer from a prepayment risk standpoint, and a few that concentrate much of the deal's prepayment risk. These risky positions are usually purchased by hedge funds and informed investors. The benefit of creating such complex structuring would be less if the underlying collateral was already fairly safe. In fact, specified pools[12] are rarely structured into CMOs, because they are considered safe enough in a pass-through form. As a result, the fact that CMOs are backed by worse pools may only be a consequence of the need for some structuring benefit to alleviate the structuring costs.

We now turn to the second important problem raised by securitization that we address in this chapter: its use as a means of regulatory arbitrage.

## 5.3 Securitization and Regulatory Arbitrage

Regulatory capital arbitrage, or **reg arb**, in the context of securitization, can be defined as the fact that banks may use securitization to reduce their capital requirements, without a corresponding reduction in risk.

In the funding of banks, one distinguishes so-called **tier 1 capital**, that is, funding that cannot be expected or requested to be paid back for a long time. Tier 1 capital is composed of equity and hybrid funding that has most of the characteristics of equity. On the assets side, recognizing that all assets do not bear the same risk, regulators define particular logic and methods to assess **risk-weighted assets**.

[11] As it would require running OASs on a large universe.

[12] Recall the discussion in Chap. 2, for example, NY pools or LLBs.

Regulators set a minimal amount of tier 1 capital that must be maintained, relative to the risk-weighted assets, generally termed the **risk-based capital ratio** or the **capital adequacy ratio**.

The regulations are varied and complex, but in a nutshell the Basel Capital Accords put forth that banks must keep a tier 1 capital ratio above 8%. Note that the notion of risk on the assets does not only include credit risk, but also all other risks, such as interest rates, operational, etc. Nevertheless, on loan portfolios, credit risk is usually by far the main concern. In addition, there are two approaches for determining risk weights: the standard approach, which relies on standardized risk multipliers set as a function of the characteristics of the assets, or the internal-ratings-based approach where the bank uses its own systems. However, in both cases, when considering securitized products, banks must use external ratings as inputs, that is, the ratings provided by the rating agencies.

In order to boost their ratio to put it in line with requirements, banks may sell risky assets (which reduces expected returns) or issue more equity (which has a high cost of funding), both leading to lower expected returns on equity. There is, therefore, an incentive to devise ways of increasing the capital ratio without too much of a detrimental impact on return on equity. One generally considers in this context that the capital requirements constitute the binding constraint in terms of funding, because banks can access very cheap financing through deposits or short- and medium-term debt. Recall Han et al. (2015) discussed in Chap. 4, where capital requirements as well as access to funding and lending opportunities all entered the bank's decision.

Finding ways of satisfying capital ratio requirements through reg arb may appear to be in the interest of bank shareholders, but it also increases the systemic risk of banks. In addition, carrying out such arbitrage involves structuring costs (such as those associated with securitization), so that the gains in return on equity through reg arb must be greater than those costs.

Following Jones (2000), we can state three general principles of regulatory arbitrage:

1. Concentrate underlying credit risk into instruments for which the maximum potential loss is much smaller than that of the underlying assets.
2. Use remote origination, so that the underlying assets are not originally created by the bank[13].
3. Use indirect credit enhancement, that is, not direct financial guarantees, which would be considered as risky as the underlying assets, but contractual arrangements.

Securitization effectively allows issuers to follow all three principles.

[13]Assets that were not originated by the bank itself are considered direct credit substitutes, and subject to a lower requirement than if they were originated, or ever owned, by the bank, in which case the retained risk is considered as recourse.

The first principle corresponds to retaining a particular junior tranche off of some risky collateral, rather than the collateral itself. The absolute expected return on the tranche may be comparable to that of the original portfolio of assets, but its maximum potential loss may be lower. By effectively selling the bulk of the amount of the original assets as senior securities at a low yield, the bank obtains a cheap financing for its assets.

The second principle can be easily followed by not having the bank itself originate the assets, but having the SPV originate them. In this case, the capital requirements are significantly reduced.

The third principle requires the sponsoring bank in a securitization to have the credit enhancements it provides not be treated as financial guarantees. This is of greater importance in certain types of transactions involving draw downs, where the assets may require more funding in the future. In this case, particular contracts provide that the banks would incur penalties in certain situations, the result of which is comparable to a financial guarantee but is not categorized as such from a regulatory standpoint.

We will first discuss the findings in Ambrose et al. (2005), who used US mortgage origination and performance data in order to determine whether issuers were selecting loans for securitization due to information asymmetry concerns or due to regulatory arbitrage. Then, we will turn to the more recent findings in Efing (2016; 2015), where the author analyzed data on ABS investment in Germany.

### 5.3.1 Is Securitization a Reg Cap Arb?

Ambrose et al. (2005) ask the question of whether securitization is driven by information asymmetry, as we have shown it may be, or by regulatory capital arbitrage. They seek to answer this question empirically, using data sourced from a unique lender on conforming and non-conforming loans.

Within the context of information asymmetry models, such as the various security design models we walked through in Chap. 4, we know that the greater the asymmetry or the loan's underlying risk, the more the issuer needs to retain junior cash flows, which creates an incentive for the issuer to retain the riskier loans and securitize the safer loans. In the reg arb context, the lender also has an incentive to retain the riskiest loans, for a given capital requirement, since these riskier loans will have higher spreads and expected returns than safer loans.

The cherry-picking argument which we discussed earlier, following Downing et al. (2009), showed us that the information asymmetry argument is not necessarily always pushing toward the securitization of higher quality loans. If the assets being sold could not be structured. Hence, if one observes that lower quality loans are retained, this would support the regulatory arbitrage argument to some extent.

Ambrose et al. obtained data on about 14,000 mortgages originated between 1995 and 1997 by a unique lender, with performance observations in 2000. While this represents very few loans, this data had the particular advantage of being comprised of both loans that were securitized and retained by the originator. In addition, further details were available distinguishing between agency securitization and private-label securitization. Overall, 5% of the loans were retained, 72% securitized through the Agencies, and 23% securitized through the non-agency market. Their tape had the usual set of loan-level characteristics.

In order to determine how the lender would have considered these loans at the time of origination, Ambrose et al. build a prepayment and credit model, predictive of future defaults or prepayments. The model has a simple linear multinomial logit structure but accounts for the bias in the data due to censoring a few years after their origination (recall that observations are as of 2000). The coefficients all have the signs and magnitude that would be intuitively expected.

Using this model, they computed projections for prepayments and defaults on the various groups of loans, and determined that the loans that were retained had a greater default likelihood.

Drilling further down, they looked into the drivers of the securitization versus retain decision. To do so, they first constructed a simple linear model for the OMS as a function of loan characteristics. Then using this model, it is possible to determine where each loan's rate came out versus the projected rate, which could be termed its fair spread. Then, they regressed the securitization decision on the loan's expected defaults, prepayments, and rate relative to the market.

They find that the loans with a higher ex ante probability of default have a significantly higher probability of being retained, and less likely to be sold into a securitization. The probability of prepayment is, on the other hand, significantly lower on retained loans; this is presumably a straightforward consequence of the worse credit quality.

Regarding loan rates, the results show that loans with greater prepayment probabilities and lower rates relative to the market are more likely to be retained. Ambrose et al. interpret this as the originator retaining discount loans that were effectively mispriced and would benefit from the higher prepayments. Ideally, it would have been better to model not so much the prepayment speed level, but rather the degree of negative convexity on the loans. The loans may prepay relatively fast, but in terms of valuation much depends on how these prepayments will vary in different interest rate environments. Still, some notion of cherry-picking may be at play for prepayment-related risks, while in contrast loans with worse credit characteristics are retained. This result seems, at least heuristically, in line with the findings from Downing et al. (2009) regarding the securitization of prepayment risk.

Interestingly, as we have mentioned earlier, prepayment risk is not the main concern of regulatory capital requirements, and in that case we see some cherry-picking, while in credit it is the opposite. This would seem to support the argument that issuers tend to retain loans with worse credit due to reg arb concerns more than due to symmetrical information considerations, and where there is less reg arb potential, in prepayment risk, then we observed cherry-picking.

### 5.3.2 Empirical Proof of Banks Arbitraging Regulations

We continue to look at the same problem, but now with a different angle, not from the perspective of the bank as an issuer of loans deciding to securitize some of them for regulatory purposes, but rather of the bank as an investor making decisions on the characteristics of the securitized products it will hold. ABS and MBS are substitutes to holding traditional bank assets from a reg arb perspective.

In a detailed empirical study in Efing (2016), the author looks at the ABS holdings, at the security level, of all banks in Germany, thanks to a national register of security ownership maintained by the Deutsche Bundesbank. In a nutshell, he finds that for a given rating category, which drives capital requirements, banks tend to buy the securities with the highest yields (and hence the highest systemic risk). Further, this behavior is more likely as the banks are more capital constrained, and is highest for those banks that are closest to the 8% minimal requirement. A first and important consideration is that the spread on securitized products reflects risks that are relevant to investors. As we know, informationally insensitive securities should not reflect particular credit risks in their valuations, as was also empirically shown.[14] Hence, variations in spread presumably represent a degree of information sensitivity. In addition, ratings may not reflect all risks precisely, and variation in spreads within the same rating level are expected to reflect variations in perceived risks by the market. Besides, as we will discuss in much detail in Chap. 8, there are various reasons why ratings may not properly capture the underlying risks of structured products. In consequence, securitized product spreads constitute a reasonable measure of the risks borne by these products, in addition to their ratings. Efing documents this situation by looking at the relationship between ABS and MBS spreads and their rating: within each rating level there is typically more variation in spreads than across ratings. This simple observation may be tainted by certain risks that are logically priced in by the market, for example, prepayment risk on certain MBS, which Efing does not account for.[15] However, given the wide variety of sectors and jurisdictions under consideration, this probably does not create a substantial bias.

As a direct consequence of this statement about spreads and risk, banks have the opportunity to gain higher expected returns, at the cost of greater risk, for a given rating and hence for a given regulatory capital requirement. Further, it is the banks that are more constrained by capital requirements that will try and increase their expected returns. The intuition does not require a formal model: consider that risk-averse banks seek to maximize their mean-variance utility. If the optimum asset allocation is such that the capital ratios are verified, then the bank is not bound by these regulations. If, on the other hand, at the optimum the bank's capital is too low, then as a function of the risk/return relationship and risk aversion, constraining by that capital requirement, the bank may have to select riskier securities at the cost of

[14]See the discussion of security design models in Chap.4.

[15]The right approach, although difficult in practice, would have been to consider OASs instead of straight spreads.

greater risk in order to reach its constrained utility maximum. This is the case unless the capital requirements are exactly adjusted as a function of the assets' true risks.

By holding ABS with the highest median spread within a given rating bucket and leveraging them to the extent possible as allowed by regulations, banks may obtain enormous returns on equity. For example, Efing mentions up to 70% in the A+ bucket. Things may not be so simple, however, because bank equity investors will typically scrutinize the bank's holdings and risk exposures and a bloated portfolio of leveraged ABS positions should not escape notice and lead to a higher cost of equity funding. Nevertheless, the fact remains that at the median spread, fully leveraged investment grade ABS and MBS promise very substantial returns (and risk, of course).

Hence, Efing expresses a testable prediction: that banks with tight regulatory constraints will aggressively pursue high ABS and MBS yields.

#### 5.3.2.1 Data

Efing gathered the Bundesbank's quarterly data on the holdings of securitized products by German Banks between 2007 and 2012, and mapped it to tranche information from Bloomberg and Dealogic. About 50% of these products were US, the rest European, and about 40% were MBS. Filtering out smaller banks and those with particular geographic investment constraints, the sample consists of 58 banks, which in total account for 65% of all German bank assets.

Then a dataset is created with every combination of bank and security, and a flag for whether the bank acquired that security within 6 months after its issuance. By focusing on bonds acquired little time after issuance, the issuance spreads (which is the only pricing information easily available) remain reasonably relevant. In addition, the spread and rating relationships also remain more relevant, since only initial ratings were provided in the data. After excluding some outliers and missing data, there are over 100,000 observations of banks/bonds pairs involving nearly 2,000 distinct bonds.

The data is joined with bank-level information, most importantly including the capital ratio, which averages out around 15%, with a standard deviation of 6%, which indicates that there are many banks for which the capital ratio is close to the 8% limit. Almost half of the bonds in the sample are AAA rated, the average spread is around 100bps, and average life about 6 years.

A first, and simple, comparison can be carried out by computing the average characteristics of the bonds bought by banks with a capital ratio above 10% with those with a ratio under 10%. The former bought bonds with a spread of 68 bps on average versus 153 bps for the latter. This is a very substantial, and significant, difference. Further, factoring in the risk weights depending on ratings and bond characteristics, the average capital requirement per face value was 1.8% for the former, and 3.3% for the latter, presumably reflecting the lower ratings on these bonds. Taking the ratio of the spread[16] over the capital requirement gives the return on equity for these

[16]Implicitly assuming that the bank's cost of funding would be the spread reference, that is, Libor. This makes sense, of course, given what the acronym stands for.

securitized products investments. It comes out at 47, and 73%, respectively, which clearly illustrates the yield grab by the more capital ratio constrained banks.

#### 5.3.2.2 Regressions

Efing runs a first test by estimating a linear[17] model for the probability that each bank buys each security as a function of all the bank- and security-level characteristics. The contribution of the spread is crossed with the risk weight category of the security, so that the effect of the selection of the class of security (the rating essentially) is separated from the selection of a spread level within that class. In addition, the interaction of capital ratio and spread is included, and found to be significantly negative: the lower the capital ratio, and the higher the spread, the more likely the bonds are purchased.

Other controls are added, such as the interaction between capital ratio and risk bucket, to capture the fact that banks with different ratios may seek different risk weight classes. The characteristics of securitized products are also added as dummy variables for sector, and average life and tranche size. The interaction between capital ratio and spread remains negative and significant. Further, adding bank fixed effects does not alter the outcome. In the regression with full controls, the interaction between total bank assets and spread becomes positive and significant, showing that all else being equal, large banks may be pursuing regulatory arbitrage more aggressively. One potentially important question that could be answered using this data and which Efing does not address is the extent to which the product category, all else being equal drove the likelihood of purchase. Consumer-loan-backed ABS, for example, tend to trade at tighter spreads than mortgage-backed securities, and CDOs at wider spreads, and as a result one could wonder if the search for wider spreads translated into riskier products within a given sector, or simply a shift in sector allocation. This shift in allocation would be consistent with the large increase in non-agency MBS and CDO issuance relative to other products through the 2000s, which we documented in Chap. 2.

Looking at the coefficients for the capital ratio and spread interaction by risk weight bucket, it appears that banks with low ratios invest more aggressively in the higher rated bonds, which is consistent with these bonds offering the largest return pickup per capital use.

An alternative specification of the model hat Efing explored is to express investment not as a binary variable, but rather as an amount, or equivalently to weigh the investment decision by the amount invested. The results remain qualitatively comparable, although some of the coefficients are less statistically significant.

One interesting remark that Efing makes is that the search for higher yield by more leveraged institutions could be unrelated to regulatory issues but instead come from a straight agency problem between the bank's stock holders and debt holders. Indeed, if the capital cushion is low, it may be optimal for the equity holders to promote risk-seeking strategies, as they are long a call option that may be near or

[17]Testing with a probit model yields the same qualitative results and a better R-square.

out of the money. How can one disambiguate this effect from the regulatory issue we are concerned with? The author computes the leverage ratio, as defined by the total unweighted assets (that is, not reflecting the regulatory risk loadings) over the bank's equity. This ratio is relevant for the agency problem, but it is not for the regulatory problem, and it is the opposite situation for the capital ratio we have been discussing thus far. Running the regression models with the unweighted leverage, it appears that leverage does not affect the reach for yield. Hence, it is not high leverage, but truly low regulatory ratios that drive the reach for higher yields.

The paradoxical conclusion from this empirical model is that the banks deemed weakest from a regulatory standpoint have a specific incentive to invest into riskier products than their safer counterparts. In order to confirm the greater degree of effective risk taken on by these more constrained banks, Efing analyzed the ex post performance of the securitized products held by the banks as a function of their capital ratio. He used 90-day delinquencies captured 9 months after issuance, while controlling for the amount of credit enhancement.[18] It appears that banks with high capital ratios tended to purchase securities with collateral that performed well after issuance, while those with a low capital ratio purchased a greater share of securities performing badly eventually.

Efing's results strike a particular chord from a practitioner's perspective, because it is highly congruent with and provides a cogent explanation for the heuristic notion that many banks, in particular European ones, would buy securitized products without much apparent concern for the analysis of the underlying risks. These banks, looking for yield pickups, purchased more complex securities such as CDOs, which for the same rating, carried greater risks than the underlying MBS as we will see in Chaps. 6 and 8.

## 5.4 Conclusion

In spite of the apparently attractive underpinnings of securitization, we have seen it was also natural to expect some issues as securitization rose to a prominent way of financing. Through some broad characterizations of the late 2000s mortgage crisis, we first saw that securitized loans exhibited abysmal credit performance. Then, focusing on a few theoretical and empirical models of loan screening and monitoring, we saw how securitization would likely go hand in hand with a lowering of credit standards. Including agency loans in the analysis gave us a much wider perspective and we observed that the data was consistent with the underlying patterns of looser

[18]Naturally, a high degree of delinquencies does not translate into worse cash flows or price performance, if it is within the expectation reflected in the structuring of the bonds.

screening. Finally, we briefly summarized the mechanics of regulatory arbitrage and saw that it was empirically confirmed to play a role in bank's lending and asset acquisition strategies.

Most of our attention so far has been on securitization as a way of selling loans, albeit with a basic layer of structure addressing information asymmetry. We now begin to delve into the details of real securitization structuring, which will be essential in understanding the economics of complex structuring decisions.

## References


Ambrose, B., LaCour-Little, M., & Sanders, A. (2005). Does regulatory capital arbitrage, reputation, or asymmetric information drive securitization? *Journal of Financial Services Research*, *28*(1), 113-01-33.

Banerjee, S., Gauthier, L., Tan, W., & Zhu, D. (2000). A study of RASC subprime loan prepayments, delinquencies, and losses. *The Journal of Fixed Income*, *10*(3), 47–67.

Boot, A., & Thakor, A. (1993). Security design. *Journal of Finance*, *48*(4), 1349–1378.

Dang, T. V., Gorton, G., & Holmström, B. (2015). The Information sensitivity of a security. Working Paper. Columbia University.

DeMarzo, P., & Duffie, D. (1999). A liquidity-based model of security design. *Econometrica*, *67*(1), 65–100.

Downing, C., Jaffee, D., & Wallace, N. (2009). Is the market for mortgage-backed securities a market for lemons? *The Review of Financial Studies*, *22*(7), 2457–2494.

Efing, M. (2016). Arbitraging the basel securitization framework: Evidence from German ABS investment. ESRB Report 22. European Systemic Risk Board.

Efing, M. (2019). Reaching for yield in the ABS market: Evidence from German bank investments. *Review of Finance*, August.

Frame, W. S. (2017). Agency conflicts in residential mortgage securitization: What does the empirical literature tell us? FRB Atlanta Working Paper 2017-1. Federal Reserve Bank of Atlanta.

Goodman, L. S. (2016). The rebirth of securitization: Where is the private-label mortgage market? *The Journal of Structured Finance*, *22*(1), 8–19.

Gorton, G., & Metrick, A. (2013). Chapter 1 - Securitization. In G. Constantinides, M. Harris, & R. M. Stulz (Eds.), *Handbook of the Economics of Finance* (pp. 2:1–70). Amsterdam: Elsevier .

Gorton, G., & Souleles, N. (2007). Special purpose vehicles and securitization. In *The Risks of Financial Institutions* (pp. 549–602). National Bureau of Economic Research, Inc.

Han, J., Park, K., & Pennacchi, G. (2015). Corporate taxes and securitization. *Journal of Finance 70* (3), 1287–1321.

Hanson, S., & Sunderam, A. (2013). Are there too many safe securities? Securitization and the incentives for information production. *Journal of Financial Economics*, *108*, 565–584.

Iacobucci, E. M., & Winter, R. A. (2005). Asset securitization and asymmetric information. *Journal of Legal Studies*, *24*(1), 161–206.

Jones, D. (2000). Emerging problems with the basel capital accord: Regulatory capital arbitrage and related issues. *Journal of Banking & Finance*, *24*(1–2), 35–58.

Keys, B. J., Mukherjee, T., Seru, A., & Vig, V. (2010). Did securitization lead to lax screening? evidence from subprime loans. *The Quarterly Journal of Economics*, *125*(1), 307–362.

Pagano, M., & Volpin, P. (2012). Securitization, transparency and liquidity. *Review of Financial Studies*, *25*(8), 2417–2453.

Paligorova, T. (2009). Agency conflicts in the process of securitization. *Bank of Canada Review*, *2009*(Autumn), 36–50.

Plantin, G. (2011). Good securitization, bad securitization. Institute for Monetary and Economic Studies 2011-E-4. Bank of Japan.

Rajan, U., Seru, A., & Vig, V. (2010). Statistical default models and incentives. *The American Economic Review*, *100*(2), 506–10.

Rajan, U., Seru, A., & Vig, V. (2015). The failure of models that predict failure: Distance, incentives, and defaults. *Journal of Financial Economics*, *115*(2), 237–2360.

# Structuring Securitized Bonds

# 6

Given a portfolio of assets, typically homogeneous enough, we are now going to see how to manufacture bonds that possess targeted characteristics, using the cash flows coming from the asset portfolio. It is generally considered that complex structuring began in the mid-1980s, with agency CMOs. Credit structuring came a few years later, in the late 1980s when the first non-agency MBS were issued. However, the techniques that were then used on these non-agencies were simple senior/subordination, a notion that had existed for centuries before.

All the various structuring techniques used in securitization deal with how one allocates cash flows. These techniques deal with attributing rights to payments to some in priority over others, and doing so in an optimal manner that satisfies all initial investors. As such, it can be seen as a particular application of contract theory, as most of the drivers of contract optimization are present: moral hazard, asymmetric information, and signaling. One could argue that although the analysis of securitized products is a part of mathematical finance, structuring is better analyzed with the logic of contract theory.

Although countless papers have referred to securitization and structures in general, there is little academic literature truly focusing on the details of securitized bonds structures. In a few rare cases, academic research papers discussing complex securitization structural details are misleading or even factually wrong if read with the attentive eye of a practitioner.

One example of a detailed academic overview of structures in the mortgage market is Gorton (2008), which offers a discussion of certain particular structures and addresses some specific aspects, citing Wall Street research reports. Ashcraft and Schuermann (2008) also briefly present some of the typical structural features of subprime securitizations, as well as a detailed account of collateral characteristics.

Some detailed aspects of structuring are exposed in Fabozzi (2006). Descriptions and analyzes of various structures in varying degrees of detail can be found



L. Gauthier, *Securitization Economics*, Springer Texts in Business and Economics,
https://doi.org/10.1007/978-3-030-50326-0_6

in analyst reports such as Kulasson (2001), Gauthier (2004), Chaudhary (2006) for agency structures, for example, and for non-agency structures Mansukhani and Qbbaj (2005), Gauthier and Zimmerman (2002a, b), or Gauthier (2002). All these reports are investment bank research intended for institutional investors.

Our objective in this chapter is to discuss the main structural features of securitization transactions in a systematic fashion and dispel any fuziness or misunderstanding about their behavior. The first section is an overview of structuring and lays the main principles of structuring logic. The second section describes a series of structuring techniques in detail, and we relate some of these structures to the basic security designs presented in Chap. 4. We also illustrate how some structures are usually combined.

## 6.1 Overview

Before stepping through a catalog of structuring techniques, we briefly discuss some useful general notions. First, we define a few key terms and concepts. Then, we examine a simple but formal framework to define structures, which will be used hereafter. Next, we list a few aspects in which structures are supposed to be optimal in practice. Finally, we define some basic collateral assumptions that will be used throughout the chapter to illustrate structural mechanisms.

### 6.1.1 Underlying Notions in Structuring

When a trading desk creates securitized bonds, the goal is to maximize the net value of the total selling price of the bonds, minus the carrying or acquisition cost of the portfolio of assets. There is, therefore, no overall theory or fundamental explanation as to what the characteristics of the bonds should be—these characteristics depend on what the investors want. The only logical assumption we can make is that the bonds that are created should have different characteristics than the initial collateral, otherwise there would not be any point for the investors to buy the bonds rather than the underlying assets.

Most often, one will tend to find common features in securitized structures: when credit is a factor, there are bonds that will tend to be particularly exposed to credit risk, and bonds that are less exposed to credit risk. The bonds that have little exposure to credit risk get a good rating, and tend to be attractive for a large class of investors, much more so than the underlying assets. The attractiveness here is not meant only in terms of relative value, or some notion of expected returns, but also because a good rating makes the bonds permissible investments, as opposed to lower rated or unrated bonds or assets.

**Credit enhancement**, which we have briefly mentioned before, is a central notion in structuring, it refers to making some bonds of better quality than the underlying collateral. We distinguish between **internal** and **external** credit enhancement. External credit enhancement is the use of a source that is external to the deal's collateral. A prime example of that is resorting to an insurer (recall that insurance on a bond creating external credit enhancement is usually called a **wrap**). Internal credit enhancement refers to credit enhancement created by particular cash flow allocation among different bonds—our main focus in structuring in this section.

The term of structuring is widely used in the derivatives markets, for example, for exotic options. The notion of designing a payoff function that is optimal for the seller and for the buyer is directly comparable with structuring securitized deals. In credit derivatives markets, the comparison can go even further since these derivatives effectively tranche an underlying reference's credit risk. The very terms of attachment and detachment points come from the credit derivatives market. **Attachment** and **detachment** points are expressed as percentages of a collateral's reference amount. As a function of that reference (for example, defaults or losses observed on a basket of corporate names after some amount of time), they specify the payments that the protection seller would have to make. If we write attachment $a$, detachment $d$, and the reference losses $l$, then the protection payments would be $\mathbb{I}_{d>l>a}\frac{l-a}{d-a} + \mathbb{I}_{l\geq d}$. The attachment represents the point from which the structure begins to take losses, and the detachment is the point at which the structure losses are at 100%. The difference detachment–attachment is called **thickness**. These notions of attachment and detachment are applicable in the world of securitization structures, but they are much more difficult to precisely define because of the overall complexity of the structures.

The so-called **pricing speed** or **pricing curve** is a particular assumption for the collateral, conventionally used in order to quotes the characteristics of some of the bonds. For example, in non-agency RMBS once used a prepayment speed of 300 PSA and 0 losses, and a bond would be labeled as a "2-year" and some other bond as a "5-year" because their average lives would be exactly equal to these values under these assumptions. Naturally, the chances that the bonds turn out to exhibit exactly these average lives are fairly slim, since the cash flow is random. Given the number of moving parts in a securitization, it is crucial to be able to fix many of them by convention, especially when quoting prices, yields, or spreads.

One usually distinguishes between **static** and **dynamic** pools. For example, a dynamic pool would be a managed portfolio of bonds in the case of a CDO, or a portfolio of all the mortgage loans on the books of a bank (including new loans being made). A static portfolio would be a set list of mortgage loans, amortizing over time. From a structuring standpoint, this does not have a large impact as it just modifies the principal and interest cash flows. When a loan is sold at a profit, for example, this creates an extra source of cash that can be attributed to principal or interest, and when loans are purchased this exchanges cash for a certain amount of principal. The only strong condition is that the portfolio be self-financed, that is not requiring any external inflow of cash flows.

Finally, it is important to realize that structures are described not in algorithmic form, but with extensive legal precision, in each deal's prospectus supplement and pooling agreement. The language below is one single paragraph stating the description of a subprime deal's payments, out of hundreds of such paragraphs.

On each distribution date, the trustee will be required to make the disbursements and transfers from the Available Funds then on deposit in the distribution account specified below in the following order of priority: (i) to the holders of each class of LIBOR Certificates in the following order of priority: (a) concurrently, (1) from the Interest Remittance Amount related to the group I mortgage loans, to the Class A-1ss and Class A-1mz certificates, prorata (based on the amounts distributable under this clause (i)(a)(1) to those classes of certificates), the related Accrued Certificate Interest and Unpaid Interest Amount for those classes of certificates, and (2) from the Interest Remittance Amount related to the group II mortgage loans, to the Class A-2a, Class A-2b and Class A-2c certificates, prorata (based on the amounts distributable under this clause (i)(a)(2) to those classes of certificates), the related Accrued Certificate Interest and Unpaid Interest Amounts for those classes of certificates; provided, that, if the Interest Remittance Amount for any group is insufficient to make the related payments set forth in clauses (i)(a)(1) or (i)(a)(2) above, any Interest Remittance Amount relating to the other group remaining after payment of the related Accrued Certificate Interest and Unpaid Interest Amounts will be available to cover that shortfall [...].

Our formal description of structures summarizes such detailed descriptions and abstracts out many details. Nevertheless in any transaction (issuing new bonds or trading existing bonds in the secondary market), notwithstanding the analytics tools that were used to come to a valuation, only the text in the legal documents (prospectus and pooling and servicing agreements in particular) prevails.

### 6.1.2 Formal Description of Structuring

We describe a simple framework for defining structures, and briefly illustrate how it can be used to define bond characteristics and stress the recursive logic in structuring. We will use the same type of assumptions as what we described in Chap. 3, tracking all the cash flows that define a loan portfolio. The collateral's outstanding balance is noted $B_t$ and its cash flow $CF_t$ at some discrete point in time $t \leq M$. With principal and interest defined as in Chap. 3, we have $CF = (P, I)$.

Structuring means creating bonds $\{1, 2, ..., n\}$ with balances $B_t^i$ and paying cash flows to their investors of $CF_t^i$, and deciding how the payments will be allocated to them so that $B_t = \sum_{j=1}^n B_t^i$ and $CF_t = \sum_{j=1}^n CF_t^i$, for all $t$. There is also an implicit constraint that $CF_t^i \geq 0$ and $B_t^i \geq 0$, since the bonds cannot take money from the investors. This means that when structuring bonds based on some underlying collateral, the sum of the bonds has to be equal to the whole. One cannot create cash from nothing, and one cannot make cash vanish.

As mentioned in Chap. 3, cash flows can also sometimes be decomposed into more categories, for example, principal payments could be coming from scheduled payments, prepayments and loss recoveries, and a particular structure could treat these sources of cash flows differently. We will not, however, go into the details of structures that distinguish between payments beyond principal and interest. Note that the core structuring constraint that $CF_t = \sum_{j=1}^n CF_t^i$ is expressed in cash flow terms, and does not necessarily translates into similar constraints on principal separated from interest. In other words, interest payments could be used to pay principal, and reciprocally.[1]

#### 6.1.2.1 Structure Definition

A structure can generally be represented as a particular function $S$ that operates on $B$ and $CF$ and returns a set of comparable pairs for the bonds that are structured. So $S(B, CF) = (B^i, CF^i)_{1 \leq i \leq n}$, subject to the constraints we have mentioned earlier: $B_t = \sum_{j=1}^{n} B_t^i$ and $CF_t = \sum_{j=1}^{n} CF_t^i$. Note that we can write $(B, CF) = \sum_{1 \leq i \leq n} (B^i, CF^i)$, as the balances and the cash flows can be summed separately.

From the basic description above there are a few degenerate cases. A first one is if we set $B_t^i = \frac{B_t}{n}$ and $CF_t^i = \frac{CF_t}{n}$. In this case, all the bonds created have the same size and exactly the same risks. There is another slightly more general degenerate case, where the $B_t^i$ are arbitrary, but $CF_t^i = CF_t \frac{B_t^i}{B_t}$. In this case, the bonds have various sizes, but relative to their sizes their cash flows are identical. The resulting bonds are **pass-throughs**, since the cash flows are just passed through to the bonds, and the bonds have the same characteristics as the collateral. In the more general case, the bonds' characteristics will tend to differ from those of the collateral, as that's the whole point in structuring.

In this expression of a structure, we consider that it operates on the aggregate cash flows of its collateral. The structure does not distinguish between loan #1 or loan #2, but considers them all as a whole. One can design structures that have specific rules for certain group of loans, in which case the structure does not operate on $(B, CF)$ but rather on $(B_k, CF_k)_{k \in \mathcal{L}}$ with $\mathcal{L}$ the set of all loans in the collateral. There are a few important specific instances where this type of approach is necessary, as we will see. Indeed there are certain structures that need to allocate cash flows differently depending on which loan they come from. This structure might not be the first that operates on the deal's underlying assets, and therefore its inputs would be some already structured cash flows. In that case, the preceding structure would keep track of its effect on every loan or group of loan as needed. For example, we might need to allocate prepayments from some loans to a bond *A1*, and prepayments from other loans to bond *A2*, but all this after a first layer of loss allocation. Hence, in order to properly define this prepayment structure the loss allocation structure needs to keep track of what it does to every loan.

#### 6.1.2.2 Collateral and Bond Characteristics

Given some asset $(B, CF)$, there might be some relevant characteristics that can be defined as functions of the entire path of balances and cash flows (or more properly speaking, functionals). For example, the average life *WAL* could be defined for each possible path $\omega$ as

[1] From a legal standpoint it is not trivial to use interest to pay principal, or principal to pay interest. In addition, both interest and principal may have a specific tax treatment. Hence, the generalized use of techniques that commingle interest and principal evolved later than other structuring techniques and dates back to the mid-1990s.

$$WAL(B, CF)(\omega) = \frac{\sum_t t P_t(\omega)}{\sum_t P_t(\omega)}$$

where of course the principal vector $P$ is just one of the coordinates of $(B, CF)$ since $CF = (P, I)$. If we were equipped with a probability then we could also define a notion of risk $R$ as the variability of average life.[2] For example:

$$R(B, CF) = \mathbb{E}[WAL^2(B, CF)] - \mathbb{E}[WAL(B, CF)]^2$$

The concept of pricing assumptions, or pricing curves, mentioned in the prior subsection can be understood as a particular $\omega_0$, used in defining the structures so that in that particular path then some characteristics are equal to a target value. Through structuring, issuers aim to maximize the aggregate selling price of the bonds, subject to constraints in terms of these characteristics.

#### 6.1.2.3 Recursive Aspect

It is important to realize that the notion of structuring can be applied recursively, as much as needed. For example, if we have a structure $S^1(B, CF) = ((B^a, CF^a), (B^b, CF^b))$ we could then apply another structure $S^2$ as follows: $S^2(B^a, CF^a) = ((B^{A1}, CF^{A1}), (B^{A2}, CF^{A2}))$. Naturally, we could also directly define some third structure as $S^3(B, CF) = ((B^{A1}, CF^{A1}), (B^{A2}, CF^{A2}), (B^b, CF^b))$ but it is usually clearer to decompose these structuring steps into logically separated operations. Hence the entire structure of a deal, from the asset portfolio to the bonds purchased by investors, can be thought of as a tree of atomic structures. Therefore, when we talk about a particular structure's collateral, this does not necessarily mean the assets portfolio, but maybe an intermediate stage in the the overall structure tree. Also, when we discuss a structure, we tend to say that it creates some bonds, while in fact they might need to be further structured into bonds that really are the end result sold to investors.

In the example above, $(B^a, CF^a)$ was the collateral to which structure $S^2$ was applied, and is presumably not the asset portfolio since it is already the result of some structuring logic. In market parlance, this tree or sequence of structures is called the **waterfall**, because structures are sometimes explained as water falling into a series of smaller and smaller buckets. Intermediate structures are sometimes called **blocks**. In Fig. 6.1, the bonds B are such a block, they would not appear in the list of all bonds eventually created (which here would be A, B1, and B2).

### 6.1.3 The Optimality of Structures

Before considering cash flow structuring per se, it is important to realize that the very choice of collateral is part of structuring too. Even though in some cases an

[2]We are not implying here that this is exactly the way structured bonds risk can be represented, this is just a simple way of presenting the concept. The metric used here could also be the yield, but it is more cumbersome to define in a concise fashion.

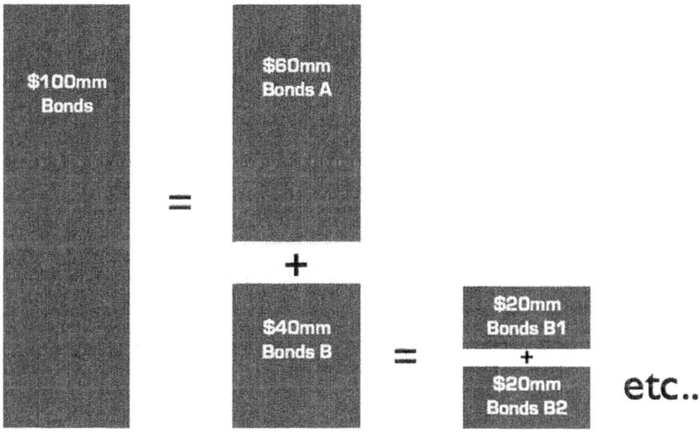


**Fig. 6.1** Simple structuring logic. *Source* Compiled by the author

issuer needs to securitize a specific pool of assets, the issuer can find it optimal to not securitize some of these assets, depending on a mix involving the characteristics of each asset, the structuring tools available, and the resulting ratings and anticipated market valuation. A Wall Street conduit may have access to a large pool of loans, from which many types of deals can be created, and a given loan may be securitized in an agency pass-through, in a prime deal, or kept longer on balance sheet, all depending on market conditions for collateral and structured bonds.

As we have mentioned earlier, structuring should be such that the bonds that are effectively created manage to optimaly satisfy a large group of market participants. However, the utility functions representing the preferences of these participants are never explicitly provided, and all their particular constraints are not always well known. In our discussion of the various types of structures, we will show to some extent why they are considered as optimal, by making a few simplifying assumptions and focusing on particular characterizations of investors' preferences.

It is worth listing and explaining a few stylized facts about structured bonds investors that we will then use in order to illustrate some aspects of structuring decisions.

**Rating/spread relationship** is a doubly important factor. First, from the standpoint of investors, setting a value for structured bonds will depend on a general notion of market spreads, modulated with the specific risks of the tranches. As we know, informationally insensitive tranches should be priced within a tight range, without a strong dependency on collateral characteristics. From the perspective of issuers, the rating and spread relationship is of paramount importance since it will drive the economics of the transaction. In order to maximize the gains in executing a deal, one normally needs to maximize the size of the highest rated tranches. As an important consequence, if we assume that all the bonds are sized maximally for a given rating (so that if they were minimally larger they could not maintain the same rating), then they have the highest degree of risk for that given rating. It follows that structured bonds should typically be expected to have more risk[3] than a typical non-structured security, which is not designed to maximize its risk given rating (such as a corporate or sovereign bond).

**Par-priced bonds** are preferred by many institutional investors, because on these bonds the coupon income will be aligned with the actual yield of the bonds. A bond at the market yield that would be priced much higher than par, say at 120, would pay a much higher coupon than required by the market (hence its high price). Over time, the holder must recognize a loss (due to the purchase premium amortizing), and an extra interest income, relative to a par-priced bond. Equivalently a bond purchased at a discount will generate income that is less than the one a par-priced bond would generate, combined with capital gains over time as the principal accrues to par. In both cases, the capital gains or losses may not cancel out from a tax standpoint with the extra or reduced income. In addition, from a reporting standpoint, the institution may need to report gains or losses that are in fact artificial.

**Rating requirements** might entice certain investors to only consider bonds with a rating above a certain level, due to their own investment charters. Some funds are only allowed to purchase AAA assets, for example. This constraint would be applicable notwithsanding the underlying risks.

**Yield** is a driving decision input for many investors, but not necessarily the "base case" yield. Indeed, a typical hedge fund will consider the yield one would obtain under a reasonable collateral behavior projection, but also and more importantly the yield under a set of stressed assumptions.

**Relative value** refers to the notion that some assets might appear cheaper in a structured form than in a non-structured form. This is typically a consequence of other, larger, investors preferences. For example, if many investors have a particular preference for a certain type of structure and bid them up, then with a given collateral purchase price, the remainder of the structure will be effectively made cheaper and could appeal to other investors. Another comparable situation could be if the market value of collateral declines, then if demand for certain parts of the structures remain strong, then as new deals are structured the remainder in these deals will become disproportionately cheaper.

### 6.1.4 Cash Flow Illustrations and Simulations

In our illustrations of various structures, it is useful to have some basic cash flow examples, and for that we will use a simple R function in order to easily create the underlying portfolio's cash flows as shown in Table 6.1.

We will also sometimes look at randomized cash flows. For this type of analysis we define two numbers in [0, 1] $h_l$ and $h_p$ such that $h_l + h_p \leq 1$, so that at every

[3]That is, if the ratings are consistent across broad sectors, which may not be the case.

**Table 6.1** Function to create basic cash flows. *Source* Compiled by the author

```
create_basic_portfolio <- function(OrigBal, Cpn, Prin, Loss) {
  prtf <- data.frame(Period = 1:length(Prin),
    BegBal = NA, Prin = Prin, Loss = Loss)
  prtf$BegBal[1] <- OrigBal
  for (k in 2:dim(prtf)[1]) {
    prtf$BegBal[k] <- prtf$BegBal[k - 1] -
      prtf$Prin[k - 1] - prtf$Loss[k - 1]
  }
  prtf$Int <- prtf$BegBal * Cpn
  return(prtf)
}
```

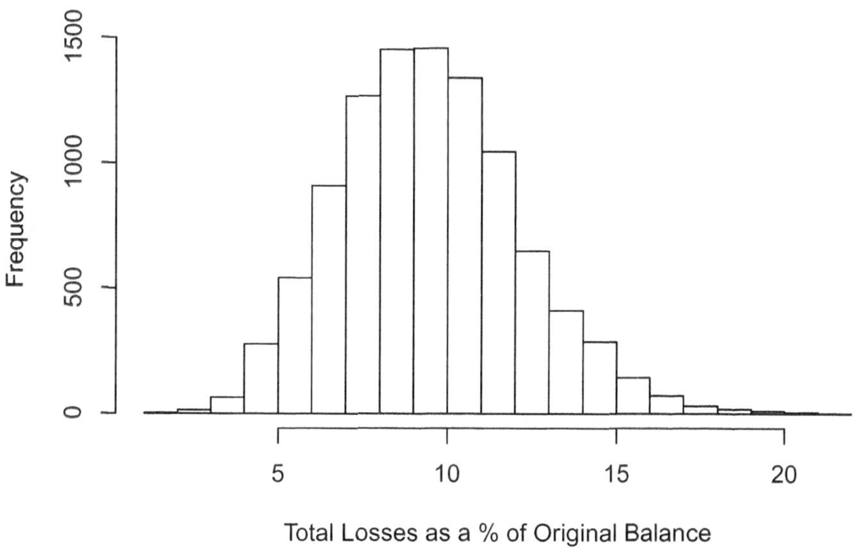


**Fig. 6.2** Distribution of total losses. *Source* Compiled by the author

period principal payments are randomly drawn in $[0, h_p]$ and losses are drawn in $[0, h_l]$. All the random variables are assumed to be uniform and independent. The function shown in Table 6.2 returns a large data frame containing realizations of cash flows. At the limit (with an increasing number of periods) one would expect that the total losses observed converge to $\frac{h_l}{h_l+h_p}$. Note that in the function definition, we leave the option of passing pre-existing vectors of uniform draws, which will be useful when we model correlation and CDOs.

With the default parameters we can run the simulations and check that the average losses are indeed close to 10%. We can also look at the distribution of these losses, as shown in Fig. 6.2. The average losses are 9.46%, with a standard deviation of 2.67%. The probability of losses exceeding 20% is 0.06%. Over 10 periods, the distribution

**Table 6.2** Function to generate random cash flows. *Source* Compiled by the author

```
make_random_examples <- function(smp = 10000, h_l = 0.05, h_p = 0.45,
                                 Cpn = 0.05, nb_per = 10, seed = 1234,
                                 ramp = 0, lossrand = NULL, ppayrand = NULL) {
  set.seed(seed)
  # Build or use random vars arrays
  if (is.null(lossrand)) {
    lossrand <- runif(smp * nb_per)
    dim(lossrand) <- c(nb_per, smp)
  }
  if (is.null(ppayrand)) {
    ppayrand <- runif(smp * (nb_per - 1))
    dim(ppayrand) <- c(nb_per - 1, smp)
  }
  all_portfolios <- list()
  for (dr in 1:smp) {
    rnd_port <- data.frame(Path = dr, Period = 1:nb_per,
      BegBal = NA, Prin = NA, Loss = NA)
    rnd_port$BegBal[1] <- 100
    loss_rd <- h_l * lossrand[, dr]
    prin_rd <- h_p * ppayrand[, dr]
    # Ramp specifies a more progressive increase in
    # principal and losses
    if (ramp > 0) {
      rmp <- c((1:ramp)/ramp, rep(1, nb_per - ramp))
      loss_rd <- loss_rd * rmp
      prin_rd <- prin_rd * rmp[-nb_per]
    }
    for (k in 1:nb_per) {
      rnd_port$Int[k] <- Cpn * rnd_port$BegBal[k]
      rnd_port$Loss[k] <- loss_rd[k] * rnd_port$BegBal[k]
      if (k < nb_per) {
        rnd_port$Prin[k] <- prin_rd[k] * rnd_port$BegBal[k]
      } else {
        rnd_port$Prin[k] <- rnd_port$BegBal[k] - rnd_port$Loss[k]
      }
      if (k < nb_per) {
        rnd_port$BegBal[k + 1] <- rnd_port$BegBal[k] -
          rnd_port$Prin[k] - rnd_port$Loss[k]
      }
    }
    all_portfolios[[length(all_portfolios) + 1]] <- data.table(rnd_port)
  }
  return(rbindlist(all_portfolios))
}
```

of losses is already relatively tight. The average cash flows on this simulated collateral show a fairly quick repayment of principal, and losses declining proportionately, as can be seen in Fig. 6.3.

If we force a ramp, then the cash flows are less front-loaded, as illustrated in Fig. 6.4. Note that since the relative proportions of losses and principal are not changed, at the limit we would still have losses converging to $\frac{h_l}{h_l+h_p}$, but a little slower than before. Hence the total losses in this case are just slightly lower than in the previous case.

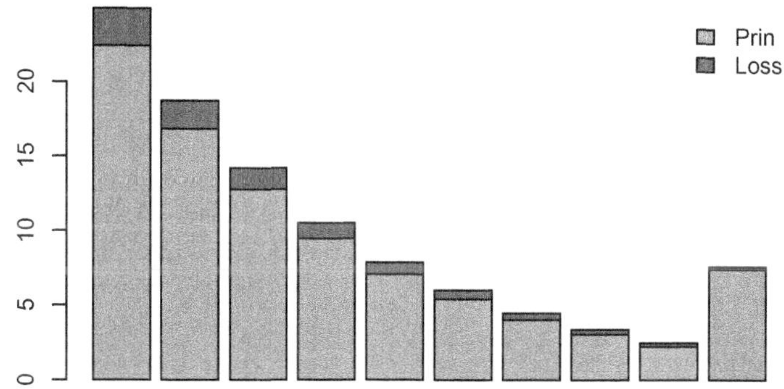


**Fig. 6.3** Average collateral cash flows over time. *Source* Compiled by the author

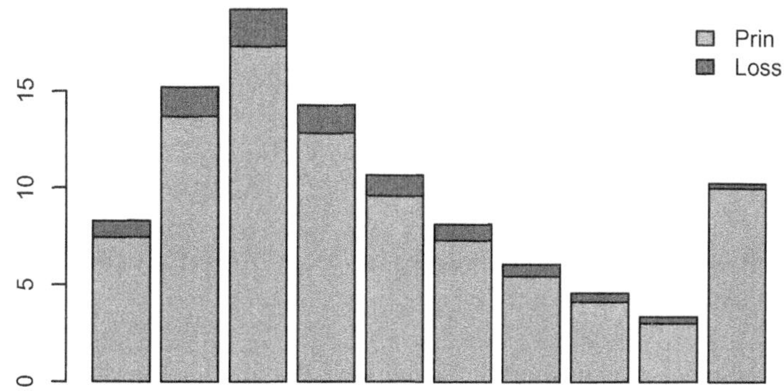


**Fig. 6.4** Average collateral cash flows over time, with 3-period ramp. *Source* Compiled by the author

## 6.2 Structure Types Descriptions

In practice, there is truly a continuum in structuring techniques, and every deal tends to have its own peculiarities in structuring logic. However, in an effort to simplify our approach, we categorize the different types of cash flow allocations into a discrete number of intended effects.

We may decompose the structures into four broad types based on what they have an impact on: **loss allocation**, **principal allocation**, **interest allocation**, and **deal behavior**.

**Loss allocation** addresses the manner in which writedowns are attributed to various bonds differently. We will cover three particular methods:

- **Subordination**, which allocates losses to some bonds in priority (which are then called **subordinated**, while those that do not get these losses are called **senior** bonds).
- **Over-collateralization**, when there are less bonds than there is collateral (hence the name).
- and **Excess-spread**, when interest payments are used to absorb losses.

**Principal allocation** deals with how quickly principal is repaid to the bonds, and we will discuss three specific methods:

- **Sequential allocation**, when some tranches get principal cash flows in priority. The bonds created that way are called **sequentials**.
- **Payment schedules**, when payments are attributed to bonds according to a predetermined schedule. The bonds created in this manner are less exposed to variations in prepayment speeds and are usually called **PACs**, i.e., planned amortization classes, while the resulting bonds that are more exposed to prepayment risk are called **supports**.
- **Shifting interest**, which delays the time until which bonds can receive their prorata amount of principal. These bonds are usually called **NAS**, non-accelerated securities.

**Interest allocation** usually refers to a method called "stripping", and strips out the interest on some bonds to give it to other bonds. This also covers the indexing of interest on some external reference. The bonds that can be created by this technique include **IOs** and **POs** (interest-only and principal-only), as well as **floaters** or **inverse floaters**.

**Deal level** structures refer to techniques or aspects of structures that have an effect on the entire deal at the same time:

- **structural breakdown**: in certain conditions, the structure on certain blocks may disappear, which changes the relative payments across many bonds.
- **grouping** refers to the allocation of the cash flows from certain loan groups to particular bonds.
- **deal calls** and **SFMCs** are particular options which allow an option holder to purchase the deal's collateral and terminate the securitization past a certain date.
- **triggers**: depending on the evolution of certain metrics regarding collateral performance, the entire structure of the deal can be affected, in an effort to protect well-rated bonds to the maximum extent possible.
- **Insurance**, in the form of **wraps** at the tranche level, or **MI** at the collateral level, use guarantees from an external third party to improve the bond's cash flows.

Finally, structures that create a **resecuritization** are a special case: they take one or several securities issued through securitization, and securitize them again. Some important particular cases are **SFCDOs**, **REREMICS**, and **NIMs**.

In the following subsections, we walk through the features of all these types of structures, and for most of them describe the algorithms in detail, and show cash flow calculations and simulations. For some structures, however, we only describe the logic. Due to their intricacies, the structural features we list here must all be at least superficially understood, if one is to carry out any form of empirical analysis using securitized bonds data. Some structures, such as sequentials, NAS, excess-spread to name a few are ubiquitous and generic enough that their existence deserves some economic explanation. We examine this question in Chap. 7. It is hence essential to study the cash flows of these important structures. Some other structures have more complex effects, such as triggers or groups, and understanding and potentially explaining their existence does not necessarily entail a fully detailed modeling of the resulting cash flows: this is why we do not delve as much on these.

Finally, note that we leave aside many structures, in particular those that leverage particular aspects of prepayment or interest rate risk. Thus, we do not drill into Zs, jump Zs, VADMs,[4] TTIBs, and many others.

### 6.2.1 Prorata Structures

Before going into the particular details of various structures, it is important to understand the notion of structures where cash flows are allocated to the **prorata**[5] of the resulting bonds' balances (balances at the beginning of the period). The idea is that the cash flows would be proportionally allocated, relative to each bond's balance at the beginning of each period. Interest, principal, or losses could be allocated in a prorata manner as follows: $I_t^i = \frac{B_t^i}{B_t} I_t$, $P_t^i = \frac{B_t^i}{B_t} P_t$, and $L_t^i = \frac{B_t^i}{B_t} L_t$. Naturally, if the bonds verify these three conditions, then they are pass-throughs, a particular and degenerate form. Bonds for which the principal and loss allocation is done on a prorata basis are said to be **pari passu**.[6]

The notion of prorata allocation might appear to imply that there is not much structure or many complicated effects at play, but this is really true only in the cases where the bonds are, and remain, true pass-throughs. For example, let us consider the case of a structure that allocates losses in a prorata manner. This would make it sound as though all the bonds out of this structure should roughly have the same credit risk, since they are all getting losses propotional to their balances. But then, what if we have principal payments structured such that one of the bonds is repaid extremely quickly, within a few months? That bond's balance will drop very quickly over time, and so will its share in loss allocation. In other words, by being repaid rapidly, this bond will effectively bear very little credit risk, while still being in some sense on an equal footing with the other bonds.

When we discuss any kind of structure, the aspects that are not explicitly addressed by that structure are assumed to be dealt with in a prorata manner. So when we discuss complex interest allocation, we are implicitly leaving $P$ and $L$ as defined above. When we discuss principal allocation, for example, with PACs, then $I$ and $L$ remain on a prorata allocation.

Also, when we structure the allocation of principal payments or losses, there is an arbitrary choice in the order in which that should be done. For example, one could first distribute losses, and then distribute principal (only to the remaining bonds).

[4] Pronounced "Vadim".

[5] From the Latin *prorata* or *prorata parte*, meaning "per the proportion under consideration".

[6] Latin, in the ablative case, meaning "based on an equal footing".

Or one could do the contrary. There are many possible variations, and in order to simplify presentation we have generally considered that losses would be allocated first.

Finally, note that if the underlying collateral had a binary outcome, and paid all principal at one instant and losses covered the entire collateral, also instantaneously, then there would be no point in structuring anything. A junior or senior tranche would have the same cash flows. It is only because principal payments and losses are progressive over time that one can use structures to make a difference between bond cash flows.

### 6.2.2 Senior/Subordinated Bonds

The notion of subordination departs from a prorata allocation of losses: when they occur, losses are applied to some bonds in priority, in order to protect the other bonds. The bonds that get the losses first are called **subordinated** or **junior**, and the bonds that get the losses last are called **senior**. Bonds in the middle are usually called **mezzanine** bonds. One can also say that a bond is junior to another one inside of a same structure if it will get losses before the other bond; and equivalently one can say a bond is senior to another one if it will get losses after that other bond.

The notion of subordination normally operates on the input block's aggregate cash flows, and not at the loan or asset level. Recall that losses are not a cash flow and are defined as a reduction in balance not compensated by a payment of principal. So when we talk about allocating losses, in fact, it means reducing the balance of certain bonds without giving them a principal payment, hence the alternative term of a **writedown** for collateral block or bond losses.

Before delving into the analysis of subordination, it is worth stressing again that in a securitization deal, the senior-most positions are not the bonds themselves, but the servicers, trustee, and potentially the manager of the deal. Indeed, these entities receive their fees at the very top of the waterfall, directly from the loan portfolio. As such, all bonds in the structure come after in the pecking order. This makes the cash flows to these third parties the safest of the entire deal.

#### 6.2.2.1 Formal Description

A senior/subordination structure can be defined by providing a series of bond sizes, an a particular ordering. Some collateral block $(B, CF)$ can be structured into a series of $n$ bonds $(B^i, CF^i)_{1\leq i\leq n}$, where the first bond would be the most junior and the last one the most senior. At this stage, we do not address the allocation of principal payments or interest, which therefore are all attributed prorata according to the balances after losses have been attributed.

We consider that for the current period, interest $I_t$ has been distributed prorata to the bonds as $I_t^i$. Each bond's balance before loss attribution is $B_t^i$. We only concern ourselves with losses now. At every payment time $t$, if there are losses, they are used to drop the balance of the junior most bond in the structure (the lowest index $i$ so that

$B_t^i > 0$); if the losses exceed that bond's remaining balance then the spill-over losses are allocated to the next one, and so on. We can express the amount of writedowns allocated to each bond as follows

$$L_t^i = \mathbb{I}_{B_t^i > 0}\left(B_t^i \mathbb{I}_{i_a \leq i < i_d} + \left(L_t - \sum_{k<i_d} B_t^k\right)\right)$$

where $i_a = \inf\{i : B_t^i > 0\}$ and $i_d = \inf\{i : \sum_{k \geq i_a}^i B_t^k \geq L_t\}$ are the index of the most junior bond at the beginning of time $t$, and the most senior bond up to which the losses rise. Most of the time one would expect that when losses are small both these indices are the same. Also recall that collateral losses verify $L_t = (B_t - B_{t+1}) - P_t$. We are implicitly assuming that $L_t \leq B_t$, so that the losses cannot exceed the total size of the bonds. The indicator $\mathbb{I}_{B_t^i > 0}$ is redundant but we want to stress that the bonds that have already reached a balance of 0 do not get any losses. Also note that in the expression one could write too $\sum_{k<i_d} B_t^k = \sum_{k<i_d} L_t^k$ due to how all the $L^i$ are defined.

After the losses have been allocated, the principal payments are attributed to the bonds according to the prorata of their remaining balances:

$$P_t^i = P_t \frac{B_t^i - L_t^i}{\sum_j (B_t^j - L_t^j)} = P_t \frac{B_t^i - L_t^i}{B_t - L_t}.$$

The writedowns defined above are applied to the bonds, some of them seeing their balances potentially dropping to zero (being **wiped out**). Some bonds also do not get any losses allocated to them. This clearly shows that when some bonds begin to be affected by losses, the amount of principal they will receive diminishes along with their balance. In cases where the collateral is composed of assets that do not amortize over time, for example, a corporate loan portfolio with concentrated maturities, the amounts of intermediate principal payments $P$ will be 0, and therefore so will all the $P^i$ until maturity.

In the general case when there are intermediate principal payments, the fact that the junior bonds that are supposed to protect the senior ones can get principal payments can be considered to weaken the structure's efficiency. One could think that the initial portfolio was composed of good loans and bad loans. The bad loans would default no matter what, and the good loans would not default, but could maybe prepay. In that case, the subordinated bonds would be getting principal cash flows from the good bonds, which would **deleverage** the structure, and make it weaker after these prepayments. This is why senior/subordination is often combined with a form of delay in principal payments to the subordinated bonds, the simplest one being sequential payment, which will be addressed later on.

Credit enhancement can be described as **hard** or **soft** in order to capture the dependency on the structure to the effect of principal repayment: credit enhancement is said to be hard if faster or slower principal repayment have no effect on the amount of losses that can be absorbed. It is said to be soft if faster repayments reduce the

**Table 6.3** Generating a bullet cash flow. *Source* Compiled by the author

```
bullet_example <- create_basic_portfolio(OrigBal = 100,
  Cpn = 0.05,
  Prin = c(rep(0, 9), 89),
  Loss = c(0, 0, 0, 1, 2, 4, 2, 1, 1, 0))
```

effective amount of credit enhancement. The credit enhancement of a senior tranche with prorata principal allocation is therefore said to be soft.

For a given tranche $i$, one could look at $a = \frac{\sum_{j<i} B^j}{B}$ and $b = a + \frac{B^i}{B}$ and consider them to be attachment and detachment points, in some sense. However, they are not "hard" attachment and detachment because due to the repayment of principal to the junior bonds there is no guarantee that loss levels below the attachment point would be effectively absorbed. In addition, if there was further structuring (such as excess-spread) before or after this senior/subordination, then the notion of attachment or detachment would be even muddier.

#### 6.2.2.2 Senior/Subordinated Structure Examples

The example in Table 6.3 creates a portfolio that behaves like a bullet bond, repaying all principal at the end of the term, with no intermediate principal cash flows.

We will apply a senior/sub structure to this asset portfolio, with three bonds (one senior, one mezzanine, one junior) called "A", "M", and "B", with sizes of 70, 20, and 10, respectively. The initial bond sizes are better defined as fractions of the portfolio amount. The logic shown in Table 6.4 is general and could handle an arbitrary list of bonds.

The structured cash flows are shown in Table 6.5. In this case, we can see that the bonds effectively have clean attachment and detachment points: A attaches at 30%, detaches at 100%, while M attaches at 10% and detaches at 30%, and B attaches at 0% and detaches at 10%. Since there is no repayment of principal, B entirely fulfills its credit protection role and gets no principal at all. M incurs a loss of 5% of its balance (1 out of 20). In this case, with no principal prepayments, there is no distinction between soft and hard credit enhancement.

**Table 6.4** Simple senior/sub structure. *Source* Compiled by the author

```
simple_senior_sub <- function(prtf, A_size = 0.7,
                              M_size = 0.2, B_size = 0.1) {
  bonds <- list("A" = A_size, "M" = M_size, "B" = B_size)
  fld_names <- c("BegBal", "Prin", "Loss", "Int")

  # Set up cash flows for the bonds
  for (bd in names(bonds)) {
    prtf[, paste0(fld_names, "_", bd)] <- NA
    prtf[1, paste0("BegBal_", bd)] <-bonds[[bd]] * prtf$BegBal[1]
  }

  # Loop over periods
  for (k in 1:dim(prtf)[1]) {
    # First determine relative balances
    rel_bal <- c()
    for (bd in 1:length(bonds)) {
      rel_bal[bd] <- prtf[k, paste0("BegBal_", names(bonds)[bd])]
    }
    rel_bal <- rel_bal / sum(rel_bal)
    # Prorata allocation of interest
    for (bd in 1:length(bonds)) {
      prtf[k, paste0("Int_", names(bonds)[bd])] <-
        rel_bal[bd] * prtf$Int[k]
    }
    # Determine loss allocation by looping through the bonds
    # in increasing seniority
    loss_alloc <- list()
    i_d_track <- 0
    i_a <- NULL
    i_d <- NULL
    for (bd in rev(names(bonds))) {
      loss_alloc[[bd]] <- 0
      rem_bal <- prtf[k, paste0("BegBal_", bd)]
      if (is.null(i_a) & rem_bal > 0) {
        i_a <- bd
      }
      if (!is.null(i_a) & is.null(i_d)) {
        loss_alloc[[bd]] <- rem_bal
        i_d_track <- i_d_track + rem_bal
        if (i_d_track >= prtf$Loss[k]) {
          i_d <- bd
          loss_alloc[[bd]] <- prtf$Loss[k] - (i_d_track - rem_bal)
        }
      }
      prtf[k, paste0("Loss_", bd)] <- loss_alloc[[bd]]
    }
```

```
    # Determine remaining relative balances
    rel_bal <- c()
    for (bd in 1:length(bonds)) {
      rel_bal[bd] <- prtf[k, paste0("BegBal_", names(bonds)[bd])] -
        prtf[k, paste0("Loss_", names(bonds)[bd])]
    }
    if (sum(rel_bal) > 0) {
      rel_bal <- rel_bal / sum(rel_bal)
    } else {
      rel_bal <- rel_bal * 0
    }
    # Prorata allocation of principal
    for (bd in 1:length(bonds)) {
      prtf[k, paste0("Prin_", names(bonds)[bd])] <-
        rel_bal[bd] * prtf$Prin[k]
    }
    # Compute next starting balance
    if (k < dim(prtf)[1]) {
      for (bd in names(bonds)) {
        prtf[k + 1, paste0("BegBal_", bd)] <-
          prtf[k, paste0("BegBal_", bd)] - prtf[k, paste0("Loss_", bd)] -
          prtf[k, paste0("Prin_", bd)]
      }
    }
  }
  return(prtf)
}
```

What if there was principal repayment? Let us consider the following example instead, shown in Table 6.6, where losses remain the same but there are some principal cash flows.

Then applying exactly the same structure, we have different cash flows, as shown in Table 6.7. Now tranche B gets some principal payment due to the prorata allocation. As a result, it is not entirely wiped out, and the losses have to be attributed elsewhere, to tranche M. M now incurs a loss of about 20% of its starting balance. As we will see later on, there are ways to ensure that the junior most bond would not receive any

**Table 6.5** Senior/subordinated cash flows on bullet assets. *Source* Compiled by the author

| Period | Beg Bal | Prin | Loss | Int | Beg Bal A | Prin A | Loss A | Int A | Beg Bal M | Prin M | Loss M | Int M | Beg Bal B | Prin B | Loss B | Int B |
|---|---|---|---|---|---|---|---|---|---|---|---|---|---|---|---|---|
| 1 | 100 | 0 | 0 | 5.0 | 70 | 0 | 0 | 3.5 | 20 | 0 | 0 | 1.00 | 10 | 0 | 0 | 0.50 |
| 2 | 100 | 0 | 0 | 5.0 | 70 | 0 | 0 | 3.5 | 20 | 0 | 0 | 1.00 | 10 | 0 | 0 | 0.50 |
| 3 | 100 | 0 | 0 | 5.0 | 70 | 0 | 0 | 3.5 | 20 | 0 | 0 | 1.00 | 10 | 0 | 0 | 0.50 |
| 4 | 100 | 0 | 1 | 5.0 | 70 | 0 | 0 | 3.5 | 20 | 0 | 0 | 1.00 | 10 | 0 | 1 | 0.50 |
| 5 | 99 | 0 | 2 | 5.0 | 70 | 0 | 0 | 3.5 | 20 | 0 | 0 | 1.00 | 9 | 0 | 2 | 0.45 |
| 6 | 97 | 0 | 4 | 4.8 | 70 | 0 | 0 | 3.5 | 20 | 0 | 0 | 1.00 | 7 | 0 | 4 | 0.35 |
| 7 | 93 | 0 | 2 | 4.7 | 70 | 0 | 0 | 3.5 | 20 | 0 | 0 | 1.00 | 3 | 0 | 2 | 0.15 |
| 8 | 91 | 0 | 1 | 4.5 | 70 | 0 | 0 | 3.5 | 20 | 0 | 0 | 1.00 | 1 | 0 | 1 | 0.05 |
| 9 | 90 | 0 | 1 | 4.5 | 70 | 0 | 0 | 3.5 | 20 | 0 | 1 | 1.00 | 0 | 0 | 0 | 0.00 |
| 10 | 89 | 89 | 0 | 4.5 | 70 | 70 | 0 | 3.5 | 19 | 19 | 0 | 0.95 | 0 | 0 | 0 | 0.00 |

**Table 6.6** Example cash flows with amortization. *Source* Compiled by the author

```
general_example <- create_basic_portfolio(OrigBal = 100,
  Cpn = 0.05,
  Prin = c(0, 2, 5, 10, 9, 7, 5, 2, 2, 47),
  Loss = c(0, 0, 0, 1, 2, 4, 2, 1, 1, 0))
```

**Table 6.7** Senior/subordinated cash flows on amortizing assets. *Source* Compiled by the author

| Period | Beg Bal | Prin | Loss | Int | Beg Bal A | Prin A | Loss A | Int A | Beg Bal M | Prin M | Loss M | Int M | Beg Bal B | Prin B | Loss B | Int B |
|---|---|---|---|---|---|---|---|---|---|---|---|---|---|---|---|---|
| 1 | 100 | 0 | 0 | 5.0 | 70 | 0.0 | 0 | 3.5 | 20.0 | 0.00 | 0.0 | 1.00 | 10.00 | 0.00 | 0.00 | 0.50 |
| 2 | 100 | 2 | 0 | 5.0 | 70 | 1.4 | 0 | 3.5 | 20.0 | 0.40 | 0.0 | 1.00 | 10.00 | 0.20 | 0.00 | 0.50 |
| 3 | 98 | 5 | 0 | 4.9 | 69 | 3.5 | 0 | 3.4 | 19.6 | 1.00 | 0.0 | 0.98 | 9.80 | 0.50 | 0.00 | 0.49 |
| 4 | 93 | 10 | 1 | 4.7 | 65 | 7.1 | 0 | 3.2 | 18.6 | 2.02 | 0.0 | 0.93 | 9.30 | 0.90 | 1.00 | 0.47 |
| 5 | 82 | 9 | 2 | 4.1 | 58 | 6.5 | 0 | 2.9 | 16.6 | 1.87 | 0.0 | 0.83 | 7.40 | 0.61 | 2.00 | 0.37 |
| 6 | 71 | 7 | 4 | 3.5 | 52 | 5.4 | 0 | 2.6 | 14.7 | 1.54 | 0.0 | 0.74 | 4.79 | 0.08 | 4.00 | 0.24 |
| 7 | 60 | 5 | 2 | 3.0 | 46 | 4.0 | 0 | 2.3 | 13.2 | 1.02 | 1.3 | 0.66 | 0.71 | 0.00 | 0.71 | 0.04 |
| 8 | 53 | 2 | 1 | 2.6 | 42 | 1.6 | 0 | 2.1 | 10.9 | 0.38 | 1.0 | 0.54 | 0.00 | 0.00 | 0.00 | 0.00 |
| 9 | 50 | 2 | 1 | 2.5 | 41 | 1.6 | 0 | 2.0 | 9.5 | 0.35 | 1.0 | 0.47 | 0.00 | 0.00 | 0.00 | 0.00 |
| 10 | 47 | 47 | 0 | 2.4 | 39 | 38.9 | 0 | 1.9 | 8.1 | 8.13 | 0.0 | 0.41 | 0.00 | 0.00 | 0.00 | 0.00 |

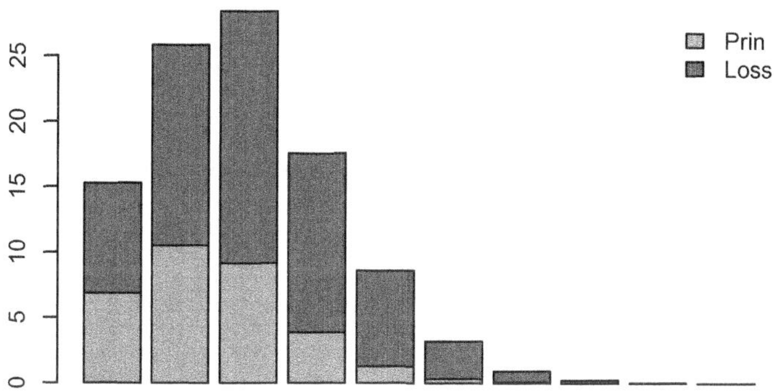


**Fig. 6.5** Average cash flows over time for Tranche B. *Source* Compiled by the author

principal, so that it can fully absorb losses as they materialize. Comparing Tables 6.5 and 6.7 clearly shows why such a structure is deemed to be "soft": it does not work as well as when there is no principal repayment.

We can also measure the efficiency of senior/subordination by looking at randomized cash flows, and comparing the probability that bonds observe a writedown, and at the expected amount of writedown. We use the function described earlier to generate random cash flows, with a 3-period ramp.

First, we can look at the average cash flows to the bonds over time shown in Figs. 6.5, 6.6, and 6.7, in the same manner as we charted them for the collateral earlier. Note that here the cash flows are scaled to the bonds' starting balances.

Looking at total losses across all paths we obtain some information about the distribution of losses, as shown in Table 6.8. In the table, the total losses refer to

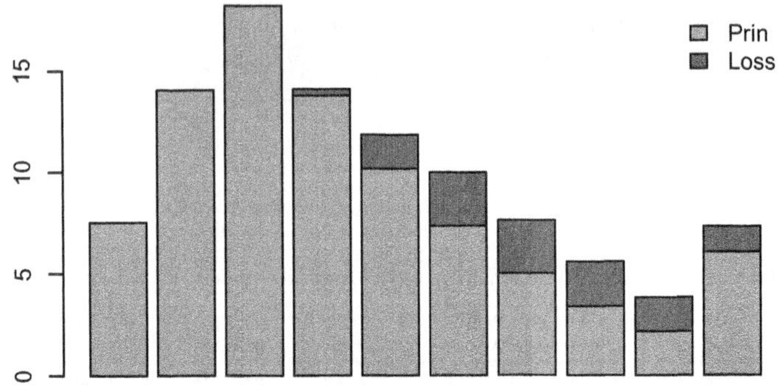


**Fig. 6.6** Average cash flows over time for Tranche M. *Source* Compiled by the author

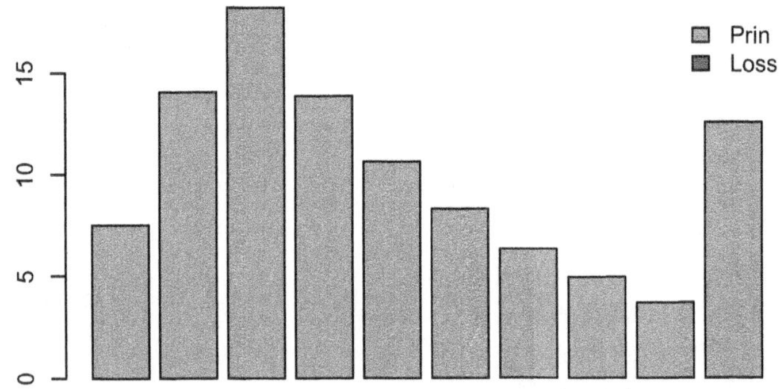


**Fig. 6.7** Average cash flows over time for Tranche A. *Source* Compiled by the author

**Table 6.8** Losses on senior/subordinated structure with randomized cash flows. *Source* Compiled by the author

| | Total loss | Total loss A | Total loss M | Total loss B |
|---|---|---|---|---|
| Min. | 2.2 | 0.0 | 0.0 | 22 |
| 1st Qu. | 7.6 | 0.0 | 7.1 | 60 |
| Median | 9.1 | 0.0 | 11.2 | 69 |
| Mean | 9.2 | 0.0 | 12.4 | 68 |
| 3rd Qu. | 10.7 | 0.0 | 16.2 | 76 |
| Max. | 19.1 | 0.3 | 46.9 | 98 |

losses relative to each bond's starting balance. We can see that even though tranche A has a substantial amount of credit enhancement, and also considering that losses are always expressed proportionately to the remaining balance, there are a few rare instances where it suffered a writedown. Tranches M and B do bear the brunt of collateral losses in the very large majority of cases. M, as a mezzanine tranche, gets some protection from B but it is far from perfect.

We may also look at loss severity at the tranche level, that is how much loss does a bond incur, conditioned by the fact that it is incurring a loss. These results

**Table 6.9** Losses on senior/subordinated structure with randomized cash flows on paths where A takes a loss. *Source* Compiled by the author

| | Total loss | Total loss A | Total loss M | Total loss B |
|---|---|---|---|---|
| Min. | 11 | 0.00 | 15 | 68 |
| 1st Qu. | 12 | 0.01 | 19 | 72 |
| Median | 12 | 0.03 | 24 | 75 |
| Mean | 13 | 0.08 | 26 | 77 |
| 3rd Qu. | 14 | 0.12 | 31 | 81 |
| Max. | 18 | 0.30 | 45 | 89 |

are presented in Table 6.9. On the collateral side, that amount is the actual losses observed, since it always incurs some losses. But this is also the case for B since the minimum loss observed on that tranche is also positive. We can look at the particular paths where A takes a loss. The probability that A takes a loss in the simulations above is 0.11%. The empirical probability that M takes a loss is very close to 100.

Although a casual description of the senior/subordination logic would make it seem like the appropriate structural design to address the creation of informationally insensitive securities, as we discussed in Chap. 4, we can clearly see that in reality it would not be the right tool in and by itself. It is necessary to create hard credit enhancement, for which additional structuring techniques are necessary.

Using the simplest formalized collateral model we presented in Chap. 3, we can further stress a paramount distinction between soft and hard credit enhancement. Recall we defined collateral with a starting balance of $B_0$, a principal payment of $P_T$ and losses of $L_T$, so that $P_T + L_T = B_0$.

Hard credit enhancement would imply that a senior bond with initial balance $B_0^S$ gets all the principal in priority (and hence the subordinated tranche gets all the losses): $P_T^S = P_T \wedge B_0^S$. In this case, mechanically, losses will reach the senior security only if $L_T > B_0^S$.

Soft credit enhancement on the contrary allows for principal to be repaid. In the dynamic structure description we have given, losses were allocated first and then principal at each time. As a result, the subordinated tranche's balance declines fast due to losses, which reduces its share into prorated principal. This effect simply cannot be captured in a single period model. As a result, it is effectively impossible to account for the simplest senior/subordination structures in a typical one-period security design model.

#### 6.2.2.3 Interest Shortfalls

In our discussion of subordination we have not really addressed how to handle interest. We simply considered that it was allocated in a prorata fashion. If the servicer fully advances interest payments then the collected interest is always synchrone with the collateral's outstanding balance and stated coupon. That is the reason for having servicers advance these cash flows, so that interest payments are not disturbed. However, servicers sometimes do not advance loan payments as we have discussed in Chap. 3, and that leads to an **interest shortfall**: there is less interest collected than what would be necessary to pay what is due to the bonds.

Dealing with an interest shortfall is akin to dealing with losses: there is less money collected than what one would need, and one needs to decide how to allocate that lack of funds. The implicit allocation of interest in the discussion above was prorata: if there was less than needed, that lack would have been shared by each tranche proportionately. One can also use senior/subordination in interest allocation excatly the same way as with loss allocation.

In order to discuss shortfall allocation, we first need to define it properly. The notion of a shortfall implies there was a reference interest that was due. Let us denote $c_t$ the expected monthly coupon from collateral at time $t$, so that the shortfall $F$ is $F_t = 0 \vee (c_t B_t - I_t)$. Then the shortfall is attributed to the bonds in increasing order of interest seniority (which may not be the same as the loss seniority). Each bond $i$'s expected interest is $c_t B_t^i$.

We express the shortfall allocation as a close parallel to the loss allocation logic. At every payment time $t$, if there is an interest shortfall, it is used to drop the balance of the junior most bond in the structure (the lowest index $i$ so that $B_t^i > 0$); if the shortfall exceed that bond's coupon then it is further allocated to the next one, and so on. We can express the amount of shortfall allocated to each bond as follows:

$$F_t^i = \mathbb{I}_{B_t^i > 0} \left( c B_t^i \mathbb{I}_{i_a \leq i < i_d} + \left( F_t - \sum_{k < i_d} c B_t^k \mathbb{I}_{i = i_d} \right) \right)$$

where $i_a = \inf\{i : B_t^i > 0\}$ and $i_d = \inf\{i : \sum_{k \geq i_a}^{i} c B_t^k \geq F_t\}$ they are the index of the most junior bond at the beginning of time $t$, and the most senior bond up to which the shortfall rises.

It is worth noting that real structures do not always fully segregate interest and principal payment. For example, in some cases if there is an interest shortfall for some senior bonds, the structure may divert principal payments that would have otherwise gone toward subordinated bonds in order to cover that shortfall.

### 6.2.3 Over-Collateralization and Excess-Spread

Over-collateralization and excess-spread are fundamentally linked, as we will see, but they can be tackled as two separate credit-enhancement techniques and as such we will first cover them separately.

#### 6.2.3.1 Over-Collateralization

As the name hints, the idea behind over-collateralization (OC) is to have more collateral than bonds, as depicted in Fig. 6.8. How does that translate into credit enhancement? One simply considers that all principal payments from the loans go toward the bonds, until they are paid off, after which whoever holds the over-collateralization tranche would receive the remaining cash flows. The coupon rate paid on the bonds in

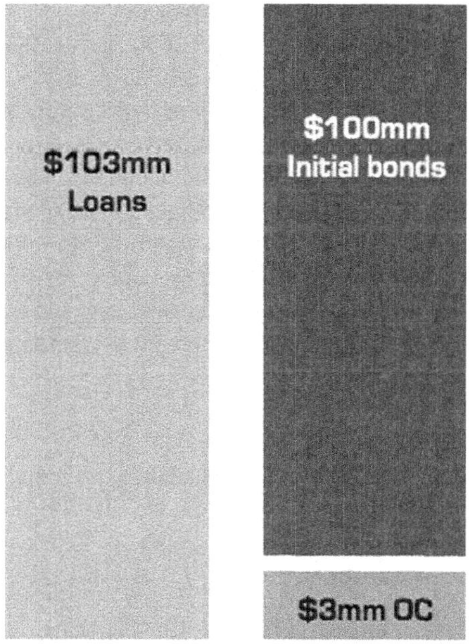


**Fig. 6.8** Over-collateralization. *Source* Compiled by the author

the example depicted would be slightly higher than on the collateral. The amount of over-collateralization is the difference in loan principal balance and bonds principal balance. In the example, we can say that initially there is $3mm of OC.

One important question is how that notion of OC is different from simply having a subordinated bond of the same size. We could create a subordinated bond, not receiving any interest, and make it so that it can never get any principal before the $100 mm senior bonds are paid down. From a cash flow standpoint that would be equivalent to over-collateralization as we have defined it here. However as we will see later on, OC is normally combined with excess-spread, and a "normal" bond, with a set principal balance that it is supposed to repay, could not receive additional cash flows from an extra source. OC is sometimes called the deal's **equity**, because it is very much like equity: it gets paid after all the bonds have been paid, and if there is any extra cash flows they act as upside. In addition, equity like OC does not have a notional balance that is supposed to be repaid. In this example, the OC tranche may have a notional amount of $100, or equal to the entire deal's balance, or equal to something else.

The attribution of losses in an OC structure is simple: while there is over-collateralization, then losses reduce the balance of the loans without affecting the balance of the bonds. Once the difference between the principal balance on both sides reaches 0 (and there is no OC anymore) then losses from the collateral pass directly to the bonds.

Based on the description so far, this OC tranche appears to correspond to the junior exposure, or equity as we described it in the security design models covered in Chap. 4.

#### 6.2.3.2 Formal Description

Given some collateral $(B, CF)$, let us define a structure that creates two tranches OC and B: $(B^{OC}, CF^{OC})$ and $(B^B, CF^B)$, where as we have mentioned above $B^{OC}$ can be arbitrary since there is no notion of principal as a distinct cash flow from interest on this tranche. Based on the description above the payment rule for interest is $I_t^B = \mathbb{I}_{B_t^B>0} I_t$. Note that the interest payments are all going to the bond here since we are not really addressing what to do with them yet. Once the bond's balance is 0 then they will be paid as cash flow to the OC tranche.

The allocation of losses is also relatively straightforward: if B has a positive balance, writedowns are attributed to B if they exceed the difference in loan principal outstanding and bond principal outstanding (the OC, that is $B_t - B_t^B$). So

$$L_t^B = \mathbb{I}_{B_t^B>0} \mathbb{I}_{L_t>(B_t-B_t^B)}(L_t - (B_t - B_t^B)).$$

After losses have been attributed, principal can be distributed, going to the bonds in priority, and limited by the remaining balance on the bonds after the allocation of losses:

$$P_t^B = (B_t^B - L_t^B) \wedge P_t$$

In a case where the OC is reduced to 0 (that is, $L_t > (B_t - B_t^B)$), then by construction the entire principal payment goes to the bonds since then $B_t^B - L_t^B = B_t - L_t$ and one must have $P_t \leq B_t - L_t$, so $P_t^B = P_t$.

The cash flows distributed to the OC tranche are simply equal to whatever is left after paying the bonds:

$$CF_t^{OC} = P_t + I_t - P_t^B - I_t^B.$$

#### 6.2.3.3 Examples of Simple OC Structures

Let us see some examples now. The simple function shown in Table 6.10 creates an OC structure following the logic exposed above.

We run this structure with an OC of 15% on the general collateral assumptions we defined earlier. We can see that the losses are totally covered, and the OC tranche gets some cash flow in Table 6.11.

Let us also look at the cash flows when the repayment of principal is more spread out over time, in Table 6.12. In that case we can see more clearly how some cash is paid out to the OC tranche. In that case, as the bond is entirely repaid before the last period, the OC receives all residual cash flows, including the interest, and the total amount is slightly higher than in the prior case.

We can compare the efficiency of the OC structure with simple subordination. We saw that with our randomized cash flows, and with 30% of subordinated bonds the senior tranche still incurred some rare losses. Also, the mezzanine was quite exposed. In both cases this is due to the repayment of principal to subordinated tranches relatively early. Now with the OC approach, we expect the structure to be more efficient. We use an OC of 20%, in order to make it more comparable to the 30% of subordination we looked at earlier, and the results are shown in Table 6.13.

**Table 6.10** Simple OC structure logic. *Source* Compiled by the author

```
simple_oc <- function(prtf, B_size = 0.85) {
  bonds <- list("B" = B_size)
  fld_names <- c("BegBal", "Prin", "Loss", "Int")
  # Set up cash flows for the bonds
  for (bd in names(bonds)) {
    prtf[, paste0(fld_names, "_", bd)] <- NA
    prtf[1, paste0("BegBal_", bd)] <- bonds[[bd]] * prtf$BegBal[1]
  }
  # Adhoc setup for OC
  prtf$BegBal_OC <- NA
  prtf$CF_OC <- NA
  prtf$BegBal_OC[1] <- (1 - B_size) * prtf$BegBal[1]

  # Loop over periods
  for (k in 1:dim(prtf)[1]) {
    # First attribute interest to bonds
    prtf$Int_B[k] <- (prtf$BegBal_B[k] > 0) * prtf$Int[k]
    # Determine loss allocation
    oc_avl <- prtf$BegBal[k] - prtf$BegBal_B[k]
    prtf$BegBal_OC[k] <- oc_avl
    prtf$Loss_B[k] <- (prtf$Loss[k] > oc_avl) * (prtf$Loss[k] - oc_avl)
    # Allocate principal
    prtf$Prin_B[k] <- min(prtf$BegBal_B[k] - prtf$Loss_B[k], prtf$Prin[k])
    # OC cash flows
    prtf$CF_OC[k] <- prtf$Prin[k] - prtf$Prin_B[k] +
      prtf$Int[k] - prtf$Int_B[k]
    # Compute next starting balance
    if (k < dim(prtf)[1]) {
      for (bd in names(bonds)) {
        prtf[k + 1, paste0("BegBal_", bd)] <-
          prtf[k, paste0("BegBal_", bd)] - prtf[k, paste0("Loss_", bd)] -
          prtf[k, paste0("Prin_", bd)]
      }
    }
  }
  return(prtf)
}
```

Although we only use 20% of OC, the probability of the bonds taking a loss is null. We can also see also that the OC does get a good amount of cash flows over time.

#### 6.2.3.4 Over-Collateralization Targets, Releases, and Floors

The over-collateralization effectively tries to protect the bonds to the maximum extent possible. In some cases, this can be "too much", in the sense that keeping a large amount of over-collateralization would not be necessary over the entire life of a deal. If losses remained low, and after a few periods the bonds were mostly paid down, one could end up with more OC than bonds outstanding, which could appear to be overkill. Naturally in a real structuring context these considerations are the result of the dealer's structuring team, the rating agencies, and investor's incentives. Allowing OC not to remain so high could still be acceptable to rating agencies and senior bonds investors, while at the same time allowing earlier returns of cash to the OC tranche and therefore a higher valuation.

**Table 6.11** Cash flows in OC structure. *Source* Compiled by the author

| Period | Beg Bal | Prin | Loss | Int | Beg Bal B | Prin B | Loss B | Int B | Beg Bal OC | CF OC |
|---|---|---|---|---|---|---|---|---|---|---|
| 1 | 100 | 0 | 0 | 5.0 | 85 | 0 | 0 | 5.0 | 15 | 0 |
| 2 | 100 | 2 | 0 | 5.0 | 85 | 2 | 0 | 5.0 | 15 | 0 |
| 3 | 98 | 5 | 0 | 4.9 | 83 | 5 | 0 | 4.9 | 15 | 0 |
| 4 | 93 | 10 | 1 | 4.7 | 78 | 10 | 0 | 4.7 | 15 | 0 |
| 5 | 82 | 9 | 2 | 4.1 | 68 | 9 | 0 | 4.1 | 14 | 0 |
| 6 | 71 | 7 | 4 | 3.5 | 59 | 7 | 0 | 3.5 | 12 | 0 |
| 7 | 60 | 5 | 2 | 3.0 | 52 | 5 | 0 | 3.0 | 8 | 0 |
| 8 | 53 | 2 | 1 | 2.6 | 47 | 2 | 0 | 2.6 | 6 | 0 |
| 9 | 50 | 2 | 1 | 2.5 | 45 | 2 | 0 | 2.5 | 5 | 0 |
| 10 | 47 | 47 | 0 | 2.4 | 43 | 43 | 0 | 2.4 | 4 | 4 |

**Table 6.12** Cash flows in OC structure, earlier principal payments. *Source* Compiled by the author

| Period | Beg Bal | Prin | Loss | Int | Beg Bal B | Prin B | Loss B | Int B | Beg Bal OC | CF OC |
|---|---|---|---|---|---|---|---|---|---|---|
| 1 | 100 | 0 | 0 | 5.00 | 85 | 0 | 0 | 5.00 | 15 | 0.0 |
| 2 | 100 | 3 | 0 | 5.00 | 85 | 3 | 0 | 5.00 | 15 | 0.0 |
| 3 | 97 | 10 | 0 | 4.85 | 82 | 10 | 0 | 4.85 | 15 | 0.0 |
| 4 | 87 | 10 | 1 | 4.35 | 72 | 10 | 0 | 4.35 | 15 | 0.0 |
| 5 | 76 | 9 | 2 | 3.80 | 62 | 9 | 0 | 3.80 | 14 | 0.0 |
| 6 | 65 | 47 | 4 | 3.25 | 53 | 47 | 0 | 3.25 | 12 | 0.0 |
| 7 | 14 | 5 | 2 | 0.70 | 6 | 5 | 0 | 0.70 | 8 | 0.0 |
| 8 | 7 | 2 | 1 | 0.35 | 1 | 1 | 0 | 0.35 | 6 | 1.0 |
| 9 | 4 | 2 | 1 | 0.20 | 0 | 0 | 0 | 0.00 | 4 | 2.2 |
| 10 | 1 | 1 | 0 | 0.05 | 0 | 0 | 0 | 0.00 | 1 | 1.1 |

**Table 6.13** Losses on simple OC structure with randomized cash flows. *Source* Compiled by the author

| | Total loss | Total loss B | Total CF OC |
|---|---|---|---|
| Min. | 2.2 | 0 | 0.87 |
| 1st Qu. | 7.6 | 0 | 9.47 |
| Median | 9.1 | 0 | 11.43 |
| Mean | 9.2 | 0 | 11.35 |
| 3rd Qu. | 10.7 | 0 | 13.33 |
| Max. | 19.1 | 0 | 19.87 |

In order to allow the structure to dynamically manage over-collateralization, we use the concept of **OC targets**. So far in the discussion of OC, the target was effectively set at the initial amount of OC. 3, which is a vector of amounts or of expressions to determine the amount, specifies what the OC should tend to at each period. The control available to the structure is how much principal is paid to the bonds (which tends to increase OC all else equal). If less principal is paid to the bonds, then it goes to the OC tranche, and by reducing the difference in balance between the collateral and the bonds, it decreases the amount of OC available. Note that the OC target does not have to be expressed in monetary units, it could just be a proportion of balance, or even set as a function of the current amount of senior and subordinated bonds (if the main block B was further structured).

In a case where the OC target is below the current level of over-collateralization, it gives rise to an **OC release**: some principal payments will go to the OC tranche in order to reduce the amount of OC (of course if there are losses the OC might be reduced just because of the losses). Such a feature is defined by a date and a target percentage. From the date in question, the OC will be allowed to **step-down** to a predetermined percentage of the then current collateral balance. For example, after 3 years, one might allow the over-collateralization to drop to the minimum between its initial size and 10% of the current collateral balance. Then, in order to not have OC decline too much one can set an **OC floor**, that is a "hard" lower limit to the OC under which it should not decline.

In securitization structures, the step-down takes place at a predetermined date, but only if certain conditions are verified regarding the collateral performance. The step-down is not systematic but requires that delinquency rates be under a certain level. As a result, the payment of principal to the OC tranche only takes place if the collateral performance at the step-down date is good enough. We do not explicitly model this trigger mechanism in our simple examples.

Let us write the OC target as $T_t^{OC}$. The amount of OC at time 0, sometimes called the **upfront OC**, is $B_0 - B_0^B$. At time 0 the OC target could be set to the actual amount of OC, so $T_0^{OC} = B_0 - B_0^B$. Then at some predetermined date $t_s$ (the **step-down date**) the target could drop to some level specified as a function of the current balance, for example, $T_{t_s}^{OC} = \frac{B_0 - B_0^B}{B_0} B_{t_s}$ so that the targeted OC level relative to the then current balance would be the same as the original OC relative to the original deal size. However this expression is not correct because it is based on the period's starting balance. The target OC should be understood in terms of the ending balance over the period, so that it includes the principal payments or losses that took place over the period. So more precisely, $T_{t_s}^{OC} = \frac{B_0 - B_0^B}{B_0}(B_{t_s} - P_{t_s} - L_{t_s})$. If losses were not very high up to that point, then this new target would be expected to give rise to an OC release. However, maybe one would set an OC floor by demanding a minimum OC level, which could be set as a fraction $\alpha$ of the initial OC target. For $t \geq t_s$, we can write the target as

$$T_t^{OC} = \left( \frac{B_0 - B_0^B}{B_0} (B_t - P_t - L_t) \right) \vee \left( \alpha (B_0 - B_0^B) \right).$$

Having an OC target changes the way the principal payments are allocated. Previously, we had $P_t^B = B_t^B \wedge P_t$. Now, if the target is lower than the current level of OC, it is going to alter this principal allocation by reducing the amount of principal going to the bonds, until the OC target is met. However we need to also account for losses (the target should be understood as the target at the end of the period after principal has been paid and losses allocated). The target is compared with the actual amount of OC after principal distribution on the collateral side, but not the distribution of principal on the bonds side, precisely because the target will drive that principal distribution.

The target as we are defining it, does not change the allocation of interest and losses, they remain as before, respectively, $I_t^B = \mathbb{I}_{B_t^B>0} I_t$ and $L_t^B = \mathbb{I}_{B_t^B>0} \mathbb{I}_{L_t>(B_t-B_t^B)}(L_t - (B_t - B_t^B))$. However with the target we now generalize the expression for the principal allocation, allowing for some to leak to the OC tranche by reducing how much is paid to the bonds. The allocation of principal depends on whether the actual OC after principal paydown is above or under the target, so it depends on the sign of $((B_t - L_t - P_t) - (B_t^B - L_t^B)) - T_t^{OC}$. The principal payment if that amount is negative is equal to the minimum between what is available and the gap to fill, that is $P_t \wedge (T_t^{OC} - ((B_t - L_t - P_t) - (B_t^B - L_t^B)))$. If that amount is positive, then the principal payment is limited so that the right amount is diverted to lower the OC toward the target, that is $0 \vee (P_t - (((B_t - L_t - P_t) - (B_t^B - L_t^B)) - T_t^{OC}))$. If we define the target gap as $TG_t = T_t^{OC} - ((B_t - L_t - P_t) - (B_t^B - L_t^B))$ then the principal payment to the bonds is

$$P_t^B = \mathbb{I}_{TG_t<0}(0 \vee (P_t + TG_t)) + \mathbb{I}_{TG_t\geq 0}(P_t \wedge TG_t).$$

In the simple case where the OC target was not specified, we had effectively $T_t^{OC} = (B_t - L_t) - (B_t^B - L_t^B)$ and the equation above boiled down to the prior version.

We can adapt the simple OC structure function from the prior subsection to work with an OC target. Since a target can be very general, we have to parameterize it somehow and choose to have it expressed as a function of a step-down period $t_s$, then have it set to the same fraction relative to deal balance as the initial OC, and subject to a floor expressed as a fraction $\alpha$ of the initial OC amount. Table 6.14 shows the algorithm for an OC structure with a target.

We can now see how the cash flows are affected by the step-down in certain cases. In the first case where the principal cash flows take place toward the end of the portfolio life, the step-down only leads to a small cash release to the OC tranche (see Table 6.15).

In the case where the collateral principal cash flows are more front-loaded, we see a different pattern, and while the OC still fulfills its role, it is getting much earlier cash flows, as illustrated in Table 6.16.

The fact that a typical OC tranche will be able to recover some principal payments early does make it somewhat different from a pure "equity-like" exposure to the collateral, and stresses the fact that OC may not be properly represented by a pure junior tranche.

**Table 6.14** OC structure with target logic. *Source* Compiled by the author

```
oc_with_target <- function(prtf, B_size = 0.85, t_s = 3, alpha = 0.2) {
  oc_initial <- prtf$BegBal[1] * (1 - B_size)
  bonds <- list("B" = B_size)
  fld_names <- c("BegBal", "Prin", "Loss", "Int")
  # Set up cash flows for the bonds
  for (bd in names(bonds)) {
    prtf[, paste0(fld_names, "_", bd)] <- NA
    prtf[1, paste0("BegBal_", bd)] <- bonds[[bd]] * prtf$BegBal[1]
  }
  # Adhoc setup for OC
  prtf$BegBal_OC <- NA
  prtf$CF_OC <- NA
  prtf$BegBal_OC[1] <- (1 - B_size) * prtf$BegBal[1]

  # Loop over periods
  for (k in 1:dim(prtf)[1]) {
    # First attribute interest to bonds
    prtf$Int_B[k] <- (prtf$BegBal_B[k] > 0) * prtf$Int[k]
    # Determine loss allocation
    oc_avl <- prtf$BegBal[k] - prtf$BegBal_B[k]
    prtf$Loss_B[k] <- (prtf$Loss[k] > oc_avl) * (prtf$Loss[k] - oc_avl)
    # Determine OC post loss and principal
    end_bal <- (prtf$BegBal[k] - prtf$Loss[k] - prtf$Prin[k])
    oc_post_loss <- end_bal - (prtf$BegBal_B[k] - prtf$Loss_B[k])
    # Determine the OC target
    oc_target <- oc_initial
    if (k >= t_s) {
      oc_target <- max((1 - B_size) * end_bal, alpha * oc_initial)
    }
    # Treatment depends on whether OC < Target
    avail_prin <- prtf$Prin[k]
    if (oc_post_loss < oc_target) {
      # Pay as much as possible to reach target
      prin_pmt <- min(avail_prin, oc_target - oc_post_loss)
    } else {
      # Divert principal payment
      prin_pmt <- max(0, avail_prin - (oc_post_loss - oc_target))
    }
    # Allocate principal
    prtf$Prin_B[k] <- min(prtf$BegBal_B[k] - prtf$Loss_B[k], prin_pmt)
    # OC cash flows
    prtf$CF_OC[k] <- prtf$Prin[k] - prtf$Prin_B[k] +
      prtf$Int[k] - prtf$Int_B[k]
    prtf$BegBal_OC[k] <- prtf$BegBal[k] - prtf$BegBal_B[k]
    # Compute next starting balance
    if (k < dim(prtf)[1]) {
      for (bd in names(bonds)) {
        prtf[k + 1, paste0("BegBal_", bd)] <-
          prtf[k, paste0("BegBal_", bd)] - prtf[k, paste0("Loss_", bd)] -
          prtf[k, paste0("Prin_", bd)]
      }
    }
  }
  return(prtf)
}
```

#### 6.2.3.5 Implied Writedowns and Under-Collateralization

The core idea of subordination or over-collateralization is to create credit enhancement for senior bonds, so that the junior securities effectively suffer some of the writedowns that the senior bonds would have otherwise suffered. When the junior

**Table 6.15** Cash flows in OC structure with target. *Source* Compiled by the author

| Period | Beg Bal | Prin | Loss | Int | Beg Bal B | Prin B | Loss B | Int B | Beg Bal OC | CF OC |
|---|---|---|---|---|---|---|---|---|---|---|
| 1 | 100 | 0 | 0 | 5.0 | 85 | 0.0 | 0 | 5.0 | 15.0 | 0.00 |
| 2 | 100 | 2 | 0 | 5.0 | 85 | 2.0 | 0 | 5.0 | 15.0 | 0.00 |
| 3 | 98 | 5 | 0 | 4.9 | 83 | 4.0 | 0 | 4.9 | 15.0 | 1.05 |
| 4 | 93 | 10 | 1 | 4.7 | 79 | 9.3 | 0 | 4.7 | 13.9 | 0.65 |
| 5 | 82 | 9 | 2 | 4.1 | 70 | 9.0 | 0 | 4.1 | 12.3 | 0.00 |
| 6 | 71 | 7 | 4 | 3.5 | 61 | 7.0 | 0 | 3.5 | 10.3 | 0.00 |
| 7 | 60 | 5 | 2 | 3.0 | 54 | 5.0 | 0 | 3.0 | 6.3 | 0.00 |
| 8 | 53 | 2 | 1 | 2.6 | 49 | 2.0 | 0 | 2.6 | 4.3 | 0.00 |
| 9 | 50 | 2 | 1 | 2.5 | 47 | 2.0 | 0 | 2.5 | 3.3 | 0.00 |
| 10 | 47 | 47 | 0 | 2.4 | 45 | 44.7 | 0 | 2.4 | 2.3 | 2.30 |

**Table 6.16** Cash flows in OC structure with target, earlier principal payments. *Source* Compiled by the author

| Period | Beg Bal | Prin | Loss | Int | Beg Bal B | Prin B | Loss B | Int B | Beg Bal OC | CF OC |
|---|---|---|---|---|---|---|---|---|---|---|
| 1 | 100 | 0 | 0 | 5.00 | 85 | 0.0 | 0 | 5.00 | 15.0 | 0.00 |
| 2 | 100 | 3 | 0 | 5.00 | 85 | 3.0 | 0 | 5.00 | 15.0 | 0.00 |
| 3 | 97 | 10 | 0 | 4.85 | 82 | 8.1 | 0 | 4.85 | 15.0 | 1.95 |
| 4 | 87 | 10 | 1 | 4.35 | 74 | 9.3 | 0 | 4.35 | 13.1 | 0.65 |
| 5 | 76 | 9 | 2 | 3.80 | 65 | 9.0 | 0 | 3.80 | 11.4 | 0.00 |
| 6 | 65 | 47 | 4 | 3.25 | 56 | 44.6 | 0 | 3.25 | 9.4 | 2.40 |
| 7 | 14 | 5 | 2 | 0.70 | 11 | 5.0 | 0 | 0.70 | 3.0 | 0.00 |
| 8 | 7 | 2 | 1 | 0.35 | 6 | 2.0 | 0 | 0.35 | 1.0 | 0.00 |
| 9 | 4 | 2 | 1 | 0.20 | 4 | 2.0 | 1 | 0.20 | 0.0 | 0.00 |
| 10 | 1 | 1 | 0 | 0.05 | 1 | 1.0 | 0 | 0.05 | 0.0 | 0.00 |

bonds are wiped out, or in any situation leading to losses being normally allocated to the senior bond, then we have explained how the senior bonds would have to suffer a writedown, since otherwise there may be less remaining collateral balance than there are senior bonds to repay.

One can, however, just not let the senior bonds recognize a writedown in this case. Quite simply this means that the balance of the senior bonds would not be going down due to collateral writedowns, but only due to principal payments. Naturally, if there is less outstanding collateral than there are senior securities, they are **under-collateralized**, a situation exactly opposite to over-collateralization. Effectively, this means that the securities have a **negative credit enhancement**. For the securities' principal to be fully repaid, it would require the collateral to pay more principal than its outstanding balance, which is typically quite unlikely.

In many deal structures, the trustees may not be allowed by the pooling agreement to ascribe a writedown to some bonds. They are then said to take **implied writedowns**, since computing a writedown as implied by the under-collateralization is the only way of measuring their degree of impairment. The real eventual writedown in this case can only be recognized at the bond's legal maturity, typically the maturity of the longest asset in the underlying collateral, very far into the future. From a cash flow standpoint the distinction between recognizing or not normal writedowns has an impact on the amount of interest that is owed to the senior bonds, since with a higher outstanding balance they should collect more coupon than they otherwise would. In a structure where all credit enhancement has been wiped out, this would essentially affect how much payment is made among the outstanding senior bonds, given that the collateral cash flows in this case would only be shared by these senior bonds.

From a practical standpoint, there is little difference whether a bond takes implied writedowns or not, since one could in all cases derive its "real" writedown level by computing its effective credit enhancement or its degree of under-collateralization. In many common tools in the industry, that difference is well accounted for and understood. However, you need to look at the right data: in all systems, there is a field for reported writedowns (which may not reflect any writedowns on the bonds that are not supposed to take writedowns), and one for calculated writedowns (which would be the proper way of measuring credit impairment). Unfortunately, some empirical papers that look into the performance of securitized products do not mention this distinction at all, and typically refer to "writedowns" or "losses" being reported. Given the prevalence of these implied writedown structures, especially in subprime MBS, it is hence impossible to determine whether their results are valid, or grossly underestimate the extent of securities losses on the bonds not already fully written down at the time of their analysis. When focusing on bonds that were not AAA rated, this is less of an issue since they commonly tend to recognize writedowns as they happen.

#### 6.2.3.6 Excess-Spread

Excess-spread refers to the use of interest payments in order to absorb losses. In the senior/subordinated or over-collateralization based structures (we discussed so far) we have not addressed interest payments, they were passed fairly untouched from the collateral to the bonds. On loans that do not have a strong credit risk, we would expect the rates to be relatively in line with broad market rates. For example, prime mortgages, or investment-grade loans, will typically pay a coupon that's less than 200 bps above the corresponding Treasury rate. In addition, structured bonds backed by such assets after some credit enhancement will pay a coupon not very far from these spread levels at issuance. For example, if mortgage rates paid by the borrower are around 5.5%, basic pass-through structures would trade at par and pay a coupon around 5%.

If we look at collateral that has a worse credit risk to start with, such as subprime mortgages, manufactured housing, subprime auto loans or leveraged loans, then one would need a lot more credit enhancement in order to create bonds that deserve a good rating. In addition, these loans will typically pay a much higher interest rate (because of their credit risk) than what the market demands for bonds once they are properly credit-enhanced. If we took subprime loans paying 8%, created enough credit enhancement and issued bonds with that coupon in a market that requires 5%, the bonds would have to trade at extremely high price levels (115 maybe), and that would make them very unpalatable for most institutional investors. Hence, finding a way to take out some of the interest and use it instead for credit enhancement has been a very useful struturing tool.

How does one use interest payments to "absorb losses"? First, we start from a situation where the assets (presumably loans) pay a coupon that is much higher than the coupon we want to see on the bonds. For example, let us consider the 8% asset coupon in a 5% market. If we are collecting 8% and only need to pay out 5%, there are 3% left over. Now suppose there are 1% of losses coming from the assets. These losses mean the balance on the assets will be declining by 1%, without a compensating principal payment. The bonds would have to be written down by that same amount. Instead, we can take a part of the extra interest, the **excess-spread**, and use it to pay extra principal on the bonds by the amount of losses. This way the decline in balance of the bonds mirrors that of the loans, but in the case of the bonds it is compensated by a payment of principal. The rest of the excess-spread cash flows (the excess-spread **residual**), 2% here, can be distributed to a special tranche often called **XS**.

Formal Description
For simplicity we are initially going to consider that the bonds pay a fixed coupon, although in reality they may often pay a floating rate indexed on Libor, for example. We also set the coupon paid by the bonds under the lowest coupon paid by the assets in the collateral, so that it can always be covered. We denote the bonds by B and the excess-spread residual tranche by XS. This tranche is not really a bond, since it does not have principal attached to it. As with the OC tranche, we can use a notional reference to to that tranche, sometimes the entire deal balance. The XS tranche will not either incur a loss, since it is not supposed to pay principal.

We write $c_B$ the constant monthly coupon intended for the bonds so that $c_B = \frac{I_t^B}{B_t^B}$. Based on our assumptions, $I_t > I_t^B$. In this excess-spread structure, allocation of interest is straightforward: $I_t^B = c_B B_t$. Excess-spread is equal to $I_t - c_B B_t$. As we have explained above, we are going to use that excess-spread in order to pay down some extra principal, so that the balance on the bonds can decline by as much as losses, without them actually incurring a loss. Hence

$$P_t^B = P_t + (L_t \wedge (I_t - c_B B_t)).$$

The loss allocation to the bonds is simply equal to whatever cannot be covered by excess-spread:

$$L_t^B = (L_t - (I_t - c_B B_t))\mathbb{I}_{L_t > I_t - c_B B_t}.$$

Excess-spread Example

The code in Table 6.17 shows the logic for a simple excess-spread structure. We consider a simple example, where the bonds are structured to pay a lower coupon than the 5% provided by our example collateral. We have the bonds paying 3%, hence generating 200 bps of excess-spread. We are looking at a cash flow with more than 5 years in average life, so intuitively this excess-spread should provide more than 10% in credit enhancement.[7]

We can compare the behavior of the XS structure in the two collateral cases we have looked at before. In the first case, even though the principal payments only come at the end, the structure does not appear to be fully efficient in order to prevent losses (see Table 6.18).

Even though the excess-spread should in principle cover about 10% of all losses, B still suffers 3.74% in losses. In the case where principal payments take place earlier the structure's efficiency is even more questionable, as can be seen in Table 6.19.

In this case losses on tranche B total 6.68% but the XS tranche receives a total of \$6.7 mm in cash flows. In fact, in both cases, the XS tranche is getting some cash flows. It seems inappropriate that this XS tranche, supposedly created to protect the bonds, would get payments which could have been used later in order to provide much needed protection. We will see later on how one can address that issue by combining excess-spread logic with over-collateralization.

If we randomize the cash flows, we can confirm our static analysis. This structure is much less efficient than the ones we have seen so far, as it pays out cash flows to the XS tranche. The losses incurred by the bonds are not negligible, as shown in Table 6.20.

In an unpublished empirical study, Bisla and Gauthier (2005) matched tranche and loan-level information on about 26,000 bonds in the jumbo and Alt-A markets issued between 1998 and 2003, in 2,100 different non-agency deals and looked into the drivers of credit enhancement. Focusing on the part of the Alt-A market using excess-spread structures, it is possible to measure how credit enhancement at the BBB tranche level related to collateral characteristics and in particular with the amount of initial excess-spread. In a regression, combining various loan-characteristics as drivers of total credit enhancement, the coefficients for excess-spread came out around −30%: for every 1% of additional excess-spread, credit enhancement declined by 0.30%. This points out that in reality, pure excess-spread was not considered as a very solid provider of credit protection, mostly because it incurs the risk of disappearing if prepayments are fast.

The Alt-A market in the mid-2000s is a good subject of enquiry regarding excess-spread, because in the 1990s, excess-spread was very rarely used in that market but

[7] That is, 5 years times 2% a year, very approximately.

**Table 6.17** Simple excess-spread structure logic. *Source* Compiled by the author

```
simple_xs <- function(prtf, c_B = 0.03) {
  bonds <- list("B" = 1.00)
  fld_names <- c("BegBal", "Prin", "Loss", "Int")
  # Set up cash flows for the bonds
  for (bd in names(bonds)) {
    prtf[, paste0(fld_names, "_", bd)] <- NA
    prtf[1, paste0("BegBal_", bd)] <-bonds[[bd]] * prtf$BegBal[1]
  }
  # Adhoc setup for XS
  prtf$CF_XS <- NA

  # Loop over periods
  for (k in 1:dim(prtf)[1]) {
    # First attribute interest to bonds
    prtf$Int_B[k] <- prtf$BegBal_B[k] * c_B
    # Available excess-spread
    avl_xs <- prtf$Int[k] - prtf$Int_B[k]
    # Determine principal allocation
    prtf$Prin_B[k] <- prtf$Prin[k] +
      min(avl_xs, prtf$Loss[k])
    # Determine loss allocation
    prtf$Loss_B[k] <- max(0, prtf$Loss[k] - avl_xs)
    # XS cash flows
    prtf$CF_XS[k] <- prtf$Prin[k] - prtf$Prin_B[k] +
      prtf$Int[k] - prtf$Int_B[k]
    # Compute next starting balance
    if (k < dim(prtf)[1]) {
      for (bd in names(bonds)) {
        prtf[k + 1, paste0("BegBal_", bd)] <-
          prtf[k, paste0("BegBal_", bd)] -
          prtf[k, paste0("Loss_", bd)] - prtf[k, paste0("Prin_", bd)]
      }
    }
  }
  return(prtf)
}
```

**Table 6.18** Cash flows in XS structure. *Source* Compiled by the author

| Period | Beg Bal | Prin | Loss | Int | Beg Bal B | Prin B | Loss B | Int B | CF XS |
|---|---|---|---|---|---|---|---|---|---|
| 1 | 100 | 0 | 0 | 5.0 | 100 | 0.0 | 0.00 | 3.0 | 2.00 |
| 2 | 100 | 2 | 0 | 5.0 | 100 | 2.0 | 0.00 | 3.0 | 2.00 |
| 3 | 98 | 5 | 0 | 4.9 | 98 | 5.0 | 0.00 | 2.9 | 1.96 |
| 4 | 93 | 10 | 1 | 4.7 | 93 | 11.0 | 0.00 | 2.8 | 0.86 |
| 5 | 82 | 9 | 2 | 4.1 | 82 | 10.6 | 0.36 | 2.5 | 0.00 |
| 6 | 71 | 7 | 4 | 3.5 | 71 | 8.4 | 2.58 | 2.1 | 0.00 |
| 7 | 60 | 5 | 2 | 3.0 | 60 | 6.2 | 0.80 | 1.8 | 0.00 |
| 8 | 53 | 2 | 1 | 2.6 | 53 | 3.0 | 0.00 | 1.6 | 0.06 |
| 9 | 50 | 2 | 1 | 2.5 | 50 | 3.0 | 0.00 | 1.5 | 0.00 |
| 10 | 47 | 47 | 0 | 2.4 | 47 | 47.0 | 0.00 | 1.4 | 0.94 |

**Table 6.19** Cash flows in XS structure, earlier principal payments. *Source* Compiled by the author

| Period | Beg Bal | Prin | Loss | Int | Beg Bal B | Prin B | Loss B | Int B | CF XS |
|---|---|---|---|---|---|---|---|---|---|
| 1 | 100 | 0 | 0 | 5.00 | 100 | 0.0 | 0.00 | 3.00 | 2.00 |
| 2 | 100 | 3 | 0 | 5.00 | 100 | 3.0 | 0.00 | 3.00 | 2.00 |
| 3 | 97 | 10 | 0 | 4.85 | 97 | 10.0 | 0.00 | 2.91 | 1.94 |
| 4 | 87 | 10 | 1 | 4.35 | 87 | 11.0 | 0.00 | 2.61 | 0.74 |
| 5 | 76 | 9 | 2 | 3.80 | 76 | 10.5 | 0.48 | 2.28 | 0.00 |
| 6 | 65 | 47 | 4 | 3.25 | 65 | 48.3 | 2.70 | 1.95 | 0.00 |
| 7 | 14 | 5 | 2 | 0.70 | 14 | 5.3 | 1.72 | 0.42 | 0.00 |
| 8 | 7 | 2 | 1 | 0.35 | 7 | 2.1 | 0.86 | 0.21 | 0.00 |
| 9 | 4 | 2 | 1 | 0.20 | 4 | 2.1 | 0.92 | 0.12 | 0.00 |
| 10 | 1 | 1 | 0 | 0.05 | 1 | 1.0 | 0.00 | 0.03 | 0.02 |

**Table 6.20** Losses on simple XS structure with randomized cash flows. *Source* Compiled by the author

| | Total loss | Total loss B | Total CF XS |
|---|---|---|---|
| Min. | 2.2 | 0.0 | 0.36 |
| 1st Qu. | 7.6 | 1.8 | 2.02 |
| Median | 9.1 | 2.6 | 2.73 |
| Mean | 9.2 | 2.7 | 2.81 |
| 3rd Qu. | 10.7 | 3.5 | 3.51 |
| Max. | 19.1 | 8.5 | 7.93 |

over time increased so that over 25% of the volume of senior bonds was backed in part by excess-spread. In that market, unlike in CLOs, in subprime or in most other securitized products sectors, structures with excess-spread coexisted with structures without excess-spread.

Available Funds Cap and Interest Rates Derivatives

In our discussion of excess-spread here we have conveniently assumed that the coupon on the collateral was systematically higher than on the bonds. This might not always be the case. For example, if one had a distribution of different coupons on the loans, some high and some low, maybe that some of them would be lower than the required coupon on the bonds. Also, if one had assets that are a mix of fixed and floating rate, and issued bonds that are all indexed on Libor, there could be at times a mismatch, if the Libor index were to increase significantly. This kind of situation is known as hitting an **available funds cap**.

The available funds cap is simply captured in the general case by setting the actual interest paid to B to the minimum between what is available and what would ideally be paid: $I_t^B = c_B B_t \wedge I_t$. This implicitly considers that the only source of cash flows to cover interest payments on the bonds should be interest (and hence exclude principal). This is generally the case, unless there is more principal outstanding on the collateral side than on the bonds side.

If B gets further structured, for example, with senior/subordination then the allocation of interest among these structures can follow any particular set of rules, for example, the subordinated bonds could absorb interest shortfalls in priority, making them effectively more exposed to an available funds cap. However this does not need to be the case, and shortfalls may be allocated in a prorata fashion.

Excess-spread is a credit enhancement mechanism, but in some cases its efficiency could be limited by the evolution of interest rates. For example, many subprime deals were backed by a portion of FRMs and a portion of ARMs. In addition, these ARMs were often in fact hybrid-ARMs, fixed for a few years, typically 2 or 3, and contained various caps (for example, a typical hybrid would be capped for life at 5% above its original rate). On the other hand the bonds issued by the structure paid floating coupons indexed on Libor. The aggregate coupon paid by the bonds was not very high, in the order of L+100 bps. Nevertheless if Libor increased significantly the difference between the interest collected and the interest needed would collapse, and threaten the excess-spread's ability to cover losses. This risk is known as **basis risk** in a deal.

One way to address this basis risk is to add derivatives to a deal's collateral:

- Interest rates swaps can be used to convert the fixed-rate loans into floating rates. The teaser period on the hybrid-ARMs when they pay a fixed rate could be covered by a 3-year swap, for example, so that the deal trustee would pay the swap counterparty a fixed coupon, and receive Libor, which would then be available for excess-spread and coupon payments.
- Interest rates caps can be used to "uncap" the floating rate loans. For example, a cap could be added to the structure with a strike set to the average life caps of all the loans minus their margins. This way, if Libor reached high enough that the coupons would be capped, the derivative would provide cash flows attenuating the difference.

Adding derivatives such as these, however, raises some difficult questions that must be addressed.

First, who is the counterparty behind these transactions? If in a subprime deal the swap counterparty was Lehman Brothers, what happens if one expects a net positive cash flow and the counterparty is in bankruptcy? This has been a difficult issue for some mortgage-backed securities a few years ago. One needs to put a process in place so that the trustee can efficiently deal with a situation where a derivatives counterparty's credit is under threat.

Then, what is the right amortization schedule for the swaps and caps? The loans in the collateral will pay principal but also prepay more or less randomly over time. One can use a pricing speed assumption in order to derive the amortizing schedule for the derivatives, however, it is likely that the actual prepayments over the deal's life will be different from that assumption. In the case of a cap, this can lead to being over covered (not necessarly bad) or under covered (in which case if rates increased much then the cap payments would not fully compensate for the caps on the loans). In the case of a swap this is a thornier issue, because unlike a cap, a swap may require the structure to pay out cash flows. In an extreme situation where all the loans in the deal prepaid suddenly, the swap would still remain and there would be an obligation to satisfy these payments, or unwind it, at some cost. One could add cancelation options to the swaps, so that the trustee could progressively adjust the swap's balance to the actual collateral; however, the pricing of such options implies an optimal exercise, and they are therefore much more expensive than they should be for the case at hand, where the observed amortization is not an efficient exercise. There have been some deals where a dealer would create an amortizing swap indexed on the actual collateral balance; however, this is not a standard swap and required pricing a complex risk. In many deals, the dealer structuring the deal simply became party to the deal and guaranteed that they would absorb residual payments, if any, due to the swap. This creates a marginal exposure in the bonds' credit to the dealer's financial health.

#### 6.2.3.7 Combining Excess-Spread and Over-Collateralization

Excess-spread and over-collateralization can be easily combined: over-collateralization can be created by using excess-spread to pay down principal on the bonds to a greater extent than to cover losses. In the examples dealing with excess-spread above, it was clear that there was an issue because excess-spread leaked outside of the structure before it could be put to use. By using it to pay down the bonds, it creates over-collateralization, which effectively "traps" the excess-spread inside the structure. At a later date, that over-collateralization may be released to the OC tranche if it is not used. Also, we can have a mechanism that diverts excess-spread toward over-collateralization until some target is reached, but once the over-collateralization is at the target then the excess-spread tranche would begin receiving some cash flows. We can keep the same mechanism as the OC target discussed earlier, but now there might be a distinction between the OC target level, and the actual over-collateralization present at the inception of the deal. The latter is called the **upfront OC**.

Traditionally, it is the tranche combining the excess-spread and the over-collateralization, or the combination of these tranches if they are separate, that is called the **equity** of a deal, or the **residual**.

Formal description
We keep the notations from the prior sections, the upfront OC is $B_0 - B_0^B$, initially the OC target is some proportion $o$ of the initial collateral balance $T_0^{OC} = oB_0$. Over time, we keep the same logic as before so for $t$ after the step-down date of $t_s$, $T_t^{OC} = oB_t \vee \alpha o B_0$. And for $t < t_s$ the OC target is constant $T_t^{OC} = oB_0$. The excess-spread is $I_t - c_B B_t$ will now be used to get the OC to its target, and if the OC is already at that target then it will be paid to the XS tranche.

First, we look at the allocation of losses. In the case where $L_t > (I_t - c_B B_t)$, that is the losses exceeded what the excess-spread could cover for this period, then the additional amount of losses will be effectively "absorbed" by the OC. Losses will be attributed to the bonds only if they exceed the excess-spread and the OC:

$$L_t^B = \mathbb{I}_{B_t^B > 0} \mathbb{I}_{L_t > (B_t - B_t^B + I_t - c_B B_t)} (L_t - (B_t - B_t^B + I_t - c_B B_t)),$$

where $B_t - B_t^B + I_t - c_B B_t$ is the total amount of OC plus excess-spread for the period. After these losses have been allocated, we can express the allocation of principal cash flows. Principal coming from the collateral is complemented with available excess-spread so that the total potential principal paid to the bonds is $P_t + (0 \vee (I_t - c_B B_t))$. Depending on the target OC versus the actual OC, some of that principal may in fact flow back to the excess-spread tranche and to the OC tranche. The principal distribution logic is very similar to the case without excess-spread, the only difference being that now the excess-spread increases the available principal payment.

To simplify notations we write the collateral end balance $E_t = 0 \vee (B_t - L_t - P_t - (I_t - c_B B_t))$. Just as in the previous case, the allocation of principal depends on whether the actual OC after principal paydown is above or under the target, so it depends on the sign of $(E_t - (B_t^B - L_t^B)) - T_t^{OC}$. The target is also expressed here as a function of the period's end balance, so

$$T_t^{OC} = \left( \frac{B_0 - B_0^B}{B_0} E_t \right) \vee \left( \alpha (B_0 - B_0^B) \right).$$

The allocation of principal payment is as follows, where we write the target gap $TG_t = T_t^{OC} - (E_t - (B_t^B - L_t^B))$

$$\begin{aligned} P_t^B = & \mathbb{I}_{TG_t < 0} (0 \vee (P_t + (I_t - c_B B_t) + TG_t)) + \\ & \mathbb{I}_{TG_t \geq 0} ((P_t + (I_t - c_B B_t)) \wedge TG_t). \end{aligned}$$

The cash flows to the excess-spread and OC tranches are, like before, based on what is left. The raw remaining cash flows are $P_t + I_t - P_t^B + I_t^B$. We need to attribute that amount between OC and XS. We simply consider that the excess-spread tranche gets all the interest-based cash flow that is not used for bond coupon payment or loss coverage, so

$$CF_t^{XS} = (P_t + I_t - P_t^B - I_t^B) \wedge \left((I_t - I_t^B - L_t) \vee 0\right),$$

and the OC tranche gets the rest

$$CF_t^{OC} = (P_t + I_t - P_t^B - I_t^B) - CF_t^{XS}.$$

Combining excess-spread and over-collateralization allows for more efficient structures, and dominates pure excess-spread structures and pure over-collateralization structures.

Examples

The code in Table 6.21 shows an implementation example of a structure combining OC and excess-spread. We consider here a combination of the prior examples with the bonds paying a 3% coupon, and an OC target of 8% with a floor at 20% of the initial target. The upfront OC is set at 1%, and the step-down date is at the 3rd period.

In the same fashion as before, let us look at the structured cash flows using the base-case collateral projection. We can see that with only 8% in OC target, the structure is able to withstand a total of 11% in losses (see Table 6.22). This is because the excess-spread is able to absorb losses over the life of the structure.

If we look at a case of faster principal payments, which reduces the absolute amount of excess-spread, then the structure does not work as well, as shown in Table 6.23.

How well does the XS-OC structure deal with random cash flows? With the same collateral cash flow assumptions as before, we can see in Table 6.24 that the combination of XS and OC, even with a fairly low OC target, works quite well in a general setting. In order to have a fairer comparison with senior/subordination structures we set the initial OC at 5%, and the target at 10%.

In Hein (2009), the author looked into the optimal trade-off between allocating losses following a pure senior/subordination, and capturing interest payment through a reserve account, which differs from over-collateralization but is nevertheless comparable. She finds that commingling interest and principal as in the case of an excess-spread structure greatly improves the senior bonds' ability to withstand collateral losses.

**Table 6.21** Combined excess-spread and OC structures logic. *Source* Compiled by the author

```
oc_xs <- function(prtf, B_size = 0.99, t_s = 3,
                  alpha = 0.2, o = 0.08, c_B = 0.03) {
  oc_initial <- prtf$BegBal[1] * (1 - B_size)
  oc_target_initial <- prtf$BegBal[1] * o
  bonds <- list("B" = B_size)
  fld_names <- c("BegBal", "Prin", "Loss", "Int")
  # Set up cash flows for the bonds
  for (bd in names(bonds)) {
    prtf[, paste0(fld_names, "_", bd)] <- NA
    prtf[1, paste0("BegBal_", bd)] <- bonds[[bd]] * prtf$BegBal[1]
  }
  # Adhoc setup for OC
  prtf$CF_OC <- NA
  # Adhoc setup for XS
  prtf$CF_XS <- NA

  # Loop over periods
  for (k in 1:dim(prtf)[1]) {
    # First attribute interest to bonds
    prtf$Int_B[k] <- prtf$BegBal_B[k] * c_B
    # Available excess-spread
    xs_avl <- prtf$Int[k] - prtf$Int_B[k]
    # Available OC
    oc_avl <- prtf$BegBal[k] - prtf$BegBal_B[k]
    # Determine loss allocation
    prtf$Loss_B[k] <- max(0, prtf$Loss[k] - (xs_avl + oc_avl))
    # Determine OC post loss and collateral principal
    end_bal <- max(0, prtf$BegBal[k] -
                   prtf$Loss[k] - prtf$Prin[k] - xs_avl)
    oc_post_loss <- end_bal - (prtf$BegBal_B[k] - prtf$Loss_B[k])
    # Determine the OC target
    oc_target <- oc_target_initial
    if (k >= t_s) {
      oc_target <- max(o * end_bal, alpha * oc_target_initial)
    }
    # Treatment depends on whether OC < Target
    avail_prin <- prtf$Prin[k] + xs_avl
    if (oc_post_loss < oc_target) {
      # Pay as much as possible to reach target
      prin_pmt <- min(avail_prin, oc_target - oc_post_loss)
    } else {
      # Divert principal payment
           prin_pmt <-max(0, avail_prin- (oc_post_loss- oc_target)) }
    # Allocate principal
    prtf$Prin_B[k] <- min(prtf$BegBal_B[k] - prtf$Loss_B[k], prin_pmt)
    # Total extra cash flow
    extra_cash <- prtf$Prin[k] + prtf$Int[k] -
      prtf$Prin_B[k] - prtf$Int_B[k]
    # XS cash flows
    max_xs <- max(0, prtf$Int[k] - prtf$Int_B[k] - prtf$Loss[k])
    prtf$CF_XS[k] <- min(max_xs, extra_cash)
    # OC cash flows
    prtf$CF_OC[k] <- extra_cash - prtf$CF_XS[k]
    # Prevent interest capitalization
    # In cases where cash flow does not even cover coupon
    if (prtf[k, paste0("Prin_", bd)] < 0) {
```

(continued)

**Table 6.21** (continued)

```
      prtf[k, paste0("Loss_", bd)] <- prtf[k, paste0("Loss_", bd)] -
        prtf[k, paste0("Prin_", bd)]
      prtf[k, paste0("Prin_", bd)] <- 0
    }
    # Compute next starting balance
    if (k < dim(prtf)[1]) {
      for (bd in names(bonds)) {
        prtf[k + 1, paste0("BegBal_", bd)] <-
          prtf[k, paste0("BegBal_", bd)] - prtf[k, paste0("Loss_", bd)] -
          prtf[k, paste0("Prin_", bd)]
      }
    }
  }
  return(prtf)
}
```

**Table 6.22** Cash flows in XS-OC structure. *Source* Compiled by the author

| Period | Beg Bal | Prin | Loss | Int | Beg Bal B | Prin B | Loss B | Int B | CF OC | CF XS |
|---|---|---|---|---|---|---|---|---|---|---|
| 1 | 100 | 0 | 0 | 5.0 | 99 | 2.0 | 0 | 3.0 | 0.00 | 0.0 |
| 2 | 100 | 2 | 0 | 5.0 | 97 | 4.1 | 0 | 2.9 | 0.00 | 0.0 |
| 3 | 98 | 5 | 0 | 4.9 | 93 | 7.1 | 0 | 2.8 | 0.00 | 0.0 |
| 4 | 93 | 10 | 1 | 4.7 | 86 | 12.1 | 0 | 2.6 | 0.00 | 0.0 |
| 5 | 82 | 9 | 2 | 4.1 | 74 | 10.1 | 0 | 2.2 | 0.78 | 0.0 |
| 6 | 71 | 7 | 4 | 3.5 | 64 | 8.6 | 0 | 1.9 | 0.00 | 0.0 |
| 7 | 60 | 5 | 2 | 3.0 | 55 | 6.3 | 0 | 1.6 | 0.00 | 0.0 |
| 8 | 53 | 2 | 1 | 2.6 | 49 | 3.2 | 0 | 1.5 | 0.00 | 0.0 |
| 9 | 50 | 2 | 1 | 2.5 | 45 | 3.1 | 0 | 1.4 | 0.00 | 0.0 |
| 10 | 47 | 47 | 0 | 2.4 | 42 | 42.3 | 0 | 1.3 | 4.74 | 1.1 |

From our analysis of an XS-OC structure, it clearly appears that there may not be much of a relationship between the sizing of the upfront OC and the total cash flows received by this equity tranche. In other words, the valuation of the equity in a deal does not have to be related to the general descriptive information typically provided about the deal's structure (such as all the various tranches' sizes). The only way of properly estimating the value or cost of an equity tranche is to run the underlying collateral cash flows with reasonable assumptions and model the structure's payments. As a result, any empirical analysis into equity tranche valuations that does not carry out detailed cash flow modeling is likely flawed, as we pointed out in Chap. 4.

In addition, depending on the relative size of the initial OC, the excess-spread and the degree of OC releases, such a tranche may not be behaving as a pure subordinated equity in the sense of the security design models. There are many potential situations in which a typical XS-OC tranche could yield a reasonable return to its holder, while more senior securities would eventually suffer principal writedowns, for example, if losses took place later in time. To some extent, diverting cash flows to the XS-OC

**Table 6.23** Cash flows in XS-OC structure, earlier principal payments. *Source* Compiled by the author

| Period | Beg Bal | Prin | Loss | Int | Beg Bal B | Prin B | Loss B | Int B | CF OC | CF XS |
|---|---|---|---|---|---|---|---|---|---|---|
| 1 | 100 | 0 | 0 | 5.00 | 99.0 | 2.0 | 0.00 | 2.97 | 0.00 | 0.00 |
| 2 | 100 | 3 | 0 | 5.00 | 97.0 | 5.1 | 0.00 | 2.91 | 0.00 | 0.00 |
| 3 | 97 | 10 | 0 | 4.85 | 91.9 | 12.1 | 0.00 | 2.76 | 0.00 | 0.00 |
| 4 | 87 | 10 | 1 | 4.35 | 79.8 | 11.7 | 0.00 | 2.39 | 0.00 | 0.29 |
| 5 | 76 | 9 | 2 | 3.80 | 68.1 | 9.9 | 0.00 | 2.04 | 0.82 | 0.00 |
| 6 | 65 | 47 | 4 | 3.25 | 58.2 | 47.3 | 0.00 | 1.75 | 1.22 | 0.00 |
| 7 | 14 | 5 | 2 | 0.70 | 10.9 | 5.4 | 0.00 | 0.33 | 0.00 | 0.00 |
| 8 | 7 | 2 | 1 | 0.35 | 5.5 | 2.2 | 0.00 | 0.17 | 0.00 | 0.00 |
| 9 | 4 | 2 | 1 | 0.20 | 3.3 | 2.1 | 0.24 | 0.10 | 0.00 | 0.00 |
| 10 | 1 | 1 | 0 | 0.05 | 1.0 | 1.0 | 0.00 | 0.03 | 0.00 | 0.02 |

**Table 6.24** Losses on XS-OC structure with randomized cash flows. *Source* Compiled by the author

| | Total loss | Total loss B | Total CF XS | Total CF OC |
|---|---|---|---|---|
| Min. | 2.2 | 0.00 | 0.00 | 0.0 |
| 1st Qu. | 7.6 | 0.00 | 0.56 | 4.3 |
| Median | 9.1 | 0.00 | 1.06 | 5.3 |
| Mean | 9.2 | 0.00 | 1.18 | 5.2 |
| 3rd Qu. | 10.7 | 0.00 | 1.66 | 6.3 |
| Max. | 19.1 | 0.99 | 5.69 | 9.7 |

tranche has the same effect as when principal is paid to a subordinated security in a straight senior/subordinated structure.

While in our examples, aiming to stress the efficacy of XS-OC we used strong OC targets, in practice, OC targets have been set up at low multiples of the initial available excess-spread, for example, typically 5% on a subprime deal with 3% in excess-spread. Because of the time it takes for losses to ramp up, the excess-spread in question is very unlikely to have to be used for loss coverage and as a result the XS-OC tranche will often receive excess-spread cash flows after little more than a year. This makes the residual cash flow quite front-loaded: some excess-spread, then potentially some OC release, and eventually at a later period the upside of whatever cash flows are left. At a high yield, appropriate for such risky equity cash flows, these front-loaded payments are valuable. As a consequence, this cash flow profile does not match with our intuition of what a true subordinated exposure should be.

These considerations stress that representing contracts in security design models as a function of a single cash flow at a future point in time is very restrictive and does not account for many variations observed in real life. Moreover, the structural features of first-loss pieces such as an XS-OC tranche may make them appear as subordinated, although they can benefit from early cash flows. This is a potential issue in any empirical study that would seek to analyze the incentives of issuers retaining such structures.

### 6.2.4 Sequential Structures

These ubiquitous structures are applicable to the distribution of principal. Interest on the resulting bonds is simply paid at the same rate as the sequential's collateral. Sequentials are generally created in order to target a particular average life, under a deal's pricing assumption. They are the simplest and most favored technique that allows for bonds with specific average lives to be created. The basic idea is that all principal payments from the collateral are diverted to a first bond, until it is entirely repaid. Then, principal payments go to another bond, until that one is entirely repaid, then to a third one, and so on. The bonds that are not yet receiving any principal payment are said to be **locked-out**, and the bond currently receiving payment is said to be the **current-pay** bond or **first cash flow** bond. The bond that is last in receiving payments is called the **last cash flow** bond. Such a structure that focuses primarily on the timing of principal repayment on the bonds is called a **time tranching** structure.

Sequential payments are generally used in two different contexts: they can help in targeting specific average lifes and make short or long bonds, and they can also be used to ensure that subordinated bonds will not be retired before they have fulfilled their credit protection role. In the first case, the sequential structure for principal payments leaves loss allocation to work in a prorata manner. In the second case, the sequential structure for principal is combined with targeted loss allocation. Note that in that second case, such a structure cannot be created by the recursive application of two different structures, such as subordination and then principal allocation, or principal allocation and then subordination. The same structure must handle the principal allocation and the loss allocation at the same time.

The existence of sequentials does raise the question of why investors would want them. The security design models we have discussed in Chap. 4 do not address the timing of cash flows directly.

#### 6.2.4.1 Formal Description

Plain Sequential

We first discuss the plain sequential structure, that does not address loss allocation. Losses are therefore allocated prorata. Obviously, if this structure is applied to an already structured block, the losses might already reflect some degree of structuring. However, within the sequential structure they would be allocated prorata. This plain sequential structure is relatively common on cash flows that have been already structured to the highest rating, on which one does not expect to observe losses.

This structure is in a way the equivalent of what a senior/subordinated structure is to losses, but to principal payments. The logic describing the allocation of cash flows will be quite similar. A sequential structure is defined by providing a series of bond sizes with a specific ordering. The collateral block $(B, CF)$ is structured into a series of $n$ bonds $(B^i, CF^i)_{1\leq i\leq n}$, where the first bond will be the first one to receive principal, and the last bond will be the last cash flow sequential. As with the other structures we have discussed so far, we will first attribute interest, losses, and then attribute principal payments.

For the current period the interest $I_t$ has been distributed prorata to the bonds as $I_t^i$, relative to their initial balances. Each bond's balance before loss attribution is $B_t^i$, and they each get a prorata share of losses. Hence $L_t^i = \frac{B_t^i}{B_t} L_t$. The bond's balance after loss attribution is

$$B_t^i - L_t^i = B_t^i \frac{B_t - L_t}{B_t}.$$

Now we distribute principal payments: at every payment time $t$, principal payments are passed to the front-most bond in the structure (in other words the lowest index $i$ so that $B_t^i > 0$); if the principal payment exceeds that bond's remaining balance then it is allocated to the next one, and so on. Note that in the case where $L_t = B_t$ then all balances are dropped to zero and we must have $P_t = 0$; we only concern ourselves here in the non-trivial cases where $P_t > 0$. Conditions that $B_t^i - L_t^i > 0$ are the same as $B_t^i > 0$. We can express the amount of principal allocated to each bond as follows:

$$P_t^i = \mathbb{I}_{B_t^i>0}\left(B_t^i \frac{B_t - L_t}{B_t}\mathbb{I}_{i_f\leq i<i_l} + \left(P_t - \frac{B_t - L_t}{B_t}\sum_{k<i_l} B_t^k\right)\right)$$

where $i_f = \inf\{i : B_t^i > 0\}$ and $i_l = \inf\{i : \frac{B_t - L_t}{B_t}\sum_{k\geq i_a}^{i} B_t^k \geq P_t\}$ which are the index of the front-most bond at the beginning of time $t$, and the longest bond up to which the prepayments are allocated.[8]

With a prorata allocation of losses, we nevertheless expect that bonds with a priority in principal payments will actually have less exposure to credit risk: they are paid off faster, before all losses materialize (in the general case where there are principal payments before maturity).

Senior/Subordinated Sequential

Let us now look into the allocation of losses and principal in the case of a senior/subordinated sequential. Now in this structure, as before, we specify an ordering of bonds but it now implies both a degree of priority in receiving principal, and in receiving losses. The front-most bonds will be the first to receive principal, but the last to receive losses. We could theoretically also structure that in the opposite fashion, where the front-most bond also receives losses in priority. This has rarely been done, because it does not really exacerbate the characteristics of the bonds.[9]

[8]We use $f$ for "front" and $l$ for "last, just like in the case of senior/subordination we used $a$ for "attachment" and $d$ for "detachment".

[9]Moving a subordinated bond into a principal priority position is known as a **turbo** feature; this not very common and typically only happens in certain conditions in a deal's life.

As before, we consider that interest has been paid based on outstanding balances. We then look at the allocation of losses, which should be exactly as defined in a standard senior/subordinate structure, with a twist: the ordering of seniority is now inverted, a low $i$ means more protection. We write

$$L_t^i = \mathbb{I}_{B_t^i > 0} \left( B_t^i \mathbb{I}_{i_a \geq i > i_d} + \left( L_t - \sum_{k > i_d} B_t^k \right) \right)$$

where $i_a = \sup\{i : B_t^i > 0\}$ and $i_d = \sup\{i : \sum_{k \leq i_a}^{i} B_t^k \geq L_t\}$. Note that now the bonds may have a zero balance with a low index $i$, or with a high index $i$. In the first case that would mean they got paid off thanks to principal allocation, in the second case they got wiped out.

Now the principal allocation works the same way as before, although we cannot simplify the expression of $B_t^i - L_t^i$ anymore. We have

$$P_t^i = \mathbb{I}_{B_t^i - L_t^i > 0} \left( \left( B_t^i - L_t^i \right) \mathbb{I}_{i_f \leq i < i_l} + \left( P_t - \sum_{k < i_l} \left( B_t^k - L_t^k \right) \right) \right)$$

with $i_f$ and $i_l$ now defined as such: $i_f = \inf\{i : B_t^i - L_t^i > 0\}$ and $i_l = \inf\{i : \sum_{k \geq i_a}^{i} (B_t^k - L_t^k) \geq P_t\}$.

#### 6.2.4.2 Examples

Plain Sequential

We first look at the behavior of the plain sequential, which does not concern itself with loss allocation explicitly. In order to best illustrate the behavior of the structure we will initially apply it to cash flows without losses. That would normally be the case if, for example, the plain sequential structure was applied to a block that already benefits from excess-spread, over-collateralization, and some senior/subordination in order to reach a AAA rating. Table 6.25 shows how we generate the cash flows we will be operating on.

In the example code shown in Table 6.26, we call the sequentials A, B, and C, although note that this plain sequential structure may be applied to senior bonds as well as junior bonds. The names with an A are usually reserved for senior bonds. It could also be applicable to a block of junior cash flows, out of which one would want to create time-tranched bonds.[10]

In Table 6.27 we can see how the collateral cash flows are allocated to the bonds, and it is quite clear that these bonds have very different average lives.

[10] Although this is not very common, because such time tranching of junior cash flows may significantly affect their credit risk and hence their likely rating.

**Table 6.25** Generating cash flows with prepays and no losses. *Source* Compiled by the author

```
general_example_noloss <- create_basic_portfolio(OrigBal = 100,
  Cpn = 0.05,
  Prin = c(0, 3, 10, 11, 11, 50, 8, 3, 3, 1),
  Loss = c(0, 0, 0, 0, 0, 0, 0, 0, 0, 0))
```

If we include losses in the collateral cash flows, using the assumptions from earlier examples, we can see in Table 6.28 that the overall behavior of the structure is the same, but the bonds do not all get the same effective exposure to losses, simply because the front bonds get repaid quickly and are not around anymore to be affected by all losses from the collateral.

Let us now look at the average cash flows across a large set of simulations (the same collateral projections as what was used for Figs. 6.5, 6.6 and 6.7). There are losses but the plain sequential structure does not specifically address those, only the timing of principal payments. The results are shown in Figs. 6.9, 6.10, and 6.11. With the randomization of the underlying collateral cash flows, the separation between the sequentials is not clear-cut, but it is nevertheless clear that they have very different average life profiles.

The distribution of losses allocated to the bonds, relative to their starting balances, clearly illustrates the impact of time tranching on credit exposure, as shown in Table 6.29. The last cash flow sequential C gets more than 5 times the losses that the front sequential A gets, on average. This is why, on junior blocks which do have a reasonable chance of being hit by losses, such time tranching is rare: it would necessarily imply different rating levels, although the bonds would technically have the same level of credit enhancement. In the case of senior bonds (rated AAA), the degree of credit protection is in principle high enough that even the last cash flows would still be protected enough in high loss scenarios.

One common way of visualizing time tranching structures (as well as other types of structures) is to look at an **average life chart**. This simply plots the average life of a particular structure as a function of a constant prepayment speed assumption (usually expressed in PSA terms). These types of charts are normally plotted with a zero loss assumption, so that it is purely the principal allocation logic of the structure that is illustrated. Figure 6.12 plots the average life for collateral (solid line) and for the three sequentials. The sequentials have clearly delineated average lives, although they all move roughly in parallel. While a front sequential will have a shorter average life than collateral, that average life will still vary significantly as the speed at which principal is returned varies.

Senior/subordinated Sequential

We now turn to the case of the senior/subordinated sequential, which combines loss allocation with principal allocation, with reversed priorities. The example code in Table 6.30 is very similar to the code for the plain sequential, but uses a part of the senior/subordinated code for loss allocation.

The example in Table 6.31 clearly shows how the losses are now all concentrated on bond C. With principal payments for C entirely shifted back, that whole bond's

**Table 6.26** Plain sequential structure logic. *Source* Compiled by the author

```
plain_sequential <- function(prtf,A_size =0.3,
                     B_size = 0.4,C_size =0.3) {
  bonds <- list("C"= C_size,"B"= B_size,"A"= A_size)
  fld_names <- c("BegBal","Prin","Loss","Int")

  # Set up cash flows for the bonds
  # Inverting order for better display
  for (bd in rev(names(bonds))) {
    prtf[, paste0(fld_names,"_", bd)] <-NA
    prtf[1,paste0("BegBal_", bd)] <-bonds[[bd]]*prtf$BegBal[1]
  }

  # Loop over periods
  for (k in 1:dim(prtf)[1]) {
    # First determine relative balances
    rel_bal <- c()
    for (bd in 1:length(bonds)) {
      rel_bal[bd] <- prtf[k, paste0("BegBal_",names(bonds)[bd])]
    }
    rel_bal <- rel_bal / sum(rel_bal)
    # Prorata allocation of interest and losses
    for (bd in 1:length(bonds)) {
      prtf[k, paste0("Int_",names(bonds)[bd])] <-
        rel_bal[bd] * prtf$Int[k]
      prtf[k, paste0("Loss_",names(bonds)[bd])] <-
        rel_bal[bd] * prtf$Loss[k]
    }
    # Determine principal allocation by looping through the bonds
    # in increasing principal priority
    prin_alloc <- list()
    i_l_track <- 0
    i_f <- NULL
    i_l <- NULL
    for (bd in rev(names(bonds))) {
      prin_alloc[[bd]] <- 0
      rem_bal <- prtf[k,paste0("BegBal_", bd)]-
        prtf[k,paste0("Loss_", bd)]
      if (is.null(i_f)& rem_bal> 0) {
        i_f <- bd
      }
      if (!is.null(i_f)& is.null(i_l)) {
        prin_alloc[[bd]] <- rem_bal
        i_l_track <- i_l_track+rem_bal
        if (i_l_track>= prtf$Prin[k]) {
          i_l <- bd
          prin_alloc[[bd]] <- prtf$Prin[k]-(i_l_track-rem_bal)
        }
      }
      prtf[k, paste0("Prin_", bd)] <- prin_alloc[[bd]]
    }
    # Compute next starting balance
    if (k < dim(prtf)[1]) {
      for (bd in names(bonds)) {
        prtf[k+ 1, paste0("BegBal_", bd)] <-
          prtf[k, paste0("BegBal_", bd)] - prtf[k,paste0("Loss_", bd)]-
          prtf[k, paste0("Prin_", bd)]
      }
    }
  }
  return(prtf)
}
```

**Table 6.27** Cash flows in plain sequential structure, no loss. *Source* Compiled by the author

| Period | Beg Bal | Prin | Loss | Int | Beg Bal A | Prin A | Loss A | Int A | Beg Bal B | Prin B | Loss B | Int B | Beg Bal C | Prin C | Loss C | Int C |
|---|---|---|---|---|---|---|---|---|---|---|---|---|---|---|---|---|
| 1 | 100 | 0 | 0 | 5.00 | 30 | 0 | 0 | 1.50 | 40 | 0 | 0 | 2.0 | 30 | 0 | 0 | 1.50 |
| 2 | 100 | 3 | 0 | 5.00 | 30 | 3 | 0 | 1.50 | 40 | 0 | 0 | 2.0 | 30 | 0 | 0 | 1.50 |
| 3 | 97 | 10 | 0 | 4.85 | 27 | 10 | 0 | 1.35 | 40 | 0 | 0 | 2.0 | 30 | 0 | 0 | 1.50 |
| 4 | 87 | 11 | 0 | 4.35 | 17 | 11 | 0 | 0.85 | 40 | 0 | 0 | 2.0 | 30 | 0 | 0 | 1.50 |
| 5 | 76 | 11 | 0 | 3.80 | 6 | 6 | 0 | 0.30 | 40 | 5 | 0 | 2.0 | 30 | 0 | 0 | 1.50 |
| 6 | 65 | 50 | 0 | 3.25 | 0 | 0 | 0 | 0.00 | 35 | 35 | 0 | 1.8 | 30 | 15 | 0 | 1.50 |
| 7 | 15 | 8 | 0 | 0.75 | 0 | 0 | 0 | 0.00 | 0 | 0 | 0 | 0.0 | 15 | 8 | 0 | 0.75 |
| 8 | 7 | 3 | 0 | 0.35 | 0 | 0 | 0 | 0.00 | 0 | 0 | 0 | 0.0 | 7 | 3 | 0 | 0.35 |
| 9 | 4 | 3 | 0 | 0.20 | 0 | 0 | 0 | 0.00 | 0 | 0 | 0 | 0.0 | 4 | 3 | 0 | 0.20 |
| 10 | 1 | 1 | 0 | 0.05 | 0 | 0 | 0 | 0.00 | 0 | 0 | 0 | 0.0 | 1 | 1 | 0 | 0.05 |

**Table 6.28** Cash flows in plain sequential structure, with losses. *Source* Compiled by the author

| Period | Beg Bal | Prin | Loss | Int | Beg Bal A | Prin A | Loss A | Int A | Beg Bal B | Prin B | Loss B | Int B | Beg Bal C | Prin C | Loss C | Int C |
|---|---|---|---|---|---|---|---|---|---|---|---|---|---|---|---|---|
| 1 | 100 | 0 | 0 | 5.00 | 30.0 | 0.0 | 0.00 | 1.50 | 40 | 0.0 | 0.00 | 2.0 | 30 | 0 | 0.00 | 1.50 |
| 2 | 100 | 3 | 0 | 5.00 | 30.0 | 3.0 | 0.00 | 1.50 | 40 | 0.0 | 0.00 | 2.0 | 30 | 0 | 0.00 | 1.50 |
| 3 | 97 | 10 | 0 | 4.85 | 27.0 | 10.0 | 0.00 | 1.35 | 40 | 0.0 | 0.00 | 2.0 | 30 | 0 | 0.00 | 1.50 |
| 4 | 87 | 10 | 1 | 4.35 | 17.0 | 10.0 | 0.20 | 0.85 | 40 | 0.0 | 0.46 | 2.0 | 30 | 0 | 0.34 | 1.50 |
| 5 | 76 | 9 | 2 | 3.80 | 6.8 | 6.6 | 0.18 | 0.34 | 40 | 2.4 | 1.04 | 2.0 | 30 | 0 | 0.78 | 1.48 |
| 6 | 65 | 47 | 4 | 3.25 | 0.0 | 0.0 | 0.00 | 0.00 | 36 | 33.9 | 2.22 | 1.8 | 29 | 13 | 1.78 | 1.44 |
| 7 | 14 | 5 | 2 | 0.70 | 0.0 | 0.0 | 0.00 | 0.00 | 0 | 0.0 | 0.00 | 0.0 | 14 | 5 | 2.00 | 0.70 |
| 8 | 7 | 2 | 1 | 0.35 | 0.0 | 0.0 | 0.00 | 0.00 | 0 | 0.0 | 0.00 | 0.0 | 7 | 2 | 1.00 | 0.35 |
| 9 | 4 | 2 | 1 | 0.20 | 0.0 | 0.0 | 0.00 | 0.00 | 0 | 0.0 | 0.00 | 0.0 | 4 | 2 | 1.00 | 0.20 |
| 10 | 1 | 1 | 0 | 0.05 | 0.0 | 0.0 | 0.00 | 0.00 | 0 | 0.0 | 0.00 | 0.0 | 1 | 1 | 0.00 | 0.05 |

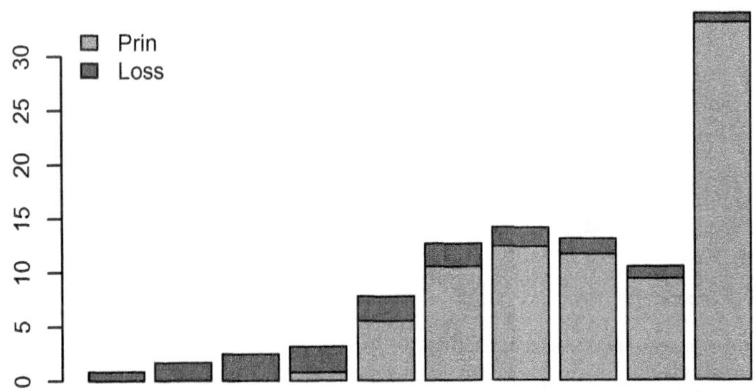


**Fig. 6.9** Average cash flows over time for Tranche C. *Source* Compiled by the author

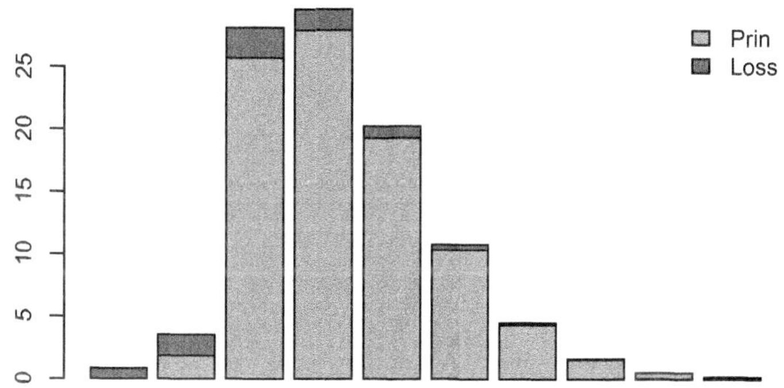


**Fig. 6.10** Average cash flows over time for Tranche B. *Source* Compiled by the author

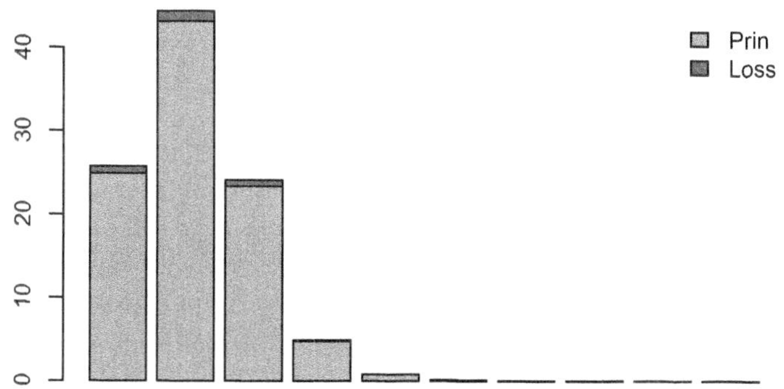


**Fig. 6.11** Average cash flows over time for Tranche A. *Source* Compiled by the author

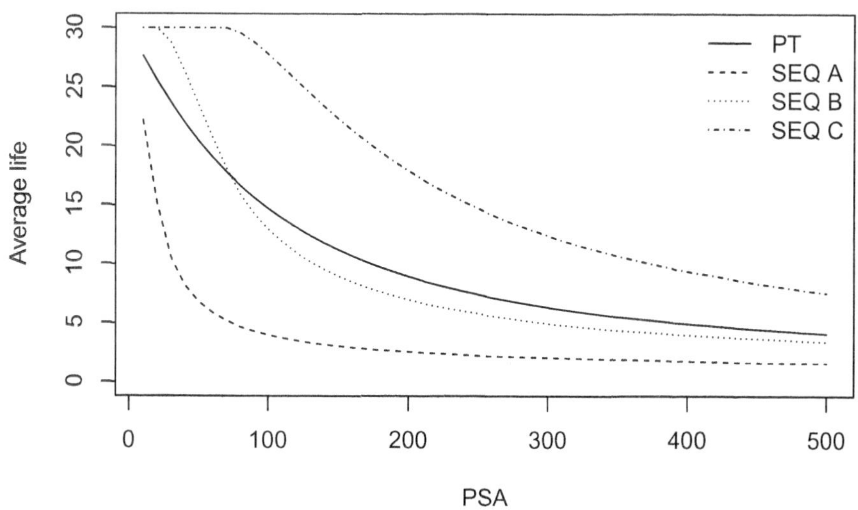


**Fig. 6.12** Average life chart for pass-through and sequentials. *Source* Compiled by the author

**Table 6.29** Losses on plain sequential structure with randomized cash flows. *Source* Compiled by the author

| | Total loss | Total loss A | Total loss B | Total loss C |
|---|---|---|---|---|
| Min. | 2.2 | 0.02 | 0.81 | 4.5 |
| 1st Qu. | 7.6 | 1.93 | 6.14 | 14.4 |
| Median | 9.1 | 2.77 | 7.95 | 16.9 |
| Mean | 9.2 | 3.00 | 8.22 | 16.9 |
| 3rd Qu. | 10.7 | 3.82 | 9.93 | 19.3 |
| Max. | 19.1 | 13.01 | 21.45 | 29.5 |

principal acts as protection for the other bonds in the structure. We can confirm that by looking at the distribution of losses at the bond level, as shown in Table 6.32. Combining principal and loss allocation in this way is a fairly standard way to create clean senior/subordination. The main issue it raises is that junior bond holders have to wait for a very long time to get some principal cash flows, and there are no mechanisms that can release principal if some threshold has been reached. As we will see, one alternative has been to combine senior/subordination with accelerated securities (using shifting interest schedules), in order to make the subordinated bonds able to release principal sooner and make them more palatable for investors.

The simple numerical examples we have discussed stress the importance of the distinction between hard and soft credit enhancement. Depending on the intensity of prepayments, a soft credit enhancement may not mean much. As a result, empirical analyzes looking, for example, at the actual performance of structured bonds depending on their credit enhancement may be flawed if they are only based on descriptive information such as tranche sizes. The only way in which one can measure the credit enhancement provided by a particular structure is to run realistic scenarios and capture under which assumptions on the collateral the bonds will absorb a first dollar of losses.

A subordinated back sequential, in the general case, is the only structure that effectively matches the pure "equity-like" junior securities we discussed in Chap. 4. As we will see in the section discussing actual combinations of structures in deals, this kind of tranche for first-loss positions is only really found in prime non-agency securitizations. In all other cases, XS-OC structures are preferred, typically due to the high coupon paid by the collateral. Subordinated back sequentials may be found as mezzanine bonds, hence supporting some senior bonds, but themselves protected by a first-loss tranche. The use of excess-spread based structures, itself driven by senior bonds investors' appetite for par-priced securities, makes it inefficient to create first-loss subordinated bonds with a hard credit enhancement. As we have mentioned earlier, the dynamics of principal payments play a crucial role in the efficacy of credit enhancement in all structures barring pure last cash flow subordinated tranches.

In Childs, Ott, and Riddiough (1996), the authors developed a model accounting for subordinated sequential structures in the CMBS market, in order to analyze the extent to which tranche characteristics impacted the fair value of the bonds. They show that senior bonds, while immune to credit risk, still are exposed to the

**Table 6.30** Senior/sub sequential structure logic. *Source* Compiled by the author

```
snrsub_sequential <- function(prtf, A_size = 0.3,
                              B_size = 0.4, C_size = 0.3) {
  bonds <- list("C" = C_size, "B" = B_size, "A" = A_size)
  fld_names <- c("BegBal", "Prin", "Loss", "Int")

  # Set up cash flows for the bonds
  # Inverting order for better display
  for (bd in rev(names(bonds))) {
    prtf[, paste0(fld_names, "_", bd)] <- NA
    prtf[1, paste0("BegBal_", bd)] <-bonds[[bd]] * prtf$BegBal[1]
  }

  # Loop over periods
  for (k in 1:dim(prtf)[1]) {
    # First determine relative balances
    rel_bal <- c()
    for (bd in 1:length(bonds)) {
      rel_bal[bd] <- prtf[k, paste0("BegBal_", names(bonds)[bd])]
    }
    rel_bal <- rel_bal / sum(rel_bal)
    # Prorata allocation of interest
    for (bd in 1:length(bonds)) {
      prtf[k, paste0("Int_", names(bonds)[bd])] <-
        rel_bal[bd] * prtf$Int[k]
    }
    # Senior/Sub allocation of losses
    loss_alloc <- list()
    i_d_track <- 0
    i_a <- NULL
    i_d <- NULL
    for (bd in names(bonds)) {
      loss_alloc[[bd]] <- 0
      rem_bal <- prtf[k, paste0("BegBal_", bd)]
      if (is.null(i_a) & rem_bal > 0) {
        i_a <- bd
      }
      if (!is.null(i_a) & is.null(i_d)) {
        loss_alloc[[bd]] <- rem_bal
        i_d_track <- i_d_track + rem_bal
        if (i_d_track >= prtf$Loss[k]) {
          i_d <- bd
          loss_alloc[[bd]] <- prtf$Loss[k] - (i_d_track - rem_bal)
        }
      }
      prtf[k, paste0("Loss_", bd)] <- loss_alloc[[bd]]
    }
    # Determine principal allocation by looping through the bonds
    # in increasing principal priority
    prin_alloc <- list()
    i_l_track <- 0
    i_f <- NULL
    i_l <- NULL
```

(continued)

**Table 6.30** (continued)

```
    for (bd in rev(names(bonds))) {
      prin_alloc[[bd]] <- 0
      rem_bal <- prtf[k, paste0("BegBal_", bd)] -
        prtf[k, paste0("Loss_", bd)]
      if (is.null(i_f) & rem_bal > 0) {
        i_f <- bd
      }
      if (!is.null(i_f) & is.null(i_l)) {
        prin_alloc[[bd]] <- rem_bal
        i_l_track <- i_l_track + rem_bal
        if (i_l_track >= prtf$Prin[k]) {
          i_l <- bd
          prin_alloc[[bd]] <- prtf$Prin[k] - (i_l_track - rem_bal)
        }
      }
      prtf[k, paste0("Prin_", bd)] <- prin_alloc[[bd]]
    }
    # Compute next starting balance
    if (k < dim(prtf)[1]) {
      for (bd in names(bonds)) {
        prtf[k + 1, paste0("BegBal_", bd)] <-
          prtf[k, paste0("BegBal_", bd)] - prtf[k, paste0("Loss_", bd)] -
          prtf[k, paste0("Prin_", bd)]
      }
    }
  }
  return(prtf)
}
```

**Table 6.31** Cash flows in senior/subordinated sequential structure. *Source* Compiled by the author

| Period | Beg Bal | Prin | Loss | Int | Beg Bal A | Prin A | Loss A | Int A | Beg Bal B | Prin B | Loss B | Int B | Beg Bal C | Prin C | Loss C | Int C |
|---|---|---|---|---|---|---|---|---|---|---|---|---|---|---|---|---|
| 1 | 100 | 0 | 0 | 5.00 | 30 | 0 | 0 | 1.50 | 40 | 0 | 0 | 2.0 | 30 | 0 | 0 | 1.50 |
| 2 | 100 | 3 | 0 | 5.00 | 30 | 3 | 0 | 1.50 | 40 | 0 | 0 | 2.0 | 30 | 0 | 0 | 1.50 |
| 3 | 97 | 10 | 0 | 4.85 | 27 | 10 | 0 | 1.35 | 40 | 0 | 0 | 2.0 | 30 | 0 | 0 | 1.50 |
| 4 | 87 | 10 | 1 | 4.35 | 17 | 10 | 0 | 0.85 | 40 | 0 | 0 | 2.0 | 30 | 0 | 1 | 1.50 |
| 5 | 76 | 9 | 2 | 3.80 | 7 | 7 | 0 | 0.35 | 40 | 2 | 0 | 2.0 | 29 | 0 | 2 | 1.45 |
| 6 | 65 | 47 | 4 | 3.25 | 0 | 0 | 0 | 0.00 | 38 | 38 | 0 | 1.9 | 27 | 9 | 4 | 1.35 |
| 7 | 14 | 5 | 2 | 0.70 | 0 | 0 | 0 | 0.00 | 0 | 0 | 0 | 0.0 | 14 | 5 | 2 | 0.70 |
| 8 | 7 | 2 | 1 | 0.35 | 0 | 0 | 0 | 0.00 | 0 | 0 | 0 | 0.0 | 7 | 2 | 1 | 0.35 |
| 9 | 4 | 2 | 1 | 0.20 | 0 | 0 | 0 | 0.00 | 0 | 0 | 0 | 0.0 | 4 | 2 | 1 | 0.20 |
| 10 | 1 | 1 | 0 | 0.05 | 0 | 0 | 0 | 0.00 | 0 | 0 | 0 | 0.0 | 1 | 1 | 0 | 0.05 |

randomness and directionality in principal payments, which then leads to a slight risk premium being assessed.

**Table 6.32** Losses on senior/subordinated sequential structure with randomized cash flows. *Source* Compiled by the author

| | Total loss | Total loss A | Total loss B | Total loss C |
|---|---|---|---|---|
| Min. | 2.2 | 0 | 0 | 7.2 |
| 1st Qu. | 7.6 | 0 | 0 | 25.4 |
| Median | 9.1 | 0 | 0 | 30.4 |
| Mean | 9.2 | 0 | 0 | 30.9 |
| 3rd Qu. | 10.7 | 0 | 0 | 35.8 |
| Max. | 19.1 | 0 | 0 | 63.8 |

### 6.2.5 Planned Amortization Classes and Supports

Planned amortization classes are much more widely known by their acronym **PACs**,[11] and were one of the earliest structures addressing variability in principal repayment. They are exclusively used at a senior level, and have not been combined with junior credit exposure. They are also typically applied to mortgage collateral, which exhibits interest rates directionality in prepayments. Indeed, while a PAC structure can stabilize random cash flows, investors have cared for stability only to the extent it cost them in terms of prepayment optionality.[12]

In a PAC structure, there are two bonds effectively created from a collateral block, the PAC and another bond, which will absorb principal payment variability, called the **support** or the **companion** (abbreviated CMP sometimes). The basic idea is to first set a principal payment schedule for the PAC, the **PAC schedule**. This will be the amount of principal that the structure will aim to pay the PAC, no more, no less. If there is more principal collected from the collateral than what is needed for the schedule, then the overflow goes to the support. If there is less principal collected than necessary, then all that is collected goes to the PAC, and there is a shortfall in the schedule which is added to the next month's scheduled payment. If at some point the support bond is fully paid down, then the PAC is the only remaining bond and it behaves like a pass-through.

When principal payments are slow, then the PAC collects all of them, or most of them, and the support gets little principal payments. In that case, the whole PAC will be repaid first, and then only later the support. That support bond hence behaves like a back sequential when principal payments are low. When principal payments are fast, the support bond gets all of them above the schedule, which makes it somewhat like a front sequential. The support's principal payment profile therefore exacerbates collateral principal payment variability: it is very short when principal payments come fast, and very long when they come slow.

PACs exhibit a particular exposure to the history of principal payments. If principal comes in fast early, then the support bond will be paid off quickly and the PAC will

[11] Pronounced "pack".

[12] The basics of prepayment optionality valuation have been addressed in Chap. 2.

have little or no support left to absorb further variations. If on the contrary principal payments come in slow, then the support will not get any principal payments and will remain available, with its full size. When a PAC's payments come off schedule, it is said to be **busted**. This is the case if, for example, principal payments were too low and the schedule could not be respected, or if they came in too fast and the support bond fully paid down.

Our presentation of PACs focuses on standard or traditional structures. There have been variations using more complex definitions in order to create bonds with very particular aspects, but we do not address them here. In their article (published in an operations research journal), Huang et al. (2007) solve a stochastic optimization program in order to show the optimality of a modified PAC structure, which would use a reserve account. The reserve account would keep some of the principal payments that would have otherwise gone to the companion, so that later slower principal payments than the schedule could be compensated. In effect, their method delays payment to the companion so that it is forced to stay around longer. It is unclear, however, whether the worse characteristics inflicted on the support would make it palatable enough for its usual buyers.

#### 6.2.5.1 Formal Description

The collateral block $(B, CF)$ is structured into two bonds, a PAC $P$ and a companion $C$. There is an initial payment schedule that has been defined for the PAC $H$, specifying the desired principal payments for each month, so that $B_0^P = \sum_{t\geq 0} H_t < B_0$ (the PAC's total scheduled principal payments should be less than the collateral's starting balance). We naturally always have $B_t = B_t^P + B_t^C$.

The PAC/support structure does not address loss allocation and therefore any losses are attributed on a prorata basis, before principal payments. Interest is also allocated on a prorata basis. So we consider that for the current period the interest $I_t$ has been distributed prorata to the bonds, and $I_t^P = I_t \frac{B_t^P}{B_t}$ and $I_t^C = I_t \frac{B_t^C}{B_t}$. For losses, $L_t^P = Lt \frac{B_t^P}{B_t}$ and $L_t^C = L_t \frac{B_t^C}{B_t}$. The condition $B_t^i - L_t^i > 0$ is equivalent to $B_t^i > 0$ for $i \in \{P, C\}$.

Over time, the actual principal payments that have been made to the PAC may have differed from the schedule, and we can measure that discrepancy at any point in time by computing $\sum_{s<t}(H_s - P_s^P)$. Note that if at any point in time $P_t^P > H_t$ it means the support has been fully repaid (otherwise it would be able to absorb the difference), and then the PAC becomes the same thing as the collateral, and the schedule does not need to be used anymore. Hence the schedule discrepancy is only going to be relevant when the terms in the sum are all positive. We note $H_t' = H_t + \sum_{s<t}(H_s - P_s^P)$ the schedule augmented with past shortfalls. It is more concise to write the support's principal payment first:

$$P_t^C = \mathbb{I}_{B_t^C > 0} \mathbb{I}_{P_t > H_t'} \left( (P_t - H_t') \wedge (B_t^C - L_t^C) \right).$$

The payment to the PAC is simply whatever is left, $P_t^P = P_t - P_t^C$.

It is important to realize there is a natural asymmetry in how fast or slow principal payments affect the support's ability to absorb variability in principal timing. For simplification, suppose there are no losses and also no backlog and hence $H_t' = H_t$. Also, $H_t = H_{t+1}$. Over two periods we have a large total principal payment $P_t + P_{t+1} = H_t + B_t^C$. We are looking at the difference between the case when the whole payment happens at $t$ and when it happens at $t + 1$.

- If $P_t = 0$ and $P_{t+1} = H_t + B_t^C$, then at time $t + 1$, the PAC should receive the backlog of $H_t$ that was not paid at time $t$, so the PAC gets a principal payment of $P_{t+1}^P = 2H_t$ and the support of $P_{t+1}^C = B_t^C - 2H_t$. The support's balance at the end of the period is therefore still positive and equal to $2H_t$.
- If $P_t = H_t + B_t^C$ and $P_{t+1} = 0$, then at time $t$ the collateral principal payment exactly covers the schedule to the PAC and fully repays the support. At time $t + 1$ the PAC has simply become a pass-through and there is no more principal payment variability protection.
- If $P_t = P_t + 1 = \frac{H_t + B_t^C}{2}$ then at time $t$ the PAC gets $H_t$ and the support gets $\frac{B_t^C - H_t}{2}$; at time $t + 1$ the PAC gets $H_t$ and the support is fully repaid. In this case, the PAC has become a pass-through at time $t + 2$.

#### 6.2.5.2 Examples

The code in Table 6.33 shows how to implement a PAC/support structure, given some schedule. Note the schedule is expressed as a fraction of total starting balance. In the examples treated here the cash flows are computed over a 30-year schedule so that they are more specifically representative of mortgage loans.

One important aspect that we have not yet detailed is the choice of the schedule. We can think of two broad parameters that drive that schedule: its total size, and its distribution over time. All else being equal, the smaller the scheduled cash flows, the larger the companion and hence the better the protection afforded to the PAC. In PAC/support structures, the PAC usually accounts for 60–70% of the total collateral. The second aspect, also quite important, is the timing of the scheduled cash flows. If these cash flows are back-loaded, so that the schedule calls for small principal payments early on, then the support will likely be paid off rapidly, and the PAC will effectively have little protection against faster principal repayments that may take place later. If on the other hand the schedule plans for large amounts of principal repayments early on, then the support will have a large balance outstanding (and hence provide contraction protection) later on.

On US mortgage-backed securities, PAC schedules are very often defined using so-called **PAC bands**. These bands are expressed in prepayment speed terms, for example, "100–250 PSA". Figure 6.13 shows the monthly principal payments on a \$100 loan at 100 PSA (dashed) and at 250 PSA (solid).[13] In this case, the PAC

[13]Note that we neglect scheduled amortization in these examples, so that the cash flows are not coupon-dependent.

**Table 6.33** PAC/support structure logic. *Source* Compiled by the author

```
pac_support <- function(prtf, sched) {
  P_size <- sum(sched)
  C_size <- 1 - P_size
  bonds <- list("P" = P_size, "C" = C_size)
  fld_names <- c("BegBal", "Prin", "Loss", "Int")
  sched <- sched * prtf$BegBal[1]

  # Set up cash flows for the bonds
  # Inverting order for better display
  for (bd in rev(names(bonds))) {
    prtf[, paste0(fld_names, "_", bd)] <- 0
    prtf[1, paste0("BegBal_", bd)] <- bonds[[bd]] * prtf$BegBal[1]
  }

  # Loop over periods
  for (k in 1:dim(prtf)[1]) {
    # First determine relative balances
    rel_bal <- c()
    for (bd in 1:length(bonds)) {
      rel_bal[bd] <- prtf[k, paste0("BegBal_", names(bonds)[bd])]
    }
    if (sum(rel_bal) > 0) {
      rel_bal <- rel_bal / sum(rel_bal)
    }
    # Prorata allocation of interest and losses
    for (bd in 1:length(bonds)) {
      prtf[k, paste0("Int_", names(bonds)[bd])] <-
        rel_bal[bd] * prtf$Int[k]
      prtf[k, paste0("Loss_", names(bonds)[bd])] <-
        rel_bal[bd] * prtf$Loss[k]
    }
    # Determine principal allocation for companion
    if (k > 1) {
      sched_prime <- sched[k] +
        sum(sched[1:(k - 1)] - prtf$Prin_P[1:(k-1)])
    } else {
      sched_prime <- sched[k]
    }
    prtf$Prin_C[k] <- 0
    if (prtf$BegBal_C[k] > 0 & prtf$Prin[k] > sched_prime) {
      prtf$Prin_C[k] <- min(prtf$Prin[k] - sched_prime,
        prtf$BegBal_C[k] - prtf$Loss_C[k])
    }
    # Apply principal allocation on PAC
    prtf$Prin_P[k] <- prtf$Prin[k] - prtf$Prin_C[k]
    # Compute next starting balance
    if (k < dim(prtf)[1]) {
      for (bd in names(bonds)) {
        prtf[k + 1, paste0("BegBal_", bd)] <-
          prtf[k, paste0("BegBal_", bd)] - prtf[k, paste0("Loss_", bd)] -
          prtf[k, paste0("Prin_", bd)]
      }
    }
  }
  return(prtf)
}
```

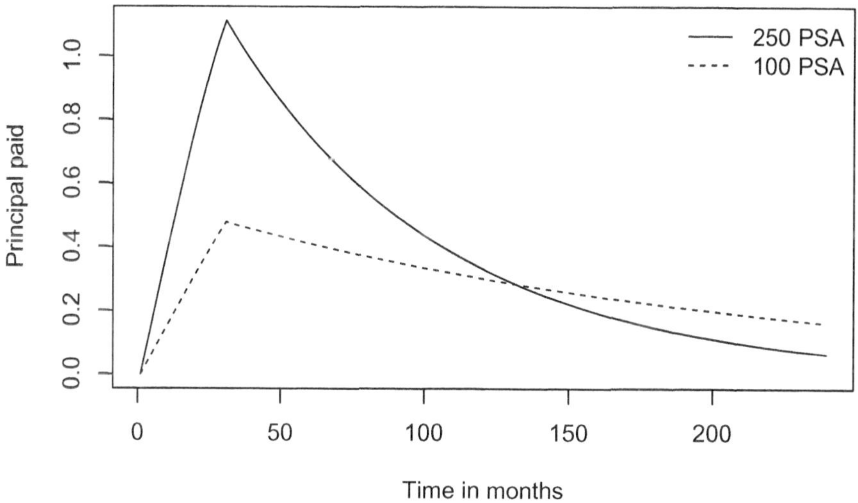


**Fig. 6.13** Principal payments at 100 and 250 PSA. *Source* Compiled by the author

schedule would be defined as the amounts that are under both curves. This way, for a *constant* prepayment speed between 100 PSA and 250 PSA, the PAC schedule would be kept. Note that the bands implicitly define the PAC's size relative to the whole collateral. If we specified very wide bands then the area underneath both bands' curves would be small. If we defined an extremely tight band range, then the area would be almost equal to the entire collateral.

In order to visualize the cash flow stability created by PAC structures, it is useful to look at an average life chart. We define a 100–250 PSA PAC schedule by taking the minimum monthly principal payment amount between the two curves at 100 and 250 PSA. In this case, the size of the PAC is about 65% of the total principal cash flow. Figure 6.14 shows the average life profile of the collateral, the PAC and the support in this example. For prepayment speeds between 100 and 300 PSA, the collateral's average life varies from 7 to 15 years approximately, which is quite substantial. The PAC, on the other hand, is much more stable and remains at about 10 years average life across these speeds. The principal payment variability is absorbed by the support, which is quite clearly riskier: its average life ranges from about 4 years to 30 years in this example.

The prepayment speeds used in an average life chart however are constant, and that makes the PAC appear more stable than it is, in a somewhat artifical manner. As we pointed out earlier, PAC structures are sensitive to the timing of principal payments, and if we introduced randomness (and therefore rather than being average, principal payments may be high and then low or reciprocally) we would expect the structure to be generally less efficient. Table 6.34 shows summary statistics on the bonds' average lives. The collateral is simulated with no losses and a yearly probability of prepayment of 12%, ramping over 3 years (which therefore roughly corresponds to 200 PSA). We can see that the PAC shows some variability in average life, due to the fact its schedule is not always respected. There is a greater degree of variability

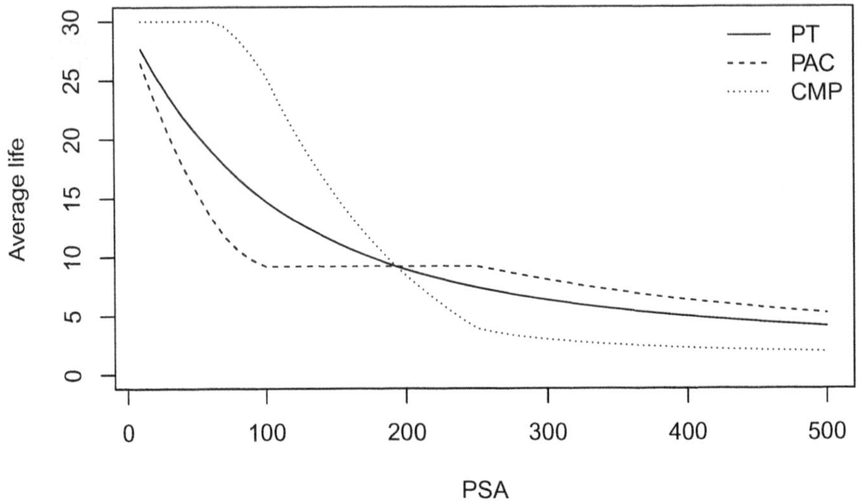


**Fig. 6.14** Average life chart for pass-through and PAC/support. *Source* Compiled by the author

**Table 6.34** Average life distribution on PAC structure with randomized cash flows. *Source* Compiled by the author

| | Avg life | Avg life P | Avg life C |
|---|---|---|---|
| Min. | 12 | 9.2 | 16 |
| 1st Qu. | 14 | 9.6 | 22 |
| Median | 15 | 9.9 | 24 |
| Mean | 15 | 10.1 | 24 |
| 3rd Qu. | 16 | 10.4 | 26 |
| Max. | 20 | 14.9 | 30 |

in terms of average life extension, which could be anticipated based on the shape of the PAC curve in Fig. 6.14: the PAC's average life extends quite significantly when the collateral prepays under 100 PSA.

### 6.2.5.3 PAC-2s

One interesting aspect of PAC structures is that it can be applied recursively. If we take a support bond, we can again apply a PAC/support structure to it. A PAC structured off of a support bond is called a **PAC-2**. The support of that PAC-2 is just called a support, but as one may expect it has much worse principal payment variability than a "normal" support.

PAC-2 schedules can be created using the same logic as for PACs. Figure 6.15 shows the projected principal cash flows on a normal PAC support, at 125 and 200 PSA. The area under both curves represents the amount that could be structured as a PAC-2. Note that the area under both curves, if these curves are wider apart than

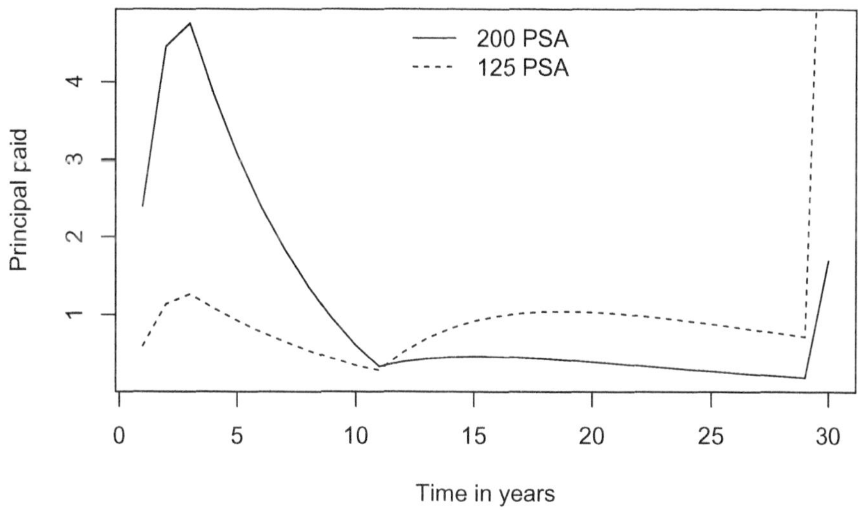


**Fig. 6.15** Principal payments on PAC support at 125 and 200 PSA. *Source* Compiled by the author

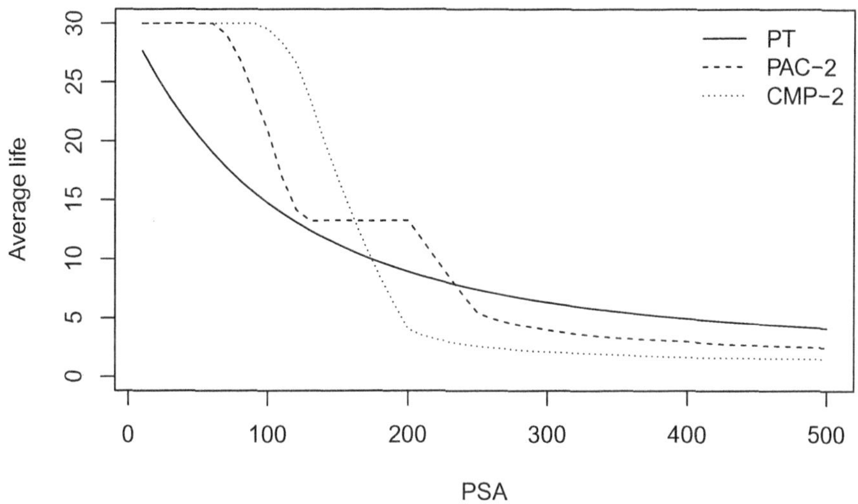


**Fig. 6.16** Average life chart for pass-through PAC-2/support. *Source* Compiled by the author

100 and 250 PSA (original PAC bands), would be zero. With these assumptions, the PAC-2 size is about 50% of the initial support size.

The average life variability characteristics of a PAC-2 are illustrated in Fig. 6.16. Even though the PAC-2 benefits from some degree of protection for constant speeds within tight bounds, the slope of its average life change relative to the PSA assumption is steeper than that of the collateral.

PACs/Supports do not directly address any credit-related structuring, and as such would seem entirely left out of the security design models that we have discussed so far in Chap. 4. Although no model has explicitly addressed the existence of these bonds, they could still be considered as less informationally sensitive than the underlying collateral, and the support appears to concentrate the informationally sensitivity. But of which sensitivity are we talking in this case? To what kind of unobserved variable exactly is the collateral exposed, to which the PAC would be less exposed?

In the case of credit enhancement, the important information could be summarized as the level of collateral losses, which has a direct impact on the cash flows investors get back, and on the value of the bonds. In the case of the principal payment speeds that PAC/Supports allocate among themselves, it is not so much the level of prepayments that is at stake but their variability, which we could express as the degree by which they could differ from the expectation. As we saw in Chap. 2, mortgage prepayments will tend to be fast/slow when we would want them to be slow/fast, respectively. Hence, the PAC bands could be seen as what both issuers and investors assume to be the maximal range of possible prepayment speeds, so that the bond's value is insensitive to the randomness in prepayments. This would make it informationally insensitive and the general ideas of basic security design models would seem applicable.

One argument in favor of this line of thought is that either issuers (for these structures, typically the investment bank structuring the deal) or hedge funds tend to own the most leveraged tranche, the PAC-2 support.[14] However, the PAC bands and even less so the PAC-2 bands are far from bracketing the typical distribution of prepayment speeds observed on collateral, and the typical PAC is hence not truly informationally insensitive.

Senior subprime bonds issued in the mid-2000s were also clearly not informational insensitive, as we discussed in Chap. 4, but that was an ex post realization. Ex ante, these AAA-rated bonds were thought to be informationally insensitive. With the PACs, the problem is that they would appear to be ex ante imperfectly informationally insensitive. There is hence the need for a gray area in security design that could address the existence of structures that are somewhat insensitive but not perfectly so. We will see in Chap. 7 how certain models may explain this situation.

### 6.2.6 Shifting Interest

The structures we have discussed so far addressing time tranching have been fairly simple: pass-throughs and sequentials. In effect, this means we can create either a front bond, getting all principal in priority, or a back bond, getting no principal, or something in the middle. These types of bonds can in fact be considered as particular examples in a much broader continuum.

A pass-through can be characterized as a bond getting at all times 100% of its prorata share of principal payments. A back sequential is a bond getting 0% of its prorata share of payments, and a front sequential is a bond getting more than 100%

[14] Maybe with further structuring as we will discuss in the section on stripping.

of its prorata share of payments.[15] Therefore, we can see that front sequential, pass-through and back sequential are just three particular settings of the bond's share in its prorata payment. In practice, this setting is normally expressed from the standpoint of the bond getting slower payments (hence less than 100% of its prorata principal), which means some other bonds are getting more than their prorata share. The practical reason is that in this expression the share is always between 0 and 100%, while the maximum range for the other bond would be changing over time as the bonds' relative balances evolve. This "dial" that sets how much a bond would postpone of its normal prorata payment is called the **shifting interest**: how much a bond is interested in its normal prorata payment gets shifted through time. The bond getting more than its normal prorata share of principal is called the **accelerated security**, and the other bond is usually called the **non-accelerated security** or **NAS**.[16] Note that this shifting interest structure logic, unlike what its name may sound like, is unrelated to interest payments.

As we pointed out above, a sequential is an extreme setting of the shifting interest, which does not vary over time. One could also set a bond to 50% of its prorata balance, for example, which would make it something between a pass-through and a back sequential, until the other bond in the structure would have been fully repaid, at which point our hybrid would be a simple pass-through. The shifting interest, however, does not need to be a constant: it can be a schedule, and increase or decrease over time. This allows for a fine control of the bond's dynamic characteristics.

Although in some sense a constant shifting interest schedule would create a bond that is somewhere between a sequential and a pass-through, this is not true in a literal sense. Indeed, the purest way in which one would create a mix between a sequential and a pass-through would be to first create two prorata blocks $A$ and $B$ with sizes $1 - \alpha$ and $\alpha$, respectively, and then cut $A$ into two pass-throughs $A1$ and $A2$, and $B$ into a front and back sequential $B1$ and $B2$. Then, $A1 + B1$ would be a mix between pass-through and front sequential with a proportion $\alpha$ of front sequential, and $A2 + B2$ would be a mix between pass-through and back sequential, with a proportion $\alpha$ of back sequential. The cash flows on $A1 + B1$, combining a pass-through and front sequential, would receive accelerate payments while the sequential $B1$ is outstanding, and then would just be the remaining pass-through $A1$. Therefore, the principal payments extend over the entire collateral's life for both $A1 + B1$ and $A2 + B2$. This is different from the behavior of an accelerated security, whose balance would reach 0 at some point before the collateral's maturity since this accelerated security would have been receiving principal payments at a faster relative rate than the collateral's.

The shifting interest schedule could in principle be arbitrary, not only increasing or decreasing over time but also going above 100%. However, given its normal use case, it can be considered to always remain between 0 and 100%, and always be

[15] More precisely it is getting 100% times the ratio of all bonds' balance over its own balance. Also note that this is subject to the implicit condition that once a bond's balance reaches zero the remainder goes to the other bond.

[16] Pronounced "naz".

increasing. The fact that it is increasing implies that we can always determine which bond is the NAS (the one getting less than its prorata share) and which one is the accelerated security (the other bond).

As with sequential structures, shifting interest is used along with prorata losses fairly exclusively on senior bonds that already have substantial credit enhancement. When it is used on more junior bonds it tends to be combined with senior/subordination. Originally, the shifting interest structure was introduced as a way of making subordinated bonds more palatable for their investors, because pure subordinated back sequentials were considered too long: the fact that one had to wait until the full repayment of the senior bonds to get any principal seemed too strong of a requirement. Non-accelerated securities were then designed as something between pure sequentials and pure pass-throughs to address this issue (although they were still closer to sequentials than to pass-throughs). The stable characteristics of the subordinated NAS then appealed to senior investors, and they began to appear as an additional structuring feature on senior blocks.

#### 6.2.6.1 Formal Description

Senior AS/NAS

In this first instance, we allocate losses in a prorata fashion. We are considering some cash flow block $(B, CF)$, which will be split into two bonds $A$ and $N$ according to a shifting interest schedule $h_t \in [0, 1]$ which would typically be increasing and such that $h_0 = 0$. In the prime mortgage market, a very common shifting interest schedule is set as follows, expressing time in years: $h_t = \sum_{k=5}^{9} \frac{k-4}{5} \mathbb{I}_{t \in [k,k+1)}$. This effectively delays the first principal payment to the NAS for 5 years, and progressively turns the NAS into a pass-through over the following 5 years. Naturally, if principal payments were so large as to fully pay off the accelerated security sooner than in 5 years, then the NAS would become a simple pass-through at that point.

First, interest and losses are allocated to the bonds, for $i \in \{A, N\}$:

$$I_t^i = \frac{B_t^i}{B_t} I_t$$

and

$$L_t^i = \frac{B_t^i}{B_t} L_t.$$

The remaining balance after loss allocation is for each bond $B_t^i - L_t^i = B_t^i \frac{B_t - L_t}{B_t}$.

We can now write the expression for the accelerated security as a function of the schedule, as it gets its own principal plus some extra amount diverted from the non-accelerated security:

$$\begin{aligned} P_t^A &= B_t^A \frac{B_t - L_t}{B_t} \wedge \frac{B_t^A \frac{B_t - L_t}{B_t} + (1 - h_t) B_t^N \frac{B_t - L_t}{B_t}}{B_t - L_t} P_t \\ &= B_t^A \frac{B_t - L_t}{B_t} \wedge \frac{B_t^A + (1 - h_t) B_t^N}{B_t} P_t. \end{aligned}$$

and the principal payment to the non-accelerated security is simply defined as the difference $P_t^N = P_t - P_t^A$. It appears from the expression of these cash flows that as far as $h$ remains between 0 and 1, there are no issues with the magnitude of the cash flows being allocated relative to the size of the entire available cash flow. Also, it is clear that with a typical schedule, the smaller the NAS, the more likely it is that it will not have to receive any principal payment for the first few years. If the NAS was very large, then the amount of extra principal diverted to the accelerated security would be large too, and that security would retire soon, transforming the NAS into a pass-through sooner than the schedule would anticipate. Senior NAS usually represent about 15% of the entire block.

Subordinated NAS

Shifting interest structures have often been used in conjunction with senior/subordination, making the non-accelerated security junior to the accelerated one. The typical shifting schedule in this case is in fact very similar to that observed on senior bonds, for the simple reason that the senior structures were directly inspired from the junior ones that predated them historically. There is one important difference in how they are structured, however: in the case of subordinated NAS, the size of the NAS is as small as possible, driven by rating agency requirements, while for senior NAS there is no such constraint. In MBS, the sizes of the subordinated NAS relative to the entire block is around 5%, corresponding to the required credit enhancement on prime mortgages.

Interest are first allocated to the bonds without any particular structural feature: $I_t^i = \frac{B_t^i}{B_t} I_t$ for $i \in \{A, N\}$. Then losses are allocated, going in priority to the non-accelerated security: $L_t^N = L_t \wedge B_t^N$ and $L_t^A = L_t - L_t^B$. The balances used to compute principal payments then reflect these losses: $B_t^N - L_t^N = (B_t^N - L_t \wedge B_t^N)$ and $B_t^A - L_t^A = B_t^A - L_t + B_t^N \wedge L_t$. Then we have

$$P_t^A = (B_t^A - L_t + B_t^N \wedge L_t) \wedge \frac{(B_t^A - L_t + B_t^N \wedge L_t) + (1 - h_t)(B_t^N - L_t \wedge B_t^N)}{B_t - L_t} P_t.$$

As before, we also express the principal payment to the NAS as $P_t^N = P_t - P_t^A$. In the case where $B_t - L_t = 0$ then principal payments are null by construction and both $P_t^A = P_t^N = 0$.

#### 6.2.6.2 Examples

In these examples we use the same inputs as for our analysis of plain and subordinated sequentials; NAS/AS are effectively comparable to a combination of sequentials and pass-throughs in some sense, as we explained earlier. We do not treat the case of subordinated NAS specifically, since they effectively behave in a comparable fashion to back sequentials.

The first step is to define a schedule; as shown in Table 6.35, we choose a typical one for mortgage securities, as mentioned earlier. The calculation of the cash flows follows the formal logic exposed above, as illustrated in Table 6.36.

**Table 6.35** NAS schedule. *Source* Compiled by the author

```
typical_si_sched <- function(per) {
  ifelse(ifelse(per > 10, 10, per) - 5 > 0, (per - 5) / 5, 0)
}
```

**Table 6.36** Shifting interest structure logic. *Source* Compiled by the author

```
plain_si <- function(prtf, hsched, N_size = 0.15) {
  bonds <- list("N" = N_size, "A" = 1 - N_size)
  fld_names <- c("BegBal", "Prin", "Loss", "Int")

  # Set up cash flows for the bonds
  for (bd in names(bonds)) {
    prtf[, paste0(fld_names, "_", bd)] <- NA
    prtf[1, paste0("BegBal_", bd)] <- bonds[[bd]] * prtf$BegBal[1]
  }

  # Loop over periods
  for (k in 1:dim(prtf)[1]) {
    # First determine relative balances
    rel_bal <- list()
    for (bd in names(bonds)) {
      rel_bal[[bd]] <- prtf[k, paste0("BegBal_", bd)]
    }
    totbal <- rel_bal$A + rel_bal$N
    if (totbal > 0) {
      rel_bal$A <- rel_bal$A / totbal
      rel_bal$N <- rel_bal$N / totbal
    }
    # Prorata allocation of interest and losses
    for (bd in names(bonds)) {
      prtf[k, paste0("Int_", bd)] <-
        rel_bal[[bd]] * prtf$Int[k]
      prtf[k, paste0("Loss_", bd)] <-
        rel_bal[[bd]] * prtf$Loss[k]
    }

    # Determine principal allocation following schedule
    full_alloc = (rel_bal$A + (1 - hsched(k)) * rel_bal$N) * prtf$Prin[k]
    prtf$Prin_A[k] <- min(full_alloc, prtf$BegBal_A[k] - prtf$Loss_A[k])
    prtf$Prin_N[k] <- prtf$Prin[k] - prtf$Prin_A[k]

    # Compute next starting balance
    if (k < dim(prtf)[1]) {
      for (bd in names(bonds)) {
        prtf[k + 1, paste0("BegBal_", bd)] <-
          prtf[k, paste0("BegBal_", bd)] - prtf[k, paste0("Loss_", bd)] -
          prtf[k, paste0("Prin_", bd)]
      }
    }
  }
  return(prtf)
}
```

Using the same simple cash flow assumptions as in prior subsections, with some prepayments and no losses, we can generate the amortization table for the accelerated and non-accelerated securities, as shown in Table 6.37. We can see that the NAS does not receive any principal for the first 5 years, and only begins to receive some at year

6. At the same time, the accelerated security still receives principal until year 7 when it is fully paid down. It is important to realize that the principal lock-out for the NAS is based on time, and not directly on the amount of principal collected, unlike a sequential. Although not absolutely fixed, it makes the NAS's average life much more stable than on a comparable standard sequential.

If we include losses in the collateral cash flows, using the assumptions from earlier examples, we can see in Table 6.38 that the exposure of the NAS to losses is roughly comparable to what it would be with a back sequential of the same amount. Initially some losses are passed prorata to the accelerated security, but since it retires relatively quickly, it does not absorb that many losses relative to its initial balance.

We apply the AS/NAS structure to the same random cash flows that we have used before, scaled to each bond's initial outstanding principal balance, as shown in Figs. 6.17 and 6.18. In spite of the randomness both in prepayments and in losses, we observe that the NAS remains properly locked-out of principal payments for the first 5 years, while the accelerated securities' principal payments span the entire range. Although principal payments from the collateral are declining over time, we can see them increasing or staying constant on the NAS, reflecting the increasing shifting interest schedule over time, after 5 years.

The seemingly strong NAS cash flow stability can be further illustrated thanks to an average life chart, as shown in Fig. 6.19. We can see the average life profile of a typical senior NAS (15% of the total bonds amount) and its corresponding AS (for 85% of the total balance), as well as a hypothetical 40% NAS with the same schedule. There are several important aspects of NAS structures that can be discussed based on this chart.

First, note how close the accelerated securities profile is to that of the collateral. Since the NAS does not account for a large part of the whole collateral, it does not have a significant effect on the remainder of the structure. The characteristics of the AS are close enough to the underlying block's that from a valuation perspective the difference will remain imperceptible. It is only in the case where one would further structure that AS that the more sensitive tranches would exhibit some differences: for example, a PAC-2 support off of an AS would show greater variability than a PAC-2 support off of the entire block.

Then, we can see that given the same schedule, the distinction between a smaller or a larger NAS is visible with faster prepayment speeds. Indeed, the faster prepayments will retire the AS sooner, and beyond a certain point will force principal payments before the end of the scheduled lock-out. In the case at hand, the average life curves show an inflection around 250 PSA for the 40% NAS and around 450 PSA for the 15% NAS.

The overall shape of the average life profile of a NAS is also reminescent of that of a long PAC: significant extension if prepayments slow down, a flat sensitivity for moderate speeds, and contraction as prepayment speeds increase beyond a certain point. Effectively, a NAS can be compared to a PAC, insofar as it offers good average life stability. Neverthless, the dynamics of the structures are quite different. Certainly both a PAC and a NAS can become "busted" following a period of last prepayments, if the bonds that absorb prepayment variability are all paid off, but a typical PAC

**Table 6.37** Cash flows in plain AS/NAS structure, no loss. *Source* Compiled by the author

| Period | Beg Bal | Prin | Loss | Int | Beg Bal N | Prin N | Loss N | Int N | Beg Bal A | Prin A | Loss A | Int A |
|---|---|---|---|---|---|---|---|---|---|---|---|---|
| 1 | 100 | 0 | 0 | 5.00 | 15 | 0.0 | 0 | 0.75 | 85.0 | 0.0 | 0 | 4.25 |
| 2 | 100 | 3 | 0 | 5.00 | 15 | 0.0 | 0 | 0.75 | 85.0 | 3.0 | 0 | 4.25 |
| 3 | 97 | 10 | 0 | 4.85 | 15 | 0.0 | 0 | 0.75 | 82.0 | 10.0 | 0 | 4.10 |
| 4 | 87 | 11 | 0 | 4.35 | 15 | 0.0 | 0 | 0.75 | 72.0 | 11.0 | 0 | 3.60 |
| 5 | 76 | 11 | 0 | 3.80 | 15 | 0.0 | 0 | 0.75 | 61.0 | 11.0 | 0 | 3.05 |
| 6 | 65 | 50 | 0 | 3.25 | 15 | 2.3 | 0 | 0.75 | 50.0 | 47.7 | 0 | 2.50 |
| 7 | 15 | 8 | 0 | 0.75 | 13 | 5.7 | 0 | 0.63 | 2.3 | 2.3 | 0 | 0.12 |
| 8 | 7 | 3 | 0 | 0.35 | 7 | 3.0 | 0 | 0.35 | 0.0 | 0.0 | 0 | 0.00 |
| 9 | 4 | 3 | 0 | 0.20 | 4 | 3.0 | 0 | 0.20 | 0.0 | 0.0 | 0 | 0.00 |
| 10 | 1 | 1 | 0 | 0.05 | 1 | 1.0 | 0 | 0.05 | 0.0 | 0.0 | 0 | 0.00 |

**Table 6.38** Cash flows in plain AS/NAS structure, with losses. *Source* Compiled by the author

| Period | Beg Bal | Prin | Loss | Int | Beg Bal N | Prin N | Loss N | Int N | Beg Bal A | Prin A | Loss A | Int A |
|---|---|---|---|---|---|---|---|---|---|---|---|---|
| 1 | 100 | 0 | 0 | 5.00 | 15 | 0.0 | 0.00 | 0.75 | 85.0 | 0.0 | 0.00 | 4.25 |
| 2 | 100 | 3 | 0 | 5.00 | 15 | 0.0 | 0.00 | 0.75 | 85.0 | 3.0 | 0.00 | 4.25 |
| 3 | 97 | 10 | 0 | 4.85 | 15 | 0.0 | 0.00 | 0.75 | 82.0 | 10.0 | 0.00 | 4.10 |
| 4 | 87 | 10 | 1 | 4.35 | 15 | 0.0 | 0.17 | 0.75 | 72.0 | 10.0 | 0.83 | 3.60 |
| 5 | 76 | 9 | 2 | 3.80 | 15 | 0.0 | 0.39 | 0.74 | 61.2 | 9.0 | 1.61 | 3.06 |
| 6 | 65 | 47 | 4 | 3.25 | 14 | 2.1 | 0.89 | 0.72 | 50.6 | 44.9 | 3.11 | 2.53 |
| 7 | 14 | 5 | 2 | 0.70 | 11 | 2.8 | 1.64 | 0.57 | 2.5 | 2.2 | 0.36 | 0.13 |
| 8 | 7 | 2 | 1 | 0.35 | 7 | 2.0 | 1.00 | 0.35 | 0.0 | 0.0 | 0.00 | 0.00 |
| 9 | 4 | 2 | 1 | 0.20 | 4 | 2.0 | 1.00 | 0.20 | 0.0 | 0.0 | 0.00 | 0.00 |
| 10 | 1 | 1 | 0 | 0.05 | 1 | 1.0 | 0.00 | 0.05 | 0.0 | 0.0 | 0.00 | 0.00 |

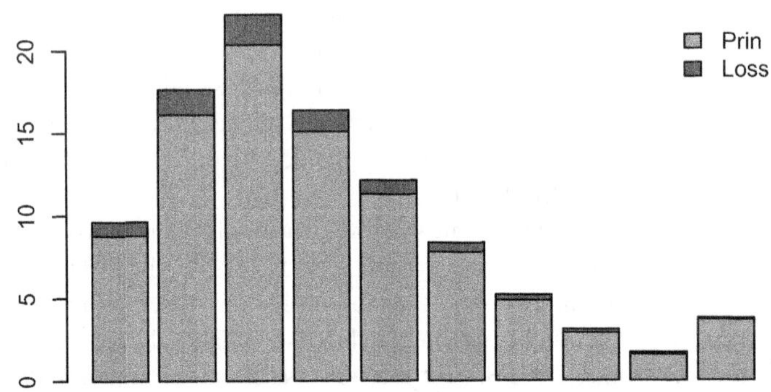


**Fig. 6.17** Average cash flows over time for Tranche A. *Source* Compiled by the author

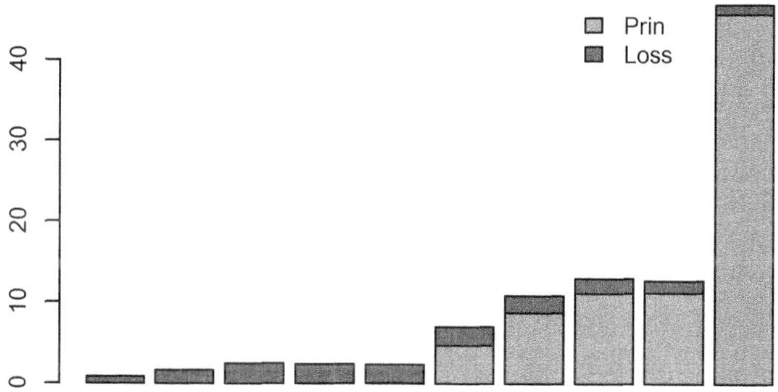


**Fig. 6.18** Average cash flows over time for Tranche N. *Source* Compiled by the author

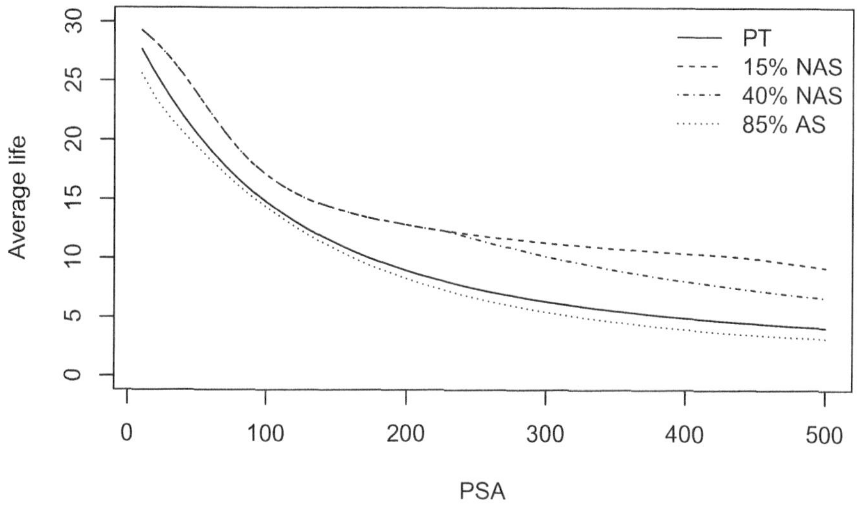


**Fig. 6.19** Average life chart for pass-through and AS/NAS. *Source* Compiled by the author

only has 30–40% of the total amount acting as protection while the typical NAS has 85% acting as protection. Hence, a NAS is much less likely to become "busted" than a PAC. On the other hand, if prepayment speeds remain moderate, a PAC will keep on benefiting from that protection going forward, and stay on schedule. However a NAS will become a pass-through at a predetermined point in time, and after that will not have any particular prepayment variability protection at all.

### 6.2.7 Stripping and Interest Allocation

In this section, we focus on several techniques that are related to the allocation of interest between bonds. We do not consider the special case of excess-spread, which we have covered already, where interest was transformed into principal. We are only dealing with interest that remains interest.

The main idea is to take interest from some bonds and give it to other bonds. If we considere a basic prorata allocation, each bond would receive its "fair" share of interest according to its relative outstanding balance. This allocation rule can be changed, and a particular bond may receive a greater share or smaller share than the prorata-based amount. This is called **stripping** interest from one bond. Another technique we will consider is called **indexing** and involves creating coupons that are indexed on some external reference, while another bond gets the inverse index payment.

We first briefly describe the creation and use of straight IOs and POs, followed by floaters and inverses, and illustrate their common uses in typical agency deals. Then we look into the mechanics of WAC IOs and WAC POs, which are more structurally complex, and illustrate their use in non-agency deals, contrasting so-called six-packs with excess-spread/OC structures.

#### 6.2.7.1 IOs and POs

A fairly simple technique is to create two pass-throughs and increase the coupon on one while decreasing it on the other. The degree by which the relative coupon on one of the bonds is altered depends on the relative sizes of the pass-throughs and on how much coupon is stripped. This technique can be applied to tranches independently from principal and loss allocation.

The algebra to determine how much interest should be paid on the bonds is very straightforward. For example \$100 mm paying 5% may become \$25 mm paying 8%, plus \$75 mm paying 4%, since $5 = .75 \times 4 + 0.25 \times 8$.

Pushing this logic to the limit we can create tranches that only pay principal and tranches that only pay interest. An **Interest-only** or **IO** tranche does not pay any principal (its prorated share is all going to some other bonds). A **Principal-only** or **PO** tranche does not pay interest (and its prorated share of interest is going to some other bonds). A block may be separated into an IO and a PO, in which case the combination of the two results into the initial block. The most common reason why IOs or POs may be created is in order to, respectively, reduce or increase the coupon on other bonds, to make them more palatable for their intended buyers. The IOs and POs themselves, being much more leveraged relative to the timing of principal payments, are typically acquired by investors who need them to hedge particular risks, or by well-informed investors who can evaluate them accurately.

#### 6.2.7.2 Floaters, Inverse Floaters, and Inverse-IOs

Another way in which interest can be allocated among bonds is through the use of an index. One bond is set to pay a coupon equal to this index plus a fixed amount. The rest of the block, called the inverse floater, pays the difference between the underlying block's available coupon, and the amount paid to the floater.

Given an amount $B$ of some fixed-rate bond with coupon $c$, one can create a floating rate bond as follows:

- Define some reference **index** $i$, such as 3-month Libor off of which the new bond's coupon should be based, and a **margin** $m$ that the floater will pay on top of the index.
- The floater's coupon will be equal to $i + m$, and that floater will have a balance of $F < B$.
- Then write the fixed-rate bond's interest payment as a decomposition including the desired floater coupon:

$$Bc = Bc + F(i + m) - F(i + m) = F(i + m) + (Bc - F(i + m)).$$

- The expression for the floater's coupon is naturally subject to a **cap**: as high as the index may be, the inverse floater could not get a negative coupon and hence $(Bc - F(i + m))$ must be positive. As a result the index $i$ when applied to the calculation of the floater coupon cannot exceed $i < \frac{B}{F}c - m$. Hence a floater created in this way can never be a "true" floating rate bond, it always must be capped.
- The inverse floater's balance is $B - F$ and hence the inverse floater's relative coupon is

$$\frac{Bc - Fm}{B - F} - \frac{F}{B - F}i.$$

This last formula clearly shows why this offshoot of the creation of the floater is called an inverse floater. The ratio $\frac{F}{B-F}$ is the inverse floater's formula leverage, normally greater than 1.

By combining floater/inverse and IO/PO logic, one can directly create from a fixed-rate bond a floater and an **inverse-IO**. In this case the floater gets all the principal payments, and the floating rate coupon (capped), while the inverse-IO gets the inverse coupon and no principal.

Since floating rate bonds have a low interest rate duration they are less subject to the problems of negative convexity which we exposed in Chap. 2 (although when rates increase and the coupon becomes capped, they locally acquire all the characteristics of a fixed-rate bond). This makes them more desirable for some investors. Inverse floaters and inverse-IOs on the other hand concentrate a good part of the negative convexity and are typically purchased by well-informed investors.

Combining stripping and indexing, as well as some of the structuring techniques we have discussed earlier, we can see two examples agency deal structures, as shown in Figs. 6.20 and 6.21.

#### 6.2.7.3 WAC IOs and POs

As we explained earlier, the use of excess-spread in credit enhancement is reserved for collateral paying a high enough coupon relative to the market. In contrast, the most popular credit enhancement structure in non-agency prime deals is typically straight senior-subordination, which includes a subordinated class and a senior class. The subordinated class is further structured into a series of six subordinated bonds

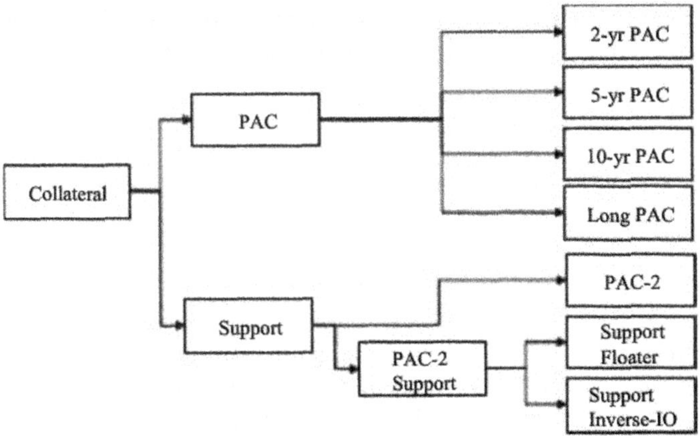


**Fig. 6.20** Illustration of a basic agency PAC deal. *Source* Compiled by the author

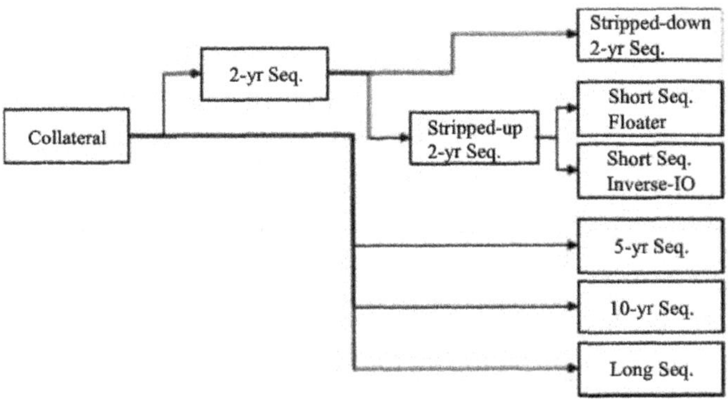


**Fig. 6.21** Illustration of a basic agency sequential deal. *Source* Compiled by the author

with ratings ranging between AA down to B and an unrated first-loss piece (hence the name **six-pack**). The subordinated class is the first-loss piece absorbing the losses and thus protecting the senior class.

Figure 6.22 shows a simple comparison of exces-spread and "six-packs" in the non-agency market. In an excess-spread/OC structure, some of the coupon payment is used to create credit enhancement. The principal allocation between senior and subordinated bonds follows a shifting interest schedule.

In a "six-pack" structure, the principal is allocated using an AS/NAS structure between senior and junior bonds; then within the junior bonds in a prorata fashion. The bottom tranche, the non-rated tranche, is the first-loss piece. Interest payments are directly distributed to the bonds. As the subordinated bonds are structured as NASs, they are locked-out from prepayments, typically for 5 years, after which they are paid prorata based on the shifting interest schedule. Additionally, to protect the senior bonds if losses and delinquencies are higher than expected, triggers are set so that no prepayments are channeled to the subordinated bonds.

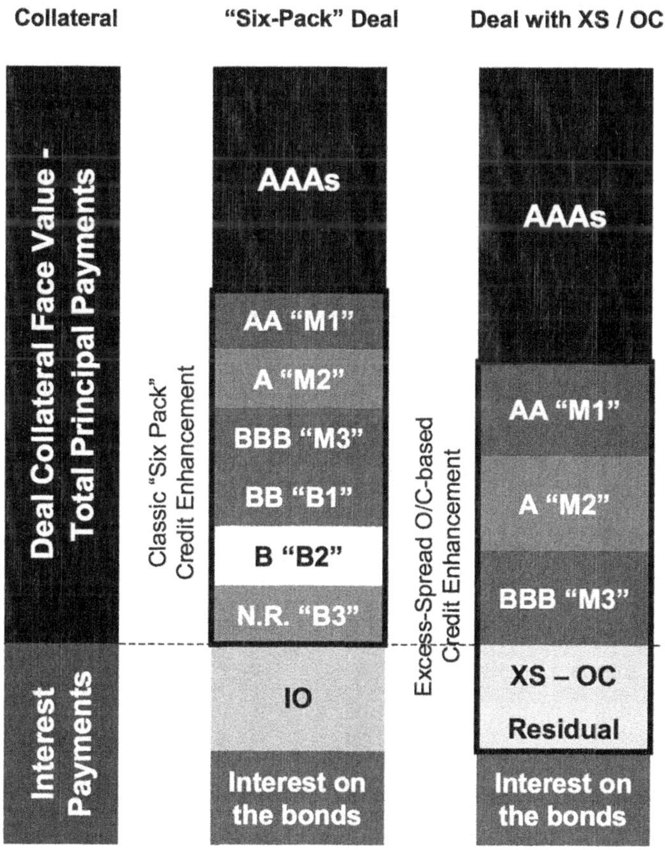


**Fig. 6.22** A comparison of excess-spread and shifting interest/senior-substructures. *Source* Compiled by the author

Looking at Fig. 6.22, we may wonder how a six-pack deal would handle the fact that all the loans do not pay exactly the same coupon. We know this would not be an issue in an excess-spread structure, but as we have described the allocation of interest in the simplest prorata case, this would be problematic. Indeed, consider the following example portfolio in Table 6.39, with a total size of $1,200,000 and an average coupon of 5.02%.

The aggregate coupon of 5.02% paid by this portfolio is not going to remain constant. It could go down if the first loan prepays, and then go up if loans 3 and 4 prepay. Typically investors want a clean coupon that does not move around. One could shave off all the coupons higher than the lowest, but then cutting all the loans down to 4% would leave a lot of cash flows on the table. How do we create a nice 5% coupon block of collateral in this case? One has to create a **WAC IO** and a **WAC PO**, since they are created for a "weighted average coupon" target. The WAC IO will receive the part of interest that is above the intended coupon on the loans that pay a higher coupon than targeted, while the WAC PO will receive a part of principal on

**Table 6.39** Loan portfolio example. *Source* Compiled by the author

| Loan Nb | Gross amt | Gross Cpn |
|---|---|---|
| 1 | 100,000 | 6.2 |
| 2 | 200,000 | 5.0 |
| 3 | 150,000 | 4.0 |
| 4 | 300,000 | 4.5 |
| 5 | 50,000 | 5.0 |
| 6 | 200,000 | 6.0 |
| 7 | 200,000 | 5.0 |

**Table 6.40** Loan portfolio with WAC IOs and POs. *Source* Compiled by the author

| Loan Nb | Gross amt | Gross Cpn | IO strip | PO amt | Net amt | Net Cpn |
|---|---|---|---|---|---|---|
| 1 | 100,000 | 6.2 | 1.2 | 0 | 100,000 | 5 |
| 2 | 200,000 | 5.0 | 0.0 | 0 | 200,000 | 5 |
| 3 | 150,000 | 4.0 | 0.0 | 30,000 | 120,000 | 5 |
| 4 | 300,000 | 4.5 | 0.0 | 30,000 | 270,000 | 5 |
| 5 | 50,000 | 5.0 | 0.0 | 0 | 50,000 | 5 |
| 6 | 200,000 | 6.0 | 1.0 | 0 | 200,000 | 5 |
| 7 | 200,000 | 5.0 | 0.0 | 0 | 200,000 | 5 |

loans that pay a coupon below the target so that their scaled interest equals the target. In the example above, loans 1 and 6 will contribute to the WAC IO, and loans 3 and 4 will contribute to the WAC PO. The initial loan portfolio is structured into a WAC IO, a WAC PO, plus a "cleaner" portfolio that is very much a pass-through (though not exactly). The computations are illustrated in Table 6.40.

In this example we obtain a total of \$60,000 in WAC PO, a WAC IO with a notional of \$300,000 paying an average coupon (initially) of 1.08%, and a portfolio of \$1,140,000 paying a constant coupon of 5%. This portfolio is in a sense a clean pass-through with a constant coupon. Note that the WAC IO could be defined relative to a notional equal to the entire underlying portfolio as well, in which case its coupon would be 0.29%, even though its cash flows only come from a particular subset of the loans.

Creating WAC IOs and POs requires a structure that operates at the loan level, and not at the aggregate cash flow level. More formally if we have a set of loans $\mathcal{L}$ with cash flows $(B_k, CF_k)_{k \in \mathcal{L}}$, each paying a coupon (assumed constant) $c_k = 100\frac{(I_k)_0}{12(B_k)_0}$ then the WAC IO/PO structure would work as follows. Note that we are only addressing fixed coupons here, because in the case of floating coupons the logic is more complex and demands defining proper indices. In fact, in the majority of cases non-agency floating rate deals that do not use excess-spread are structured as pass-throughs for interest payments (and hence have a nonconstant random coupon). We set a target coupon of $c_{\mathcal{S}}$, which would normally be equal to the initial weighted average coupon of the whole portfolio

$$c_\delta = \frac{\sum_k (B_k)_0 c_k}{\sum_k (B_k)_0}$$

We can obviously decompose $\mathcal{L}$ as follows: $\mathcal{L} = \{k : c_k = c_\delta\} \bigcup \{k : c_k > c_\delta\} \bigcup \{k : c_k < c_\delta\}$. The WAC IO *WIO* is defined as a strip of coupon from a particular subset of loans, all the ones that pay more than $c_\delta$:

$$(I_{WIO})_t = \sum_{k:c_k > c_\delta} (c_k - c_\delta)(B_k)_t$$

and

$$(P_{WIO})_t = 0 \text{ and } (B_{WIO})_t = \sum_{k:c_k > c_\delta} (B_k)_t.$$

The WAC PO is defined as collecting principal payments on the loans $\{k : c_k < c_\delta\}$ such that the on each one of these loans the coupon relative to the remaining balance is exactly equal to the target:

$$(I_{WPO})_t = 0 \text{ and } (P_{WPO})_t = \sum_{k:c_k < c_\delta} (1 - \frac{c_k}{c_\delta})(P_k)_t$$

and

$$(B_{WIO})_t = \sum_{k:c_k < c_\delta} (1 - \frac{c_k}{c_\delta})(B_k)_t.$$

Then, by construction the clean pass-through is expressed as follows:

$$(B_{CPT})_t = \sum_{k:c_k \geq c_\delta} (B_k)_t + \sum_{k:c_k < c_\delta} \frac{c_k}{c_\delta}(B_k)_t$$

and

$$(I_{CPT})_t = c_\delta( \sum_{k:c_k \geq c_\delta} (B_k)_t + \sum_{k:c_k < c_\delta} \frac{c_k}{c_\delta}(B_k)_t)$$

and

$$(P_{CPT})_t = ( \sum_{k:c_k \geq c_\delta} (P_k)_t + \sum_{k:c_k < c_\delta} \frac{c_k}{c_\delta}(P_k)_t).$$

The WAC IO/WAC PO structure may be applied after credit enhancement has been addressed in which case the interest and principal payments arc "clcancd" of crcdit-related effects: interest shortfalls would be addressed by some dedicated subordinated bonds, and writedowns would be allocated to junior bonds as well, so that at the senior level where the WAC IO and PO are structured losses would appear as prepayments. In non-agency MBS, if the subordinated bonds need to pay constant coupons then the WAC IO/WAC PO must be structured at a lower level.

### 6.2.8 Senior Structural Breakdown

Deal structures may sometimes contain provisions for their own disappearance in certain particular conditions, buried in the hundreds of pages of the PSA. In all generality there is nothing against this logic, but in practice, this came as a surprise to some during the mortgage crisis when certain bonds ended up behaving in a surprising fashion.

We focus on a particularly important case of cash flows by-passing structuring logic, the so-called **stay-sequential** versus **go-prorata** deal structures. As we have extensively discussed so far, senior bonds are typically created using a complex range of internal credit enhancement techniques. A priori, the AAA-rated senior bonds are supposed to only suffer writedowns in the most extreme of scenarios. In addition, one may consider that within the set of bonds that receive the best rating, there should not be significant differences in credit risk. As a result, in some deals, provisions exist to the effect that once the senior-most block of bonds sees any writedown, then within that block principal and loss allocation rules disappear. Deals with such a feature are termed "go-prorata" deals, while deals that on the contrary retain all principal allocation logic of the senior block are called "stay-sequential".[17]

An ill-informed bond holder with a senior front sequential in a go-prorata deal may discover that as collateral losses will increase, the senior structure will disappear and hence the sequential will become a pass-through. Symmetrically, a last cash flow sequential holder may be happy to realize the bond will then become a pass-through, improving its principal payment perspectives relative to the initial structure.

#### 6.2.8.1 Formal Description

First, note that the structure's switch to a prorata allocation is normally not reversible, because once the senior block has suffered a writedown, this loss cannot be taken away. Also, note that both principal and loss allocation rules become prorata, since there is in principle no other form of subordination, and within the senior block all the bonds are expected to be on a prorata loss allocation among themselves. Finally, we consider that the interest allocation rules within the senior group only potentially depend on external indices, and not on principal or loss related metrics from the structure itself.

Assume $\left(B^A, (P^A, I^A)\right)$ are the cash flows for a senior block, and it is structured with some particular principal and interest allocation (losses are assumed to be prorata) with a structure $S_S$. We have our stay-sequential structure

$$S_S\left(B^A, (P^A, I^A)\right) = \left(B^{A_i}, (P^{A_i}, I^{A_i})\right)_{i\leq n}.$$

[17]Note that in spite of the name this is not just applicable to sequential deals stricto sensu, but to all aspects of principal allocation.

We can define the go-prorata version of this structure $S_P$ as follows:

$$S_P\left(B^A,(P^A,I^A)\right)=\left(B^{\bar{A}_i},(P^{\bar{A}_i},I^{\bar{A}_i})\right)_{i\le n}.$$

In any case, losses are always prorata and can be expressed as $L_t^{\bar{A}_i}=L_t^A\frac{B_t^{\bar{A}_i}}{B_t^A}$. Let us now define a metric tracking the senior block writedowns:

$$W_t^A=(B_0^A-B_t^A)-\sum_{s<t}P_s^A$$

which simply expresses that the drop in balance of the senior block is more than the cumulated principal payment it has received. The go-prorata bonds' cash flows can now be expressed. Principal payment is dependent on whether the event $W^A>0$ has taken place at time $t$, so

$$P_t^{\bar{A}_i}=\mathbb{I}_{W_t^A>0}P_t^A\frac{B_t^{\bar{A}_i}}{B_t^A}+\mathbb{I}_{W_t^A=0}P_t^{\bar{A}_i}.$$

Interest payments have to be defined based on what they would be in the underlying structure:

$$I_t^{\bar{A}_i}=\mathbb{I}_{W_t^A>0}B_t^{\bar{A}_i}\frac{I_t^{A_i}}{B_t^{A_i}}+\mathbb{I}_{W_t^A=0}I_t^{A_i}.$$

#### 6.2.8.2 Stay-Sequential and Go-Prorata Examples

Using the algorithms we have presented earlier for hard subordination and for PAC/Support principal allocation, we can easily build an entire stay-sequential structure.[18] We represent the subordinated tranches, protecting the senior, as subordinated sequentials. The senior structure itself ($S_S$ in the formal description) is a basic PAC/Support. For the underlying collateral cash flows we will use comparable static assumptions as in the discussion of sequential structures, and the same parameters for simulated cash flows.

Our static base case is set up as shown in Table 6.41, with fairly spread out prepayments.

We use two pure subordinated sequentials to provide credit protection, so that there is a total of 7% hard enhancement. The block A thus created is further structured into a PAC/Support combination (tranches P and C, respectively), where the PAC schedule uses 100–250 PSA bands. The PAC therefore amounts to about 65% of the whole senior block.

[18] In this case the senior structure is not a sequential but a PAC, but the term "stay-sequential" is still applicable.

**Table 6.41** Generating example cash flows. *Source* Compiled by the author

```
general_example_alt <- create_basic_portfolio(OrigBal = 100,
  Cpn = 0.05,
  Prin = c(0, 4, 8, 13, 12, 10, 9, 8, 13, 12),
  Loss = c(1, 3, 4, 2, 1, 0, 0, 0, 0, 0))
```

**Table 6.42** Senior PAC stay-sequential cash flows on amortizing assets. *Source* Compiled by the author

| Period | Beg Bal | Prin | Loss | Int | Beg Bal C | Prin C | Loss C | Int C | Beg Bal P | Prin P | Loss P | Int P |
|---|---|---|---|---|---|---|---|---|---|---|---|---|
| 1 | 93 | 0 | 0 | 4.7 | 31.7 | 0.00 | 0.00 | 1.59 | 61 | 0.0 | 0.00 | 3.1 |
| 2 | 93 | 4 | 0 | 4.7 | 31.7 | 0.00 | 0.00 | 1.59 | 61 | 4.0 | 0.00 | 3.1 |
| 3 | 89 | 8 | 1 | 4.5 | 31.7 | 0.23 | 0.36 | 1.59 | 57 | 7.8 | 0.64 | 2.9 |
| 4 | 80 | 13 | 2 | 4.0 | 31.1 | 8.13 | 0.78 | 1.56 | 49 | 4.9 | 1.22 | 2.4 |
| 5 | 65 | 12 | 1 | 3.2 | 22.2 | 7.42 | 0.34 | 1.11 | 43 | 4.6 | 0.66 | 2.1 |
| 6 | 52 | 10 | 0 | 2.6 | 14.5 | 5.69 | 0.00 | 0.72 | 38 | 4.3 | 0.00 | 1.9 |
| 7 | 42 | 9 | 0 | 2.1 | 8.8 | 4.95 | 0.00 | 0.44 | 33 | 4.0 | 0.00 | 1.7 |
| 8 | 33 | 8 | 0 | 1.6 | 3.8 | 3.82 | 0.00 | 0.19 | 29 | 4.2 | 0.00 | 1.5 |
| 9 | 25 | 13 | 0 | 1.2 | 0.0 | 0.00 | 0.00 | 0.00 | 25 | 13.0 | 0.00 | 1.2 |
| 10 | 12 | 12 | 0 | 0.6 | 0.0 | 0.00 | 0.00 | 0.00 | 12 | 12.0 | 0.00 | 0.6 |

With the principal payment and loss assumptions explicited above, the collateral losses amount to 11%, so the senior block suffers 4 units of losses. Table 6.42 shows the cash flows for the stay-sequential structure, where even after losses reach the senior block in period 7, the PAC and support continue to behave according to their specific logic. In the case at hand, the PAC suffers the bulk of the losses from the underlying block, and has a fairly long average life of 6.8 years, since the support gets paid off early as it absorbs fast prepayments.

The algorithm in Table 6.43 represents the alteration of the structure in a go-prorata case, directly implementing the formal description we presented earlier.

We used the go-prorata algorithm on the cash flows generated by the stay-sequential structure, and the results are shown in Table 6.44. The losses on the PAC are slightly higher than in the prior case, but its average life shortens to 6.3 years, a shortening which, in the context of distressed product trading at a high yield, is significant.

Simulating across a large number of paths as we have done for other structures, we can measure the extent to which the stay-sequential versus go-prorata alter the loss profile as well as the average life profile of the bonds in our example. Table 6.45 shows these distributions in the stay-sequential case, and Table 6.46 in the go-prorata case. Over many random paths, the average total loss is affected slightly, and the average life of the bonds moves by approximately a quarter of a year. While these effects do not appear enormous, it is worth noting that they would be applicable on distressed securities, and that the PAC/support structure we have chosen as an illustration is not one that would exhibit the strongest sensitivity to a structural breakdown.

**Table 6.43** Go-prorata/stay-sequential structure logic. *Source* Compiled by the author

```
go_prorata <- function(prtf, tr_nms = c("C", "P")) {
  metrs <- c("BegBal", "Prin", "Loss", "Int")
  newprtf <- prtf[, c("Period", metrs)]
  for (trn in tr_nms) {
    for (met in metrs) {
      newprtf[, paste0(met, "_", trn)] <- 0
    }
  }
  # Loop over periods
  for (k in 1:dim(newprtf)[1]) {
    # Determine if there are losses or not
    if (sum(newprtf$Loss[1:k]) == 0) {
      # Copy over CFs from stay-seq case
      for (trn in tr_nms) {
        for (met in metrs) {
          newprtf[k, paste0(met, "_", trn)] <-
            prtf[k, paste0(met, "_", trn)]
        }
      }
    } else {
      # Switch to pro-rata
      for (trn in tr_nms) {
        if (k > 1) {
           newprtf[k, paste0("BegBal_", trn)] <-
             newprtf[k - 1, paste0("BegBal_", trn)] -
             newprtf[k - 1, paste0("Prin_", trn)] -
             newprtf[k - 1, paste0("Loss_", trn)]
        } else {
           newprtf[k, paste0("BegBal_", trn)] <-
             prtf[k, paste0("BegBal_", trn)]
        }
      }
      rel_bal <- c()
      for (bd in 1:length(tr_nms)) {
        rel_bal[bd] <- newprtf[k, paste0("BegBal_", tr_nms[bd])]
      }
      rel_bal <- rel_bal / sum(rel_bal)
      # Prorata allocation
      for (bd in 1:length(tr_nms)) {
        newprtf[k, paste0("Int_", tr_nms[bd])] <-
          rel_bal[bd] * newprtf$Int[k]
        newprtf[k, paste0("Loss_", tr_nms[bd])] <-
          rel_bal[bd] * newprtf$Loss[k]
        newprtf[k, paste0("Prin_", tr_nms[bd])] <-
          rel_bal[bd] * newprtf$Prin[k]
      }
    }
  }
  return(newprtf)
}
```

**Table 6.44** Senior PAC stay-sequential cash flows on amortizing assets. *Source* Compiled by the author

| Period | Beg Bal | Prin | Loss | Int | Beg Bal C | Prin C | Loss C | Int C | Beg Bal P | Prin P | Loss P | Int P |
|---|---|---|---|---|---|---|---|---|---|---|---|---|
| 1 | 93 | 0 | 0 | 4.7 | 31.7 | 0.0 | 0.00 | 1.59 | 61.3 | 0.0 | 0.00 | 3.06 |
| 2 | 93 | 4 | 0 | 4.7 | 31.7 | 0.0 | 0.00 | 1.59 | 61.3 | 4.0 | 0.00 | 3.06 |
| 3 | 89 | 8 | 1 | 4.5 | 31.7 | 2.9 | 0.36 | 1.59 | 57.3 | 5.2 | 0.64 | 2.86 |
| 4 | 80 | 13 | 2 | 4.0 | 28.5 | 4.6 | 0.71 | 1.43 | 51.5 | 8.4 | 1.29 | 2.57 |
| 5 | 65 | 12 | 1 | 3.2 | 23.2 | 4.3 | 0.36 | 1.16 | 41.8 | 7.7 | 0.64 | 2.09 |
| 6 | 52 | 10 | 0 | 2.6 | 18.5 | 3.6 | 0.00 | 0.93 | 33.5 | 6.4 | 0.00 | 1.67 |
| 7 | 42 | 9 | 0 | 2.1 | 15.0 | 3.2 | 0.00 | 0.75 | 27.0 | 5.8 | 0.00 | 1.35 |
| 8 | 33 | 8 | 0 | 1.6 | 11.8 | 2.9 | 0.00 | 0.59 | 21.2 | 5.2 | 0.00 | 1.06 |
| 9 | 25 | 13 | 0 | 1.2 | 8.9 | 4.6 | 0.00 | 0.45 | 16.1 | 8.4 | 0.00 | 0.80 |
| 10 | 12 | 12 | 0 | 0.6 | 4.3 | 4.3 | 0.00 | 0.21 | 7.7 | 7.7 | 0.00 | 0.39 |

**Table 6.45** Losses and average life distributions in stay-sequential structure. *Source* Compiled by the author

| | Total loss P | Total loss C | AvgL P | AvgL C |
|---|---|---|---|---|
| Min. | 0.0 | 0.00 | 3.9 | 1.6 |
| 1st Qu. | 1.0 | 0.00 | 5.2 | 2.2 |
| Median | 3.4 | 0.00 | 5.7 | 2.6 |
| Mean | 3.7 | 0.50 | 5.8 | 2.8 |
| 3rd Qu. | 5.8 | 0.25 | 6.2 | 3.1 |
| Max. | 15.1 | 16.76 | 7.8 | 10.0 |

**Table 6.46** Losses and average life distributions in go-prorata structure. *Source* Compiled by the author

| | Total loss P | Total loss C | AvgL P | AvgL C |
|---|---|---|---|---|
| Min. | 0.0 | 0.0 | 3.9 | 1.6 |
| 1st Qu. | 1.0 | 0.0 | 5.2 | 2.2 |
| Median | 3.3 | 0.0 | 5.6 | 2.6 |
| Mean | 3.4 | 1.0 | 5.6 | 3.0 |
| 3rd Qu. | 5.4 | 1.1 | 6.1 | 3.4 |
| Max. | 15.2 | 14.0 | 8.2 | 8.9 |

The presence of this particular feature on many deals, but not all, makes it difficult to precisely relate the eventual performance of bonds to their initial target average lives. If one were to look at how different types of bonds performed throughout the mortgage crisis, as a function of their initial average life targets, one would a priori expect that the shorter bonds would be more protected than longer bonds, by a degree commensurate with their average lives. The structural breakdown feature we have discussed could significantly muddy these waters and reduce the strength of that relationship, on some deals but not all.

### 6.2.9 Other Deal-Level Structural Features

In this section, we briefly review various aspects of structuring that concern the organization of the entire deal. They are important, but are generally specified in an adhoc fashion and fairly varied. As a result, we only describe their general features without drilling down into detailed cash flow analysis. These structuring techniques are fairly ubiquitous nevertheless.

We first discuss grouping, that is how subsets of loans are allocated to specific bonds. Then we describe deal calls, followed by deal triggers. Finally we look into wraps and a mortgage-specific sort of insurance, LPMI.

#### 6.2.9.1 Grouping

In structuring, grouping refers to the allocation of cash flows from particular loans to particular bonds. In effect, this is a deviation from the kind of full commingling of cash flows we have generally discussed so far. The reason for grouping could be to create bonds that satisfy particular constraints. For example, subprime deals sometime contained so-called conforming tranches, which would be backed only by the loans inside the collateral that had a conforming balance.

First, note that the notion of grouping is just a point on a continuum of degrees of commingling between subsets of collateral. Between two entirely separate deals, and one single deal holding the same assets as the two deals, one could distinguish the following cumulative thresholds:

1. Two entirely separate deals
2. Two entirely separate deals on the same shelf done by the same sponsor and placed by the same investment bank
3. One deal, with two separate collateral blocks, each serviced by a different servicer and issuing entirely separate securities, with a single trustee and a single PSA
4. One deal, with two separate collateral blocks, serviced by the same issuer where servicing expenses are pooled, issuing separate securities
5. One deal, with two separate collateral blocks where excess-spread is common, issuing separate securities
6. One deal, with two separate collateral blocks where excess-spread and subordinated tranches are common, issuing separate senior securities
7. One deal, with a single collateral block.

Usually, the main distinction is between what is called an **H-structure** and a **Y-structure**, which correspond to the distinction between items 4 or 5 for the H, and item 6 for the Y. When bonds in one group benefit from the credit enhancement from bonds in another group, this is called **cross-collateralization**, as is the case with a Y-structure.

In order to create a Y-structure, where separate groups of senior bonds are backed by a common group of subordinated bonds, one can think of the junior tranches as working the same way as in a deal without grouping. In a deal with excess-spread, one would also expect that to be commingled. For the senior bonds, however, collateral principal payments are allocated each to their own group.

The use of grouping logic matters greatly when one analyzes deal-level information or bond-level information. The categorization of the bonds indeed needs to be that of the underlying groups (which may not be straightforward to determine). An H-structure deal that combines a large group of jumbo prime loans and a small group of subprime loans would appear as a prime deal on an aggregate basis. However the bonds backed by the small subprime group would definitely need to be categorized as subprime.

#### 6.2.9.2 Deal Calls

In this section, we discuss particular rights or obligations that are attached to certain tranche holders, which force a purchase of the deal's collateral at a certain price, typically predetermined. These **deal calls**, also known as **clean-up calls**, are effectively call options. They are typically designed to "clean up" a small remaining balance on a deal so that it does not linger on for a long time although its outstanding balance may be very small. They generally become exerciceable once the deal's outstanding balance has reached a certain small percentage of its entire starting balance. The exercise price is par on performing loans and (depending on deal language) a lower value for non-performing loans.

The residual tranche or the most junior bond in a deal almost systematically possesses this call option on the collateral. Once the deal balance reaches a certain fraction of the original deal balance (generally 10%, 5%, or sometimes 1%) then the call holder has a right to buy back the remaining collateral at any time.

After the clean-up date, coupons on the remaining bonds often have a **step-up**, and they increase by a certain amount, in order to create a greater incentive for a residual holder to call the deal. Indeed, the greater coupon paid to the bond holders means less excess-spread, and in turn lower cash flow releases to the XS-OC tranche holder.

The valuation of clean-up calls themselves is complex, see Gauthier (2006), for example. Indeed, the time at which the call will be exerciseable is random (depending on cumulative prepayments). In addition, the call is an option on interest rates: if rates go down, the value of the collateral will typically go up and reciprocally. Finally, the call is an option on credit: if credit performance is good then the collateral value will be higher.

Factoring in the impact of a clean-up call potential exercise in the analysis of a securitized bond has also been difficult because the exercise of the call may seem random. Certain issuers tend not to efficiently exercise their calls, while others exercise them quite often. Empirically, the exercise of deal calls has appeared to be relatively rational, once one reflected the expected drivers, credit and interest rates. In many cases, issuers wait until enough exercisable calls have been accumulated, then exercise them and sell the loans or find the most profitable exit strategy for these loans. Sometimes, the call rights themselves can be offered for sale, in which case the buyer takes a risk on their own optimality regarding the call exercise decision.

There are some particular instances of deal calls, called **SFMCs** or stated final maturity classes, which are akin to clean-up calls with a forced exercise at a particular point in time (effectively, a forward contract on the remainder of the collateral pool). The logic of such structures is to ensure a maximum maturity to a bond. The party committing to calling the deal is typically the deal's sponsor. See Chaudhary and Gauthier (2002) for a detailed analysis of these products.

#### 6.2.9.3 Triggers

A deal trigger is a mechanism that modifies the deal structure based on dynamic performance measures and certain thresholds. These performance measures can be **absolute performance measures**, such as comparing delinquency rates with a threshold, or **relative performance measures** such as comparing delinquency rates with the size of subordinated bonds relative to senior bonds.

The thresholds may be **reversible** or **irreversible**: if delinquencies are above a certain amount, they may go down later, but if cumulative losses are above a certain amount they will not go back down.

For example, a trigger might be active if the amount of 60+ delinquent loans represents more than 1.5 times the amount of subordinated tranches (non-agency MBS). Another mechanism would be for a trigger to be active if cumulative losses represented more than 5% of the deal's original collateral amount (subprime). The types of mechanisms are adapted to the nature of the collateral as well: in CLOs, a trigger is active is the collected interest represents less than the coupon due to all the bonds.

Trigger effects are very diverse. In many deals, there are conditions in which more junior bonds get some principal payment before the more senior bonds are fully paid off. Triggers generally revert that, and force principal to be paid to the bonds strictly in order of seniority, in order to preserve the senior-most securities.

#### 6.2.9.4 Insurance: Wraps and LPMI

A **wrap** is an insurance contract that the SPV purchases with a third party, in order to guarantee the payments on a bond, akin to a CDS. The insurance permits a higher rating based on the insurer's rating, usually AAA. The insurance does normally not apply on an unstructured bond but typically requires the unwrapped bond to be enhanced at the single-A level. The SPV pays the insurance premium to the insurer over time. Resorting to a wrap is a simple structuring decision: comparing the amount for which a naked A-rated bond wrapped up to a AAA would be sold in the market, minus the insurance cost, to the amount for which an internally enhanced and smaller AAA along with the necessary mezzanine bonds would be sold.

One important case of insurance wraps which we have already mentioned several times is that of **agency guarantees**: they follow the same principle as a wrap but work slightly differently. Issuers of MBS pay an insurance premium specific to each loan according to a precise grid, the loan-level price adjustment or **LLPA**. The entire pool (without pre-existing credit enhancement) receives an agency guarantee. The underlying bond that is wrapped is a pure pass-through.

The credit risk of the wrapped bonds is a combination of that of the underlying bond and of the insurer. During the mortgage crisis many insurers were unable to face their guarantee payments, and some wrapped bonds did not fully repay the principal and interest they owed.

One particular type of insurance, not bearing on the bonds but on the underlying collateral, is mortgage insurance in the case of RMBS. We have already discussed private mortgage insurance, taken by a borrower in order to alleviate their credit risk, often in order for their high LTV loan to be securitizable by the agencies. This PMI is normally a given, and while one can decide to securitize certain loans or not, it is not a structuring technique. There is however lender-paid mortgage insurance, **LPMI**, which as the name indicates is paid for by the lender. When structuring a deal, one might decide to obtain insurance on high LTV loans in order to reduce the credit enhancement requirements for the pool. The trade-off between the cost of the insurance and the gain from selling a larger amount of AAA-rated bonds is the driving force behind the use of such a structuring tool.

In order to measure the exposure of a particular bond to the LPMI provider(s), one typically measures the sensitivity of the bond to the performance of each underlying loan, scaled by the expected contribution of the mortgage insurance to that loan's performance.

### 6.2.10 Resecuritizations

As the name implies, resecuritization is the securitization of already securitized bonds. By construction, it should happen some amount of time after the underlying bonds' securitization (otherwise it would be part of the same initial structure). We will first discuss net-interest-margin securitizations (NIMs) and analyze their typical cash flows with the same toolset as what we have used so far. Then, we will look into structured finance CDOs and reremics.

Note that the notion of securitizing again does raise some theoretical issues. If, as we saw in our discussion of security design in Chap. 4, creating subordinated tranches is optimally carried out so as to alleviate some information asymmetry costs, then if resecuritizing, or changing the structure of these bonds, was optimal it should be done from the outset. We will see in Chap. 7 how this problem can be addressed with an extension of the theoretical framework of security design.

#### 6.2.10.1 NIMs

**Net-interest margin** securitizations appeared in the late 1990s and were aimed at monetizing the shorter and presumably safer part of residual cash flows. Indeed, the collateral for a NIM consists mainly of a basket of residuals (XS-OC tranches, which we have discussed extensively earlier). As shown in Fig. 6.23 as a basic illustration, the residual, which is akin to the equity in a structure that uses excess-spread, by being securitized can be turned into a short rated bond followed by another, smaller, residual. This second residual, naturally more leveraged than the first one, is called the **baby-equity**. In reality, NIMs include other residual-like tranches as part of their

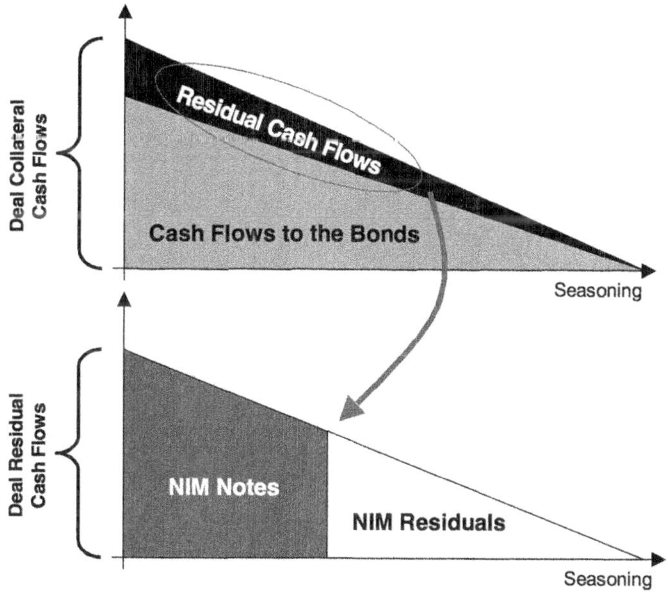


**Fig. 6.23** A simple overview of NIMs. *Source* Compiled by the author

collateral, such as prepayment penalty tranches or NAS IOs, but for our discussion we can leave these details aside.

Since the XS-OC tranches entering a NIM securitization do not have a principal amount attached to them, the NIM's senior bonds are sized based on the amount of cash flows that are likely to be paid by the residual under various stress scenarios. NIMs have been structured off of many types of collateral on which it made sense to use excess-spread, which therefore resulted in the presence of some residual.

From a structure standpoint, the NIM is simple: it simply pays interest to the senior note first, then all the remainder of the cash flow as principal to the senior note, until it is fully paid down. This can be represented as an excess-spread structure with no upfront OC, and with an OC target equal to the senior note's starting balance. The example code in Table 6.47 shows how we defined a basic NIM (using the XS/OC structure function) off of a very basic pure XS residual.

Table 6.48 displays the cash flow on the underlying collateral (that of the XS tranche), and the cash flows on the NIM senior note and NIM own residual (the baby-equity). The assumptions are the same one we have used several times (see Table 6.18 for the corresponding underlying residual XS cash flows), with losses of 11% in total, and relatively slow principal payments. The NIM note is sized at \$1.5 mm, pays a coupon of 3%, and does not incur any loss.

Table 6.49 shows the same structure when the principal payments take place earlier (see Table 6.19 for the corresponding underlying residual XS cash flows). Total losses remain the same at \$11m. We can see that in this case, the NIM's principal and interest are unchanged, and only the baby-equity sees some variations in its cash flows, which are reduced (a lesser amount of eventual OC release). In this prepayment stress

**Table 6.47** NIM structure logic. *Source* Compiled by the author

```
nim <- function(prtf, c_B = 0.03,
                nim_cpn = 0.03, nim_snr_sz = 0.010) {

  # Get XS residual
  res_cf <- simple_xs(prtf, c_B)

  # Create NIM structure by applying OC structure to altered CFs
  nimsr <- prtf$BegBal[1] * nim_snr_sz
  res_cf_alt <- prtf
  res_cf_alt$BegBal <- nimsr
  res_cf_alt$Prin <- 0
  res_cf_alt$Loss <- 0
  res_cf_alt$Int <- res_cf$CF_XS
  res_cf_alt$Loss[dim(res_cf_alt)[1]] <- nimsr

  nim_cf <- oc_xs(res_cf_alt, B_size = 1.0, t_s = 0,
                  alpha = 0.0, o = 1.0, c_B = nim_cpn)

  for (fld in c('BegBal', 'Prin', 'Loss', 'Int')) {
    nim_cf[, fld] <- prtf[, fld]
    names(nim_cf)[names(nim_cf) == paste0(fld, '_B')] <-
      paste0(fld, '_NIM')
  }
  nim_cf$CF_RES <- nim_cf$CF_OC + nim_cf$CF_XS
  nim_cf <- nim_cf[, !(names(nim_cf) %in% c('CF_OC', 'CF_XS'))]

  return(nim_cf)
}
```

scenario, the faster prepayments do not take place very early in the collateral's life, and since the NIM note is such a short cash flow it is essentially unaffected by such stresses.

Simulating prepayments and losses across a large number of paths, as we have done for other structures, we obtain the NIM notes and residuals cash flow distribution statistics, as shown in Table 6.50. These results correspond to the simulations shown in Table 6.20 for the underlying XS tranche cash flows. We can see that both on average and at least up to the 3rd quartile, losses at the NIM note level are very low. However, they become massive in the extreme.

NIM notes typically received investment-grade ratings so that if one considers the entire securitization of a typical subprime deal, much of it ended up with a rating above BBB, and only the small NIM baby-equity was effectively non-investment grade.

#### 6.2.10.2 SFCDOs and Reremics

We now turn to structured finance CDOs and reremics, which share some common characteristics relevant for our analysis. The main difference between these CDOs and reremics is that the latter is static, while the former is dynamic and managed.

The CDOs typically acquire securitized bonds in the market for the purpose of securitizing them. They normally constitute an arbitrage between the ABS or MBS markets, and the CDO liability market (the **tranched** market). The managed

**Table 6.48** Cash flows on NIM structure. *Source* Compiled by the author

| Period | Beg Bal | Prin | Loss | Int | Beg Bal NIM | Prin NIM | Loss NIM | Int NIM | CF RES |
|---|---|---|---|---|---|---|---|---|---|
| 1 | 100 | 0 | 0 | 5.0 | 1.5 | 1.5 | 0 | 0.04 | 0.46 |
| 2 | 100 | 2 | 0 | 5.0 | 0.0 | 0.0 | 0 | 0.00 | 2.00 |
| 3 | 98 | 5 | 0 | 4.9 | 0.0 | 0.0 | 0 | 0.00 | 1.96 |
| 4 | 93 | 10 | 1 | 4.7 | 0.0 | 0.0 | 0 | 0.00 | 0.86 |
| 5 | 82 | 9 | 2 | 4.1 | 0.0 | 0.0 | 0 | 0.00 | 0.00 |
| 6 | 71 | 7 | 4 | 3.5 | 0.0 | 0.0 | 0 | 0.00 | 0.00 |
| 7 | 60 | 5 | 2 | 3.0 | 0.0 | 0.0 | 0 | 0.00 | 0.00 |
| 8 | 53 | 2 | 1 | 2.6 | 0.0 | 0.0 | 0 | 0.00 | 0.06 |
| 9 | 50 | 2 | 1 | 2.5 | 0.0 | 0.0 | 0 | 0.00 | 0.00 |
| 10 | 47 | 47 | 0 | 2.4 | 0.0 | 0.0 | 0 | 0.00 | 0.94 |

**Table 6.49** Cash flows on NIM structure, earlier principal payments. *Source* Compiled by the author

| Period | Beg Bal | Prin | Loss | Int | Beg Bal NIM | Prin NIM | Loss NIM | Int NIM | CF RES |
|---|---|---|---|---|---|---|---|---|---|
| 1 | 100 | 0 | 0 | 5.00 | 1.5 | 1.5 | 0 | 0.04 | 0.46 |
| 2 | 100 | 3 | 0 | 5.00 | 0.0 | 0.0 | 0 | 0.00 | 2.00 |
| 3 | 97 | 10 | 0 | 4.85 | 0.0 | 0.0 | 0 | 0.00 | 1.94 |
| 4 | 87 | 10 | 1 | 4.35 | 0.0 | 0.0 | 0 | 0.00 | 0.74 |
| 5 | 76 | 9 | 2 | 3.80 | 0.0 | 0.0 | 0 | 0.00 | 0.00 |
| 6 | 65 | 47 | 4 | 3.25 | 0.0 | 0.0 | 0 | 0.00 | 0.00 |
| 7 | 14 | 5 | 2 | 0.70 | 0.0 | 0.0 | 0 | 0.00 | 0.00 |
| 8 | 7 | 2 | 1 | 0.35 | 0.0 | 0.0 | 0 | 0.00 | 0.00 |
| 9 | 4 | 2 | 1 | 0.20 | 0.0 | 0.0 | 0 | 0.00 | 0.00 |
| 10 | 1 | 1 | 0 | 0.05 | 0.0 | 0.0 | 0 | 0.00 | 0.02 |

**Table 6.50** Losses on NIM structure with randomized cash flows. *Source* Compiled by the author

| | Total loss | Total loss NIM | Total CF RES |
|---|---|---|---|
| Min. | 2.2 | 0.0 | 0.00 |
| 1st Qu. | 7.6 | 0.0 | 0.47 |
| Median | 9.1 | 0.0 | 1.18 |
| Mean | 9.2 | 3.9 | 1.31 |
| 3rd Qu. | 10.7 | 1.4 | 1.96 |
| Max. | 19.1 | 82.7 | 6.38 |

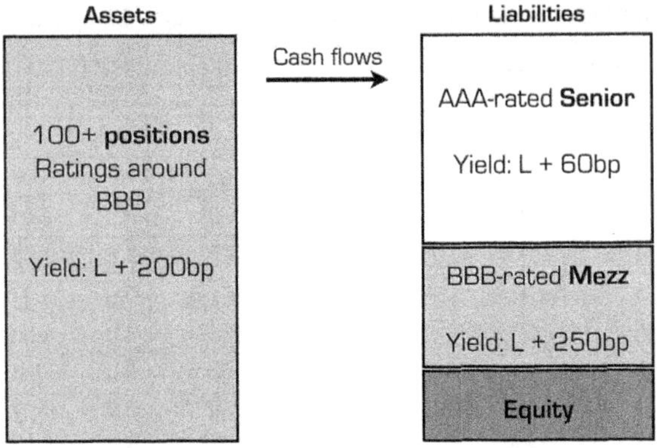


**Fig. 6.24** A simple overview of an ABS CDO. *Source* Compiled by the author

CDO structures are quite complex, including many different tranches issued (seniors, mezzanine, and junior debt), excess-spread, over-collateralization, complex trigger mechanics as well as fully detailed trading and position limits for the manager. See Fig. 6.24 for a simplified view of a structured finance CDO.

Reremics on the other hand do not normally concern very liquid bonds, and are typically motivated by funding and leverage needs, combined with regulatory requirements in some cases. They are essentially applied to RMBS positions.

A first type of reremic, related to regulations, would be applicable to a bank holding an impaired RMBS position. For example, a bond with an initial rating of AAA has suffered some writedowns and is then very costly for the bank in terms of regulatory capital.[19] It may make sense for the bank to resecuritize the bond and only keep a senior position with a high rating, while a hedge fund may hold the junior position.

A second type of reremic, less driven by a regulatory requirement and more akin to a NIM, would be applicable for an investment bank holding a portfolio of deeply subordinated RMBS. These positions would be in a sense equivalent to the non-agency XS/OC residuals that the bank may have owned and subsequently NIM'd, but composed of six-pack bonds. Putting them in a basket and issuing senior notes allow the bank to retain a cheap residual, and effectively fund the positions by selling a senior note. See Fig. 6.25 for an example of such a structure.

The typical structured finance CDO and the basket reremic differ significantly in two respects, which tend to make the CDO more exposed to changes in the underlying collateral performance:

- The reremic's collateral is composed of very junior positions which mostly have upside, while the CDO's typically show a higher (initial) rating, and are mezzanine bonds.

[19]See the discussion in Chap. 5.

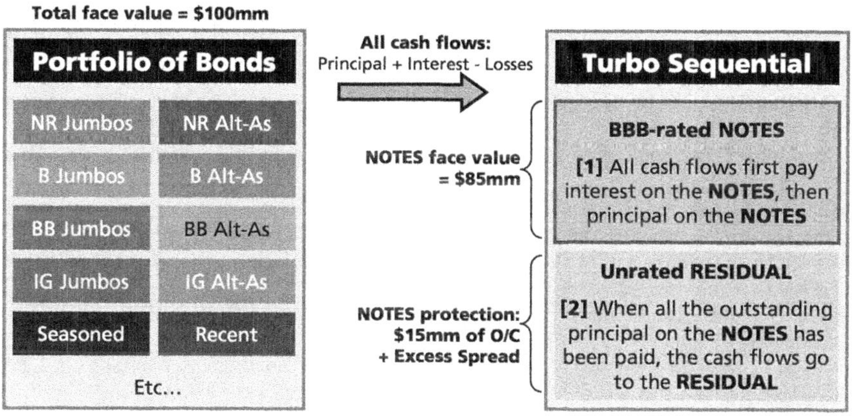


**Fig. 6.25** A simple example of Reremic. *Source* Compiled by the author

- The reremic has a very simple structure with only a senior note and a residual, so that the tranches, either senior or junior, are fairly thick. In contrast, the CDO's mezzanine bonds may be fairly thin.

Nevertheless, they share an important feature: since they combine a basket of bonds and tranche it, they become exposed to the degree of correlation in the performance of these various bonds. We will analyze the impact of correlation on performance in more detail in Chap. 8, when we discuss how structural complexity leverages risks.

## 6.3 Conclusion

In this discussion of structuring, we have addressed some general concepts and notions, including the motivations and reasoning behind many structural choices. We reviewed a selection of structuring techniques in a good amount of detail, even though they remained fairly stylized. We have also observed how these techniques are typically combined into some real securitized products.

Many of the features we have discussed in this chapter, albeit in a simplified framework, do appear to be quite complex. There is a quantum jump between the types of "structures" we began discussing as part of security design in Chap. 4 and the mechanics we have just reviewed. The next chapter, focusing on the economics of structuring, will attempt to bridge some of that gap.

## References

Ashcraft, A., & Schuermann, T. (2008). Understanding the securitization of subprime mortgage credit. FRB New York Staff Reports 318. Federal Reserve Bank of New York.

Bisla, Ambika, & Gauthier, Laurent. (2005). *An Introduction to Non-Agency MBS*. Morgan Stanley: Unpublished Research Report.

Chaudhary, S. (2006). Introduction to agency CMO structures. Research Report, Bank of America.

Chaudhary, S., & Gauthier, L. (2002). Jumbo hybrid ARM securities. *The Journal of Fixed Income, 11*(4), 64–77.

Childs, Paul D., Ott, Steven H., & Riddiough, Timothy J. (1996). The pricing of multiclass commercial mortgage-backed securities. *Journal of Financial and Quantitative Analysis, 31*(4), 581–603.

Fabozzi, F. J. (Ed.) (2006). The handbook of mortgage-backed securities, (6th ed.). New York: McGraw-Hill Education.

Gauthier, L. (2002). *The secrets of NIMs*. UBS: Research Report.

Gauthier, L. (2004). An introduction to CMOs. Research Report, Morgan Stanley.

Gauthier, L. (2006). Analysis of clean-up calls. In F. J. Fabozzi (Ed.), *The handbook of mortgage-backed securities* (6th ed.). McGraw-Hill Education.

Gorton, G. (2008). The subprime panic. NBER Working Papers 14398. National Bureau of Economic Research, Inc.

Gauthier, L., & Zimmerman, T. (2002a). *Introduction to the home-equity loan market*. UBS: Research Report.

Gauthier, L., & Zimmerman, T. (2002b). *The analysis of non-agency mortgage credit*. UBS: Research Report.

Hein, J. (2009). "Four Essays on Credit Securitization, PhD Thesis." University of Konstanz.

Huang, Dashan, Kai, Yoshitaka, Fabozzi, Frank, & Fukushima, Masao. (2007). An Optimal design of collateralized mortgage obligation with PAC-companion structure using dynamic cash reserve. *European Journal of Operational Research, 177*(2), 1134–52.

Kulasson, B. (2001). An introduction to CMO cashflow structures. Research Report, Salomon Smith Barney.

Mansukhani, S., & Qbbaj, M. (2005). *CSFB's starter kit for non-agency residential mortgage-backed securities*. CSFB: Research Report.

# The Economics of Securitization Structuring

# 7

Chapter 4 exposed some of the justifications for the existence of securitization as a way of segregating assets.[1] We also looked into the reasons why these segregated assets may be optimally issued as a form of debt, rather than equity. The models that we looked into generally gave us good reasons why securitization was optimal for issuers, investors, and investment banks under certain conditions. Some of these models' predictions have been tested and while the results sometimes need to be carefully qualified, they generally agreed with the models.

Now, after a reasonably detailed description and analysis of structuring in Chap. 6, it should be apparent that a general distinction between debt and equity cannot explain securitization structures. In the present chapter, we specifically focus on the economics of the complex structures that have been observed in securitization. What can justify the existence of arcane cash flow allocations such as the ones we have analyzed, while the theory so far simply suggests there should be debt and equity?

In the following section, we begin by discussing pooling and tranching models. Pooling models look into the reasons for grouping assets together in a securitization as opposed to securitizing them separately. In these models, we also discuss some simple tranching: in fact, it usually makes sense to pool assets together and at the same time create basic senior and junior securities. We also look into models that specifically address tranching and look into some reasons for multi-layered tranche structures in securitizations. We analyze and compare several models from the literature that justify the existence of multiple tranches, including mezzanine bonds, for example.

Then, we turn to investors' desire for par-valued bonds and the specific structuring of interest and principal. As we will see, the simple security design models we have

[1] Although sometimes implicit recourse was provided.



L. Gauthier, *Securitization Economics*, Springer Texts in Business and Economics,
https://doi.org/10.1007/978-3-030-50326-0_7

analyzed so far do not properly account for the way in which interest and principal are allocated in basic securitization structures and they need to be extended.

Finally, we discuss some empirical findings on the complex structures observed in the securitized markets.

## 7.1 Pooling and Tranching Models

In this section, we first focus on the mechanics of **pooling**, the simple fact of packaging assets together without necessarily adding further structure. It does appear, as we will see, that simple pooling often needs to be combined with some tranching in order to be optimal.

We discuss extensions of the models from Boot and Thakor (1993) and Dang et al. (2015) that can explain the pooling of multiple assets, rather than creating different securities for each asset separately. Further optimality can be gained by issuing claims on a pool of underlying assets rather than on a more granular level. We then discuss DeMarzo (2005), where the author proposes an extension of DeMarzo and Duffie (1999) including both pooling and simple tranching: through pooling, risk is diversified, and by tranching the bonds are made more informationally insensitive. Then, we walk through the model of Gaur et al. (2011), which explains pooling in a no-arbitrage context. Although these models are particularly concerned about pooling, tranching also plays a role but remains fairly simple. The first models we discuss in detail in the following subsections are extensions of the security design models which were exposed in Chap. 4.

Some research has looked into **tranching**, which tries to explain the multiplicity of structures observed in structured finance deals. One important article on the optimal design of debt contracts; Diamond (1993) showed that both maturity and seniority could be engineered optimally in order to alleviate the negative effects of information asymmetries. However, this research is not applicable in the case of securitization, as the author considers debt that can be refinanced, and cases when debt holders could take over the issuer's control, situations which are not applicable to the large majority of securitizations.

We focus on two models related to tranching, which represent fairly different angles in explaining multiple tranches. In Fender and Mitchell (2009), tranching is useful as a way for the buyers of the loans to induce proper screening by the originator, in a regulatory context. In a more complex model, Plantin (2003) focused only on tranching, but showed through an endogenous bidding mechanism that multiple seniority tranching is optimal when investors have diverse sophistication and are more or less able to acquire information on asset quality.

The issue of tranching has been analyzed from many other angles. For example, Ortner and Schmalz (2019) consider that belief disagreements between investors and issuers about the assets can make pooling and tranching optimal. In particular, belief disagreement between issuer and investors can be alleviated by pooling, while tranching allows the issuer to exploit belief disagreement between investors. Guo et al. (2014) also look into how diverse beliefs in investors leads to an optimal tranching. Specifically looking into tranching for heterogeneous investors with various time and risk preferences, and without information asymmetries, Malamud et al. (2010) show that it is optimal to create multiple categories of tranches. With CARA utility functions, the tranching is shown to be linear at the optimum. The same authors also analyzed the incentives for the issuer to monitor quality in Malamud et al. (2012), where they modeled optimal contracts depending on the form of the utility functions of market participants.

The tranching involved in this section is more complex than the type of tranching we have discussed so far as part of security design, as we are trying to explain the emergence of advanced structures, that go beyond a simple dichotomy between a senior and a junior bond.

### 7.1.1 Pooling Without Structuring

We first discuss the pooling of assets in a securitization by following the model from Boot and Thakor (1993), which has the advantage of being reasonably simple. The assumptions are the same as in our discussion in Chap. 4.

Boot and Thakor look at the benefits of pooling by considering the case of multiple firms, for which the signal is not perfect but noisy. In that case, a single security backed by multiple firms or projects maximizes revenue because through diversification the uncertainty is reduced for informed traders. We are following a slightly different approach and will consider the case of noisy signals, when the issuer only creates a single security. Instead of observing $Y$ directly, informed traders will be able to observe $\phi = Y + N$ where $N$ is a random variable with a continuous distribution representing the noise, such that $\mathbb{E}[N] = 0$ and $\mathbb{V}[N] = \sigma^2$. $N$ is independent of $L$ and $Y$. We write the cumulative distribution $k(x) = \mathbb{P}[N < x]$, which we assume strictly increasing. Further, $N$ is assumed to be unimodal and symmetric around 0.

We consider that the informed trader will specify a threshold $\bar{y}$ for $\phi$ so that the probability of observing a positive while the underlying value is negative is equal to the probability of observing a negative while the underlying value is positive, in other words, a threshold so that the probabilities of type 1 and type 2 errors are the same, so that the probability of an error in general is minimal. We define $q(\sigma) = \mathbb{P}[\phi > \bar{y} | Y = y_b]$ (this can naturally be expressed as a function of the noise's dispersion). The condition on type 1 and 2 errors implies that

$$q(\sigma) = \mathbb{P}[\phi > \bar{y} | Y = y_b] = \mathbb{P}[\phi \leq \bar{y} | Y = y_g].$$

We can write these expressions explicitly as a function of the distribution of $N$:

$$\begin{aligned} q(\sigma) &= 1 - \mathbb{P}[N \leq \bar{y} - y_b] = \mathbb{P}[N \leq \bar{y} - y_g] \\ &= 1 - k(\bar{y} - y_b) = k(\bar{y} - y_g). \end{aligned}$$

Since $N$ is symmetric around 0, $k(-x) = 1 - k(x)$ and therefore $k(y_b - \bar{y}) = k(\bar{y} - y_g)$. Since $k$ is strictly monotonic, then this is equivalent to $y_b - \bar{y} = \bar{y} - y_g$ and hence $\bar{y} = \frac{y_b + y_g}{2}$. We can now write $q$ more explicitly as

$$q(\sigma) = \mathbb{P}\left[N \leq -\frac{y_g - y_b}{2}\right].$$

Therefore, $q$ is increasing in $\sigma$: a greater dispersion in $N$ increases the probability of a wrong signal.

We can now look at the equilibrium price under these assumptions. As we did previously, we write $P^\sigma(D)$ for the price set by the uninformed discretionary traders (the investment banks, presumably), with $D = L + \theta \mathbb{I}_{\phi > \bar{y}}$. Following the same logic as before, we have

$$P^\sigma(D) = y_b + (y_g - y_b)\mathbb{P}[Y = y_g|D].$$

The term $\mathbb{P}[Y = y_g|D]$ can be expressed formally as a limit, where one can now also condition as a function of $N$. We obtain

$$\begin{aligned}
&\mathbb{P}[Y = y_g|D] \\
&= \lim_{\varepsilon \to 0} \frac{\mathbb{P}\left[Y = y_g \cap \delta \leq L + \theta \mathbb{I}_{\phi > \bar{y}} \leq \delta + \varepsilon\right]}{\mathbb{P}\left[\delta \leq L + \theta \mathbb{I}_{\phi > \bar{y}} \leq \delta + \varepsilon\right]} \\
&= \frac{A(p,\sigma) f(D - \theta)}{A(p,\sigma) f(D - \theta) + (1 - A(p,\sigma))\, f(D)}.
\end{aligned}$$

with $A(p, \sigma) = p + q(\sigma) - 2pq(\sigma)$. One can recognize the same type of expression as previously for the price, if $q$ is set to zero. $A$ represents the probability that the signal is positive and the loan performs $p(1 - q(\sigma))$ or the signal is negative and the loan does not perform $(1 - p)q(\sigma)$.

The price can now be written explicitly

$$P^\sigma(D) = \frac{y_g A(p,\sigma) f(D - \theta) + y_b (1 - A(p,\sigma))\, f(D)}{A(p,\sigma) f(D - \theta) + (1 - A(p,\sigma))\, f(D)}.$$

**Proposition 7.1** (Boot–Thakor Impact of Noisy Signals on Issuer Gains) *At the equilibrium, the fraction of traders choosing to acquire information is strictly decreasing as a function of the noise's variance. The good quality issuer's expected revenue is strictly decreasing as a function of the noise's variance.*

***Proof*** As we have the expression for the price, we can look at the value for the informed investor to acquire information

$$
\begin{aligned}
V^{\sigma}(\theta) &= \mathbb{E}\left[\mathbb{I}_{\phi>\bar{y}}\frac{Y - P^{\sigma}(D)}{P^{\sigma}(D)} - c\right] \\
&= \mathbb{E}\left[\mathbb{I}_{Y=y_g}\mathbb{I}_{N>\bar{y}-y_g}\frac{y_g - P^{\sigma}(L+\theta)}{P^{\upsilon}(L+\theta)}\right] \\
&+ \mathbb{E}\left[\mathbb{I}_{Y=y_b}\mathbb{I}_{N>\bar{y}-y_b}\frac{y_b - P(^{\sigma}L+\theta)}{P^{\sigma}(L+\theta)}\right] - c \\
&= p(1-q(\sigma))\mathbb{E}\left[\frac{y_g - P^{\sigma}(L+\theta)}{P^{\sigma}(L+\theta)}\right] \\
&+ (1-p)q(\sigma)\mathbb{E}\left[\frac{y_b - P^{\sigma}(L+\theta)}{P^{\sigma}(L+\theta)}\right] - c \\
&= -c - A(p,\sigma) + \mathbb{E}\left[\frac{p(1-q(\sigma))y_g + (1-p)q(\sigma)y_b}{P^{\sigma}(L+\theta)}\right].
\end{aligned}
$$

We know that

$$
\mathbb{E}\left[\frac{1}{P^{\sigma}(L+\theta)}\right] = \mathbb{E}\left[\frac{A(p,\sigma)f(L) + (1-A(p,\sigma))\,f(L+\theta)}{y_g A(p,\sigma)f(L) + y_b\,(1-A(p,\sigma))\,f(L+\theta)}\right],
$$

so $V^{\sigma}$ has the same form as $V$ as a function of $\theta$, and the sign of $\frac{\partial V^{\sigma}}{\partial\theta}$ is that of $f'(l+\theta)$ for $l>0$, which is negative.

Boot and Thakor then look a $V - V^{\sigma}$ and after simplifications show that it is positive. In addition, they show that $\frac{\partial(V^{\sigma}-V)}{\partial q} < 0$ and therefore $\frac{\partial V^{\sigma}}{\partial q} < 0$. Since $q$ is increasing in $\sigma$, then $\frac{\partial V^{\sigma}}{\partial\sigma} < 0$. This shows that the presence of noise reduces the informed traders' gains when they acquire information. Set $\theta^{**}$ such that $V^{\sigma} = 0$, the optimum number of traders that choose to buy information when there is noise. Since $V^{\sigma}$ is decreasing in $\sigma$ and in $\theta$, then $\theta^{**}$ is decreasing in $\sigma$ and noise discourages the acquisition of information.

Then, the expected revenue of an issuer with a good quality loan can be shown to be strictly decreasing in $\sigma$ with some algebra. □

In this noisy information context, let us consider a group of $n$ issuers all holding good quality loans. They may each issue a security backed by each loan, in which case the revenue is strictly lower than when there is no noise in the signals as we have just seen. Alternatively, if they all commingled their securities and issued a single security, the cash flows to the investors purchasing the securities would be identical. Each issuer would contribute a fraction $\frac{1}{n}$ of the pooled security, and the investors who would have purchased their securities would be able to purchase the same amount as a share of the pool.

We can consider that in this case the signals acquired by each informed investor would be also pooled, so that they would observe the total of signals relative to each individual issuer $\sum_{i\leq n}\phi_i = \sum_{i\leq n}(Y_i + N_i)$. If we consider that issuing firms would always pool together if they have the same type (or in other words issuers know other issuers' types), then the distribution of $\frac{1}{n}\sum_{i\leq n} Y_i$ is the same as that of any given $Y$, good with probability $p$. However, the distribution of $\frac{1}{n}\sum_{i\leq n} N_i$ will converge toward a single mass at zero as $n$ grows. Therefore, the effective $\sigma$ of the distribution of the noise on which the investors will base their decision will converge to 0, and the value to each issuer increases.

This could justify the existence of pooling in securitization, when multiple assets are grouped in a single deal. Typically, however, it is not multiple issuers who pool assets for a securitization, but a single issuer who gathers some of its assets for a securitization. The reasoning could only be applicable if all the issuer's assets are of the same quality, since otherwise the issuer may want to include some bad quality assets in the mix. Hence, it makes sense to think of the notion of loan quality in this model not as the quality of each particular loan or portfolio that a bank may originate, but rather as the quality of their lending process, so that presumably all of their production is of similar quality. In mortgage parlance, one could describe such an originator as having a particularly tight lending box.

Boot and Thakor's model as applied to pooling suffers from the same limitations as we already underlined: being somewhat simplistic it does not capture well the complex reality of securitization.

### 7.1.2 Pooling and Structuring

We now extend the security design model of Dang et al. (2015) presented in Chap. 4 to the pooling and tranching of multiple assets. We will see that the information sensitivity is minimized by creating debt backed by a pool of assets.

We keep the same notations from the single asset model: there are $n$ assets indexed by $0 \leq i \leq n$, paying a positive cash flow $Y_i$ at the end of the period. The $Y_i$ all have the same distribution as $Y$, with their support in $[y_b, y_g]$ and are independent. We assume that the cost of information acquisition is null, so that the issuer is informed. It may be possible to relax these assumptions, but the proof would become more cumbersome.

We write $Y_{(n)} = \frac{1}{n}\sum_{i\leq n} Y_i$, and $F_{(n)}$ for the inverse cumulative distribution of this random variable.

**Proposition 7.2** (Dang-Gorton-Holmström Optimality of Pooling and Tranching) *If the number of assets is large enough, then it is optimal for the issuer to pool the assets and create debt securities.*

***Proof*** With a portfolio of assets as described in the assumptions, and the context of Dang-Gorton-Holmström, we assume there are two structuring alternatives: sell $n$ debt securities, or sell one debt security backed by the pool of assets. We do not consider the case of selling arbitrary securities, since we know that thanks to Corollary 4.1 it is not optimal.

Recall that the investors decide which contract to offer to the issuer, and hence the solution that gets chosen needs to be optimal in terms of maximizing the investors' utility. We will write the buyers' utility $U_S$ when they are buying $n$ separate securities, and $U_P$ when they are buying a single security collateralized by the entire pool. In order to simplify notations, we only focus on the analysis of a single contract when $n$ securities are issued, and on the value of one $n$th of the pooled contract.

In the first case, $n$ securities are created each with the same price and the same security design function $g_i = g$ since if some design is optimal for one it must be for the others, given our assumptions. We know that the utility in this case is

$$U_S = \alpha \mathbb{E}[Y \wedge p_0^S] - p_0^S,$$

with the optimal price, for the separate securities defined as

$$p_0^S = w \wedge F\left(1 - \frac{1}{\alpha}\right).$$

Note that $\mathbb{P}[Y < p_0^S] > 0$. Indeed if $p_0^S = w$, then this comes from the fact that we have explicitly assumed $\mathbb{P}[Y < w] > 0$. If $p_0^S = F\left(1 - \frac{1}{\alpha}\right)$, then by definition $\mathbb{P}[Y < p_0^S] = 1 - \frac{1}{\alpha}$ which is positive. As a result, $\mathbb{E}[Y \wedge p_0^S] < p_0^S$ and hence $U_S < p_0^S(\alpha - 1)$.

In the same fashion, we have for the pooled security

$$U_P = \alpha \mathbb{E}[Y_{(n)} \wedge p_0^B] - p_0^B$$

with

$$p_0^B = w \wedge F_{(n)}\left(1 - \frac{1}{\alpha}\right).$$

In order to show the result, we will consider that there have to be enough separate assets being pooled: based on the strong law of large numbers, given any $\varepsilon$ we can pick $n$ so that $\mathbb{P}\left[\left|Y_{(n)} - \mathbb{E}[Y]\right| < \varepsilon\right] = 1$. We give ourselves such an $\varepsilon$ and a $n$. Note that this implies that $\left|F_{(n)}\left(1 - \frac{1}{\alpha}\right) - \mathbb{E}[Y]\right| < 2\varepsilon$, since the entire distribution of $Y_{(n)}$ is concentrated around $\mathbb{E}[Y]$.

We want to show that the utility from the pooling case is higher than in the segregated case. We need to look into several cases depending on the wealth $w$ in relation to $\mathbb{E}[Y]$ and to $F\left(1 - \frac{1}{\alpha}\right)$.

First, let us consider the case when $w < \mathbb{E}[Y]$. In this case, we consider that $n$ was picked so that $\mathbb{E}[Y] - 2\varepsilon > w$ and hence $w < F_{(n)}\left(1 - \frac{1}{\alpha}\right)$, and $p_0^B = w$. In addition, since almost surely $\left|Y_{(n)} - \mathbb{E}[Y]\right| < \varepsilon$ and $\mathbb{E}[Y] - w > 2\varepsilon$, then almost surely $\left|Y_{(n)} - w\right| > \varepsilon$.

Hence we can write

$$U_P = \alpha \mathbb{E}[Y_{(n)} \wedge w] - w = w(\alpha - 1).$$

If $w < F\left(1-\frac{1}{\alpha}\right)$, then $p_0^S = w$ and as we have seen above, $U_S < w(\alpha-1)$. If $p_0^S = F\left(1-\frac{1}{\alpha}\right)$, then we can write

$$U_S < F\left(1-\frac{1}{\alpha}\right)(\alpha-1) < w(\alpha-1).$$

Since $U_P = w(\alpha-1)$, we have in both cases $U_S < U_P$.

Now, let us consider the case when $w > \mathbb{E}[Y]$. We now will consider that $n$ was picked so that we have a symmetrical situation to the previous case: $\mathbb{E}[Y] + 2\varepsilon < w$ and hence $w > F_{(n)}\left(1-\frac{1}{\alpha}\right)$, and $p_0^B = F_{(n)}\left(1-\frac{1}{\alpha}\right)$. In addition, since almost surely $\left|Y_{(n)} - \mathbb{E}[Y]\right| < \varepsilon$ and $\left|F_{(n)}\left(1-\frac{1}{\alpha}\right) - \mathbb{E}[Y]\right| < 2\varepsilon$, then almost surely $\left|Y_{(n)} - F_{(n)}\left(1-\frac{1}{\alpha}\right)\right| < 3\varepsilon$. Since $w > F_{(n)}\left(1-\frac{1}{\alpha}\right)$, then we have $p_0^B = F_{(n)}\left(1-\frac{1}{\alpha}\right)$ so we can write

$$\begin{aligned} U_P &= \alpha\mathbb{E}\left[Y_{(n)} \wedge F_{(n)}\left(1-\frac{1}{\alpha}\right)\right] - F_{(n)}\left(1-\frac{1}{\alpha}\right) \\ &> \alpha(\mathbb{E}[Y]-2\varepsilon) - \mathbb{E}[Y] - 2\varepsilon \\ &> (\alpha-1)(\mathbb{E}[Y]-2\varepsilon). \end{aligned}$$

Looking at $U_S$, we first distinguish the case where $w > F\left(1-\frac{1}{\alpha}\right)$. Then we know we can express $U_S$ as a conditional expectation:

$$U_S = (\alpha-1)\mathbb{E}\left[Y|Y \le F\left(1-\frac{1}{\alpha}\right)\right].$$

We know that $\{Y \le F\left(1-\frac{1}{\alpha}\right)\}$ has a positive probability by construction, so the conditional expectation is strictly less than $\mathbb{E}[Y]$, and hence we can choose $\varepsilon$ and $n$ such that $U_S < U_P$.

Finally, if $w < F\left(1-\frac{1}{\alpha}\right)$, then we first note that $U_S$ is strictly smaller than its value if $w$ was not the binding constraint, which itself can be expressed as a conditional expectation, so

$$U_S < (\alpha-1)\mathbb{E}\left[Y|Y \le F\left(1-\frac{1}{\alpha}\right)\right].$$

As we have just seen, this quantity is less than $U_P$ and therefore $U_P > U_S$ and this concludes the proof. □

In Dang et al. (2015), the authors have more relaxed assumptions but do not in fact show the optimality, because they only prove that the set on which $p - \left(\frac{1}{n}\sum_{i\le n} Y_i\right) \wedge p$ vanishes is larger than the set on which all $p - Y_i \wedge p$ vanishes, which does not imply the expectation would follow the same order and does not reflect the fact that the optimal price $p$ is chosen as a function of whether there is pooling or not.

The benefit of pooling comes from the diversification it offers: as there is less uncertainty, the cost of asymmetrical information is reduced and this makes pooling optimal. This is effectively very comparable to the situation in the model of Boot and Thakor.

In this model, however, we used a richer setting, and both tranching and pooling worked together in making pooling optimal. We now turn to the more complex model of DeMarzo and Duffie and consider its extension to pooling. This approach is important because, as we will later see, it can be further extended to account for the existence of more complex structures.

### 7.1.3 Pooling, Information Destruction, and Structuring

In DeMarzo (2005) and in DeMarzo (2002), the author extends DeMarzo and Duffie (1999) to the case of multiple assets that may be pooled together.

We place ourselves in the same context as the model from DeMarzo and Duffie which we have presented in Chap. 4, where instead of having a single asset there are now a series of them. We will also apply slightly more constraining assumptions concerning the cash flows generated by these assets. The issuer will seek to design securities backed by these assets in order to optimally sell them to uninformed investors.

There are $n$ assets indexed by $0 \leq i \leq n$, paying a cash flow $Y_i$ at the end of the period. The information on them is simplified; we assume that the cash flow is the sum of privately observed information and a noise term: $Y_i = Z_i + N_i$ where the vector $Z$ represents private information and $N$ the noise terms. To be consistent with the model from DeMarzo and Duffie (1999), $N$ and $Z$ are assumed to be continuous. We write $Y^n = \sum_{i\leq n} Y_i$, and a vector $X$ of variables where the $i$th element is excluded is written $X_{-i}$. In the same way, we write $Z^n = \sum_{i\leq n} Z_i$. The conditional structure of the $Y$ relative to the private information is simpler than in the underlying model. We have for all $i$ $Y_i \geq 0$, and $\mathbb{E}[N_i|Z] = 0$ so $\mathbb{E}[Y_i|Z] = Z_i$.

We further assume that conditioned upon $Z_{-i}$, the support of $Z_i$ is a closed interval. This effectively means that, given an asset, whatever information one might have on the other assets, some risk on the asset is still present. In addition, still conditioned upon $Z_{-i}$, the support of $Z_i$ has a lower bound $z_L^i$, or in other words the worst-case outcome of $Z_i$ conditioned on the information on the other assets is a given level independent of $Z_{-i}$. As a consequence, the support of $Z^n$ is an interval with a lower bound $z_L^{(n)} = \sum_{i\leq n} z_L^i$. Note that with the particular assumption that $Y_i = Z_i + N_i$ and that $Z_i$ has $z_L^i$ for lower bound, then $z_L^i$ is a worst-case outcome for $Y_i$.

Investors and issuers are all assumed to be risk-neutral, as in the original model in DeMarzo and Duffie (1999), and the interest rate applicable in the market is 0. The issuer, however, applies a discount rate of $\frac{1}{1+r}$, which provides an incentive for it to sell the assets.

Propositions 4.12 and 4.13 are applicable: the profit function for the seller of the assets verifies the same properties, and the solution to the signaling equilibrium has the same expression. We know that for an asset $Y$ with private information $Z$ with a lower bound $z_L$ then the quantity of security sold is as follows.

#### 7.1.3.1 Pooling and Information Destruction

As a first step, we can look at the case when there is no structuring, and the entire asset is offered for sale. However, the issuer can choose to either sell it as an entire pool at a unique price or sell the $n$ assets separately at $n$ potentially different prices. We will see that selling the portfolio as a unique transaction reduces the benefit to the issuer, because it takes away its ability to optimally determine the price of each asset separately.

The following proposition shows the optimality of segregating the assets:

**Proposition 7.3** (DeMarzo Optimality of Segregated Asset Sales) *The issuer prefers a separate sale of the unstructured assets to an unstructured pooled sale.*

***Proof*** In the case where an individual asset $Y_i$ is sold without any structure, then its expected value to the issuer is given by Proposition 4.13:

$$V(Y_i) = \frac{r}{1+r}\mathbb{E}[Y_i|Z_i = z_L^i]\mathbb{E}\left[\left(\frac{\mathbb{E}[Y_i|Z_i = z_L^i]}{\mathbb{E}[Y_i|Z_i]}\right)^{\frac{1}{r}}\right]$$
$$= \frac{r}{1+r}z_L^i\mathbb{E}\left[\left(\frac{z_L^i}{Z_i}\right)^{\frac{1}{r}}\right].$$

In this case, the value of selling all the assets is

$$\sum_{i=1}^{n} V(Y_i) = \frac{r}{1+r}\sum_{i=1}^{n} z_L^i\mathbb{E}\left[\left(\frac{z_L^i}{Z_i}\right)^{\frac{1}{r}}\right].$$

If the assets are sold as a pooled unit, then the same proposition applies and the expected value to the issuer is

$$V\left(Y^n\right) = \frac{r}{1+r}z_L^{(n)}\mathbb{E}\left[\left(\frac{z_L^{(n)}}{Z^n}\right)^{\frac{1}{r}}\right],$$

where $z_L^{(n)} = \sum_{i\leq n} z_L^i$ and $Z^n = \sum_{i\leq n} Z_i$.

We know the function $x \mapsto x^{-\frac{1}{r}}$ for $x \in [0, 1]$ is convex and therefore $\sum_i \theta_i x_i^{-\frac{1}{r}} \geq \left(\sum_i \theta_i x_i\right)^{-\frac{1}{r}}$ for a set of positive weights $\theta_i$ summing to 1. Hence using $\frac{z_L^i}{z_L^{(n)}}$ for these weights, we can write

$$\sum_{i=1}^{n} \frac{z_L^i}{z_L^{(n)}} \left(\frac{Z_i}{z_L^i}\right)^{-\frac{1}{r}} \geq \left(\sum_{i=1}^{n} \frac{z_L^i}{z_L^{(n)}} \frac{Z_i}{z_L^i}\right)^{-\frac{1}{r}}$$
$$= \left(\frac{Z^n}{z_L^{(n)}}\right)^{-\frac{1}{r}},$$

and therefore taking the expectations we obtain

$$\frac{r}{1+r} \sum_{i=1}^{n} z_L^i \mathbb{E}\left[\left(\frac{z_L^i}{Z_i}\right)^{\frac{1}{r}}\right] \geq \frac{r}{1+r} z_L^{(n)} \mathbb{E}\left[\left(\frac{z_L^{(n)}}{Z^n}\right)^{\frac{1}{r}}\right].$$

This result shows that $V(Y^n) \leq \sum_{i=1}^{n} V(Y_i)$. □

We can see that by pooling, some value is lost because the ability to use knowledge on each asset is lost: this is the **information destruction effect**.

#### 7.1.3.2 Subordination and Risk Diversification

While unstructured assets are best sold one by one, structuring a more complex security will lead to a greater optimum, which is improved by pooling.

We now allow the issuer to sell security designs $g_i$, a function of each of the cash flows, such that $g_i(Y_i) \leq Y_i$, as well as a design $g$ depending on the sum of the cash flows $Y^n$. We will compare the two cases. Also, we are first considering the case where the security design is decided before the specifics of each collateral are known, that is, before the $Z_i$ are observed. This case of ex ante design is more typical of the decisions facing the issuer of a securitization deal, because the types of structures are normally known and accepted by investors in advance. We will also look into the optimal security design when it is determined after the private information is observed.

The following lemma tells us that the maximum attainable value with the assumptions is equal to the retention value of the worst-case expected outcome.

**Lemma 7.1** (DeMarzo Maximum Value to Issuer) *Given any security design $g_i$ the maximum issuer value verifies $V(g_i(Y_i)) < \frac{r}{1+r} z_L^i$.*

***Proof*** The results from DeMarzo and Duffie (1999) are applicable directly in this case. We define $s_L^i = \inf_z \mathbb{E}[g_i(Y_i)|Z_i = z]$, and then according to Proposition 4.13, we have the value to the issuer of

$$V(g_i(Y_i)) = \frac{r}{1+r} s_L^i \mathbb{E}\left[\left(\frac{s_L^i}{\mathbb{E}[g_i(Y_i)|Z_i]}\right)^{\frac{1}{r}}\right].$$

Recall that $V$ is defined as a functional, it depends on the entire definition of $g_i(Y_i)$, not on a particular outcome.

Note that if the $N_i$ and $Z_i$ are independent, then $s^i_L = \mathbb{E}[g_i(Y_i)|Z_i = z^i_L]$. Also, since $s^i_L \leq \mathbb{E}[g_i(Y_i)|Z_i]$, and noting that $s^i_L \leq z^i_L$ we know that

$$V(g_i(Y_i)) \leq \frac{r}{1+r} z^i_L.$$

If $s^i_L < z^i_L$ then the inequality would be strict. If $s^i_L = z^i_L$, that is, $\mathbb{E}[g_i(Y_i)|Z_i = z^i_L] = \mathbb{E}[Y_i|Z_i = z^i_L]$, since $g_i$ cannot explicitly depend on $Z_i$, then it must imply that $g_i(Y_i) = Y_i$. Hence, $\mathbb{E}[g_i(Y_i)|Z_i = z] = z$ and since $Z_i$ is continuous, there exists some $z$ such that $\mathbb{E}[g_i(Y_i)|Z_i = z] > \mathbb{E}[g_i(Y_i)|Z_i = z^i_L]$. As a result,

$$\frac{\mathbb{E}[g_i(Y_i)|Z_i = z^i_L]}{\mathbb{E}[g_i(Y_i)|Z_i]} < 1$$

and $V(g_i(Y_i)) < \frac{r}{1+r} z^i_L$. □

We will now make further assumptions about the noise terms $N_i$: we express them as the sum of a systemic risk, and a risk specific to each asset, such that $N_i = \varepsilon_i + \eta$ where each $\varepsilon_i$ is independent of $\varepsilon_{-i}$, $\eta$, and $Z$. The common risk $\eta$ is assumed to be independent of $\varepsilon$ and $Z$. Finally, assume that $\varepsilon$ and $\eta$ are log-concave.

These assumptions capture a situation where there is some common risk that cannot be diversified away, unknown by the issuer, and some idiosyncratic risk.

We can show the following lemmas:

**Lemma 7.2** (DeMarzo Optimality of Standard Debt on Segregated Assets) *The optimal monotone security design for each asset $g_i$ is standard debt with a face value $D^i$ that maximizes issuer value.*

***Proof*** Thanks to the assumptions about the composition of the noise terms, the density of $N_i$ is log-concave. Hence, it satisfies the maximum likelihood ratio property, and as a result $Z_i + N_i$ admits a uniform worst-case in $z^i_L$, as we showed in Chap. 4. Therefore, according to Proposition 4.19, the optimal debt structure is standard debt. □

**Lemma 7.3** (DeMarzo Optimality of Standard Debt on Pooled Assets) *The optimal monotone security design $g$ for the pooled assets is standard debt with a face value $D$ that maximizes issuer value.*

***Proof*** With our assumptions, $N^n = \sum_{i=1}^n N_i + n\eta$ is log-concave. Also, $Y^n$ has a uniform worst case of $\sum_{i=1}^n z^i_L = z^{(n)}_L$. The conditions for the application of Proposition 4.19 are satisfied, considering the total cash flow $Y^n$ and a security design $g$, and the optimal security design is hence a standard debt contract. □

We write the optimal issuer value as a functional of the asset cash flow

$$F(Y) = \sup_D V(Y \wedge D),$$

where $Y$ can be understood as each asset, or the sum, and the corresponding optimal face value

$$D^*(Y) = \arg\max_D V(Y \wedge D).$$

Hence, with this notation $D^*(Y^n)$ and $D^*(Y_i)$ are the optimal face values for the pooled assets and for each asset.

In order to look into the comparison of the pooled and segregated securities, we make further assumptions about the limit behavior of some quantities. We assume that at the limit the worst case for the private information is properly defined:

$$\lim_{n\to\infty} \frac{1}{n} \sum_{i=1}^{n} z_L^i = z_L,$$

and that there is always some losses that cannot be diversified away, so that for each asset $Y_i$ the following is verified:

$$\limsup_{n\to\infty} \frac{F(Y_n)}{z_L^n} < \frac{r}{1+r}.$$

This assumption implies that the optimum is not degenerate (setting the face value to the minimum outcome) on all assets at the same time. The following proposition shows that in some conditions, pooling and creating a senior/subordinated structure is optimal. In particular, when the noise around the private information $Z$ is entirely idiosyncratic to each asset, that is, $\eta = 0$, then pooling tranched assets is optimal at the limit.

**Proposition 7.4** (DeMarzo Optimality of Pooling and Tranching with Idiosyncratic Risk) *If* $\eta = 0$ *and the* $\mathbb{E}[Y_i^2]$ *are bounded, then*

$$\lim_{n\to\infty} F\left(\frac{1}{n}\sum_{i=1}^{n} Y_i\right) = \frac{r}{1+r} z_L$$

*and*

$$\lim_{n\to\infty} D^*\left(\frac{1}{n}\sum_{i=1}^{n} Y_i\right) = z_L.$$

***Proof*** We define

$$h_n(d,z) = \mathbb{E}\left[d \wedge \left(z + \frac{1}{n}\sum_{i=1}^{n}\varepsilon_i\right)\right] = \mathbb{E}\left[d \wedge \left(\frac{1}{n}\sum_{i=1}^{n} Y_i\right) | \frac{1}{n}\sum_{i=1}^{n} Z_i = z\right].$$

This function is continuous and increasing in $d$ and $z$. Thanks to the strong law of large numbers, we know that $\frac{1}{n}\sum_{i=1}^{n}\varepsilon_i$ converges to zero almost surely, which implies convergence in expectation since $d \wedge \left(z + \frac{1}{n}\sum_{i=1}^{n}\varepsilon_i\right)$ is bounded and continuous relative to $\frac{1}{n}\sum_{i=1}^{n}\varepsilon_i$. Hence $\lim_{n\to\infty} h_n(d,z) = d \wedge z$.

Define $f^d$ as $f^d(y) = y \wedge d$. In other words, now $F(Y) = \sup_D V(f^D(Y))$. We have

$$\begin{aligned}
&\inf_{(z_i)_{1\le i\le n}} \mathbb{E}\left[f^d\left(\frac{1}{n}\sum_{i=1}^{n} Y_i\right) | Z = (z_i)_{1\le i\le n}\right] \\
&= \mathbb{E}\left[f^d\left(\frac{1}{n}\sum_{i=1}^{n} Y_i\right) | \forall i, Z_i = z_L^i\right] \\
&= \mathbb{E}\left[d \wedge \left(\frac{1}{n}\sum_{i=1}^{n} Y_i\right) | \frac{1}{n}\sum_{i=1}^{n} Z_i = \frac{1}{n} z_L^{(n)}\right] \\
&= h_n\left(d, \frac{1}{n} z_L^{(n)}\right).
\end{aligned}$$

Since $h_n$ is continuous and converges, and since we know that by definition $\frac{1}{n} z_L^{(n)}$ goes to $z_L$, we infer that

$$\lim_{n\to\infty} \inf_{(z_i)_{1\le i\le n}} \mathbb{E}\left[f^d\left(\frac{1}{n}\sum_{i=1}^{n} Y_i\right) | Z = (z_i)_{1\le i\le n}\right] = d \wedge z_L.$$

If we consider the case when $d = z_L$, we see that the expression goes to $z_L$.

Note that

$$z_L \ge h_n\left(z_L, \frac{1}{n}\sum_{i=1}^{n} Z_i\right) \ge h_n\left(z_L, \frac{1}{n}\sum_{i=1}^{n} z_L^i\right),$$

and therefore $h_n\left(z_L, \frac{1}{n}\sum_{i=1}^{n} Z_i\right)$ converges to $z_L$. Hence, we have shown that

$$\lim_{n\to\infty} \mathbb{E}\left[z_L \wedge \left(\frac{1}{n}\sum_{i=1}^{n} Y_i\right) | \frac{1}{n}\sum_{i=1}^{n} Z_i\right] = z_L$$

almost surely.

Now we can write the issuer value:

$$V\left(f^{z_L}\left(\frac{1}{n}\sum_{i=1}^{n}Y_i\right)\right) = \frac{r}{1+r}h_n\left(z_L, \frac{1}{n}z_L^{(n)}\right)$$
$$\mathbb{E}\left[\left(\frac{h_n\left(z_L, \frac{1}{n}z_L^{(n)}\right)}{\mathbb{E}\left[z_L \wedge \left(\frac{1}{n}\sum_{i=1}^{n}Y_i\right) | \frac{1}{n}\sum_{i=1}^{n}Z_i\right]}\right)^{\frac{1}{r}}\right].$$

As we have shown above, all these terms converge and we obtain

$$\lim_{n\to\infty} V\left(f^{z_L}\left(\frac{1}{n}\sum_{i=1}^{n}Y_i\right)\right) = \frac{r}{1+r}z_L.$$

We now turn to the optimal face value. We show that it is equal to $z_L$ at the optimum by proving that any other choice leads to a lower value to the issuer.

Assume we set a face value $d < z_L$. Then we know that

$$\lim_{n\to\infty}\inf_{(z_i)_{1\le i\le n}} \mathbb{E}\left[f^d\left(\frac{1}{n}\sum_{i=1}^{n}Y_i\right) | Z = (z_i)_{1\le i\le n}\right] = d \wedge z_L = d.$$

Also, we know that

$$\frac{h_n\left(d, \frac{1}{n}z_L^{(n)}\right)}{\mathbb{E}\left[d \wedge \left(\frac{1}{n}\sum_{i=1}^{n}Y_i\right) | \frac{1}{n}\sum_{i=1}^{n}Z_i\right]} \le 1$$

and therefore

$$\lim_{n\to\infty} V\left(f^{d}\left(\frac{1}{n}\sum_{i=1}^{n}Y_i\right)\right) \le \frac{r}{1+r}d < \frac{r}{1+r}z_L.$$

Hence, a face value $d < z_L$ is suboptimal.

Now assume that we have $d > z_L$, in which case

$$\lim_{n\to\infty}\inf_{(z_i)_{1\le i\le n}} \mathbb{E}\left[f^d\left(\frac{1}{n}\sum_{i=1}^{n}Y_i\right) | Z = (z_i)_{1\le i\le n}\right] = d \wedge z_L = z_L.$$

We now want to show that under this assumption,

$$\lim_{n\to\infty} V\left(f^{d}\left(\frac{1}{n}\sum_{i=1}^{n}Y_i\right)\right) < \frac{r}{1+r}z_L.$$

Note that for any $n$, $f(Y_n) \geq V(Y_n)$ by definition. In addition, $V(Y_n) = \frac{r}{1+r} z_L^n \mathbb{E}\left[\left(\frac{z_L^n}{\mathbb{E}[Y_n|Z_n]}\right)^{\frac{1}{r}}\right]$ and hence thanks to Jensen's inequality $V(Y_n) \geq \frac{r}{1+r} z_L^n \left(\frac{z_L^n}{\mathbb{E}[Y_n]}\right)^{\frac{1}{r}}$. However, we have assumed that $\limsup_{n\to\infty} \frac{F(Y_n)}{z_L^n} < \frac{r}{1+r}$. Therefore

$$\limsup_{n\to\infty} \frac{r}{1+r} \left(\frac{z_L^n}{\mathbb{E}[Y_n]}\right)^{\frac{1}{r}} < \frac{r}{1+r},$$

which is equivalent to $\liminf_{n\to\infty} \frac{\mathbb{E}[Y_n]}{z_L^n} > 1$. Hence, we have

$$\lim_{n\to\infty} \frac{1}{n} \sum_{i=1}^{n} \mathbb{E}[Y_i] > \lim_{n\to\infty} \frac{1}{n} \sum_{i=1}^{n} z_L^i = z_L.$$

From this limit, we infer that there exists $n_0$ and $\varepsilon$ such that $\forall n > n_0$, $\frac{\mathbb{E}[\sum_{i=1}^n Y_i]}{n} > z_L + \varepsilon$. Since we assumed that $\mathbb{E}[Y_n^2]$ is bounded, then $\left(\frac{\mathbb{E}[\sum_{i=1}^n Y_i]}{n}\right)^2$ is also bounded.

Note that for a random variable $A$, if $\mathbb{E}[A] \geq a$ and $\mathbb{E}[A^2] \leq b$, then we can write for all $c \in [0, a]$, $\mathbb{P}[A \geq c] = \mathbb{P}[A \geq \theta \mathbb{E}[A]]$ with $\theta \in [0, 1]$, by setting $\theta = \frac{c}{\mathbb{E}[A]}$. Thanks to the Paley–Zygmund inequality, we know that then $\mathbb{P}[A \geq c] \geq (1-\theta)^2 \frac{\mathbb{E}[A]^2}{\mathbb{E}[A^2]}$, which simplifies into $\mathbb{P}[A \geq c] \geq \frac{(\mathbb{E}[A]-c)^2}{b}$. Hence, $\mathbb{P}[A \geq c] \geq \frac{(a-c)^2}{b}$.

Applying this result to $A = \frac{1}{n}\sum_{i=1}^n Y_i$ and $c = z_L + \frac{\varepsilon}{2}$, we obtain that there exists some number $\lambda$ so that

$$\mathbb{P}\left[\frac{1}{n}\sum_{i=1}^{n} Y_i \geq z_L + \frac{\varepsilon}{2}\right] \geq \lambda.$$

We have shown earlier that $\lim_{n\to\infty} h_n(d, z) = d \wedge z$, and we are assuming that $d > z_L$, hence we can find $n_1 > n_0$ such that for all $n > n_1$, $h_n\left(d, z_L + \frac{\varepsilon}{2}\right) \geq z_L + \frac{\varepsilon}{4}$. We also know that $\lim_{n\to\infty} h_n\left(d, \frac{1}{n} z_L^{(n)}\right) = d \wedge z_L$, and hence $n_1$ can also be picked so that for $n > n_1$, $h_n\left(d, \frac{1}{n} z_L^{(n)}\right) \leq z_L + \frac{\varepsilon}{6}$.

Thus, for all $n > n_1$,

$$\mathbb{P}\left[\frac{\frac{1}{n} z_L^{(n)}}{\mathbb{E}\left[f^d\left(\frac{1}{n}\sum_{i=1}^n Y_i\right)|Z = (z_i)_{1\leq i\leq n}\right]} \leq \frac{z_L + \frac{\varepsilon}{6}}{z_L + \frac{\varepsilon}{4}}\right] > \lambda.$$

This indicates that one can find an $n$ large enough so that the value to the issuer is less than the optimal value with a nonzero probability. □

We know that by pooling, there is an information destruction effect, which reduces the value to the issuer. However, at the same time, the proposition shows that there is a **risk diversification effect** whereby the risk of the debt can be reduced, and a larger amount can be issued thansame would be the case otherwise.

Note that for any security design, and in particular for the optimal one of value $F$, and for all $n$, we have $F(Y_n) < \frac{r}{1+r} z_L^n$. Hence, multiplying by $\frac{1}{n}$ and taking the limit we see that thanks to the proposition:

$$\lim_{n\to\infty} F\left(\frac{1}{n}\sum_{i=1}^{n} Y_i\right) > \lim_{n\to\infty} \frac{1}{n}\sum_{i=1}^{n} F(Y_i).$$

This shows the strict benefit gained by tranching a pool, rather than pooling tranches. With the assumptions from the proposition, by pooling the assets, the issuer can issue more informationally insensitive debt than by summing the debt that could be issued off of each asset separately.

We can confirm that the benefits of pooling and tranching come from the diversification effect, by considering the case where there is no idiosyncratic risk, but a single common risk, as shown in the following proposition.

**Proposition 7.5** (DeMarzo Optimality of Not Pooling with Systemic Risk) *If, for all $i$, $\varepsilon_i = 0$ and $z_L^i = z_L$ then for any $n$, pooling is not optimal.*

***Proof*** According to our assumptions, we have $Y_i = Z_i + \eta$, so that $\frac{1}{n}\sum_{i=1}^{n} Y_i = \eta + \frac{1}{n}\sum_{i=1}^{n} Z_i$.

Given $n$, define $d_n = D^*\left(\frac{1}{n}\sum_{i=1}^{n} Y_i\right)$ the optimal debt face value if the assets are pooled, and define the function $h(d, z) = \mathbb{E}[d \wedge (z + \eta)]$. This function is concave in $z$ and $d$.

Separately, note that based on the expression for $h$ and for $Y_i$, we can write

$$\mathbb{E}\left[d_n \wedge \left(\eta + \frac{1}{n}\sum_{i=1}^{n} Z_i\right) | Z_i = z_L\right] = h(d_n, z_L).$$

Now let us consider the expected value to the issuer of the pooled and tranched issuance:

$$F\left(\frac{1}{n}\sum_{i=1}^{n} Y_i\right) = V\left(d_n \wedge \frac{1}{n}\sum_{i=1}^{n} Y_i\right)$$

$$= \mathbb{E}\left[d_n \wedge \left(\eta + \frac{1}{n}\sum_{i=1}^{n} Z_i\right) | Z_i = z_L\right]\mathbb{E}\left[\left(\frac{\mathbb{E}\left[d_n \wedge \left(\eta + \frac{1}{n}\sum_{i=1}^{n} Z_i\right) | Z_i = z_L\right]}{\mathbb{E}\left[d_n \wedge \left(\eta + \frac{1}{n}\sum_{i=1}^{n} Z_i\right) | Z_i\right]}\right)^{\frac{1}{r}}\right]$$

$$= h(d_n, z_L)\mathbb{E}\left[\left(\frac{h(d_n, z_L)}{h\left(d_n, \frac{1}{n}\sum_{i=1}^{n} Z_i\right)}\right)^{\frac{1}{r}}\right].$$

Since $h$ is concave, then for a vector of realizations $(y_i)_{i\leq n}$ we have

$$h\left(d, \frac{1}{n}\sum_{i=1}^{n} y_i\right) \geq \frac{1}{n}\sum_{i=1} h(d, y_i),$$

and as a result

$$\mathbb{E}\left[\left(\frac{h(d_n, z_L)}{h\left(d_n, \frac{1}{n}\sum_{i=1}^{n} Z_i\right)}\right)^{\frac{1}{r}}\right] \leq \mathbb{E}\left[\left(\frac{h(d_n, z_L)}{\frac{1}{n}\sum_{i=1}^{n} h\left(d_n, Z_i\right)}\right)^{\frac{1}{r}}\right].$$

In addition, as we have already noted the function that maps $x$ to $x^{-\frac{1}{r}}$ is convex, and hence by Jensen's inequality,

$$\mathbb{E}\left[\left(\frac{h(d_n, z_L)}{\frac{1}{n}\sum_{i=1}^{n} h\left(d_n, Z_i\right)}\right)^{\frac{1}{r}}\right] \leq \frac{1}{n}\sum_{i=1}^{n} \mathbb{E}\left[\left(\frac{h(d_n, z_L)}{h\left(d_n, Z_i\right)}\right)^{\frac{1}{r}}\right].$$

Therefore, we have

$$\begin{aligned} F\left(\frac{1}{n}\sum_{i=1}^{n} Y_i\right) &\leq \frac{1}{n}\sum_{i=1}^{n} h(d_n, z_L)\mathbb{E}\left[\left(\frac{h(d_n, z_L)}{h\left(d_n, Z_i\right)}\right)^{\frac{1}{r}}\right] \\ &= \frac{1}{n}\sum_{i=1}^{n} V\left(Y_i \wedge d_n\right) \\ &\leq \frac{1}{n}\sum_{i=1}^{n} F(Y_i). \end{aligned}$$

The last inequality comes from the fact that $F(Y) = \sup_d V(Y \wedge d)$. It is clear, then, that there is more value in issuing the securities separately than in pooling them. □

The gains from pooling and then tranching clearly appear as a function of the degree of diversification in the collateral performance. We can also consider it from the standpoint of the nature of private information. Indeed, separately from the structure of the noise affecting the assets independently from the issuer's information, that information may itself be more concentrated or more dispersed.

Given a random variable $\hat{X}$, a variable $X$ is called a **mean-preserving spread** if there exists a random variable $M$ such that $X$ has the same distribution as $\hat{X} + M$ and $\mathbb{E}[M|\hat{X}] = 0$. In other words, both $X$ and $\hat{X}$ have the same expectation but $X$ is more spread out.

Let us consider a situation with two types of poolable assets, $Y_i = Z_i + \eta + \varepsilon_i$ and $\hat{Y}_i = \hat{Z}_i + \eta + \varepsilon_i$ where the aggregate private information is such that $Z^n = \frac{1}{n}\sum_{i=1}^{n} Z_i$ is a mean-preserving spread of $\hat{Z^n} = \frac{1}{n}\sum_{i=1}^{n} \hat{Z}_i$. This represents a case where the expectation of aggregate private information is the same in both cases, but it is more dispersed in the first case. Since both expressions are means of $n$ observations, this would be the case if the $Z_i$ have common factors driving them, while the $\hat{Z}_i$ have more independent factors driving them, so that once they are summed up they end up more concentrated around the average.

The following proposition shows that the gains from pooling are greater when the private information on the assets shares more common factors.

**Proposition 7.6** (DeMarzo Optimality of Pooling for More Concentrated Information) *Set* $Y_i = Z_i + \eta + \varepsilon_i$ *and* $\hat{Y}_i = \hat{Z}_i + \eta + \varepsilon_i$*. If* $Z^n = \frac{1}{n}\sum_{i=1}^n Z_i$ *is a mean-preserving spread of* $\hat{Z}^n = \frac{1}{n}\sum_{i=1}^n \hat{Z}_i$*, then*

$$F\left(\frac{1}{n}\sum_{i=1}^{n} Y_i\right) \geq F\left(\frac{1}{n}\sum_{i=1}^{n} \hat{Y}_i\right).$$

***Proof*** Define the concave and increasing function $h$ as

$$h(d,z) = \mathbb{E}\left[d \wedge \left(z + \eta + \frac{1}{n}\sum_{i=1}^{n} \varepsilon_i\right)\right].$$

As in the prior proof, and recalling that we defined $z_L^{(n)} = \sum_{i=1}^n z_L^i$, we can write for some $d$:

$$V\left(d \wedge \frac{1}{n}\sum_{i=1}^{n} Y_i\right) = h\left(d, \frac{1}{n} z_L^{(n)}\right) \mathbb{E}\left[\left(\frac{h\left(d, \frac{1}{n} z_L^{(n)}\right)}{h\left(d, \frac{1}{n} Z^n\right)}\right)^{\frac{1}{r}}\right].$$

Similarly, we can write

$$V\left(d \wedge \frac{1}{n}\sum_{i=1}^{n} \hat{Y}_i\right) = h\left(d, \frac{1}{n} z_L^{(n)}\right) \mathbb{E}\left[\left(\frac{h\left(d, \frac{1}{n} z_L^{(n)}\right)}{h\left(d, \frac{1}{n} \hat{Z}^n\right)}\right)^{\frac{1}{r}}\right].$$

Since $h$ is increasing and concave, and $x \mapsto x^{-\frac{1}{r}}$ is decreasing and convex, then the compounded function is convex. Since we assumed that $Z^n$ was a mean-preserving spread of $\hat{Z}^n$, then for any convex function $g$ we have $\mathbb{E}[g(Z^n)] \geq \mathbb{E}[g(\hat{Z}^n)]$. As a result, we can see that for a given $d$,

$$V\left(d \wedge \frac{1}{n}\sum_{i=1}^{n} Y_i\right) \geq V\left(d \wedge \frac{1}{n}\sum_{i=1}^{n} \hat{Y}_i\right).$$

This is hence true for $D^*\left(\frac{1}{n}\sum_{i=1}^n \hat{Y}_i\right)$, so that

$$V\left(D^*\left(\frac{1}{n}\sum_{i=1}^n \hat{Y}_i\right) \wedge \frac{1}{n}\sum_{i=1}^n Y_i\right) \geq F\left(\frac{1}{n}\sum_{i=1}^n \hat{Y}_i\right).$$

However, we have by definition

$$F\left(\frac{1}{n}\sum_{i=1}^n Y_i\right) \geq V\left(D^*\left(\frac{1}{n}\sum_{i=1}^n \hat{Y}_i\right) \wedge \frac{1}{n}\sum_{i=1}^n Y_i\right),$$

and we can conclude that $F\left(\frac{1}{n}\sum_{i=1}^n \hat{Y}_i\right) \leq F\left(\frac{1}{n}\sum_{i=1}^n Y_i\right)$. □

Propositions 7.4, 7.5, and 7.6 are important as they provide rationale for the pooling logic that has been observed in securitization, which we pointed out in Chap. 4: in securitizations, assets of the same type have always been pooled together, but separately from other asset types. Indeed, private information on assets of a very different nature is unlikely to be correlated, which according to Proposition 7.6 would reduce the benefits of pooling and tranching.

### 7.1.4 No-Arbitrage and Pooling

We now consider an alternative approach to justifying pooling that does not rely on information asymmetry but on no-arbitrage considerations. The models presented in Gaur et al. (2003) initially and then in Gaur et al. (2011), consider market completeness and show that pooling, by completing the market, accrue value to issuers and investors. The approach relies on no-arbitrage pricing theory, which is somewhat different from the information asymmetry perspective of the majority of other models we have discussed so far.

In spite of this fundamental difference, there are substantial commonalities between these approaches. When in an asymmetrical information framework, for example, that of an informed issuer, we know that investors will effectively start from a form of worst-case assumption, and update their beliefs at the equilibrium in order to reflect the informed issuer's optimal issuance strategy. The valuation of the securities therefore typically reflects the expected cash flows conditioned by the worst-case private information, as can be seen in our discussion of DeMarzo and Duffie (1999), for example. This worst case in fact corresponds to the best one could collect assuming the information was the worst. In the context of no-arbitrage pricing in an incomplete market, as we will see in this section, one can argue that the valuation of a claim is the lower bound of its most valuable replication portfolio. In other words, it is the best valuation one can get with a portfolio of tradable assets that pays less than the new claim. Thus, in both cases, one uses a lower bound, which effectively minimizes the investor's worst case.

One important difference in Gaur et al. (2011) with the other models of security design is that the economy is discrete, and there are no continuous variables. The results rely on linear programming theory heavily, and extending them to a continuous economy would raise substantial issues. We know thanks to general no-arbitrage valuation theory that in order to avoid trivial valuations in a continuous model with discrete time periods, one would need bounded distributions for the noise driving future cash flows. Having to specify a finite (and hence bounded) set of possible outcomes is therefore not much more restrictive.

The model proposed by Gaur et al. is more general than strictly required: in particular, it can be applied to real investment valuations. Also, the structure of randomness is not specifically adapted to securitization. The examples given in the original article are simplistic and do not really capture the reality of securitization. As such, as we go through the model, we develop a more narrowly defined setup to better account for the realistic patterns in loan securitization and use it to show how the more complex general model can shed light on some aspects of securitization structuring.

Also, in their paper Gaur et al. not only address pooling, but also tranching. However, the way Gaur et al. envision tranching contrasts with the practical structuring logic such as what we covered in Chap. 6. In fact, they define a tranche as the sum of all the cash flows going to all the investors while in fact, from the standpoint of normal securitization, this would rather be defined as the total structured issuance. The actual tranches would be the sum of the distinct cash flows going to each investor class. In addition, the approach requires very specific assumptions on investors' utility functions in order to be tractable, and hence we are leaving these results aside.

#### 7.1.4.1 No-Arbitrage Pricing Overview

We consider a discrete economy with two time periods 0 and 1, where at period 1 there exist $K$ possible states of the world denoted $\Omega = \{\omega_1, \omega_2, ..., \omega_K\}$. We write $\omega_0$ for the unique state of the world at time 0. We assume that the risk-free rate is 0. There exist $N$ primary securities traded on a market so that each security $n$ has a unique price $p_n$, and payoffs $S_n(\omega_k)$ in the $k$th state. Without specifying the state payoff, the security can be written $S_n$. Note that the risk-free rate being zero means that there is no security returning a strictly positive cash flow in all possible outcomes; otherwise, that security could be the bank account, and the risk-free rate would not be zero.

For the definitions of terms pertaining to this discrete securities market, and for the most important results allowing us to characterize valuations, we are referring to Pliska (1997). Also, this reference covers all the necessary background in linear programming and duality theory, which is used extensively not only to prove the core results in discrete no-arbitrage pricing theory, but also in the proofs for Gaur et al. (2011, 2003).

A **trading strategy** $H$ is a portfolio allocation $(H_1, ..., H_N)$ purchase at time 0 and kept until time 1. Each element $H_n$ of the vector $H$ represents the number of securities $n$ purchased: the portfolio's initial cost at time 0 is $H_0 = \sum_{n=1}^{N} H_n p_n$ and its payoff at time 1, a function of the state, is $\sum_{n=1}^{N} H_n S_n$. The **value of the strategy** $V(H)$ is the payoff at time 1: $V(H) = \sum_{n=1}^{N} H_n S_n$. A strategy $\hat{H}$ is a **dominant strategy** if there exists another strategy $H$ such that $H_0 = \hat{H}_0$ and $V(\hat{H}_0)(\omega_k) > V(H_0)(\omega_k)$ for all $k \in [1..K]$. Note that the dominant strategy must strictly beat the other strategy.

A **linear pricing measure** is a non-negative vector $\pi = (\pi_1, ..., \pi_K)$ such that for all $n$:

$$p_n = \sum_{k=1}^{K} \pi_k S_n(\omega_k),$$

and in this case it verifies $\sum_{k=1}^{K} \pi_k = 1$. Theorem 1.9 in Pliska (1997) states that there exists a linear pricing measure if and only if there are no dominant strategies.

An **arbitrage** is a trading strategy $H$ such that $H_0 = 0$, $V(H)(\omega_k) \geq 0$ for all $k \in [1..K]$, and there exists $j$ such that $V(H)(\omega_j) > 0$. It is a less narrow condition than for a dominant strategy, as some zero-gain states are allowed. When arbitrages are not possible, we will see that it leads to a more restrictive set of linear pricing measures. A **risk-neutral measure** is a linear pricing measure such that all the weights $\pi_k$ are strictly positive. Theorem 1.16 in Pliska (1997) tells us that there are no-arbitrage opportunities if and only if there exists a risk-neutral probability measure. We note $\mathbb{E}_m$ the expectation operator under probability measure $m$. One important consequence is also that if $m$ is a risk-neutral measure then for any trading strategy $H$, one has $H_0 = \mathbb{E}_m[V(H)]$, and the constant $H_0$ does not depend on the choice of $m$.

A **contingent claim** is a random variable $X$ representing some payoff at time 1, depending on each state of the world $\omega_k$. It may be a new asset yet untraded, or represent a contract promising some payment depending on future outcomes. The value of a contingent claim in all generality would be a function of market participants' utility, or private or common information as well. However, thanks to arbitrage pricing theory, one can find valuations or bounds that would always be applicable. A contingent claim is said to be **attainable** if there exists a strategy $H$, a replication portfolio, such that $V(H) = X$. When there are no-arbitrage opportunities the value of an attainable claim is unique and given by the value at time zero of its replication portfolio. Assume that there are no arbitrages, and there exists a set $\mathbb{M}$ of risk-neutral measures. Theorem 1.23 in Pliska (1997) states that a contingent claim $X$ is attainable if and only if $\mathbb{E}_m[X]$ is constant for all $m \in \mathbb{M}$.

Some contingent claims may not be attainable, in which case there is no replication portfolio and one cannot obtain an unequivocal valuation. A market where there are unattainable claims is said to be **incomplete**, and complete if all claims are attainable. One important result is that a market is complete if and only if the set $\mathbb{M}$ of risk-neutral measures is a singleton. If a market is incomplete, then there is a continuous infinity of risk-neutral measures.

In an incomplete market, one cannot determine a unique value for an unattainable contingent claim but specific bounds can be determined. Write $\mathbb{A}$ the set of all attainable claims (that is, those that can be written as $\sum_{n=1}^{N} H_n S_n$). We define the best approximations of the contingent claim with attainable securities as follows:

$$V^{+}(X) = \inf_{m \in \mathbb{M}} \{\mathbb{E}_m[Y] : Y \geq X, Y \in \mathbb{A}\},$$

and

$$V^{-}(X) = \sup_{m \in \mathbb{M}} \{\mathbb{E}_m[Y] : Y \leq X, Y \in \mathbb{A}\}.$$

The price bounds $V^{+}$ and $V^{-}$ are such that the value of the unattainable contingent claim cannot be under $V^{-}$ or above $V^{+}$ without the existence of arbitrage. Indeed, if that was the case one could build an arbitrage based on the replication portfolio for the bound.

Theorem 1.28 in Pliska (1997), shown using linear programming duality, states that if $\mathbb{M}$ is the set of risk-neutral measures in an arbitrage-free market, then for any contingent claim $X$,

$$V^{+}(X) = \sup_{m \in \mathbb{M}} \mathbb{E}_m[X],$$

and

$$V^{-}(X) = \inf_{m \in \mathbb{M}} \mathbb{E}_m[X].$$

For both optimization programs, the optimum is reached in the closure of $\mathbb{M}$ because it is a linear pricing measure (with some potentially null weights), which is a linear combination of a set of independent risk-neutral probabilities in $\mathbb{M}$. The set of risk-neutral pricing measures $\mathbb{M}$ is, hence, spanned by a set of independent linear pricing measures, which is finite. We label these linear pricing measures $Q = \{q_1, q_2, \ldots, q_L\}$.

We assume that the market for the securities in our model is without frictions, and that there are no arbitrages, so that all the results presented above hold. The first result shown by Gaur et al. is an extension of some of the results discussed by Pliska.

**Lemma 7.4** (Gaur–Seshadri–Subrahmanyam Value Bounds) $V^{+}(X) = \max_{q \in Q} \mathbb{E}_q[X]$ *and* $V^{-}(X) = \min_{q \in Q} \mathbb{E}_q[X]$. *In addition, if for all* $k$ $X(\omega_k) \geq 0$ *then the bounds are unaffected by the inability of agents to short sell securities.*

***Proof*** We first prove $V^{+}(X) = \max_{q \in Q} \mathbb{E}_q[X]$. We consider the following linear program:

$$\min_{z \in \mathbb{R}} z$$

$$\forall l \in [1..L], z \geq \sum_{k=1}^{K} q_l(\omega_k) X(\omega_k).$$

This program effectively computes $\max_{q\in Q} \mathbb{E}_q[X]$. If $z \geq \sum_{k=1}^{K} q_l(\omega_k)X(\omega_k)$, then for all $(\delta_l)_{l\in[1..L]}$ such that $\delta_l \geq 0$ and $\sum_{l=1}^{L} \delta_l = 1$, we have

$$\sum_{l=1}^{L} \delta_l z \geq \sum_{l=1}^{L}\sum_{k=1}^{K} \delta_l q_l(\omega_k)X(\omega_k).$$

However, since the $q_l$ span $\mathbb{M}$, any element $m \in \mathbb{M}$ can be written as a linear combination of the elements in $Q$ such that $m$ is a probability measure with strictly positive weights. Hence $z \geq \sup_{m\in\mathbb{M}} \mathbb{E}_m[X]$. Therefore, the optimal solution to the linear program $z^*$ is such that $z^* \geq V^+(X)$. At the same time, $\max_{q\in Q} \mathbb{E}_q[X]$ is a feasible solution to the linear program, and $\max_{q\in Q} \mathbb{E}_q[X] \leq \sup_{m\in\mathbb{M}} \mathbb{E}_m[X]$. As a result, $\max_{q\in Q} \mathbb{E}_q[X] = V^+(X)$.

The proof for $V^-(X)$ is exactly symmetrical.

We now prove that the bounds are not affected by the agents' ability to sell short as far as for all $k$ $X(\omega_k) \geq 0$. We first consider the linear program that expresses the maximum attainable value of a claim $X$, that is, finding the trading strategy with the highest present value such that its payoff value is less than the claim. If we restrict the strategies to those with positive weights, the linear program writes

$$\max_{H\in\mathbb{R}^N} \sum_{n=1}^{N} H_n p_n$$

$$\forall k \in [1..K], \sum_{n=1}^{N} H_n S_n(\omega_k) \leq X(\omega_k)$$

$$\forall n \in [1..N], H_n \geq 0.$$

The dual of this problem is

$$\min_{\lambda\in\mathbb{R}^K} \sum_{k=1}^{K} \lambda_k X(\omega_k)$$

$$\forall n \in [1..N], \sum_{k=1}^{K} \lambda_k S_n(\omega_k) \geq p_n$$

$$\forall k \in [1..K], \lambda_k \geq 0.$$

However, since the $\lambda_k$ are constrained to be positive, if $X(\omega_k) \geq 0$ then the first set of constraints must be $\sum_{k=1}^{K} \lambda_k S_n(\omega_k) = p_n$. These conditions, however, imply that the $\lambda_k$ constitute a linear pricing measure, and hence $\lambda \in \overline{\mathbb{M}}$, that is, the closure of $\mathbb{M}$. Therefore, the solution to this dual is $\inf_{q\in\mathbb{M}} \mathbb{E}_q[X]$, and by duality theory, that is the same solution as for the primal problem. In addition, thanks to the first part of the proof, we know that this solution equals $V^-(X)$.

The result for $V^+$ can be shown symmetrically. Thus, under our assumption, constraining trading to prevent short sales does not affect the bounds $V^-$ and $V+$. □

#### 7.1.4.2 Assets, Firms, Intermediaries

We can now begin to focus on the different market participants in the model. There are originators (firms) and issuers (intermediaries). In our version of the model, investors do not need to be modeled explicitly. We'll designate as **primary securities** the $S_n$ that are traded in the market, and as **secondary securities** contingent claims that may be created and traded. We have also changed the denomination of these market participants relative to Gaur et al. (2011) in order to better capture their typical roles. In the context of securitization, our approach allows us to stress the difference between loan origination and securities issuance.

- Investors can invest in securities and collect the eventual payoff. They can buy or sell primary securities, but they cannot sell or create secondary securities. Investors may be hedge funds, mutual funds, insurance companies, or banks, for example.
- Originators are the firms which own real assets and have issued primary securities backed by the cash flows from their assets. They can also create new assets (originating loans, for example) and sell claims on these new assets to issuers (intermediaries). They try to get the highest value possible for these new assets, and will have a reservation price that depends on their characteristics. Originators may be commercial banks, large car manufacturers with a financing branch, or credit card companies, for example.
- Issuers repackage the claims purchased from the originators and issue secondary securities. Issuers are investment banks or conduits, for example.

Short selling of secondary securities is not allowed, as it would not possible in reality to short an asset or mortgage-backed security. In addition, the primary securities cannot be repackaged by investors or issuers: debt, stocks, or any other primary securities issued by firms are set and not to be altered. In the framework under study, market incompleteness would be trivially addressed by cutting up the primary securities enough times and trading them if primary securities could be repackaged freely.

In addition, we assume the **small firm argument** is applicable: the originators are small enough that creating secondary securities does not have an impact on the value of primary securities. Note that this is not entirely innocuous: we know from the discussion in Chap. 4 that securitizing assets would have an impact on the value of existing securities; see Iacobucci and Winter (2005) or Gorton and Souleles (2007), for example.

Originators or Firms

We assume there exist $J$ firms that might invest and originate new assets. Each firm will seek to maximize the expected value of its investment at time 0. Firm $j \in [1..J]$ creates a unique asset $Y_j$, which pays a positive cash flow $Y_j(\omega_k)$ in each state $k$ at time 1. The firm may sell claims fully backed by $Y_j$ to the intermediary. The reservation price of firm $j$ for the asset it can create is written $r_j$ and is exogenous: it depends on the specifics of the project and of the firm. The firm only invests if the price at which it can sell the asset is greater than the reservation price. The authors note in the original article that considering the asset effectively gets sold allows us to avoid the issue of determining how the firm can value cash flows in a way that satisfies all its shareholders optimally.

The total cash flow produced by all firms $\sum_{j=1}^{J} Y_j$ is assumed to be small, so that the small firm argument can be used, and each firm behaves as a price taker. Since there may not be an unequivocal price due to market incompleteness, the firm will still try to get the highest value for its project.

The fact that the market model in Gaur et al. (2011) is discrete may appear as a restrictive assumption, but in fact it can account for a good variety of situations. As we will see, such a model can account for a variety of asset portfolios, each with either a good or a bad outcome. This would contain the models by Gorton and Metrick (2013), Gorton and Souleles (2007), or Boot and Thakor (1993). We narrow the model setup from Gaur et al. in order to make its applicability to securitization more direct, within a reasonably tractable model. In order to capture the essence of risks and hedging for pools of assets, we will consider that interest rates are a common underlying driver, affecting the assets as well as some reference Treasury bond. In addition, each asset or portfolio will have its own individual risk.

Our instantiation of the model in a framework applied to securitization works as follows. There is a security representing the bank account with a constant value $B = 1$ and a security $S_0$ representing a Treasury or market index bond with price $p_0$. The Treasury returns $(1 + R)$ at maturity, with $R \in \{y_l, y_h\}$ where $y_l < y_h$ such that $y_h > 0$.

The $J$ originators create assets so that for all $j \in [1..J]$, $Y_j = R + X_j$, with $X_j \in \{d_j, 1\}$ and $d_j < 1$. These assets can be considered as loans or portfolios of loans, such that they return their face value and some interest at the same rate as Treasurys, but may also default in which case a lower amount is recovered. The dependence of the $Y_j$ on $R$ can be understood as a simple interest rate collection, or also as a common credit risk driver across all projects. We have $\Omega = \{y_l, y_h\} \times \prod_{j=1}^{J}\{p_j, 1\}$, and $|\Omega| = 2^{J+1}$. We do not need to formally express each $\omega_k$ for $k \in [1..2^{J+1}]$. For some probability measure $m$ on $\Omega$, we also define the probability of a default by asset $j$ is $\pi_{m,j}^{X} = m[X_j = d_j]$.

Further, we assume that the production cost of these loans for each originator is $r_j = 1 + y_j$. We can think of $y_j$ as the coupon at which the originator is able to extend the loan with these characteristics.

Note that we have $V^-(Y_j) = (1 + y_l)d_j$ and $V^+(Y_j) = 1 + y_h$. With our conditions, we know that Lemma 7.4 is applicable and hence preventing short selling, as would naturally be the case with pools of assets, does not affect the valuation bounds $V^+$ and $V^-$.

Issuers or Intermediaries

These agents possess knowledge about the requirements of the firms and of investors. They do not have private information on future outcomes $\omega_k$ but know the investors and originators' preferences.

The issuers seek to benefit from gains by repackaging the cash flows from the originators and selling them to investors. We assume that intermediaries pay the same price for the same asset, because there is enough competition from other intermediaries. This competition is not explicitly modeled, and one simply needs to consider the case of a single intermediary optimizing claim.

The secondary securities created by issuers may reflect pooling. In this context, pooling is combining the cash flows from different originators into a single security. Note that the issuers sell packaged securities to investors, but they are not arbitraging them by simply selling replicable cash flows at a marked-up price based on the investor's preferences. This is in contrast with the model from Brennan et al. (2009) in continuous time, for example, where replicable cash flows are sold to investors for a profit because the investors consider all products with the same rating to be priced the same way. In the context of Gaur et al. (2011), it would be possible to represent a comparable situation by specifying investors' preferences accordingly, and then having the issuers package securities that would benefit from a lower credit risk, thanks to diversification and tranching.

For our particular model application, we will consider there exist $N$ primary securities that pool the loans in a simple fashion. We consider $N$ disjoint sets (groups of assets) $G_1, G_2, ..., G_I$ that form a partition of $[1..J]$, with cardinals $K_n = |G_n|$. We will write for all $j \in [1..J]$, $n(j) = \{n : j \in G_n\}$. The $N$ securities are defined as, for all $n \in [1..N]$, $S_n = \sum_{j \in G_n} Y_j$. These securities capture the aggregate credit performance of each of the $N$ pools of assets. We assume that these securities pool assets with comparable risks, so that for all $n \in [1..N]$ there exists $\delta_n$ such that for all $j \in G_i$, $d_j = \delta_{n(j)}$. We will also assume that $d_j + y_l \geq 0$ so that the asset cash flows are always positive even in bad states. Note that the prices of the asset pools must be such that $\frac{p_n}{K_n} \leq p_0$ and $\frac{p_N}{J} \leq p_0$, since their cash flows are lesser or equal to those of the Treasury or benchmark reference bond.

We will also analyze an alternative set of assumptions where the loan groups are the same, but are not traded as securities, and instead only a pool across all assets is traded. We will in this case simply write

$$S_N = \sum_{j \in [1..J]} Y_j = \sum_{n \in [1..N]} \sum_{j \in G_n} Y_j$$

for this security.

### 7.1.4.3 Pooling

With the model at hand, we will consider the problem of pooling the cash flows from several originators. The new cash flows that are created by the issuer are valued by replication in the securities market. The lower bound $V^-$ is used as the right valuation measure. First, we know that using this bound there are no-arbitrage opportunities on the new claim. Second, securities can be sold at this price notwithstanding the investors' preferences and utility functions. Third, even if there is adverse selection (for example the originator has private information), the valuation cannot be lower than this lower bound. Finally, this bound is transparent and can be computed by all market participants without particular knowledge of the originators or other investors' characteristics.

Consider a firm $j$. If $r_j \leq V^-(Y_j)$, then the firm can profitably invest and create asset $j$, since even without further structuring it would be attractive to investors. If $r_j \geq V^+(Y_j)$, then there is no condition where creating the asset would be attractive. If $V^-(Y_j) \leq r_j \leq V^+(Y_j)$, then the situation is ambiguous. In our securitization model, we will assume that for all $j \in [1..J]$, $(1+y_l)d_j - 1 < y_j < y_h$ so that all originators are in this ambiguous situation.

Before looking into the optimality of pooling, we characterize the valuation of different assets and pools in our illustrative model. We have the following proposition.

**Proposition 7.7** (No-Arbitrage Valuation of Securitizable Assets) *If the pools $S_n$ are traded at prices $p_n$, assuming $\frac{K_n p_0 - p_n}{1-\delta_n} \leq K_n$, then for all $j \in [1..J]$,*

$$V^-\left(Y_j\right) = p_0 - \left(1 - \delta_{n(j)}\right) \wedge \left(K_n p_0 - p_n\right).$$

*If only the entire pool $S_N$ is traded, assuming $\sum_{n\in[1..N]}(1-\delta_n)K_n - Jp_0 + p_N \geq 0$, then for all $j \in [1..J]$,*

$$V^-\left(Y_j\right) = p_0 - \left(1 - \delta_{n(j)}\right) \wedge \left(Jp_0 - p_N\right),$$

*and*

$$V^-\left(\sum_{j\in G_n} Y_j\right) = K_n p_0 - \left(1-\delta_n\right) K_n \wedge \left(Jp_0 - p_N\right).$$

In order to show these results, we will use the following lemma.

**Lemma 7.5** *Define $L \subset [1..J]$ a non-empty set and $A$ and $(\alpha)_{j\in[1..J]}$ such that $0 \leq A \leq \sum_{j\notin L} \alpha_j + \beta|L|$, and such that $\forall l \in L$, $\alpha_k = \beta$. The solution $m^*$ to the following program*

$$\max_{(m_j)_{j\in[1..J]}} \sum_{l\in L} m_l$$

$$\forall j \in [1..J], m_j \in [0,1]$$

$$\sum_{1\leq j\leq J} \alpha_j m_j = A$$

*verifies $\sum_{l\in L} m_l^* = \frac{A}{\beta} \wedge |L|$.*

***Proof*** Note that thanks to the assumptions,

$$\sum_{1\leq j\leq J} \alpha_j m_j = \sum_{j\in L} \alpha_j m_j + \sum_{j\notin L} \alpha_j m_j = \beta \sum_{j\in L} m_j + \sum_{j\notin L} \alpha_j m_j.$$

We can rewrite the program

$$\max_{(m_j)_{j\in[1..J]}} \sum_{l\in L} m_l$$
$$\forall j \in [1..J], m_j \in [0, 1]$$
$$\sum_{l\in L} m_l = \frac{1}{\beta}\left(A - \sum_{j\notin L} \alpha_j m_j\right).$$

If $\frac{A}{\beta} > |L|$, then since $A \leq \sum_{j\notin L} \alpha_j$, $(m_j^*)_{j\notin L}$ can be set so that $\frac{1}{\beta}\left(A - \sum_{j\notin L} \alpha_j m_j\right) = |L|$, and for all $l \in L$, $m_l^* = 1$ is feasible. If $\frac{A}{\beta} \leq |L|$, then the program can be directly solved by setting $m_l^* = 0$ for all $l \notin L$.

The term $\sum_{l\in L} m_l^*$ hence verifies $\sum_{l\in L} m_l^* = \frac{A}{\beta} \wedge |L|$. □

We can now turn to the proof of Proposition 7.7.

***Proof*** We begin by characterizing the linear pricing measures that are consistent with the prices given on the pooled assets in the two cases, either a series of $p_n$ or a single $p_N$.

Any pricing measure $q$ consistent with the prices $p_n$ verifies for all $n \in [1..N]$

$$\begin{aligned} p_n &= \mathbb{E}_q\left[\sum_{j\in G_n} Y_j\right] \\ &= \mathbb{E}_q\left[\sum_{j\in G_n} (S_0 - 1 + X_j)\right] \\ &= K_n(p_0 - 1) + \sum_{j\in G_n} \mathbb{E}_q\left[X_j\right] \\ &= K_n(p_0 - 1) + \sum_{j\in G_n} \left(\delta_n \pi_{q,j}^X + (1 - \pi_{q,j}^X)\right). \end{aligned}$$

The condition for the measure $q_s$ to be a pricing measure consistent with $p_n$, hence, writes

$$\sum_{j\in G_n} \pi_{q_s,j}^X = \frac{K_n p_0 - p_n}{1 - \delta_n}.$$

Thanks to the assumption that $\frac{K_n p_0 - p_n}{1-\delta_n} \leq K_n$, then $\sum_{j\in G_n} \pi_{q_s,j}^X \leq K_n$, and hence is possible with $\pi_{q_s,j}^X \in [0, 1]$ for all $j \in G_n$. We define $\mathbb{M}_s$ as the set of all pricing measures verifying this condition.

Let us now examine the case where a single valuation is provided for the entire pool, $p_N$. We have

$$\begin{aligned} p_N &= \mathbb{E}_q\left[\sum_{j\in[1..J]} Y_j\right] \\ &= J(p_0-1)+\sum_{n\in[1..N]}\sum_{j\in G_n}\mathbb{E}_q\left[X_j\right] \\ &= Jp_0-\sum_{n\in[1..N]}(1-\delta_n)\sum_{j\in G_n}\pi^X_{q,j}, \end{aligned}$$

so the condition for the measure $q_a$ to be a pricing measure consistent with $p_N$ is

$$\sum_{n\in[1..N]}(1-\delta_n)\sum_{j\in G_n}\pi^X_{q_a,j}=Jp_0-p_N.$$

Thanks to the assumption in the proposition, this equality can be verified with $\pi^X_{q_a,j}\in[0,1]$. We define $\mathbb{M}_a$ as the set of all pricing measures verifying this condition.

Thanks to these characterizations, we can now compute the lower value bounds for particular assets. If the pools $S_n$ are traded at prices $p_n$ then for all $k\in[1..J]$, $V^-(Y_k)=\min_{q\in\mathbb{M}_s}\mathbb{E}_q[Y_k]$. We assume $k\in G_n$, so using the characterization of $\mathbb{M}_s$ we have obtained, $V^-(Y_k)$ is equal to

$$\begin{aligned} &\min_{\left(\pi^X_{q_s,j}\right)_{j\in[1..J]}} \quad p_0-(1-\delta_n)\pi^X_{q_s,k} \\ &\forall j\in[1..J],\ \pi^X_{q_s,j}\in[0,1] \\ &\sum_{j\in G_n}\pi^X_{q_s,j}=\frac{K_n p_0-p_n}{1-\delta_n}. \end{aligned}$$

The solution is the same as for

$$\begin{aligned} &\max_{\left(\pi^X_{q_s,j}\right)_{j\in[1..J]}} \quad \pi^X_{q_s,k} \\ &\forall j\in[1..J],\ \pi^X_{q_s,j}\in[0,1] \\ &\sum_{j\in G_n}\pi^X_{q_s,j}=\frac{K_n p_0-p_n}{1-\delta_n}. \end{aligned}$$

We can use Lemma 7.5, setting $L=\{k\}$ and $\alpha_j=1$ and $\beta=1$. The condition $\frac{K_n p_0-p_n}{1-\delta_n}\le K_n$ in the assumptions ensures that $A\le\sum_{j\notin L}\alpha_j+\beta|L|$. We obtain the characterization of the solution:

$$\pi^X_{q_s^*,k}=\frac{K_n p_0-p_n}{1-\delta_n}\wedge 1.$$

Then by substitution we have

$$\begin{aligned} V^-(Y_k) &= p_0 - (1-\delta_{n(k)})\pi^X_{q_s,k} \\ &= p_0 - \left(1-\delta_{n(j)}\right) \wedge (K_n p_0 - p_n) . \end{aligned}$$

We now consider the case where only the total set of pools is traded at price $p_N$. Assuming again that $k \in G_n$, we use the characterization of $\mathbb{M}_a$ to write the value of $V^-(Y_k)$ as

$$\begin{aligned} &\min_{\left(\pi^X_{q_a,j}\right)_{j\in[1..J]}} \quad p_0 - (1-\delta_n)\pi^X_{q_a,k} \\ &\forall j \in [1..J], \pi^X_{q_a,j} \in [0,1] \\ &\sum_{n\in[1..N]} (1-\delta_n) \sum_{j\in G_n} \pi^X_{q_a,j} = J p_0 - p_N . \end{aligned}$$

We apply Lemma 7.5, with $L = \{k\}$ and $\alpha_j = (1-\delta_{n(j)})$ and $\beta = (1-\delta_{n(k)})$. The condition $\sum_{n\in[1..N]}(1-\delta_n)K_n - J p_0 + p_N \geq 0$ ensures that $A \leq \sum_{j\notin L} \alpha_j + \beta|L|$. At the optimum,

$$\pi^X_{q_a^*,k} = \frac{J p_0 - p_N}{1-\delta_n} \wedge 1.$$

Then, substituting in the expression for $V^-(Y_k)$, we obtain the result from the proposition.

The value of $V^-\left(\sum_{l\in G_n} Y_l\right)$ is

$$\begin{aligned} &\min_{\left(\pi^X_{q_a,j}\right)_{j\in[1..J]}} \quad K_n p_0 - (1-\delta_n) \sum_{l\in G_n} \pi^X_{q_a,l} \\ &\forall j \in [1..J], \pi^X_{q_a,j} \in [0,1] \\ &\sum_{n\in[1..N]} (1-\delta_n) \sum_{j\in G_n} \pi^X_{q_a,j} = J p_0 - p_N . \end{aligned}$$

We can apply Lemma 7.5 again, with $\alpha_j = 1-\delta_{n(j)}$ and $\beta = 1-\delta_n$ and $A = J p_0 - p_N$, and $L = G_n$. At the optimum, we have

$$\sum_{l\in G_n} \pi^X_{q_a^*,j} = \frac{J p_0 - p_N}{1-\delta_n} \wedge K_n .$$

Hence, $V^-\left(\sum_{l\in G_n} Y_l\right) = K_n p_0 - (J p_0 - p_N) \wedge K_n(1-\delta_n)$. □

The proposition verifies that in the securitization model with a single market price for all assets together $p_N$, the lower bound valuation of a pool of assets is greater than the sum of the assets' lower bound values:

$$V^-\left(\sum_{j\in G_n} Y_j\right) \geq \sum_{j\in G_n} V^-(Y_j) .$$

While there would be more value in grouping these projects than otherwise, this does not tell us if it would be beneficial for the originators, because it depends on the cost of originating the assets. We will now look into a precise definition of pooling and the conditions in which it will take place, in the general model of Gaur et al.

The Value of Pooling
We say there is value to pooling if there exists a linear combination of assets $(\alpha_j)_{j\in[1..J]}$ such that $\alpha_j \in [0,1]$ for all $j$ so that $V^-\left(\sum_{j=1}^J \alpha_j Y_j\right) \geq \sum_{j=1}^J \alpha_j r_j$ and $\alpha_j > 0$ and $V^-(Y_j) < r_j$ for at least one $j$. This condition says that even if at least one firm is strictly losing in investing in its project, still one can create a pool so that in aggregate all firms in the pool benefit. Given this definition, we have the following result.

**Proposition 7.8** (Gaur–Seshadri–Subrahmanyam Value to Pooling) *If there is $q \in \mathbb{M}$ such that for all $j \in [1..J]$, $r_j \geq \mathbb{E}_q[Y_j]$ then value cannot be created by pooling the $Y_j$. If there is no $q \in \mathbb{M}$ such that for all $j \in [1..J]$, $r_j \geq \mathbb{E}_q[Y_j]$, then value can be created by pooling the $Y_j$.*

***Proof*** To prove the first part of the proposition, we will show that if value can be created by pooling, then there exists no $q \in \mathbb{M}$ such that for all $j \in [1..J]$, $r_j \geq \mathbb{E}_q[Y_j]$.

We consider now the determination of the optimal set of weights given the projects $Y_j$, so that the value of these projects minus the total reservation prices is maximal. This expression uses the fact that the value of the asset pool is defined as $V^-\left(\sum_{j=1}^J \alpha_j Y_j\right)$, which in turn thanks to Lemma 7.4 can be written as the minimum value across all linear pricing measures $q_l$, $l \in [1..L]$. The value of the pool $v$ and the optimal weights $\alpha$ can be expressed as solutions to the following linear program:

$$\max_{v\in\mathbb{R}^+,(\alpha_j)_{j\in[1..J]}} \quad v - \sum_{j=1}^J \alpha_j r_j$$

$$\forall j \in [1..J], \alpha_j \in [0,1]$$

$$\forall l \in [1..L], -\mathbb{E}_{q_l}\left[\sum_{j=1}^J \alpha_j Y_j\right] + v \leq 0.$$

If value can be created by pooling, based on our definition, then there exist weights $\alpha$ such that the linear program is feasible and $v - \sum_{j=1}^J \alpha_j r_j > 0$. We assume this is the case.

Let $\theta_l \geq 0$ be a set of weights such that $\sum_{l=1}^L \theta_l = 1$. Then, we multiply all the last $L$ constraints by the corresponding $\theta_l$, and sum. We obtain

$$-\sum_{l=1}^L \theta_l \mathbb{E}_{q_l}\left[\sum_{j=1}^J \alpha_j Y_j\right] + v \leq 0.$$

Note that $q = \sum_{l=1}^{L} \theta_l q_l$ is a linear pricing measure. Since the $\theta$ are arbitrary, it is an arbitrary linear pricing measure and the set of all such pricing measures necessarily contains $\mathbb{M}$. The arbitrary pricing measure can therefore be chosen in $\mathbb{M}$ arbitrarily.

Also, we have thanks to our assumption:

$$\mathbb{E}_q\left[\sum_{j=1}^{J} \alpha_j Y_j\right] \geq v > \sum_{j=1}^{J} \alpha_j r_j.$$

For this inequality to be true, there must exist $j$ such that $r_j < \mathbb{E}_q\left[Y_j\right]$. Hence, we have shown that if there is value to pooling then there are no pricing measures $q$ in $\mathbb{M}$ such that for all $j \in [1..J]$, $r_j \geq \mathbb{E}_q\left[Y_j\right]$, and the first part of the proposition is proved.

Now to prove the second part of the proposition, we consider the dual linear program. We write $\mu_l$ the variables corresponding to the last $L$ constraints.

$$\min_{(\mu_l)_{l\in[1..L]}} \quad 0$$

$$\sum_{l=1}^{L} \mu_l = 1$$

$$\forall l \in [1..L], \mu_l \geq 0$$

$$\forall j \in [1..J], \sum_{l=1}^{L} \mu_l \mathbb{E}_{q_l}[Y_j] \leq r_j.$$

We need to show that if no value can be created by pooling, then there exists $q \in \mathbb{M}$ such that $\mathbb{E}_q[Y_j] \leq r_j$ for all $j \in [1..J]$.

First, note that the primal problem is feasible, since one can find a solution setting all the $\alpha_n$ to zero, and in that case $v$ is also zero. Hence, the solution to the primal problem is bounded below at zero. Also, since the dual's solution is 0, then if the dual is feasible and the primal has a bounded solution, then that solution is zero. This corresponds to the case where no value can be created by pooling, since then $v - \sum_{j=1}^{J} \alpha_j r_j = 0$. Hence, if no value can be created by pooling then the primal has a bounded solution and the dual is feasible.

If the dual problem is feasible, it means that there exist weights $\mu_l$ so that under the pricing measure $b = \sum_{l=1}^{J} \mu_l q_l$, for all $j$ we have $\mathbb{E}_b[Y_j] \leq r_j$. Therefore, if no value can be created by pooling then this condition is verified, and the second part of the proposition is proved. □

The proposition tells us what the conditions are so that there would be value in pooling. We can see now that in the securitized assets illustrative model, pooling will be beneficial, and assets will be created, as far as the prices that are given by the market on the pools it trades are above the aggregate production cost.

**Proposition 7.9** (No-Arbitrage Pooling Conditions for Securitizable Assets) *If prices $p_n$ are provided for pooled securities $S_n$, then if for some $n_0$ $p_{n_0} \geq \sum_{j \in G_{n_0}} (1 + y_j)$ then value can be created by pooling. If only a price $p_N$ is provided for the whole set of assets, then if $p_N \geq \sum_{j \in [1..J]}(1 + y_j)$ then value can be created by pooling.*

***Proof*** According to Proposition 7.8, in order to show this proposition we need to find conditions so that no measure $q \in \mathbb{M}$ exists such that for all $j \in [1..J]$ $1 + y_j \geq \mathbb{E}_q[Y_j]$.

For the first part of the proposition, a measure $q_s \in \mathbb{M}_s$ would need to satisfy all the conditions $1 + y_j \geq \mathbb{E}_{q_s}[Y_j]$ in order for no value to be created by pooling. Assume for some $n_0$ we have $p_{n_0} \geq \sum_{j \in G_{n_0}} (1 + y_j)$. By definition, this is equivalent to $\sum_{j \in G_{n_0}} \left(\mathbb{E}_{q_s}\left[Y_j\right] - (1 + y_j)\right) \geq 0$, and hence there exists some $j \in G_{n_0}$ such that $\mathbb{E}_{q_s}\left[Y_j\right] \geq (1 + y_j)$. Hence, there is no measure $q_s$ that verifies the conditions.

For the second part of the proposition, we assume $p_N \geq \sum_{j \in [1..J]}(1 + y_j)$. We write $p_N$ as an expectation under a pricing measure $q_a \in \mathbb{M}_a$, so the inequality becomes $\mathbb{E}_{q_a}\left[\sum_{j \in [1..J]} Y_j\right] \geq \sum_{j \in [1..J]}(1 + y_j)$. Hence, there must be some $j$ such that $\mathbb{E}_{q_a}\left[Y_j\right] \geq 1 + y_j$ and as a consequence there is no measure satisfying the conditions of Proposition 7.8, and there is value in pooling. □

Propositions 7.8 and 7.9 tell us that value may be created by pooling but do not characterize how much value, and which assets would be grouped together. For pooling to take place, it has to be optimal for a group of issuers at the same time. This will be analyzed as a cooperative game.

The Pooling Game

We now look into the relationship between reservation prices and the incentives that the originators will have in having their cash flows pooled in a particular way. We will consider a cooperative game where originators can form coalitions, and benefit from the pooling of their cash flows within that coalition. We write $J_w$ a subset of all firms $[1..J]$ where each firm $j$ contributes a fraction $w_j \in [0, 1]$ of its cash flows, with a proportional reservation price $w_j r_j$. We write the complement $J_w^c = J - J_w$, where the contribution of each firm $j$ is $(1 - w_j)Y_j$ with reservation price $(1 - w_j)r_j$. We write $Y(J_w) = \sum_{j \in J_w} w_j Y_j$.

In the coalition game, the value of a coalition $V(J_w)$ is defined as $V^-(Y(J_w))$. In all generality, we allow coalitions to be formed with fractional assets. We will consider that there is a solution to this game if the grand coalition of all firms together cannot be blocked. Recall that the **core** of a cooperative game is the set of feasible allocations that cannot be further improved by a subset of the agents.

We have the following proposition.

**Proposition 7.10** (Gaur–Seshadri–Subrahmanyam Pooling Coalition Value) *If for all $j \in [1..J]$, $r_j \leq V^-(Y_j)$ then the core of the game is not empty. In addition, there* *is a solution in the core such that the payments to all firms exceed their reservation prices if and only if for every subset $J_w$ of $J$ we have*

$$V(J) \geq V(J_w) \vee \sum_{j \subset J_w} w_j r_j + V(J_w^c) \vee \sum_{j \subset J_w} (1 - w_j) r_j.$$

***Proof*** In order to show the result, we first only consider partitions $w_j \in \{0, 1\}$ and later generalize to fractional partitions. With this assumption, the cash flows can be simply written as $\sum_{j \in J_w} Y_j$, with reservation price $\sum_{j \in J_w} r_j$.

We first prove the first part of the proposition that the core of the game is not empty. We assume that for all $j$, $r_j \leq V^-(Y_j)$.

Consider the valuation of the portfolio constituted of the assets in coalition $J_w$ as the highest value of a replication portfolio based on primary securities:

$$\max_{(\beta_n)_{n \in [1..N]}} \sum_{n=1}^{N} \beta_n p_n$$

$$\forall k \in [1..K], \sum_{n=1}^{N} \beta_n S_n(\omega_k) \leq \sum_{j \in J_w} Y_j(\omega_k)$$

$$\forall n \in [1..N], \beta_n \geq 0.$$

The dual of this linear program is

$$\min_{(\lambda_k)_{k \in [1..K]}} \sum_{k=1}^{K} \lambda_k \sum_{j \in J_w} Y_j(\omega_k)$$

$$\forall n \in [1..N], \sum_{k=1}^{K} \lambda_k S_n(\omega_k) \geq p_n$$

$$\forall k \in [1..K], \lambda_k \geq 0.$$

Note that the constraints of the dual do not depend on the specific coalition. In addition, the dual is feasible since setting $\lambda$ to any $q \in \mathbb{M}$ will satisfy the constraints, as $q$ is a linear pricing measure and $\sum_{k=1}^{K} q_k S_n(\omega_k) = p_n$. Also, since $Y_j \geq 0$ and $\lambda \geq 0$, the solution is finite and bounded by zero below. Finally, since the program is a minimization and $S_n \geq 0$, the first constraints are saturated at the optimum: for all $n \in [1..N]$, $\sum_{k=1}^{K} \lambda_k S_n(\omega_k) = p_n$.

We assume that we solve the dual problem for the grand coalition $J$ and obtain $(\lambda_k^*)_{k \in [1..K]}$. Since $\sum_{k=1}^{K} \lambda_k^* S_n(\omega_k) = p_n$ and $\lambda_k^* > 0$, $\lambda^*$ is a linear pricing measure and belongs to the closure $\overline{\mathbb{M}}$.

It is now possible to propose a solution to the cooperative game: each firm $j$ receives the payment $\sum_{k=1}^{K} \lambda_k^* Y_j(\omega_k)$, that is, the expectation of $Y_j$ under the pricing measure $\lambda^*$. By definition, this payment is greater than $V^-(Y_j)$. Also, because of our assumption, $V^-(Y_j) \geq r_j$, and hence the payment is greater than $r_j$. In the grand coalition, the firms belonging to a subset $J_w$ receive in total the sum of the payments $\sum_{j \in J_w} \mathbb{E}_{\lambda^*}[Y_j]$. For the grand coalition to be stable, this payment needs to be greater than the payment that this subset would obtain by forming their own coalition, that is, $\sum_{j \in J_w} \mathbb{E}_{\lambda^*_w}[Y_j]$ where we write $\lambda^*_w$ the solution to the linear program where the objective function applies to $J_w$. To show that the core of the game is not empty, we therefore need to show that

$$\sum_{j \in J_w} \mathbb{E}_{\lambda^*}[Y_j] \geq \sum_{j \in J_w} \mathbb{E}_{\lambda^*_w}[Y_j].$$

Consider the dual problem for the subset $J_w$. By definition $\sum_{j \in J_w} \mathbb{E}_{\lambda^*_w}[Y_j]$ is the solution to that minimization problem. However, the constraints of the dual do not depend on the subset $J_w$, but only the objective function, so $\lambda^*$ satisfies the constraints for the dual problem with any coalition $J_w$. Hence, $\sum_{j \in J_w} \mathbb{E}_{\lambda^*}[Y_j]$ is the value of the objective function for a particular set of values $\lambda^*$. Since $\lambda^*_w$ is the minimum argument, the inequality is proved. Hence, the possible solution we have proposed cannot be improved by a subset of the agents, and the core contains the grand allocation.

To prove the second part of the proposition, we need to demonstrate that there exists a payment scheme that works for all coalitions simultaneously. We alter the definition of the value of a coalition in order to reflect the reservation prices: $V(J_w) = V^-(J_w) \vee \sum_{j \in J_w} r_j$. We first show that when the condition in the proposition is verified for a partition of $J$ with two subsets, then it is verified for a partition of arbitrary length.

Assume that the condition does not hold for some partition $J_1, J_2, \ldots, J_r$ of $J$, that is,

$$V(J) < \sum_{i=1}^{r} \left( V^-(J_i) \vee \sum_{j \in J_i} r_j \right).$$

For each $i$, the value of the coalition $V(J_i)$ may be equal to the lower bound or to the reservation prices, so we separate the indices without loss of generality: for $i \in [1..h]$, we have $V(J_i) = V^-(J_i)$ and for $i \in [h+1..r]$ we have $V(J_i) = \sum_{j \in J_i} r_j$. Now note that $V^-$ is super-additive, as for claims $X$ and $Y$, $V^-(X+Y) \geq V^-(X) + V^-(Y)$. Hence, we have

$$V^- \left( \bigcup_{i=1}^{h} J_i \right) \geq \sum_{i=1}^{h} V^-(J_i).$$

Let us write $J_w = \bigcup_{i=1}^{h} J_i$, so that $J_w^c = \bigcup_{i=h+1}^{r} J_i$. Then, if the condition in the proposition applicable to any partition with two elements is true, then $V(J) \geq V(J_w) + V(J_w^c)$. Hence,

$$V(J) \geq \sum_{i=1}^{h} V^-(J_i) + \sum_{j=h+1}^{r} \sum_{j \in J_i} r_j,$$

and this term is also equal to $\sum_{i=1}^{r} V^{-}(J_i) \vee \sum_{j \in J_i} r_j$, itself assumed to be strictly greater than $V(J)$. We have thus arrived to a contradiction, and this proves that if the proposition condition is verified then it is also true for any partition of size greater than two.

In any solution to the cooperation game, the grand coalition therefore offers a greater value than that of any set of partitions, since each coalition $J_w$ gets at least $V^{-}(J_w) \vee \sum_{j \in J_w} r_j$. While we have shown this is true given any coalition, it needs to be shown to be true for all coalitions at the same time.

We define the following primal linear program:

$$\begin{aligned} &\min_{(\pi_j)_{j \in [1..J]}} \quad 0 \\ &\forall J_w \subseteq J, \sum_{j \in J_w} \pi_j \geq V(J_w) \\ &\sum_{j=1}^{J} \pi_j = V(J) \\ &\forall j \in [1..J], \pi_j \geq 0. \end{aligned}$$

This program, if it is feasible, defines the simultaneous payments $\pi_j$ to all the firms, so that the total payment is the value of the grand coalition, and the sum of payments is greater or equal to the value to each subcoalition.

The dual problem is

$$\begin{aligned} &\max_{\lambda \in \mathbb{R}, (\lambda_{J_w})_{J_w \subseteq J}} \sum_{J_w \subseteq J} \lambda_{j_w} V(J_w) + \lambda V(J) \\ &\forall j \in [1..J], \sum_{J_w \subseteq J} \mathbb{I}_{j \in J_w} \lambda_{j_w} + \lambda \leq 0 \\ &\forall J_w \subseteq J, \lambda_{J_w} \geq 0. \end{aligned}$$

The variables $(\lambda_{J_w})_{J_w \subseteq J}$ correspond to the series of constraints in the primal program, while $\lambda$ corresponds to the equality constraint. The dual is feasible, since setting all variables to 0 verifies the constraints. The dual solution will equal zero if the primal is feasible, since the primal's solution is zero. Therefore, one must have $\lambda \leq 0$ for there to be a bounded solution on the dual. Indeed, the dual could be unbounded if the solution is above 0, as the variables can be arbitrarily scaled.

Therefore, if we show that there is a bounded solution to the dual, then its solution is 0 and the primal is feasible, and there exist payments to all firms at the same time so that the grand coalition is more attractive than sub-coalitions.

Note that

$$\sum_{J_w \subseteq J} \mathbb{I}_{1 \in J_w} \lambda_{j_w} V(J_w) \leq \sum_{J_w \subseteq J} \mathbb{I}_{1 \in J_w} \lambda_{j_w} \max\{V(J_w) : 1 \in J_w, J_w \subseteq J\}.$$

Therefore, if we multiply the first constraint of the dual by $\lambda V(J) \geq \lambda \max\{V(J_w) : 1 \in J_w, J_w \subseteq J\}$, we obtain

$$\sum_{J_w \subseteq J} \mathbb{I}_{1 \in J_w} \lambda_{j_w} V(J_w) + \lambda \max\{V(J_w) : 1 \in J_w, J_w \subseteq J\} \leq 0.$$

More generally, we can multiply every constraint for $j$ by

$$\max\{V(J_w) : j \in J_w, \forall i \in [1..j-1], i \in J_w^c, J_w \subseteq J, J_w^c \subseteq J\},$$

we obtain

$$\sum_{j \in J_w, \forall i \in [1..j-1], i \in J_w^c, J_w \subseteq J, J_w^c \subseteq J} \mathbb{I}_{j \in J_w} \lambda_{j_w} V(J_w)$$
$$+ \lambda \max\{V(J_w) : j \in J_w, \forall i \in [1..j-1], i \in J_w^c, J_w \subseteq J, J_w^c \subseteq J\} \leq 0.$$

The sets $A_j = \{j \in J_w, \forall i \in [1..j-1], i \in J_w^c, J_w \subseteq J, J_w^c \subseteq J\}$ are disjoint and $\bigcup_{j=1}^J A_j = J$ and therefore adding the inequalities across all $j \in [1..J]$ yields

$$\sum_{J_w \subseteq J} \lambda_{j_w} V(J_w) + \lambda \sum_{j=1}^{J} \max\{V(J_w) : j \in A_j\} \leq 0.$$

However, due to super-additivity, we know that $V(J) \geq \sum_{j=1}^J \max\{V(J_w) : j \in A_j\}$, so that

$$\sum_{J_w \subseteq J} \lambda_{j_w} V(J_w) + \lambda V(J) \leq 0.$$

This shows that the dual's objective function is bounded above, and since it is a maximization then the linear program's solution is bounded. Hence, the primal problem has a feasible solution, and there exists an allocation such that the grand coalition is stable.

The proof was given for weights $w_j \in \{0, 1\}$. If we consider that the $w_j$ could be fractional, then the same proof would still apply, by treating each fractional exposure to an asset as an asset itself. □

While it is positive to be able to characterize the cases where originators will have an interest in pooling, one issue with Proposition 7.10 is that verifying the second condition for every possible partition, including those using fractional weights, is difficult.

However, it is possible to show that an easier set of conditions are equivalent to the ones from that proposition.

**Proposition 7.11** (Gaur–Seshadri–Subrahmanyam Simpler Conditions for Pooling Coalition) *Let $q \in \mathbb{M}$ be a pricing measure such that $\sum_{j=1}^{J} \mathbb{E}_q[Y_j] = V^-\left(\sum_{j=1}^{J} Y_j\right)$. If $\mathbb{E}_q[Y_j] \geq r_j$ for all $j \in [1..J]$, then the second condition of Proposition 7.10 is verified, and the opposite is true as well.*

***Proof*** We first show the sufficiency part of the proposition. Assume that$q \in \mathbb{M}$ is a pricing measure such that $\sum_{j=1}^{J} \mathbb{E}_q[Y_j] = V^-\left(\sum_{j=1}^{J} Y_j\right)$, and $\mathbb{E}_q[Y_j] \geq r_j$ for all $j \in [1..J]$. We consider a fractional partition with two elements, such that one coalition pools $\sum_{j=1}^{J} w_j Y_j$ and the other pools $\sum_{j=1}^{J}(1-w_j)Y_j$, with reservation prices of $\sum_{j=1}^{J} w_j r_j$ and $\sum_{j=1}^{J}(1-w_j)r_j$, respectively.

By assumption, $\sum_{j=1}^{J} \mathbb{E}_q[w_j Y_j] \geq \sum_{j=1}^{J} w_j r_j$, and due to the definition of $V^-$, we infer that $\sum_{j=1}^{J} \mathbb{E}_q[w_j Y_j] \geq V^-\left(\sum_{j=1}^{J} w_j Y_j\right)$, and as a consequence of both inequalities,

$$\sum_{j=1}^{J} \mathbb{E}_q[w_j Y_j] \geq V^-\left(\sum_{j=1}^{J} w_j Y_j\right) \vee \sum_{j=1}^{J} w_j r_j.$$

With the same logic, we also get

$$\sum_{j=1}^{J} \mathbb{E}_q[(1-w_j)Y_j] \geq V^-\left(\sum_{j=1}^{J}(1-w_j)Y_j\right) \vee \sum_{j=1}^{J}(1-w_j)r_j.$$

Adding both inequalities, and using the assumption that $\sum_{j=1}^{J} \mathbb{E}_q[Y_j] = V^-\left(\sum_{j=1}^{J} Y_j\right)$, we have:

$$V^-\left(\sum_{j=1}^{J} Y_j\right) \geq V^-\left(\sum_{j=1}^{J} w_j Y_j\right) \vee \sum_{j=1}^{J} w_j r_j + V^-\left(\sum_{j=1}^{J}(1-w_j)Y_j\right) \vee \sum_{j=1}^{J}(1-w_j)r_j.$$

Since the $w_j$ were arbitrary, we have shown that

$$V(J) \geq V(J_w) \vee \sum_{j \in J_w} w_j r_j + V(J_w^c) \vee \sum_{j \in J_w}(1-w_j)r_j,$$

and this concludes the proof of the sufficiency of the condition.

Now we turn to the proof of the necessity. We assume that the solution where $w_j = 1$ for all $j$ is in the core, but the condition in the proposition does not hold: for each $q \in \mathbb{M}$ such that $\sum_{j=1}^{J} \mathbb{E}_q[Y_j] = V^-\left(\sum_{j=1}^{J} Y_j\right)$, there exists $j$ such that $\mathbb{E}_q[Y_j] < r_j$.

Now we consider the following linear program, which looks for the optimal weights $w_j$ of all assets, if the originators can produce these assets at the reservation prices, such that the value of the pool is highest:

$$\max_{v \in \mathbb{R}, (w_j)_{j \in [1..J]}} \quad v - \sum_{j=1}^{J} w_j r_j$$

$$\forall l \in [1..L], v - \sum_{j=1}^{J} w_j \mathbb{E}_{q_l}[Y_j] \leq 0$$
$$\forall j \in [1..J], w_j \leq 1$$
$$\forall j \in [1..J], w_j \geq 0.$$

The dual of this linear program writes

$$\min_{(\gamma_j)_{j \in [1..J]}, (\lambda_l)_{l \in [1..L]}} \sum_{j=1}^{J} \gamma_j$$

$$\sum_{l=1}^{L} \lambda_l = 1$$

$$\forall j \in [1..J], -\sum_{l=1}^{L} \lambda_l \mathbb{E}_{q_l}[Y_j] + \gamma_j \geq -r_j$$
$$\forall j \in [1..J], \gamma_j \geq 0$$
$$\forall l \in [1..L], \lambda_l \geq 0.$$

We suppose this dual is solved by $\lambda^*$ and $\gamma^*$. Define $q^* \in \overline{\mathbb{M}}$ such that $q^* = \sum_{l=1}^{L} \lambda_l q_l$. We have assumed earlier that the solution with $w_j = 1$ was in the core, so the optimal solution of the primal linear program must be $w_j^* = 1$ for all $j \in [1..J]$, in which case we also obtain $v^* = V^-\left(\sum_{j=1}^{J} Y_j\right) - \sum_{j=1}^{J} r_j$. In addition, since the second constraints are binding in the primal (the $w_j$ are 1), the corresponding constraints in the dual are also binding for all $j$ at the optimum. Hence, for all $j \in [1..J]$, $\gamma_j^* = \mathbb{E}_{q^*}[Y_j] - r_j$, and since the $\gamma^*$ are constrained to be positive, we have $\mathbb{E}_{q^*}[Y_j] \geq r_j$. Therefore, the optimal solution to the dual is $\mathbb{E}_{q^*}\left[\sum_{j=1}^{J} Y_j\right] - \sum_{j=1}^{J} r_j$.

Since the primal problem has the same solution as the dual, we infer that the optimal value $v^*$ solution to the primal program is also equal to $\mathbb{E}_{q^*}\left[\sum_{j=1}^{J} Y_j\right] - \sum_{j=1}^{J} r_j$, and therefore

$$\mathbb{E}_{q^*}\left[\sum_{j=1}^{J} Y_j\right] = V^-\left(\sum_{j=1}^{J} Y_j\right).$$

By assumption, this implies that there must be some firm $i$ for which $\mathbb{E}_{q^*}[Y_j] < r_j$, but that is a contradiction since all these constraints must be binding in the dual. Therefore, we have proved the necessity in the proposition. □

The proposition shows that there are payment schemes so that all firms are willing to participate in pooling, so the next step is to determine what exactly these payment schemes are. While there may be many schemes, we will require an optimal scheme for our analysis to be fair, or in other words such that all firms are paid the same amount in the scheme for the same cash flow contribution. Therefore, the payment should be defined as a linear pricing measure. The following proposition shows us how to define such a pricing measure.

**Proposition 7.12** (Gaur–Seshadri–Subrahmanyam Pooling Pricing Measure) *If there exists a pricing measure $q_p \in Q$ with $q_p \notin \mathbb{M}$, or a linear combination of such measures, such that $\sum_{j=1}^{J} \mathbb{E}_{q_p}[Y_j] = V^-\left(\sum_{j=1}^{J} Y_j\right)$, and $r_j \leq \mathbb{E}_{q_p}[Y_j]$ for all $j \in [1..J]$, then the grand coalition of all firms can be sustained when firm $j$ is paid $\mathbb{E}_{q_p}[Y_j]$.*

***Proof*** Thanks to Lemma 7.4 we know, we can find $q \in Q$ so that $\mathbb{E}_{q_p}[W] = V^-(W)$ with $W = \sum_{j=1}^{J} Y_j$, and if there are more than one $q$ for which this is true, then it is also true for any linear combination of them with positive weights summing up to 1. Hence, we know that one can find such a measure $q_p$.

We know that if for all $j$ we have $r_j \leq \mathbb{E}_{q_p}[Y_j]$ then $r_j \leq V^-(Y_j)$. Hence, thanks to Proposition 7.10, the core of the game is not empty, that is, there exists a set of feasible allocations that cannot be further improved by a subset of the agents. For the grand allocation to be sustained, its optimization problem must yield the highest value that can be obtained by pooling all the assets, which is $\mathbb{E}_{q_p}\left[\sum_{j=1}^{J} Y_j\right]$. Also, any linear pricing measure so that the grand coalition is in the core must be an optimal dual solution to the problem of determining $V^-\left(\sum_{j=1}^{J} Y_j\right)$.

Since all optimal solutions to the dual problem are obtained as convex combinations of optimal extreme points in $Q$, then one pricing measure can be found so that each firm $j$ gets paid more than $r_j$, and the grand coalition is in the core. □

Note that according to this result, the measure $q_p$ used to determine whether the expectation is above the reservation cost does not depend on the specific project only but on the entire set of projects.

With the conditions of this proposition, all firms will pool all of their assets. However, there may be situations, as characterized by Propositions 7.10 or 7.11 such that some firms may only make fractional contributions, and the choice of optimal amount pooled may not be unique. The following proposition shows that there exists an optimal amount $w_j^*$ that maximizes the value of the pool. In addition, if we consider the $w_j^* Y_j$ as the assets themselves as opposed to the $Y_j$, then the results from Propositions 7.10, 7.11, and 7.12 are applicable.

**Proposition 7.13** (Gaur–Seshadri–Subrahmanyam Optimal Pooling Fraction) *If the conditions in the second part of Proposition 7.8 are verified, then the value of pooling is maximized by solving*

$$\max_{(w_j)_{j\in[1..J]}} \quad V^-\left(\sum_{j=1}^{J} w_j Y_j\right) - \sum_{j=1}^{J} w_j r_j$$

$$\forall j \in [1..J], 0 \leq w_j \leq 1.$$

*An optimal solution of this program exists in the core of the pooling game. The assets of firms whose value is higher than the corresponding reservation price will be fully included in the pool. Also, the remaining cash flows* $(1 - w_j^*)Y_j$ *do not give any value in pooling.*

***Proof*** The expression is the highest surplus over the reservation price, so it is the highest value that can be achieved by pooling, while ensuring that all reservation prices are met.

Set $q$ a pricing measure under which the pooled assets reach their minimum value, that is, $\mathbb{E}_q\left[\sum_{j=1}^{J} w_j^* Y_j\right] = V^-\left(\sum_{j=1}^{J} w_j^* Y_j\right)$. Then if asset $j$ is at a strictly positive allocation in the pool then $\mathbb{E}_q[Y_j] > r_j$; otherwise, it would be more optimal to set its allocation to zero. In addition, the assets $w_j^* Y_j$ verify the conditions of Proposition 7.11.

Since the $w^*$ are optimal, then the expected value of the unpooled assets must be below the reservation price, and hence thanks to Proposition 7.8, they do not have any value in pooling. □

Propositions 7.11 and 7.13 are consistent because if for all $j$ we have $\mathbb{E}_{q_p}[Y_j] \geq r_j$ then setting $w_j^* = 1$ gives an optimal solution to the optimization problem in Proposition 7.13.

The grand coalition achieves the highest value in pooling in certain conditions, and it includes all the assets when further specific conditions are verified, and only fractional assets otherwise. We have also shown that a linear pricing measure can define the optimal payments.

We apply a further simplification of the securitized assets illustration model, by considering only two groups $G_1$ and $G_2$ representing loans with different credit risks, so $K_1 + K_2 = J$, with $\delta_1 > \delta_2$, and different origination costs $y_1$ and $y_2$.

We assume that the loans in the second group cannot be originated at a gain relative to the aggregate price so that $\frac{p_N}{J} < 1 + y_2$. We also assume that $\frac{p_N}{J} > \frac{K_1}{J}(1 + y_1) + \frac{K_2}{J}(1 + y_2)$, and hence according to Proposition 7.9 there is value in pooling. Finally, the size of the good loans bucket is assumed to be large enough, so that $K_1 \geq \frac{(K_1+K_2)p_0 - p_N}{1-\delta_1}$.

Since all the assets that belong within each group $G_1$ or $G_2$ have the same characteristics, there is no reason to expect they would be treated differently in any optimal pooling. Hence, we will only consider two fractional pooling parameters $w_1$ and $w_2$.

Besides, because of our assumptions on costs, we will only consider the case where $w_1 > w_2$.

**Proposition 7.14** (No-Arbitrage Optimal Pooling of Securitizable Assets) *With our assumptions, the optimal pooling in the core of the pooling game will involve all the assets of group 1 if* $p_N \geq K_2 p_0 + (1 + y_1)K_1$ *and none otherwise, and if* $p_0 \geq 1 + y_2$ *all the assets of group 2 and none otherwise.*

***Proof*** We first calculate $V^-\left(w_1 \sum_{j\in G_1} Y_j + w_2 \sum_{j\in G_1} Y_j\right)$ by definition as

$$\min_{\left(\pi^X_{q_a,j}\right)_{j\in[1..J]}} \quad (w_1 K_1 + w_2 K_2)p_0 - w_1(1-\delta_1)\sum_{j\in G_1} \pi^X_{q_a,j} - w_2(1-\delta_2)\sum_{j\in G_2} \pi^X_{q_a,j}$$

$$\forall j \in [1..J], \pi^X_{q_a,j} \in [0,1]$$

$$(1-\delta_1)\sum_{j\in G_1} \pi^X_{q_a,j} + (1-\delta_2)\sum_{j\in G_2} \pi^X_{q_a,j} = (K_1 + K_2)p_0 - p_N.$$

The solution to this program is the same as

$$\max_{\left(\pi^X_{q_a,j}\right)_{j\in[1..J]}} \quad w_1(1-\delta_1)\sum_{j\in G_1} \pi^X_{q_a,j} + w_2(1-\delta_2)\sum_{j\in G_2} \pi^X_{q_a,j}$$

$$\forall j \in [1..J], \pi^X_{q_a,j} \in [0,1]$$

$$(1-\delta_1)\sum_{j\in G_1} \pi^X_{q_a,j} = (K_1 + K_2)p_0 - p_N - (1-\delta_2)\sum_{j\in G_2} \pi^X_{q_a,j}.$$

By substitution, it has the same solution as

$$\max_{\left(\pi^X_{q_a,j}\right)_{j\in[1..J]}} \quad (w_2 - w_1)(1-\delta_2)\sum_{j\in G_2} \pi^X_{q_a,j}$$

$$\forall j \in [1..J], \pi^X_{q_a,j} \in [0,1]$$

$$(1-\delta_1)\sum_{j\in G_1} \pi^X_{q_a,j} = (K_1 + K_2)p_0 - p_N - (1-\delta_2)\sum_{j\in G_2} \pi^X_{q_a,j}.$$

Since $w_2 - w_1$, and by assumption $K_1(1-\delta_1) \geq (K_1 + K_2)p_0 - p_N$, a solution with for all $j \in G_2$ $\pi^X_{q_a^*,j} = 0$ and $(1-\delta_1)\sum_{j\in G_1} \pi^X_{q_a^*,j} = (K_1 + K_2)p_0 - p_N$ is feasible.

Substituting the optimum probabilities into the original expression, we have

$$
\begin{aligned}
V^{-} & \left( w_1 \sum_{j \in G_1} Y_j + w_2 \sum_{j \in G_1} Y_j \right) \\
&= (w_1 K_1 + w_2 K_2) p_0 - w_1 (1 - \delta_1) \sum_{j \in G_1} \pi^X_{q^*_a, j} - w_2 (1 - \delta_2) \sum_{j \in G_2} \pi^X_{q^*_a, j} \\
&= (w_1 K_1 + w_2 K_2) p_0 - w_1 ((K_1 + K_2) p_0 - p_N) \\
&= w_1 p_N - (w_1 - w_2) K_2 p_0.
\end{aligned}
$$

Then, to find the optimal fraction of assets to be pooled, we need to solve

$$
\begin{aligned}
& \max_{w_1, w_2} V^{-} \left( w_1 \sum_{j \in G_1} Y_j + w_2 \sum_{j \in G_1} Y_j \right) - K_1 w_1 (1 + y_1) - K_2 w_2 (1 + y_2) \\
& 0 \leq w_2 \leq w_1 \leq 1.
\end{aligned}
$$

Hence, the program writes

$$
\begin{aligned}
& \max_{w_1, w_2} w_1 (p_N - K_2 p_0 - (1 + y_1) K_1) + w_2 (K_2 p_0 - K_2 (1 + y_2)) \\
& 0 \leq w_2 \leq w_1 \leq 1.
\end{aligned}
$$

This program is trivially solved depending on the sign of $p_N - K_2 p_0 - (1 + y_1) K_1 \geq 0$ and of $K_2 p_0 - K_2 (1 + y_2) \geq 0$, with $w_1^* = \mathbb{I}_{p_N - K_2 p_0 - (1+y_1) K_1 \geq 0}$ and $w_2^* = \mathbb{I}_{K_2 p_0 - K_2 (1+y_2) \geq 0}$. Note that with our assumptions, if $w_2^* = 1$ then $w_1^* = 1$. □

Since the higher aggregate valuation of the whole market $p_N$ the greater the incentive to pool, we can also see, in a way, how a generalized yield grab would induce the pooling of some bad or expensive assets as far as their relative weight remains limited. The presence of second lien mortgages in subprime pools could potentially be explained in that manner.

Our implementation of Gaur, Seshadri, and Subrahmabyam's model illustrates how in certain conditions issuers will be willing, to their benefit, to sell assets to be securitized. The model does not make any assumptions on preferences or on any information structure, which makes it fairly general. By completing the market, the pooled assets bring value to all participants. We also illustrated conditions in which it made sense even for loans that were more expensive than the market aggregate to be pooled, in particular, if their origination cost was less than Treasurys. This resonates well with the large range of loan quality and relative value generally observed within a securitized pool.

### 7.1.5 Retention and Tranching

We now shift our focus to tranching and begin with the model by Fender and Mitchell (2009), which looks into different types of incentives that can lead the originator to carry out screening efforts on the loans that are originated. We will see that in certain conditions it is best for the originator to retain a mezzanine tranche, which hence justifies more complex structuring than simply a senior and a junior tranche.

Since the goal in this model is to analyze loan screening incentives, the assumptions are comparable to the ones from the models of Gorton and Souleles (2007) and Han et al. (2015), which accounted for screening and which we discussed in Chap. 4. There are some differences, however: while in these prior models the effort directly reduced the probability of default, we will now consider screening reduces the proportion of bad loans that are acquired by the originator.

We assume that an originator makes loans which are either kept on balance sheet or securitized. When they are securitized, the originator may be required by regulations to retain certain tranches and only sell the rest to investors. The originator can decide how much effort they put into the screening process for the loans, but this amount of effort is not contractible and is not observable by the investors. The investors cannot make their valuation of the securities contingent on an effort that would explicitly depend on that valuation. In other words, the issuer acts in its interest without factoring in any anticipation of effort by the investors.

#### 7.1.5.1 Loan Screening Model

We consider there are loans of type "good" and "bad", and the proportion of good loans in the population is $\theta$. The risk-free rate is null, and all market participants are risk-neutral. While Fender and Mitchell assume that there is a unique loan, this is in fact not consistent with how the probability distribution of the cash flows is used. We need to assume that a large number $n$ of loans are made, but can scale their total face value to be 1. When loans default, they generate a cash flow of 0, and when they do not default, they generate a cash flow of $\frac{y}{n}$, with $y > 1$.

We write $T$ the type of a loan, which can be good or bad, and hence $T \in \{b, g\}$. The good and bad loans cannot be distinguished from screening, but screening allows the originator to reduce the probability that a loan is bad: effort reduces the probability of type-2 errors, accepting a bad borrower. Efforts also come at a cost: given an effort level $e \in [0, 1]$, the cost is $c(e)$ such that $c(0) = 0$, $c'(e) > 0$, and $c''(e) > 0$.

The effect from screening is modeled by parameterizing the probability of getting a good or bad loan: $\alpha_b(e) = \mathbb{P}[T = b] = 0 \vee ((1 - \theta) - e)$ and $\alpha_g(e) = \mathbb{P}[T = g] = 1 \wedge (\theta + e)$. The effort $e$ directly increases the probability of obtaining a good loan. Note that for $e \in [0, 1 - \theta]$, $\frac{\partial \alpha_b}{\partial e} = -1$ and $\frac{\partial \alpha_g}{\partial e} = 1$. The screening effort does not have any impact for $e > 1 - \theta$, and therefore we can assume that the originator will never select $e > 1 - \theta$.

One significant difference with the models mentioned before is that we introduce a systemic risk factor driving defaults in addition to loan quality. The systemic risk factor $Z$ cannot be observed in advance by the originator or investors, and can be a "high" or "low" economic output, which we write $Z \in \{h, l\}$. We have $\mathbb{P}[Z = l] = p_l$ and $\mathbb{P}[Z = h] = 1 - p_l = p_h$. $Z$ is assumed to be independent of the loan quality.

Based on the loan quality and the economic context, the probability of default varies. Writing $D$ for the event of loan default, we assume that $\mathbb{P}[D|\{T = b\} \cap \{Z = l\}] = 1$ and $\mathbb{P}[D|\{T = g\} \cap \{Z = h\}] = 0$, and $d_h = \mathbb{P}[D|\{T = b\} \cap \{Z = h\}] > 0$ and $d_l = 1 - \mathbb{P}[D|\{T = g\} \cap \{Z = l\}] < 1$. The quantity $d_h$ indicates by how much the probability of default in a good environment is reduced by having a good loan, and $d_l$ indicates by how much the probability of default is reduced by having a good loan in a bad environment. We would expect that in a realistic setting $d_l > d_h$, that is, the gain in performance of a good loan in a bad environment is more than the loss in performance probability of a bad loan in a good environment, because loan selection would matter more in a constrained environment.

We assume that the loan portfolio is large enough and all the random variables relative to each loan are independent, so that the law of large numbers applies to the total portfolio cash flow $Y$.

With these elements we can show the following lemma:

**Lemma 7.6** (Loan Payment Distribution) *Given a screening effort of e by the originator, the distribution of the portfolio payment Y can be characterized, for all measurable f, by*

$$\mathbb{E}[f(Y)] = p_l f\left(y\alpha_g(e)d_l\right) + p_h f\left(y(\alpha_g(e) + \alpha_b(e)d_h)\right).$$

***Proof*** For any given effort $e$, and some measureable function $f$, we can write for the total portfolio payment $Y$:

$$\mathbb{E}[f(Y)] = \mathbb{E}[f(Y)|Z = l]p_l + \mathbb{E}[f(Y)|Z = h]p_h.$$

In addition, since we assumed that the portfolio cash flow converged to its expected value by the law of large numbers, we have $\mathbb{E}[f(Y)|Z = l] = f\left(\mathbb{E}[Y|Z = l]\right)$. Note that in the low economic outcome, only good loans perform and hence

$$\mathbb{E}[Y|Z = l] = y\alpha_g(e)\left(1 - \mathbb{P}[D|\{T = g\} \cap \{Z = l\}]\right) = y\alpha_g(e)d_l.$$

Following the same logic and noting that $\mathbb{P}[D|\{T = g\} \cap \{Z = h\}] = 0$, we also have

$$\begin{aligned}\mathbb{E}[Y|Z = h] &= y\alpha_g(e) + y\alpha_b(e)\left(1 - \mathbb{P}[D|\{T = b\} \cap \{Z = h\}]\right) \\ &= y(\alpha_g(e) + \alpha_b(e)d_h).\end{aligned}$$

Hence, $\mathbb{E}[f(Y)|Z = h] = f\left(y(\alpha_g(e) + \alpha_b(e)d_h)\right)$ and $\mathbb{E}[f(Y)|Z = l] = f\left(y\alpha_g(e)d_l\right)$, and we can infer the characterization of the distribution of $Y$:

$$\mathbb{E}[f(Y)] = p_l f\left(y\alpha_g(e)d_l\right) + p_h f\left(y(\alpha_g(e) + \alpha_b(e)d_h)\right),$$

which concludes the proof. □

#### 7.1.5.2 Portfolio Retention, Securitization, and Screening

We first consider the screening incentive that the originator has if it keeps the entire loan port folio, and compare it with the securitization of the entire pool.

The originator's expected profit $\Pi_p$ in this case, for a given effort $e$, is equal to the expected cash flow from the loan minus screening costs and minus the loan's face amount. Using Lemma 7.6, we can write

$$\Pi_p(e) = y\left[p_h - d_h\alpha_b(e)p_h + d_l\alpha_g(e)p_l\right] - c(e) - 1$$

The first-order condition tells us that the optimal effort $e_p$ verifies $\frac{\partial \Pi_p}{\partial e} = 0$, which for $e_p \in [0, 1-\theta]$ simplifies to

$$c'(e_p) = y(p_l d_l + p_h d_h).$$

The value $e_p$ represents the maximum effort that could be observed.

In order to induce securitization, Fender and Mitchell do not use an endogenous approach but in a fashion somewhat similar to DeMarzo and Duffie (1999) (discussed in Chap. 4) assume that securitized cash flows are more valuable to the originator by a factor $1 + r$. They justify its multiplier as capturing the attractiveness of lower regulatory capital, or a higher cost of funding for no-balance sheet assets holding.

Since the effort is not contractible and not observable by the investors, their valuation of the securities that are issued cannot depend on the effort that is chosen by the originator, and hence in its own decision the originator is assumed to treat the investors' valuation of the securities as a constant relative to its choice of $e$. We write $S_s$ the investors' valuation of the securities.

The profit for the issuer if the entire pool is securitized, as a function of its effort, writes

$$\Pi_s(e) = (1 + r)S_s - c(e) - 1.$$

The optimal screening effort in this case is $e_s = 0$: the issuer has no incentive to apply any screening. The investors value the pool reflecting the null effort and we have

$$S_s = y\left[p_h - d_h(1-\theta)p_h + d_l\theta p_l\right].$$

This lack of effort by the originator in the case of securitization presents a problem, due to the social cost of lending without screening. The so-called "originate to distribute" mortgage lending model has been widely criticized as one of the reasons for the late 2000s mortgage crisis. Nevertheless, as we stressed in our discussion of Plantin (2011), this issue is not so important if the valuation of the loans properly reflects the lack of screening, which is the case in the model at hand.

Between these two extremes of no securitization of maximally screened loans, or full securitization of unscreened loans, we now look into how certain structures retained by the originator can induce screening while still allowing securitization.

#### 7.1.5.3 Mechanism Design to Induce Screening

Fender and Mitchell (2009) places itself in a regulation context: the eventual goal is to analyze the types of regulatory requirements that could incite originators to carry out proper loan screening while still allowing securitization. If an originator is forced by regulations to retain a particular tranche, then the tranche's structure needs to be simple enough. Hence, Fender and Mitchell are not looking for an optimal security design in absolute, as we did, for example, in Chap. 4, but assume specific simple shapes: a vertical slice of the portfolio, an equity tranche, or a mezzanine tranche.

We have the following proposition:

**Proposition 7.15** (Fender Mitchell Vertical Slice) *Holding a vertical slice of size $w$ of the assets induces less screening than when the entire portfolio is retained: the optimal effort $e_v$ in this case verifies $c'(e_v) = wc'(e_p)$.*

***Proof*** Assume that $S_v$ is the valuation of the remainder of the portfolio by investors, which as before is independent of the effort $e$. Using Lemma 7.6, we can write the profit to the originator retaining a vertical slice of a fraction $w < 1$ as

$$\Pi_v(e) = (1+r)S_v + wy\left[p_h - d_h\alpha_b(e)p_h + d_l\alpha_g(e)p_l\right] - c(e) - 1.$$

The first-order condition amounts to

$$c'(e_v) = wy(p_l d_l + p_h d_h) = wc'(e_p).$$

Hence, since $c'$ is increasing, the optimal effort $e_v$ when a vertical slice is retained is less than the optimal effort when the whole portfolio is retained. □

We now turn to the case where an equity tranche is retained. The senior bond size is set to $\beta$, so the senior tranche pays $Y \wedge \beta$ and the equity tranche pays $(Y - \beta) \vee 0$. We assume that the equity tranche is sized so that a particular condition is verified when there is no effort:

$$y\alpha_g(0)d_l - \beta \le 0 < y(\alpha_g(0) + \alpha_b(0)d_h) - \beta,$$

which can be written explicitly as

$$y\theta d_l \le \beta < y\theta + y(1-\theta)d_h.$$

We also assume that the senior bond size verifies $\beta \le yd_l$, which is not implied by the inequalities above.

**Proposition 7.16** (Fender Mitchell Equity Tranche) *Define $e_1 = \frac{\beta}{yd_l} - \theta$. If $c'(e_1) < y\,(p_h d_h + p_l d_l)$, then the optimal effort level $e_q$ for the originator holding the equity tranche verifies $c'(e_q) = y\,(p_h d_h + p_l d_l)$, and is the same as the effort $e_p$ when holding the whole pool. If $c'(e_1) > y\,(p_h d_h + p_l d_l)$, then the optimal effort* *level $e_q$ verifies $c'(e_q) = yp_h d_h$ and is strictly lower than $e_p$. In addition, holding the equity of size $1-\beta$ will lead to less screening than holding a portfolio share of size $1-\beta$ if $1-\beta > \frac{p_h d_h}{p_h d_h + p_l d_l}$.*

***Proof*** We write $S_q$ the investor's valuation of the senior securities, again assumed to be independent of the effort $e$. We know the distribution for $Y$ from Lemma 7.6, so we can write the expected equity tranche cash flow as

$$\begin{aligned}\mathbb{E}[(Y-\beta)\vee 0] &= p_l\left(y\alpha_g(e)d_l - \beta\right)\vee 0\\ &\quad + p_h\left(y(\alpha_g(e)+\alpha_b(e)d_h) - \beta\right)\vee 0.\end{aligned}$$

Note that this is where assuming only a single loan is made would lead to only the probability of the loan not defaulting being affected by the effort, and hence the equity and the senior tranche would have the same probability of cash flowing, which leads to trivial results. In order to resolve this inconsistency, we had to assume a large number of loans were made.

Hence, the originator's expected profit as a function of the effort can be written as

$$\begin{aligned}\Pi_q(e) &= (1+r)S_q + p_l\left(y\alpha_g(e)d_l - \beta\right)\vee 0\\ &\quad + p_h\left(y(\alpha_g(e)+\alpha_b(e)d_h) - \beta\right)\vee 0 - c(e) - 1.\end{aligned}$$

We can see that if $y\alpha_g(e)d_l - \beta \leq 0$ then in the low outcome, the equity tranche is wiped out. Similarly, if $y(\alpha_g(e)+\alpha_b(e)d_h) - \beta \leq 0$, then in the high outcome the equity tranche is also wiped out. The specific assumption we made earlier states that when no effort is spent, the equity tranche is wiped out in the low outcome but generates cash flows in the high outcome.

We define the effort level $e_1$ such that $\alpha_g(e_1) = \frac{\beta}{yd_l}$, so that for all efforts greater than $e_1$, the equity tranche is not wiped out in the low outcome. Since we have assumed that $\beta \geq y\theta d_l$, we know that $\frac{\beta}{yd_l} - \theta \geq 0$. In addition, since $\beta \leq yd_l$, then $\frac{\beta}{yd_l} - \theta \leq 1-\theta$. As a result $e_1 = \frac{\beta}{yd_l} - \theta$, and it is a feasible effort, since $e_1 \in [0, 1-\theta]$.

We can then write

$$\frac{\partial\Pi_q(e)}{\partial e} = y\left(p_h d_h + p_l d_l \mathbb{I}_{e>e_1}\right) - c'(e).$$

The marginal impact of the effort on revenue is, hence, discontinuous. Whether at the optimum where $\frac{\partial\Pi_q(e)}{\partial e} = 0$, the effort is greater or less than $e_1$ depends on the value of $c'(e_1)$.

If $c'(e_1) > y\left(p_h d_h + p_l d_l\right)$ then since $c'$ is increasing, the optimal effort $e_q$ must be less than $e_1$, so that the equality $\frac{\partial\Pi_q(e)}{\partial e} = 0$ may be verified. Then, at the optimum the first-order condition becomes $c'(e_q) = yp_h d_h$. In this case, the cost is increasing too fast, the originator decides on a low effort level and in the low outcome, the equity is wiped out.

If on the other hand $c'(e_1) < y(p_h d_h + p_l d_l)$, then the $e_q$ such that $c'(e_q) = y(p_h d_h + p_l d_l)$ is necessarily greater than $e_1$, and in that case the first-order condition translates into that equality. The cost is increasing slowly enough that it is optimal for the originator to apply a higher level of screening, and the equity tranche is not wiped out. Note that in this case the level of screening is the same as when the entire pool is retained.

Finally, recall the expression for $e_v$: $c'(e_v) = wy(p_h d_h + p_l d_l)$. So in the case where $c'(e_1) > y(p_h d_h + p_l d_l)$ and $c'(e_q) = yp_h d_h$, then $e_v > e_q$ is equivalent to $c'(e_v) > c'(e_q)$, and to $w > \frac{p_h d_h}{p_h d_h + p_l d_l}$. □

Interestingly, the size of the equity tranche $1 - \beta$ does not enter the expression for the optimal effort level directly. It enters it indirectly through the way $e_1$ is defined, which depends on $\beta$: as the equity tranche increases, the senior tranche decreases and the threshold $e_1$ decreases, which makes it more likely that the conditions are verified so that the maximum level of screening is applied.

While we have only considered senior or junior bonds so far, it makes sense to also consider mezzanine tranches. Indeed, from the analysis above we could see that when the equity is wiped out in a low economic outcome, the screening incentive is not optimal from a social standpoint. By considering a mezzanine tranche instead, which presumably should be less likely to be entirely wiped out, maybe that the originator's having more skin in the game could lead to a higher screening incentive.

The mezzanine tranche's size is set to that of the equity, so that one can make a more direct comparison of the impact on incentives. As before, we will assume that the originator sells all the other tranches and only retains this mezzanine of size $1 - \beta$. The cash flow to the senior bond is now $Y \wedge (2\beta - 1)$, and the cash flow to the equity is the same as before, $(Y - \beta) \vee 0$. The cash flow to the mezzanine is therefore $((Y - (2\beta - 1)) \vee 0) \wedge (1 - \beta)$. Note also that the sum of the cash flow to the mezzanine and to the new senior bond is the same as the cash flow to the senior bond from the prior case when there were only two tranches, equity and senior.

We keep the assumptions from the prior case, which allowed $e_1$ to be defined as a feasible effort level, $y\theta d_l \leq \beta < y\theta + y(1 - \theta)d_h$, but we also require that

$$\frac{yd_l\theta + 1}{2} \leq \beta < \frac{yd_l + 1}{2}.$$

**Proposition 7.17** (Fender Mitchell Mezzanine Tranche) *If $c'(e_1) > y(p_h d_h + p_l d_l)$, then the originator would choose a low effort level $e_q$ if it held the equity tranche, so that it is wiped out in the low economic state. If instead the originator holds the mezzanine tranche, it will also choose an effort level such that the equity is wiped out in the low state but that effort level $e_m$ will be greater than $e_q$ if $p_l d_l > p_h d_h$. In addition, holding the mezzanine of size $1 - \beta$ will lead to less screening than holding a portfolio share of size $1 - \beta$ if $1 - \beta > \frac{p_l d_l}{p_h d_h + p_l d_l}$.*

***Proof*** We write $S_m$ the value of the securities purchased by the investors (the senior bond and the equity), so that the originator's expected profit given its effort $e$ is

$$\Pi_m(e) = (1+r)S_m + \mathbb{E}[((Y-(2\beta-1)) \vee 0) \wedge (1-\beta)] - c(e) - 1.$$

We can write the expected cash flow from the mezzanine, using the distribution for $Y$:

$$\begin{aligned}
&\mathbb{E}[((Y-(2\beta-1)) \vee 0) \wedge (1-\beta)] \\
&= p_l\left(\left(y\alpha_g(e)d_l-(2\beta-1)\right) \vee 0\right) \wedge (1-\beta) \\
&+ p_h\left(\left(y(\alpha_g(e)+\alpha_b(e)d_h)-(2\beta-1)\right) \vee 0\right) \wedge (1-\beta).
\end{aligned}$$

The conditions under which the equity tranche may be wiped out are the same as in the previous case, since its size is unchanged. There are now, however, two possible cases if the equity is wiped out in the low economic outcome: the mezzanine may also be wiped out, or may be receiving some cash flows. Finally, when the equity receives cash flows, then we know that the mezzanine tranche is fully paid. Under our assumptions, we know that the equity tranche does receive cash flows in the high economic case, and hence the mezzanine is fully paid.

We have defined $e_1$ earlier so that $y\alpha_g(e_1)d_l - \beta = 0$, and for efforts above $e_1$ the equity receives payments in the low state, and the mezzanine is fully paid. We now also define $e_2$ so that $y\alpha_g(e_2)d_l - (2\beta-1) = 0$. Since we have assumed that $\frac{yd_l\theta+1}{2} \le \beta < \frac{yd_l+1}{2}$, we find that $e_2 = \frac{2\beta-1}{yd_l} - \theta$ is a feasible effort level, and $e_2 \in [0, 1-\theta]$. The threshold effort level $e_2$ is such that for $e \le e_2$, the mezzanine tranche receives no cash flows and is wiped out in the low state. Note that since $\beta < 1$, $2\beta - 1 < \beta$ and $e_2 < e_1$.

It is possible to write the derivative of the expected profit, using $e_1$ and $e_2$ to condition the cash flows. Since in the high state the tranche is always fully paid, there is sensitivity to the effort only for the low state. And in the low state, efforts above $e_1$ do not yield any increase in expected profit, and efforts below $e_2$ do not yield any profit either. Hence, we have

$$\frac{\partial \Pi_m(e)}{\partial e} = \mathbb{I}_{e_1>e>e_2} y p_l d_l - c'(e).$$

We can therefore distinguish three cases.

In the first case, $c'(e_1) > yp_ld_l$ and $c'(e_2) \le yp_ld_l$. In this case, there exists $e_m \in [e_1, e_2]$ such that $c'(e_m) = yp_ld_l$ at the first-order condition. The optimal effort is such that the equity gets wiped out in the low state, but the mezzanine receives some cash flow.

In the second case, $c'(e_1) > yp_ld_l$ and $c'(e_2) > yp_ld_l$. Then there is no $e \in [e_1, e_2]$ such that $c'(e) = yp_ld_l$, and the optimal effort is 0. The equity and the mezzanine are wiped out in the low outcome case.

In the third case, $c'(e_1) \le yp_ld_l$, and this implies that $c'(e_2) \le yp_ld_l$ as well. The originator chooses the maximum available effort level of $e_1$, and the mezzanine pays its full cash flow in both states of the world.

We can now compare the effort levels obtained when retaining the mezzanine tranche with those when retaining the equity tranche. Recall that according to Proposition 7.16 if $c'(e_1) > y(p_h d_h + p_l d_l)$, then the originator holding equity decides to apply an effort that verifies $c'(e_q) = y p_h d_h$. In this case, we also have $c'(e_1) > y p_l d_l$ and hence the originator holding a mezzanine tranche will choose an effort $e_m < e_1$, such that $c'(e_m) = y p_l d_l$. If $p_l d_l > p_h d_h$, then $e_m > e_q$.

For the comparison with holding a vertical slice of the assets, note that $c'(e_v) = wy(p_h d_h + p_l d_l)$. So in the case where $c'(e_1) > y p_l d_l$ and $c'(e_2) \leq y p_l d_l$, so that $c'(e_m) = y p_l d_l$, then $e_v > e_m$ is equivalent to $c'(e_v) > c'(e_m)$, and to $w > \frac{p_l d_l}{p_h d_h + p_l d_l}$. □

The model from Fender and Mitchell shows that if the issuer needs to screen, it makes sense for it to hold the mezzanine tranche, which hence explains the existence of a more complex structure than the pure senior/equity dichotomy. However, in reality issuers rarely retained mezzanine tranches rather than equity exposure. Paradoxically, the fundamental reasons why Fender and Mitchell see mezzanine as a good candidate for regulatory tranche retention could explain why such a tranche may have been issued. Indeed, while we know issuers may have reasons to hold equity and issue informationally insensitive bonds to some investors, mezzanine tranches by being particularly exposed to loan quality could have been strong candidates for selling: if there is pure upside from equity, its higher end, that is, the mezzanine, dilutes it.

### 7.1.6 Optimal Bidding and Tranching

In Plantin (2003), the author developed a model that could explain the presence of multiple tranches in a securitization structure as a consequence of investors having different degrees of sophistication. While in Dang et al. (2015), DeMarzo and Duffie (1999) and DeMarzo (2005) the issuer had private information, Plantin considers the case of investors acquiring private information, more or less efficiently. In that regard, the model is closer in philosophy to that of Boot and Thakor (1993), which we discussed earlier, or Axelson (2007). As in all the other models, investors and issuers are risk-neutral. The discount rate is also set to 0.

There are three time periods indexed by $t \in \{0, 1, 2\}$. There is an asset or portfolio of assets with a payoff $Y$ at time 2, such that $Y$ is bounded and has support $[0, y_H]$. This collateral may be good or bad, which we represent as a random variable $T$ for the type which may take the values of $g$, for "good", or $b$, for "bad" and $Y$ is not independent of $T$. We write $\mu_g$ and $\mu_b$ the density of $Y$ conditional on $T = g$ and $T = b$, and $M_g(x) = \mathbb{P}[Y \geq x | T = g]$, and $M_b(x) = \mathbb{P}[Y \geq x | T = b]$.

We assume that $\frac{M_g(x)}{M_b(x)}$ is increasing in $x$. One consequence is that $\mathbb{E}[Y|T = g] \geq \mathbb{E}[Y|T = b]$. There exists a common knowledge prior $q = \mathbb{P}[T = g]$.

The owner of the asset, the issuer, does not have private information and can sell this collateral in a structured form, by splitting it into $n$ securities $S_i = g_i(Y)$ for $1 \leq$

$i \leq n$, so that each $g_i$ is piece-wise differentiable and increasing, and $\sum_{i=1}^{n} g_i(Y) = Y$. Given some security design $S$, we write $S_g = \mathbb{E}[S|T = g]$ and $S_b = \mathbb{E}[S|T = b]$.

The investors who can buy these securities have the ability to screen the collateral with more or less efficiency, and must also retail the securities they buy after time 1. These investors are institutional intermediaries, distributing the bonds they purchase to their own investors. For example, such an investor may be a mutual fund, or a hedge fund, or a commercial bank offering an investment fund to its clients. Note that the case of a commercial bank holding securitized products for its own asset/liability management or an insurance company holding them in its reserves would not fit this context. One may alternatively consider that the issuer is a conduit or a bank, and the investors are investment banks each purchasing a particular security which it then sells to its own clients, which may include many types of institutions such as commercial banks, investment funds, insurance companies, or hedge funds.

The investors all have a certain sophistication $k \in [k_1, 1]$, which is the probability of learning that the collateral is good conditioned on it being good. We write $O_j$ the event that the investors know that the collateral is of good quality, $G_j$ the event that investor $j$ learns whether the collateral is of good quality and $k_j$ is that investor's sophistication. Then $O_j = G_j \cap \{T = g\}$, or in other words for the investor to know the collateral is of good quality, the collateral must actually be of good quality and the investor must learn it. We know $k_j = \mathbb{P}[G_j|T = g]$ and therefore $\mathbb{P}[O_j] = qk_j$. Hence, the event that investor $j$ does not know the collateral is good is $\overline{O_j} = \{T = b\} \cup \left(\{T = g\} \cap \{\overline{G_j}\}\right)$ with probability $1 - qk_j$.

There is a cost attached to retailing, which is a function of sophistication. The cost $c(k)$ is applied proportionally to the expected security payoff when the collateral is good: $\mathbb{E}[g_i(Y)|T = g]$ for some design $g_i$. The more sophisticated the investors are, the more expensive it is to retail the securities purchased: this cost $c$ is assumed to be such that $c(k)\frac{1-k}{k}$ is increasing. We scale the costs so that $c(k_1) = 0$.

The investors are assumed to be partitioned into a finite number $N$ of classes having each the same sophistication. For each class $i$, there is a number of investors $n_i > 1$ with a common sophistication $k_i$, where $k_i$ is non-decreasing in $i$. We write $N_i = \sum_{j=i}^{N} n_j$, so that $N = N_1$, and $N_i$ is the number of investors in classes $i$ and above.

#### 7.1.6.1 Securities Auction Optimal Strategies

We begin by examining the way generic securities will be valued by the investors as a whole. There is a bidding process, whereby the issuer will offer securities for sale, and investors bid on the securities in a sealed auction process. Investors will announce the securities they bid for starting with class 1, then 2, etc.

Define $K_1 = 1$ and for all $i \in [2..N + 1]$, $K_i = \prod_{j=1}^{i-1}(1 - k_j)^{n_j}$. These products can be written as $\mathbb{P}\left[\bigcap_{j=1}^{i-1}\bigcap_{l=1}^{n_j}\overline{G_l}\right]$; in other words, the probability that no investor in the $i - 1$ least sophisticated classes knows that the collateral is good.

We define the expected value of the security if no one knows that the collateral is good:

$$P_1 = S_g - \frac{1-q}{1-q(1-K_{N+1})}(S_g - S_b).$$

For all $i \in [1..N]$, we further define

$$P_{i+1} = \left(1 - K_i(1-k_i)^{N_i-1}\right) S_g + K_i(1-k_i)^{N_i-1} P_1.$$

**Proposition 7.18** (Plantin Auction Game for a Generic Security) *Given a security design $S$, the issuer organizes a sealed bid auction. Assume all classes participate in the auction. There exists a unique mixed strategy equilibrium. There is an increasing series $(P_i)_{i\in[1..N+1]}$ included in $[S_b, S_g]$ such that*

- *If the investor does not know if the collateral is good, it bids $P_1$.*
- *If an investor in class $i \in [j..N]$ knows the collateral is good, it randomizes its bid over $[P_1, P_{i+1}]$ with the following cumulative distribution:*

$$F_i(p) = \frac{1-k_i}{k_i}\left(\left(K_i\frac{S_g - P_1}{S_g - p}\right)^{\frac{1}{N_i-1}} - 1\right).$$

- *The expected profit is the same for each member of the same class and is increasing with sophistication:*

$$\frac{(1-q)qK_{N+1}}{1-q+qK_{N+1}}(S_g - S_b)\frac{k_i}{1-k_i}.$$

In order to show the proposition, we need some preliminary results. We start with the following lemma.

**Lemma 7.7** (Auction Game For Class 1) *An investor of class 1 must bid $p \in [P_1, P_2]$ with the following randomization mix:*

$$F_1(p) = \frac{1-k_1}{k_1}\left(\left(\frac{S_g - P_1}{S_g - b}\right)^{\frac{1}{N_1-1}} - 1\right).$$

***Proof*** Let us assume that a bid $p$ done by an investor of class $i$ is such that it is a possible bid for all classes of investors.

For there to be an equilibrium with a mixed strategy, a given investor must be made indifferent across its possible choices in the mix's support, conditioned on its available information. Hence, conditioned on its own information, the expected gain of a given investor must be constant whether the others are informed or not, when it plays a best response based on their information. We write $po_{j\neq i}$ a response by the investor of class $i$ knowing that other investors are informed or not. Then, we can write $H_i^{(p_j(O_j))_{j\neq i}}\left(p_{O_{j\neq i}}\right)$ the gain when bidding some response $p_{O_{j\neq i}}$, and given the set of bids of the other investors $(p_j(O_j))_{j\neq i}$.

So we must have for any possible Boolean vector $o$ stating whether other investors know or not that the collateral is good:

$$\mathbb{E}\left[H_i^{(p_j(O_j))_{j\neq i}}(p_o)\mathbb{I}_{O_{j\neq i}=o}|O_i\right]=c_O$$

for some constant $c_O$ depending only on $O_i$. In particular, we have

$$\mathbb{E}\left[H_i^{(p_j(O_j))_{j\neq i}}\left(p_{\exists j:O_j}\right)\mathbb{I}_{\exists j:O_j}|O_i\right]=\mathbb{E}\left[H_i^{(p_j(O_j))_{j\neq i}}\left(p_{\bigcap_{j\neq i}\overline{O_j}}\right)\mathbb{I}_{\bigcap_{j\neq i}\overline{O_j}}|O_i\right].$$

In other words, the value on the set where others are informed or not, conditioned by the investor being informed, is the same when the investor plays a deterministic best response knowing whether they are informed.

When no other investor is informed, and the investor of class $i$ knows it, the investor's best response is to bid an infinitesimal amount more than $P_1$, which is what all the others are bidding, and win the auction, so that

$$H_i^{(p_j(O_j))_{j\neq i}}\left(p_{\bigcap_{j\neq i}\overline{O_j}}\right)=S_g-P_1,$$

and

$$\begin{aligned}\mathbb{E}\left[H_i^{(p_j(O_j))_{j\neq i}}\left(p_{\bigcap_{j\neq i}\overline{O_j}}\right)\mathbb{I}_{\bigcap_{j\neq i}\overline{O_j}}|O_i\right]&=(S_g-P_1)\mathbb{P}\left[\bigcap_{j\neq i}\overline{O_j}|O_i\right]\\&=\frac{K_{N+1}}{1-k_i}(S_g-P_1).\end{aligned}$$

When some other investors are informed, the investor's response is to bid some $p>P_1$, as a function of which the gain will depend. Given this bid $p$, the investor of class $i$ will win the auction only if the other investors who know the collateral is good draw a random bid lower than that of the given investor of class $i$. Therefore, we have

$$H_i^{(p_j(O_j))_{j\neq i}}\left(p_{\exists j:O_j}\right)=(S_g-p)\mathbb{I}_{p_j(O_j)_{j\neq i}<p}.$$

From this, we can write

$$\mathbb{E}\left[H_i^{(p_j(O_j))_{j\neq i}}\left(p_{\exists j:O_j}\right)\mathbb{I}_{\exists j:O_j}|O_i\right]=(S_g-p)\mathbb{E}\left[\mathbb{I}_{p_j(O_j)_{j\neq i}<p}\mathbb{I}_{\exists j:O_j}|O_i\right].$$

In order to calculate $\mathbb{P}\left[p_j(O_j)_{j\neq i}<p\bigcap\exists j:O_j|O_i\right]$, we first note that for all $j$, $F_j(p)$ is the probability that an investor of class $j$ draws a bid lower than $p$. Hence,

$k_j F_j(p) + 1 - k_j$ is the probability that, knowing the collateral is of good quality, an investor of class $j$ learns it and bids randomly less than $p$. Therefore, we have

$$\mathbb{P}\left[p_j(O_j)_{j \neq i} < p \bigcap \exists j : O_j | O_i\right] = \frac{\prod_{l=1}^{N}(k_l F_l(p) + 1 - k_l)^{n_l}}{k_i F_i(p) + 1 - k_i}.$$

As a result, we can write the following equation for all $i \in [1..N]$:

$$\frac{\prod_{l=1}^{N}(k_l F_l(p) + 1 - k_l)^{n_l}}{k_i F_i(p) + 1 - k_i}(S_g - p) = \frac{K_{N+1}}{1 - k_i}(S_g - P_1).$$

If this is true for all $i$, it is also true for all $j$, and given the same $p$, taking the ratio of both equations yields

$$\frac{k_i F_i(p) + 1 - k_i}{k_j F_j(p) + 1 - k_j} = \frac{1 - ki}{1 - k_j},$$

so that we can write for all $i \in [1..N]$:

$$\begin{aligned}
\prod_{l=1}^{N}(k_l F_l(p) + 1 - k_l)^{n_l} &= \prod_{l=1}^{N}\left((k_i F_i(p) + 1 - k_i)\frac{1 - k_j}{1 - k_i}\right)^{n_l} \\
&= \left(\frac{k_i F_i(p) + 1 - k_i}{1 - k_i}\right)^{\sum_{l=1}^{N} n_l} \prod_{l=1}^{N}(1 - k_l)^{n_l} \\
&= \left(\frac{k_i F_i(p) + 1 - k_i}{1 - k_i}\right)^{N_1} K_{N+1}.
\end{aligned}$$

Replacing the new expression for the product in the original equation, we obtain

$$\left(\frac{k_i F_i(p) + 1 - k_i}{1 - k_i}\right)^{N_1 - 1}(S_g - p) = S_g - P_1,$$

which is equivalent to

$$F_i(p) = \frac{1 - k_i}{k_i}\left(\left(\frac{S_g - P_1}{S_g - b}\right)^{\frac{1}{N_1 - 1}} - 1\right).$$

Now note that according to the definition given earlier,

$$P_2 = \left(1 - (1 - k_1)^{N_1 - 1}\right) S_g + (1 - k_1)^{N_1 - 1} P_1.$$

If we set $i = 1$, we can see that $F_1(P_1) = 0$ and $F_1(P_2) = 1$, so that for $F_1$ to be a proper cumulative distribution we must have $p \in [P_1, P_2]$. As a result, an investor from class 1 must bid at or below $P_2$, following the randomization mix given by $F_1$.

□

Note that the expression of the mix distribution $F_i$ in the domain where all classes participate is such that for a given $p$, $F_i$ is decreasing in $i$ since $k_i$ is increasing. The more sophisticated investors have a lesser incentive to bid low than the less sophisticated investors.

Let us now show that uninformed investors do not bid above $P_1$.

**Lemma 7.8** (Uninformed Bids) *An uninformed investor makes no expected profit by bidding above* $P_1$.

***Proof*** Let us express the expected outcome from a bid $p > P_1$, such that all classes participate, by an investor of class $i$ who does not know if the collateral is good. There are two cases in which that investor does not know about the collateral: either the collateral is bad or it is good but the investor did not learn it. We write the gain $H_i(p)$, and recalling that $\overline{O_i} = \{T = b\} \cup \left(\{T = g\} \cap \{\overline{G_i}\}\right)$:

$$\mathbb{E}\left[H_i(p)|\overline{O_i}\right] = \frac{\mathbb{E}\left[H_i(p)\mathbb{I}_{\overline{O_i}}\right]}{\mathbb{P}\left[\overline{O_i}\right]}$$

$$= \frac{\mathbb{E}\left[H_i(p)\mathbb{I}_{\{T=b\}}\right]}{\mathbb{P}\left[\overline{O_i}\right]} + \frac{\mathbb{E}\left[H_i(p)\mathbb{I}_{\{T=g\}\cap\{\overline{G_j}\}}\right]}{\mathbb{P}\left[\overline{O_i}\right]}.$$

We know that $\mathbb{P}\left[\overline{O_i}\right] = 1 - qk_i$. Also, we know that the gain on the set where the collateral quality is good will only be positive if the investor wins the auction, and

$$\begin{aligned}
\mathbb{E}\left[H_i(p)\mathbb{I}_{\{T=g\}\cap\{\overline{G_j}\}}\right] &= q(1-k_i)\frac{\prod_{l=1}^{N}(k_l F_l(p) + 1 - k_l)^{n_l}}{k_i F_i(p) + 1 - k_i}(S_g - p) \\
&= q(1-k_i)\frac{K_{N+1}}{1-k_i}(S_g - P_1) \\
&= qK_{N+1}(S_g - P_1).
\end{aligned}$$

The simplification is due to the result in the proof of Lemma 7.7, which must be valid in a Nash equilibrium.

In addition, the gain can be computed easily if the collateral is bad:

$$\mathbb{E}\left[H_i(p)\mathbb{I}_{\{T=b\}}\right] = (1-q)(S_b - p).$$

Gathering all these parts, we obtain

$$\mathbb{E}\left[H_i(p)|\overline{O_i}\right] = \frac{qK_{N+1}(S_g - P_1) + (1-q)(S_b - p)}{1 - qk_i}.$$

After some simplifications, we find that $\mathbb{E}\left[H_i(p)|\overline{O_i}\right] \leq 0$ is equivalent to

$$p \geq S_b + \frac{qK_{N+1}}{1 - q(1 - K_{N+1})}(S_g - S_b) = P_1.$$

Therefore, the expected gain for an uninformed investor bidding above $P_1$ is negative. By bidding $p = P_1$, the uninformed investor has a null expected profit. □

We are now in a position to prove Proposition 7.18.

***Proof*** Let us now assume that the strategies of the informed agents are as stated in the proposition for classes up to and including $j - 1$, for some $j \in [2..N]$. We will see that it implies that investors of class $j$ will also follow the same strategy.

Let us consider an informed investor from class $i \geq j$ at the equilibrium, bidding an amount $p > P_j$. We can follow the same reasoning as in the proof of Lemma 7.7:

$$\mathbb{E}\left[H_i^{(p_j(O_j))_{j\neq i}}\left(p_{\exists j:O_j}\right)\mathbb{I}_{\exists j:O_j}|O_i\right] = \mathbb{E}\left[H_i^{(p_j(O_j))_{j\neq i}}\left(p_{\bigcap_{j\neq i}\overline{O_j}}\right)\mathbb{I}_{\bigcap_{j\neq i}\overline{O_j}}|O_i\right],$$

with a difference since now we know from our assumption that the classes up to $j - 1$ do not bid above $P_j$. The determination of the probability of winning the auction is therefore adjusted to reflect this situation. On the right-hand side, in the case where no other investor is informed the expression remains the same.

As a result we can write

$$\mathbb{P}\left[p_j(O_j)_{j\neq i} < p \bigcap \exists j : O_j|O_i\right] = \frac{\prod_{l=j}^{N}(k_l F_l(p) + 1 - k_l)^{n_l}}{k_i F_i(p) + 1 - k_i},$$

and hence for all $i \in [j..N]$, we have

$$\frac{\prod_{l=j}^{N}(k_l F_l(p) + 1 - k_l)^{n_l}}{k_i F_i(p) + 1 - k_i}(S_g - p) = \frac{K_{N+1}}{1 - k_i}(S_g - P_1).$$

From this, we infer that for all $i \in [j..N]$ and $l \in [j..N]$

$$k_l F_l(p) + 1 - k_l = (k_i F_i(p) + 1 - k_i)\frac{1 - k_l}{1 - k_i},$$

and therefore

$$\prod_{l=j}^{N}(k_l F_l(p) + 1 - k_l)^{n_l} = \left(\frac{k_i F_i(p) + 1 - k_i}{1 - k_i}\right)^{N_j}\frac{K_{N+1}}{K_j}.$$

Replacing in the equation yields

$$\left(\frac{k_i F_i(p) + 1 - k_i}{1 - k_i}\right)^{N_j}(S_g - p) = K_j(S_g - P_1),$$

and solving for $F_i$ we find

$$F_i(p) = \frac{1-k_i}{k_i}\left(\left(K_j \frac{S_g - P_1}{S_g - p}\right)^{\frac{1}{N_j-1}} - 1\right).$$

Setting $i = j$, we obtain the expression from the proposition. We can see that $F_i(P_1) = 0$, and $F_i(P_{i+1}) = 1$ and therefore the investor of class $i$ does not bid above $P_{i+1}$. We have shown that the property being true for classes up to $j - 1$ implies it is true for class $j$, and this is therefore the case for all classes.

If the investor is uninformed, we know the expected profit is null so $\mathbb{E}\left[H_i(p)|\overline{O_i}\right] = 0$, and we can write the expected profit as follows:

$$\begin{aligned}
\mathbb{E}\left[H_i(p)\right] &= \mathbb{E}\left[H_i(p)|O_i\right]\mathbb{P}[O_i] \\
&= \frac{qk_i K_{N+1}}{(1-k_i)}(S_g - P_1) \\
&= \frac{k_i}{1-k_i}\frac{q(1-q)K_{N+1}}{1-q(1-K_{N+1})}(S_g - S_b),
\end{aligned}$$

as stated in the proposition. □

Now that we have established how any security offered up for sale would be bid by all the investors, we shift our focus to how these investors will analyze the securities, and how they will maximize their gains given their own specific constraints.

#### 7.1.6.2 Investors Bidding Preferences

So far we have only considered how investors would bid if they wanted to do so, but we also need to analyze whether they would gain something by participating in the auction.

**Proposition 7.19** (Plantin Auction Participation Strategy) *For all $i \in [2..N]$, if class $i$ participates in the auction for a security $S$, then all classes $j \leq j$ also participate. Set*

$$t_i = \left(1 - \frac{1 - q + qK_{i+1}}{q(1-q)K_{i+1}} qc_i \frac{1-k_i}{k_i}\right)^{-1},$$

*then the number of classes $I$ participating in the auction for $S$ verifies*

$$I = \max\{i \in [1..N] : S_g \geq t_i S_b\}.$$

***Proof*** Given a subset $S$ of $[1..N]$, we define $K_S = \prod_{s\in S}(1 - k_s)^{n_s}$. Also, set $A_i$ the event that investors of class $i$ participate in the auction. Since all the investors have the same characteristics, if one participates they all do. Finally, set $I = \{i \in [1..N] : A_i\}$ and $m = \max I$.

We now look into the expected profit from investors of class $m$. Consider the proof for the formula for the expected gains from Proposition 7.18: if only a subset of investors were participating in the auction, it would simply change the indexing in the whole analysis where a new index $i'$ would span $I$ instead of $[1..N]$. As a result the expected gain of investors of class $m$ if indeed only the classes in $I$ participate is

$$\frac{k_m}{1-k_m}\frac{q(1-q)K_I}{1-q(1-K_I)}(S_g - S_b).$$

In order for class $m$ to participate, this expected gain must be greater than the cost $c(k_m)$ and hence

$$\frac{S_g}{S_b} \geq \left(1 - \frac{1-q+qK_I}{q(1-q)K_I} qc_m \frac{1-k_m}{k_m}\right)^{-1}.$$

Then, for all $l \in [1..m]$ we know that $K_{I\cap[1,l]} \geq K_I, k_l \leq k_m$, and also by assumption $c(k_l)\frac{1-k_l}{k_l} \leq c(k_m)\frac{1-k_m}{k_m}$. In addition for $q \in [0,1]$, we can easily check that $\frac{1-q-qx}{q(1-q)x}$ is decreasing in $x$. As a result,

$$\left(1 - \frac{1-q+qK_I}{q(1-q)K_I} qc_m \frac{1-k_m}{k_m}\right)^{-1} \geq \left(1 - \frac{1-q+qK_{I\cap[1..l]}}{q(1-q)K_{I\cap[1..l]}} qc_l \frac{1-k_l}{k_l}\right)^{-1}.$$

In consequence, for all $l \in [1..m]$,

$$\frac{S_g}{S_b} \geq \left(1 - \frac{1-q+qK_{I\cap[1..l]}}{q(1-q)K_{I\cap[1..l]}} qc_l \frac{1-k_l}{k_l}\right)^{-1}.$$

Hence, given a set of participation $I \cap [1..l]$, we know that class $l$ participates and therefore $l = \max\{I \cap [1..l]\}$, and as a result $l \in I$. Since this is true for every $l$, we have shown that $I = [1..m]$.

The second part of the proposition is a straightforward consequence. □

The ratio $\frac{S_g}{S_b}$ is defined as a measure of information sensitivity by Plantin, a definition that is similar to the ones we have discussed so far in Chap. 4, in the models from Boot and Thakor (1993), DeMarzo and Duffie (1999), and Dang et al. (2015), for example. The $t_i$ are increasing in $i$, so Proposition 7.19 shows that participation increases with informational sensitivity.

#### 7.1.6.3 Issuer Optimal Strategy

Issuance is a zero-sum game: anything the investors gain, the issuer loses. Hence, the bank's expected loss is the expected investors' gain. If investors up to class $i$ participate, we define the total expected gain as

$$G_i = (S_g - S_b)\frac{q(1-q)K_{i+1}}{1-q(1-K_{i+1})}\sum_{j=1}^{i} n_j \frac{k_j}{1-k_j} = l_i(S_g - S_b).$$

The quantity $l_i$ is therefore a coefficient driving the bank's loss for a given security design, if investors up to class $i$ participate.

**Proposition 7.20** (Plantin Tranching) *Assume that for some $i \in [2..N]$, $\frac{\mathbb{E}[Y|T=g]}{\mathbb{E}[Y|T=b]} < t_i$ so that the collateral itself is not strongly informationally sensitive, and that the $l_i$ are decreasing in $i$. Then the issuer maximizes its profits by creating $N$ claims in the form of debt, mezzanine debt, or equity, such that the more sophisticated the investors are, the most junior the tranches they bid on.*

We follow a different approach from Plantin and make the optimal issuer strategy explicit.

***Proof*** It is clear that given a security design, the only parameter driving the issuer's loss is the number of investors participating in the auction. If class $i$ participates in the bid for a given design, we know that all classes under $i$ participate too according to Proposition 7.19. Hence, the parameter driving the bank loss given a single security design is simply the highest class participating. If a set of security designs $(g_i)_{i\geq 1}$ such that $Y = \sum_i g_i(Y)$ is optimal for the bank, then there are not more than $N$ different securities: indeed, if all classes are already the highest participating class for some security, then any additional security will simply add to the security design chosen by one of these highest classes. Therefore, the issuer will minimize the investors' expected gains over a set of $N$ possible security designs.

Now note that for a derivable function $f$ such that $f(0) = 0$, we have

$$
\begin{aligned}
\mathbb{E}[f(Y)|T=g] &= \int_0^{y_H} f(x)\mu_g(x)dx \\
&= \left[ f(x) \int_0^x \mu_g(z)dz \right]_0^{y_H} - \int_0^{y_H} f'(x) \int_0^x \mu_g(z)dzdx \\
&= f(y_H) - \int_0^{y_H} f'(x) \left( 1 - \int_x^{y_H} \mu_g(z)dz \right) dx \\
&= \int_0^{y_H} f'(x) M_g(x)dx.
\end{aligned}
$$

Therefore, given a differentiable security design $g_i$, we have

$$
\begin{aligned}
S_g - S_b &= \mathbb{E}[g_i(Y)|T=g] - \mathbb{E}[g_i(Y)|T=b] \\
&= \int_0^{y_H} g_i'(x)(M_g(x) - M_b(x))dx.
\end{aligned}
$$

For a security design $g_i$, the investors' expected gain is positive only if they are participating, or in other words if there is one class which is the highest participating class for this security. Since the cost $c(k_1)$ is null by assumption, we know the first class always participates. Recall that there is an increasing series $(t_i)_{i>1}$ so that class $j$ participates if the security design verifies $S_g \geq t_j S_b$, which we can write

$$\int_0^{y_H} g_i'(x)(M_g(x) - t_j M_b(x))dx \geq 0.$$

Since $(t_i)_{i>1}$ is increasing, as $j$ increases the investors may not want to participate. Define the highest class number willing to participate for a design $g_i$:

$$I[g_i] = \min\left\{k : \int_0^{y_H} g_i'(x)(M_g(x) - t_k M_b(x))dx \geq 0\right\},$$

which may be greater than $N$ in which case nobody participates, or 1 in which case all participate. Since the set of designs $g_i$ are arbitrary, they can be ordered according to $I[g_i]$, so that $I[g_{i+1}] \geq I[g_i]$ without any loss of generality. Also, note that $i \geq I[g_i]$ is equivalent to

$$\int_0^{y_H} g_i'(x)(M_g(x) - t_i M_b(x))dx \geq 0.$$

We write for some measurable function $f$: $H_i[f] = \int_0^{y_H} f(x)(M_g(x) - t_i M_b(x))dx$.

The investor gain coming from a particular design can only be positive if there is participation, so that effectively any design $g_i$ can be written as $g_i(x)\mathbb{I}_{H_i[g_i'] \geq 0}$. Given a set of $N$ designs $(g_i)_{i \in [1..N]}$, the total investor gain or issuer loss across all designs is therefore

$$\sum_{i=1}^{N} l_i \int_0^{y_H} g_i'(x)\mathbb{I}_{H_i[g_i'] \geq 0}(M_g(x) - M_b(x))dx.$$

The issuer's optimization program is

$$\min_{(g_i)_{i \in [1..N]}} \sum_{i=1}^{N} l_i \mathbb{I}_{H_i[g_i'] \geq 0} \int_0^{y_H} g_i'(x)(M_g(x) - M_b(x))dx$$

$$\forall x \in [0, y_H], \sum_{i=1}^{N} g_i'(x)\mathbb{I}_{H_i[g_i'] \geq 0} = 1$$

$$\forall x \in [0, y_H], \forall i \in [1..N], g_i'(x) \in [0, 1].$$

After some simplifications, the objective function reduces to

$$V[(g_i)_{i \in [1..N]}] = \sum_{i=2}^{N} \mathbb{I}_{H_i[g_i'] \geq 0} (l_i - l_1) \int_0^{y_H} g_i'(x)(M_g(x) - M_b(x))dx,$$

skipping the term $l_1 \int_0^{y_H} (M_g(x) - M_b(x))dx$, which is constant with respect to the design choice.

Since the $l_i$ are decreasing in $i$, we know that all the terms $l_i - l_1$ are negative and decreasing. The issuer, hence, can reach the minimum by maximizing the weight of $g_i'$ for high $i$, as far as $H_i[g_i'] \geq 0$.

We now define a series of points $(x_i^0)_{i\in[1..N+1]}$, with $x_{N+1}^0 = y_H$ and

$$x_{i-1}^0 = \inf\left\{y \in [0, x_i^0] : \int_y^{x_i^0} M_b(x)\left(\frac{M_g(x)}{M_b(x)} - t_i\right) dx \geq 0\right\}.$$

By construction, $x_{i-1}^0 \leq x_i^0$, and hence the series is increasing in $i$.

Now set $h_i$ such that $h_i'(x) = \mathbb{I}_{x_i^0 \leq x < x_{i+1}^0}$. By construction, we have $H_i[h_i'] \geq 0$ for all $i$, and for all $x \in [0, y_H]$, $\sum_{i=1}^N h_i'(x) = 1$. The value function of the optimization, up to a constant, writes

$$V[(h_i)_{i\in[1..N]}] = \sum_{i=2}^{N} (l_i - l_1) \int_{x_i^0}^{x_{i+1}^0} (M_g(x) - M_b(x))dx.$$

For a given $k$ and $j$, we now apply a perturbation. For all $i$, set $A_i$ a closed subset of the interval $[x_i^0, x_{i+1}^0]$, so that $\int_{A_i}(M_g(x) - t_i M_b(x))dx = 0$. We define a series of designs $(m_{k\to j,i})_{i\in[1..N]}$, given $\varepsilon > 0$, such that

- for all $i \neq k$ and $i \neq j$, $m_{k\to j,i} = h_i$,
- and $m_{k\to j,k}$ is such that $m_{k\to j,k}'(x) = h_k'(x) - \varepsilon\mathbb{I}_{A_k}(x)$, and $m_{k\to j,j}'(x) = h_j'(x) + \varepsilon\mathbb{I}_{A_k}(x)$.

The $m$ represent a perturbation of the presumably optimal set of designs $h$, by transferring cash flows from $h_k$ to $h_j$. We distinguish the cases when $j < k$ and $j > k$.

If $j < k$, then since $\frac{M_g}{M_b}$ is increasing, $t_j < t_i$ and $\int_{A_i}(M_g(x) - t_i M_b(x))dx = 0$, we know that $\int_{A_i}(M_g(x) - t_j M_b(x))dx \geq 0$. As a result, $H_j[m_{k\to j,j}] > 0$ and $H_k[m_{k\to j,k}] \geq 0$, so both securities are still bid on by investors.

Hence, using the general expression of the value function, we have

$$V[(m_{k\to j,i})_{i\in[1..N]}] - V[(h_i)_{i\in[1..N]}] = \varepsilon(l_j - l_k)\int_{A_k}(M_g(x) - M_b(x))dx,$$

which is positive.

If $j > k$, then we know that $H_j[m_{k\to j,j}] < 0$ and therefore investors do not participate in the auction for this security. This is true for all $j > k$, so that either $A_k$ must have a measure of zero, or the additional cash flow must be transferred to one of the securities with $j \leq k$.

Hence, any alteration to the design $h$ results in a higher value function, and therefore $h$ is optimal. The series of $h_i$ characterize debt, mezzanine, and equity-shaped cash flows. □

This model by Plantin does not make specific assumptions about investors' utility functions, only on their ability to access information and to redistribute cash flows to their own investors. This is difficult to quantify in reality, but it is a plausible differentiation factor among them. In effect, more sophisticated investors such as hedge funds have a higher cost of raising investment funds than banks, for example, since their investors typically require greater returns. The model captures the optimal allocation of risks and returns among these varied investors, and we can see how the emergence of thin mezzanine tranches may be justified.

## 7.2 Interest and Principal Structuring

In the current literature, there has not been any particular theoretical construct that can specifically explain excess-spread rather than senior/subordination, or IOs and POs, for example. Before delving into the economic analysis of structures addressing interest allocation, we first look into an important driving force behind certain structures, the preference that some investors have for par-priced debt securities. We will see eventually that this may drive many of the structural aspects that have not been discussed in the literature. It is worth noting that in Childs et al. (1996), the authors introduced a model for CMBS structures that accounted for interest payment, but did not specifically discuss the optimality in interest allocation structures. In the context of an arbitrage-free pricing model, they numerically analyzed the relationship between tranche characteristics and the spreads required on the different tranches.

Before specifically focusing on interest allocation, we begin, however, by looking at the importance of par valuation for bonds for certain institutions, and will later analyze the extent to which it may drive structuring. We develop a model explaining the requirement for par due to dividend signaling, by following Miller and Rock (1985). We then discuss extensions of the model from DeMarzo and Duffie (1999) that can explain the particular allocation of interest in simple stripped-down structures as well as in excess-spread structures.

### 7.2.1 Why Do Investors Want Par Bonds?

As we have mentioned in Chap. 6, there is a significant effort in structure design specifically aimed at manufacturing par-priced bonds. This implies allocating interest in relation to principal and expected losses, so that the bonds' coupon exactly matches its required net yield. Excess-spread (typically accompanied by overcollateralization) as well as interest stripping (IOs/POs) are the usual structural methods of choice to build par-priced bonds. Looking at the range of securities typically issued in a securitization deal, making par-priced bonds will appear as important as creating senior/subordinated exposure. However, there has not been much specific literature looking at this particular feature of structures. Lack of information about the details of structures is a likely explanation for this lack of academic interest.[2]

The literature and research we discussed in Chap. 4 gave us good fundamental explanations for why we would expect to find senior and junior securities in securitizations. These models, in turn, can provide background on which the more advanced models we discuss in the present chapter are built, explaining certain senior/subordinated complex mechanisms. Just as we needed fundamental explanations for investors' desire for senior or junior securities, we need to find some fundamental reason why par-priced bonds would be so important that they drive so much of the structuring effort.

One first remark, which is important to realize, is that it is mostly for senior bonds that institutions will focus on par valuation. Indeed, junior securities have a non-negligible probability of becoming impaired, and the magnitude of that credit risk is large relative to coupon variations that could get these bonds valued at par. Mezzanine securities (investment-grade bonds that are, however, not AAA-rated) could be an exception to that logic, but in an effort to simplify our analysis we will only consider senior bonds in the discussion.

Not all investors typically require par pricing. Hedge fund or sophisticated investors generally only care about the cash flows. Mutual funds or more broadly speaking investment management companies are not either particularly worried about the price at which securitized bonds may be issued. In fact, these types of institutional investors could be seen as **investment vehicles**. They channel their own investors' money into the particular types of securities their funds are supposed to invest into. As such, they have limited discretion in terms of what they can trade. If their investors needed them to buy par-priced bonds, then that would be part of the funds' investment parameters. Funds with such a particular constraint are far from the norm. Such investment vehicles may buy par-priced securities at issuance, if these bonds are structured this way. If they want a higher or a lower coupon, they will buy IOs or POs and have an aggregate cash flow with the characteristics they desire.

Which type of institutions tends to require par pricing? Commercial banks and insurance companies will generally fall into that category. These types of securitized bond buyers are particular in that they are businesses (as opposed to simple investment vehicles), and owning securitized bonds is part and parcel of their businesses. In fact, banks and insurers are the only types of operating companies that will typically own substantial amounts of securitized bonds as part of their activity. Some other types of companies may hold securitized bonds in the same way as they may own other bonds as part of their cash management, but that is not an integral part of their business. The securitized bond holdings of banks and insurance companies are substantial and can have a non-negligible impact on their earnings. We argue that they will have a preference for par-priced securities because they are operating companies, and need to distribute dividends.

[2]As we mentioned before, there have been few research papers mentioning actual structures, even less looking into the details of structures specifically.

#### 7.2.1.1 Par-Priced Bonds

The first step in our analysis is to look into how par-priced bonds differ from those priced away from par. Valuing bonds would seem a trivial exercise in the light of modern financial theory; however, these modern tools all assume a no-arbitrage world where all sorts of cash flows can be freely bought or sold. In such a framework where all cash flows can be efficiently replicated, it would be pointless to look into a preference for par pricing. Therefore, we set ourselves in a framework consistent with the way fixed-income instruments may be traded by operating businesses:

- Trading can only take place at certain times; we'll consider a 2 or 3 periods economy;
- Information on certain random variables is only observed at certain times, but their distributions are known;
- Shorting for hedging purposes is only possible on certain securities.

We consider bonds that are assumed to not take losses. Indeed, the issue of par pricing is most pregnant with bonds that would be designed to have the lowest yield, relative to the amount of coupon typically paid by collateral. In addition, bonds with any ex ante substantial credit risk would not be considered the typical long-term investment for a commercial bank or insurance company.

Unhedged Positions

Without much loss in generality, we will consider a bond capitalizing interest, making a single payment at maturity. We write $T$ for the maturity, $B_0$ for the initial outstanding amount, and $c$ for the annualized coupon. In order to improve tractability, we consider that capitalization is continuous, so that the bond's payment at maturity is $B_0e^{cT}$. We are considering fixed-rate bonds; in the case of floating-rate bonds the logic would be similar but would require to model a dynamic short rate process on which the coupons would be indexed.

In the context of a Treasury bond or a safe corporate bond, the maturity would not be random. Here, however, in order to encompass securitized bonds, $T$ is a random variable. We consider that a bond's price is given by the present value of its expected cash flow as investors are risk-neutral and apply the appropriate yield for this type of cash flow to express inter-temporal preferences. The present value is calculated using continuous discounting, again for better tractability. Hence, given the relevant reference rate $y$ we have at time 0

$$P_0 = B_0\mathbb{E}\left[e^{(c-y)T}\right].$$

We say the bond is par priced if $P_0 = B_0$.

The performance of the bond's collateral if it is a securitized bond, or in the case of a corporate bond the evolution of the issuer's financial health, will progressively provide information on the eventual value of $T$. To simplify matters, we consider there is a date $t$ such that $\mathbb{P}[t < T] = 1$ from which $T$ is known, or more formally there is a filtration $\mathcal{F}$ and $T$ is $\mathcal{F}_t$-measurable.

**Proposition 7.21** (Benefit of Par Pricing 1) *A bond with a random maturity will have a deterministic future price, if it is initially par priced.*

***Proof*** We can write the bond price at time $t$ as a conditional expectation (since by then $T$ is known)

$$P_t(T) = B_0 \mathbb{E}\left[e^{cT-y(T-t)}|T\right] = B_0 e^{yt} e^{(c-y)T}.$$

Let us look at the evolution of the value of a bond that is sold at par at time 0. For the bond to be issued at par, the bond's price is such that $1 = \mathbb{E}\left[e^{T(c-y)}\right]$. Since $c$ and $y$ are constant, we need to set $c = y$ so that the bond is priced at par. In this case, at time $t$ the bond's price relative to its price at time 0 is deterministic

$$\frac{P_t(T)}{P_0} = e^{yt}.$$

If the bond was not initially par priced, we would have $c \neq y$, and hence the simplification above could not work. Writing $\gamma = e^{c-y}$, we have

$$\frac{P_t(T)}{P_0} = e^{yt} \frac{\gamma^T}{\mathbb{E}\left[\gamma^T\right]},$$

which is not deterministic and depending on $\gamma$ may vary substantially as a function of the value taken by $T$. □

For example, if $T$ could be equal to 5 or 15, with the same probability, and $\gamma = 1.03$ (the bond pays a coupon approximately 3% higher than the discount rate), then the bond's price would be 0.85 or 1.15 times $e^{yt}$. If we set the coupon lower than the risk-free rate, and $\gamma = 0.97$, then the bond's price at time $t$ would vary by the same degree.

If $T$ follows a distribution with a compact support in $[T_L, T_H]$, then the lowest value that $P_t(T)$ can take is a direct function of the distance between the coupon and the yield:

$$\inf P_t(T) = B_0 e^{yt} \left(\mathbb{I}_{c>y} e^{(c-y)T_L} + \mathbb{I}_{c<y} e^{(c-y)T_H}\right).$$

A bond that is not priced at par can be seen as a par-priced bond, plus or minus a strip of interest the value of which will be very dependent on the time it takes for the bond to be paid off. We have shown that even on bonds without any credit risk, the variability in time to maturity (or more realistically, average life for securitized bonds) leads to significant changes in the value of the bonds. At time $T$, the bond's value will be exactly par, so at time $t$ after $T$ is known one knows that the bond's value may increase back up or go down.

The discussion above would be applicable to bonds for which no losses at all are expected. While that may be applicable for AAA-rated CMOs that commercial banks will often hold, this model would not cover the long average life subordinated bonds (still investment grade) that insurance companies tend to hold. Also, for floating-rate bonds, the underlying logic would remain the same, where a bond priced away from par would include a long or short stream of interest, the value of which would change as a function of changes in the bond's maturity.

Treasury Bonds and Hedging
In some cases, fixed-income positions may be hedged for their interest rate risk, which in our framework can be defined as the risk of a change in the discount rate $y$. The discount rate could be seen as the sum of a risk-free discount rate $r$ and some premium, a spread $s$, specific to the bond: $y = r + s$. Introducing this risk-free rate allows us to define Treasury bonds that could be used for hedging.

We consider a highly simplified risk-free discount rate random process $(r_t)_{t \geq 0}$, as it can only be observed at time zero and at time $t$ when information becomes available. The risk-free rate stays at the level $r_t$ until a given time $M$ when it reverts back to $r_0$. We are considering that the risk of changes in the valuation of Treasury bonds is concentrated in the medium term. We assume that $\mathbb{E}\left[e^{-r_t(M-t)}\right] = e^{-r_0(M-t)}$, so that in expectation discounting by $r_t$ over the period when it is applicable is the same as discounting with $r_0$.

We also only focus on Treasury bonds of maturity $M$ paying a continuously capitalized coupon $c_M$. Such a bond with a face value of 1 has the following value at time 0:

$$R_0 = \mathbb{E}\left[e^{c_M M - r_0 t - r_t(M-t)}\right].$$

If $c_M = r_0$, and thanks to the relationship between $r_t$ and $r_0$, then the Treasury bond is par priced:

$$R_0 = \mathbb{E}\left[e^{r_0 M - r_0 t - r_t(M-t)}\right] = 1.$$

At time $t$, the value of the initially par-priced Treasury bond writes $R_t(r_t) = e^{r_0 M - r_t(M-t)}$.

Now we consider the structured bond we analyzed earlier in this framework. The random maturity $T$ is now assumed to be greater than $M$ with probability 1. In other words, we may be hedging some interest rate exposure, but we do not address the interaction between the randomness in the discount rate and the randomness in the structured bond's maturity.

**Proposition 7.22** (Benefit of Par Pricing 2) *If a bond with a random maturity is hedged for interest rate risk, the net position value is deterministic if both the bond and the hedge are par priced.*

***Proof*** The bond is valued at the appropriate spread $s$ over Treasurys:

$$P_0 = B_0 \mathbb{E}\left[e^{cT} e^{-(r_0+s)t-(r_t+s)(M-t)-(r_0+s)(T-M)}\right].$$

We rewrite this in the following manner:

$$P_0 = B_0 \mathbb{E}\left[e^{(c-r_0-s)T+(r_0-r_t)(M-t)}\right],$$

which stresses that choosing $c = r_0 + s$ makes the bond par priced, since we have assumed $\mathbb{E}\left[e^{-r_t(M-t)}\right] = e^{-r_0(M-t)}$.

At time $t$, the value of the initially par-priced bond is

$$P_t(T, r_t) = B_0 e^{(r_0+s)T-(r_0+s)t-(r_t+s)(M-t)-(r_0+s)(T-M)}.$$

The notion of hedging we are applying here is that the holder of the bonds will want to minimize the variation in net position at the intermediate period due to changes in the risk-free discount rate, by selling short the Treasury bond with maturity $M$. The value of the total position at time 0 is 0 (both bonds being par priced), and we can look at the value at time $t$.

The ratio of the value of the bond, with a coupon $c$ to the par-priced Treasury bond used for hedging at time $t$, is

$$\begin{aligned} V_t(T, r_t) &= \frac{P_t(T, r_t)}{R_t(r_t)} \\ &= \frac{e^{cT-(r_0+s)t-(r_t+s)(M-t)-(r_0+s)(T-M)}}{e^{r_0 M - r_t(M-t)}} \\ &= e^{(c-r_o-s)T-r_0 t}. \end{aligned}$$

We can see that the hedging is efficient, since the value of $V_t$ does not depend on $r_t$. In addition, by picking the same coupon that made the bond par priced $c = r_0 + s$, we eliminate the noise in $V_t$ and make the value at time $t$ deterministic. □

In this case, we can see that if $T$ follows a distribution with a compact support $[T_L, T_H]$ then the lowest value that the hedged position $P_t(T, r_t) - R_t(r_t)$ can take is

$$e^{-r_0 t}\left(\mathbb{I}_{c>r_0+s} e^{(c-r_0-s)T_L} + \mathbb{I}_{c<r_0+s} e^{(c-r_0-s)T_H}\right) - 1,$$

again a direct function of the distance of the coupon to the par coupon.

Whether for hedged or unhedged positions, in our simplified framework with limited trading and information being revealed suddenly, par-priced bonds minimize the positions' value variability and can even eliminate it.

#### 7.2.1.2 Par-Priced Bonds Reducing Under Investment

The fact that the value of some asset would vary as it reflects information or knowledge of its underlying cash flows is not an issue in and by itself, in particular, if we consider that all agents are risk-neutral. There needs to be some explanation for the underlying desire of some firms to minimize the variations in the value of some of the assets they hold.

As mentioned earlier, we are considering firms holding securitized products, and unlike investment funds these firms have managers with inside information and shareholders. For the managers, all else being equal choosing projects with less noise reduces the costs attached to information asymmetries between them and the market. In order to show this result, we extend the original model from Miller and Rock (1985).

In the model from Miller and Rock, the firm's project returns a random amount at time 1, with a noise $\varepsilon_1$ centered at zero. With perfect information, the firm decides on its investments optimally and will size them so that the marginal return on investment is equal to the firm's risk-adjusted discount rate. The distribution of dividends or access to additional financing is driven by the optimal amount to be invested. If information is asymmetric and the firm's managers have inside information, they use dividends as a way of signaling the quality of the projects they can invest in, and the market values the firm based on that signal. As a result, now the amount of dividend drives the amount of investment, which is therefore not optimal as in the perfect information case anymore. By reducing the noise around the projects' returns, the difference between the ideal investment level and the one that is selected to signal optimally is reduced.

In the cases we are focusing on, the entities holding securitized products such as banks, insurance companies, or mortgage REITs typically hold a very substantial amount of assets relative to the magnitude of their income. As such, variations in the value of these assets are significant for their business.

Investment Decision in Full Information

Following Miller and Rock (1985), we consider a firm with an earnings stream expressed as

$$Y_t = f(I_{t-1}) + \varepsilon_t,$$

for $t = 1$ or $t = 2$, where the series of $Y_t$ represents the earnings, $I_{t-1}$ is the investment realized in the prior period, and $f(I_{t-1})$ is the output from that investment, with $f$ positive, infinitely differentiable, $f' > 0$ and $f'' < 0$. The investment $I$ is always assumed to be positive or null. The series of $\varepsilon$ are random terms, assumed to follow a distribution with a compact support in $[\varepsilon_L, \varepsilon_H]$ such that $\mathbb{P}[\varepsilon \leq z]$ is strictly increasing in $z$ and $\mathbb{E}[\varepsilon] = 0$. We do not consider a resilience effect as in Miller and Rock's original article as it is not necessary to capture the main effects at play in our approach.

The firm can raise additional funds during the period noted $B_t$, and pays a dividend $D_t$. The firm's value to the original stockholders at time 1 is

$$V_1 = D_1 + e^{-y}\mathbb{E}[Y_2] - B_1$$

where $y$ represents the discount factor required by investors applied over one period.

In the full information case, the firm chooses $D_1$, $B_1$, and $I_1$ to maximize $V_1$ subject to the funding condition $Y_1 + B_1 = I_1 + D_1$. The variable $\varepsilon_1$ is known to the market and hence we can write

$$V_1 = Y_1 - I_1 + e^{-y} f(I_1).$$

This is consistent with the result from Modigliani and Miller, as the value of the firm does not depend on the amount of financing. The only choice to address for optimality is that of the investment:

$$\max_i Y_1 - i + e^{-y} f(i),$$

and at the optimum $f'(I_1^*) = e^y$.

Let us now introduce the exposure to a portfolio of bonds in the firm's business. We consider that the firm has to possess this exposure, in order to satisfy its regulatory requirements for reserves. These assets can be seen as a way for the firm to be able to carry out its normal production function. The size of the portfolio is given, and the yield on these assets is the market required yield for the firm $y$. We will allow a choice of coupon $c$ such that $c \in [c_L, c_H]$ with $c_L < y < c_H$, which the firm makes public at or before the dividend announcement. We can also consider that the investment strategy is decided in advance at the prior period and made public at that time. The securities have a random maturity $T_t$ with support in $[T_L, T_H]$ with $T_L > 1$ such that $\mathbb{P}[T_t \leq z]$ is strictly increasing, and all the $T_t$ are independent of the other sources of noise. We will consider that at the end of each period the securities are rolled, i.e., they are sold at their market value and new ones are purchased. Rolling position is a typical way of keeping an aggregate maturity roughly constant while benefiting from the higher yields of longer instruments. The value of the securities is revealed at the end of the period, just as in our prior treatment of par-priced bonds. Also, the funding cost of the securities portfolio is taken into account, and its cost is the same as for the firm, $y$. As a result, the contribution of the portfolio to the earnings comes from any potential differences in valuation of the securities, as a positive or as a negative.

For a given amount $\alpha$ of such securities acquired in portfolio, the contribution to earnings at each period can be written as a function of the coupon choice $\pi_t(c) = \alpha\left[e^{(c-y)T_t} - \mathbb{E}[e^{(c-y)T_t}]\right]$ so that the output at period 1 is

$$Y_1 = f(I_0) + \varepsilon_1 + \pi_1(c).$$

Note that the choice of the securities' coupon is made ex ante, so that $c$ cannot depend on the observation of $T_1$. Since $\mathbb{E}\left[\left[e^{(c-y)T_1} - \mathbb{E}[e^{(c-y)T_1}]\right]\right] = 0$, introducing this additional noise term does not change the result from Miller and Rock in the full information case. The managers' investment strategy remains optimal.

Asymmetrical Information and Impact of Securities Coupons

We now turn to the asymmetrical information case, where investors cannot observe the random components in earnings nor the in the securities portfolio's performance directly. Right after the information is made public, the information sets are $\phi_d = \{I_0, \varepsilon_1, \pi_1(c), I_1, D_1\}$ for the firm's directors and $\phi_m = \{I_0, D_1\}$ for the market. Then, as explained in Miller and Rock (1985), there is an earnings announcement effect when the total earnings are communicated by the firm. Also, since dividends are constrained by the amount of available earnings, if the market assumes that the firm's investment decision is optimal, then the dividend announcement carries the same information as the earnings announcement.

**Proposition 7.23** (Miller–Rock with Securities Portfolio) *Under asymmetrical information, the firm managers will under invest and use dividends as a signal of their earnings. The optimal dividend schedule depends on coupon choice through the boundary condition so that at the lowest possible earnings there is no under investment.*

***Proof*** With our assumptions, and if the firm invested the optimal amount $I_1^*$, the difference between the actual net dividend and the expected net dividend is

$$(D_1 - B_1) - \mathbb{E}[D_1 - B_1] = \varepsilon_1 + \pi_1(c).$$

The price change triggered by the dividend's announcement is

$$V_1 - \mathbb{E}[V_1] = \varepsilon_1 + \pi_1(c).$$

There may be an incentive for the firm to inflate the dividend in order to increase its value: the managers may benefit by then selling stock at an inflated price, or they may have received a monetary incentive from some stockholders to do the detriment of other investors. If such gains can be garnered, then one cannot make the assumption that the firm will invest the optimal amount in its production but will rather pay more dividends.

In this case, the investors will need to assume that the firm is under investing, and the firm itself will need to under invest in a consistent fashion, the signaling of its strategy being based on the choice of dividend.

From the standpoint of the directors, the value of the firm at time 1 is $V_1^d(Y_1, D_1) = D_1 + e^{-y} f(I_1) = D_1 + e^{-y} f(Y_1 - D_1)$, which is simply the full information value, while the value of the firm from the standpoint of investors is $V_1^m(D_1) = D_1 + e^{-y}\mathbb{E}[f(I_1)|D_1, I_0]$. Note that conditioning by $\{Y_1, D_1\}$ is the same as conditioning by $\{I_1, D_1\}$ due to the fact that $D_1 + I_1 = Y_1$. The firm director's objective to maximize the wealth of shareholders is now ambiguous since there may be shareholders wishing to sell after the announcement, and some wishing to hold their shares, and the value of the firm to each is different. Miller and Rock propose to solve this problem by using a social welfare function where the interest of each group is weighted according to their amount of stock holdings.

We write $k$ the share of stockholders who wish to sell, and then the aggregate wealth is $W_1(Y_1, D_1) = kV_1^m(D_1) + (1 - k)V_1^d(Y_1, D_1)$, which depends on both the total earnings and the dividend choice.

The directors control the coupon $c$ of the structured securities purchased at the beginning of the period. Given $\varepsilon_1$ and $T_1$, which are observed by the firm directors, and the coupon, the earnings are uniquely determined. Since the coupon choice is made before time 1, before all random variable realizations are known, we can first consider it is a given, and then find its optimal value. We write the firm's optimization program as a function of the earnings it observes, with coupon choice a given:

$$
\begin{aligned}
W^*(v, c) &= \max_d W_1(v, d, c) \\
&= \max_d \left[ k V_1^m(d, c) + (1 - k) V_1^d(v, d, c) \right]
\end{aligned}
$$

Note that the market's valuation of the firm explicitly depends on the coupon choice, which is known.

Given a coupon choice $c$, we can write $D^*(v, c) = \arg\max_d W_1(v, d, c)$. This expression of the dividend as a function of the total earnings states how the firm will choose dividends optimally based on the information it possesses, given a prior choice of coupon. Inverting this relationship, we define $\Upsilon$ such that $\Upsilon(D^*(v, c), c) = v$, and $\Upsilon$ gives us the earnings that correspond to a given dividend and coupon level.

Both parties (the stockholders who remain and the firm) in this game establish their valuation as a function of the other party's estimated firm valuation. At any equilibrium, the investors and the firm will have rational expectations if $D_c^*$ is single valued and hence

$$
V_1^m(d, c) = V_1^d(\Upsilon(d, c), d, c).
$$

Now recall that we made specific assumptions about the distribution of $\varepsilon_1$ and $T_1$, so that $\varepsilon_1 + \pi_1(c)$ has a strictly increasing cumulative distribution function and a compact support. We can compute the lower bound for $\varepsilon_1 + \pi_1(c)$. Both variables are independent and the minimum for $\pi_1(c)$ depends on the structured bond's coupon choice relative to the required yield. We have

$$
\begin{aligned}
m(c) &= \inf_\omega \left(\varepsilon_1 + \pi_1(c)\right) \\
&= \varepsilon_L + \alpha \left[ \mathbb{I}_{c<y} e^{(c-y)T_H} + \mathbb{I}_{c>y} e^{(c-y)T_L} - \mathbb{E}[e^{(c-y)T}] \right].
\end{aligned}
$$

Using this definition, the lowest possible value for $Y_1^c$ is $f(I_0) + m(c)$. We also write $M(c) = \max_\omega \left(\varepsilon_1 + \pi_1(c)\right)$.

Miller and Rock in their original article then use the fact that the distribution for the noise has a minimum and has a strictly increasing cumulative distribution, and assuming rational expectations, conclude there exist infinitely many informationally consistent equilibria following Riley (1979).

In the case where a firm observes this minimal value for its earnings, whatever dividends it pays would be less than the dividend paid by the firm if it observed any higher level of earnings, because the equilibrium is informationally consistent. Hence, there is no reason for a firm in this situation to depart from the full information optimal level of investment $I_1^*$ (which, as we pointed out earlier, does not depend on $c$). As a consequence, $D^*\left(f(I_0) + m(c)\right) = f(I_0) + m(c) - I_1^*$ or in other words the optimal dividend for this lowest realization is the one corresponding to the optimal investment in the full information case. Equivalently, if $d_c^* = f(I_0) + m(c) - I_1^*$ is the optimal dividend, $\Upsilon(d_c^*, c) = f(I_0) + m(c)$.

Separately, and still following Miller and Rock (1985), we can express the first-order conditions by substituting the rational expectations equality in the optimization program (dropping the time subscript for clarity and using subscripts to denote derivatives), and using $\Upsilon(d, c) = v$ we obtain

$$kV_v^d(\Upsilon(d, c), d, c)\Upsilon_d(d, c) + V_d^d(\Upsilon(d, c), d, c) = 0.$$

The function $V^d$ is known: $V^d(v, d, c) = d + e^{-y} f(v - d)$ and does not depend on $c$ as a separate variable from $v$. In effect, the earnings schedule given dividends $\Upsilon$ only depends on the coupon through the initial condition $\Upsilon(f(I_0) + m(c) - I_1^*) = f(I_0) + m(c)$. The differential equation can, hence, be rewritten as

$$\Upsilon_d(d) = \frac{f'(\Upsilon(d) - d) - e^y}{kf'(\Upsilon(d) - d)}.$$

and effectively as is common in signaling equilibria, this schedule only depends on the worst-case outcome of the variable unobserved by the uninformed party.

The second-order condition writes

$$\Upsilon_d(d)e^{-y} f''(v - d) < 0,$$

which implies that for a maximum to be obtained $\Upsilon$ must be strictly increasing. If $\Upsilon_d > 0$, then this also implies that $f'(\Upsilon(d) - d) - e^y > 0$ and as a result under investment occurs since $\Upsilon(d) - d$ is not large enough for $f'(\Upsilon(d) - d)$ to reach 0. □

While we have seen that the noise in the earnings distribution leads to under investment, we have not clearly captured the relationship between the extent of the noise and the extent of the resulting under investment. This question is in fact not addressed by Miller and Rock.

In order to look into this issue, we first define the investment function $H$ as a function of $\delta$, the additional dividend beyond the lowest observed dividend: $H(\delta) = \Upsilon(d^* + \delta) - (d^* + \delta)$. The differential equation for $\Upsilon$ can be rewritten for $H$ as follows:

$$H_\delta(\delta) = \frac{(1 - k)f'(H(\delta)) - e^y}{kf'(H(\delta))}.$$

The boundary conditions are now given in the same manner, notwithstanding the coupon choice:

$$H(0) = \Upsilon(d_c^*, c) - d_c^* = I_1^*.$$

Hence, $H$ does not depend on $c$ in any way. The function $H$ follows the same curve, given a starting point defined as $\Upsilon(d_c^*, c) - d^* = I_1^*$. If we vary $c$, that starting point's abscissa is shifted but the curve of $H$ remains the same.

**Proposition 7.24** (Optimality of Par-Priced Securities) *Assume that the production functions $f$ and $M(c)$ are such that if $f'(H(\delta)) = \frac{e^y}{1-k}$ then $\delta > M(c) - m(c)$. Then the firm managers choose $c = y$, and the cost of not choosing a par-priced coupon is an increasing function of $|c - y|$.*

***Proof*** With a given dividend $c$, we know that $Y_1 \in [f(I_0) + m(c), f(I_0) + M(c)]$ and therefore the earnings inferred from the optimal schedule must also verify $\Upsilon(d, c) \in [f(I_0) + m(c), f(I_0) + M(c)]$.

Based on the definition of $H$, we can determine that $H_\delta(0) = -1$. Also, we can compute the first-order condition for the minimum reached by $H$, $H_\delta(\delta_0) = 0$:

$$f'(H(\delta_0)) = \frac{e^y}{1-k}.$$

Hence, starting from the smallest possible additional dividend, $H$ is downward sloping and reaches a minimum of $[f']^{-1}\left(\frac{e^y}{1-k}\right)$. The additional dividend level $\delta_0$ for which this minimum is reached does not depend on $c$, but we have assumed it is greater than $M(c) - m(c)$. Note that for a logarithmic production function of the form $f(x) = a\ln(x + b)$, for example, this condition is verified as the solution $H$ is decreasing with an asymptotic minimum.

In addition, $f'$ is a positive function the input of which is also positive and therefore $H$ is necessarily positive. As a result $\Upsilon(d, c) \geq d$ and hence the possible dividends from the schedule $D^*(\upsilon)$ are in $[f(I_0) + m(c), f(I_0) + M(c)]$. Since $H$ is decreasing, the maximal investment of $I_1^*$ is reached at $\delta = 0$ and the minimal investment at $\delta = M(c) - m(c)$.

For the managers, the ex ante (at the time of coupon choice) expected level of investment is $\mathbb{E}[H^c|\phi_m]$, that is, where $\varepsilon_1$ and $T_1$ are random variables and not yet known. The managers will look to maximize the level of investment, since it increases firm value, and hence will determine the coupon $c*$ that maximizes

$$\max_c \mathbb{E}[H^c|\phi_m].$$

Starting from a coupon equal to the required yield $c = y$, we look at how the expectation varies for a small perturbation. Without a loss in generality, we will consider an increase in coupon (since the calculations are symmetrical for a decrease). We write for a coupon $c = y + \epsilon$

$$\pi_1(c) = \alpha\epsilon(T_1 - \mathbb{E}[T_1]) + o(\epsilon).$$

The full expression for the expectation can be simplified by using a development around the coupon at $y$:

$$\begin{aligned}
\mathbb{E}[H^c|\phi_m] &= \int \mathbb{P}[\varepsilon_1 \in d\varepsilon] \int \mathbb{P}[T_1 \in dt] H\left(D^*(Y_1) - (f(I_0) + m(c))\right) \\
&= \int \mathbb{P}[\varepsilon_1 \in d\varepsilon] \int \mathbb{P}[T_1 \in dt] \\
& H\left(D^*(f(I_0) + \varepsilon + \alpha\varepsilon(t - \mathbb{E}[T_1])) - (f(I_0) + m(c))\right) \\
&= \int \mathbb{P}[\varepsilon_1 \in d\varepsilon] \int \mathbb{P}[T_1 \in dt] H\left(D^*(f(I_0) + \varepsilon) - (f(I_0) + m(c))\right) \\
&+ \epsilon \int \mathbb{P}[\varepsilon_1 \in d\varepsilon] \int \mathbb{P}[T_1 \in dt] \left[\alpha(t - \mathbb{E}[T])D_\upsilon^*(f(I_o) + \varepsilon) + \alpha(\mathbb{E}[T] - T_L))\right] \\
& H_\delta\left[D^*(f(I_0) + \varepsilon) - (f(I_0) + \varepsilon_L)\right].
\end{aligned}$$

Replacing, integrating with respect to $t$ and simplifying we get

$$\mathbb{E}[H^c|\phi_m] = \mathbb{E}[H^y|\phi_m] \\ + \epsilon \int \mathbb{P}[\varepsilon_1 \in d\varepsilon]\alpha(\mathbb{E}[T] - T_L))H_\delta \left[D^*(f(I_0) + \varepsilon) - (f(I_0) + \varepsilon_L)\right].$$

But we know that $H_\delta$ is negative and $\mathbb{E}[T] - T_L$ is positive, and conclude that

$$\mathbb{E}[H^c|\phi_m] \leq \mathbb{E}[H^y|\phi_m],$$

with the difference locally proportional to the distance between the coupon and the market yield $\epsilon$. □

Equipped with this result, we can now look at the impact such a requirement for par coupons has on structures and collateral.

### 7.2.2 Allocation of Interest and Principal

Maybe the most fundamental discrepancy between the security design models, we have discussed earlier in Chap. 4 and the structuring logic from Chap. 6 is the fact that interest and principal are very systematically segregated in many structures. The model by DeMarzo and Duffie, which has the most complete representation of the underlying collateral noise and information structure, considers cash flows as an aggregate. In consequence, the structuring is applied to the total cash flow, and the typical optimal debt-like contract would commingle all interest payments with the principal. Since this is quite different from standard structuring logic, it makes sense to look closer into the application of security design models to cash flows more closely representative of a loan portfolio.

We follow the model from Gauthier (2019) closely. In order to capture differential behaviors between interest and principal, we choose to model a random coupon, and separately collateral losses. The coupon's randomness may come from the fact it is indexed on an external reference, such as 3-month Libor. We assume that the coupon as a random variable is independent of the credit performance. This is a reasonable assumption because the dynamics of coupon indices are typically not strongly related to the credit performance of a particular pool of loans. In addition, the coupon has a multiplicative effect on the principal returned: indeed, the loans that default do not pay their interest, so credit losses effectively lower the total amount of interest recovered.

#### 7.2.2.1 Framework and Assumptions

The collateral balance is set to 1 for simplicity, and the portfolio maturity is fixed at time 1. The underlying losses $L$ are assumed to follow a distribution with a compact support included in $[0, 1]$. The coupon $c$ is a positive random variable. The interest payment comes from the coupon rate $c$ and is made at maturity. Since there may be credit losses and the loans that default do not pay a coupon, the total cash flow from the collateral is $Y = (1 - L)(1 + c)$.

We consider we are in the framework of the security design model from DeMarzo and Duffie[3]: an issuer with a higher retention cost than investors and with information on the assets' credit risk is looking to sell optimal securities. We assume that the issuer observes information that conditions $L$ privately, as it can access information relevant to the quality of the loans, but does not know $c$ in advance. Although the issuer of loans may be aware of or control some of the drivers of the quality of the loans, it cannot control or know in advance the value of interest rate indices. While the model from DeMarzo and Duffie can be extended to account for a nonzero discount rate for investors, it makes calculations more extensive and does not add to our analysis. Hence, as in their original model, we assume that investors do not discount cash flows, and the issuer discounts them at a rate $y$. To investors, without discounting, the value of an asset paying principal $1 - L$ and coupon $c$ is $\mathbb{E}[(1 + c)(1 - L)]$.

In the model by DeMarzo and Duffie, the entire cash flow $Y$ is the contractible variable, and it is only assumed that $Y$ is not independent of the privately observed $Z$. In order to account for the distinction between interest and principal payments, we will write $Y = XV$ where $X = (1 + c)$ is the interest multiple, $X$ is independent of $V$ and $X \geq 1$.[4] The variable $V$, representing the principal recovered, is assumed to possess a conditional distribution $\mu_V(v, z)$ relative to $Z$, that is, continuous as a function of $z$. Also, we assume that $V \in [0, 1]$, as one cannot recover more than the initial balance.

The extension of the model from DeMarzo and Duffie to an investor-specific discount rate, along with a random payment time $T$ independent of $Z$ but not independent of $Y$ is difficult, because then the cash flows evaluated by the issuer would have the form $g(Y)(1 + y)^{-T}$. This makes the extension of the model much more complex and potentially intractable. However, the simple random coupon approach we follow can represent the maturity randomness if the investors' discount rate is null: we can just consider that the cash flows have the form $V(1 + cT)$ where $c$ may be a random coupon, and $T$ is a positive continuous variable representing the random maturity. The issuer's discounting of the future cash flows is assumed to be independent of the time over which the cash flows take place, for example, if all interest payments to the issuer are kept in escrow until a legal maturity equal to the maximum possible $T$. Also note that the time $T$ may represent the average life of cash flows taking place over time, rather than a maturity at which a full bullet payment takes place. The fact that the issuer does not have any privileged information on timing, but only on credit, is consistent with the notion that prepayments may be driven by factors independent of the issuer's control, unlike loan origination.

---

[3] See Chap. 4.

[4] We are assuming investors do not discount cash flows, so implicitly we are requiring that the collateral coupon is higher than the yield required by the market.

One important technical aspect is that, as in the original model, we assume that $V$ has a uniform worst-case $z_L$: there exists a value $z_L$ and an increasing function $\nu_z(v)$ such that for all measurable $g$,

$$\int g(v)\mu_V(v,z)dv = \int g(v)\nu_z(v)\mu_V(v,z_L)dv.$$

Because of this, for any increasing function $g$, $z_L$ is the minimum argument of $\inf_z \mathbb{E}[g(Y)|Z=z]$. We also assume that $Y = XV$ has the same uniform worst-case $z_L$.

A most important extension of the original model is to consider that interest is contractible separately from principal. In other words, a security design can be expressed as $g(X, V)$ rather than $g(XV)$. Note that although we represent $V$ as $WZ$ explicitly, neither of these two variables can be contracted upon since $Z$ is private. We will assume that all security designs we consider are continuous and increasing (in $y$ or in both $x$ and $v$), and in all cases $g(Y) \leq Y$.

As in the model by DeMarzo and Duffie, the issuer decides on an optimal design before being able to observe $Z$ or the other variables, although the distributions of all the random variables are known in advance.

We note $V(g(Y))$ for the value to the issuer of a particular security design, following DeMarzo and Duffie, with

$$V(g(Y)) = \frac{y}{1+y}\mathbb{E}[g(Y)|Z=z_L]\mathbb{E}\left[\left(\frac{\mathbb{E}[g(Y)|Z=z_L]}{\mathbb{E}[g(Y)|Z]}\right)^{\frac{1}{y}}\right],$$

where we use the fact that $\mathbb{E}[g(Y)|Z=z_L] = \min_z \mathbb{E}[g(Y)|Z=z]$. Note that the value $V$ is defined as a functional of $g(Y)$, not as a function of a particular $g(Y)$-measurable outcome.

#### 7.2.2.2 Dynamic Rather Than Standard Debt

**Standard debt** can be defined as a particular security design of the form $g(y) = y \wedge D$, for a face value $D$. It has been shown to be an optimal security design under some particular conditions. We define **dynamic debt** with face value $D$ as a design of the form $g(x, v) = f(x)(v \wedge D)$; the term dynamic means that the actual total cash flow that is paid is random even if the full face value is repaid.

Standard debt of the form $g(XV) = XV \wedge D$ goes against the grain of practice in securitization, because it commingles interest and principal cash flows, in such a way that interest may effectively compensate for a shortfall in principal, and principal may compensate for a shortfall in interest. This is very different from the typical designs in securitizations, where in most cases interest is paid in a prorated fashion relative to the expected principal payments. In effect, designs in the form of dynamic debt are much more common in securitization than standard debt, as defined in DeMarzo and Duffie (1999) or DeMarzo (2005).

We will see, under our assumptions, that if interest is contractible then a standard debt contract is not optimal, but rather a dynamic debt contract allowing for a prorated coupon payment of the form $g(xv) = x(v \wedge D)$ for a face value $D$.

We have the following proposition.

**Proposition 7.25** (Optimality of Dynamic Debt) *Among all contracts of the form $g(xv)$, standard debt $g(xv) = xv \wedge D$ is optimal for some $D$. Among all contracts of the form $g(x, v)$, which include those of the form $g(xv)$, dynamic debt $g(x, v) = x(v \wedge D)$ is optimal for some $D$, and therefore dominates standard debt.*

***Proof*** First, since we have assumed $Y$ has a uniform worst-case $z_L$, then using Proposition 4.19 we know that among all contracts of the form $g(Y)$, where interest is not contractible separately, the optimal contract has the form $g(Y) = Y \wedge D$ for some $D$.

Let us now show that optimal contracts have the form $f(x)k(v) = (x \wedge D_0)(v \wedge D_1)$. We consider a generic design with contractible interest $g(x, v) \leq xv$. We assume $g$ is increasing and continuous relative to $x$ and $v$. Given $g$, we define a dynamic debt contract $d(x, v) = (x \wedge D_0)(v \wedge D_1)$. Note that as a function of $D_1$ and as a function of $D_0$, $d$ is increasing and continuous. We set $D_0$ and $D_1$ such that

$$\mathbb{E}[d(X, V)|Z = z_L] = \mathbb{E}[g(X, V)|Z = z_L].$$

Finding such values for $D_0$ and $D_1$ is possible since $d$ is continuous and increasing relative to them, and varying $D_0$ and $D_1$, $0 \leq d(x, v) \leq xv$, and $0 \leq g(x, v) \leq xv$.

Then, comparing $V(d(X, V))$ and $V(g(X, V))$ only depends on the difference between $\mathbb{E}[d(X, V)|Z]$ and $\mathbb{E}[g(X, V)|Z]$. We write $e(x, v) = g(x, v) - d(x, v)$, which may be positive or negative, but is continuous in $x$ and in $v$. In addition, for $V \geq D_1$ and $X \geq D_0$, $e(x, v)$ is increasing in $v$. Hence, there exists a continuous function $v^*$ depending on $g$, $D_0$ and $D_1$ such that $v > v^*(x)$ is equivalent to $e(x, v) > 0$.

Now, we write

$$\begin{aligned}
\mathbb{E}[e(X, V)|Z = z] &= \mathbb{E}[\mathbb{I}_{e(X,V)>0} e(X, V)|Z = z] + \mathbb{E}[\mathbb{I}_{e(X,V)\leq 0} e(X, V)|Z = z] \\
&= \mathbb{E}[\mathbb{I}_{V>v^*(X)} e(X, V)\nu_z(V)|Z = z_L] \\
&\quad + \mathbb{E}[\mathbb{I}_{V\leq v^*(X)} e(X, V)\nu_z(V)|Z = z_L],
\end{aligned}$$

where we know that $\nu_z$ is increasing. Noting that the second term in the sum is negative, we can write

$$\mathbb{E}[e(X, V)|Z = z] \geq \mathbb{E}[\nu_z(v^*(X))]\mathbb{E}[e(X, V)|Z = z_L].$$

However, we set $D_0$ and $D_1$ so that $\mathbb{E}[e(X, V)|Z = z_L] = 0$ and therefore $\mathbb{E}[e(X, V)|Z = z] \geq 0$. As a consequence, given a generic contract $g$, we have determined a superior contract of the form $(x \wedge D_0)(V \wedge D_1)$.

Now, we consider contracts of this form $g(x, v) = f(x)k(v)$, with $f(x) = (x \wedge D_0)$ and $k(v) = (v \wedge D_1)$. We can write

$$V(g(X, V)) = \frac{y}{1+y}\mathbb{E}[f(X)]\mathbb{E}[k(V)|Z = z_L]\mathbb{E}\left[\left(\frac{\mathbb{E}[k(V)|Z = z_L]}{\mathbb{E}[k(V)|Z]}\right)^{\frac{1}{y}}\right].$$

This value is maximal for $f$ set as the identity, and therefore the optimal contract takes the form: $X(V \wedge D)$ for some $D$ that maximizes $V(X(V \wedge D))$. □

For specific contracting of interest cash flows, we therefore find that the optimal security design is consistent with the structures observed in securitization. Prorated interest is paid to the senior bonds.

We note

$$m(D) = \mathbb{E}[V \wedge D|Z = z_L]\mathbb{E}\left[\left(\frac{\mathbb{E}[V \wedge D|Z = z_L]}{\mathbb{E}[V \wedge D|Z]}\right)^{\frac{1}{y}}\right].$$

We will then note $D^*$ the optimal face value that maximizes $m$:

$$D^* = \arg\max_D m(D).$$

This optimal $D^*$ is a function of $y$ and of the distribution of $V$ and $Z$, and is the optimal face value that maximizes the value of the dynamic debt contract $x(v \wedge D)$ for the issuer. We will write the optimal dynamic debt contract $g_{PR}(x, v) = x(v \wedge D^*)$. Also for simplicity we write $m = m(D^*)$ since $D^*$ depends on the same inputs as $m$.

Note that the senior tranche is not entirely sold to investors, and the issuer retains part of it. The quantity sold, according to DeMarzo and Duffie (1999), is expressed as

$$Q^*(\mathbb{E}[g_{PR}(X, V)|Z]) = \left(\frac{\mathbb{E}[V \wedge D^*|Z = z_L]}{\mathbb{E}[V \wedge D^*|Z]}\right)^{\frac{1+y}{y}} < 1.$$

For convenience, we will write the expected quantity as

$$\mathbb{E}\left[Q^*(\mathbb{E}[g_{PR}(X, V)|Z])\right] = q,$$

since $D^*$ depends on the same inputs as well. The expected price corresponding to this quantity is

$$\mathbb{E}\left[P^*\left(Q^*(\mathbb{E}[g_{PR}(X, V)|Z])\right)\right] = \mathbb{E}\left[\mathbb{E}[g_{PR}(X, V)|Z]\right] = \mathbb{E}[g_{PR}(X, V)] = p\mathbb{E}[X].$$

Both $q$ and $p$ as expectations represent either the investors estimates or the issuer's own estimates before knowing the private information $Z$.

We can make some further assumptions to potentially simplify the expression of the optimal securities, but they are not essential to obtaining our results. In particular, it is reasonable to assume that the principal amount $V$ is the product of two independent variables: $V = WZ$, where $Z$ is the issuer's private information, and $W$ represents the common information on credit risk. We assume that $W \in [w_L, 1]$ and $Z \in [z_L, 1]$. Using a multiplicative relationship to represent private information is consistent with the issuer's knowledge of credit risk being expressed in odds ratios: the characteristics of a particular portfolio of loans only known to the issuer may make it worse or better than the typical portfolio.

We can characterize how to satisfy the uniform worst-case condition when the cash flows behave multiplicatively relative to the issuer's information, as we have assumed above.

**Proposition 7.26** (Conditions for Uniform Worst Case) *If the distribution $\mu_A$ of a random variable $A$ is log-concave and such that $\frac{\mu'_A(a)}{\mu_A(a)}$ vanishes at zero, or if $\frac{\mu'_A(a)}{\mu_A(a)}$ goes to infinity and $\frac{\mu'_A(a)}{\mu_A(a)} \geq \alpha \frac{\mu'_A(\alpha a)}{\mu_A(\alpha a)}$ for $\alpha \geq 1$, then the uniform worst case of $AZ$ is $z_L$.*

***Proof*** We want to show that $AZ$ has a uniform worst case $z_L$ for any independent random variable $A$ with a distribution $\mu_A$ verifying the conditions of the Proposition.

In this case, we can write the conditional expectation $\mathbb{E}[g(AZ)|Z = z]$ as follows:

$$\begin{aligned}
\int g(y)\mu(y,z)dy &= \int g(za)\mu_A(a)da \\
&= \int g(y)\mu_A\left(\frac{y}{z}\right)\frac{dy}{z} \\
&= \int g(y)\frac{z_L\mu_A\left(\frac{y}{z}\right)}{z\mu_A\left(\frac{y}{z_L}\right)}\mu_A\left(\frac{y}{z_L}\right)\frac{dy}{z_L} \\
&= \int g(z_L a)\frac{z_L\mu_A\left(\frac{z_L}{z}a\right)}{z\mu_A(a)}\mu_A(a)\,da.
\end{aligned}$$

And therefore the Radon–Nikodym derivative is

$$\nu_z(y) = \frac{z_L\mu_A\left(\frac{y}{z}\right)}{z\mu_A\left(\frac{y}{z_L}\right)}.$$

Since the $z_L$ is a lower bound of $Z$, any value $z$ in the domain of $Z$ verifies $z \geq z_L$ and $\frac{z}{z_L} > 1$.

For $\nu_z(y)$ to be increasing, the first derivative needs to be positive. If we write $a = \frac{y}{z}$ and $\alpha a = \frac{y}{z_L}$ for simplicity (with $\alpha > 1$), the condition is

$$\mu'_A(a)\mu_A(\alpha a) \geq \alpha\mu_A(a)\mu'_A(\alpha a).$$

Now we show that if $\mu_A$ is log-concave, along with another condition, then the condition

$$\frac{\mu'_A(a)}{\mu_A(a)} \geq \alpha \frac{\mu'_A(\alpha a)}{\mu_A(\alpha a)}$$

is verified.

Assume that $\mu_A$ is log-concave. In this case, $\frac{\mu'_A}{\mu_A}$ is decreasing. We also assume that the ratios are defined and vanish at zero, so that $\frac{\mu'_A(a)}{\mu_A(a)}$ goes to zero when $a$ goes to zero. With $a = 0$, we see that this is necessary for the inequality to be verified; otherwise, we would arrive at $\alpha \leq 1$. Therefore, we see that $\frac{\mu'_A}{\mu_A} \leq 0$, so this ratio must be decreasing and also negative.

Now, we note that thanks to log-concavity

$$\frac{\mu'_A(a)}{\mu_A(a)} \geq \frac{\mu'_A(\alpha a)}{\mu_A(\alpha a)},$$

but both sides of this inequality are negative so

$$\frac{\mu'_A(\alpha a)}{\mu_A(\alpha a)} \geq \alpha \frac{\mu'_A(\alpha a)}{\mu_A(\alpha a)},$$

and the condition is verified.

If on the other hand we do not assume that $\frac{\mu'_A(a)}{\mu_A(a)}$ goes to zero when $a$ goes to zero, then we need to assume that $\frac{\mu'_A(a)}{\mu_A(a)}$ goes to infinity when $a$ goes to zero, again so that $\alpha \leq 1$ is not implied. In this case, $\frac{\mu'_A}{\mu_A} \geq 0$ at least on some of its domain. In the cases where this quantity is negative, we can infer the condition as we have above. Where $\frac{\mu'_A}{\mu_A}$ is positive, and $\mu'_A$ is positive, the condition of log-concavity is not sufficient and we need a stronger specific assumption, that

$$\frac{\mu'_A(a)}{\mu_A(a)} \geq \alpha \frac{\mu'_A(\alpha a)}{\mu_A(\alpha a)}.$$

This implies that the second derivative of $\frac{\mu'_A(a)}{\mu_A(a)}$ be negative enough.

Hence, the variables of the form $ZA$ admit a uniform worst-case equal to $\inf Z$ when $A$ has a log-concave distribution $\mu_A$ either with $\frac{\mu'_A(a)}{\mu_A(a)}$ vanishing in zero, or if $\frac{\mu'_A(a)}{\mu_A(a)}$ goes to infinity in zero, then the stronger condition that $\frac{\mu'_A(a)}{\mu_A(a)} \geq \alpha \frac{\mu'_A(\alpha a)}{\mu_A(\alpha a)}$ is required. □

We can apply this proposition to $A = W$ and $A = WX$, in which case $V$ and $Y$ admit a uniform worst-case $z_L$, if $W$ and $WX$ verify one of the conditions of the proposition. For example, the distribution of density $\mu_A(a) = (\beta + 1)a^\beta$ on $[0, 1]$ satisfies the second condition. A uniform distribution satisfies the first condition.

#### 7.2.2.3 Targeted Coupon, Strip Down, and Excess-Spread

We can now see to what extent more complex structures such as stripping or excess-spread may be optimally used. In the optimal designs we have discussed so far, the need for structured securities to have a specific coupon. In particular, structured securities are typically issued at par, so that their initial valuation equals their face value. In other words, they are designed so that the expected coupon they pay exactly compensates for the discount rate demanded by investors. In our simple construct, we are assuming that investors do not have a discount rate, so we are setting the structural requirement in terms of a coupon target: an interest rate such that the expected value of the cash flows capitalizes at that rate.

In order to properly define the notion of coupon on a structured security, we need to also define its principal. Given any design $g$ such that $g(x, v) = f(x, v)k(x, v)$ and $f(x, v) \geq 1$, we call $f(x, v)$ the coupon and $k(x, v)$ the principal.

The requirement for a specific expected coupon $s$ implies that a security design $g = fk$ must verify

$$\mathbb{E}\left[f(X, V)k(X, V)\right] = (1+s)\mathbb{E}\left[k(X, V)\right].$$

We are interested in the most common case in securitization, where the coupon collected on collateral is greater than the coupon required by investors, so we assume that $1 + s < \mathbb{E}[X]$.

We will also need to define the notion of excess-spread more formally. The standard structuring method, without the use of excess-spread, allocates principal and interest separately: the interest paid on the structured bond comes from the collateral's interest payment, and the principal paid on the structured bond comes from the collateral's principal payment.

A standard structure can therefore be defined as a security design $g$ such that $g(x, v) = f(x)k(v)$ with $f(x) \leq x$ and $k(v) \leq v$. In other words, one cannot pay more interest or principal than the interest or principal, respectively, that is collected.

In contrast, an excess-spread structure allows for the use of interest to repay principal, and therefore does not have the particular restriction above: it can be defined as a security design $g$ such that $g(x, v) = f(x, v)k(x, v)$ with the only constraint that coupon is positive, so $f(x, v) \geq 1$.

Based on these definitions, we have the following proposition:

**Proposition 7.27** (Optimal Standard Structure) *With a target coupon of $s$, the standard structure $g_{SS(s)}$ paying principal of $V \wedge D^*$ and a coupon of $\frac{X(1+s)}{\mathbb{E}[X]}$ is optimal.*

***Proof*** First, we can verify that a standard structure with a coupon as defined satisfies the condition for the target coupon. The design stated in the proposition is a standard structure of the form $g(x, v) = \frac{x(1+s)}{\mathbb{E}[X]}k(v)$. We have

$$\mathbb{E}[g(X, V)] = (1+s)\mathbb{E}[k(V)]$$

so this security effectively pays the target coupon.

Once the coupon condition is verified, the value of this design to the issuer only depends on $k$. Finding the optimal $k$ is equivalent to finding an optimal design structured off of a cash flow $V$. Since we have assumed that $V$ had a uniform worst-case $z_L$ (the same as $VX$), then we know thanks to Proposition 4.19 that the optimal design $k$ is of the form $k(v) = v \wedge D$ for some $D$ maximizing

$$V(V \wedge D) = \frac{y\mathbb{E}[V \wedge D|Z = z_L]}{1+y}\mathbb{E}\left[\left(\frac{\mathbb{E}[V \wedge D|Z = z_L]}{\mathbb{E}[V \wedge D|Z]}\right)^{\frac{1}{y}}\right].$$

However, we know that this expression is maximized by $D^*$, and the proposition is proved. □

Under the constraint that a target coupon should be reached, and if one can only create standard structures, the common technique of stripping down the coupon is an optimal design.

However, this structure is not absolutely optimal. We can easily see that

$$V\left(g_{PR}(X, V)\right) - V\left(g_{SS(s)}(X, V)\right) = \frac{ym}{1+y}\left(\mathbb{E}[X] - (1+s)\right),$$

which is positive since $1 + s < \mathbb{E}[X]$.

Using excess-spread will allow us to circumvent this issue of suboptimality, as the following proposition illustrates.

**Proposition 7.28** (Optimal Excess-Spread Structure) *With a target coupon of $s$, the excess-spread structure $g_{XS(s)}$ paying principal of $\frac{X}{1+s}(V \wedge D^*)$ and a coupon of $(1 + s)$ is optimal. In addition,*

$$V\left(g_{XS(s)}(X, V)\right) = V\left(g_{PR}(X, V)\right).$$

***Proof*** We can verify that the design respects the target coupon constraint: with the principal set to $k(x, v) = \frac{x}{1+s}(v \wedge D^*)$, we have

$$\mathbb{E}\left[g_{XS(s)}(X, V)\right] = (1+s)\mathbb{E}\left[k(X, V)\right].$$

In addition, $g_{XS(s)}(x, v) = x(v \wedge D^*)$ and hence $g_{XS(s)} = g_{PR}$, so we know that $g_{XS(s)}$ is optimal. □

Whether the issuer creates a standard structure or uses excess-spread, the entire tranche is not sold. In both cases, the quantity sold is the same since it only depends on the distribution of $V$ and of $D^*$. We have

$$Q^*(\mathbb{E}[g_{SS(s)}(X, V)|Z]) = Q^*(\mathbb{E}[g_{XS(s)}(X, V)|Z]) = Q^*(\mathbb{E}[g_{PR}(X, V)|Z]).$$

In expectation, all these quantities are equal to $q$.

The total cash flow retained by the issuer can be seen equivalently as collateral minus $q$ shares of senior bonds, or 1 unit of subordinated cash flow plus $1 - q$ units of senior bond. The share of senior cash flows that is retained by the issuer can be paralleled with the typical principal return mechanisms that exist for subordinated tranches in securitization structures:

- In the case of standard structures, subordinated bonds are normally not pure last cash flow sequentials and receive some early principal payments. The subordinated bonds are said to deleverage in this case.
- In the case of excess-spread structures, the excess-spread residual retained by the issuer is typically paired with an over-collateralization tranche acting as a kind of subordinated tranche, which can also receive an over-collateralization release: an early principal payment. The share of senior cash flow retained by the issuer effectively works as such a release of safe principal cash flow.

Let us now see how both standard and excess-spread structures may coexist in the same market. The targeted coupon can be set so that the securities are par priced, which with our assumption regarding the investors' discount rate translates into $s = 0$. Also, in order to capture the more common reasons for randomness in total coupon cash flow, we consider that the coupon rate $c$ is fixed, but the timing is random, so that $X = (1 + cT)$ for some positive variable $T$ (such that the assumptions on $X$ are still valid).

In this case, the difference between the issuer's gain using an excess-spread structure and a standard structure, if securities have to be par priced, is

$$V\left(g_{XS(0)}(X, V)\right) - V\left(g_{SS(0)}(X, V)\right) = \frac{cy\mathbb{E}[T]m}{1+y}.$$

Since an excess-spread structure uses interest to pay principal, obtaining a rating would be expected to require more work, as the analysis of interest payments needs to be factored in, although in the case of a standard structure it is not necessary. As a result it is reasonable to assume there is a cost $k$ in executing such a structure. We consider this cost, paid by the issuer, to be proportional to the entire collateral balance (set to 1).

As a consequence, the issuer will choose to execute an excess-spread structure if

$$V\left(g_{XS(0)}(X, V)\right) - V\left(g_{SS(0)}(X, V)\right) > k.$$

This condition simplifies into

$$c > \frac{k(1+y)}{y\mathbb{E}[T]m}.$$

Hence, for low collateral coupons, we will expect to see standard structures, while high collateral coupons will lead to excess-spread structures. This is exactly consistent with the patterns that have been observed in securitization structures. In the prime market, securitizations are mostly based on standard structures, in the subprime market mostly on excess-spread structures, and in the Alt-A market both have been observed.

#### 7.2.2.4 NIM Structures

Net-interest margin structures have been quite common in the subprime market, and to a lesser extent in the Alt-A market. They are applied to the residual of an excess-spread securitization, which contains a stream of interest commingled with some principal.

Since a NIM is a further securitization of the cash flows kept by the issuer in the first place, we should be able to explain how a presumably optimal contract, the original structure, could be further improved. We know that NIM securitizations have for the most part been backed by several underlying residuals. Typically, NIMs combined two or three separate residuals, sometimes more, from similar deals, and not always the entirety of the residual cash flows.

We considered that the issuer designed the initial optimal excess-spread structure $g_{XS}(X, V) = X(V \wedge D^*)$ ex ante, before gaining access to the private information $Z$. At the time the structure is sold, the investors will be able to observe the amount issued $Q^*(Z)$, which is a function of the private information. In particular, if $\mathbb{E}[Y \wedge D^*|Z = z]$ is increasing as a function of $z$, investors will recoup the private information $Z$ from the observation of the quantity of bonds for sale.

In order to capture the logic in NIM securitizations, we will assume there are $n$ deals being structured, all in the same sector with the same distributional characteristics $Y_i = X_i W_i Z_i$ with $0 < i \leq n$, where there is the same uniform worst case $z_L$ for all $Y_i$. The $X_i$, $W_i$, and $Z_i$ are all independent with the same distributions as $X$, $W$, and $Z$. We have assumed that $X$ and $WX$ verified the conditions of Proposition 7.26, but we will further assume that $XWZ$ is log-concave, so that the uniform worst-case property is stable by summing variables of the form $X_i W_i Z_i$.

The issuer observes all the $Z_i$ and the deals' optimal structures are the same $D^*$. The tranches have not yet been sold, so that investors are not yet aware of the optimal quantities selected by the issuer for each deal $Q^*(Z_i)$. For each deal, the issuer retains the following cash flow, which is a combination of a slice of collateral and excess-spread structure residual:

$$C_i = (1 - Q^*(Z_i))X_i(W_i Z_i \wedge D^*) + X_i(W_i Z_i - D^*)\mathbb{I}_{W_i X_i - D^* \geq 0}.$$

The first term in this expression is the retained senior exposure, and the second one is the residual subordinated exposure. Since the retained senior exposure is not known at the time when the structure is created (before observing private information), it cannot be used as part of the NIM structure, and only the excess-spread structure residual $R_i = X_i(W_i Z_i - D^*)\mathbb{I}_{W_i Z_i - D^* \geq 0}$ is used to create a NIM.

Creating a NIM off of each deal separately cannot be optimal. Indeed, this would simply be equivalent to altering the initial structure, which we have shown to be optimally designed as $g_{XS}(x, v) = x(v \wedge D^*)$. As a result, a single NIM defined as $g_{NIM}(x, v) = f\left(x(v - D^*)\mathbb{I}_{v-D^*\geq 0}\right)$ for some design $f$ would only be optimal for $f = 0$. We will show that by pooling different residuals together, the NIM resecuritization further improves the issuer's value.

Since a NIM is based on an excess-spread structure, we can assume that it is possible to commingle interest and principal as needed in order to create par-valued securities, just as we did in the case of senior bonds relying on excess-spread.

**Proposition 7.29** (Optimality of NIM Resecuritization) *Creating a NIM structure off of a series of excess-spread residuals further improves the issuer's value. At the limit, the optimal structure is*

$$g_{NIM}\left(\frac{1}{n}\sum_{i=1}^{n} R_i\right) = \left(\frac{1}{n}\sum_{i=1}^{n} R_i\right) \wedge \mathbb{E}\left[(z_L XW - D^*)\mathbb{I}_{z_L XW - D^*\geq 0}\right],$$

*and the value to the issuer verifies*

$$\lim_{n\to\infty} V\left(g_{NIM}\left(\frac{1}{n}\sum_{i=1}^{n} R_i\right)\right) = \frac{y}{1+y}\mathbb{E}\left[(z_L XW - D^*)\mathbb{I}_{z_L XW - D^*\geq 0}\right].$$

***Proof*** We know that $V = WZ$ and $Y = XWZ$ have $z_L$ as a uniform worst case, and so does $(ZXW - D^*)\mathbb{I}_{ZXW-D^*\geq 0}$ as an increasing function. Thanks to the log-concavity assumption, $\sum_i (Z_i X_i W_i - D^*)\mathbb{I}_{Z_i X_i W_i - D^*\geq 0}$ also admits a uniform worst-case relative to the $Z_i$ and since the distribution is the same for all $i$ it is equal to $z_L$.

Hence, thanks to Proposition 4.19, we know that among all security designs of the form

$$g\left(\frac{1}{n}\sum_{i\geq 1}^{n}(Z_i X_i W_i - D^*)\mathbb{I}_{Z_i X_i W_i - D^*\geq 0}\right),$$

a standard debt contract

$$\begin{aligned} g^d_{NIM}&\left(\frac{1}{n}\sum_{i\geq 1}^{n}(Z_i X_i W_i - D^*)\mathbb{I}_{Z_i X_i W_i - D^*\geq 0}\right) \\ &= \left(\frac{1}{n}\sum_{i\geq 1}^{n}(Z_i X_i W_i - D^*)\mathbb{I}_{Z_i X_i W_i - D^*\geq 0}\right) \wedge d \end{aligned}$$

is optimal.

Let us now define

$$\begin{aligned} j_n(d,z) &= \mathbb{E}\left[\left(\frac{1}{n}\sum_{i\geq 1}^{n}(Z_iX_iW_i - D^*)\mathbb{I}_{Z_iX_iW_i-D^*\geq 0}\right)\wedge d|\forall i\leq n: Z_i = z\right] \\ &= \mathbb{E}\left[\left(\frac{1}{n}\sum_{i\geq 1}^{n}(zX_iW_i - D^*)\mathbb{I}_{zX_iW_i-D^*\geq 0}\right)\wedge d\right]. \end{aligned}$$

As $z_L$ is the uniform worst case for all the $Z_iX_iW_i$, we have

$$\begin{aligned} &\inf_{(z_i)_{1\leq i\leq n}} \mathbb{E}\left[\left(\frac{1}{n}\sum_{i\geq 1}^{n}(Z_iX_iW_i - D^*)\mathbb{I}_{Z_iX_iW_i-D^*\geq 0}\right)\wedge d|\forall i\leq n: Z_i = z_i\right] \\ &= \mathbb{E}\left[\left(\frac{1}{n}\sum_{i\geq 1}^{n}(Z_iX_iW_i - D^*)\mathbb{I}_{Z_iX_iW_i-D^*\geq 0}\right)\wedge d|\forall i\leq n: Z_i = z_L\right] \\ &= j_n(d,z_L). \end{aligned}$$

The value to the issuer of the contract $g^d_{NIM}$ is therefore as follows (we did not write the full random variable expression on the left-hand side for brevity):

$$\begin{aligned} V(g^d_{NIM}) &= \frac{y}{1+y} j_n(d,z_L) \\ \mathbb{E}&\left[\left(\frac{j_n(d,z_L)}{\mathbb{E}\left[\left(\frac{1}{n}\sum_{i\geq 1}^{n}(Z_iX_iW_i - D^*)\mathbb{I}_{Z_iX_iW_i-D^*\geq 0}\right)\wedge d|(Z_i)_{1\leq i\leq n}\right]}\right)^{\frac{1}{y}}\right]. \end{aligned}$$

The $X_iW_i$ are independent and identically distributed, so thanks to the weak law of large numbers, we know that $j_n(d,z)$ converges and

$$\lim_{n\to\infty} j_n(d,z) = \mathbb{E}\left[(zWX - D^*)\mathbb{I}_{zWX-D^*\geq 0}\right]\wedge d.$$

We define $r_L = \mathbb{E}\left[(z_LWX - D^*)\mathbb{I}_{z_LWX-D^*\geq 0}\right]$, so that if we set $d = r_L$ then

$$\lim_{n\to\infty} j_n(r_L,z) = \mathbb{E}\left[(zWX - D^*)\mathbb{I}_{zWX-D^*\geq 0}\right]\wedge r_L = r_L,$$

since $z_L$ is the uniform worst case of $WXZ$.

In addition, note that

$$r_L \geq \mathbb{E}\left[\left(\frac{1}{n}\sum_{i\geq 1}^{n}(Z_iX_iW_i - D^*)\mathbb{I}_{Z_iX_iW_i-D^*\geq 0}\right)\wedge r_L|(Z_i)_{1\leq i\leq n}\right]$$

as well as

$$\mathbb{E}\left[\left(\frac{1}{n}\sum_{i\geq 1}^{n}(Z_iX_iW_i - D^*)\mathbb{I}_{Z_iX_iW_i-D^*\geq 0}\right) \wedge r_L|(Z_i)_{1\leq i\leq n}\right] \geq j_n(r_L, z_L).$$

Since $j_n(r_L, z_L)$ goes to $r_L$, then the conditional expectation converges to $r_L$ as well.

As a result, we see that

$$\lim_{n\to\infty} V(g_{NIM}^{r_L}) = \frac{y}{1+y}r_L.$$

Now let us verify that setting $d$ to $r_L$ is the optimal contract. If $d > r_L$ then we know that the value to the issuer $V(g_{NIM}^d)$ verifies

$$V(g_{NIM}^d) \leq \frac{y}{1+y}j_n(d, z_L),$$

and $j_n(d, z_L)$ goes to $d \wedge r_L$, which by our assumption is $r_L$. If $d < r_L$, then we can also write $V(g_{NIM}^d) \leq \frac{y}{1+y}j_n(d, z_L)$ but now $j_n(d, z_L)$ goes to $d$ which is smaller than $r_L$. Hence, setting the NIM size to $r_L$ is optimal at the limit. □

Resecuritization appears as an efficient way of exploiting diversification to further increase the issuer's value.

#### 7.2.2.5 Impact of Securitization on Collateral Valuation

Without a NIM securitization, the issuer creates senior bonds, necessarily priced at par, and retains the junior securities and some of the senior bonds. This issuer may originate the loans itself or buy them, but in any case we will assume that there are many such issuers in competition and therefore, at a marginal profit of 0, the valuation of the loans is driven by the valuation of the structured securities that are issued.

We consider the valuation before the issuer knows the private information $Z$, since potential choices between different types of collateral would have to be made before the specifics are known. For example, an issuer may choose to concentrate on prime borrowers rather than subprime borrowers before the details of a particular prime loan portfolio that the issuer originates are known. Also, note that we implicitly assume that the investors do not have access to this primary market but must go through the issuer.

We write $p = \mathbb{E}[V \wedge D^*]$, since as in the expression for $q$ and $m$, this quantity just depends on the distributions of $V$, $Z$ and on $y$.

The valuation of the collateral based on a securitization execution can be written as follows, in the two cases depending on the type of structure satisfying the par valuation requirement:

$$P_{XS} = \left(q + \frac{1-q}{1+y}\right) p\mathbb{E}[X] + \frac{\mathbb{E}[V] - p}{1+y}\mathbb{E}[X],$$

and

$$P_{SS} = \left(q + \frac{1-q}{1+y}\right)p + \frac{\mathbb{E}[V]\mathbb{E}[X] - p}{1+y}.$$

The difference can be written as

$$P_{XS} - P_{SS} = (\mathbb{E}[X] - 1)\frac{1 + qy - p}{1+y},$$

which is positive since $\mathbb{E}[X] > 1$ and $p \leq 1$.

We consider that the collateral is a portfolio of loans, and when these loans are made they typically are valued at par. Also recall that we can write $X = 1 + cT$. Therefore, there are coupons $c_{SS}$ and $c_{XS}$ such that $P_{SS} = 1$ and $P_{XS} = 1$. Solving for these coupons and after some simplifications, we find

$$c_{SS} = \frac{1 + y - pqy - \mathbb{E}[V]}{\mathbb{E}[V]\mathbb{E}[T]}$$

and

$$c_{XS} = \frac{1 + y - pqy - \mathbb{E}[V]}{(pqy + \mathbb{E}[V])\mathbb{E}[T]}.$$

All else being equal, we can see that the collateral coupon if an excess-spread structure is used is lower than if a standard structure is used. In both cases, a longer expected time to repayment leads to a lower coupon.

Both par coupons could be compared to the par coupon obtained if the collateral was valued by the issuer under the assumption it did not result in a securitization. In this case, the collateral would be worth

$$P_I = \frac{\mathbb{E}[X]\mathbb{E}[V]}{1+y},$$

and solving for the par coupon gets us

$$c_I = \frac{1 + y - \mathbb{E}[V]}{\mathbb{E}[V]\mathbb{E}[T]}.$$

As could be expected, the par coupon is higher in the case when there is no securitization execution: $c_I \geq c_{XS} \geq c_{SS}$.

As we will see, it is unfortunately not possible to express the relationships between collateral characteristics and pricing through securitization in a tractable manner, but we can illustrate some patterns using numerical calculations.

We can substitute the collateral par coupon expression in the ex ante issuer's expected value. In the case of a standard structure with par-valued bonds, the gain to the issuer is

$$V\left(g_{SS(0)}(X, V)\right) = \frac{ym}{1+y}$$

and does not depend on the coupon. This expression only depends on the distribution of $V$ through $m$ and $D^*$ (on which $m$ depends).

In the case of an excess-spread structure, we find that

$$V\left(g_{XS(0)}(X,V)\right)=\frac{ym}{ypq+\mathbb{E}[V]}.$$

The ratio, capturing how much more is gained by using excess-spread securitization over a standard structure, simplifies to

$$\frac{V\left(g_{XS(0)}(X,V)\right)}{V\left(g_{SS(0)}(X,V)\right)}=\frac{1+y}{ypq+\mathbb{E}[V]}.$$

As $y$ goes to zero, this quantity converges to $\frac{1}{\mathbb{E}[V]}$. Hence, if the discount rate of the issuer is close to that of the investors, being able to use an excess-spread structure is all the more so attractive as the collateral's expected recoveries are low. This pattern could explain how the use of excess-spread in the mortgage-backed securities market drove an ever increasing preference for worse-quality underlying loans.

#### 7.2.2.6 Numerical Examples

The interaction between the known credit risk $W$ and the privately observed credit risk $Z$ leads to complex calculations. In order to look at patterns in the pricing of collateral as driven by optimal structure execution, we need to make simplifying assumptions.

First, we assume that $V=ZW$, with $W$ independent of $Z$. For $W$, we choose a density such that $V$ has a uniform worst case and which gives more probability to high principal payment outcomes. It seems normal to expect that low loss observations are the most common. We pick the distribution

$$\mu_W(w)=\frac{\beta+1}{1-w_L}\left(\frac{w-w_L}{1-w_L}\right)^{\beta}\mathbb{I}_{w\in[w_L,1]},$$

with $\beta\in(0,1)$ and $w_L\in[0,1]$, which we know satisfies the conditions of Proposition 7.26. The parameter $\beta$ is related to how more likely high loss observations are than low loss observations, and $w_L$ is the lowest possible amount of principal recovery. Then, we have

$$\mathbb{E}[W]=w_L+(1-w_L)\frac{\beta+1}{\beta+2}$$

and for $d\in[w_L,1]$,

$$\mathbb{E}[W\wedge d]=d-\frac{d-w_L}{\beta+2}\left(\frac{d-w_L}{1-w_L}\right)^{\beta+1}.$$

Hence

$$\mathbb{E}[V \wedge D|Z = z_L] = z_L \mathbb{E}\left[W \wedge \frac{D}{z_L}\right] = D - \frac{D - z_L w_L}{\beta + 2}\left(\frac{\frac{D}{z_L} - w_L}{1 - w_L}\right)^{\beta+1}.$$

If we use $\mu_Z$ to write the density of $Z$ on $[z_L, 1]$, then the expression for $m$ cannot be readily simplified:

$$m(D) = (\mathbb{E}[V \wedge D|Z = z_L])^{\frac{1+y}{y}} \int_{z_L}^{1} dz \mu_Z(z) \left(\mathbb{E}[V \wedge D|Z = z]\right)^{-\frac{1}{y}}.$$

Even with the simplest distribution assumption for $Z$, the first-order condition for the maximum of $m$ cannot be solved formally for $D$, so we compute numerical solutions.

We pick the following parameters for the distribution of $W$: $\beta = 0.5$ and $w_L = 0.85$. For $Z$, we use a uniform distribution on $[z_L, 1]$ with $z_L = 0.8$, and define $X = 1 + cT$, where $T$ is a uniform distribution on $[T_L, T_H]$ with $T_L = 1$ and $T_H = 10$. The coupon is set as $c = 0.05$ initially but will later be determined implicitly so that the collateral is priced at par through an excess-spread structure execution.

We first look a the shape of $m(D)$ as a function of $D$, varying $w_L$ in Fig. 7.1, with all the other variables set as described above. We can see that the higher the maximum losses (or equivalently the lowest the minimum recovered principal) the less marked the optimal face value is, and the lower $m$ is at the optimum relative to $D$. In Fig. 7.2, we fix $w_L$ and vary $z_L$ instead. We can see that the overall shape of $m$ then remains approximately the same when we change $z_L$, with the optimum $m$ being close to, and slightly lower than, $D$.

Numerically solving for the optimum $D^*$, we can plot that optimum as a function of the minimum recovery $w_L$ and varying the issuer's minimum observation $z_L$, as

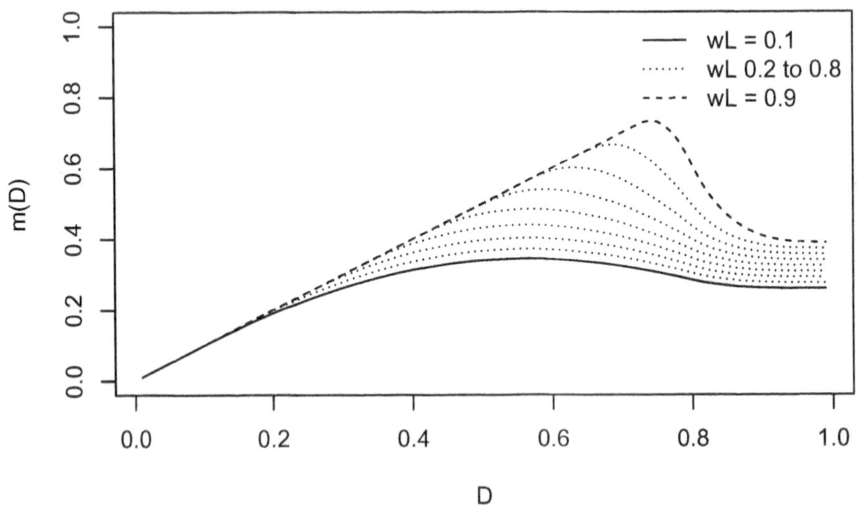


**Fig. 7.1** $m(D)$ versus face value $D$ Varying $w_L$. *Source* Compiled by the author

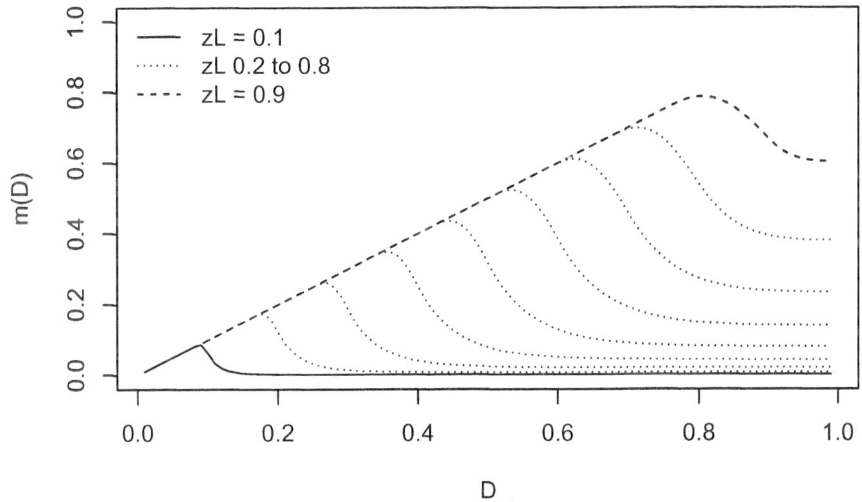


**Fig. 7.2** $m(D)$ versus face value $D$ Varying $z_L$. *Source* Compiled by the author

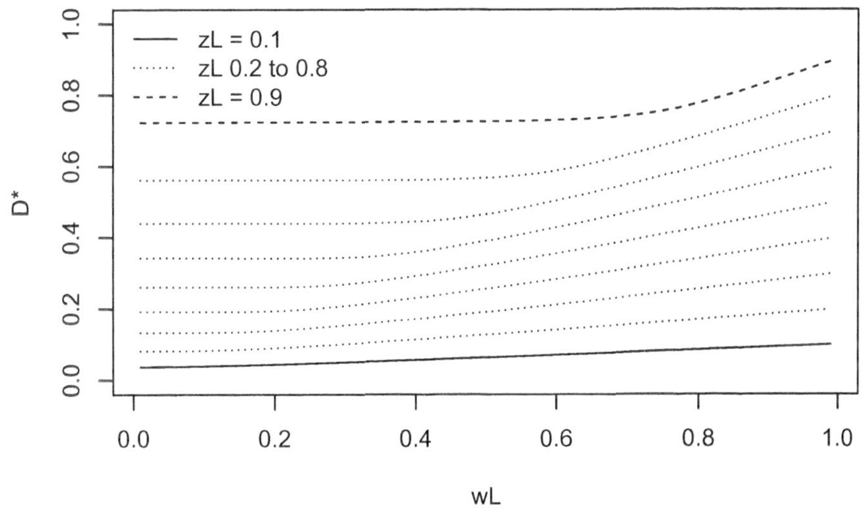


**Fig. 7.3** Optimal face value $D^*$ as a function of $w_L$ varying $z_L$. *Source* Compiled by the author

shown in Fig. 7.3. With our parameters, the optimum $D^*$ is not very sensitive to the collateral's worst-case outcome independent of the issuer's private observation. The influence of the worst case as observed by the issuer is much stronger as we can see.

The resulting value to the issuer is shown in Fig. 7.4. Here again, altering the distribution of $W$ does not have a very strong impact on the issuer's gain, although altering the worst-case outcome $z_L$ affects the issuer gain much more strongly.

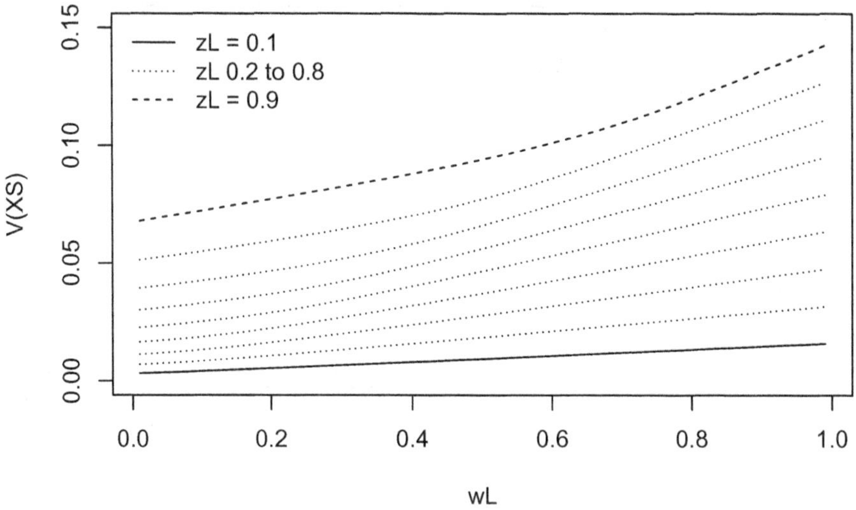


**Fig. 7.4** Maximal issuer value as a function of $w_L$ varying $z_L$. *Source* Compiled by the author

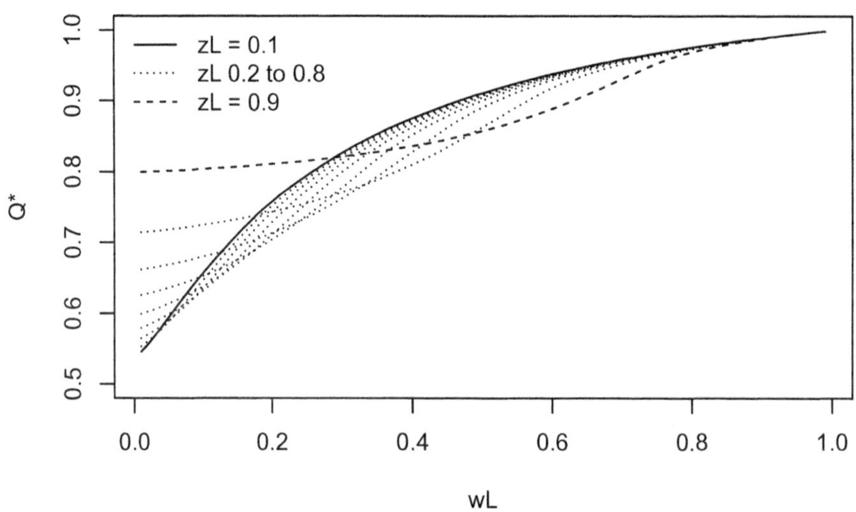


**Fig. 7.5** Optimal quantity sold as a function of $w_L$ varying $z_L$. *Source* Compiled by the author

With the optimal excess-spread structure, the quantity of senior securities sold $Q^*$ exhibits a more complex relationship to both $w_L$ and $z_L$, as shown in Fig. 7.5. In particular, when the potential loss increases, the issuer ends up keeping a larger principal release.

As we have seen in Fig. 7.4, with high-enough $w_L$ and $z_L$, the securitization gain to the issuer is in the order to 0.10. Figure 7.6 shows that the limiting gain from a NIM resecuritization is fairly substantial in relation. We can also see that depending on $z_L$, there is a maximum to the value of a NIM as a function of the worst case $w_L$.

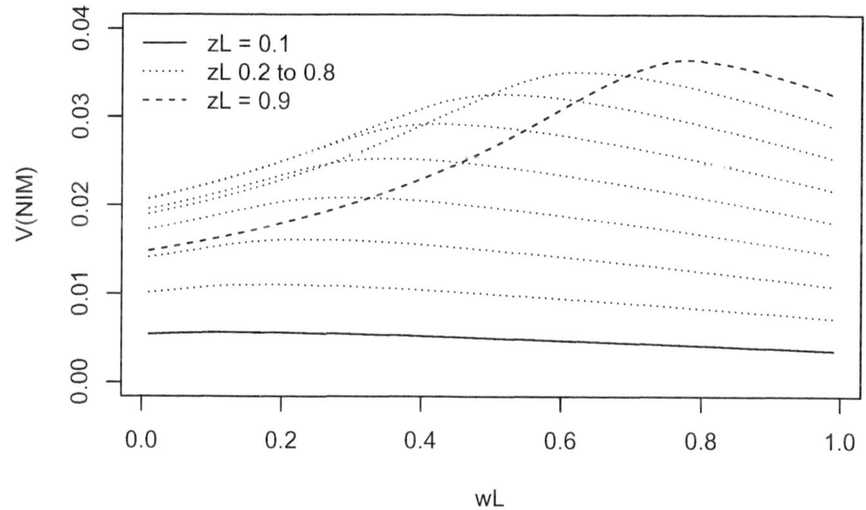


**Fig. 7.6** Gain from NIM issuance as a function of $w_L$ varying $z_L$. *Source* Compiled by the author

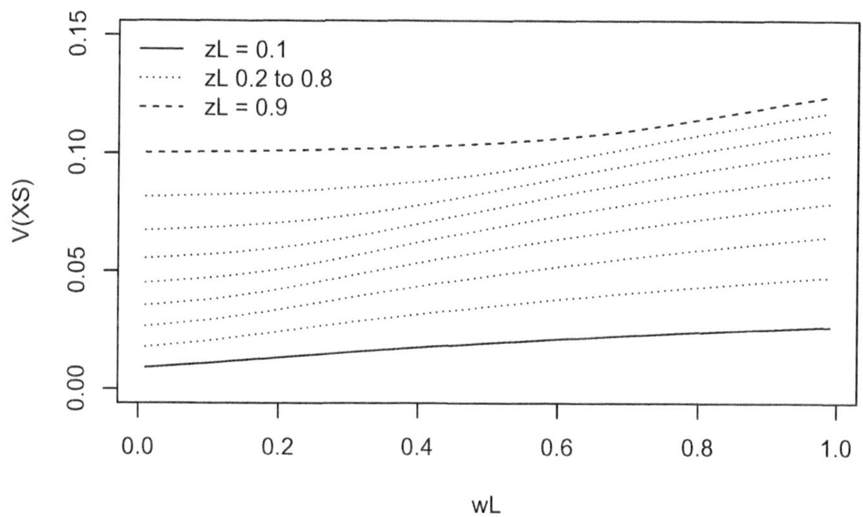


**Fig. 7.7** Gain from XS structure off par price collateral as a function of $w_L$ varying $z_L$. *Source* Compiled by the author

As the minimal recovery declines, and expected losses increase, the value to the issuer of an excess-spread securitization declines, but Fig. 7.7 shows us that the slope of this decline is quite small. In effect, the collateral's coupon increases, for it to be par priced, as expected losses increase, and the excess-spread structure is able to make use of that higher coupon. A standard senior/subordination structure is not able to use the extra coupon, and its value to the issuer declines to a greater extent as expected losses increase.

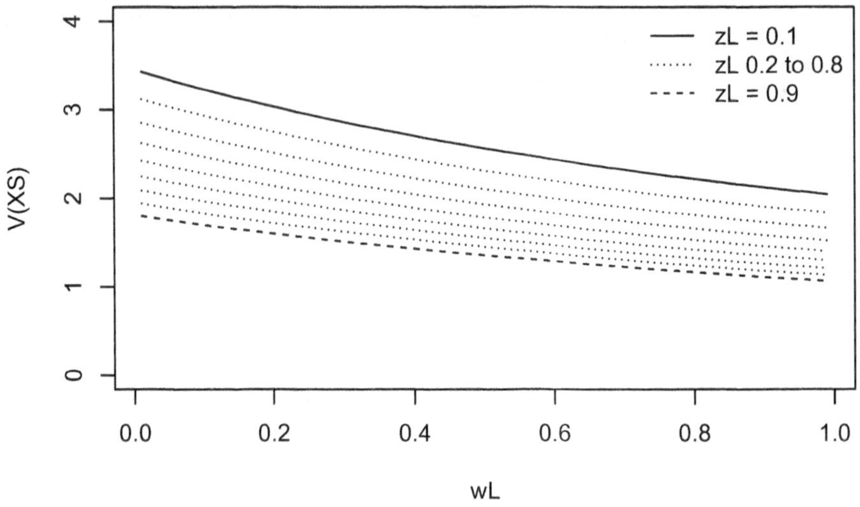


**Fig. 7.8** Ratio of gains from XS structure to SS structure off par price collateral as a function of $w_L$ varying $z_L$. *Source* Compiled by the author

Looking at the ratio of the value to the issuer of an excess-spread structure to the value of a standard structure as shown in Fig. 7.7, we can see how par-priced collateral with a low credit quality will be much more efficiently securitized through an excess-spread structure (Fig. 7.8).

As we have seen, it is not easy to explain some of the most common securitization structures, and scratching the surface already becomes nearly intractable. Nevertheless, broadly speaking we have been able to account for some designs that would have otherwise seemed arbitrarily arcane. We now turn to some empirical research into the economics of structuring.

## 7.3 Discussion of Pooling and Tranching Models

As we have seen in the first section, the simplest effect of structuring, that is, to select and pool assets together, can be explained within all three security design models we had introduced in Chap. 4. In addition, we saw with DeMarzo (2005) that there was a justification for what we had remarked on in that same chapter, that assets of the same nature tended to be pooled together.

When we looked into tranching, the research landscape was somewhat different; indeed, the models that explained tranching mainly had to resort to particular assumptions about investors and had different fundamental setups from the security design models from Chap. 4. This stresses the difficulty in explaining real-life structuring, as it would imply modeling a combination of investor preferences with issuers' private information or investors' information acquisition.

We saw along Gauthier (2019), however, that reflecting some particular constraints in investor's requirements, although not emanating from preferences strictly speaking, allowed us to account for several structural features in securitization, such as stripping, excess-spread, and NIMs. This model, with a single period and a fairly simple representation of information and collateral along DeMarzo and Duffie (1999), is still far from explaining dynamic structural aspects such as OC floors and triggers. Still, looking at structural complexity from the perspective of simple investor constraints rather than arbitrary differences in preferences may be more fruitful, presumably because it greatly simplifies the representation of these investors' choices.

There have been a few empirical studies that specifically sought to explain tranching and structuring based on the theoretical underpinnings we have discussed in this chapter.[5] We discuss the findings from Firla-Cuchra and Jenkinson (2006), Franke and Weber (2009), and Pena-Cerezo et al. (2019), which in all three cases find that the data agrees with most of the hypotheses derived from theoretical models.

We know that structuring is a complex affair, and there are multiple ways in which a senior block may be created. In addition, the structuring of that senior block can take several forms depending on the desired characteristics of the resulting bonds. The bonds may have more or less average life variability, be longer or shorter, pay more or less coupon... In the empirical studies that have tried to explain this diversity, there is nevertheless no such distinction of the nature of the structuring that has been applied. Structuring is typically only measured in terms of the number of bonds that are created. Categorizing the bonds in sufficient detail would be difficult, not only because it requires a good understanding of structuring logic, but also because the data usually available is limited. This is particularly true on the European market, which happens to be the focus of the three studies discussed below.

The theoretical analyses we carried out so far have told us that creating senior and junior securities may be related to information asymmetry or to market completion, while tranching within a given seniority level could be related to investors' specific preferences. Figure 7.9, inspired by Pena-Cerezo et al. (2019), illustrates some of the hypotheses regarding tranching and pricing that can be tested with the data.

### 7.3.1 Explaining Tranching with Market Segmentation and Asymmetric Information

Firla-Cuchra and Jenkinson (2006) was the first research paper to systematically test theoretical explanations for tranching. The authors explored the relationships between asset type and quality, securitized bonds pricing, and the degree of tranching in the deals.

They test the following hypotheses about tranching:

[5] Some studies, such as Vink and Thibeault (2008), have analyzed the pricing of tranched and structured securities, but not from the perspective of accounting for tranching.

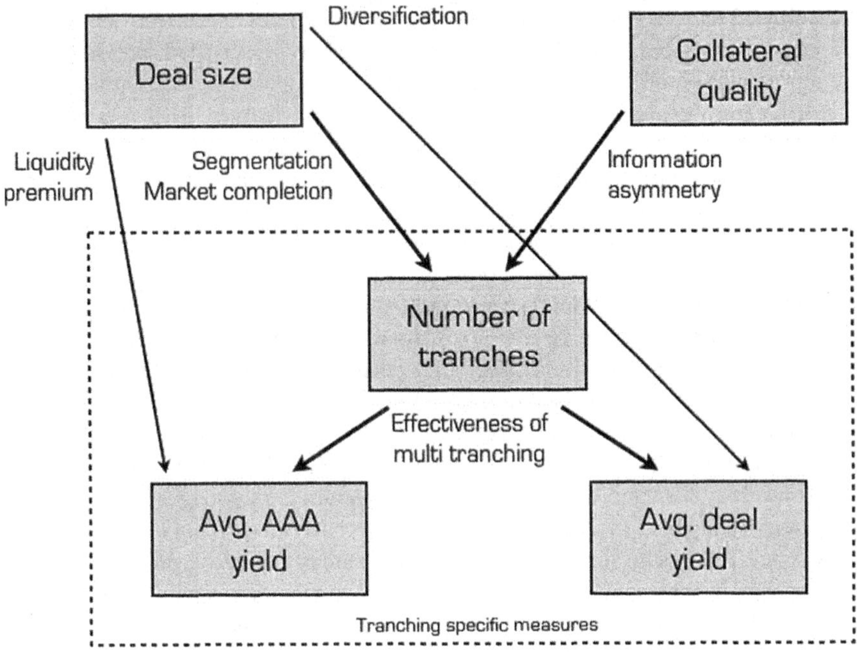


**Fig. 7.9** Possible data relationships related to tranching. *Source* Pena-Cerezo et al. (2019)

1. Tranching should be associated with investor sophistication, following Plantin (2003), and the tranching of less informationally sensitive assets should be increasing with sophistication;
2. Tranching should be more prevalent at times when there is less market liquidity, and there are more opportunities for arbitrage, according to Gaur et al. (2011);
3. If the market is segmented, then larger issues would be beneficially cut into separate tranches in order to avoid suffering from a downward sloping demand curve, while fixed costs in securitization and ex post trading liquidity would favor larger tranches. In total, one would expect a relatively stable optimal tranche size;
4. Following DeMarzo and Duffie (1999) or DeMarzo (2005), one would expect more tranching on collateral that is more likely to exhibit exposure to private information;
5. The tranching of securities within a rating level should be related to clientele effects and exploit market incompleteness;
6. Tranching should improve the valuation of the overall transaction.

#### 7.3.1.1 Data

Firla-Cuchra and Jenkinson obtained comprehensive data on European securitizations between 1987 and 2003 from JP Morgan. They also extracted deal-level and bond-level metrics from Bloomberg and other sources. In total, they gathered information on over 5000 tranches in over 1600 separate deals, across the ABS, MBS,

**Table 7.1** Summary of tranche data. *Source* Firla-Cuchra Jenkinson (2006) and author's own calculations

| Product type | Deal size | Pct AAAs |
|---|---|---|
| Cards | 571 | 95 |
| Auto | 405 | 87 |
| Public agencies | 2029 | 47 |
| Equip | 420 | 83 |
| RMBS | 659 | 80 |
| CMBS | 594 | 74 |
| Other | 362 | 57 |
| Consumer | 377 | 68 |
| Whole business | 828 | 37 |
| CDO | 727 | 66 |
| Aggregate | 630 | 73 |

and CDO sectors. Table 7.1 shows a summary of the product types used in their data along with average deal sizes and share of AAAs.

The information collected included the variables that one would expect, such as underlying asset type, issuance spread, rating, size, etc... For many bonds, this data also included the average life.[6] Pricing information is not available on all tranches, but on a majority of them: keeping only the deals where pricing is provided there are over 2500 tranches in the dataset issued on over 800 deals.

Time tranching is one of the essential aspects of structuring, as we know, and hence it is important to be able to compare the average life of various securities in the same structure. The authors determine that, in their dataset, 73% of the bonds have in the same deal at least another bond with exactly the same average life. In other words, for atleast 27% of the tranches, a form of time tranching is at play.

More generally, Firla-Cuchra and Jenkinson compute for each deal the number of rating classes, that is, the number of distinct ratings, in contrast with what they term the number of market classes, that is, the number of tranches with the same rating. The rating classes effectively capture the number of structure blocks with different credit enhancement levels, while the market classes capture the number of structure blocks within identical credit enhancement levels.

#### 7.3.1.2 Tranching, Market Incompleteness, and Sophistication

In order to test the first three hypotheses, it is necessary to define certain approximations for the metrics of interest, in particular, for sophistication.

As mentioned earlier, one of the parameters that may drive tranching is the degree of investor sophistication, which raises the challenge of how to measure that notion.

[6]In many instances of empirical studies, this essential piece of information is not collected, or, worse, the legal maturity is collected instead.

Firla-Cuchra and Jenkinson proposed to tackle this approximation in a simple, but reasonable, fashion: with the development of the securitization market. Indeed, the tools and techniques of risk analysis and modeling have progressed over time, and in particular of the period that their data covers, from the late 1980s to early 2000s. In parallel, securitization issuance has steadily grown over that period of time. Hence, in the regressions explaining tranching, they measure investor sophistication with a time trend. They also note that the relationship between sophistication and market development can be applied when comparing the US and European securitization markets: the US market is considered as more mature, and is larger than the European market, and tranching is more prevalent in the US market.

Another proxy for sophistication proposed by the authors is the flag for European structures sold into the US market; however, this information is not often available and this reduces the sample significantly. A third, potentially cumulative, measure for sophistication is to take each country's rank in total securitization issuance.

The extent of tranching itself is measured as the number of tranches per deal. It is also important to specify controls in the regressions, so that the contributions of the effects under study can be properly captured: dummies by product type, tranche average life, issue size, and average launch spread. Controlling by average life accounts for the fact that longer collateral may offer more opportunities for time tranching than shorter collateral, and hence we would expect a relationship. The average issuance spread of a deal is a proxy for the market conditions. Finally, small issue size could prevent tranching simply because of fixed costs.

The first regression takes the form:

$$N_{i(k)} = \gamma_1 . C^1_{i(k),k} + \beta_1 t_{i(k)} + \varepsilon^1_k,$$

where the index $k$ represents all the tranches in the dataset, and $i(k)$ is the index of the deal on which tranche $k$ was issued. $N_{i(k)}$ is the number of tranches issued by deal $i(k)$, and $C^1_{i(k),k}$ is the vector of controls for that tranche and this deal, including product type, average life, average spread, etc. The time trend $t_i$ is simply the year in which the deal was issued, and $\varepsilon^1$ is the series of noise terms.

Controlling for all these effects, Firla-Cuchra and Jenkinson find that their simple approximation of sophistication (the time trend) has a significant and positive impact $\beta_1$ on the extent of tranching, providing empirical support for hypothesis 1 above. This is also true if the country-specific sophistication measure is also included in the regression.

As we know, credit enhancement is not the only reason for tranching, and in many cases blocks with a given level of enhancement are further structured along various dimensions. As we stressed earlier, about a third of the sample has some form of time tranching at play, for example. While information asymmetry has provided us with good explanations for creating credit enhancement, market completion would seem to provide better support to explain structuring within a given rating level.

In consequence, it should make sense to look for increased tranching at times when market liquidity is limited, since this would be associated with greater arbitrage potential, thus creating opportunities.

Separately, one would also expect that larger issues are more likely to be split up into smaller pieces in order to exploit different investor preferences: the issuer, by creating separate products, is less subject to the downward sloping demand curve for a single one. However, there are certain costs associated with tranching, which limit the benefit of structuring to a certain point. These considerations would point toward a relatively stable tranche size across issues, and logically the larger the issue, the greater the number of tranches.

The relevant coefficients in the regression above support hypotheses 2 and 3. Among the controls $C^1$, the measure of the average issuance spread at the deal level has a significant and positive coefficient, which can be interpreted as worse market conditions leading to more tranching. Note, however, that this could also be interpreted as riskier collateral leading to more tranching, which may be expected too. A more appropriate way of measuring market conditions could be an aggregate issuance spread across all deals within a certain product, bucketed by issuance quarter. Finally, the control for the deal size is also positive and significant, and as one would expect according to the market segmentation logic, larger deals are more tranched.

#### 7.3.1.3 Tranching and Asymmetrical Information

As we have discussed at length so far, information asymmetry is expected to drive credit tranching, following the analyses of DeMarzo and Duffie (1999), DeMarzo (2005), or Plantin (2003), to name a few. How can one test this empirically? If the issuer's profits are related to the information sensitivity of the junior tranches and there is some cost to tranching, then we would expect that assets with more information sensitivity would be more tranched. Following DeMarzo more particularly, we know that tranching is more attractive when the issuer's private information is more pool-specific and associated with the particular type of asset.

In order to construct a measure of information sensitivity of different asset types, Firla-Cuchra and Jenkinson use the dispersion of issuance spreads: they compute a ranking of asset types based on the standard deviation of tranche issuance spread within each rating level, relative to the average standard deviation for each rating level. By this metric, it appears that corporate collateral such as CMBS, CDOs, or WBs exhibits more dispersion than pools backed by consumer loans.

The new regression can be expressed as

$$N_{i(k)} = \gamma_2 . C^2_{i(k),k} + \beta_2 a_{\tau(i(k))} + \varepsilon^2_k,$$

where $\tau(i(k))$ is the type of deal $i$ which issued tranche $k$, and $a_\tau$ is the issuance spread dispersion rank for product type $\tau$. $C^2$ are the new controls, now including investor sophistication as proxied in regression 1, and excluding product type dummies.

The fit shows that there is a strong and significant relationship between the information asymmetry proxy and the degree of tranching, and this relationship remains significant notwithstanding which controls are entered, in particular, tranche average life. Increasing asset spread dispersion ranking by 3 or 4 toward more information sensitivity leads to adding 1 tranche to a securitization, all else being equal.

Firla-Cuchra and Jenkinson also study the relationship between the quality of the assets, as measured by a weighted average rating, and the degree of tranching. They do not find any significant effect. However, they computed aggregate ratings using the simple order of these ratings (AAA being 1, AA 2, etc.) and given what we know of the order of magnitude of a typical rating factor,[7] this simplified manner in which they aggregate ratings is not realistic.

As we stressed earlier, one issue with basing tranching explanations on asymmetrical information is that it cannot properly account for tranching within a rating level, and market incompleteness can help fill that void. In order to further empirically investigate tranching, the tranches are grouped according to rating classes and market classes, which were defined earlier. The number of rating classes in a deal is the number of separate rating levels, and the number of market classes is the number of separate tranches within a credit enhancement block.

Since the market classes are not differentiated by rating, we assume that their tranching is not due to asymmetrical information but rather to clientele or segmentation effects, and are presumably designed to exploit market incompleteness. We can now specify a regression that could capture both effects separately:

$$M_{i(k)} = \gamma_3^m . C_{i(k),k}^3 + \beta_1^m t_{i(k)} + \beta_2^m a_{\tau(i(k))} + \varepsilon_k^3$$
$$R_{i(k)} = \gamma_3^r . C_{i(k),k}^3 + \beta_1^r t_{i(k)} + \beta_2^r a_{\tau(i(k))} + \varepsilon_k^3,$$

where $M_{i(k)}$ is the number of market classes in the deal containing tranche $k$, and $R_{i(k)}$ is the number of rating classes. The other variables and controls are the same as described earlier. In particular, the log of the issue size is included as one of the controls.

The regression results support hypotheses 4 and 5: the index for collateral information sensitivity obtains a much larger coefficient for the number of rating classes than for the number of market classes. However, the deal size's coefficient exhibits the opposite pattern, being larger for the number of market classes (and the deal size is a proxy for segmentation possibility). The measure for the quality of assets (which, we pointed out, is unfortunately flawed) shows a positive coefficient for the number of rating classes, but a negative coefficient for the number of market classes. This is interpreted by the authors as the sign that lower quality assets, more difficult to place, may require more structuring within a given rating. Finally, the year index, a proxy for sophistication, is only significant for the number of rating classes.

The impact of market conditions, which capture times of potentially strained liquidity, illustrates that there are more market classes created when spreads were wide, which would be consistent with expectations.

[7] As explained in Chap. 3, the rating factor is an approximation for an odds-ratio type of credit risk metric based on rating.

#### 7.3.1.4 Tranching and Pricing

While the regressions discussed so far related the extent of tranching to various collateral and market characteristics, we have not yet addressed whether tranching could lead to improved pricing.

The metric of interest in this case is the valuation of the whole issue, which can be captured by computing the aggregate spread of the entire deal. Besides, there are various well-known determinants of bond valuations that should be accounted for as control variables, such as interest rate levels, the slope of the yield curve, implied volatility of interest rates derivatives, and collateral average life.

A first regression of the aggregate spreads with these control variables and the issue size shows a negative coefficient for that issue size, which implies that larger deals would price better in aggregate, presumably due to improved liquidity. The other factors such as volatility or slope all have signs and magnitudes as would be expected. This regression is simply expressed as

$$S_{i(k)} = \gamma_4.C^4_{i(k),k} + \varepsilon^4_k,$$

where $S_i$ is the aggregate spread of deal $i$.

Then, in order to properly account for the effect of tranching, we need to include the predicted number of tranches according to the other regressions discussed above: given each tranche's characteristics, we project the estimated number of tranches that should be structured in the deal and use that as an additional input to explain the aggregate spread. This last regression can hence be written as

$$S_{i(k)} = \gamma_5.C^5_{i(k),k} + \beta^5\overline{N}_{i,k} + \varepsilon^5_k,$$

where $\overline{N}_{i,k}$ is the estimated number of tranches, using year index, issue size, and collateral spread dispersion as explanatory variables in addition to various controls.

The predicted total number of tranches is highly significant and negative, so that the more tranches there are, the better the valuation. In addition, once the number of tranches is included in the regression, then the coefficient for the issue size is significant and positive, which is consistent with a downward sloping demand curve. This also illustrates that in effect, structuring allows to mitigate the negative effect of a large deal size. Hence, there is support for hypothesis 6.

With these results, we can say that the drivers of tranching in general, which we explored in the more theoretical parts of the present chapter, have found empirical support. While the research by Firla-Cuchra and Jenkinson analyzed multiple products on a large market, we now more briefly discuss two other studies which concentrated on particular subsets: a specific product for one and a specific country for the other.

### 7.3.2 Optimal Tranching in CLO/CBO Transactions

Focusing on a particular market, the authors in Franke and Weber (2009) test a number of hypotheses on 169 European CLOs and CBOs between 2000 and 2004.

By focusing on these particular structures, they benefit from a more thorough understanding of the underlying risks. Indeed, as we have discussed in Chap. 3, corporate loans or bonds generally offer more precise information on their ex ante risks than consumer loans: their market prices are often available, as are ratings or rating factors. This wealth of information allows for a more precise understanding of the relationships between collateral characteristics and tranching, relative to the more general analysis that could be carried out in Firla-Cuchra and Jenkinson (2006). Among other metrics, Franke and Weber exploit the diversity score provided by Moody's on these deals, as well as the weighted average default probability, which can be derived from the assets' rating factors along with recovery assumptions.

They identify the following hypotheses, among others:

1. Given collateral quality and equity size, a higher number of tranches reduces the spread on these tranches. The argument stems, for example, from Plantin (2003): depending on investors' preferences, it is necessary to create tranches of various levels of credit enhancement. Also following Gaur et al. (2011), each cash flow is divided into optimal pieces that each go to the investors with the highest marginal price for that particular cash flow. In either case, the issuer stands to make more profit by splitting the cash flows into more tranches.
2. A larger tranche size reduces the tranche's spread. The argument, which has to some extent been addressed by Firla-Cuchra and Jenkinson (2006), is that all else being equal, a larger tranche should benefit from a lesser liquidity premium.
3. The number of rated tranches increases with deal size. While the prior hypothesis would imply that issuers want to minimize the number of tranches, it is also possible that the benefits from the lower liquidity premium decline beyond a certain size, for example, because investors require a certain diversification. The data in Firla-Cuchra and Jenkinson (2006) also supported this hypothesis. Further, if one considers there are fixed costs in issuing the marginal tranche, then there would be an optimal tranche size factoring in these costs as well as the liquidity premium benefits.
4. Credit tranching increases with collateral information asymmetry. Based on the security design and pooling literature such as Boot and Thakor (1993), Dang et al. (2015), DeMarzo and Duffie (1999), or DeMarzo (2005), we expect the issuer to retain the most information-sensitive tranches. While it only explains a simple senior/subordination structure, this argument combined with multiple investor preferences could lead to multiple tranching, as with Plantin (2003). One important additional point is that for uninformed investors, the actual structure (such as attachment and detachment points in a simplified setting), as it satisfies various requirements due to the tranches' ratings, carries information about the underlying collateral. When buying a AA tranche, an uninformed investor gains by looking at the structure of the AAAs, As, or BBBs.[8]

[8]This does assume, however, that the rating agencies would have access to more information than the investors.

5. The risk premium of a tranche increases with collateral information asymmetry. Although senior tranches should be considered informationally insensitive in theory, as was empirically shown by Park (2013), Franke and Weber point out that on more junior bonds there should be such a relationship.
6. The risk premium of a tranche is better explained by its rating than by collateral quality and structure details. A rating may not capture all the features and risks of a tranche, and within that given rating there may be significant variation, but the expectation would be that the rating captures most of these variations.

Since issuer characteristics may affect tranching, they categorized the data in order to distinguish banks or investment firms, and gathered detailed information on the banks (while such information is scarcer on investment management firms). The information on banks, such as equity capital ratios, capital, or assets structure, profitability, was used as a set of controls in the regressions.

First testing the drivers of the number of tranches, Franke and Weber find that the average default probability and the overall deal size significantly and positively affect tranching, while the diversity score and the equity size negatively affect the number of tranches. In other words, a lower portfolio quality leads to more tranches, which is consistent with hypothesis 4. There is little to be gained by tranching high-quality collateral, and the inverse holds true. In addition, the size of the equity, which is related to collateral quality, may contribute a mechanical effect in that a larger equity piece leaves less room to create tranches. Hypothesis 3 is also supported.

Next, one can look at the weighted average spread on the tranches issued in a deal in order to analyze valuations. Franke and Weber also propose a measure of the risk premium, by multiplying the average spread over the maturity of the deal, minus the expected losses on the deal (which is obtained from the default probability). This naturally raises the issue of the meaning of the maturity of a securitized transaction—typically quite limited. In the case at hand, however, factoring in the fact that these deals are normally managed to ramp down rapidly after some time, and composed of bullet loans or bonds, this gross approximation for the average life may not be entirely wrong. As a result, while such an approach raises some issues, we can hope that Franke and Weber's measure of the risk premium is not too biased. In any case, looking at a risk premium rather than a spread is a better way to capture the valuation of the deal, since it adjusts for the collateral's underlying default risk.

What are the empirical drivers of the weighted average risk premium on cash CLOs and CBOs? First, Franke and Weber find significant coefficients, positive for the collateral default probability and negative for deal size. This provides support for hypothesis 5, and in some sense to hypothesis 2 if it was understood at the deal level. Further, in a separate regression, the number of tranches has a significant impact and a negative coefficient, while average market credit spreads have a positive coefficient. The explanatory power of the regression is increased by using the number of tranches, rather than the overall deal size. Issuing more tranches allows for more precise signals on collateral quality, and for a more optimal adjustment of securities to investor preferences. As a result, the authors find support for hypothesis 1.

The risk premium for a rated tranche can be expressed in a similar fashion to the risk premium for the entire deal, where the expected loss on the tranche is computed by simulation using the tranche's attachment and detachment points as well as the collateral's distribution of characteristics. Equipped with this measure, that risk premium can be regressed over the collateral's default probability, diversity score, number of tranches, and other measures of interest. Carrying out this regression, Franke and Weber find that the collateral's risk and market credit spreads are both significant and positive contributors, while the collateral diversity, and number of subordinated tranches reduce the risk premium. Hypothesis 5 is supported by these findings too. Adding rating in the regression instead of the characteristics mentioned above does not improve the explanatory power, and as a result hypothesis 6 should be rejected. In addition, tranche size is not significant in explaining the tranche's risk premium, so that hypothesis 2 should be rejected at the tranche level.

In summary, this study confirms that the main motivation for an issuer of a securitization to issue multiple tranches is to reduce the weighted average funding cost, although fixed costs in creating tranches, including lesser liquidity, leads to an optimal number of securities structured. This optimal number of tranches increases with the degree of information asymmetry in the collateral's performance, and that information asymmetry is inversely related to asset quality.

### 7.3.3 Tranching and the Valuation of Structured Products

Pena-Cerezo et al. (2019) consider Spanish securitization across sectors and look to explain the valuation of structured securities as a function of tranching and other factors. Figure 7.9 shows some of the relationships set out to test empirically, which are comparable to those studied by Firla-Cuchra and Jenkinson (2006) and Franke and Weber (2009). The data is, however, original, as it is a comprehensive list of all ABS and MBS securitization tranches that were issued in Spain between 1993 and 2011. While the focus is on a very specific market, and not a particularly large one, including every possible product, and covering the periods before and during the mortgage crisis makes the study particularly relevant.

Some potentially significant issues in the treatment of the data include the following, on which we have commented before:

- Applying a linear scale for ratings: Instead of using rating factors, average ratings are computed on a scale of 1 to 22 from bankruptcy to AAA, while the differences in expected default or losses are explosive as one goes down the rating scale;
- Using the legal maturity of the securities as opposed to their average life, or simply not using the data (which would be, of course, much better than using this misleading metric), in cases where the collateral is not composed of pure bullet bonds with similar maturities.

Excluding the results that rely on these particular data, the findings in the article provide further support for and help qualify the various hypotheses we have mentioned so far concerning pooling and tranching.

One interesting innovation proposed by the authors is to distinguish two forms of tranching effectiveness. They define the notion of strong and weak effectiveness of tranching. The weak effectiveness hypothesis is that a higher number of tranches in a deal reduces the yield on the senior bonds. The strong effectiveness hypothesis is that the number of tranches in a deal reduces the yield on the entire deal. If the strong effectiveness hypothesis were to be true, then one could qualify securitization as more than a zero-sum game, where some strictly positive value is created.

While Pena-Cerezo et al. find that most of the hypotheses from Firla-Cuchra and Jenkinson (2006) or Franke and Weber (2009) which we discussed earlier bore out on the Spanish market, one significant discrepancy is that they only found support for the weak hypothesis of tranching effectiveness, and rejected the strong hypothesis. This was true considering pre-crisis or post-crisis data. While the greater complexity of deals reduced yield on senior bonds, it did not reduce it for the entire structure, hence simply reallocating risk rather than reducing it entirely.

The discrepancy could be attributed to the fact that in their article, Pena-Cerezo et al. included the entire tranche stack in the calculation of the aggregate deal spread, while in the other studies the junior most tranches, typically the cheapest by far, were excluded from the calculation due to the lack of data.

Another incremental contribution from the article is that it included analysis of securitization during the mortgage crisis. In particular, they found that before the crisis there was no relationship between the number of tranches and risk premia, while a significant relationship appeared afterward: perceived deal complexity was presumably driving the risk premium. In addition, while the weak effectiveness of tranching was strongly significant in pre-crisis securitizations, it became much less so during the crisis, stressing that the considerations at play in securitizations had evolved.

## 7.4 Conclusion

With this chapter, we have been able to establish some fundamental justifications for securitization structures that ranged from the pooling of homogeneous assets to the tranching of cash flows. We saw that the creation of multiple layers of similar structures could be associated with different investor preferences. Further, we analyzed the reasons why investors may prefer par-priced bonds, and in turn we were able to explain certain complex structures such as excess-spread as a way of efficiently creating par-priced bonds. Finally, we discussed empirical evidence that supports the use of tranching to satisfy a range of investor preferences. However, as we will see in the next chapter, structuring does raise important issues.

## References

Axelson, U. (2007). Security design with investor private information. *Journal of Finance*, *62*(6), 2587–2632.

Boot, A., & Thakor, A. (1993). Security design. *Journal of Finance*, *48*(4), 1349–78.

Brennan, M., Hein, J., & Poon, S.-H. (2009). Tranching and rating. *European Financial Management*, *15*(5), 891–922.

Childs, P. D., Ott, S. H., & Riddiough, T. J. (1996). The pricing of multiclass commercial mortgage-backed securities. *Journal of Financial and Quantitative Analysis*, *31*(4), 581–603.

Dang, T. V., Gorton, G., & Holmström, B. (2015). The information sensitivity of a security. Working paper. Columbia University.

DeMarzo, P. (2002). Portfolio liquidation and security design with private information. Working paper. SSRN.

Dang, T. V., Gorton, G., & Holmström, B. (2005). The pooling and tranching of securities: A model of informed intermediation. *The Review of Financial Studies*, *18*(1), 1–35.

DeMarzo, P., & Duffie, D. (1999). A liquidity-based model of security design. *Econometrica*, *67*(1), 65–100.

Diamond, D. (1993). Seniority and maturity of debt contracts. *Journal of Financial Economics*, *33*(3), 341–68.

Fender, I., & Mitchell, J. (2009). Incentives and tranche retention in securitisation: A screening model. CEPR discussion papers 7483. C.E.P.R. discussion papers.

Firla-Cuchra, M., & Jenkinson, T. (2006). Why are securitization issues tranched? Working paper. Oxford University.

Franke, G., & Weber, T. (2009). Optimal tranching in CDO transactions. Working paper. SSRN.

Gaur, V., Seshadri, S., & Subrahmanyam, M. G. (2003). Market incompleteness and super value additivity: Implications for securitization. LSE research online documents on economics OM-2005-07. New York University.

DeMarzo, P., & Duffie, D. (2011). Securitization and real investment in incomplete markets. *Management Science*, *57*(12), 2180–96.

Gauthier, L. (2019). Securitization structures and security design. Working paper. SSRN.

Gorton, G., & Metrick, A. (2013). Chapter 1 - securitization. In G. Constantinides, M. Harris, & R. M. Stulz (Eds.), *Handbook of the economics of finance* (pp. 2:1–70). Amsterdam: Elsevier.

Gorton, G., & Souleles, N. (2007). Special purpose vehicles and securitization. In *The risks of financial institutions*, (pp. 549–602). National Bureau of Economic Research, Inc.

Guo, G., Wang, F. Y., & Wei, X. (2014). Optimal tranching with diverse beliefs. *Economics Letters*, *124*, 222–26.

Han, J., Park, K., & Pennacchi, G. (2015). Corporate taxes and securitization. *Journal of Finance*, *70*(3), 1287–1321.

Iacobucci, E. M., & Winter, R. A. (2005). Asset securitization and asymmetric information. *Journal of Legal Studies*, *24*(1), 161–206.

Malamud, S., Rui, H., & Whinston, A. (2010). Optimal securitization with heterogeneous investors. Working paper. SSRN.

Malamud, S., Rui, H., & Whinston, A. (2012). Optimal incentives and securitization of defaultable assets. Working paper. SSRN.

Miller, M., & Rock, K. (1985). Dividend policy under asymmetric information. *Journal of Finance*, *40*(4), 1031–51.

Ortner, J., & Schmalz, M. (2019). Pooling and tranching under belief disagreement. Working paper. SSRN.

Park, S. (2013). The design of subprime mortgage-backed securities and information insensitivity. *International Economic Journal*, *27*(2), 249–84.

Pena-Cerezo, M. A., Rodriguez-Castellanos, A., & Ibanez-Hernandez, F. J. (2019). Multi-tranche securitisation structures: More than just a zero-sum game? *European Journal of Finance*, *25*(2), 167–89.

Plantin, G. (2003). *Tranching*. LSE Research Online Documents on Economics: London School of Economics; Political Science.

Han, J., Park, K., & Pennacchi, G. (2011). Good securitization, bad securitization. Institute for Monetary and Economic Studies 2011-E-4. Bank of Japan.

Pliska, S. R. (1997). *Introduction to mathematical finance: Discrete time models*. New Jersey: Wiley.

Riley, J. G. (1979). Informationally consistent equilibrium. *Econometrica*, *47*(2), 331–59.

Vink, D., & Thibeault, A. (2008). An empirical analysis of asset-backed securitization. Working paper. SSRN.

# Problems in Securitization Structuring 8

Having discussed how complex securities are structured in securitization deals, and having looked into certain economic justifications for the existence of these complex structures, we now turn to the issues specifically raised by structuring. We discuss issues in the sense that structuring may only work toward the welfare of some market participants to the detriment of others, and also in the sense that the theoretical models claiming to explain structuring may not work empirically.

We begin by examining some fundamental symptoms and explanations of issues in structuring. With the help of a simple theoretical model, we first address the issue that it may be expected that investors purchase low-quality structured products in certain conditions, in the sense that the products may not have the characteristics that the investors desire or need. Then we show that structures were effectively inefficient through the mortgage crisis, and in some cases they were knowingly made so.

Next, we address the detrimental effects of complexity on investor welfare. We first focus on the manner in which structural complexity may hide risks for investors. We discuss some tests compiled in Brennan et al. (2009), Coval et al. (2009), and Hull and White (2010), and propose a detailed simulation model capturing the structural leverage of a CDO, relying on the algorithms from Chap. 6. Next, we consider some empirical findings relating complexity to the negative performance of the collateral and of the securitized bonds.

Finally, we turn to some negative effects in structured products rating. We first discuss the effect of relationships, influence, and shopping on ratings, with a simple theoretical model followed by some empirical analyses'. Then, we look specifically at rating analysts' individual choices and go through two empirical studies that related the hiring of rating analysts by investment banks to prior or subsequent fairness in ratings.

 
L. Gauthier, *Securitization Economics*, Springer Texts in Business and Economics,
https://doi.org/10.1007/978-3-030-50326-0_8

## 8.1 Some Fundamental Problems in Structuring

In this first section, we focus on some fundamental symptoms and explanation about the failings of structuring. Indeed, "it did not work" could be the main issue one would raise about structuring. Separately from the fact that many structured securities suffered enormous writedowns in the late 2000s, one essential problem is that these losses were maybe not what they should have been, had structuring, tranching, and pooling carried out their function as expected.

We start with a formal model that shows how investors would settle for lower quality products if the access to better products is competitive. This model serves to illustrate that we should not necessarily expect that all products be perfectly structured, although investors in that context would be assumed to knowingly value these imperfections. If many such lower quality products are created, how would it have transpired? One perspective is that in fact structuring has been mostly useless. Using the empirical study in Ospina and Uhlig (2018) on bond performance through the mortgage crisis, we offer an interpretation that structuring has simply not worked. Finally, relying on the research by Chernenko (2017), we discover some motivations why certain products may have been created in a fashion that is best described as "toxic".

### 8.1.1 Optimal Purchase of Low-Quality Products

With the help of a simple model, we can show that even products with inferior characteristics would be structured when the structural benefits of these products are shared among investors. We consider the case of a number of investment banks arranging securities with various degrees of quality, while investors want to maximize the quality of the bonds they buy. The banks issuing these products incur an exogenously defined cost that is increasing with quality.

We assume there are $K + 1$ investment banks and $n$ institutional investors. Each investment bank $k \in [0..K]$ manufactures securities with a quality $m_k$; we do not need to precisely define this measure of quality; it may be the bonds' ability to withstand losses or the underwriting effort that went into the loans, for example. However, we consider that if there are $h_k$ investors buying securities from bank $k$ with quality $m_k$, they each receive a benefit of $\frac{m_k}{h_k}$: the quality needs to be shared among the investors. This is a simplification of the structuring constraints: having to tailor securities to many investors with varying preferences reduces the bank's ability to cater to all of them at the same time.

Each investor $i \in [1..n]$ is assumed to be risk-neutral and seeks to maximize their share of bond quality. As a result, and since we do not make any particular preference assumptions that would distinguish one investor from another, the situation is represented by a symmetric game with perfect information. In particular, the problem of optimally accessing a resource shared in common is well known, a form of "El Farol Bar" or "Kolkata Paise" problem, as discussed in Arthur (1994) or Chakrabarti et al. (2009). We have the following result for the way investors will choose banks when $n$ is large.

**Proposition 8.1** (Optimal Choice of Investment Bank) *The Nash equilibrium in the game for the investors is a symmetric mixed strategy with a probability distribution* $(\pi_k)_{k\in[0..K]}$ *across banks, and* $\forall k \in [0..K]$*:*

$$\lim_{n\to\infty} \pi_k = \frac{m_k}{\sum_{i=0}^{K} m_i}.$$

***Proof*** We assume a symmetrical Nash equilibrium in the game in the form of a mixed strategy: all players draw their choice for the god to choose from the same distribution $(\pi_k)_{k\in[0..K]}$ where $\pi_k > 0$. The equilibrium is characterized by the fact that the expected gain for any player is independent of the specific choice they make.

Set $e_k$ the expected share in quality received from choosing bank $k$ when all others follow the optimal strategy and can hence be expressed as a function of $\pi_k$. The number of other investors choosing the same bank follows a binomial distribution and

$$e_k = \sum_{i=0}^{n-1} C_i^{n-1} \pi_k^i (1-\pi_k)^{n-1-i} \frac{m_k}{i+1}.$$

This quantity is known, see Chao and Strawderman (1972), for example, and simplifies to

$$e_k = m_k \frac{1-(1-\pi_k)^n}{n\Pi_k}.$$

Since the Nash equilibrium is characterized by $e_k = e_0$ for all $k$, we have

$$\frac{1-(1-\pi_0)^n}{n\Pi_0} = \frac{m_k}{m_0} \frac{1-(1-\pi_k)^n}{n\Pi_k}.$$

As $n$ becomes large, both $(1-\pi_0)^n$ and $(1-\pi_k)^n$ go to zero and the equation becomes

$$\pi_k = \frac{m_k}{m_0}\pi_0.$$

By definition $\sum_{k=0}^{K} \pi_k = 1$, so $1 = \pi_0 + \sum_{k=1}^{K} \pi_k$ and hence $1 = \pi_0 + \sum_{k=1}^{K} \frac{m_k}{m_0} \pi_0$. Solving for $\pi_0$, we obtain after simplification

$$\pi_0 = \frac{m_0}{\sum_{i=0}^{K} m_i}.$$

Similarly, we also obtain that $\pi_k = \frac{m_k}{\sum_{i=0}^{K} m_i}$.

Note that scaling the share received up or down by the same factor has no impact on the optimal probabilities.

So far we have considered that the quality $m_k$ was a given for every bank. Now, we reflect the fact that it is manufactured by the banks at some internal cost. We assume that the banks want to maximize the proportion of investors who buy their products, because they gain a share of their investments.

We assume that the banks are risk-neutral and know how investors will make their optimal choices and seek to maximize their gains in the form of the probability of being chosen minus a proportional cost relative to quality, attached to creating the securities. The bank $k$'s gain, as a function of the quality $m_k$, can therefore be written as $g_k(m_k) = \pi_k(m_k) - c_k m_k$, where $c_k$ is the exogenously given proportional cost. All banks will seek to maximize their gains at the same time, reflecting their knowledge of each other's strategy.

The following proposition characterizes the endogenously determined quality of the bonds issued by the banks, the probability of being chosen, and the expected gain at the equilibrium where all banks and investors act optimally.

**Proposition 8.2** (Optimal Structuring Strategy) *The optimal strategy for all banks is for the quality they offer to verify for all $k$ in $[0..K]$ and with $M = \{i : c_i = \max_{k\in[0..K]}\{c_k\}\}$:*

$$m_k^* = \frac{(c_M - c_k)(K+1) + \sum_{j=0}^{K}(c_M - c_j)}{4(K+1)\left(\sum_{j=0}^{K}(c_M - c_j)\right)^2}.$$

*At this optimum, the probability of being chosen is*

$$\pi_k^* = \frac{c_M - c_k}{2\sum_{j=0}^{K}(c_M - c_j)} + \frac{1}{2(K+1)},$$

*and the gain for banks is*

$$g_k^* = \pi_k^* \left(1 - \frac{c_k}{2\sum_{j=0}^{K}(c_M - c_j)}\right).$$

***Proof*** We first note that

$$\frac{\partial \pi_k}{\partial m_k}(m_k) = \frac{\sum_{i=0}^K m_i - m_k}{\left(\sum_{i=0}^K m_i\right)^2}.$$

Further, $\sum_{i=0}^K m_i - m_k$ does not depend on $m_k$ so that $\frac{\partial \pi_k}{\partial m_k}(m_k)$ is decreasing, and the second-order condition is verified for the existence of a maximum.

The first-order conditions for each priest $k$'s gain optimization writes $\frac{\partial \pi_k}{\partial m_k}(m_k) - c_k = 0$, which based on Proposition 8.1 simplifies into

$$\sum_{i=0}^K m_i - m_k = c_k \left(\sum_{i=0}^K m_i\right)^2.$$

Since the costs $c_k$ are arbitrary, without loss of generality we choose to rank them so that $c_0$ is the highest and $c_K$ the lowest. Taking differences for all $l$ and $k$ in $[0..K]$, we hence have

$$m_k - m_l = (c_l - c_k)\left(\sum_{i=0}^K m_i\right)^2,$$

and, in particular, at the optimum,

$$m_k = (c_0 - c_k)\left(\sum_{i=0}^K m_i\right)^2 + m_0.$$

Using that expression, we can write

$$\begin{aligned}\sum_{j=0}^K m_j &= \sum_{j=0}^K \left((c_0 - c_j)\left(\sum_{i=0}^K m_i\right)^2 + m_0\right)\\ &= (K+1)m_0 + \left(\sum_{i=0}^K m_i\right)^2 \sum_{j=0}^K (c_0 - c_j).\end{aligned}$$

Hence, taking the square and writing $X = \left(\sum_{i=0}^K m_i\right)^2$, we obtain

$$X = (K+1)^2 m_0^2 + 2(K+1)m_0 \sum_{j=0}^K (c_0 - c_j)X + \left(\sum_{i=0}^K (c_0 - c_j)\right)^2 X^2.$$

Since all the $(m_k)$ are determined up to a scalar, bank 0 can choose $m_0$ arbitrarily: there is a continuum of possible optimal equilibria depending on $m_0$. We consider that they always choose the highest $m_0$, that is, the highest quality compatible with the existence of optimal solutions. Hence, $m_0$ is set so that the determinant of the equation is null, that is,

$$1 - 4(K+1)m_0 \sum_{j=0}^{K}(c_0 - c_j) = 0.$$

In that case we obtain the solution

$$X = \left(\sum_{i=0}^{K} m_i\right)^2 = \frac{1}{4\left(\sum_{j=0}^{K}(c_0 - c_j)\right)^2}.$$

Replacing in the equation for the optimality, we can write after some simplifications:

$$m_k^* = \frac{(c_0 - c_k)(K+1) + \sum_{j=0}^{K}(c_0 - c_j)}{4(K+1)\left(\sum_{j=0}^{K}(c_0 - c_j)\right)^2},$$

and

$$\frac{m_k^*}{m_0^*} = \frac{(c_0 - c_k)(K+1) + \sum_{j=0}^{K}(c_0 - c_j)}{\sum_{j=0}^{K}(c_0 - c_j)}.$$

Replacing into the expression for $\pi_k$, we obtain at the optimum

$$\pi_k^* = \frac{c_0 - c_k}{2\sum_{j=0}^{K}(c_0 - c_j)} + \frac{1}{2(K+1)}.$$

Finally, the optimal expected gain for banks writes

$$\begin{aligned} g_k^* &= \pi_k^* - c_k m_k^* \\ &= \frac{c_0 - c_k}{2\sum_{j=0}^{K}(c_0 - c_j)} + \frac{1}{2(K+1)} - c_k \frac{(c_0 - c_k)(K+1) + \sum_{j=0}^{K}(c_0 - c_j)}{4(K+1)\left(\sum_{j=0}^{K}(c_0 - c_j)\right)^2} \\ &= \left(\frac{c_0 - c_k}{2\sum_{j=0}^{K}(c_0 - c_j)} + \frac{1}{2(K+1)}\right)\left(1 - \frac{c_k}{2\sum_{j=0}^{K}(c_0 - c_j)}\right) \\ &= \pi_k^*\left(1 - \frac{c_k}{2\sum_{j=0}^{K}(c_0 - c_j)}\right). \end{aligned}$$

We have specified the ranking of the banks as a function of costs ($c_k$) with the only effective requirement that $c_0$ should be the largest. As a result, all the expressions at the optimum can be written by replacing the index 0 with $M = \{i : c_i = \max_{k\in[0..K]}\{c_k\}\}$, so that $c_M = \max_{k\in[0..K]}\{c_k\}$. □

We can see that all the banks will sell securities to investors, even if the quality of these securities is low, and even if they are known to be of low quality. Also, the optimal probability $\pi_M^*$, which is the lowest among all the $\pi_k^*$, is not affected by changes in the costs $(c_k)_{k\in[0..K]}$ and is constant with $\pi_M^* = \frac{1}{2(K+1)}$.

A particular case is to specify $c_k = 1 - (k_\delta + k)\delta$, for some positive numbers $\delta$ and $k_\delta$ such that $\frac{1}{K+k_\delta} < \delta \leq \frac{1}{K(K+1)+k_\delta}$ so that all the banks' optimal expected gains are positive. We have $M = 0$. Then, it is easy to see that $c_0 - c_k = k\delta$ and $\sum_{j=0}^{K}(c_0 - c_j) = \frac{1}{2}\delta K(K+1)$. As a result, we have

$$\pi_k^* = \frac{K+2k}{2K(K+1)}$$

$$\frac{m_k^*}{m_0^*} = \frac{k+K}{K}$$

$$g_k^* = \frac{(K+2k)\,(\delta(K(K+1)+k+k_\delta)-1)}{2\delta K^2(K+1)^2}.$$

In this simplified context, with linearly decreasing costs of producing quality bonds as a function of the bank's rank, the optimal probability of choosing bank $k$ is linearly increasing in $k$ and does not depend on the slope of the relationship between cost and rank, and neither is the ratio of quality to the lowest quality $m_0^*$. The total gain is a quadratic form in $k$.

Figure 8.1 shows the distribution of market shares for the first 10 issuers in the ABS and MBS markets at two points in time, rescaled to sum up to 1. These distributions can be compared with the formula for $\pi_k^*$ with a linear cost assumption and $K = 9$, shown as the dotted line on the chart. This simple model, which predicts a very particular linear distribution, appears to account for observed league tables fairly well.

While we cannot conclude that securitized products issuance league tables are driven by differences in quality, the important conclusion from this model is that lower quality products may not be shunned by investors, and knowingly, in cases where they compete for access to tailored quality products.

### 8.1.2 Useless Structuring

The point of structuring is to allocate differential cash flows to various classes of investors, in order to optimally alleviate information asymmetry as well as satisfy investor preferences. In particular, creating tranches with different credit enhancement levels allows structurers to finely tailor the degree of protection required by each buyer of the bonds. As we will see, however, structured products in the mortgage market have not behaved as one would anticipate given the intentions with which they were presumably manufactured. The argument here is not that they have not performed well, but that their performance has not been differentiated enough.

In Ospina and Uhlig (2018), the authors carried out an extensive study of the ex post performance of mortgage-backed securities. They gathered data from

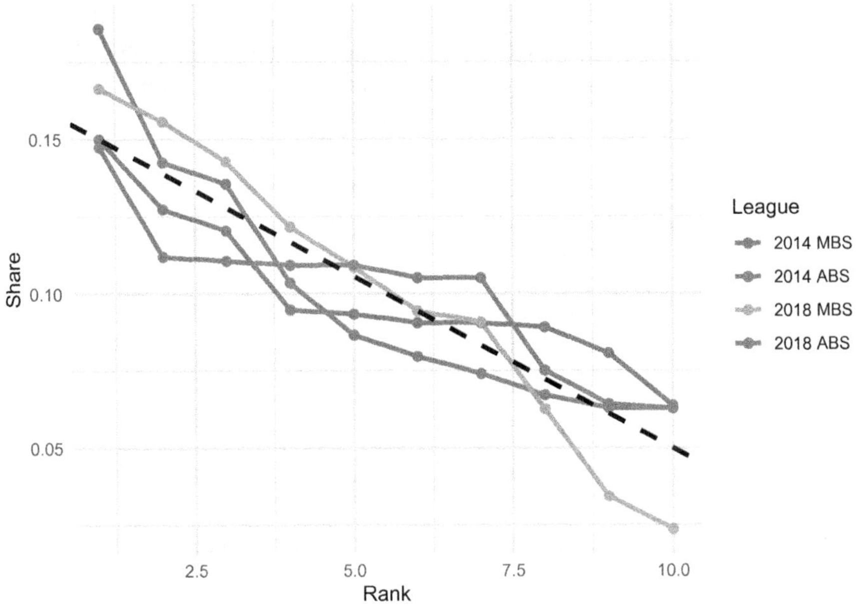


**Fig. 8.1** Securitized products issuance league table examples. *Source* Thomson Reuters Debt Capital Markets Review and author's own calculations

Bloomberg on an impressive 143 thousand mortgage securities across the prime, Alt-A, and subprime markets issued between 1987 and 2013, added categorization information, and computed writedowns at the bond level. There is, however, a potential critical problem in their work, as they did not appear to have accounted for implied writedowns. As we know, securities that do not recognize writedowns are common in US MBS and, in particular, in subprime. Hence, the losses that one might calculate at the securities level can be significantly biased. One of the conclusions in the paper is that subprime AAA bonds did surprisingly well (less than 0.5% losses, versus over 6% for Alt-As); unless a correct calculation is assured, this may be an artifact. However, for the discussion at hand we are mostly interested in the non-AAA securities, which are normally not affected by these implied writedowns.

Their data consists of 87% of AAA-rated bonds, 11% mezzanine, and 2% below-investment-grade tranches. Non-AAA tranches represent about $700bb of cumulative issuance. Table 8.1 shows the aggregate amount of securities in their data and the cumulative loss amounts they calculated, along with the corresponding rating factor.[1] A star marks the total writedown amount that may be significantly underestimated, as we remarked above.

Based on the data from this paper, we can also compute the proportion of securities reported to have taken a loss, by rating category and by sector. The results

[1]Recall from Chap. 3 that the rating factor gives a numerical approximation to the credit risk attached to a rating.

**Table 8.1** Aggregate securities issued and performance. *Source* Ospina and Uhlig (2018) and author's own calculations

| Rating | Total issued | Cum. losses | Rating factor |
|---|---|---|---|
| AAA | 4531 | 2.2%* | 1 |
| AA | 297 | 33.1% | 20 |
| A | 212 | 38.8% | 120 |
| BBB | 118 | 46.9% | 360 |
| BIG | 58 | 52.6% | 2000+ |

**Table 8.2** Proportion of defaulted securities. *Source* Ospina and Uhlig (2018) and author's own calculations

| Sector | AAA | IG (%) | BIG (%) |
|---|---|---|---|
| Prime | 35% | 59 | 80 |
| Alt-A | 51% | 81 | 88 |
| Subprime | 9%* | 68 | 89 |

are shown in Table 8.2. It is worth noting that the proportion of subprime bonds reported to have incurred writedowns is surprisingly low, given the extent to which the investment-grade bonds supporting them have incurred losses, an effect potentially due to unrecognized under-collateralization, as mentioned earlier.

We can see from these numbers that apart from AAA bonds, the level of losses ranges from 35 to 50%, and the probability of incurring a loss across all rating levels ranges from 60 to 90%. There are some variations, and indeed AAs have performed a little better than BBBs, but that differential is nowhere close to the differential in rating factors. It is neither the case that all bonds under a certain rating level would be fully wiped out and that all these bonds would behave similarly because they are all equally wiped out.

Besides, if we consider the AAA-level reported losses as an underestimate or consider the probability of a loss in the prime market for which unrecognized under-collateralization is less likely, the ratio of BBB bonds losses to AAA bonds losses comes out around 25, to be compared with 360 in terms of rating factor. In spite of all the structuring that has taken place, it is apparent that there are no significant differences among the various levels of subordination. In addition, the ability of AAA bonds to withstand losses relative to that of subordinated bonds is much less than would have been implied by the ratings.

This does raise the question of why one should bother creating multiple tranches finely differentiated by credit risk, if they all end up behaving the same way. We can therefore argue that, at least based on the performance data of mortgage securities through the mortgage crisis, fine structuring did not serve any directly observable purpose.

### 8.1.3 Toxic Pooling

While structuring may have not served any useful purpose ex post, could it also be the case that it was even detrimental to investors? With an illuminating piece of empirical research, Chernenko (2017) documents and proves the common narrative that CDO managers were "front men" for the investment banks and served to place structured securities that the banks could not easily otherwise distribute. As a result, the very act of pooling collateral was stacked against investors from the outset. As Chernenko shows, delegating management of the CDO to an asset manager in many cases was simply a front.

Chernenko indeed shows that, among other things:

- Investment banks effectively rewarded specialized CDO managers who were willing to invest in low-quality assets with future management assignments;
- The specialized CDO managers' underperformance was due to their willingness to buy assets from the investment banks' unsold inventory.

Chernenko gathered data on ABS CDOs issued between 2002 and 2007 amounting to 517 deals for a total of $469bb, using Bloomberg, Moody's, Barclays Live and the open model published by Pershing Square Capital Management. This data is mapped to detailed information on each one of the 136 different collateral managers, based on various public sources. Using the deal prospectuses, the details of management fees can too be derived on a majority of these deals.

In order to measure these asset managers' degree of specialization, he used the CDO share, that is, how much CDO management represented in the asset manager's overall business. This information is also combined with a categorization of these asset managers, such as hedge fund, insurance company, etc. For example, the CDO share of asset managers in the specialized CDO manager category is 72%, while it is only 1% for insurance companies.

The performance of the CDOs at the deal level is computed by first gathering all the data relative to the tranches they issued, and computing their aggregate cash flows. As of the time of the analysis, there are still cash flows that could be paid in the future; however, Chernenko assumes them to be worth zero. This effectively addresses the potential issue of writedowns not being recognized by some of these securities. From the cash flows, an IRR can be derived. Simple statistics show that the average IRR ranges from –24 to –37% depending on CDO deal type.

The CDOs' underlying assets are also listed and analyzed, so that useful aggregate metrics can be computed at the deal level. In particular, Chernenko calculated the collateral average spread, the share of subprime RMBS in the collateral, the share of CDO assets structured by the same investment bank arranging the CDO, and the share of collateral that belonged to the list of bonds shorted by hedge fund Magnetar. This last metric is a proxy for identifying assets which were generally considered of particularly bad quality.

The first step in the analysis is to establish whether investment banks selected good managers for their CDO deals, or those who were willing to buy the low-quality collateral they could not place. A Poisson regression of the following form helps answer this question:

$$\ln\left(N_{t,i}^{d}\right) = \sum_{j} \alpha_j X_{t-1,i} + \varepsilon_i,$$

where $N_{t,i}^{d}$ is the number of deals closed by manager $i$ during period $t$, and $X_{t-1,i}$ is the vector of average characteristics of the deals closed by manager $i$ up to period $t$. Among the deal characteristics, the collateral performance is included. The performance of the CDOs being computed several years later than when the CDOs were issued, its use in this regression analysis does not imply the managers or the banks would have known in advance what the performance would be, but it is used as an ex post measure of the quality of the collateral that was selected.

The main significant variables in the regression are the number of deals issued up to time $t$, the number of tranches, and the performance of these deals (IRR), with a negative coefficient. An eventual performance higher by one standard deviation led to a decline in 20% in the number of deals closed. In addition, the contribution of the collateral IRR can be made non-significant by adding the share of collateral made up of CDOs sponsored by the arranger, and the share of bad quality collateral as measure by the proportion of collateral shorted by hedge fund Magnetar, in the regression, which both have a significant positive coefficient.

The results from this regression suggest that investment banks directed business toward those managers who were willing to buy lower quality paper. Chernenko also carried out further analysis showing that the greater the share of CDOs in the manager's overall business, the worse the IRR of their deals. In other words, those managers who had little reputational value to lose in their other asset management businesses tended to purchase lower quality collateral. Additional analyses show that the worse performance of the collateral selected by those managers was not significantly related to the fund manager's characteristics in terms of experience and education quality but was to some extent related to the incentives, such as retained equity, and in all cases to the proportion of CDO management in the managers' business.

The performance of each collateral asset over several years is also shown to not only be very significantly related to the share of CDO management in the manager's business, but also to its coupon spread, and to the fact it was issued by the same arranging bank as the CDO.

Finally, controlling for many collateral characteristics under control of the asset manager, such as asset spread or sector, the deal's performance remains significantly affected mostly by the manager's dedication to the CDO business, and the extent to which the collateral was provided by the arranger.

In the very act of pooling collateral, CDO issuers therefore placed bad quality assets that they could not otherwise sell, by using certain CDO managers in a *quid pro quo*[2] relationship.

[2]From the Latin, "something for something else".

## 8.2 The Problem of Structural Complexity

An issue that has been raised over time, and, in particular, since the mortgage crisis, is the particular complexity of securitization structures. From the perspective of Chesney and Seele (2017), complex structures have the characteristics of **financial toxicity**, which they define as the degree to which financial products or practices can systematically harm their buyers or users and on a large scale. This notion of complexity is considered by many to be one of the root problems that caused the mortgage crisis.

We discussed some of the aspects of structural convolutions in Chap. 7 and proposed reasonable explanations for a certain degree of complexity in structures. Empirical studies provided support for these theories, and tranching could be explained as a function of collateral characteristics in relation with tranche pricing. Nevertheless, as we will see in the current section, not only does the complexity of securitization structures go beyond what we were able to explain, but it also appears to lead to worse collateral and tranche performance.

In the present section, we first discuss Brennan et al. (2009), Coval et al. (2009), and Hull and White (2010), who focused on how complexity hides some arbitrages and risks. In order to study more precisely this question of complexity, we create a reasonably detailed cash flow model for a CDO using the algorithms from Chap. 6 and show how its structure amplifies small collateral performance deteriorations. Then, we walk through empirical findings in Furfine (2014) that show to what extent the quality of loans has been related to structural complexity. Then, following Ghent et al. (2019), we examine the empirical evidence on the relationship between complexity and bond performance. Finally, we discuss some of the interactions between security design and structural complexity. As we have mentioned earlier, there are no formal models that purely explain the reasons for complexity in structures to such a high degree.

### 8.2.1 Complexity Hiding Arbitrage and Risk

In this section, we address some of the most salient issues with complexity in structured finance, the fact that complexity may be in the interest of investment banks and not investors, and that it hides a magnified exposure to important risks. We discuss the findings of Brennan et al. (2009), Coval et al. (2009), and Hull and White (2010), as they show how

- When investors use ratings as an indication of value in a no-arbitrage model context, the more tranches there are (and hence complexity), the more the investment bank can gain by creating structured securities;
- The multiplicity of structural layers, as with CDOs and CDO-squared, introduces an extreme sensitivity to the underlying collateral performance assumptions, in particular, on correlation and probability of default;

- Highly structured securities are particularly sensitive to systemic risk;
- Securities based on less layers of structuring do not have so many negative features.

#### 8.2.1.1 Complexity Allows Investment Bank Arbitrage

Brennan et al. (2009) consider a model where products are priced based on their rating, which is itself a function of either the probability of default or the expected default loss. For the underlying assets, the valuation is given. For structured assets, the investment bank may acquire the collateral (the valuation of which is rating-based) and create tranches that are sold to investors, who value them based on their rating. They study the conditions in which the investment bank can gain from the arbitrage, stemming from the higher value allocated by investors to the sum of the tranches relative to the acquisition cost. They place themselves in a continuous no-arbitrage setting, where the investment bank is nevertheless allowed its own arbitrage. Note that the modeling of complexity in this approach focuses on the multiplicity of tranches in a given deal, for a given collateral.

They formalize the basic logic of creating mezzanine and super senior tranches: given some senior bond, if the rating only depends on the probability of incurring a loss, then a junior bond created off of the senior bond will have the same rating (and hence, in their assumptions the same spread) as the original senior bond. In addition, the super senior thus created will presumably trade at a tighter spread, so that the value of the whole is greater for the issuer.

It is somewhat paradoxical to use a no-arbitrage model where without particular transaction costs or information asymmetries a class of participants would just base their investment decisions on a limited vision of risks and returns. One could argue that investors have to resort to the rating as a pricing input precisely because of the complexity of the structured bond.

The results in Brennan, Hein, and Poon show that under some conditions, the arbitrage gains increase as the number of tranches increases in a securitization: it is optimal to have as many tranches as there are rating levels. If the above argument about complexity is valid, then it is easy to see how both complexity and the possibility of arbitraging ratings would have gone hand in hand. Picking reasonable market-based risk and valuation assumptions for the collateral, they obtain a net gain of about 5% for an entire securitization. This gain is concentrated in the junior tranches, because in this example the senior bonds benefit from a large level of credit enhancement as well as substantial thickness and are hence fairly immune to credit risk. Also, the optimal sizing of the tranches and the total arbitrage gain differ to some extent depending on whether the rating logic is based on the probability of default or on the expected default loss. The arbitrage gain increases as a function of the systemic risk in the collateral and decreases as a function of the noise in collateral value.

One issue in the analysis from Brennan, Hein, and Poon is that in reality structured bonds have generally not been issued at the same spread as comparably rated collateral, but at higher spreads. The measures for arbitrage that they propose are therefore most likely over-estimated.

#### 8.2.1.2 Multiple Layers of Complex Structures Obfuscate Risks

We now consider complexity at a higher level that involves resecuritizations. Coval et al. (2009) look specifically at CDOs and stress the importance of assessing the joint default probability distribution of all assets in the collateral pool, rather than for each corporation independently.

They conduct a simple and realistic simulation in order to measure the sensitivity of a CDO-square's default probability to parameter assumptions. They simulate the performance of 40 CDOs each with 100 underlying bonds with a probability of default of 5% and severity of 50% (which would give these bonds roughly a BB+ rating). Within each CDO, the pairwise default correlation is set to 20%. Further, the collateral pools of different CDOs are assumed to be uncorrelated.[3] Each CDO issues a junior tranche (with attachment and detachment 0–6%), a mezzanine (6–12%), and a senior (12–100%). Then, the CDO-square is created by taking the 40 CDO mezzanine tranches, pooling them, and structuring equity, mezzanine and senior bonds with the same attachment and detachment points as mentioned before.

Based on the simulation results, the CDO and CDO-square senior bonds have essentially zero default probability and would hence receive a AAA rating. The CDO mezzanine has a default probability of about 2%, which would correspond to a BBB rating, while the CDO-square mezzanine has a zero default probability, which would correspond to a AAA: this bond would have been a mezzanine AAA. The CDO-square mezzanine with these assumptions has an expected principal payment of 100%.

These results, however, are crucially dependent on the choice of parameters. The expected default performance of the collateral pools underlying the 40 CDOs does not depend on correlation: only the shape of the distribution is affected, not the expected value. The tranches, on the contrary, are affected and the more junior tranches benefit while the senior tranches see their expected principal payment decline. This effect is amplified by the structure layers: the CDO-square mezzanine sees its expected principal payment drop by 25% if the underlying correlation assumption shifts from 20 to 60%. Leaving correlation unchanged, a shift in the probability of default from 5 to 10% leads to a decline by 8% of the expected principal payment of the CDO-square mezzanine. In these cases, the mezzanine AAA would be seriously downgraded.

Coval, Jurek, and Stafford point out that due to the diversification inherent in large asset pools, the underlying performance is mainly driven by systemic factors. As a result, the tranched securities off of this collateral are less affected by idiomatic risk, and mostly driven by systemic risk. This is amplified by further tranching, and hence the most complex securities such as CDO-square effectively have a digital outcome, either returning all their principal or failing entirely.

One important issue in the approach developed in Coval et al. (2009) is that they assume no correlation across the collateral pools of various CDOs. This does not appear to be an appropriate assumption, because in the case of mortgage securities (a large subset of the whole market), home prices would be expected to affect the

[3]Note this is not a particularly conservative assumption.

loans notwithstanding of their belonging to one pool or the other. In addition, while they account for the performance of CDOs and CDO-squares, they do not look at the performance of the first layer of mortgage securities, the MBS themselves.

In Hull and White (2010), the authors set out to address these questions. They developed a different model to account for the correlation structure of loan defaults, using a copula model, which can account for correlations within pools and across pools. They consider two measures of credit risk that would be used for rating purposes, the probability of suffering a loss, and the expected loss, and using these criteria find out the credit enhancement required on complex securities.

With their assumptions, including more realistic and conservative correlation, as well as various base-level default parameters, they show that AAA-rated CDO tranches do have substantial risk, effectively more than was implied in Coval et al. (2009). Also, they point out that even if the MBS mezzanine tranches that went into the CDOs had been made wider, the results would still be comparable. Interestingly, they also show that the credit risk on MBS AAAs, those directly backed by the underlying loans, was not markedly different from that of AAA-rated corporate loans. This is due to the large thickness of these senior tranches.

Using a more detailed model of CDO cash flows, we can now see that the patterns mentioned in Coval et al. (2009) are quite significant on a more realistic collateral pool with layers of structures.

#### 8.2.1.3 A Detailed Model of a CDO

In order to be able to analyze the effect of correlation within the basket of underlying securitized products that enter a resecuritization, we adapted the random simulation infrastructure as illustrated in Table 8.3. With this logic, we can specify a degree of correlation in yearly prepayments and in yearly losses in the simulations. If every separate deal entering the collateral of a resecuritization was independent of the rest, the correlation inputs would be set to zero. However, as we know that prepayments are strongly driven by interest rates, which affect all loans the same way, it would make sense to have a fairly high correlation in prepayments among deals. Credit in mortgages is also driven by an important common factor, house prices. However, it seems reasonable to anticipate a lesser degree of correlation in yearly losses than in yearly prepayments, because local housing rarely evolves in synchrony (apart from extreme situations such as during the mortgage crisis).

Equipped with this logic in order to generate correlated paths at the deal level in our simulations, we can construct an example resecuritization collateral portfolio using the code shown in Table 8.4. With the default parameters, we combine 30 securities across 500 paths, each with a wide range of attachment points (from 10 to 15%) and thickness (from 1 to 10%). All these underlying securities are intended to represent basic non-agency mezzanine tranches structured as pure subordinated back sequentials, for simplicity. In the simulations with our default parameters, these securities suffer about 6% of losses in aggregate, which represents about 100bps per year over 6 years, a spread that would be commensurate with the lower end of investment-grade credit.

**Table 8.3** Example code for correlated paths generation. *Source* Compiled by the author

```
make_correlated_paths_rand <- function(smp = 500, nb_sec = 30,
                                       ppay_cor = 0.75, loss_cor = 0.25,
                                       nb_per = 10, seed = 1234) {
  set.seed(seed)
  # Generate correlated Gaussians
  ppay_cormat <- matrix(ppay_cor, nrow = nb_sec, ncol = nb_sec) +
    diag(nb_sec) * (1 - ppay_cor)
  loss_cormat <- matrix(loss_cor, nrow = nb_sec, ncol = nb_sec) +
    diag(nb_sec) * (1 - loss_cor)
  norm_ppay <- mvrnorm(n = smp * (nb_per - 1), mu = rep(0, nb_sec),
                       Sigma = ppay_cormat)
  norm_loss <- mvrnorm(n = smp * nb_per, mu = rep(0, nb_sec),
                       Sigma = loss_cormat)

  # Convert Gaussians to uniform
  unif_ppay <- pnorm(norm_ppay)
  unif_loss <- pnorm(norm_loss)

  # Structure output
  unif_ppay <- t(unif_ppay)
  dim(unif_ppay) <- c(nb_sec, nb_per - 1, smp)
  unif_loss <- t(unif_loss)
  dim(unif_loss) <- c(nb_sec, nb_per, smp)

  return(list(
    lossrand = unif_loss,
    ppayrand = unif_ppay
  ))
}
```

Based on this collateral, we created a simplified version of a CDO by first applying an excess-spread/OC structure with 1% of upfront OC, followed by senior/sub-pure sequential tranching where the mezzanine has 8% of credit enhancement (the tranche C and upfront OC), and its thickness is 12%. The CDO mezzanine tranche B we created, hence, attaches at 8% and detaches at 20%. The CDO senior bond A attaches at 20% and detaches at 100%.

Apart from some minor variations due to sampling, changing the correlation assumptions does not change the average outcome of losses for the collateral. It does, however, affect the probability that very high or very low aggregate losses may be realized, which in turn affects the CDO mezzanine's ability to repay its principal.

Table 8.5 shows statistics on the 500 paths, assuming 0 correlation in prepayments and in losses. The total loss column refers to the losses observed on the collateral portfolio of 30 securities itself. The total losses are about 6%, as we mentioned above, and we can see that under these assumptions the maximum losses are under 20%. Recall that the underlying collateral's expected losses are around 9% with a maximum of 18% (see Fig. 6.2, for example). The bond portfolio hence benefits from some credit enhancement and from a lower risk exposure than the underlying loans, if there is no correlation among the bonds. The senior and mezzanine CDO tranches

**Table 8.4** Example code to create CDO collateral. *Source* Compiled by the author

```
make_cdo_b_collat <-function(smp =
500, nb_sec =
30,
                                attvec = c(10, 12, 15) / 100,
                                thickvec = c(1, 3, 5, 7, 10) / 100,
                                ppay_cor = 0.75, loss_cor = 0.25,
                                h_l = 0.05, h_p = 0.45, Cpn = 0.05,
                                nb_per = 10, seed = 1234, ramp = 3
                                ) {

  # Generate correlated uniform variables on some collateral pools
  uni_paths <-make_correlated_paths_rand(
    smp = nbsamp, nb_sec = nbsec,
    ppay_cor = ppay_cor, loss_cor = loss_cor)

  # Create cash flows on all paths for all underlying collateral
  allcolcf <-list()
  for (ksec in 1:nbsec) {
    allcolcf[[ksec]] <-make_random_examples(
      smp = nbsamp, ramp = ramp,
      h_l = h_l, h_p = h_p, Cpn = Cpn,
      lossrand = uni_paths$lossrand[ksec,,],
      ppayrand = uni_paths$ppayrand[ksec,,])
  }

  # Create structured bond cash flows
  strinp <-expand.grid(attvec, thickvec) strinp <-data.frame(attvec =
rep(strinp$Var1,
                            nbsec /(length(attvec)*length(thickvec))),
                          thickvec = rep(strinp$Var2,
                            nbsec /(length(attvec)*length(thickvec))))

  coreflds <-c("BegBal_B","Prin_B", "Loss_B","Int_B")   struct_list<- list()
  for (ksec in 1:nbsec) {
    for (dr in 1:max(allcolcf[[ksec]]$Path)) {
      # Compute structured CFs
      cfdt <-snrsub_sequential(data.frame(allcolcf[[ksec]][Path== dr]),
        A_size = 1 - strinp$thickvec[ksec] - strinp$attvec[ksec],
        B_size = strinp$thickvec[ksec], C_size = strinp$attvec[ksec])
      cfdt <- cfdt[,c("Path","Period", coreflds)]
      # Rescaling
      cfdt[, coreflds] <- cfdt[,coreflds] /strinp$thickvec[ksec]
      cfdt$Bond <-ksec struct_list[[length(struct_list)+ 1]]<- data.table(cfdt)
    }   }   allseccf<- rbindlist(struct_list)

  # Create CDO-level Aggregated Collateral with B tranches
  cdocollat <- allseccf %>% group_by(Path, Period) %>%
summarise(BegBal =
sum(BegBal_B) /nbsec,
              Prin = sum(Prin_B) / nbsec,
              Loss = sum(Loss_B) / nbsec,
              Int = sum(Int_B) / nbsec) %>%
    data.table()

  return(cdocollat)
}
```

**Table 8.5** Losses on CDO structures with randomized cash flows with correlations of 0. *Source* Compiled by the author

| | Total loss | Total loss A | Total loss B | Total loss C | Positive loss B | Severity loss B |
|---|---|---|---|---|---|---|
| Min. | 0.00 | 0 | 0.00 | 0.00 | 0.0 | 4.61 |
| 1st Qu. | 3.85 | 0 | 0.00 | 0.00 | 0.0 | 4.61 |
| Median | 6.10 | 0 | 0.00 | 0.00 | 0.0 | 4.61 |
| Mean | 6.34 | 0 | 0.01 | 2.37 | 0.2 | 4.61 |
| 3rd Qu. | 8.72 | 0 | 0.00 | 0.00 | 0.0 | 4.61 |
| Max. | 18.59 | 0 | 4.61 | 100.00 | 100.0 | 4.61 |

**Table 8.6** Losses on CDO structures with randomized cash flows with correlations of 0.75 for prepayments and 0.25 for losses. *Source* Compiled by the author

| | Total loss | Total loss A | Total loss B | Total loss C | Positive loss B | Severity loss B |
|---|---|---|---|---|---|---|
| Min. | 0.00 | 0.00 | 0.00 | 0.00 | 0.0 | 2.51 |
| 1st Qu. | 0.55 | 0.00 | 0.00 | 0.00 | 0.0 | 29.38 |
| Median | 3.95 | 0.00 | 0.00 | 0.00 | 0.0 | 64.08 |
| Mean | 6.72 | 0.26 | 6.03 | 13.74 | 9.8 | 61.49 |
| 3rd Qu. | 9.05 | 0.00 | 0.00 | 0.00 | 0.0 | 100.00 |
| Max. | 44.36 | 18.99 | 100.00 | 100.00 | 100.0 | 100.00 |

A and B in this example therefore fare very well and experience essentially no losses. The probability of a positive loss for B is just 0.2%, that is, a single path. On this path where the mezzanine takes a loss, its severity is low, under 5%.

As we alluded to before, assuming no correlation among different mortgage securities does not make sense, because we know prepayments are largely affected by common factors and so is credit, albeit to a lower extent. Table 8.6 shows the outcome from a more realistic correlation structure, where the underlying portfolio's performance distribution is now significantly affected. The CDO mezzanine tranche is unaffected in about 92% of all paths, but when it does suffer a loss that loss is substantial with an average severity of 60%. This scenario could be understood as a base case starting point for a mezzanine CDO, as it captures its performance profile: in a nutshell, it is fine most of the time but suffers substantial writedowns in a few rare cases.

**Table 8.7** Losses on CDO structures with randomized cash flows with correlations of 0.90 for prepayments and 0.60 for losses. *Source* Compiled by the author

| | Total loss | Total loss A | Total loss B | Total loss C | Positive loss B | Severity loss B |
|---|---|---|---|---|---|---|
| Min. | 0.00 | 0.00 | 0.00 | 0.0 | 0.0 | 3.99 |
| 1st Qu. | 0.00 | 0.00 | 0.00 | 0.0 | 0.0 | 38.92 |
| Median | 1.29 | 0.00 | 0.00 | 0.0 | 0.0 | 100.00 |
| Mean | 6.52 | 0.74 | 8.52 | 14.8 | 11.4 | 74.72 |
| 3rd Qu. | 8.11 | 0.00 | 0.00 | 0.0 | 0.0 | 100.00 |
| Max. | 60.83 | 40.04 | 100.00 | 100.0 | 100.0 | 100.00 |

**Table 8.8** Losses on CDO structures with randomized cash flows with correlations of 0.90 for prepayments and 0.60 for losses, and increased baseline losses. *Source* Compiled by the author

| | Total loss | Total loss A | Total loss B | Total loss C | Positive loss B | Severity loss B |
|---|---|---|---|---|---|---|
| Min. | 0.00 | 0.00 | 0.00 | 0.00 | 0.0 | 0.04 |
| 1st Qu. | 2.85 | 0.00 | 0.00 | 0.00 | 0.0 | 47.41 |
| Median | 10.37 | 0.00 | 0.00 | 0.00 | 0.0 | 100.00 |
| Mean | 16.56 | 4.40 | 26.08 | 40.34 | 34.8 | 74.95 |
| 3rd Qu. | 24.21 | 0.00 | 53.92 | 100.00 | 100.0 | 100.00 |
| Max. | 84.73 | 72.44 | 100.00 | 100.00 | 100.0 | 100.00 |

Let us now consider two layers of moderate stresses from this starting point. First, we increase correlation further, setting prepayment correlation to 90% and credit to 60%. This would capture the case where the lending environment affects all the loans in a similar way, in addition to interest rates incentives. Further, this would be consistent with home prices becoming more correlated across geography, both in growth as in downturns. Second, still within this increased correlation, we increase the yearly maximum loss rate from 5 to 6%, a 20% relative increase.

Tables 8.7 and 8.8 show the performance statistics in both scenarios. While the increase in correlation by itself does not have a dramatic impact on the loss probability or on the expected losses for the CDO mezzanine, the minor increase in collateral losses has magnified consequences. Expected losses jump to 26% for that CDO tranche, an increase by a factor close to 6 relative to the base case, while the expected losses on the bond portfolio increased by a factor of less than 3. Further, this is in response to an increase of losses by a factor of only 1.2 at the collateral level.

This more detailed CDO model confirms that across securitization structural complexity has likely led to a significant underestimation of credit risk, while at the level of the first layer of securitization, this does not appear to be the case. We can now turn to empirical studies of complexity within deals and of the relationships between complexity and loan and bond performance.

### 8.2.2 Complexity and Loan Performance

In Furfine (2014), the author uses data from the US CMBS market in order to test whether structural complexity is related to subsequent collateral performance. The data covers nearly 360 CMBS deals issued between 2001 and 2007, with performance information as of 2010. Details on the bonds and on the collateral, including prospectuses, were obtained from Bloomberg. There are over 40,000 loans underlying these deals.

The collateral metrics of importance include deal-level average DSCR, LTV, loan pricing at issuance (spread to Treasurys), an index-based estimation of the change in property value, a flag indicating whether the loan is interest only, and a flag for whether the loan is non-performing as of the observation period.

The structure-related metrics include deal size, number of tranches in the deal, number of AAA bonds, number of investment-grade bonds, as well as number of below-investment-grade bonds. There is also a flag for whether only two rating agencies rated the bonds in the structure as opposed to three. A flag is also included to mark the case when the deal sponsor included some loans they originated themselves into the collateral.

Over the period from 2001 to 2007, the average LTV increased slightly and DSCR stayed roughly stable. More strikingly, the average deal size increased steadily from about \$1.5bb to around \$2.5bb. The average number of tranches in these deals, as well as the number of AAA tranches, also increased over the period.

With this data, Furfine sets out to show the following empirical patterns:

- Loans in more complex securitizations defaulted more than expected;
- Neither the price of the securities issued nor the amount of securities retained reflect the relationship between complexity and loan quality;
- Sponsor-originated loans were placed in deals exhibiting this complexity/loan quality relationship, not in others.

Furfine carries out a probit regression, of the following form, for each loan $i$ belonging to deal $j$:

$$\mathbb{P}[D_i] = \phi\left(\alpha.A_j + \beta.B_i\right),$$

where $D_i$ is the event where loan $i$ is delinquent or in default, $A_j$ represents the vector of deal-level metrics, including complexity, and $B_i$ represents the vector of loan-level metrics which were mentioned earlier. Period dummies are also included.

The loan-level metrics in the regression exhibit the patterns that one would anticipate, apart from a few minor exceptions. LTV, property value change, DSCR, and loan spread all have significant coefficients with appropriate signs and magnitudes. A one standard deviation increase in LTV leads to a 3.2% higher probability of default, while a one standard deviation increase in DSCR leads to a decline in defaults by 2.6%. A greater spread at origination by 100bps leads to a 2.3% increase in default probability. The fact that a loan is interest only reduces the probability of default slightly, but this could be understood in two opposite ways: an interest only loan is self-selected to choose to pay less and have a principal payment shock at a later date; but it also implies that the borrower faces less cash flow strain during the mortgage's life.

In this model, the number of AAA tranches in the deal is a significant contributor to loan defaults: a one standard deviation increase in the number of such tranches leads to an increase in defaults by about 2.5% in absolute terms. Coefficients for the other potential measures of convexity considered by Furfine are not significantly different from zero (number of other investment-grade tranches or total deal size, for example).

These results are consistent with the case where the deal issuers place more loans with low quality relative to their hard characteristics (low unobservable quality) in more complex deals. This could be seen as a sign that lower quality collateral required more structuring in order to be rendered palatable for the market. This, Furfine then points out, begs the question of whether investors obtained better pricing due to the lower collateral quality.

The question is addressed by regressing the yield spread on the AAA tranches over the pool characteristics and the complexity measures. It appears that the complexity measures are not significantly different from zero. This is the case even when including a small tranche flag in the regression: when small AAA bonds are structured, they are presumably tailored for specific investor needs and therefore are sold more expensively to them.

We can determine that there were some issues in the regression of AAA spreads as described. First, these AAA tranches may have very diverse levels of credit enhancement, which would presumably be set as a function of the collateral characteristics. As we have already discussed a few times, in particular, in Chap. 4, the senior bonds are in principle structured so as to be informationally insensitive, and hence at the first order their valuation would not be expected to be strongly dependent on collateral characteristics. Second, without including probably the most important driver of issuance spreads, the bonds' average life, the results may be picking up spurious relationships. For example, if more complex deals are used to create more short-term bonds, then their spreads would all come out tighter, and this could show a certain pricing/complexity relationship that would not mean anything.

### 8.2.3 Complexity and Bond Performance

We now turn toward the relationship between complexity and bond performance rather than loan performance. In an interesting study, Ghent et al. (2019) focus on the empirical relationships between structural complexity and tranche performance. They also address connex issues, such as whether collateral performance is related to complexity, and how complexity affects bond pricing. By focusing on the performance of securities, rather than the underlying collateral, they address some of the issues in the analysis of Furfine (2014).

Their findings are in line with those of Griffin et al. (2014) (which we do not discuss in detail), who showed that banks with a good reputation, as measured by their presence in the equity IPO market, did not issue better products but rather that the products they issued had a worse outcome in negative environments.

The authors used Bloomberg to obtain data on all US non-agency MBS issued between 1999 and 2007, including numerical data on the collateral, on the structure, as well as textual data from the deal prospectuses. Fixed-rate securities were dropped from the sample, in order to simplify the analysis and focus on credit aspects more than prepayment risk. Tranches backed by collateral with a high share of fixed-rate loans were also excluded for the same reason. The data contains some data at the deal level, at the collateral group level, and at the tranche level.

The most important deal-level variable is complexity. In order to carry out their empirical analysis, they defined a measure of complexity in five dimensions (which are all correlated to some extent or formally related): the number of collateral groups, the number of tranches, the number of pages in the prospectus supplement, the number of pages in the prospectus supplement describing collateral, and the number of pages in the prospectus supplement describing structure. Taking the first component of a PCA on these metrics across all their data, they created a complexity index.

Over the period from 1999 to 2007, the data shows that the average number of loan groups remained roughly constant, while the number of securities and the number of pages in the prospectuses (both for collateral and structure) increased steadily. The complexity index therefore raised significantly over that period of time. As could be expected, the components of the complexity index are correlated.

Control variables are necessary in order to properly account for the role of complexity, some of them at the deal level. These include the total deal size, excess-spread amount, and the sponsor's total volume for that year. This latest metric should capture the issuer's importance, which could be related to how much sway they might have in obtaining favorable ratings. In addition, a flag is reported for whether the deal used cross-collateralization.

At the securities level, the control variables include rating, rounded to the closest notch (AAA, AA, A, BBB), as well as a flag for split ratings. Tranche performance is captured by a measure of security default as a binary outcome, as of 2013. Default is defined as an event when a tranche has suffered a principal loss, or has a rating of CCC or less. The aggregate observed default rate comes out at 37% on AAAs, 80% on AAs, 96% on As, and 95% on BBBs. The data also include a measure of initial credit enhancement (typically, hard credit enhancement is reported). It is worth stressing that the presence of a wrap is not one of the variables, and the data is not filtered to exclude wrapped bonds.

There could have been a major issue in the treatment of the data: whether implied writedowns are accounted for is not made explicit in the paper, and as a result many bonds could be reporting no writedowns although they are grossly under-collateralized. However, since the authors state that they used the rating as well in order to qualify default (and an under-collateralized bond would naturally be rated as defaulted), we can hope that the issue of implied writedowns is circumvented. With as many as 37% of the bonds showing an impairment at the AAA level, this order of magnitude seems to indicate that the implied writedown problem is avoided.

The pricing data for the securities is the bonds' coupon margin, which assuming they are issued at par should be a good approximation for their yield spread. Since the securities included in the sample are all investment grade, this is a reasonable assumption.

Collateral group-level data includes some geographic concentration measures (the five largest states weights), as well as common collateral credit risk metrics such as FICO score, LTV, documentation, and principal balance. Note that the data does not include lien information, and that the LTV may or may not be CLTV. The collateral data also include a flag for whether the collateral is conforming and satisfies the underwriting constraints of the GSEs. Finally, collateral performance is measured as the share of foreclosures at the collateral group level as of 2013.

#### 8.2.3.1 Defaults and Complexity

Equipped with this data, Ghent, Torous and Valkanov specify a probit model. They consider security $i$ in deal $j$ issued at time $t$, and $D_{i,t}$ the event where that security was in default at the fixed observation time. Then, the regression model writes, with $\phi$ the cumulative distribution of the standard normal distribution,

$$\mathbb{P}[D_{i,t}] = \phi\left(\beta_1.M_{i,j,t} + \beta_2.N_{i,j,t}\right),$$

where $\beta_1$ and $\beta_2$ are coefficient vectors, $M_{i,j,t}$ is a vector of the complexity variables for security $i$ in deal $j$ known at time $t$, and $N_{i,j,t}$ is a vector of control variables for security $i$ in deal $j$ known at time $t$.

Initially, the core control variables in this model only reflect deal and security-level data:

- At the deal level: the deal size, the cross-collateralization flag, the excess-spread, the sponsor's issuance, and issuance vintage dummies;
- At the security level: rating category dummies, subordination, spread at issuance, and a dummy for split rating.

The regressions show that either each one of the complexity metrics or all of them together have a positive and significant coefficient whereby more complexity leads to a greater probability of tranche default. Adding one loan group increases the probability of default by 3%, adding 37 pages to the prospectus increases the probability of default by 2%, and adding one unit to the complexity index leads to a 3% increase, for example. In relative terms, a one standard deviation increase in complexity leads to a 17% increase in tranche default probability on AAA bonds.

Another interesting aspect of the regression is that even though rating enters the control variables, the spread is positively correlated with the probability of default. All else being equal, a 100bps increase in spread at issuance leads to a 3% increase in probability of default. Carrying out the regression only for AAA securities, a 100bps increase in spread leads to a 7% increase in the probability of default, which is quite significant since without conditioning the AAA bonds had a 37% probability of default across the entire sample. It is interesting that this result seems to be opposite to what Park (2013) found, which we discussed in Chap. 4, that until the onset of the mortgage crisis the AAA securities were informationally insensitive. However, Park looked at collateral characteristics at the time of issuance, not at the subsequent performance.

Still focusing on AAA securities only, the same pattern regarding complexity as with the entire data is observed, but with even stronger coefficients: adding one loan group leads to a 6.5% increase in default probability, and adding one unit to the complexity index leads to a 7% increase in default probability. Since the base case expected probability of default is less for AAA securities than for the others, these percentages are even more important in relative terms.

Having established these empirical relationships, it makes sense to check whether they remain stable as more control variables are added, in particular, variables related to collateral quality. Including all the group-level collateral data in the regression, complexity continues to explain defaults with the same degree of significance, but with a lower magnitude by about one-third.

Another test consists in excluding all the conforming collateral pools and related securities, and recomputes the number of collateral groups and securities used as predictors. The rationale is that these pools were typically structured in order to cater to the GSEs, and hence their presence artificially added to the complexity measure. The results, after this transformation, remain very similar.

Controlling by the deal sponsor, namely, with fixed effects (for the top 10 at least), the results still remain largely unaffected. The bonds in more complex deals by the same sponsor, all else being equal, remain more likely to default than those in less complex deals. This also implies that based on this data, it is not that there would be good and bad underwriters, the bad ones using more complexity.

#### 8.2.3.2 Complexity as Structural or Collateral Related

Ghent, Torous and Valkanov point out that there may be two separate and potentially cumulative reasons why complexity may lead to higher securities defaults:

- Complexity may be a way of hiding lower collateral quality, in which case one would expect to see worse collateral performance on more complex deals;
- Complexity may be disadvantaging senior bonds (sold to investors) to the advantage of junior bonds (retained by the issuer), by diverting more cash flows toward them, in which case the collateral performance should not be affected.

In order to test the first one of these possible explanations, one should carry out a regression of a measure of collateral performance, the foreclosure rate in the case at hand, as a function of the collateral characteristics and the complexity measures.

The coefficients for the particular complexity measures are not statistically significant, although the complexity index coefficient is significant at the 1% level. A one standard deviation increase of the index leads to a 0.6% increase in collateral foreclosure rate. This finding is analogous to that of Furfine (2014), which we discussed earlier. However, Ghent, Torous and Valkanov stress that one could also interpret this result as the consequence of the fact that worse collateral requires more complex structuring. This perspective is questionable, because the regression includes many collateral-specific metrics which all strongly condition performance. Hence, their argument is that more complex structuring would be necessary in order to address the credit risk beyond that which can be explained by usual collateral characteristics, which could seem far-fetched.

The second potential explanation for how complexity affects eventual bond defaults can be then tested by entering actual collateral performance as a control in the probit model for the probability of tranche default. In this regression, the coefficient for the foreclosure rate is high and significant, as could be expected: the bonds are more likely to default when the collateral performance is bad. More importantly, the coefficient for the complexity index is barely affected by the addition of this control: complexity affects the probability of default notwithstanding the contribution of eventual collateral performance. As a result, the second explanation for the reason of the impact of complexity appears to be the most aligned with the data.

#### 8.2.3.3 Complexity, Pricing, and Rating

Given how complexity has been shown to affect ex post tranche performance, it raises the question of whether tranche pricing or tranche rating is affected by complexity.

Ghent, Torous and Valkanov first analyze the impact of complexity on pricing using the following regression:

$$Y_{i,t} = \gamma_1.M_{i,j,t} + \gamma_2.N_{i,j,t} + \varepsilon_i,$$

where $Y_i$ is the spread of tranche $i$ of deal $j$ issued at time $t$, and the $\varepsilon$ are the noise terms.

The control coefficients in that regression show intuitive directions and magnitudes: the higher the rating, the tighter the spread, there is a higher spread with a split rating, bonds issued by larger sponsors or in large deals trade slightly tighter, and more subordination leads to tighter spreads. Interestingly, the complexity measures mostly obtain negative coefficients, albeit with a small magnitude and low degree of significance. Still, this analysis suffers from a similar issue as that in Furfine (2014): differences in bond average life are not accounted for, and they are significant and account for a substantial part of pricing variation among securities.

Then turning to the impact on ratings: were more complex deals required to provide more credit enhancement all else being equal? One potential issue is the case of rating shopping, or competition between rating agencies, which could lead to inflated ratings, as we will discuss in more details in the following section.

The following model gives some insights into this question:

$$S_{i,t} = \eta_1.M_{i,j,t} + \eta_2.N_{i,j,t} + \epsilon_i,$$

where $S_i$ is the subordination amount of tranche $i$ of deal $j$ issued at time $t$, and $\epsilon$ the noise term.

Strikingly, the coefficient for the complexity index is negative and significant: more complex deals (although they led to worse performance) benefited from less credit enhancement requirements all else being equal. A one standard deviation increase in complexity leads to a 0.6% decline in subordination. Adding one loan group leads to a decline of 0.8% in subordination levels. Based on this data, one can reject the hypothesis that ratings would be unbiased and accurate measures of the quality of complex tranches.

Further distinguishing among securities, the authors separated senior AAAs and junior AAAs, by defining the senior ones as those with the tightest issuance spread in a deal. Note that the tighter spread could be due to explicit structuring (a super senior security, for example), or just to a much shorter repayment window. In both cases, the bond would be less exposed to credit risk due to a form of structuring. For the senior AAAs thus defined, the impact of complexity is close to zero. In contrast, for the junior AAAs (either longer or more subordinated AAA bonds), a one standard deviation increase in complexity leads to 0.6% less subordination, with a significant coefficient.

#### 8.2.3.4 Relationship with Security Design

Based on the empirical findings pointed out so far, complexity did not work toward the welfare of investors, rather the opposite. This raises the question of the extent to which these results are consistent with security design models.

As we have discussed in Chaps. 4 and 7, where we addressed some aspects of security design, there were two main justifications to structuring securities: due to market completion through arbitrage as in Gaur et al. (2011), for example, or due to asymmetrical information, as in DeMarzo and Duffie (1999), for example.

In theory, informationally insensitive tranches (the AAAs) are created so that investors can value them more efficiently without the downside of issuer private information. This approach, however, as we also discussed at length in Chap. 7, does not directly explain why there may be many different tranches, or why they might have particularly complex features. We addressed some aspects of that question in the discussion of Gauthier (2019), but this is not sufficient to explain the full complexity we are analyzing in this section.

Ghent, Torous and Valkanov argue that if structuring exists in order to cater to different investor preferences, then one should expect that loan groups should contain dissimilar collateral. If the group characteristics were very close to each other, then they would not be able to behave differently across future outcomes. Hence, the loan characteristics across groups in the same deal must be different enough. This can be measured by computing the intra-deal dispersion: the average dispersion of the group-level average loan characteristic relative to the deal-level average; and the inter-deal dispersion: the average dispersion of the group-level average loan characteristic relative to the vintage-level average. If collateral groups allocate loans in a discriminant manner, exacerbating their differences in some way, then we would expect that the differences intra-deals would on average be greater than the differences inter deals. Otherwise, there would be no point in creating these loan groups; they would just as well be securitized in different deals.

Carrying out the calculation, it turns out that there is much more variation across deals than within deals. The argument that structuring complexity inside deals would be related to the need to tailor to different investor preferences therefore does not appear to hold up to the data.

## 8.3 Ratings and Rating Analysts

As we know, structuring goes hand in hand with ratings, since all structures are designed to minimally satisfy the constraints that the rating agencies set for each rating level. The structuring exercise is an optimization of cash flow allocation to maximize the value of the resulting bonds, which depends on the ratings they obtain. In these conditions, it is natural to expect that structurers may exploit all the resources at their disposal, including the selection of the most favorable rating agency for any particular bond. Further than that, since investment banks are the rating agencies' clients, one may wonder to what extent they could exert some influence on the rating outcomes. In addition, by hiring analysts from the rating agencies, investment banks may be able to obtain better information on their analyses and better optimize their structures.

To address these questions, we begin by discussing ratings in the light of relationships and influence. We present a simple theoretical model followed by some empirical studies on the way in which ratings may be optimally selected or influenced by investment banks accounting for a large share of the agencies' business.

Then, we consider the individual career path of rating analysts, with two empirical studies: one concentrating on the potential prospects of switching jobs to an investment bank and the other one on the extent to which former rating analysts at investment banks had an impact of the ratings that the banks obtained for their products.

### 8.3.1 Relationships, Ratings, and Influence

While the logic in rating shopping, magnified by the complexity of structured bonds, can explain certain stylized facts concerning the efficiency of ratings, another way to consider the relationship between issuers and rating agencies is through the prism of influence. We discuss the empirical findings from two papers, Riddiough and Zhu (2009) and Efing and Hau (2015), which both try to sort out the issue, after some introductive theoretical considerations.

#### 8.3.1.1 A Theoretical Model for Rating Shopping

Riddiough and Zhu (2009) develop a model explaining optimal structuring with specific assumptions, in order to justify why issuers select the highest face value that makes a senior security risk-free. Then, they lay out a less formal model of rating shopping and influence.

We do not follow the same initial model, because we can directly justify this result using the tools we have already developed. First, note that this is one of the results of the model by Boot and Thakor (1993) in Chap. 4 (see Proposition 4.11), but in their case it is a rather direct consequence of the assumptions. However, we can show that it is a consequence of the model from DeMarzo and Duffie (1999), in particular, Proposition 4.19, in certain conditions.

**Proposition 8.3** (Optimal Structuring Strategy for a Perfectly Informed Issuer) *In a model with a perfectly informed issuer with a higher cost of capital than the market, the optimal structure is to sell senior debt with face value set to the maximum safe amount.*

***Proof*** First, recall that with the same assumptions as in Proposition 4.19, we have

$$V(D \wedge Y) = \frac{r}{1+r}\mathbb{E}[Y \wedge D|Z = z_L]\mathbb{E}\left[\left(\frac{\mathbb{E}[Y \wedge D|Z = z_L]}{\mathbb{E}[Y \wedge D|Z]}\right)^{\frac{1}{r}}\right],$$

where $V(V \wedge Y)$ is the value to the issuer of creating a debt contract that pays a face value of $D$ off of the collateral $Y$. One of the conditions is that there is a uniform worst case $z_L$ for the noise variable $Z$, which the issuer can observe.

In order to roughly adjust this model to the one developed in Riddiough and Zhu (2009), we will assume that $Y = Z$ and that $Z$ has a lower bound $z_L$. In this case, there is no additional noise beyond the one observed by the issuer.

In the expression for the value of a debt contract to the issuer, we have $\mathbb{E}[Z \wedge D|Z = z_L] = D \wedge z_L$ and $\mathbb{E}[Z \wedge D|Z] = Z \wedge D$. Note that therefore if we define $D^* = z_L$, then $\mathbb{E}[Z \wedge D^*|Z] = z_L$. In this case

$$V(Z \wedge D^*) = \frac{r}{1+r}z_L.$$

Besides, for any $D$, $\mathbb{E}[Z \wedge D|Z = z_L] \leq z_L$. Hence, $\mathbb{E}[Z \wedge D|Z = z_L]$ is maximal when $D$ is set at $D^* = z_L$. Further, for any $D \geq z_L$, $\mathbb{E}[Z \wedge D|Z] \geq z_L$ and consequently for $D \geq z_L$, $V(Z \wedge D^*) \geq V(Z \wedge D)$.

Then, for $D \leq z_L$, we know that $\mathbb{E}[Z \wedge D|Z = z_L] \leq z_L$, and that we always have $\frac{\mathbb{E}[Z \wedge D|Z=z_L]}{\mathbb{E}[Z \wedge D|Z]} \leq 1$. Then, it follows that $D \leq z_L$, $V(Z \wedge D^*) \geq V(Z \wedge D)$.

The optimal face value is therefore $D^* = z_L$ in this model. □

Following Riddiough and Zhu, we now introduce the rating agencies' role. There are several rating agencies, which can observe the collateral quality, but not perfectly. Each agency will analyze the collateral with specific tools, to which investors are not supposed to have access to and compute a lower bound for the collateral performance, which is necessarily higher than the worst-case outcome. Hence, each agency $a$ can determine a lower performance bound $z_L^a$, which is a function of that agency's information and of the actual $Z$, and verifies that for all $a$, $z_L^a > z_L$. The value $z_L^a$ can be communicated to investors, in which case the senior securities are not sized based on $z_L$ but based on $z_L^a$, and the issuer extracts more value.

In these conditions, and if the cost of obtaining the rating is not large, then it is optimal for the issuer to obtain as many as possible and communicate the highest one to investors.

One aspect of the distribution of the $z_L^a$ that deserves to be considered closely is its correlation structure. If the differences between the $z_L^a$ as a function of $Z$ are random and independent, then the way in which the issuer will benefit from shopping is strictly that from picking the maximum of a set of independent random variables. Riddiough and Zhu call it **randomized rating shopping**. If, however, there are systematic biases in the $z_L^a$ as a function of $Z$, then this may be termed **relationship rating shopping**: an issuer could be resorting to the same agency more often because of a particular bias in their favor.

A further mechanism to consider is **issuer influence**, in which the issuer communicates with the rating agency, and may be able to influence the rating. The extreme outcome of this situation would be a case where for some particular $a^*$, $z_L^{a^*} > Z$. This influence could be exerted through promises of future rating business.

#### 8.3.1.2 Influence and Ratings

According to the theoretical framework mentioned above, for a systematic resource misallocation to take place, Riddiough and Zhu argue that more than rating shopping is necessary, and there must be influence at play. Implicitly, the manner in which the rating agencies would estimate without influence $z_L^{a^*}$ would be assumed to necessarily lead to $z_L^{a^*} \leq Z$. Note that Skreta and Veldkamp (2009) look at that same issue differently, and in their model they explicitly account for the situation where shopping, in and by itself, leads to misallocation due to ratings.

Riddiough and Zhu list the following empirical consequences from the theoretical framework :

1. The amount of senior bonds structured off of the collateral is maximized. This would seem rather obvious at this stage, since this is very much a structurer's job definition, but it is interesting to list it as one of the facts to test empirically.
2. The way in which the rating agencies analyze pools does not differ significantly. This would also imply that, given that senior securities should be held to be risk-free, the valuation of the senior bonds depends neither on the rating agency nor on the collateral's credit characteristics. The latter effect has been well documented, as we discussed in detail in Chaps. 4 and 7, in particular, Park (2013) and Franke and Weber (2009).
3. Subordination levels are not affected by the pair issuer/agency; otherwise, that would be an indication of some influence.

4. Rating agencies are randomly selected. Even if there is shopping, if the rating agencies' characteristics are comparable, then selection should be random. If it is not random, this could indicate relationship rating shopping.
5. Investors naively trust the rating agencies. This stronger hypothesis demands that pricing would not be affected by the pair issuer/agency, showing that investors would not account for any knowledge of the potential relationship or influence effects.

The authors consider the pool of collateral as a given, and once it has been specified the optimal structure is determined in relation with the rating agencies. This actually represents a strong hypothesis and is typically not verified in reality. As we mentioned in Chap. 6, the choice of collateral is part of structuring, and issuers will add or subtract loans from pools as part of the structure optimization, as a function of the rating agencies' requirements and analyses. In the case at hand, it is fairly difficult to estimate whether this situation could create a significant bias in the results.

Riddiough and Zhu used data from the commercial mortgage market: a set of AAA CMBS issued on over 550 deals between 1998 and 2008, sourced from the Commercial Mortgage Alert database. It contains information on each issuance, with pool characteristics, spread, some structural information (in particular, credit enhancement at the AAA level), and spreads. Using CMBS brings some advantages over MBS. Since most of the loans have prepayment penalties (often in the form of defeasance requirements), principal payments on these loans are by far much lower and less variable and directional than those on residential mortgages. As a result, the credit exposure is much more directly identifiable and more straightforward to address structurally. It gives a cleaner reading of the relationship between structuring and credit risk.

Descriptive statistics on the data show, among other things, that issuance was concentrated, with 15 issuers accounting for 85% of the volume. These are all conduits, some of them from commercial banks and some from investment banks, issuing loans for the purpose of securitization. The rating agencies' market shares were variable over time.

The empirical models to be tested require us to address both at the same time how the rating agencies are selected, and how certain unobservable factors may explain subordination levels. To this end, the authors use selection models.

The data is organized with one line for each possible AAA security. Note that the securities on the same deal may not be all rated by the same agencies. Then, given a rating agency $j$, one can analyze the drivers of the likelihood for it to be selected. The first-stage regressions write, for each security $i$, and given the rating agency $j$:

$$I_{ij} = \left(X_{ij}, Y_{ij}, Z_{ij}\right) \cdot \Phi_j + \varepsilon^1_{ij},$$

where $X$ is a vector of credit characteristics on the pool, $Y$ is a vector of bond characteristics, $Z$ is a vector of issuer characteristics, and $\varepsilon^1$ is an error term. $I$ is an indicator, taking values in $\{0, 1\}$, of whether agency $j$ rated security $i$.

A first series of regressions is carried out for Moody's, S&P and Fitch. Using the asset pool credit characteristics, year of issuance, and issuer name as explanatory variables, Riddiough and Zhu find that many of the credit characteristics are significant for each of the agencies. They interpret it to suggest that issuers would pick particular rating agencies based on the pool characteristics. We could go further and consider that the agencies may have been selected because of a weakness in assessing some aspects of risks, which would be exploited by the issuers. We could also interpret in an entirely opposite way, as the rating agencies requiring particular pool characteristics, and the issuers obliging them. The dummies for issuer names are significant too, which points toward some issuer and rating agency pair preferences.

In second-stage regressions (one for each agency), the authors look at the level of credit enhancement, using comparable variables as in the first regression, plus a form of adjustment accounting for the selection bias in whether a given agency supplied a rating. As could be anticipated, many of the pool's credit risk characteristics have significant weights, generally consistent across rating agencies. The dummies for issuance year point to a uniform tendency toward lower credit enhancement, which has been also documented in other markets (see Efing and Hau 2015 which we discuss in the next subsection, for example). This may be interpreted as rating agencies becoming more familiar with the analysis of CMBS collateral, or improving their models over time. Importantly, the coefficients for issuer name dummies as well as for the first-stage regression are significant, which points to shopping or relationship building. The results also point toward unobserved factors affecting rating agency selection, and leading to lower credit enhancement requirements, all else being equal.

Finally, Riddiough and Zhu examined the valuation of the AAA tranches, with typical drivers such as the spread over 10-year Treasury yield.[4] The coefficients show that there is no significant relationship between the subordination level and credit spreads. Since, as mentioned above, the subordination levels were presumably driven down by shopping or relationships, one could have expected the market to reflect that knowledge in valuations. This is apparently not the case.

This study, hence, shows that at least in the CMBS market, there was a degree of rating shopping and potential relationship building, and that senior bond valuations did not reflect this effect.

#### 8.3.1.3 Relationships and Rating Inflation

In an empirical article, Efing and Hau (2015) analyze the influence that the amount of business brought by securitized product issuers to rating agencies may have had on these agencies' ratings. Since an inflation of ratings was observed over the years leading to the mortgage crisis, it is natural to ask whether this may have been linked to the way the rating requests were allocated by investment banks. The hypothesis is that the rating agencies may have been more lenient with issuers who sent them

[4]It is worth noting that for anything that has to do with the valuation of structured securities, and if one tries to identify the pricing of risk specific to these products, it is usually best to use the spread to swaps. See Collin-Dufresne and Solnik (2001), for example.

large amounts of business, and as we will see the data clearly supports it. This study uses a much more extensive dataset than Riddiough and Zhu (2009), and effectively confirms and generalizes their main findings.

The authors gathered tranche-level data from DCM Analytics on over 7,000 European and US ABS, MBS, and CDO deals issued between 1999 and 2011. The data covered a large range of countries and products. They obtained various tranche and deal-level-specific metrics, which were also augmented with data from Bloomberg, including the appropriate average life at pricing and issuance spreads and issuance prices on a majority of bonds. The data also included ratings from the main three agencies. Further, pool-level collateral quality data was obtained from Moody's (such as delinquency rates observed several months after issuance) and various structural enhancement-related measures, such as over-collateralization. The data included information on each deal's issuer or sponsor.

In order to carry out this study, it is necessary, however, to properly control for all the deal or tranche characteristics that could have affected the rating. In fact, since from the issuer's standpoint the gains from a securitization are measured at the level of the entire deal, one first step is to compute a form of deal-level rating. As we have pointed out earlier, in particular, in our discussion of Vink and Thibeault (2008) and Pena-Cerezo, et al. (2019) in Chap. 7, it is not appropriate for this purpose to allocate a rank to each rating. A reasonable approach may be to use rating factors.[5] Efing and Hau developed and used a new and efficient measure of aggregate rating: they computed, for each rating level, an average issuance spread, and calculated an aggregate issuance spread for each deal combining all the tranches.

Determining the relevant spread for each rating level is not a matter of a simple aggregation: the rating on each tranche may depend on many of its characteristics such as average life, tranche size, or the shape of the yield curve. Efing and Hau then use a simple pricing model

$$S_i = \alpha_D.D_i + \alpha_C.C_i + \varepsilon_i,$$

where for each tranche $i$, $S_i$ is the issuance spread, the $D_i$ are dummies by rating and the $C_i$ are linear controls. Then, they define rating-implied spread as the coefficient $\alpha_D$ for each rating level. It captures the contribution of the rating to spreads, net of other tranche characteristics that may affect that rating. This rating-implied spread, after being aggregated for an entire deal, results in a deal-level aggregate rating-implied spread, $R_{a,d}$, the aggregate rating-implied spread of deal $d$ according to agency $a$. Efing and Hau point out that the resulting deal-level aggregate spread exhibits a correlation of only 0.55 with the deal's AAA subordination level. This means that, while AAA enhancement levels are important, they are only half the story when the entire rating of a deal is concerned: the subordinated tranches, although being smaller in size, concentrate much of the relative value in a deal.

[5] And in fact, Efing and Hau also carried out their tests using rating-implied capital charges from the US insurance industry, akin to rating factors, and obtained similar results.

Another metric of import necessary in analyzing issuer and rating agency relations is that of shared business, a metric at the deal and rating agency level. The shared business $B_{d,a}$ for a deal $d$ and an agency $a$ at some month $t$ is the sum of securitized product face value rated by that agency and sponsored by the issuer of deal $d$, issued between $t - 6$ and $t + 6$. This measure, aggregated over issuers, is quite variable among dealers and rating agencies, with in some cases twice as much business being allocated to one agency versus the others.

Equipped with these useful metrics, the following regression can be specified, where the use of logarithms helps in flattening out the significant skew observed on many of these variables:

$$\ln(R_{a,d}) = \beta_B \ln(B_{d,a}) + \beta_C.C_d + \varepsilon_{d,a},$$

where $C_d$ is a large set of controls related to the credit risks of the deals, including delinquencies, OC, number of tranches, asset type, and several others. In this regression, as well as variations with dummies by issuers or including deal size, the coefficient for shared business is significant and negative. An increase in the logarithm of shared business by one standard deviation leads to a decline in aggregate spread by 4bps, relative to an average of 10bps. On a \$1bb deal, a cost reduction by 4bps, with an average life of 5 years (as in the case in the dataset at hand), translates into savings of \$2mm for the issuer.

One important test is to include the number of tranches in the regression, which we know we can use as a proxy for deal and structural complexity. The variable $\ln(B_{d,a})N_d$ where $N_d$ is the number of tranches in the deal gains a significant and negative coefficient, showing that both greater business and deal complexity lead to better ratings. This is in fact consistent with the empirical work of Ghent et al. (2019), as well as the theoretical model of Skreta and Veldkamp (2009). Further, robustness testing in Efing and Hau (2015) includes different time periods and shows that in boom periods, where reputational costs of inflated ratings may be less severe, the effect is stronger.

Finally, no single rating agency drives the results by itself, but there are differences among them: It appears that Fitch and Moody attributed stricter ratings, all else being equal, when rating favors are controlled for, than S&P. On the other hand, rating favors were more pronounced for S&P and Fitch.

While Efing and Hau's interpretation of their results is that the rating agencies offered favors to banks that sent them more business, it is worth pointing out that there are other explanations that would be consistent with their results. From the investment bank's standpoint, the reasoning behind the ratings given by the agencies is not always very clear. There is a benefit in understanding that reasoning, because it allows the bank to reverse engineer it to some extent. This understanding necessarily improves from rating more deals with that agency. As a result, the rating favors mentioned by Efing and Hau may simply be a more efficient arbitrage of the rating agencies by the issuers, as they learn more details about the rating process. Alternatively, we could also consider that once a dealer believes it understands better one of the agencies, it would be natural for it to favor that agency going forward. In both of these alternate explanations, we would observe the same end result, without a conflict of interest being at play due to the rating agencies' business.

### 8.3.2 Rating Analysts and Revolving Doors

To what extent may the career paths of the individuals working in rating agencies explain some aspects of structured products rating inflation? The very detailed and interesting studies by Kempf (2019) and Jiang et al. (2018) deserve a particular focus. Both look at the career paths of rating analysts who went from rating agencies to become structurers at investment banks, and try to measure empirically whether ratings were inflated, either before the analysts were hired or after they were hired.

In the structured products markets, the degree of technicality required to work as a structurer on the sell side or as a rating analyst is not that different. In the boom years, however, a sell-side position would have paid a large multiple of a rating analyst's salary. While former rating analysts may not have accounted for a large population on a securitized product's trading floor, they would have represented a significant share of the smaller pool of analysts working for rating agencies.

#### 8.3.2.1 Impact of Job Prospects on Ratings

In Kempf (2019), the author carries out an empirical study and focuses on the work of rating analysts before they may move on to an investment bank, and asks whether their ratings could have been influenced by the prospect of being hired by the investment bank.

Rating analysts may be tempted to show leniency in their ratings in a quid pro quo, where the investment bank would hire them in return for the favor. This effect is termed **capture** by Kempf, in opposition with **incentive** whereby the analysts may be incited to exert a stronger effort at their job in order to be hired by an investment bank.

In order to empirically test for the presence of these effects, specific data is required on rating analysts, the deals they rated, and the investment banks that potentially hired them. One particular challenge is to measure the analysts' performance at rating. Kempf focuses on the career paths of 245 analysts at Moody's between 2000 and 2009 along with over 24,000 ratings they directed and uses published rating updates,[6] which are ex post rating adjustments, in order to measure whether a particular analyst's ratings had to be corrected after some amount of time. Since the period of time covers the mortgage crisis, many of these ratings and, in particular, the later ones are expected to have been adjusted downward; in order to correct for this bias, any particular analyst's rating adjustments are considered only relative to the average rating adjustment for the same period and the same sector. An analyst's rating accuracy is defined as the average absolute rating adjustments after 3 years,

[6] These are carried out by a committee independent of the initial rating analyst.

in notches.[7] In addition to the relative adjustments, Kempf controls for a variety of metrics that may affect the difficulty in establishing a rating, such as deal complexity (number of tranches), deal size, over-collateralization, credit score and LTV, and others.

Using LinkedIn, she tracked the job changes of the rating analysts, in order to flag cases where they went to work at investment banks (specifically one of the top 20 banks in Bloomberg league tables). One immediate conclusion that could be gathered from the data is that the probability of being hired by a bank was very strongly related to rating accuracy. One standard deviation of greater accuracy led to a 78% increase in the probability of being hired by an investment bank. In aggregate, for the first quartile of accurate analysts, the probability of moving to a bank was 9% per semester versus less than 4% for the last quartile. Note that the measure of accuracy potentially looks into the future relative to when the hiring takes place. It is assumed that while the bank may not observe the future rating adjustments, it would be able to observe the professional quality of the analyst, which is related to these future adjustments.

First focusing on the incentive effect, Kempf ran the following regression:

$$H_{i,z,t} = \lambda_{z,t} + \delta I_{i,z,t} + \beta . X_{i,z,t} + \varepsilon_{i,z,t},$$

where $H_{i,z,t}$ is an indicator for analyst $i$ having worked on product $z$ being hired by an investment bank at time $t$, $I_{i,z,t}$ is the measure of inaccuracy of the analyst, $X_{i,z,t}$ is a vector of controls, and $\lambda_{z,t}$ are fixed effects by sector and semester. $X$ includes various deal characteristics, as well as the total number of deals rated by the analyst (for the product and period), tenure at Moody's, and others.

Inaccuracy has a strongly significant and negative coefficient in the regression, with a decrease of 1 standard deviation in inaccuracy leading to a 33% increase in the probability of being hired, after accounting for all the control variables. While this analysis tells us that banks are more likely to hire accurate analysts, it does not address to what extent analysts may exert a particular effort to increase their accuracy in order to increase the likelihood of being hired by a bank.

In order to empirically answer this question, Kempf, among other things, looked at the impact on analyst accuracy of particular events. Indeed, banks often enter a particular sector in which they have not been active before. This can be tracked by seeing which bank issues deals in which sector. If a bank issues the first deal in a particular sector, this should count as a signal that bank will be active and, in that particular sector, there may be employment opportunities at that time. She identified 16 such sector entry events in 7 separate sectors, and observed that subsequent to these events there was an increase in the rate of analysts departing to banks. Then, in order to test the relationship between efforts and such incentive, she ran a regression

[7] This measure does not factor in the differences in relative credit risk implied by different rating levels, but in the context at hand it is not an issue. We are reasoning in rating space, not in credit risk space.

relating inaccuracy to fixed effects and dummy variables attached to the occurrence of a market entry up to three semesters before or after each point in time:

$$I_{i,z,t} = \lambda_{z,t} + \lambda_i + \sum_{\tau=-3}^{3} \delta_\tau E^\tau_{z,t} + \beta.X_{i,z,t} + \varepsilon_{i,z,t},$$

where the $\lambda$ are fixed effects, $X$ are controls as before, and $E^\tau_{z,t}$ is a flag for a bank's entry into sector $z$ at time $t + \tau$. The regression is run on all analysts, only the analysts that have a low predicted probability of going to a bank, and only the analysts that have a high probability of going to a bank.

The results show that before the event, for $\tau < 0$, the coefficients $\delta_\tau$ are close to zero, but they jump to a very negative value for $\tau \in \{0, 1\}$ and revert to zero for higher $\tau$. Further, the analysts with a low ex ante probability of being hired do exhibit this strong pattern, it is mostly concentrated on these analysts with a high ex ante probability of being hired.

It appears therefore that the incentive effect is at play, where not only do investment banks hire the most accurate analysts, but these analysts tend to display greater accuracy at times when banks may be hiring. One consequence that could play a significant role is the impact of investment bank hiring on the pool of rating agency analysts. While it is understandable that banks may want to hire more qualified personnel (and hence more accurate analysts), these banks may not have had a need to hire from rating agencies in the first place, as they have had a steady inflow of candidates from the best schools across the world. At the rate of 9% a semester, the pool of good analysts at the agencies depletes fast, due to their hiring by investment banks. If this depletion led to a decrease in accuracy of one standard deviation over time, then this greater variability in agencies could have been efficiently arbitraged by banks, leading to greater gains. If we assume that it would lead to an increase in the aggregate rating by one notch, it would translate, according to Kempf, to about \$10bb in pricing value over the period under consideration. This can be estimated to represent about 40 times the cost of hiring the best 50 rating analysts of the sample over 5 years, assuming a typical compensation at the Vice-President level at the time, in an MBS/ABS structuring role, of \$1 mm per year.

Looking next at the capture effect, Kempf defined a measure of relative optimism, that is, the average difference between a given analyst's ratings and the rest of the sample. Such a term added to the regression for $H_{i,z,t}$ does not obtain a significant coefficient. However, if it is further qualified by measuring optimism only for the deals that the hiring bank has issued, then the coefficient is significant and positive. The magnitude of this capture effect is small, however, at about a quarter of that of the incentive effect.

In summary, the main impact of investment bank hiring appears to be in thinning out the pool of most competent rating analysts in rating agencies, with a limited induced bias in the resulting ratings.

#### 8.3.2.2 Impact of Job Changes on Ratings

Tackling the issue with a slightly different angle, Jiang et al. (2018) considered the extent to which rating analysts helped investment banks obtain better ratings on their structures after they were hired. The reason for such an effect could be, for example, that these analysts understand better the inner workings of ratings and allow investment banks to more optimally tailor the structures to reach a certain rating. Another perspective could be that these analysts were generally better at structuring than the average investment bank staff, and hence would improve its ability to optimize structures. As we just discussed, Kempf (2019) showed that the rating analysts hired by banks were at least the best ones within rating agencies.

In Jiang et al. (2018), the authors used LinkedIn, as well as other sources such as ZoomInfo, historical rating reports, or Google, in order to track about 300 rating analysts who joined investment banks between 1997 and 2007. They identified the banks that they joined and mapped them to securitization deals and shelves the banks sponsored, and the ratings on these structures as of 2013. About two-thirds of the rating analysts who moved to a bank went to the top 10 issuers of securitized products.

One first question addressed in this article is that of the characteristics of the investment banks that hire the most rating analysts. In order to control for various effects, a measure of experience is introduced, as the logarithm of rating experience for each analyst. The relevant metric at the bank level is not considered to be the number of analysts hired, but rather the sum of this logarithm. Other important variables are the bank's market share in the ABS and MBS market, the issuer's own rating (capturing its reputation), and its overall size as the logarithm of its market value. Further flags are added, such as the type of institution (depositary or broker/dealer).

The data shows that the larger an issuer's market share in the ABS/MBS markets, the higher the total rating analyst experience they tend to have, and this is true for various model specifications. In particular, controlling for issuer fixed effects, the coefficient for market share is the only one remaining significant, showing an increase of 10–20% in total rating analyst experience when market share is raised by one standard deviation.

The second question addressed in the article is an important one: can one relate an inflation in ratings to the hiring of structured finance rating analysts? Since rating inflation is a difficult quantity to measure directly, Jiang et al. compare the intensity of eventual rating downgrades that took place later as an indication of initial rating inflation. Note that the downgrades are measured in number of notches, not using a rating factor difference. This may not be the most appropriate approach,[8] but given the intent behind the measure, where rating inflation may be looked at as a binary situation, tracking changes in number of notches may not be a critical issue. In aggregate, the AAA securities in the sample used by Jiang et al. were downgraded by 7 notches, while more junior bonds were downgraded by 10 notches.

[8]Looking at the change in the weighted average rating factor of all securities issued in a deal would have seemed better, as we commented in the discussion of Efing and Hau (2015).

It is worth expliciting the logic with which the data is organized for regression analysis. The table combining rating analysts with securities and issuer information has one line for every tranche, with bond-specific information (which includes future downgrades) as well as the issuer's own information. The data on analysts is aggregated at the tranche level by summing up the logarithms of the experience of all the analysts working at that bank at the time of the transaction who had worked at one of the agencies that rated the bond. In addition, metrics related to deal complexity, such as the number of tranches, or rating/issuer relationships, such as the amount of business done by a bank and a particular agency for an issuer, are included in the data.

Regressing the extent of downgrades over the logarithm of rating experience, it appears there is a significant positive coefficient, so that a one standard deviation increase in rating experience leads to further downgrades by about one notch. Jiang et al. applied various controls for tranche complexity and for issuer/agency relationships, since these effects have been documented to be significant for future performance, as we saw earlier with Furfine (2014), Ghent et al. (2019) or Efing and Hau (2015). They not only confirmed these effects on their sample, but also show that the relationship between total experience from rating analyst and rating downgrades remains positive and significant. Whether measuring the occurrence of downgrades, or tranche writedowns, or the price return, the outcome also remains the same, and securities structured by banks with a greater total rating analyst experience exhibited worse performance all else being equal.

In order to further explore this effect, the authors also considered the impact of hiring rating analysts without specific experience in structured finance. In that case, the coefficients in the relationship between the sum of logarithms of experience and future downgrades, defaults, or performance were not significant. In addition, they carried out cross-sectional analysis bucketing by deal complexity, as approximated by the number of tranches. The impact of hiring rating analysts remained robusts, and the coefficient for more complex deals is significantly higher than for less complex deals.

In summary, it appears that controlling for several effects which we discussed in the prior section, namely, that complexity and stronger business relationships with rating agencies led to a worse structural quality, the hiring of analysts from rating agencies further contributed to lowering the effective quality of structuring.

## 8.4 Conclusion

We have seen that for a variety of reasons, securitized products have been suboptimally structured from the standpoint of their investors. Further, this suboptimality has generally not been captured in pricing. It was clear throughout this chapter that there were some fundamental flaws in structuring, both theoretically and empirically. In some respects, one can say that pooling and structuring did not work on many of the bonds structured in the mid- to late 2000s. We discussed empirical evidence that shows how structuring complexity hides risks and leads to worse ex post performance. Finally, we discussed evidence that ratings were arbitraged by deal sponsors and influenced, potentially through the hiring of rating analysts.

## References

Arthur, W. B. (1994). Inductive reasoning and bounded rationality. *The American Economics Review*, *84*(2), 406–11.

Boot, A., & Thakor, A. (1993). Security design. *Journal of Finance*, *48*(4), 1349–78.

Brennan, M., Hein, J., & Poon, S.-H. (2009). Tranching and rating. *European Financial Management*, *15*(5), 891–922.

Chakrabarti, A.-S., Chakrabarti, B., Chatterjee, A., & Mitra, M. (2009). The Kolkata paise restaurant problem and resource utilization. *Physica A: Statistical Mechanics and Its Applications*, *388*(12), 2420–2426.

Chao, M. T., & Strawderman, W. E. (1972). Negative moments of positive random variables. *Journal of the American Statistical Association*, *67*(338), 429–31.

Chernenko, S. (2017). The front men of wall street: The role of CDO collateral managers in the CDO boom and bust. *Journal of Housing Economics*, *72*(5), 1893–1935.

Chesney, M., & Seele, P. (2017). Toxic sustainable companies: A critique on the shortcomings of current corporate sustainability ratings and a definition of 'financial toxicity. *Journal of Sustainable Finance & Investment*, *7*(2), 139–46.

Coval, J., Jurek, J., & Stafford, E. (2009). The economics of structured finance. *Journal of Economic Perspectives*, *23*(1), 3–25.

Collin-Dufresne, P., & Solnik, B. (2001). On the term structure of default premia in the swap and libor markets. *The Journal of Finance*, *56*(3), 1095–1115.

DeMarzo, P., & Duffie, D. (1999). A liquidity-based model of security design. *Econometrica*, *67*(1), 65–100.

Efing, M., & Hau, H. (2015). Structured debt ratings: Evidence on conflicts of interest. *Journal of Financial Economics*, *116*(1), 46–60.

Franke, G., & Weber, T. (2009). Optimal tranching in CDO transactions. Working paper. SSRN.

Furfine, C. (2014). Complexity and loan performance: Evidence from the securitization of commercial mortgages. *Review of Corporate Finance Studies*, *2*(2), 154–87.

Gaur, V. Sridhar, S. and Marti G. (2011). Securitization and real investment in incomplete markets. *Management Science*, *57*(12), 2180–96.

Gauthier, L. (2019). Securitization structures and security design. Working paper. SSRN.

Ghent, A., Torous, W., & Valkanov, R. (2019). Complexity in structured finance. *Review of Economic Studies*, *86*(2), 467–722.

Griffin, J., Lowery, R., & Saretto, A. (2014). Complex securities and underwriter reputation: Do reputable underwriters produce better securities? *The Review of Financial Studies*, *27*(10), 2872–2925.

Hull, J., & White, A. (2010). The risk of tranches created from mortgages. *Financial Analysts Journal*, *66*(5), 54–67.

Jiang, J.X., Wang, I.Y., & Philip Wang, K. (2018). Revolving rating analysts and ratings of mortgage-backed and asset-backed securities: Evidence from Linkedin. *Management Science*, *64*(12).

Kempf, E. (2019). The job rating game: The effects of revolving doors on analyst incentives. *Journal of Financial Economics*, To appear.

Ospina, J., & Uhlig, H. (2018). *Mortgage-backed securities and the financial crisis of 2008: A post mortem*. NBER Working Papers 24509. National Bureau of Economic Research, Inc.

Park, S. (2013). The design of subprime mortgage-backed securities and information insensitivity. *International Economic Journal*, *27*(2), 249–84.

Pena-Cerezo, M. A., Rodriguez-Castellanos, A., & Ibanez-Hernandez, F. J. (2019). Multi-tranche securitisation structures: More than just a zero-sum game? *European Journal of Finance*, *25*(2), 167–89.

Riddiough, T., & Zhu, J. (2009). Shopping, relationships, and influence in the market for credit ratings. Working paper. University of Wisconsin.

Skreta, V., & Veldkamp, L. (2009). Ratings shopping and asset complexity: A theory of ratings inflation. *Journal of Monetary Economics*, *56*(5), 678–95.

Vink, D., & Thibeault, A. (2008). An empirical analysis of asset-backed securitization. Working paper. SSRN.

# 9 Conclusion of Securitization Economics

This work has taken the reader through a deeper and deeper foray into the economic drivers of securitization. We began with a simple overview of securitization, which covered the basic mechanics, the naming conventions, the markets and trading of securitized products, and an introduction to valuation approaches. This was followed by a rapid discussion of loan portfolio analysis, in which the common thread has been to gain just enough details to make the close reading of many empirical papers in the field accessible, in addition to opening the door of an advanced discussion of structuring techniques. The high-level description of mortgage data and of sometimes opaque characteristics or definitions for the uninitiated came in handy when later we drilled into some empirical research.

Having established a good background, we have begun to explore the economic drivers of the existence of securitization, and of the issuance of senior and junior structured products. We first saw how securitization should not exist in theory and how a series of plausible explanations in terms of optimal funding could justify its existence, in contrast with the simple Modigliani–Miller model. We found some empirically motivated benefits in securitization. Then, we turned our attention to the reason why securitized products should be at least simply structured. A few security design models, with various assumptions, all showed that information asymmetries explained the necessity for equity and debt structures. Empirical research offered some validation for these theoretical models. Then, we were in a position to start asking what the issues were with the simple fact of securitizing. Through some broad characterizations of the late 2000s mortgage crisis, we first saw that securitized loans exhibited abysmal credit performance. Then, focusing on a few theoretical and empirical models of loan screening and monitoring, we saw how securitization would likely go hand in hand with a lowering of credit standards. Finally, we briefly summarized the mechanics of regulatory arbitrage and saw that it was empirically confirmed to play a role in bank's lending and asset acquisition strategies.



L. Gauthier, *Securitization Economics*, Springer Texts in Business and Economics,
https://doi.org/10.1007/978-3-030-50326-0_9

We continued with a dive into structuring. We addressed some general concepts and notions, including the motivations and reasoning behind many structural choices. We then reviewed a selection of structuring techniques in a good amount of detail. We also observed how these techniques are typically combined into real securitized products. This allowed us to seize the common complexity of actual securitization structures, quite different from the simplified models from the security design literature. We then looked into some fundamental justifications for the complexity of securitization structures that ranged from the pooling of homogeneous assets to the tranching of cash flows. We saw that the creation of multiple layers of similar structures could be associated with different investor preferences. We also analyzed the reasons why investors may prefer par-priced bonds, and in turn we were able to explain certain complex structures such as excess-spread as a way of efficiently creating par-priced bonds. Then, we discussed empirical evidence that supports the use of tranching to satisfy a range of investor preferences. Finally, we discussed the problems raised by structuring. The justifications for structuring do not prevent some flaws that can be shown both fundamentally and empirically. In some respects, one can say that pooling and structuring did not work on many of the bonds structured in the mid- to late 2000s. We also discussed empirical evidence that shows how structuring complexity hides risks and leads to worse ex post performance. Finally, we discussed evidence that ratings were arbitraged by deal sponsors and influenced, potentially through the hiring of rating analysts.

To come back to the question we raised in the introduction, to what extent is securitization inherently bad? We could say, based on this work, that it is bad to the extent that anything that is made and sold by an informed agent, or an agent who does not suffer any consequences related to the product's subsequent performance, is potentially bad.